P9-ELF-934

The Atlas of African-American History and Politics

From the Slave Trade to Modern Times

Arwin D. Smallwood
with
Jeffrey M. Elliot

McGraw Hill

Boston Burr Ridge, IL Dubuque, IA Madison, WI New York San Francisco St. Louis
Bangkok Bogotá Caracas Lisbon London Madrid
Mexico City Milan New Delhi Seoul Singapore Sydney Taipei Toronto

McGraw-Hill
A Division of The McGraw-Hill Companies

THE ATLAS OF AFRICAN-AMERICAN HISTORY AND POLITICS
FROM THE SLAVE TRADE TO MODERN TIMES

Copyright © 1998 by The McGraw-Hill Companies, Inc. All rights reserved. Printed in the United States of America. Except as permitted under the United States Copyright Act of 1976, no part of this publication may be reproduced or distributed in any form or by any means, or stored in a data base or retrieval system, without the prior written permission of the publisher.

This book is printed on recycled acid-free paper containing 10% postconsumer waste.

Printed in the United States of America
11 12 QDB/QDB 15 14 13 12

ISBN-13: 978-0-07-058436-5
ISBN-10: 0-07-058436-2

Publisher: *Jane Vaicunas*
Sponsoring editor: *Lyn Uhl*
Marketing manager: *Annie Mitchell*
Project manager: *Terry Routley*
Production supervisor: *Laura Fuller*
Designer: *Joseph A. Piliero*
Cover designer: *Joan Greenfield*
Cartographer: *University Cartographic Laboratory at the University of Wisconsin, Madison*
Project supervision: *The Total Book*
Compositor: *GTS Graphics*
Typeface: *Times Roman*
Printer: *Quad/Graphics, Dubuque*

Library of Congress Cataloging-in-Publication Data

Smallwood, Arwin D.
The atlas of African-American history and politics: from the slave trade to modern times / Arwin D. Smallwood with Jeffrey M. Elliot.
p. cm.
Includes bibliographical references and index.
ISBN 0-07-058436-2
1. Afro-Americans—History. 2. Afro-Americans—Politics and government. 3. Afro-Americans—History—Maps. 4. Afro-Americans—Politics and government—Maps. I. Elliot, Jeffrey M. II. Title.
E185.S574 1998
973'.0496073—dc21

97-25485
CIP

Dedication

I dedicate this book to my family and friends, and to all the people who have made a difference in my life, especially my mother and great aunt

Mrs. Lois Marie Cherry Smallwood
Mrs. Catherine Walton Bond

and

In memory of loved ones who have passed on

Mrs. Lottie Beatrice Walton Cherry, 1918–1984
Mrs. Glossie Rascoe Smallwood, 1913–1985
Mr. Bart Fearing Smallwood, 1935–1985
Mr. Jesse Thurston McPhail, 1906–1994
Mrs. Drucilla Nixon Hemphill, 1935–1994
Mr. George Lewis Bond, 1921–1996
Dr. Max H. Kele, 1936–1996

About the Authors

Arwin D. Smallwood is the director of African-American studies and assistant professor of history at Bradley University. He has also served as acting chair of the department of history during the summer of 1997, and a visiting lecturer of history at North Carolina Agricultural and Technical State University, in Greensboro. Born in Windsor, North Carolina in 1965, he earned his bachelor of arts degree in political science, in 1988 and the master of arts degree *cum laude,* in history, in 1990, from North Carolina Central University. The Ohio State University awarded him the Ph.D. in history in 1997. He is a member of Phi Alpha Theta, the national history honor society, and Pi Gamma Mu, the national honor society for the social sciences. He also holds membership in several major historical associations including the Association for the Study of African American Life and History, the Southern Historical Association, the Organization of American Historians, and the American Historical Association.

While at Bradley he has updated and revised the curriculum and developed study abroad programs to Africa for the African-American Studies program. He has also lectured to and worked with a number of state and local groups and organizations including the Institute for Learning in Retirement at Bradley University, the American Association of University Women, Illinois Central College, the Tri-County (Peoria) Urban League, the Illinois Department of Corrections, and Peoria area schools. He has served as a Faculty Research Mentor for the 1996–97 and 1997–98 academic years where he assists undergraduate students in researching and writing presentable and publishable papers and directs them in contributing to books such as this one.

He has received a number of awards including the First Year Faculty Teaching Award from Bradley University in 1996 and an Outstanding Service Award from the Foreign Service Institute of the United States Department of State. He has also been a pioneer in the study of rural landscapes and their historical and contemporary impact on African Americans and has helped organize several national conferences and sessions on the topic, including a session for the 1996 meeting of the Association for the Study of African-American Life and History in Charleston, South Carolina.

Jeffrey M. Elliot is professor of political science at North Carolina Central University. A distinguished scholar, Dr. Elliot is a specialist in American politics and government, foreign policy and national security, civil rights and civil liberties, and political economy and global development. Dr. Elliot received his bachelor of arts and master of arts degrees in political science from the University of Southern California (1969, 1970), and his doctor of arts degree in government from the Claremont Graduate School (1978). A recipient of numerous honorary degrees, he also holds a Certificate in Conflict Resolution (1997), a Certificate in International Trade and Development (1995), and a Certificate in Grantsmanship (1980). In 1986, California State University-San Bernardino established The Jeffrey M. Elliot Collection, a permanent archive of his published works. Dr. Elliot is also the subject of a book-length study entitled, The Work of Jeffrey M. Elliot: An Annotated Bibliography and Guide (1986, 1998). A celebrated scholar, he has four times been selected as the "Outstanding Researcher" by North Carolina Central University.

A prolific writer, Dr. Elliot has authored, co-authored, or edited nearly 100 books and 550 articles, reviews, and interviews. His work has appeared in over 250 publications, both in the United States and abroad, and has been nominated for more than 125 academic and literary awards. Among his many published works are *The Encyclopedia of African-American Politics* (1998), *The Historical Dictionary of OPEC* (1998), *Fidel By Fidel* (1997), *The Brown and Benchmark Reader in American Government* (1993), *Annual Editions: The Third World* (1992), *Into the Flames: The Life Story of a Righteous Gentile* (1992), *Voices of Zaire: Rhetoric or Reality?* (1990), *Conversations with Maya Angelou* (1989), *The Arms Conrol, Disarmament, and Military Security Dictionary* (1989), *Fidel Castro: Nothing Can Stop the Course of History* (1986), *Black Voices in American Politics* (1985), *Deathman Pass Me By: Two Years on Death Row* (1983), *Educational Opportunity: Equal for Everyone?* (1981), *Getting and Using Power: Political Access Without Discrimination* (1981), and *Keys to Economic Understanding* (1977).

Table of Contents

Unit 3: Free Blacks, Slaves, and Slavery in the New American Republic

Unit 4: The "Peculiar Institution" and Sectionalism in Antebellum America

Unit 5: The Civil War, Its Impact on African Americans, and the End of Slavery in the Western Hemisphere

Unit 6: Reconstruction, the West, and the Black Struggle Against Colonialism and American Racism

Unit 7: The Rise of Jim Crow, World War I, the Harlem Renaissance, and the Great Migration from the American South

Unit 8: The Growth of Black Political Power in the North, the Great Depression, and Blacks during World War II

Unit 9: African Americans during the Cold War and the Civil Rights Movement (1945–1965)

Unit 10: Black Power, Black Nationalism, and the Rise of the African American Counterculture

Unit 11: African Americans and the Challenges of the 1990s

Preface

In this work I have attempted to give students of history and political science an opportunity to better understand the history and politics of African Americans through the use of maps. This volume was not meant to be studied by itself, but instead, to be used in conjunction with the numerous scholarly volumes written on the various aspects of African-American history and political science referenced in this work. The volume traces the African and African-American experience throughout the world, with special attention paid to those Africans who were forcibly brought to the Americas. It vividly illustrates the major African kingdoms, the various African slave trades, and the subsequent African diaspora. The work demonstrates that people of African descent in the Western Hemisphere (the Caribbean, Central America, and North and South America) have a common place of origin, which is West Africa. The volume also highlights the relationships of these Africans to Native Americans, Europeans, and other peoples around the world. By doing so the work paints a clearer picture of the contributions made by people of African descent to the entire world and acknowledges those peoples who have befriended them, harbored them, and welcomed them into their communities. In this work, maps are used to graphically reinforce historical facts and show the worldwide movement of African peoples. The volume adds a new dimension to the fields of history and political science and aids the historical pedagogy by giving teachers and students of these disciplines the opportunity to learn historical and political geography as it pertains to people of African descent.

This work is the result of four years of research and a lifetime of experiences, disappointments, and successes. Throughout my life I have gleaned as much knowledge and understanding from my failures and disappointments as from my successes, for they have helped me maintain my humility and developed in me a strong desire to end ignorance through teaching and learning. I have been taught this humility by my family, friends, and the many courageous people around this country and world that I have had the privilege of knowing—people like Ann Alling Long, Lee Lacy, Majorie Manning, Lawrence A. Bray, and Wolfram Scharrer. As an undergraduate student and later graduate student at North Carolina Central University in Durham, I became fascinated by my courses in African-American, European, and American history. A number of professors there—David W. Bishop, E. E. Thorpe, Helen G. Edmonds, and Percy E. Murray—challenged me and inspired me to learn all I could about African Americans. Later as a doctoral student at The Ohio State University, in Columbus, I was once again challenged to expand my knowledge by my professors: John C. Burnham, Joan Cashin, John A. M. Rothney, and Warren R. Van Tine. Both of these experiences and the freedom given through independent study by Percy Murray and Warren Van Tine allowed me to broaden my reading to include material from fields outside African-American history to answer questions of concern to African Americans.

I would like to thank God for allowing me to go this far in life and blessing me with a loving family and friends, and for bringing into my life all the people who have encouraged and inspired me throughout my life. Their assistance in my professional, social, and spiritual growth will never be forgotten. In completing this research, I am indebted to a number of research libraries including Perkins Library of Duke University; the Wilson and Davis Libraries of the University of North Carolina at Chapel Hill, particularly the North Carolina Collection and the Southern Historical Collection; the James E. Shepard Memorial Library of North Carolina Central University, the North Carolina State Archives and History; and the Black Studies Library of The Ohio State University. I am also indebted to several outstanding scholars who agreed to review this work and offer suggestions on how to improve and refine it. They include John Hope Franklin, James B. Duke Professor Emeritus, Duke University; Darlene Clark Hine, John A. Hannah Professor of History, Michigan State University; Gerald Smith, Associate Professor of History, University of Kentucky; Patience Essah, Auburn University; William Van Deburg, University of Wisconsin; Arthur Harris, Penn State University; Robert Pratt, University of Georgia; and Sylvia Jacobs, North Carolina Central University. Their support of this work was much needed and greatly appreciated. Finally, I would also like to thank several outstanding students in my African-American history classes at Bradley University.

I must also note the work of my nine research students for the spring 1997 semester at Bradley University; Butch A. Acena, Jamaal R. Buchanan, Dakia L. Hargrett, Arletha Johnson, Charles F. Kittendorf, Juan Martinez, Harold L. McCampbell, Jr., Brenda M. McFadden, and Layla K. Willingham all of whom were undergraduates completing work in the African-American Studies Program. Their questions, comments, and criticisms helped me to refine this work for classroom use. The students include Shaotia J. Artis, Eva Braxton, Sarlanda R. Calip, La' Shay Y. Carter, Preshell Carter, Lee A. Copeland, Amie L. Dosemann, Nicole R. Foster, Oni Harris, Amber M. Maynard, Tina Moyer, Ernestine Muhammad, Anthony Parker, Nesby Rodriguez, Shauna L. Sever, Ginnye-Claire C. Thomas, and Alesia Wilkinson.

I would also like to thank several of my colleagues in the Department of History at Bradley University who suggested works that expanded my knowledge and filled gaps in my research especially Lester Brune, retired Oglesby Professor of American Heritage, who gave me an excellent list of works on black troops in Korea and the cold war; Timothy Maga, current Oglesby Professor of American Heritage, who suggested the superb two-volume work of Samuel Eliot Morrison on early European exploration and colonization of the Americas, and informed me of the role of African Americans in shaping U.S. foreign policy in the Philippines; and the late Max Kele, Director of the Berlin-Prague Seminar, who as my faculty mentor encouraged my teaching and research and asked engaging questions about this work that forced me to find answers through additional research. I would also like to thank one of the most extraordinary people I have ever met, Barbara Penelton, Chair of the Department of Education at Bradley University. Dr. Penelton is responsible for my decision to accept my current position as Director of African-American Studies at Bradley University. She personally saw to it that my wife and I were made a part of the university and neighboring community. Her kindness, intelligence, and sincerity have profoundly impacted my wife and me, and forever won her a place in our hearts. These individuals have established as their goal creating a university that is an international center of learning, and one that encourages lifelong learning. Their support of my teaching, research, and community service has been unyielding, and I thank them and the Peoria community for their support of the African-American Studies Program at Bradley University.

In closing, I would like to acknowledge the work of the talented team from the University Cartographic Laboratory at the University of Wisconsin, Madison: Onno Brouwer, director; Daniel Maher, project manager; Qingling Wang, Richard Worthington, and Katherine Sopa, graduate students in cartography; and Ryan Meyer and Michael Des Barres, undergraduate students in cartography. They did an outstanding job of moving many of my ideas from the abstract to the real.

I would also like to thank a number of people at McGraw-Hill including Lyn Uhl, Monica

Freedman, Kate Scheinman, Terry Routley, and David Yelton, whose hard work and planning helped to keep this work on schedule and affordable for students without sacrificing quality. I would like especially to acknowledge the assistance of Mr. Yelton. I first approached him with the idea for this work in 1993. He thought it was an excellent idea, and he presented it to his superiors at McGraw-Hill. He then worked diligently to have this volume published. Without his efforts this work may have never been published. I would also like to thank our gifted copy editor Judy Duguid.

Finally, and most importantly, I would like to acknowledge the contributions of my wife, Alisa Mayfield Smallwood. When I had given up hope of bringing together all of the talented people necessary to produce this type of work, she constantly encouraged me to push on and suggested alternatives that proved most beneficial. Therefore this volume is as much hers as mine, and is for all the people the world over who daily live lives of learning.

Arwin D. Smallwood

Unit 1 Africa, the African Slave Trades, and the Beginnings of African Slavery in the Americas

MAP 1

Africa: The Origin of Humans

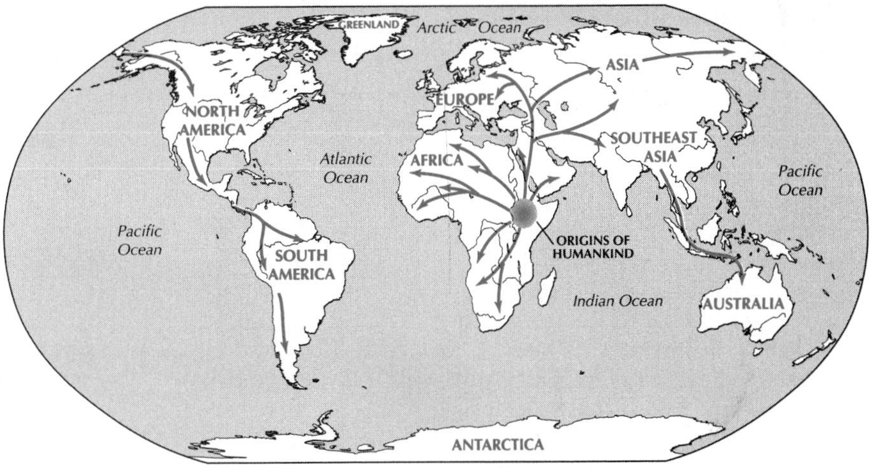
GREENLAND
Arctic Ocean
ASIA
EUROPE
NORTH AMERICA
SOUTHEAST ASIA
Atlantic Ocean
AFRICA
Pacific Ocean
Pacific Ocean
SOUTH AMERICA
ORIGINS OF HUMANKIND
Indian Ocean
AUSTRALIA
ANTARCTICA

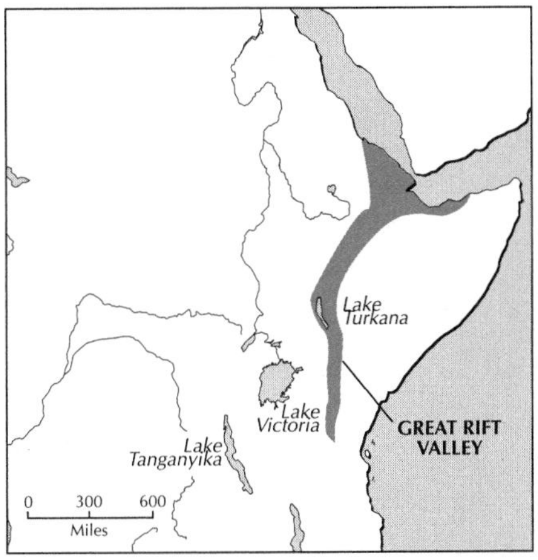
Lake Turkana
Lake Victoria
Lake Tanganyika
GREAT RIFT VALLEY
0 300 600
Miles

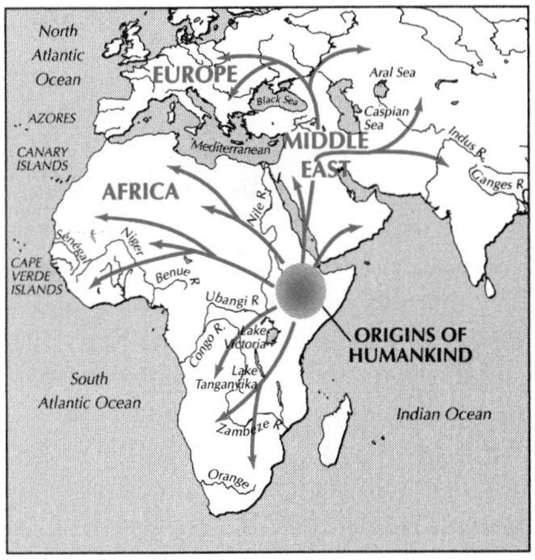
North Atlantic Ocean
EUROPE
Aral Sea
Black Sea
Caspian Sea
AZORES
MIDDLE EAST
Mediterranean
Indus R.
CANARY ISLANDS
Ganges R.
AFRICA
Nile R.
Senegal
Niger
Benue R.
CAPE VERDE ISLANDS
Ubangi R.
Congo R.
Lake Victoria
ORIGINS OF HUMANKIND
South Atlantic Ocean
Lake Tanganyika
Indian Ocean
Zambeze R.
Orange

Anthropologists have unearthed the oldest human remains in the world in the East African countries of Kenya and Ethiopia. Beginning with the discovery by Louis Leakey in 1959, numerous fossilized remains have been found in the Great Rift Valley of East Africa. The Leakeys—Louis, his wife Mary, and their son Richard—continued to unearth remains that predated human remains on other continents and dated human origins at about 1.7 million years ago. Until the discovery of "Lucy" in November 1974 in Hadar, Ethiopia, their discoveries were the oldest. Lucy's remains are of a female and are approximately 3.5 million years old. Lucy was discovered, and named, by anthropologist Dr. Donald Johanson of the Cleveland Museum of Natural History. Leading anthropologists agree that these early humans migrated from East Africa, settling in South Africa, West Africa, Central Africa, North Africa, and the Middle East. Anthropologists contend that from the Middle East, these early humans migrated to Europe and Asia. From Asia, most likely pursuing caribou or other food sources, early humans migrated across the Bering Strait to the Western Hemisphere, arriving in North America around 10,000 B.C. Traveling through what is known as the "ice corridor," these early peoples populated North America, South America, and the Caribbean. As human settlements began to become more permanent, one of the world's earliest great empires, Egypt, was founded in Northeast Africa, along the Nile River around 3200 B.C. ■

MAP 2

Africa: Its Climate and Geography

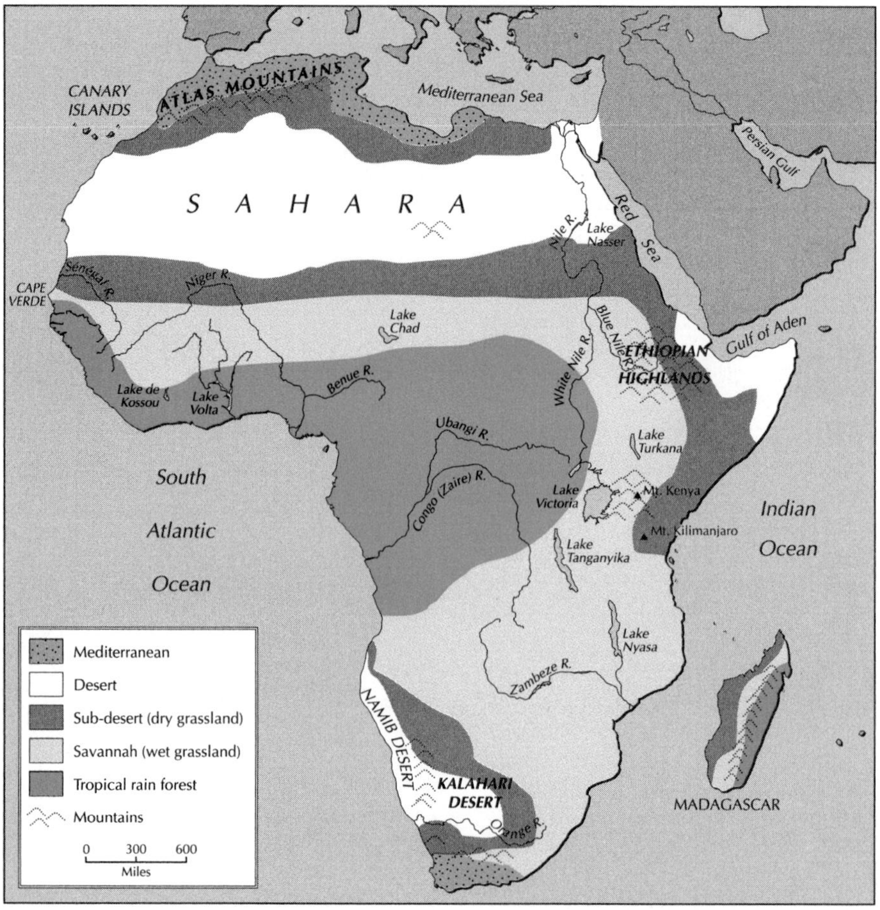
CANARY ISLANDS
ATLAS MOUNTAINS
Mediterranean Sea
Persian Gulf
S A H A R A
Red Sea
Lake Nasser
Nile R.
CAPE VERDE
Senegal R.
Niger R.
Lake Chad
Blue Nile R.
White Nile R.
ETHIOPIAN HIGHLANDS
Gulf of Aden
Lake de Kossou
Lake Volta
Benue R.
Ubangi R.
Lake Turkana
South Atlantic Ocean
Congo (Zaire) R.
Lake Victoria
Mt. Kenya
Mt. Kilimanjaro
Indian Ocean
Lake Tanganyika
Lake Nyasa
Zambeze R.
NAMIB DESERT
KALAHARI DESERT
Orange R.
MADAGASCAR
Mediterranean
Desert
Sub-desert (dry grassland)
Savannah (wet grassland)
Tropical rain forest
Mountains
0 300 600
Miles

Africa is the second largest continent in the world at 12,000,000 square miles; only Asia is larger. Africa is three times larger than the continental United States, which is 3,615,102 square miles, and six times larger than Europe, which is 1,906,176 square miles. It is surrounded by several islands, including Madagascar, the largest, the Madeira Islands, the Canary Islands, the Azores, the Cape Verde Islands, and the São Tomé and Principe Islands. Africa has four major lakes: Chad, Victoria, Tanganyika, and Nyasa. It has thirteen major rivers: the Nile, Atbara, Blue Nile, White Nile, Ubangi, Congo (Zaire), Zambezi, Limpopo, Vaal, Orange, Benue, Niger, and Senegal. The continent is bordered to the west by the Atlantic Ocean, to the southeast by the Indian Ocean, to the northeast by the Red Sea, and to the north by the Mediterranean Sea. Africa covers 20 percent of the Earth's surface, and contains five major climatic zones, including the Mediterranean, Sub-Desert, Desert, Savanna, and Tropical Rain Forest. The Mediterranean zone is located in North Africa on the Mediterranean Sea and in South Africa on the Cape of Good Hope. The Sub-Desert zone, characterized by dry grassland and sparse vegetation, borders the Desert zone and the Savanna. The Desert zone consists of three deserts, the Sahara (the world's largest) in North Africa and the Namib and Kalahari in Southwest Africa. The Savanna zone (or flat wet grassland) constitutes the largest part of Africa. It abounds in the lowlands of South, Central, East, and West Africa. The Savanna also includes several highlands located in South and East Africa, as well as the Atlas Mountains (the only mountain range located in North Africa), which are situated between the Mediterranean and the Sub-Desert zones. The Tropical Rain Forest zone runs along the west coast and on both sides of the equator in Central Africa and encompasses the island of Madagascar. Owing to the diversity of the continent, the lives of African peoples varied in important ways. For example, Africans in the Savanna hunted wild animals for food; those who lived in the drier Sub-Desert regions favored herding; in the wetter Savanna region people developed a grain-based agriculture; finally, the Tropical Rain Forest inhabitants favored hunting and gathering and, eventually, raised root-based crops, while those who lived in areas around rivers or lakes fished. ■

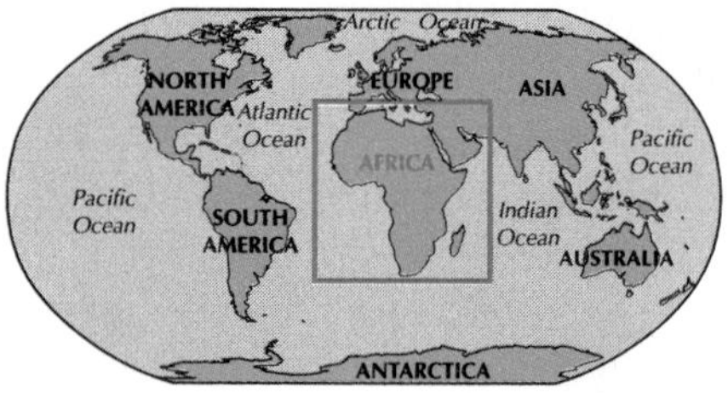
Arctic Ocean
NORTH AMERICA
EUROPE
ASIA
Atlantic Ocean
AFRICA
Pacific Ocean
Pacific Ocean
SOUTH AMERICA
Indian Ocean
AUSTRALIA
ANTARCTICA

MAP 3

Africa: Its Peoples before European Intrusion

Today, Africa consists of countless ethnic groups, including the Europeans, who have for the past 500 years greatly influenced the continent's indigenous peoples. Africa is and has always been a very diverse continent. In addition to the Europeans, historically there have been more than 800 African ethnic and linguistic groups, each maintaining its own culture, language, and religion. These peoples can be grouped into five major ethnic and linguistic groups: (1) the Afro-Asiatics, who populate North Africa, (2) the Nilotics, who populate East Africa, (3) the Bantu, who populate Central Africa, (4) the Khoisan, who populate South Africa, (5) the Malagasy (Malayo-Polynesian), who populate the island of Madagascar, and (6) the many different ethnic and linguistic groups of West Africa. On the whole, Africa's history has not been unlike that of Europe or the Americas. At various times, different ethnic groups have warred with each other and struggled for power. This was also true of the Europeans, who fought one another for centuries before the first nation-states were created, and equally true of the various Native American peoples. Ethnic, cultural, religious, and linguistic differences pitted Africans against one another, allowing the Europeans to use these differences to further divide, conquer, and enslave them, as they would Native Americans in the Caribbean and North and South America. By 1993 Africa contained 53 ethnically, linguistically, and religiously diverse African-ruled countries with a total population of 817,000,000. ■

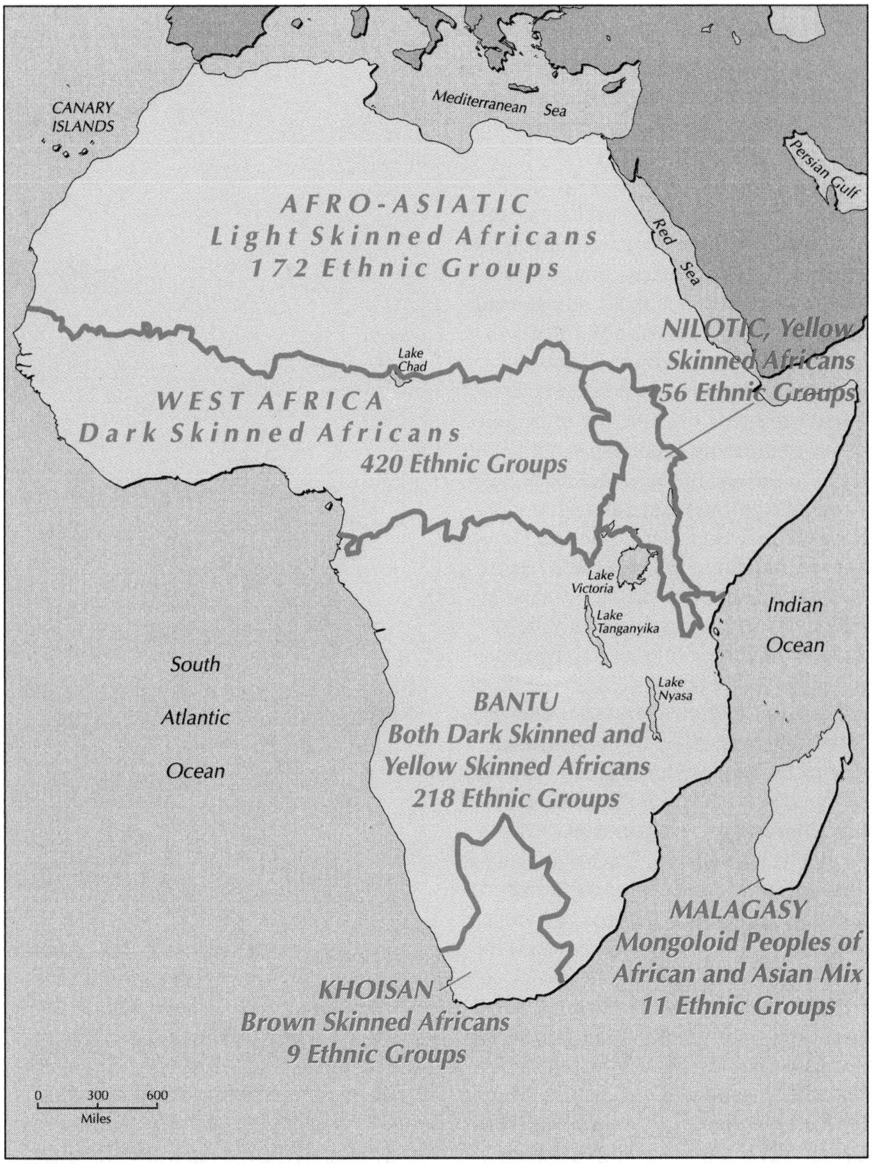
CANARY ISLANDS
Mediterranean Sea
Persian Gulf
Red Sea
AFRO-ASIATIC
Light Skinned Africans
172 Ethnic Groups
NILOTIC, Yellow Skinned Africans
56 Ethnic Groups
Lake Chad
WEST AFRICA
Dark Skinned Africans
420 Ethnic Groups
Lake Victoria
Lake Tanganyika
Lake Nyasa
Indian Ocean
South Atlantic Ocean
BANTU
Both Dark Skinned and Yellow Skinned Africans
218 Ethnic Groups
MALAGASY
Mongoloid Peoples of African and Asian Mix
11 Ethnic Groups
KHOISAN
Brown Skinned Africans
9 Ethnic Groups
0 300 600
Miles

MAP 4

The North African Muslims (Moors) and Their Influence in Portugal, Spain, and France (610–1492)

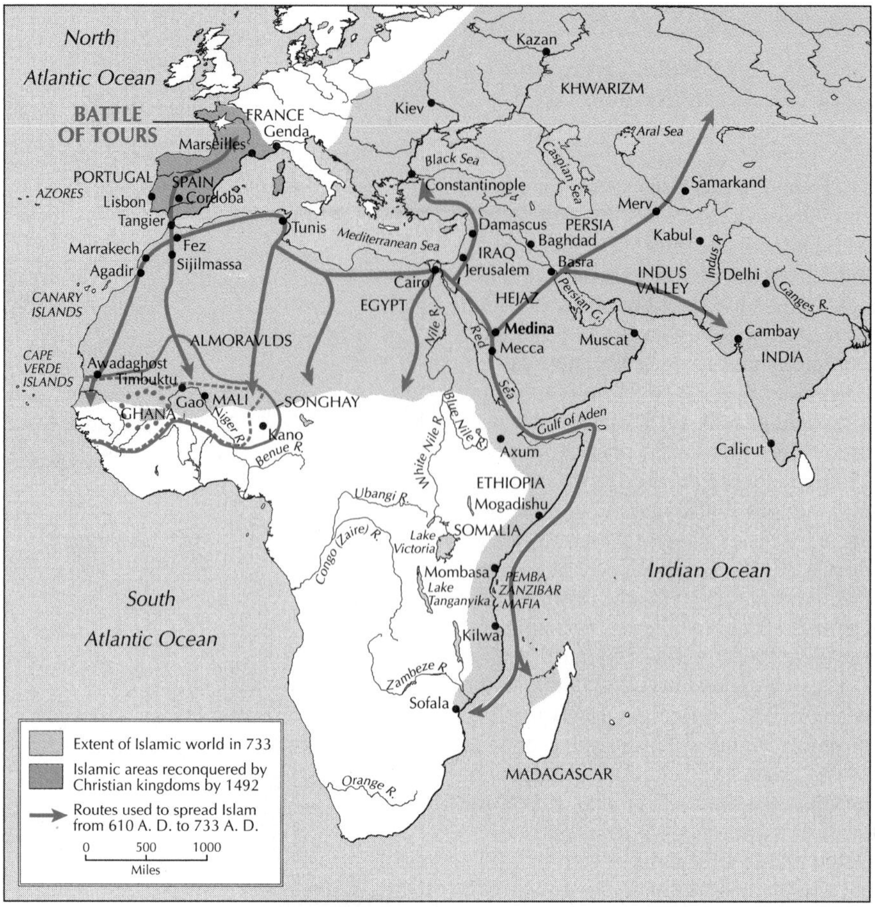

North Atlantic Ocean
BATTLE OF TOURS
FRANCE
Genda
Marseilles
PORTUGAL
SPAIN
Cordoba
AZORES
Lisbon
Tangier
Marrakech
Agadir
Fez
Sijilmassa
CANARY ISLANDS
CAPE VERDE ISLANDS
Awadaghost
Timbuktu
GHANA
Gao
MALI
SONGHAY
Niger R.
Kano
Benue R.
ALMORAVLDS
Tunis
Mediterranean Sea
Cairo
EGYPT
Nile R.
Red Sea
Kiev
Kazan
KHWARIZM
Aral Sea
Black Sea
Caspian Sea
Constantinople
Damascus
IRAQ
Jerusalem
PERSIA
Baghdad
Basra
Persian G.
HEJAZ
Medina
Mecca
Muscat
Merv
Samarkand
Kabul
Indus R.
INDUS VALLEY
Delhi
Ganges R.
Cambay
INDIA
Calicut
Gulf of Aden
Blue Nile R.
White Nile R.
Axum
ETHIOPIA
Mogadishu
SOMALIA
Ubangi R.
Congo (Zaire) R.
Lake Victoria
Mombasa
Lake Tanganyika
PEMBA
ZANZIBAR
MAFIA
Kilwa
Zambeze R.
Sofala
MADAGASCAR
Orange R.
South Atlantic Ocean
Indian Ocean
Extent of Islamic world in 733
Islamic areas reconquered by Christian kingdoms by 1492
Routes used to spread Islam from 610 A. D. to 733 A. D.
0 500 1000
Miles

In A.D. 610 the Prophet Muhammad began to preach the Islamic faith. His goal was to unite the Arabs and spread the "true faith." Through the Jihad, or Holy War, within two decades of his death in 632 his followers had conquered and forcibly converted the people of the Middle East, including Persia, Syria, Palestine, and North Africa, including Egypt, Algiers, and Morocco. Between 652 and 733, these conquerors converted people in the islands of the Mediterranean including the Balearic Islands, Corsica, Sardinia, and Sicily and also much of southern Italy. The Muslims were successful in building an empire that included southern Europe, North and East Africa, and Asia as far east as India. Converted Moors in North Africa carried Islam into southern Europe through conquest and to West Africa through trade. The Moors pushed through southern Europe, including Portugal and Spain and across the Pyrenees Mountains into southwestern France, where in 733 they were halted by Charles Martel at the Battle of Tours and Poitiers. Through trade with West Africa across the Sahara Desert, the Moors also spread Islam to the West African kingdoms of Ghana, Mali, and Songhay. During southwestern Europe's occupation by the Moors, the inhabitants were exposed to the education, culture, and riches of these West African kingdoms. As Islam spread throughout North and West Africa, the Moors developed trading ties with these nations which significantly benefited Spain and Portugal. The Moors and West Africans regularly traded gold, ivory, and slaves, and many of these prized commodities easily found their way into Muslim-held Portugal, Spain, and western France. This is significant in that long after the Moors were driven out of Spain and Portugal, trade between these two countries and West Africa continued. In fact, Portugal and Spain emerged from Muslim rule as major European mercantile powers, expanding and developing new trade routes to Africa, Asia, and eventually the Americas. ■

MAP 5

North and West African Empires (900–1800)

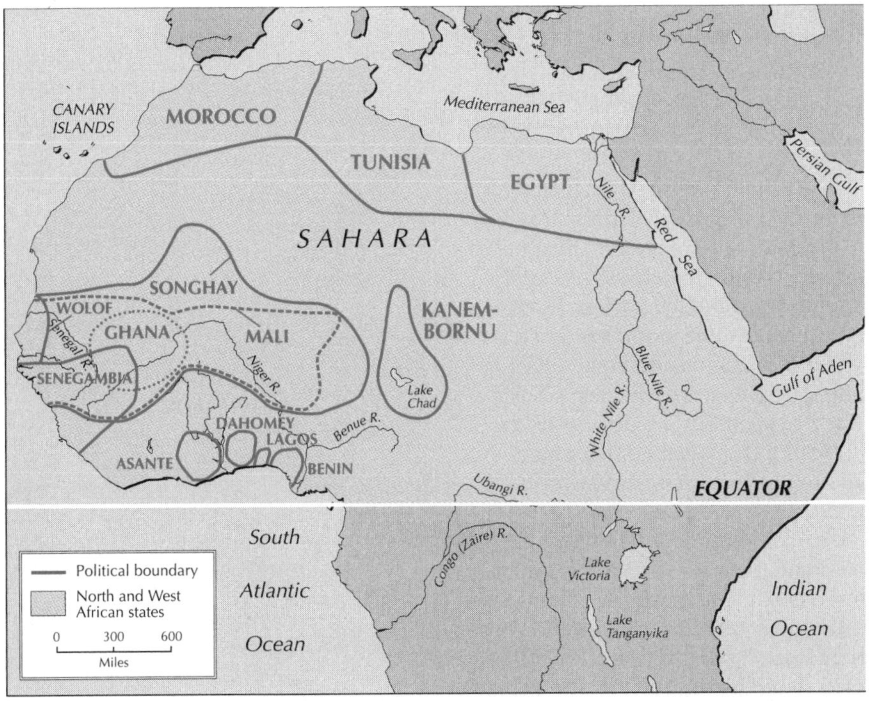
CANARY ISLANDS
MOROCCO
Mediterranean Sea
TUNISIA
EGYPT
Persian Gulf
Nile R.
SAHARA
Red Sea
SONGHAY
WOLOF
KANEM-BORNU
Senegal R.
GHANA
MALI
SENEGAMBIA
Niger R.
Lake Chad
Blue Nile R.
White Nile R.
Gulf of Aden
DAHOMEY
Benue R.
LAGOS
ASANTE
BENIN
Ubangi R.
EQUATOR
South Atlantic Ocean
Congo (Zaire) R.
Lake Victoria
Indian Ocean
Lake Tanganyika
Political boundary
North and West African states
0 300 600
Miles

During the medieval period, while the feudal system held sway in Europe, several great North and West African empires became major powers. In North Africa the empire of Morocco, controlled by the Almoravids, the empire of Algiers, controlled by the Almohads, and the Egyptian Empire, controlled by the Fatimids, dominated Southern Europe and the Mediterranean Sea. These three empires ruled North Africa unencumbered until their absorption from 1520 to 1566 by the Ottoman Empire. Since they all were Muslim states, they maintained military alliances with each other that enabled them to dominate the lucrative trade in gold, ivory, silks, and spices with Africa and the Orient. While the North Africans were thriving, several West African kingdoms rose and fell, beginning with the kingdom of Ghana around 900. In Ghana scholars practiced astronomy and developed advanced mathematics, and its leaders controlled one of Africa's most powerful militaries. The Ghanaian Empire, with its centralized government and strong economy, lasted for nearly 300 years (900 to 1200), until it was conquered by Mali. Ultimately, Mali created one of the world's richest and most advanced civilizations, from 1200 to 1450. Heavily involved in the trans-Saharan trade, Mali spread its wealth and influence throughout North Africa, Southern Europe, and the Middle East. Mansa-Musa, Mali's most famous leader, ruled that kingdom from 1312 to 1337. He is especially well known for his historic pilgrimage to Mecca in 1324. While on this pilgrimage, he visited many parts of his kingdom, as well as neighboring nations, including the lands of the Berbers and Egyptians and the great holy Arab cities of Mecca and Medina. In 1468, Mali was conquered by Sonni Ali and became part of the greatest West African kingdom, Songhay, which lasted from 1450 to 1800. Encompassing the territories of both Ghana and Mali, Songhay stretched throughout West Africa. It expanded the trans-Saharan trade and boasted one of the world's most renowned universities in Timbuktu. Songhay's decline as a major world power signaled the end of African independence and the rise of modern European nation-states as world powers. Several additional West African kingdoms that rose and fell during this period are also worth noting. They include Nok, Kanem, Bornu, Hausa, Asante, Ibo, Oyo, Dahomey, Lagos, Senegambia, Benin, Wolf, Yoruba, and Walata. ■

MAP 6

South and East African Empires (900–1800)

As with the West African empires, there were many East African empires that were quite impressive. Egypt was the oldest and greatest of these early civilizations. In fact, ancient Egypt was one of four of the world's oldest river valley civilizations (the other three being Mesopotamia, India, and China). The Egyptian Empire dates back to 3000 B.C. It saw three kingdoms rise and fall before the birth of Christ: the Old Kingdom, 3100 B.C. to 2100 B.C.; the Middle Kingdom, 2060 B.C. to 1785 B.C.; and the New Kingdom, 1580 B.C. to 1085 B.C. The towering pyramids of modern Egypt are a testament to the extraordinary skill of these early Egyptians. Until its conquest by the Romans in 100 B.C., Egypt stood alone as the master of the Mediterranean and the Middle East. South of Egypt was the kingdom of Nubia, which stretched from Egypt's borders to the borders of Ethiopia. Nubia and Ethiopia not only controlled a lucrative trade with the Mediterranean and the Middle East, but were among the first African nations to convert to Christianity. A myriad of city-states and nations dotted the East African coast: Somalia, Zanj or Zanzibar, Tanganyika, Katanga, Kiteve, Monomatapa, Marave, Cheva, Buvuma, Buganda, Rwanda, and Ankole. In South Africa a number of great kingdoms also rose and fell from 900 to 1800, including the Congo, the Zulu, the Khoisan, and Great Zimbabwe. Great Zimbabwe is perhaps the best known of these South African kingdoms. Rising around the year 900, this remarkable and nearly lost kingdom was built on the gold trade between East Africa, the Middle East, and Asia. Much of the gold that found its way into the Middle East and Mediterranean during this period originated in Great Zimbabwe. ■

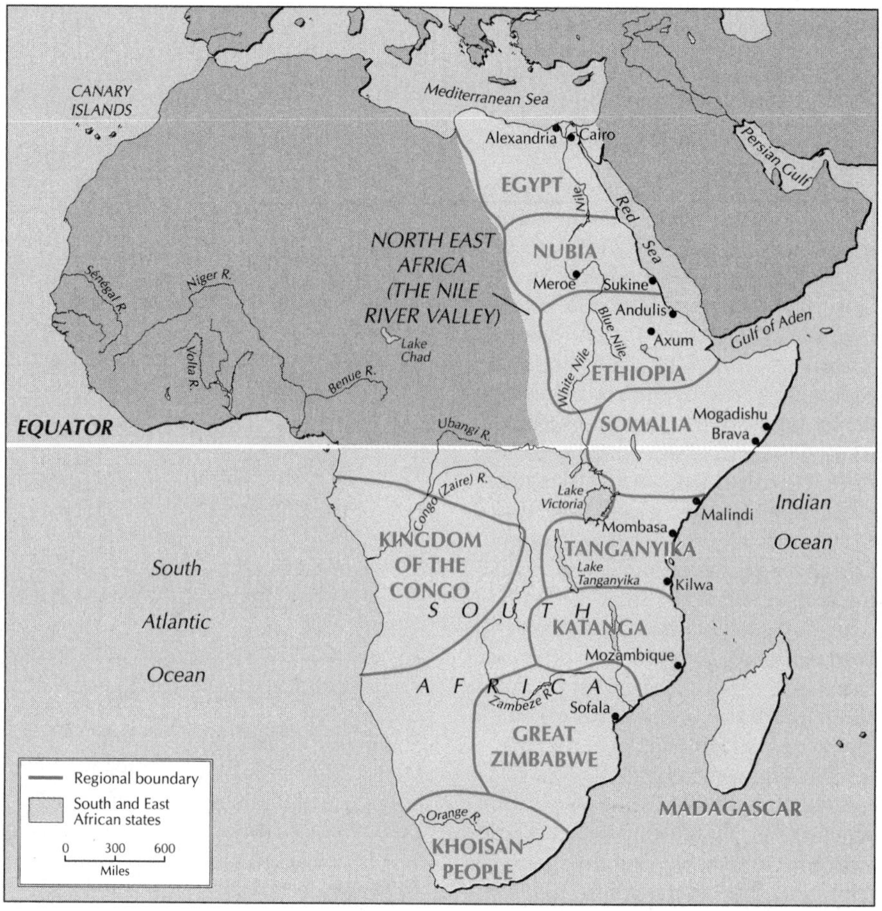
CANARY ISLANDS
Mediterranean Sea
Alexandria
Cairo
Persian Gulf
EGYPT
Nile
Red Sea
NORTH EAST AFRICA (THE NILE RIVER VALLEY)
NUBIA
Meroe
Sukine
Andulis
Axum
Gulf of Aden
Sénégal R.
Niger R.
Volta R.
Benue R.
Lake Chad
Blue Nile
White Nile
ETHIOPIA
SOMALIA
Mogadishu
Brava
EQUATOR
Ubangi R.
Congo (Zaire) R.
Lake Victoria
Mombasa
Malindi
Indian Ocean
KINGDOM OF THE CONGO
TANGANYIKA
Lake Tanganyika
Kilwa
South Atlantic Ocean
SOUTH AFRICA
KATANGA
Mozambique
Zambeze R.
Sofala
GREAT ZIMBABWE
MADAGASCAR
Orange R.
KHOISAN PEOPLE
Regional boundary
South and East African states
0 300 600
Miles

MAP 7

The Trans-Saharan Slave Trade (900–1500)

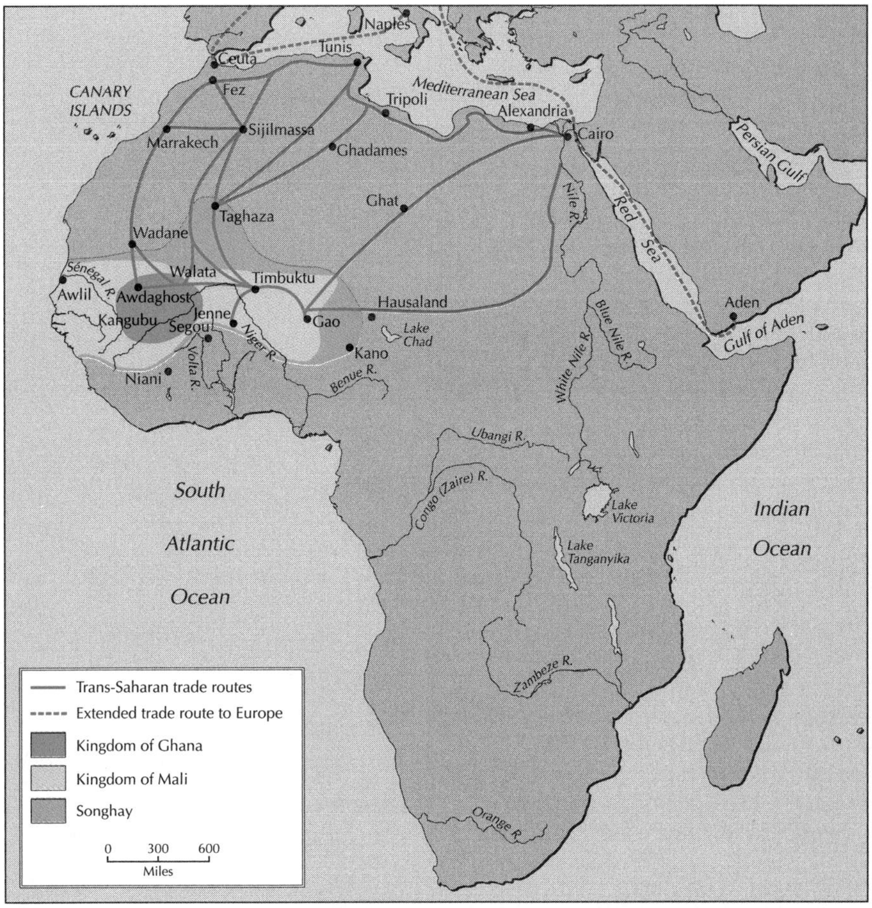
Naples
Tunis
Ceuta
Fez
CANARY ISLANDS
Mediterranean Sea
Tripoli
Alexandria
Cairo
Sijilmassa
Marrakech
Ghadames
Persian Gulf
Nile R.
Red Sea
Ghat
Taghaza
Wadane
Walata
Timbuktu
Sénégal R.
Awlil
Awdaghost
Kangubu
Jenne
Segou
Hausaland
Gao
Lake Chad
Kano
Niger R.
Volta R.
Niani
Benue R.
White Nile R.
Blue Nile R.
Aden
Gulf of Aden
Ubangi R.
South Atlantic Ocean
Congo (Zaire) R.
Lake Victoria
Lake Tanganyika
Indian Ocean
Zambeze R.
Orange R.
Trans-Saharan trade routes
Extended trade route to Europe
Kingdom of Ghana
Kingdom of Mali
Songhay
0 300 600
Miles

During the fifth century, the North African Berbers used the camel and saddle to dominate the Sahara Desert and control several lucrative trade routes from southern Europe and North Africa to West Africa. The Berbers controlled these routes from 700 to 900. This lucrative network of trade routes economically connected the Mediterranean coast, Southern Europe, the Middle East, and Asia to West Africa. There were four major routes: (1) the Morocco to Ghana-Mali-Songhay route, which ran from Fez to Awdaghost, Walata, Timbuktu, and Gao, with routine stops for water at Sijilmassa and Taghaza; (2) the Algeria to Ghana-Mali-Songhay route, which began at Sijilmassa and ended at Timbuktu, with a stop at Taghaza on the return trip; (3) the Egypt to Bornu route, which started at Cairo and ended at Lake Chad, with stops at Ghat, Agades, and Takedda; and (4) the Axum to Bornu route, which originated in East Africa, went through the Middle East (Persia) and Asia (India), and also included a route west to Lake Chad. On these trade routes merchants carried silk, cotton, cloth, beads, mirrors, dates, and salt to West Africa. In return, they received gold, ivory, gum, kola nuts, and slaves. Eventually, slaves became West Africa's major export (along with gold). The trans-Saharan trade eventually became the trans-Saharan slave trade and lasted from 650 to 1500. As many as 4 million West African slaves were sold to North Africa, Morocco, Egypt, Southern Europe (Portugal, Spain), the Middle East (Persia), and Southwestern Asia (India). The trans-Saharan slave trade impacted West Africa in three major ways: It stimulated gold mining, expanded the search for additional slaves, and fostered new economic growth in many West African cities engaged in the trade. ■

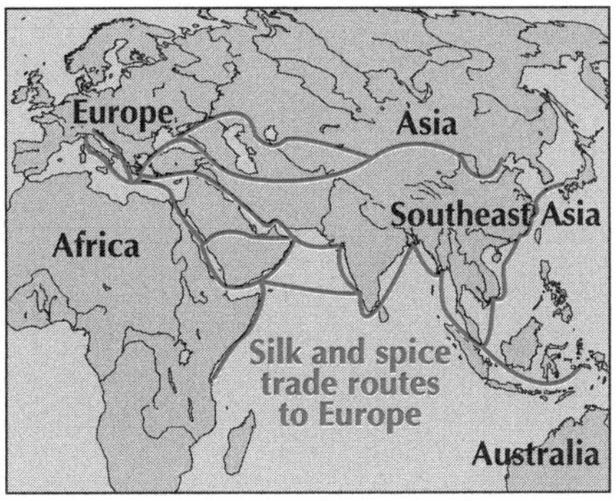
Europe
Asia
Southeast Asia
Africa
Silk and spice trade routes to Europe
Australia

MAP 8

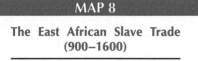

The East African Slave Trade (900–1600)

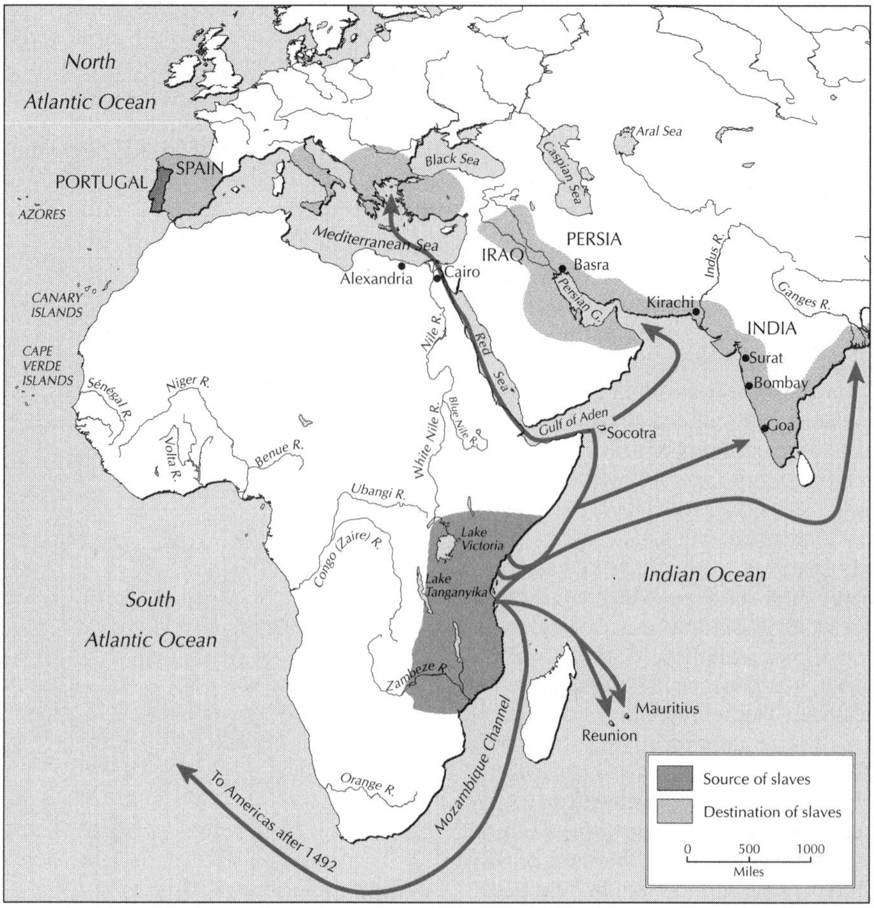
North
Atlantic Ocean
PORTUGAL
SPAIN
AZORES
Black Sea
Aral Sea
Caspian Sea
Mediterranean Sea
Alexandria
Cairo
IRAQ
PERSIA
Basra
Persian G.
Indus R.
Ganges R.
Kirachi
INDIA
Surat
Bombay
Goa
CANARY ISLANDS
CAPE VERDE ISLANDS
Sénégal R.
Niger R.
Volta R.
Benue R.
Nile R.
Red Sea
White Nile R.
Blue Nile R.
Gulf of Aden
Socotra
Ubangi R.
Congo (Zaire) R.
Lake Victoria
Lake Tanganyika
Indian Ocean
South
Atlantic Ocean
Zambeze R.
Mauritius
Reunion
Mozambique Channel
Orange R.
To Americas after 1492
Source of slaves
Destination of slaves
0 500 1000
Miles

While the trans-Saharan slave trade was thriving in North and West Africa, the East African slave trade was also doing a lucrative business. This trade took place between East Africa, the Middle East, and Asia. East African slaves were traded as far east as Malaysia and Indonesia. Slaves were traded for silk and spices as well as for gold and silver. Asians also traveled to Africa along the same trade routes and established settlements on the east coast of Africa and the island of Madagascar. Today Madagascar has a population of mixed peoples who are descendants of African, Asian, and Arab settlers who traded on this island during the East African slave trade. Nearly 2 million Africans were taken from East Africa during this limited but profitable trade. East African slaves were also traded to Persia, Egypt, Arabia, and India. By 1500, the Portuguese established ports on the African coast from Cape Bojador, in North West Africa, to Axum, in North East Africa. After 1500 the Portuguese also began trading East African slaves, whom they sold to the Spanish in the Americas, particularly in Brazil to Portuguese colonists, Argentina, and Uruguay, instead of the traditional markets in Asia and the Middle East. The East African slave trade persisted well into the eighteenth century. ■

MAP 9

Africans in the Caribbean and Central America Before Christopher Columbus

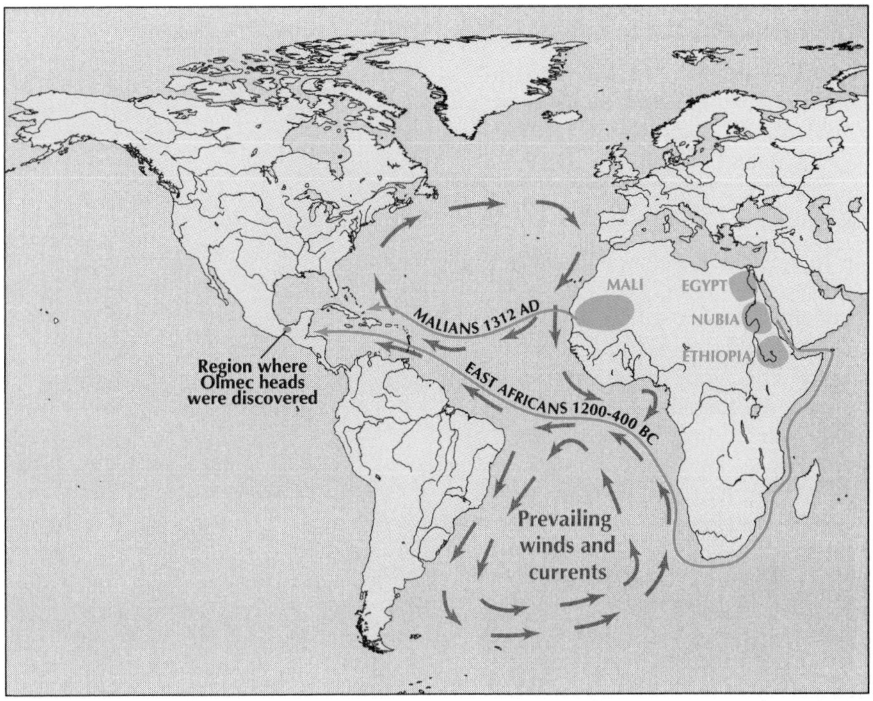
MALIANS 1312 AD
MALI
EGYPT
NUBIA
ETHIOPIA
Region where Olmec heads were discovered
EAST AFRICANS 1200-400 BC
Prevailing winds and currents

The Spanish were not the first explorers to establish contact with the indigenous populations of the Caribbean and Central America. Many scholars have argued that when Columbus reached the Americas in 1492, Africans were already there. Harvard professor Leo Wiener in his book *Africa and the Discovery of America,* published in 1920, was one of the first to put forth this argument. His position has subsequently been supported by a number of noted scholars, including Ivan Van Sertima, Cheikh Anta Diop, and Michael Bradley. Columbus's own logs along with archeological evidence have strongly reinforced the contention that Africans had explored and traded with people in the Americas long before the Spanish. Columbus noted that when he established communication with the natives, they indicated that the Spanish had arrived from the south, while the Africans who preceded them arrived from the southeast. Furthermore, Columbus and his crew reported that when they arrived in the Americas, they found Africans already there. They also reported that on their arrival on Hispaniola, ports had already been established. Finally, Columbus wrote in his journal that while on his third voyage to the Americas, he observed a ship loaded with goods leaving the coast of Guinea and headed west in the direction of the Americas. West African records also document efforts of Africans to cross the Atlantic and trade with the Americas. Arabic documents reveal that Abu Bakari II, the king of Mali from 1305 to 1312, sent two expeditions across the Atlantic. The first expedition consisted of more than 200 ships, only 3 of which returned. The second numbered over 2,000, led by Abu Bakari himself after relinquishing his throne to Mansa-Musa (who, as noted earlier, became one of Africa's greatest leaders). On this expedition, no ships returned. Archeological evidence supports the presence of East Africans even before the Malian expeditions. According to the evidence, Central American civilization was heavily influenced by East African Olmec culture, specifically from Ethiopia, Kemet, or Meroë. It is believed that one or more of these civilizations crossed the Atlantic between 1200 and 400 B.C. Upon arriving in Central America these early explorers significantly altered the developing Central American cultures of the Maya, Teotihuacán, Monte Albán, and Aztecs by introducing these Native Americans to the technology used to erect their pyramids, Olmec heads, and

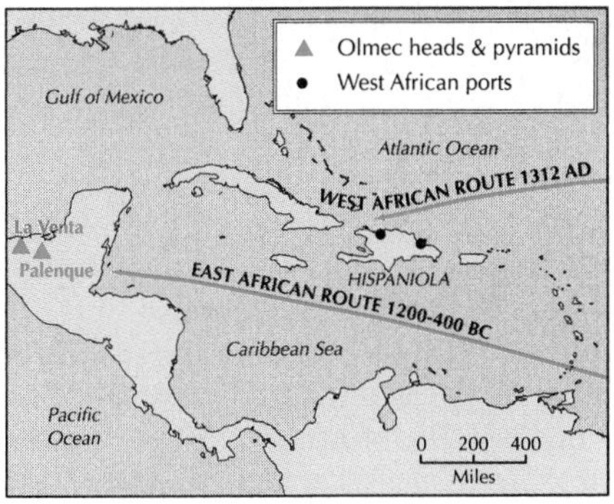
Olmec heads & pyramids
West African ports
Gulf of Mexico
Atlantic Ocean
WEST AFRICAN ROUTE 1312 AD
La Venta
Palenque
EAST AFRICAN ROUTE 1200-400 BC
HISPANIOLA
Caribbean Sea
Pacific Ocean
0 200 400
Miles

hieroglyphics, which are similar in many ways to those of the Nile River Valley and the renowned East African empires of Egypt, Nubia, Ethiopia, Kemet, and Meroë. Further evidence can be seen in the faces carved into the Olmec heads, whose features are African rather than Native American and which date around 1200 to 400 B.C. ■

MAP 10

The Expulsion of the Moors from Portugal and Spain, and Portugal's Exploration of the African Coast (1393–1492)

In 1393 the Portuguese drove the North African Moors out of Portugal and united the Portuguese people to create the first modern European nation-state. Following their unification the Portuguese ushered in the Age of European Exploration and Colonization, when Prince Henry the Navigator opened his school to train seamen in 1400. Prince Henry's students from 1415 to 1474 would explore the Madeira Islands, Canary Islands, Azores, and Cape Verde Islands for Portugal. These students would also be responsible for exploring the west coast of Africa from Cape Bojador to Cape St. Catherine. The Portuguese, as would the Spanish in 1492, initiated their explorations in search of a more expeditious trade route to Asia. They were especially interested in the spices and silks of the Orient. From 1415 to 1498, the Portuguese slowly made their way down along the West African coast, founding trading ports as they went, and eventually reaching the Cape of Good Hope in 1493. From Good Hope, they sailed to Madagascar and up the East African coast to Axum, and then on to the Orient. Meanwhile in Spain, King Ferdinand of Aragon and Queen Isabella of Castille married to unite the peoples of Spain in 1479. In 1492, their combined armies defeated the Moors at Obo and drove them out of Spain. Soon thereafter, Queen Isabella and King Ferdinand issued an edict expelling all Muslims, Jews, and non-Christians from Spain. In late 1492, following this edict Columbus secured financing from Queen Isabella to find a quicker trade route to India. Instead of finding India, Columbus established contact with a continent previously unknown to Europeans which he claimed for Spain. ■

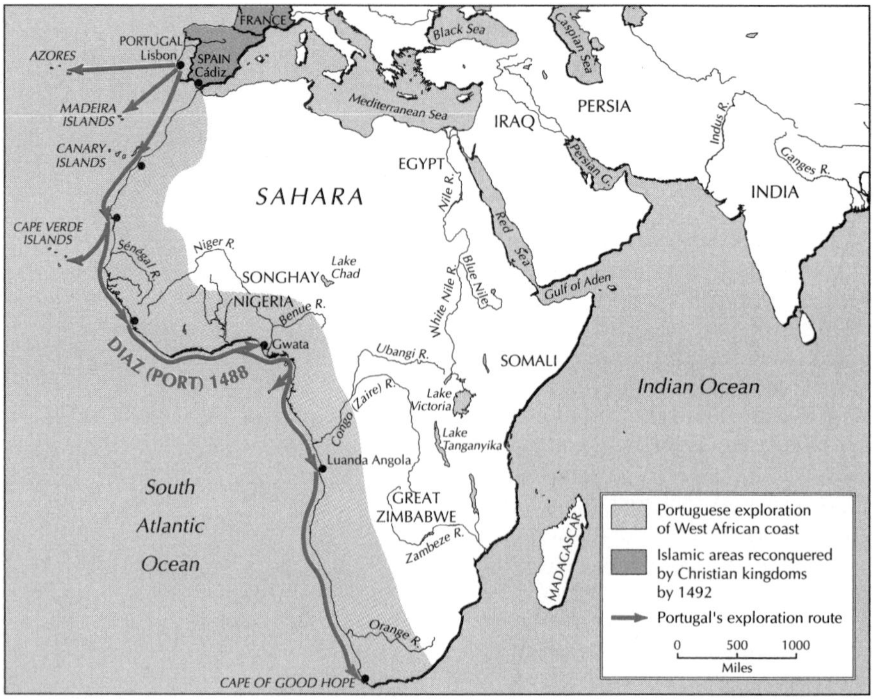
FRANCE
PORTUGAL
Lisbon
SPAIN
Cádiz
AZORES
MADEIRA ISLANDS
CANARY ISLANDS
CAPE VERDE ISLANDS
Black Sea
Caspian Sea
Mediterranean Sea
IRAQ
PERSIA
Persian G.
Indus R.
Ganges R.
INDIA
EGYPT
SAHARA
Nile R.
Red Sea
Niger R.
Sénégal R.
Lake Chad
SONGHAY
NIGERIA
Benue R.
Blue Nile
White Nile R.
Gulf of Aden
DIAZ (PORT) 1488
Gwata
Ubangi R.
SOMALI
Indian Ocean
Congo (Zaire) R.
Lake Victoria
Lake Tanganyika
Luanda Angola
South Atlantic Ocean
GREAT ZIMBABWE
Zambeze R.
MADAGASCAR
Orange R.
CAPE OF GOOD HOPE
Portuguese exploration of West African coast
Islamic areas reconquered by Christian kingdoms by 1492
Portugal's exploration route
0 500 1000
Miles

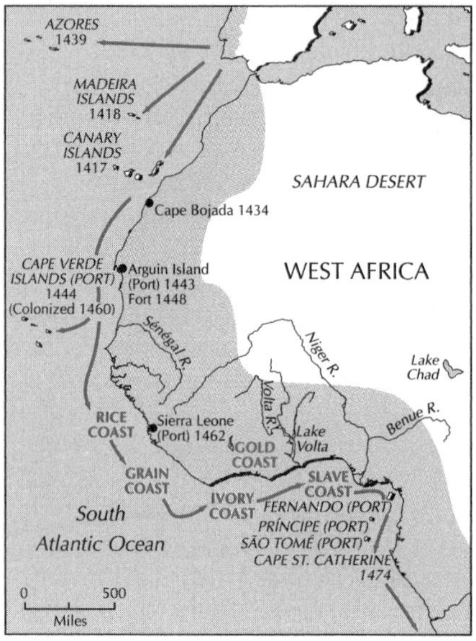
AZORES 1439
MADEIRA ISLANDS 1418
CANARY ISLANDS 1417
SAHARA DESERT
Cape Bojada 1434
CAPE VERDE ISLANDS (PORT) 1444 (Colonized 1460)
Arguin Island (Port) 1443 Fort 1448
WEST AFRICA
Sénégal R.
Niger R.
Lake Chad
Benue R.
Volta R.
Lake Volta
RICE COAST
Sierra Leone (Port) 1462
GOLD COAST
GRAIN COAST
SLAVE COAST
IVORY COAST
FERNANDO (PORT)
PRÍNCIPE (PORT)
SÃO TOMÉ (PORT)
CAPE ST. CATHERINE 1474
South Atlantic Ocean
0 500
Miles

MAP 11

The Role of Africans in the Exploration and Settlement of the Caribbean and the Americas (1492–1520)

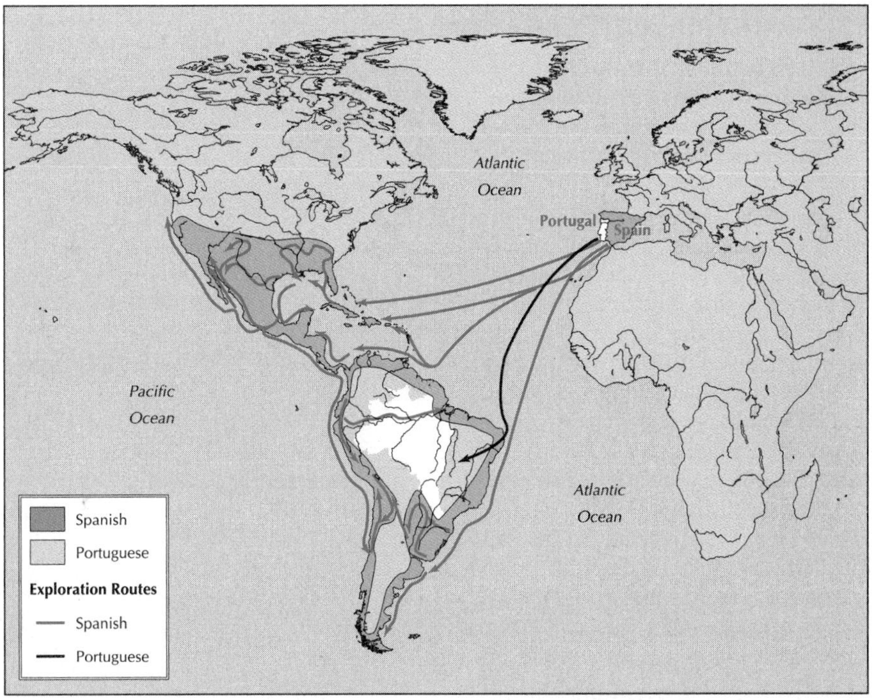
Atlantic Ocean
Portugal
Spain
Pacific Ocean
Atlantic Ocean
Spanish
Portuguese
Exploration Routes
Spanish
Portuguese

When Columbus arrived in the Bahamas on October 12, 1492, and anchored near the island of San Salvador, he immediately began to explore and catalog this unknown land for Spain. He first mapped the Bahamas, and through developing relations with the native peoples found out from them more about the Caribbean islands. He then moved along the southern and western coasts of Florida into the Gulf of Mexico. He also explored the rest of the Caribbean, including the Greater Antilles, Lesser Antilles (or Caribbees) and Central America. The islands Columbus mapped in the Greater Antilles are known as the Cayman Islands, Cuba, Jamaica, Puerto Rico, and Hispaniola (now Haiti and the Dominican Republic). The islands mapped in the Lesser Antilles included the Leeward Islands (the Virgin Islands, Saba, St. Christopher, Nevis, Antigua, and Barbuda), the Windward Islands (Martinique, St. Lucia, St. Vincent, Grenadines, and Grenada), Barbados, Trinidad, Tobago, and the Netherland Antilles (Aruba, Curacao, and Bonaire). When Columbus landed in the Bahamas in October of 1492, he was accompanied by an African, Pedro Alonso Niño, who helped him to navigate the Atlantic and explore these uncharted islands. Two years after Columbus's first voyage in 1494, the Spanish established their first permanent settlement on the island of Cuba. Among these early settlers were African soldiers and explorers, many of whom were from Spain and assisted the Spanish in exploring and conquering the native peoples of the Americas. Both because of the influence of the North African Muslims on Portugal and Spain from 733 to 1492 and because of the West African slave trade which the Portuguese had been conducting since 1441, Africans had become a well-established part of Portuguese and Spanish society by 1492. Some Africans had acquired wealth and fame, and even retained high-ranking positions in the Portuguese and Spanish governments and military. As a result, many of the first Africans who arrived in the Americas from Spain were soldiers, explorers, and sailors. A sizable number of the conquistadors who conquered the Aztecs, Mayas, Incas, and the Southwestern Indians were also African. When Vasco Nuñez de Balboa discovered the Pacific Ocean in 1513, he was aided by Nuflo de Olano, an African, who played an important role in the expedition. Africans were both explorers and conquistadors, traveling with such well-known Spanish adventurers as Cortés, Valas, Alvardo, Pizarro, Almagro, Valdivia, Alarcon, Coronado, Narváez, and Cabeza de Vaca, as they explored and conquered the Americas. Among the most famous of these Africans was an explorer named Little Stephen ("Estevanico"). Little Stephen

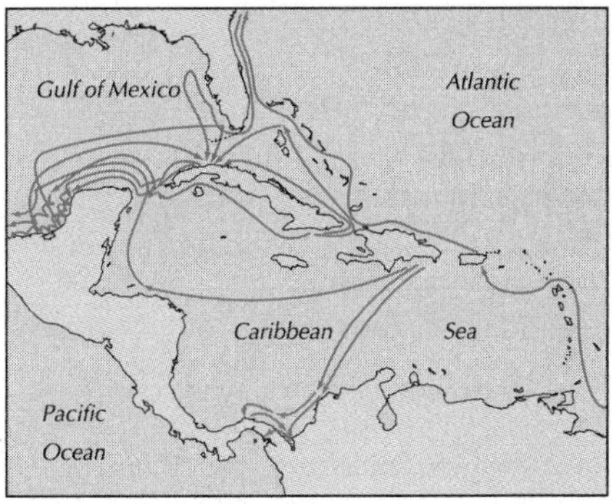
Gulf of Mexico
Atlantic Ocean
Caribbean
Sea
Pacific Ocean

was responsible for exploring present-day Florida, Mississippi, Alabama, Texas, New Mexico, and Arizona for the Spanish before he was killed by the Indians, who inhabited the Arizona territory. Thus, the Spanish, with the assistance of Africans, became the first Europeans to explore and colonize the Americas. By 1502 these early Africans would be joined by slaves who were imported into the Caribbean from West Africa to work on the sugar plantations of the Caribbean and Americas. ■

MAP 12

The Treaty of Tordesillas: The Line of Demarcation between Portugal and Spain (1494)

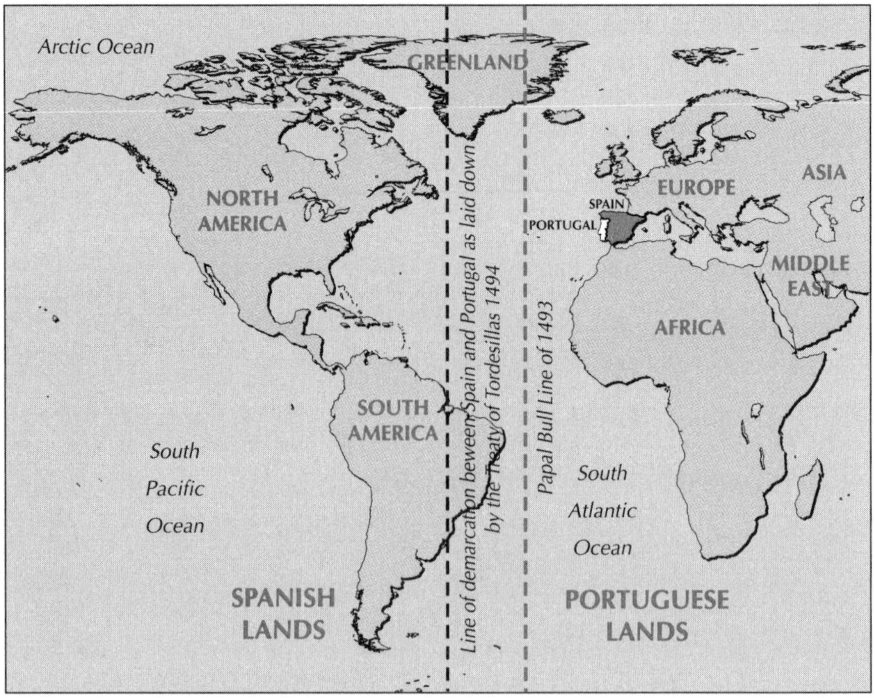
Arctic Ocean
GREENLAND
NORTH AMERICA
EUROPE
ASIA
SPAIN
PORTUGAL
MIDDLE EAST
AFRICA
SOUTH AMERICA
South Pacific Ocean
South Atlantic Ocean
Line of demarcation between Spain and Portugal as laid down by the Treaty of Tordesillas 1494
Papal Bull Line of 1493
SPANISH LANDS
PORTUGUESE LANDS

When the Portuguese became aware of Columbus's contact with the Americas they began to demand access to this uncharted region. The Spanish refused; and it appeared that these two nations, the most powerful in the world at the time, were poised to go to war with each other. To prevent war between these two Catholic states, Pope Alexander VI in 1493 issued a proclamation creating the "Line of Demarcation" between lands explored and claimed by Spain in the Americas and those explored and claimed by Portugal. Unhappy with the original decree, Portugal negotiated with Spain for more favorable terms. As a result Spain and Portugal signed the Treaty of Tordesillas in 1494. This treaty basically divided the world into halves. Under the treaty the Americas, with the exception of present-day Brazil, were given to Spain, while Africa, Asia, and Brazil were consigned to Portugal. This treaty is important for two reasons. First, it gave the vast lands of the Americas to the Spanish to explore and plunder. Second, by giving Africa to Portugal, the Portuguese gained control over the African slave trade and all other trade with the continent. Thus as a result of this treaty, the Portuguese held the exclusive right to export slaves to the Spanish colonies in the Americas. As Spain expanded its settlements in the Caribbean and the Americas, the need for slave labor multiplied. Thus, the Portuguese reaped huge profits from their trade in human flesh. Their dominance over the slave trade was soon challenged, however, by other European nations that were emerging out of the Dark Ages as newly unified nation-states, including France, England, the Netherlands, Denmark, and Sweden. ■

MAP 13

Slave Revolts and Maroon Communities in the Spanish and Portuguese Colonies of the Caribbean and the Americas (1502–1600)

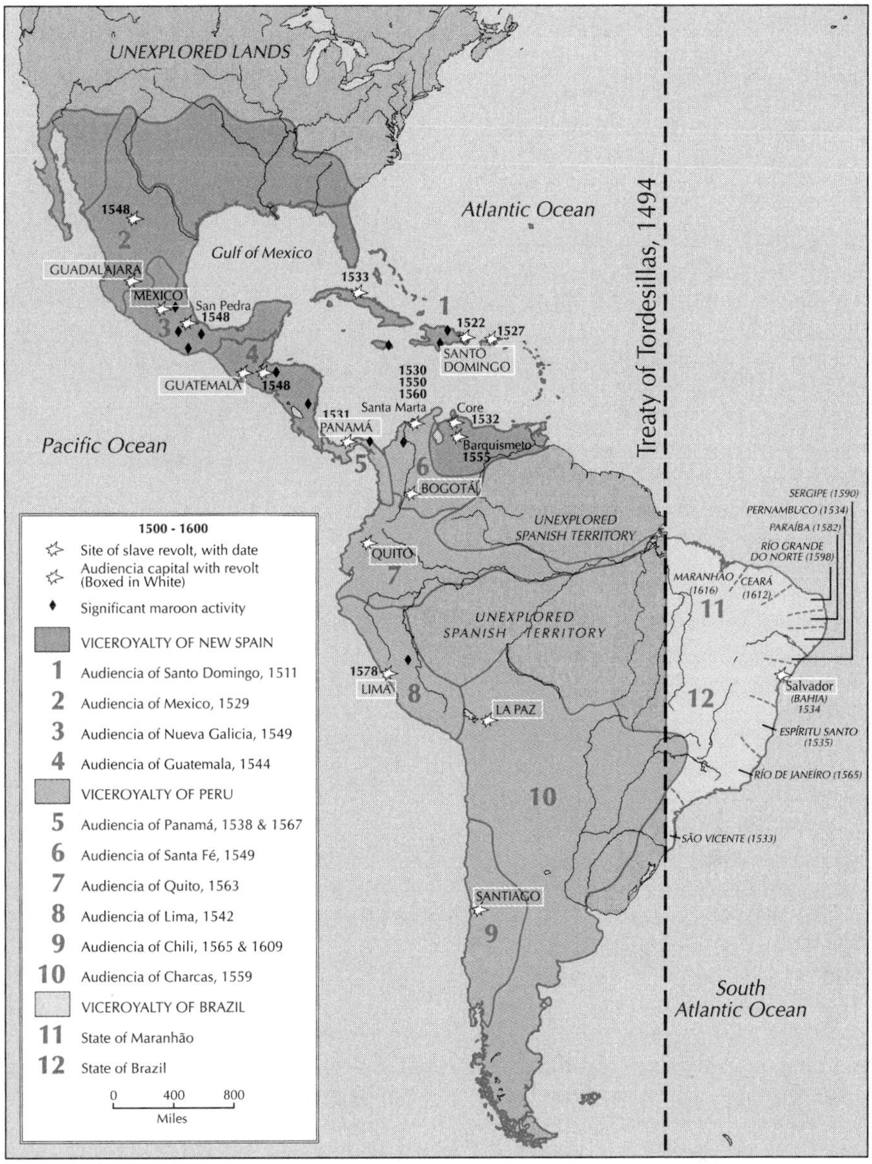
UNEXPLORED LANDS
Atlantic Ocean
Gulf of Mexico
Pacific Ocean
Treaty of Tordesillas, 1494
1548
GUADALAJARA
MEXICO
San Pedra 1548
GUATEMALA
1548
1533
1522
1527
SANTO DOMINGO
1530
1550
1560
1531
Santa Marta
Core 1532
PANAMÁ
Barquisimeto 1555
BOGOTÁ
UNEXPLORED SPANISH TERRITORY
QUITO
UNEXPLORED SPANISH TERRITORY
1578
LIMA
LA PAZ
SANTIAGO
South Atlantic Ocean
SERGIPE (1590)
PERNAMBUCO (1534)
PARAÍBA (1582)
RÍO GRANDE DO NORTE (1598)
MARANHÃO (1616)
CEARÁ (1612)
Salvador (BAHIA) 1534
ESPÍRITU SANTO (1535)
RÍO DE JANEIRO (1565)
SÃO VICENTE (1533)
1500 - 1600
Site of slave revolt, with date
Audiencia capital with revolt (Boxed in White)
Significant maroon activity
VICEROYALTY OF NEW SPAIN
1 Audiencia of Santo Domingo, 1511
2 Audiencia of Mexico, 1529
3 Audiencia of Nueva Galicia, 1549
4 Audiencia of Guatemala, 1544
VICEROYALTY OF PERU
5 Audiencia of Panamá, 1538 & 1567
6 Audiencia of Santa Fé, 1549
7 Audiencia of Quito, 1563
8 Audiencia of Lima, 1542
9 Audiencia of Chili, 1565 & 1609
10 Audiencia of Charcas, 1559
VICEROYALTY OF BRAZIL
11 State of Maranhão
12 State of Brazil
0 400 800
Miles

The Spanish were the first Europeans to practice African slavery in the Americas. They would be followed by the Portuguese and eventually the Dutch, French, and English. At first, to satisfy their labor needs the Spanish enslaved the natives of the Caribbean islands and Central and South America, beginning in 1492. However, since the natives were not resistant to European diseases, they quickly perished from illnesses like smallpox; they also died from being overworked. In 1502, ten years after Columbus's landing, the first African slaves were brought to Cuba from West Africa to replace Indian slaves who were dying by the millions. In 1504, the Spanish began their first sugar plantations on Hispaniola. From that point on, countless Indian and African slaves were forced to grow and process sugar and its by-products. By the mid-1500s, the entire Caribbean, Central America, South America (except for Brazil), and the southern United States were settled by the Spanish and contained large Indian and African slave populations. Upon their arrival in the Americas, many slaves outwitted their overseers by escaping at their first opportunity. These runaway slaves created Indian and black or all-black communities, which became known as *maroon communities*. The first runaway, or maroon, was among the first shipment of African slaves brought to the Spanish colony of Hispaniola in 1502. This slave fled to the mountains, where he found refuge with the Indians who resided there. It can be inferred from this account that Africans never accepted the institution of slavery. From its earliest beginnings, they defied the practice of slavery by either revolting or escaping. Maroon communities were established throughout the Caribbean and the Americas, including Spanish America, Portuguese America, and, after 1600, the French Caribbean, British Caribbean, and United States. Some maroon communities were so well organized and defended that Europeans were forced to sign treaties with them granting their independence. The most powerful of these maroon states were in Cuba, Brazil, Colombia, Ecuador, Hispaniola, Jamaica, Mexico, Florida, the Great Dismal Swamp of North Carolina and Virginia, and Surinam. Blacks built their maroon communities in the swamps, mountains, and jungles. They chose these hostile and unproductive lands because they were virtually inaccessible to whites and because they were easier to defend from attacking whites. To defend themselves, the maroons laid deadly traps for whites and their dogs. They also developed armies, trained by escaped slaves with military experience, many of whom employed guerrilla tactics. The maroon armies proved extremely effective in repelling and defeating the European armies. In response to those successes, the Europeans often resorted to conscripting Indians and blacks—called "Rangers"— to defeat the maroon armies. These Rangers were used against the maroons in Brazil, Dominica, Guatemala, Guiana, Mexico, and the United States. The Rangers proved more adroit than their European counterparts, as they were better trackers than whites and were superb guerrilla fighters. Over fifty maroon communities were built in the United States and hundreds in South America and the Caribbean. Although many maroon communities were eventually destroyed, some existed into the twentieth century. ■

MAP 14

The Establishment of French, English, Dutch, and Swedish Colonies in the Americas and Caribbean (1600–1720)

As the rest of Europe became conscious of the riches the Spanish and Portuguese were reaping from the Americas, they began to race against each other to establish colonies there. Between 1580 and 1620 England, Holland, Sweden, and France would join Spain and Portugal in laying claim to land in the Americas. In 1587, for example, the English founded the colony of Roanoke in North Carolina, while the French established the colonies of Quebec and New Orleans in Canada and Louisiana, respectively. The Dutch founded New Netherlands in New York and northern New Jersey, and the Swedes followed suit in southern New Jersey and Delaware in founding New Sweden. By the mid-1600s, the European nations of France, England, Holland, Sweden, Spain, and Portugal shared control of the Americas. As soon as colonies were founded, the need for labor became apparent. The Spanish and Portuguese satisfied their labor needs with African slaves as early as 1502. The Dutch soon followed, as did the French and the English. During this period not only did the Europeans expand the institution of slavery in the Americas, but they also battled each other for control of the Americas, using slaves, maroons, and free blacks to assist their militaries in these wars for world domination. In fact, as Peter M. Volez points out in his work *Slave and Soldiers: The Military Impact of Blacks in the Colonial Americas,* both free and enslaved Africans were used by the Spanish and Portuguese to defend and protect their colonial possessions in the Americas during this period. As well, they were used by the Dutch, English, and French, who allied themselves with maroons, slaves, and free blacks, promising them weapons and freedom for fighting

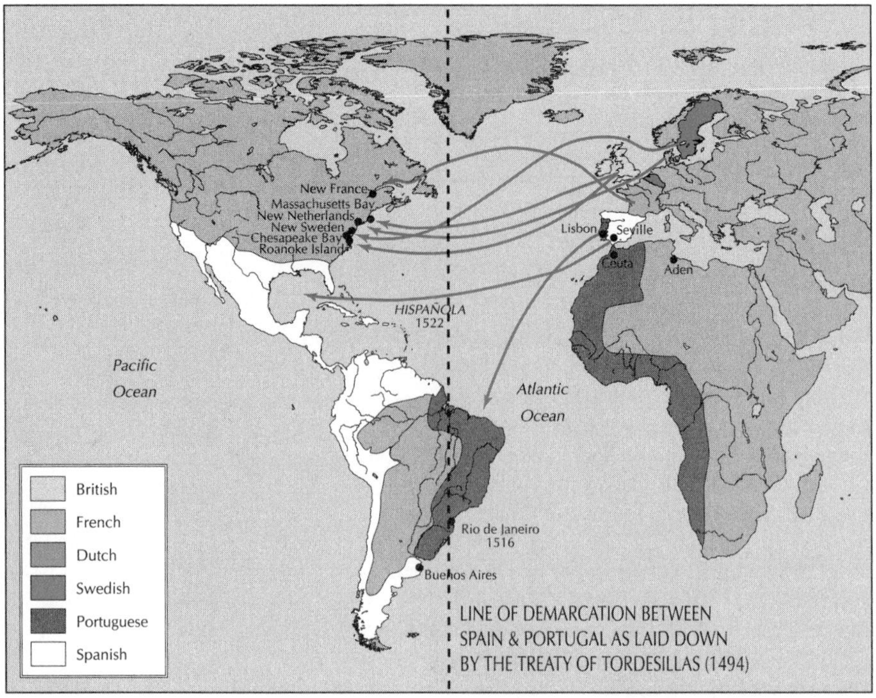

New France
Massachusetts Bay
New Netherlands
New Sweden
Chesapeake Bay
Roanoke Island
Lisbon
Seville
Ceuta
Aden
HISPAÑOLA
1522
Pacific Ocean
Atlantic Ocean
Rio de Janeiro
1516
Buenos Aires
British
French
Dutch
Swedish
Portuguese
Spanish
LINE OF DEMARCATION BETWEEN
SPAIN & PORTUGAL AS LAID DOWN
BY THE TREATY OF TORDESILLAS (1494)

against the Spanish and Portuguese. Throughout the colonial period thousands of maroons, slaves, and free blacks assisted in the defense and conquest of the Americas by the Europeans, battling for control of the Western Hemisphere, from 1492 to the late 1800s. Africans fought in Cuba, Peru, Brazil, New Amsterdam, Surinam, Bermuda, Panama, Virginia, Jamaica, St. Kitts, South Carolina, Louisiana, North Carolina, Nova Scotia, Argentina, and Venezuela. They continued to also be employed in Indian wars as well, two of the most notable being the Tuscarora War of 1711 and the Yamasee War of 1715 in North and South Carolina. When the British defeated the Spanish Armada in 1588, they acquired control of not only the sea, but also the sea trading routes. Soon, English settlements dotted the entire North American coast. The British began with two settlements, one in Massachusetts and the other in Virginia. Through conquest from 1624 to 1690 the British added the Dutch settlements of New York and northern New Jersey, and the once Swedish (then Dutch) settlements of Delaware and

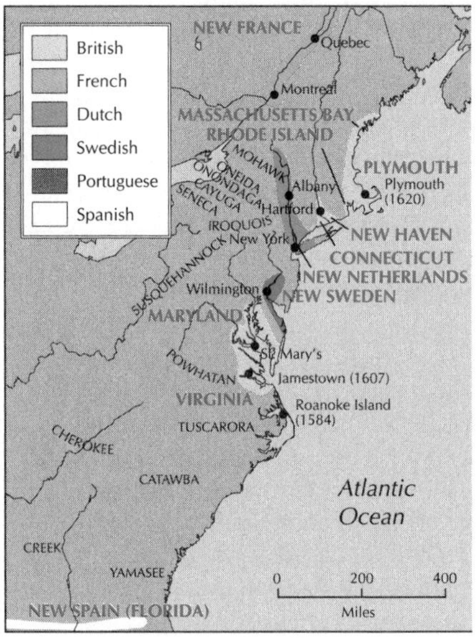

British
French
Dutch
Swedish
Portuguese
Spanish
NEW FRANCE
Quebec
Montreal
MASSACHUSETTS BAY
RHODE ISLAND
PLYMOUTH
Plymouth
(1620)
MOHAWK
ONEIDA
ONONDAGA
CAYUGA
SENECA
Albany
Hartford
IROQUOIS
New York
NEW HAVEN
CONNECTICUT
NEW NETHERLANDS
NEW SWEDEN
SUSQUEHANNOCK
Wilmington
MARYLAND
St. Mary's
POWHATAN
Jamestown (1607)
VIRGINIA
Roanoke Island
(1584)
TUSCARORA
CHEROKEE
CATAWBA
Atlantic Ocean
CREEK
YAMASEE
0
200
400
Miles
NEW SPAIN (FLORIDA)

southern New Jersey. The British also gained control of several Spanish islands in the Caribbean, along with Belize in Central America and Guyana in South America, and, following the French and Indian War from 1755 to 1763, became heir to the French settlement in Canada. ■

Map and Text Sources

1. Harris, Joseph E. *Africans and Their History.* New York: New American Library, 1987.
   Johanson, Donald, and Maitland Edey. *Lucy, The Beginnings of Human Kind.* New York: Simon & Schuster, 1990.
   Leakey, Louis. *Adam, or Ape: A Sourcebook of Discoveries about Early Man.* Cambridge, Mass.: Schenkman, 1982.
   Leakey, Richard E. *Human Origins.* London: Phoenix, 1996.
   Oxnard, Charles E. *Fossils, Teeth, and Sex: New Perspectives on Human Evolution.* Seattle: University of Washington Press, 1986.
   Snow, Dean R. *The Archaeology of North America.* Norman: University of Oklahoma Press, 1989.
   Wiedner, Donald L. *A History of Africa South of the Sahara.* New York: Random House, 1962.
2. Pritchard, J. M. *Africa: The Geography of a Changing Continent.* New York: Africana Publishing Corporation, 1971.
   Stamp, L. Dudley, and W. T. W. Morgan. *Africa: A Study in Tropical Development*, 3rd ed. New York: Wiley, 1972.
3. Bohannan, Paul, and Philip Curtin. *Africa and Africans.* Prospect Heights, IL: Waveland Press, 1995.
   Hiernaux, Jean. *The People of Africa.* New York: Scribner, 1975.
   Murdock, George P. *Africa: Its Peoples and Their Culture History.* New York: McGraw-Hill, 1984.
4. Donner, Fred. McGraw. *The Early Islamic Conquests.* Princeton, NJ: Princeton University Press, 1981.
   Kaegi, Walker E. *Byzantium and the Early Islamic Conquests.* Cambridge: Cambridge University Press, 1995.
   Lewis, Bernard. *The Muslim Discovery of Europe.* New York: Norton, 1982.
   Savage, Elizabeth. *A Gateway to Hell, a Gateway to Paradise: The North African Response to the Arab Conquest.* Princeton, NJ: Darwin Press, 1996.
5. Ajayi, J. F. Ade, and Ian Espie, eds. *A Thousand Years of West African History: A Handbook for Teachers and Students.* New York: Humanities Press, 1972.
   Harris, Joseph E. *Africans and Their History.* New York: New American Library, 1987.
   Oliver, Roland A. *The Dawn of African History*, 2nd ed. London: Oxford University Press, 1968.
6. Harris, Joseph E. *Africans and Their History.* New York: New American Library, 1987.
   Maxon, Robert M. *East Africa: An Introductory History*, 2nd ed. Morgantown: West Virginia University Press, 1994.
   Oliver, Roland A., *The Dawn of African History.* 2nd ed. London: Oxford University Press, 1968.
   Oliver, Roland A., and Gervase Mathew, eds. *History of East Africa*, vol. 1. Oxford: Clarendon Press, 1968.
   Oliver, Roland A., and Caroline Oliver, eds. *Africa in the Days of Exploration.* Englewood Cliffs, NJ: Prentice-Hall, 1965.
7. Bovill, Edward W. *The Golden Trade of the Moors*, 2nd ed. Princeton, NJ: Weiner Publishers, 1994.
   Bulliet, Richard W. *The Camel and the Wheel.* New York: Columbia University Press, 1990.
   Lewis, Bernard. *Race and Slavery in the Middle East: An Historical Enquiry.* New York: Oxford University Press, 1992.
   Manning, Patrick. *Slavery and African Life: Occidental, Oriental, and African Slave Trades.* Cambridge: Cambridge University Press, 1990.
8. Chittick, H. Neville, and Robert I. Rotberg. *East Africa and the Orient: Cultural Syntheses in Pre-Colonial Times.* New York: Africana Publishing Co., 1975.
   Manning, Patrick. *Slavery and African Life: Occidental, Oriental, and African Slave Trades.* Cambridge: Cambridge University Press, 1990.
   Oliver, Roland A. and Caroline Oliver, eds. *Africa in the Days of Exploration.* Englewood Cliffs, NJ: Prentice-Hall, 1965.
9. Bradley, Michael A. *The Columbus Conspiracy.* New York: A & B Books, 1992.
   Bradley, Michael A. *Dawn Voyage: The Black African Discovery of America.* New York: A & B Books, 1992.
   Diop, Cheikh Anta. *Precolonial Black Africa: A Comparative Study of the Political and Social Systems of Europe and Black Africa, from Antiquity to the Formation of Modern States.* Trenton, NJ: Africa World Press, 1987.
   Van Sertima, Ivan. *African Presence in Early America.* New Brunswick, NJ: Transaction Publishers, 1992.
   Van Sertima, Ivan. *They Came Before Columbus.* New York: Vintage Books, 1989.
   Wiener, Leo. *Africa and the Discovery of America.* New York: A & B Books, 1992.
10. Bitterli, Urs. *Cultures in Conflict: Encounters between European and Non-European Cultures, 1492–1800.* Cambridge: Polity, 1989.
    Lewis, Bernard. *Cultures in Conflict: Christians, Muslims, and Jews in the Age of Discovery.* New York: Oxford University Press, 1996.
    Oliver, Roland A. and Caroline Oliver, eds. *Africa in the Days of Exploration.* Englewood Cliffs, NJ: Prentice-Hall, 1965.
    Scammell, Geoffrey Vaughn. *The World Encompassed: The First European Maritime Empires, c. 800–1650.* London: Methuen, 1981.
    Thompson, Vincent Bakpetu. *The Making of the African Diaspora in the Americas, 1441–1900.* White Plains, NY: Longman, 1986.
    Vogt, John. *Portuguese Rule on the Gold Coast, 1469–1682.* Athens: University of Georgia Press, 1979.
11. Davis, Darien J. ed. *Slavery and Beyond: The African Impact on Latin America and the Caribbean.* Wilmington, DE: SR Books, 1995.
    Galloway, J. H. *The Sugar Cane Industry: An Historical Geography from Its Origins to 1914.* Cambridge: Cambridge University Press, 1989.
    Hoetink, H. *Slavery and Race Relations in the Americas: Comparative Notes on Their Nature and Nexus.* New York: Harper & Row, 1973.
    Mintz, Sidney Wilfred, and Richard Price. *An Anthropological Approach to the Afro-American Past: A Caribbean Perspective.* Philadelphia: Institute for the Study of Human Issues, 1976.
    Morison, Samuel Eliot. *The European Discovery of America, the Northern Voyages A.D. 500–1600.* New York: Oxford University Press, 1971.
    Morison, Samuel Eliot. *The European Discovery of America, the Southern Voyages A.D. 1492–1616.* New York: Oxford University Press, 1974.
    Price, Richard. *Ethnographic History, Caribbean Pasts.* College Park: University of Maryland, 1990.
    Toplin, Robert B. *Slavery and Race Relations in Latin America.* Westport, CT: Greenwood Press, 1974.
    Voelz, Peter M. *Slave and Soldier: The Military Impact of Blacks in the*

Colonial Americas. New York: Garland, 1993.

12. Catholic Church. *The Earliest Diplomatic Documents on America; the Papal Bulls of 1493 and the Treaty of Tordesillas*. Berlin: P. Gottschalk, 1927.

Dawson, Samuel E. *Lines of Demarcation of Pope Alexander VI and the Treaty of Tordesillas, A.D. 1493 and 1494*. Ottawa: J. Hope & Sons, 1899.

Harrisse, Henry. *The Diplomatic History of America: Its First Chapter 1452–1493–1494*. London: B. F. Stevens, 1897.

13. Burns, E. Bradford. *A History of Brazil*, 3rd ed. New York: Columbia University Press, 1993.

Bush, Barbara. *Slave Women in Caribbean Society, 1650–1838*. Bloomington: Indiana University Press, 1989.

Conrad, Robert E. *Childern of God's Fire: A Documentary History of Black Slavery in Brazil*. University Park: Pennsylvania State University Press, 1994.

Curtin, Philip D. *Latin America*. Morristown, NJ: Silver Burdett, 1970.

Genovese, Eugene D. *From Rebellion to Revolution: Afro-American Slave Revolts in the Making of the Modern World*. Baton Rouge: Louisiana State University Press, 1992.

Hine, Darlene Clark and David Barry Gaspar, editors. *More Than Chattel: Black Women and Slavery in the Americas*. Bloomington: Indiana University Press, 1996.

Klein, Herbert S. *African Slavery in Latin America and the Caribbean*. Oxford: Oxford University Press, 1994.

Mattoso, Katia M. de Queiros. *To Be a Slave in Brazil, 1550–1888*. New Brunswick, NJ: Rutgers University Press, 1986.

Mellafe, R. Rolando. *Negro Slavery in Latin America*. Berkeley: University of California Press, 1975.

Morner, Magnus. *Recent Research on Negro Slavery and Abolition in Latin America*. Pittsburgh: Center for Latin American Studies, University of Pittsburgh, 1979.

Okihiro, Gary Y., ed. *In Resistance: Studies in African, Caribbean and Afro-American History*. Amherst: University of Massachusetts Press, 1987.

Price, Richard. *Maroon Societies: Rebel Slave Communities in the Americas*. Baltimore: Johns Hopkins University Press, 1979.

Rout, L. B. *The African Experience in Spanish America*. New York: Cambridge University Press, 1977.

Voelz, Peter M. *Slave and Soldier: The Military Impact of Blacks in the Colonial Americas*. New York: Garland, 1993.

Weber, David J. *The Spanish Frontier in North America*. New Haven, CT: Yale University Press, 1992.

14. Morison, Samuel Eliot. *The European Discovery of America: the Northern Voyages A.D. 500–1600*. New York: Oxford University Press, 1971.

Morison, Samuel Eliot. *The European Discovery of America: the Southern Voyages A.D. 1492–1616*. New York: Oxford University Press, 1974.

Voelz, Peter M. *Slave and Soldier: The Military Impact of Blacks in the Colonial Americas*. New York: Garland, 1993.

MAP 15

The Trans-Atlantic Slave Trade and the European Nations Enriched by the Trade (1502–1888)

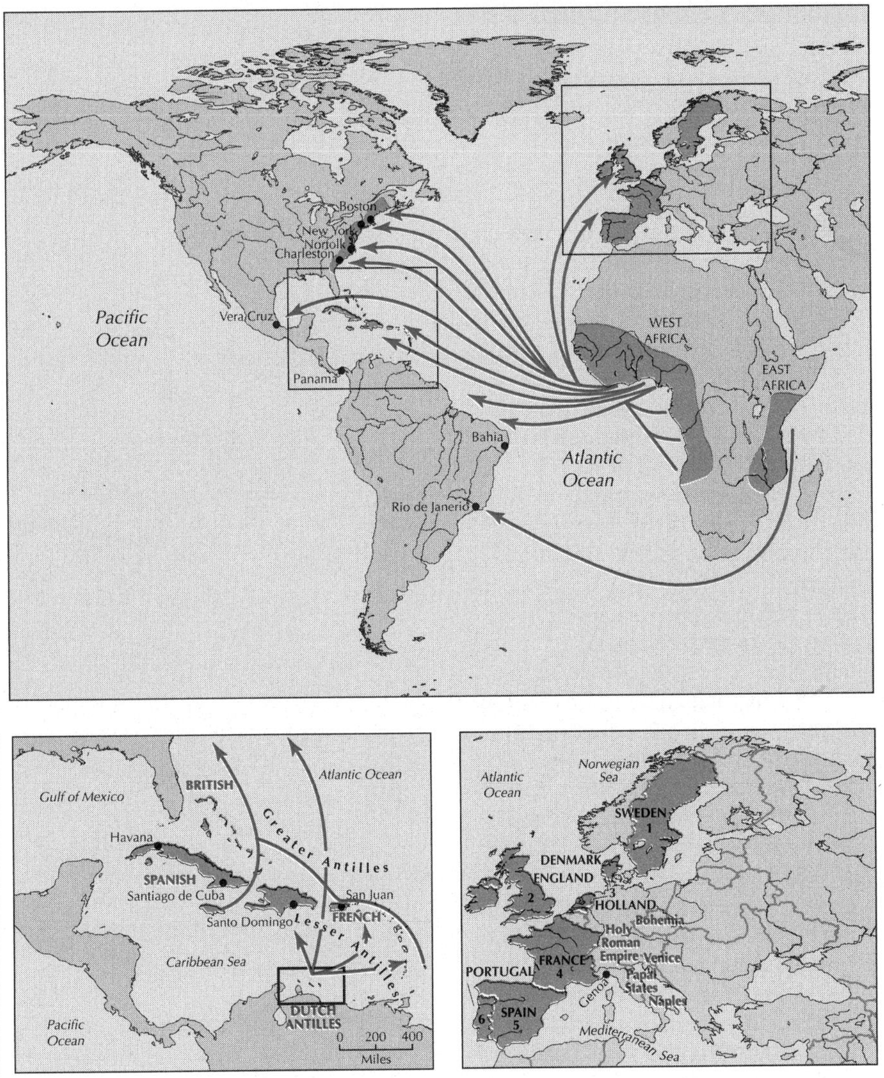
Boston
New York
Norfolk
Charleston
Pacific Ocean
Vera Cruz
Panama
WEST AFRICA
EAST AFRICA
Bahia
Atlantic Ocean
Rio de Janerio
Gulf of Mexico
BRITISH
Atlantic Ocean
Havana
Greater Antilles
SPANISH
Santiago de Cuba
San Juan
Santo Domingo
FRENCH
Lesser Antilles
Caribbean Sea
Pacific Ocean
DUTCH ANTILLES
0 200 400
Miles
Atlantic Ocean
Norwegian Sea
SWEDEN 1
DENMARK
ENGLAND
2
3
HOLLAND
Bohemia
Holy Roman Empire
Venice
PORTUGAL
FRANCE 4
Genoa
Papal States
Naples
6
SPAIN 5
Mediterranean Sea

The trans-Atlantic slave trade began in 1502 and lasted until 1888. During the period 1502–1620, most of the slaves were transported to the Spanish colonies in the Caribbean and South America and to the Portuguese colony of Brazil. In 1619, however, the English became acutely aware of this seemingly endless labor supply and began to import African slaves into their colonies. By the end of the slave trade, an estimated 9 million to 12 million Africans had been taken from their homeland, only to become forced laborers in the Americas. In what has become known as the "middle passage," an estimated 4 million slaves perished, never making it to the Americas. Of those slaves who were exported to the Americas from 1502 to 1810, 33 percent (approximately 2,451,000) went to Portuguese Brazil, 22.5 percent (approximately 1,664,700) to the British Caribbean, 20.3 percent (approximately 1,504,200) to the French Caribbean, 11.7 percent (approximately 871,000) to Spanish America, 6.7 percent (approximately 500,000) to the Dutch Caribbean, 5.4 percent (approximately 400,000) to British North America, and 0.4 percent (approximately 28,000) to the Danish Caribbean. Slavery practiced in the Caribbean and in North and South America by the Spanish, Portuguese, French, and Dutch requires special mention, however, due to the differences in the way slavery was practiced by these Europeans and by the British in the Caribbean and North America. Interestingly, the labor requirements and basic attitudes of the Spanish, Portuguese, French, and Dutch toward Africans paralleled those of the British in North America. However, in contrast to the British, these other Europeans often intermarried with their Africans and cared for the children they fathered by slaves, creating a mixed-blooded class of people including mulattos and mestizos and developing a social-economic system based on various shades of skin color. As a result, their society evolved very differently from that of British North America, most of which would become the United States. ■

MAP 16

The Trans-Atlantic Slave Trade and the West African Kingdoms Enriched by the Trade (1500–1800)

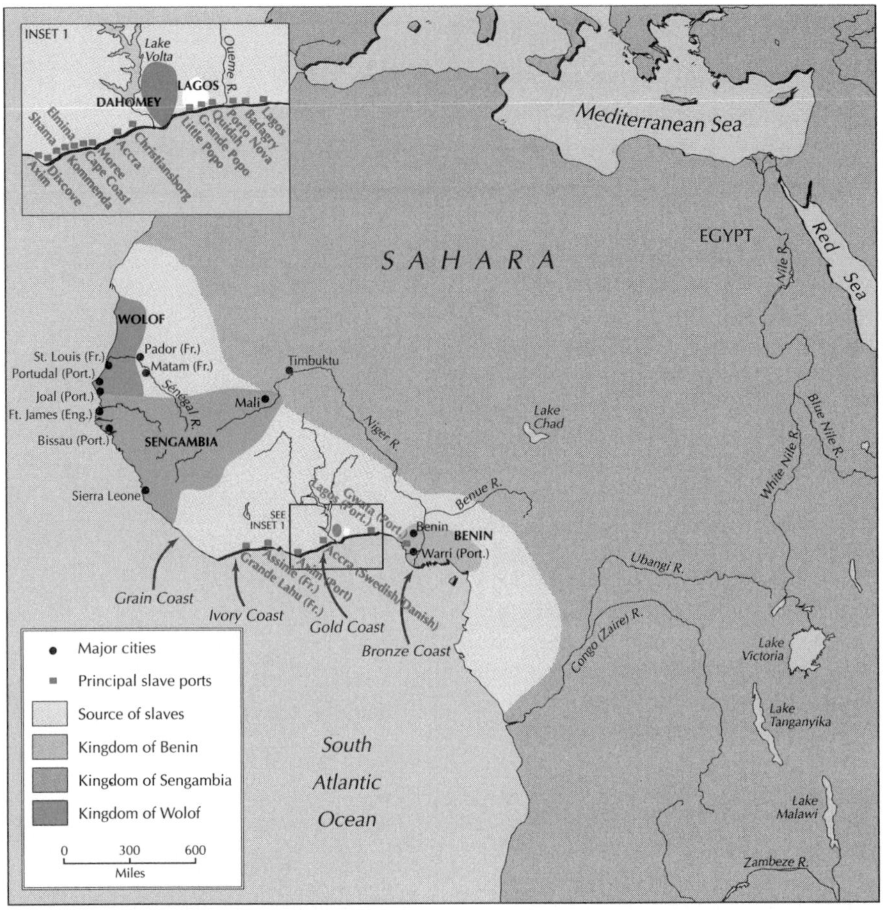
INSET 1
Lake Volta
LAGOS
DAHOMEY
Oueme R.
Elmina
Shama
Axim
Dixcove
Kommenda
Cape Coast
Morée
Accra
Christiansborg
Little Popo
Grande Popo
Ouidah
Porto Nova
Badagry
Lagos
Mediterranean Sea
EGYPT
Red Sea
SAHARA
Nile R.
WOLOF
St. Louis (Fr.)
Portudal (Port.)
Joal (Port.)
Ft. James (Eng.)
Bissau (Port.)
Pador (Fr.)
Matam (Fr.)
Senegal R.
Timbuktu
Mali
SENGAMBIA
Niger R.
Lake Chad
Blue Nile R.
White Nile R.
Sierra Leone
SEE INSET 1
Benue R.
Lagos (Port.)
Gwato (Port.)
Benin
BENIN
Warri (Port.)
Assinie (Fr.)
Grande Lahu (Fr.)
Axim (Port.)
Accra (Swedish/Danish)
Grain Coast
Ivory Coast
Gold Coast
Bronze Coast
Ubangi R.
Congo (Zaire) R.
Lake Victoria
Lake Tanganyika
Lake Malawi
Zambeze R.
South Atlantic Ocean
Major cities
Principal slave ports
Source of slaves
Kingdom of Benin
Kingdom of Sengambia
Kingdom of Wolof
0 300 600
Miles

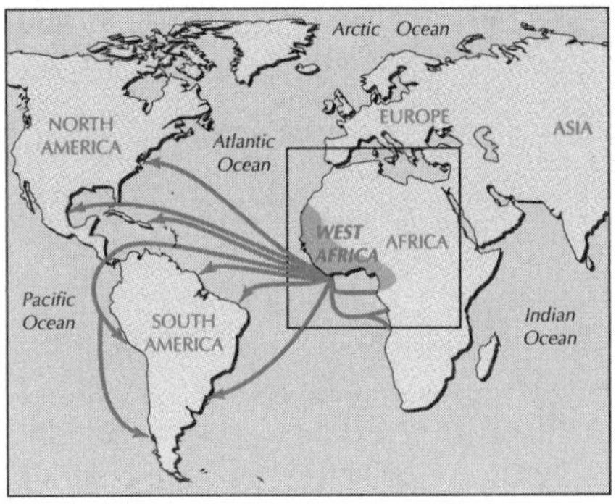
Arctic Ocean
NORTH AMERICA
EUROPE
ASIA
Atlantic Ocean
WEST AFRICA
AFRICA
Pacific Ocean
SOUTH AMERICA
Indian Ocean

By 1492, Portugal had developed a lucrative trade with West Africa that included the trading of slaves. As early as 1502, the Portuguese were shipping West African slaves to Spanish colonies in the Caribbean to work on sugar plantations. The trade continued to increase, and by the mid-1500s, thousands of slaves were being sold to cultivate the large sugar plantations and to fill the other labor needs in the Americas and the Caribbean. By the late 1600s millions of slaves were being used to grow sugar cane in the Caribbean; cultivate coffee and mine gold and silver in South America; run haciendas in Mexico; cultivate rice, indigo, and tobacco in North America; and act as servants and skilled and unskilled laborers throughout the Western Hemisphere. As the trade in slaves mushroomed, the coastal nations of Senegambia, Benin, and Wolof profited and grew by creating a sophisticated slave-gathering system from the interior regions of Africa and by establishing major slave ports. Two other slaving nations that grew and prospered in West Africa were Dahomey and Lagos. These two nations were made up of former Brazilian slaves who were freed and who returned to Africa to become slave traders. ■

MAP 17

Slave Revolts and the Maroon Communities in the Caribbean and the Americas (1600–1700)

Although slavery flourished in the Americas for more than 300 years, it was not without incident and cost. As of the preceding 100 years, /as not expanded without oppo- ɹring the period 1600–1700, North America, South America, and the Caribbean were sites of several major slave revolts, which caused tremendous loss of property and life. One of the most successful of these revolts occurred in Brazil, where the Africans were not only able to win their freedom, but also to create the African state of Palmares in 1630. Although most of the other insurrections were not as successful, they did demonstrate Africans' hatred of their servitude and their willingness to risk their lives rather than submit to slavery. These insurrections created widespread fear among the colonists, regardless of the European nation(s) involved. As a result of these rebellions, slave codes, which existed in all of the slaveholding colonies, were strengthened and harsh treatment of slaves increased. Even so, slaves continued to flee and establish or join maroon communities in the mountains, swamps, and forests of the Americas and the Caribbean. Many were also taken in by friendly Native Americans who intermarried with them and accepted them as members of their nations; in some cases Africans and their descendants rose to become warriors, chiefs, and even great shamans. ■

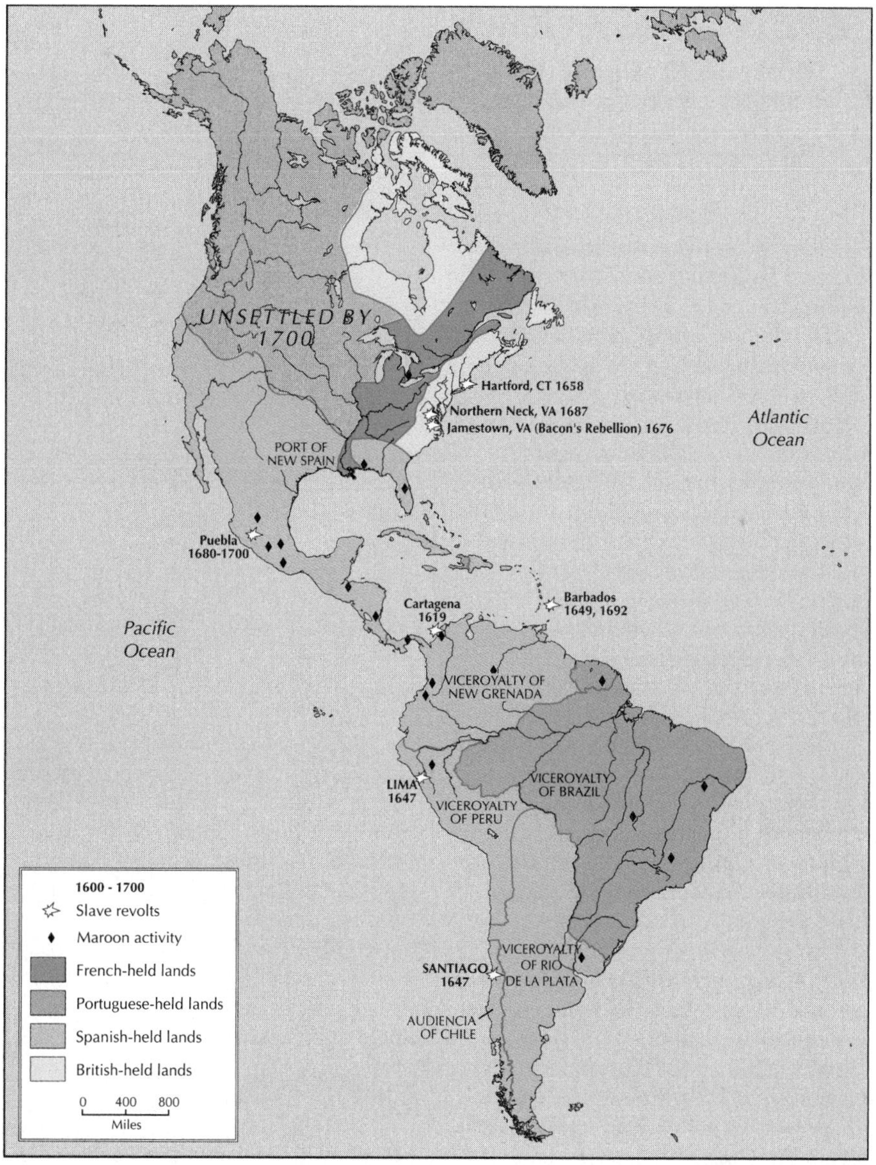
UNSETTLED BY 1700
Hartford, CT 1658
Northern Neck, VA 1687
Jamestown, VA (Bacon's Rebellion) 1676
Atlantic Ocean
PORT OF NEW SPAIN
Puebla 1680-1700
Pacific Ocean
Cartagena 1619
Barbados 1649, 1692
VICEROYALTY OF NEW GRENADA
VICEROYALTY OF BRAZIL
LIMA 1647
VICEROYALTY OF PERU
SANTIAGO 1647
VICEROYALTY OF RIO DE LA PLATA
AUDIENCIA OF CHILE
1600 - 1700
Slave revolts
Maroon activity
French-held lands
Portuguese-held lands
Spanish-held lands
British-held lands
0 400 800
Miles

MAP 18

Territorial and Political Changes in North America and the Caribbean (1600–1700)

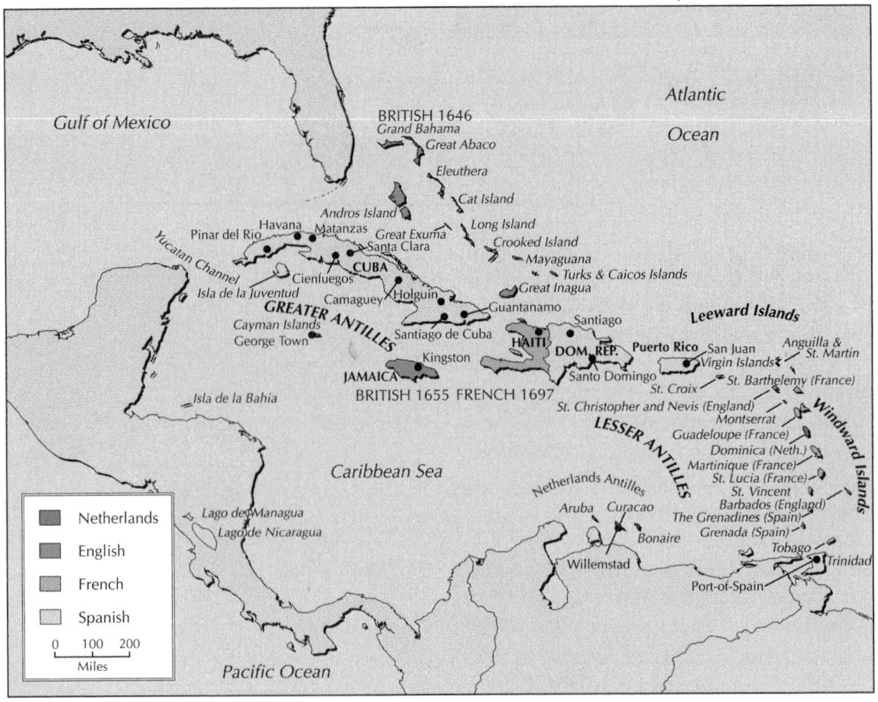
Gulf of Mexico
Atlantic Ocean
BRITISH 1646
Grand Bahama
Great Abaco
Eleuthera
Cat Island
Andros Island
Long Island
Crooked Island
Mayaguana
Turks & Caicos Islands
Great Inagua
Havana
Matanzas
Pinar del Rio
Great Exuma
Santa Clara
Yucatan Channel
Cienfuegos
CUBA
Isla de la Juventud
Camaguey
Holguin
Guantanamo
GREATER ANTILLES
Cayman Islands
George Town
Santiago de Cuba
Santiago
Leeward Islands
HAITI
DOM. REP.
Puerto Rico
San Juan
Virgin Islands
Anguilla & St. Martin
Kingston
JAMAICA
BRITISH 1655 FRENCH 1697
Santo Domingo
St. Croix
St. Barthelemy (France)
Isla de la Bahia
St. Christopher and Nevis (England)
Montserrat
LESSER ANTILLES
Guadeloupe (France)
Dominica (Neth.)
Windward Islands
Caribbean Sea
Martinique (France)
St. Lucia (France)
St. Vincent
Netherlands Antilles
Barbados (England)
Aruba
Curacao
The Grenadines (Spain)
Bonaire
Grenada (Spain)
Lago de Managua
Lago de Nicaragua
Tobago
Trinidad
Willemstad
Port-of-Spain
Netherlands
English
French
Spanish
0 100 200
Miles
Pacific Ocean

As a result of the English Reformation and the political turmoil in Central Europe, Spain ruled the Americas virtually unchallenged from 1492 to 1588. Although most European nations did not abide by the Treaty of Tordesillas and explored and established settlements in the Americas, no nation was strong enough to challenge Spain for control of the sea. By 1588, however, after the British defeat of the Spanish Armada, England became the preeminent naval power. Between 1600 and 1680, the British began through conquest to consolidate their landholdings in North America and the Caribbean. By 1660, three European nations could lay claim to control of North America: England enjoyed preeminence from the Appalachian Mountains to the east coast, from present-day Maine to Georgia; France, from the Appalachians to the Mississippi River including central Canada; and Spain, from the western United States to South America. Through a series of European world wars, which were waged in the Americas and Europe, these lands and islands would change hands several times before Britain became the dominant power in Europe and North America. During these world wars Africans played a major military role in the armies of all the combatants. Maroons, slaves, and free blacks were used by the English, French, Dutch, Portuguese, and Spanish to protect their colonies from invasion and to disrupt and harass the economic interest of their enemies. The Portuguese and the Spanish were the first to use Africans as soldiers, enlisting their aid as early as 1441 in Europe to defeat and drive out the North African Moors from Portugal and Spain. By the early 1500s these soldiers were marching through the Aztec, Mayan, and Incan Empires, conquering these peoples for Spain. African soldiers would also be used by the Portuguese to conquer Brazil and protect their colony from Spain. Africans would also fight in the Spanish colonial civil wars on both sides from 1545 to 1548. They were later used in Cuba to turn back the French, who began their assault on the Spanish in the Caribbean in 1555. Sir Francis Drake used Spanish maroons, slaves, free blacks, and Indians in the interest of England in Central America and the Caribbean as early as 1572 and later in the 1580s. African soldiers were used by the Spanish against the Dutch in Peru in 1615 and by the Dutch against the Indians in New Amsterdam (New York) in 1641. Africans were used as soldiers by France, England, the Netherlands, Portugal, and Spain for control of the Caribbean and North America. They would continue to be called upon to defend territory, put down slave revolts, and subdue unfriendly Indians throughout the colonial period and beyond. ■

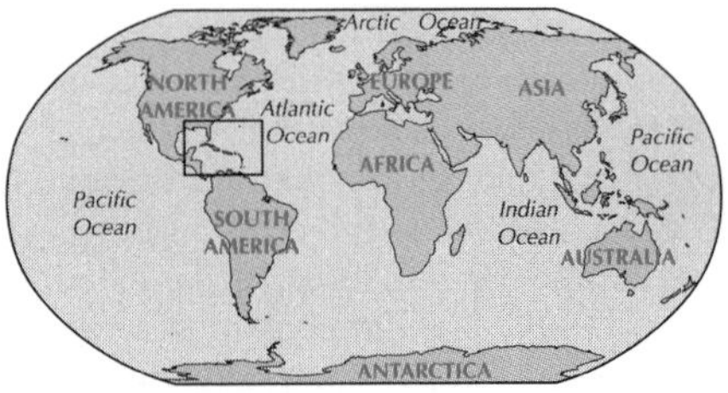
Arctic Ocean
NORTH AMERICA
EUROPE
ASIA
Atlantic Ocean
AFRICA
Pacific Ocean
Pacific Ocean
SOUTH AMERICA
Indian Ocean
AUSTRALIA
ANTARCTICA

MAP 19

The Arrival of the First Blacks into English-Held North America and the First English Colonial Census in 1620

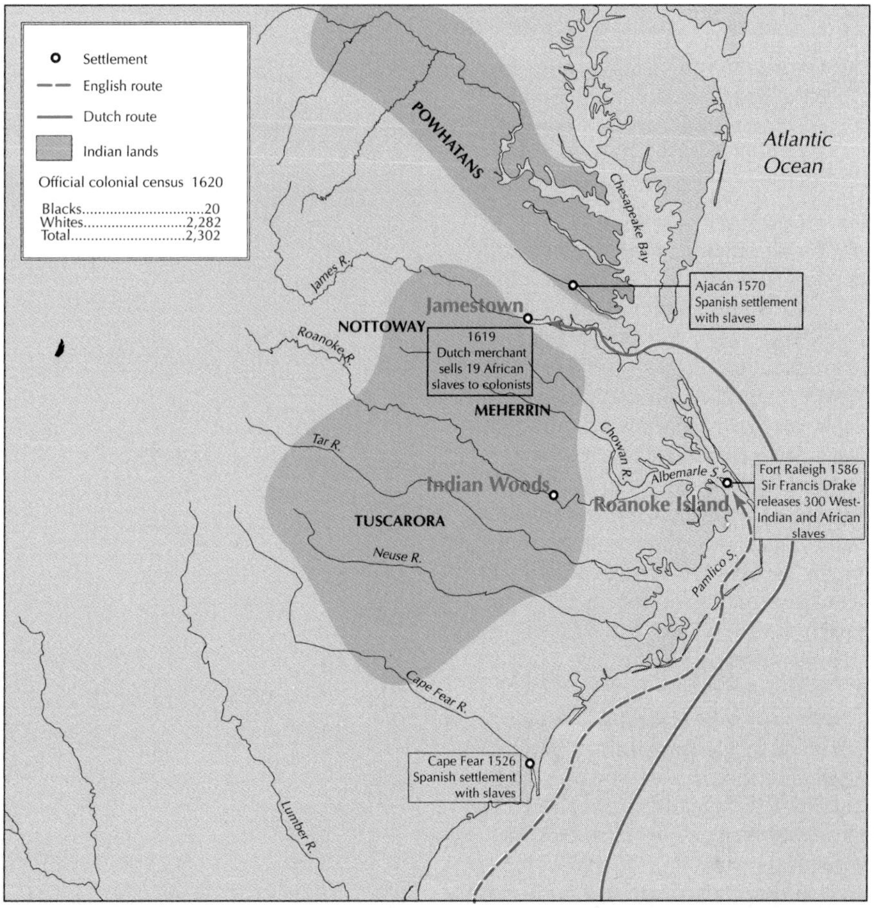
Settlement
English route
Dutch route
Indian lands
Official colonial census 1620
Blacks....20
Whites....2,282
Total....2,302
Atlantic Ocean
POWHATANS
Chesapeake Bay
James R.
Jamestown
NOTTOWAY
Roanoke R.
1619 Dutch merchant sells 19 African slaves to colonists
MEHERRIN
Chowan R.
Tar R.
Albemarle S.
Indian Woods
Roanoke Island
TUSCARORA
Neuse R.
Pamlico S.
Cape Fear R.
Lumber R.
Ajacán 1570 Spanish settlement with slaves
Fort Raleigh 1586 Sir Francis Drake releases 300 West-Indian and African slaves
Cape Fear 1526 Spanish settlement with slaves

In 1619, a Dutch merchant arrived in the colony of Jamestown, Virginia, bringing with him nineteen Africans, whom he subsequently sold to the colonists. Thus began African slavery in British North America. The English colonists were cognizant of slavery in the Caribbean and South America, but had given little thought to the introduction of the institution into their colonies. However, as the need for labor became more acute, the colonists saw the necessity of having a dependable labor supply. Initially, they conscripted the Indians, but discovered that they were susceptible to a variety of European diseases and often died. The Indians were also extremely familiar with the countryside and would run away at the first opportunity. Rarely were they ever found. The colonists also experimented with indentured servitude, an experiment that proved to be both inadequate and problematic. Indeed, the first Africans brought by the Dutch to Virginia were indentured servants. As tobacco became increasingly popular in Europe, and the need to cultivate tobacco and clear land grew, slavery became the "perfect" solution. In 1620, in their first colonial census the British recorded 20 Africans out of a total population of 2,302, showing Africans making up only 1 percent of the Virginia colony's population. There had, however, been other blacks. In 1586 Sir Francis Drake, rewarded more than 300 African and West-Indian maroons and slaves for their help in raiding the Spanish Caribbean by giving them their freedom and releasing them on Roanoke Island in North Carolina. As best as can be determined, these maroons and Indians were absorbed by the North Carolina Indian nations. ■

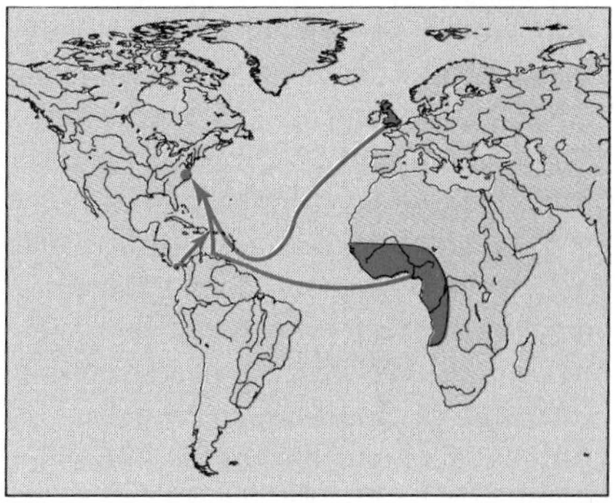

MAP 20

English Colonial Slavery in the New England Colonies, Middle Colonies, Southern Colonies, and the Caribbean (1620–1776)

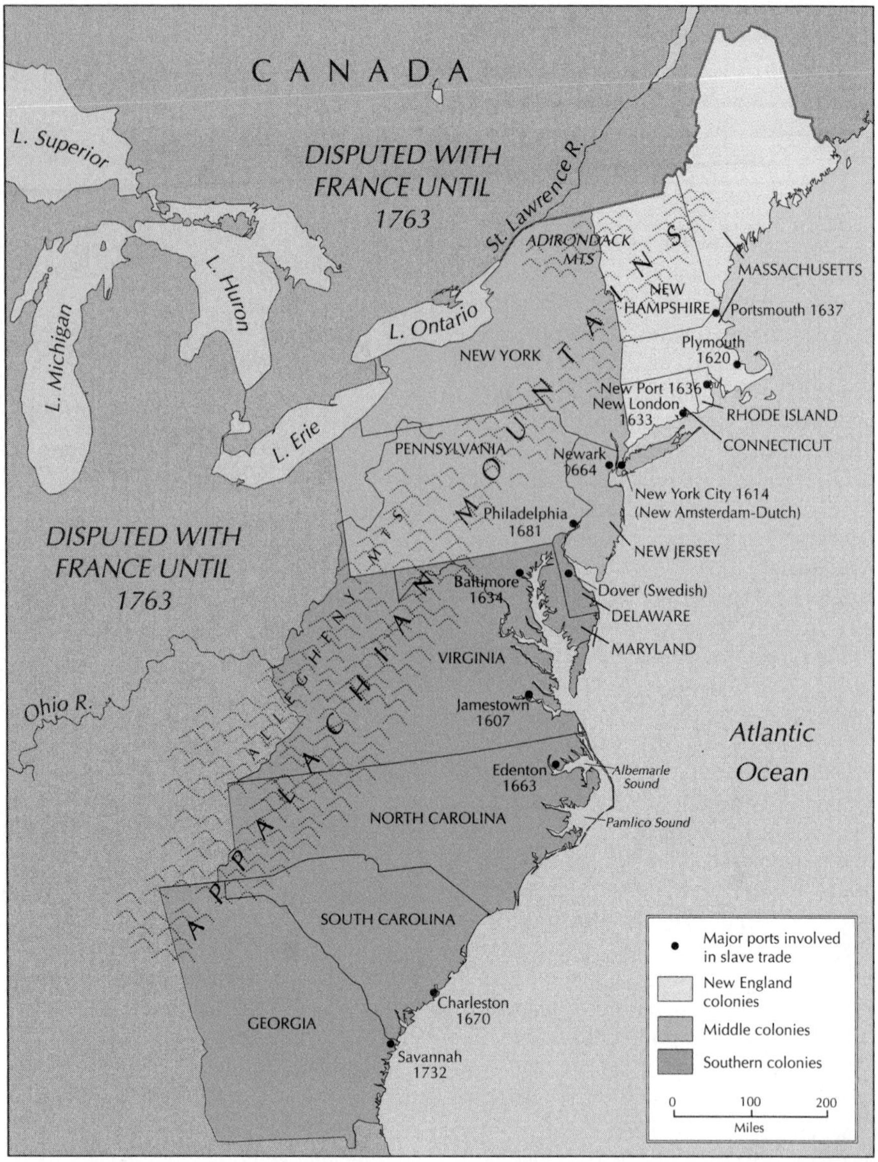
CANADA
DISPUTED WITH FRANCE UNTIL 1763
L. Superior
L. Michigan
L. Huron
L. Ontario
L. Erie
St. Lawrence R.
ADIRONDACK MTS
NEW HAMPSHIRE
Portsmouth 1637
MASSACHUSETTS
Plymouth 1620
NEW YORK
New Port 1636
New London 1633
RHODE ISLAND
CONNECTICUT
PENNSYLVANIA
Newark 1664
New York City 1614 (New Amsterdam-Dutch)
Philadelphia 1681
NEW JERSEY
DISPUTED WITH FRANCE UNTIL 1763
Baltimore 1634
Dover (Swedish)
DELAWARE
MARYLAND
VIRGINIA
ALLEGHENY MTS
APPALACHIAN MOUNTAINS
Ohio R.
Jamestown 1607
Atlantic Ocean
Edenton 1663
Albemarle Sound
NORTH CAROLINA
Pamlico Sound
SOUTH CAROLINA
Charleston 1670
GEORGIA
Savannah 1732
Major ports involved in slave trade
New England colonies
Middle colonies
Southern colonies
0 100 200
Miles

By the middle of the seventeenth century, slavery had become an important part of the economic life of the English colonies. Slavery spread rapidly throughout the English colonies in North America and the Caribbean, but especially in the Caribbean and southern colonies. In these two regions, sugar, molasses, and rum, along with rice, indigo, tobacco, and naval stores such as pitch and turpentine, were the major exports, and the labor-intensive nature of these exports required large numbers of workers. The more slaves that were brought to the Americas, the more entrenched the system became. Slavery spread into four main regions occupied by the British—the Caribbean, southern, middle, and New England colonies. In each of these regions, slavery developed its own characteristics. It took its harshest form in the Caribbean. In a series of wars from 1600 to 1660, Britain was successful in capturing a number of islands from Spain, including the Bahamas, Jamaica, Nevis, St. Kitts, Antigua, and Barbados. Soon thereafter, England fashioned a lucrative sugar trade. As a result of its successes, large sugar plantations were established in Jamaica and Barbados. Clearly, this increased the need for slaves. The slave trade in the Caribbean proved to be both cruel and perilous. Despite this fact, it thrived there unabated until 1838. Slavery also burgeoned in the southern colonies, which included Georgia, South Carolina, North Carolina, Virginia, Delaware, and Maryland. Like Jamaica and Barbados, the southern colonies also employed plantation slavery. In the lower South—Georgia and South Carolina—slaves were used to grow rice and indigo; in the upper South—North Carolina—Virginia, Delaware, and Maryland—slaves were employed to cultivate tobacco. The slave trade in this region was often brutal, but not as severe as in the Caribbean. In the middle colonies, New Jersey, Pennsylvania, and New York, slaves were used primarily as servants, but were later employed as skilled and unskilled urban laborers, such as carpenters, shipbuilders, and dockworkers. As a result, slaves in this region tended to be better treated than southern or Caribbean slaves. They had more contact with whites and other blacks and more freedom. Finally, the New England region, which comprised Connecticut, Rhode Island, Massachusetts, and New Hampshire, held the fewest number of slaves, as they had scant need for them. This region was dominated by the Puritans, who preferred to do their own farming. As a result, most of the slaves were found in the cities, where they tended to be servants. Although the Puritans chose not to own slaves themselves, they were quite willing to ship slaves to the South, where they were in demand, and thus the Puritans dominated the intercolonial shipping of slaves. Slaves were also used to defend the English colonies from foreign and domestic threats. Many were armed to fight Indians, to repulse European invaders, and to put down slave revolts. This would continue to be the case during the period of English slavery. ■

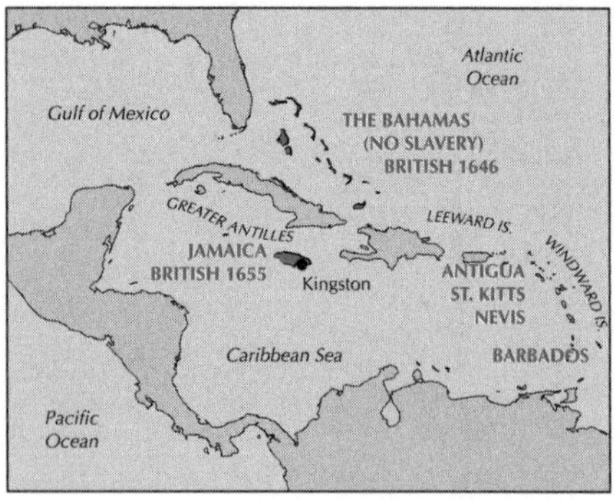
Atlantic Ocean
Gulf of Mexico
THE BAHAMAS (NO SLAVERY) BRITISH 1646
GREATER ANTILLES
LEEWARD IS.
WINDWARD IS.
JAMAICA BRITISH 1655
Kingston
ANTIGUA
ST. KITTS
NEVIS
Caribbean Sea
BARBADOS
Pacific Ocean

MAP 21

The Native American Slave Trade, the Legalization of Slavery, the Rise of Slave Codes, and the Growth of the African Slave Population in the English Colonies (1650–1755)

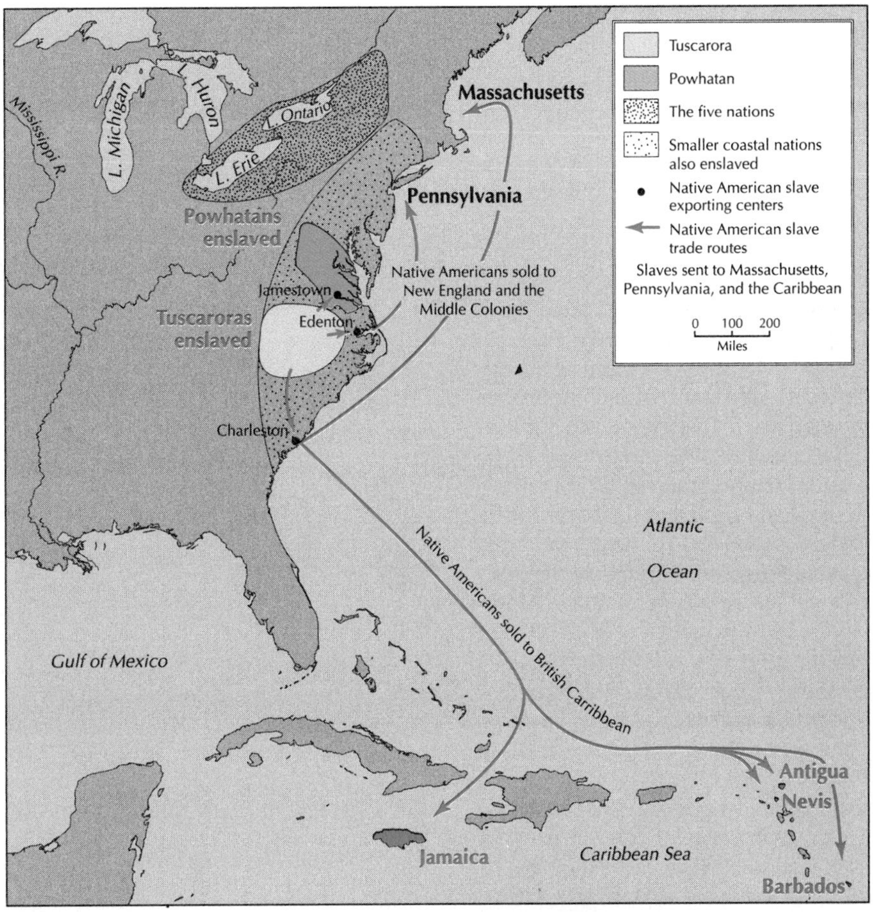
Tuscarora
Powhatan
The five nations
Smaller coastal nations also enslaved
Native American slave exporting centers
Native American slave trade routes
Slaves sent to Massachusetts, Pennsylvania, and the Caribbean
0 100 200
Miles
Massachusetts
Pennsylvania
Native Americans sold to New England and the Middle Colonies
Mississippi R.
L. Michigan
L. Huron
L. Ontario
L. Erie
Powhatans enslaved
Jamestown
Tuscaroras enslaved
Edenton
Charleston
Native Americans sold to British Caribbean
Atlantic
Ocean
Gulf of Mexico
Antigua
Nevis
Jamaica
Caribbean Sea
Barbados

Slavery had been practiced by the English in Virginia as early as 1610. Many of the early slaves were Native Americans, mostly the Algonquians of coastal Virginia and North Carolina. By the 1680s English settlers were routinely kidnaping Native American women and children in the coastal plains of North Carolina and Virginia in order to sell them. This Native American slave trade involved a number of colonies, including Virginia, the Carolinas, Pennsylvania, Massachusetts, Jamaica, Barbados, St. Kitts, and Nevis. So many Indian slaves were being traded to Pennsylvania that Pennsylvania passed a law in 1705 forbidding the importation of Carolina Indian slaves. This law came about to avoid conflict with the Iroquois confederacy, who threatened to militarily intervene to stop the trade. From 1680 to 1715 thousands of Indians were sold into slavery by the English; some were sent as far away as the Caribbean. Indian slavery, however, was filled with problems, not the least of which were Indian attacks, and by 1720 Indian slavery was abandoned for African slavery. Although in 1640 there were only 1,600 Africans in the thirteen colonies (New York contained the majority, with 500), over the next three decades the number would continue to grow with the legalization of the institution and the introduction of race-based slavery. The first colonies to legalize slavery were Massachusetts in 1641, Connecticut in 1650, Virginia in 1661, Maryland in 1663, New York in 1665, and South Carolina in 1682. The southern and Caribbean colonies unlike the northern colonies became increasingly dependent on slaves to run large tobacco, rice and indigo, and sugar plantations. Although the laws of Massachusetts, Connecticut, and Virginia recognized the institution of slavery, Maryland held the distinction of being the first colony in 1661—to mandate slavery as a lifelong condition for Africans and their children, a step that preceded its actual statutory recognition of the institution in 1663. Virginia followed suit in 1670, defining slavery as a lifelong inheritable "racial" status. As settlements spread along the Atlantic coast, so did the need for slave labor and the legalization of slavery. With the onset of the eighteenth century, the remaining colonies legalized slavery, beginning with Pennsylvania in 1700 and followed closely by New Jersey in 1702 and Rhode Island in 1703. The legalization of slavery in Pennsylvania, New Jersey, and Rhode Island was especially surprising, considering that these colonies were heavily populated by the Quakers, who disapproved of the institution of slavery. The last colonies to legalize slavery were New Hampshire in 1714; North Carolina, also a Quaker haven, in 1715; Delaware in 1721; and finally Georgia in 1755. Initially, when it was established in 1732, Georgia was conceived as a penal colony. Its purpose was to rehabilitate criminals for England, as well as serve as a defensive buffer between South Carolina and

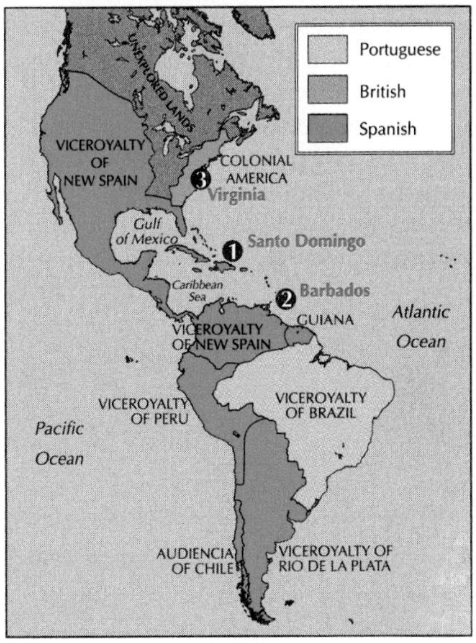
Portuguese
British
Spanish
UNEXPLORED LANDS
VICEROYALTY OF NEW SPAIN
COLONIAL AMERICA
Virginia
Gulf of Mexico
Santo Domingo
Caribbean Sea
Barbados
GUIANA
Atlantic Ocean
VICEROYALTY OF NEW SPAIN
VICEROYALTY OF PERU
VICEROYALTY OF BRAZIL
Pacific Ocean
AUDIENCIA OF CHILE
VICEROYALTY OF RIO DE LA PLATA

Spanish Florida. Led by James Oglethorpe, the colony remained alcohol-free and slave-free until 1750. Oglethorpe harbored a strong dislike for slavery, not only because he viewed it as cruel, but because he thought it caused many whites to be lazy and unproductive. By 1755, however, slavery was legalized throughout the colonies and spread rapidly. As the number of African slaves increased, it became necessary to develop a system to regulate the growing slave population. Many colonies looked to the Spanish. The Spanish were the first to pass codes to prevent slave revolts in the Caribbean. Following the Spanish model, Virginia, South Carolina, North Carolina, Georgia, and Maryland fashioned slave codes that regulated every aspect of the slaves' lives. The codes forbade teaching slaves to read and write, and outlawed group gatherings. The codes also required slaves to carry passes and prohibited them from affiliating with free blacks, who were often viewed as instigators of slave revolts. Despite the comprehensiveness of the slave codes, the severity of punishment and the level of enforcement varied from colony to colony. Georgia and South Carolina developed and enforced the most brutal slave codes in British North America. South Carolina, which had the largest population of slaves in the colonial period—often larger than the white population—enacted the strictest codes. Soon thereafter, Georgia adopted many of the same practices. Scholars have advanced numerous theories to explain the harshness of these codes, one prominent theory being that the codes were precipitated by white fears of the large numbers of enslaved Africans, whom they did not like or trust. ■

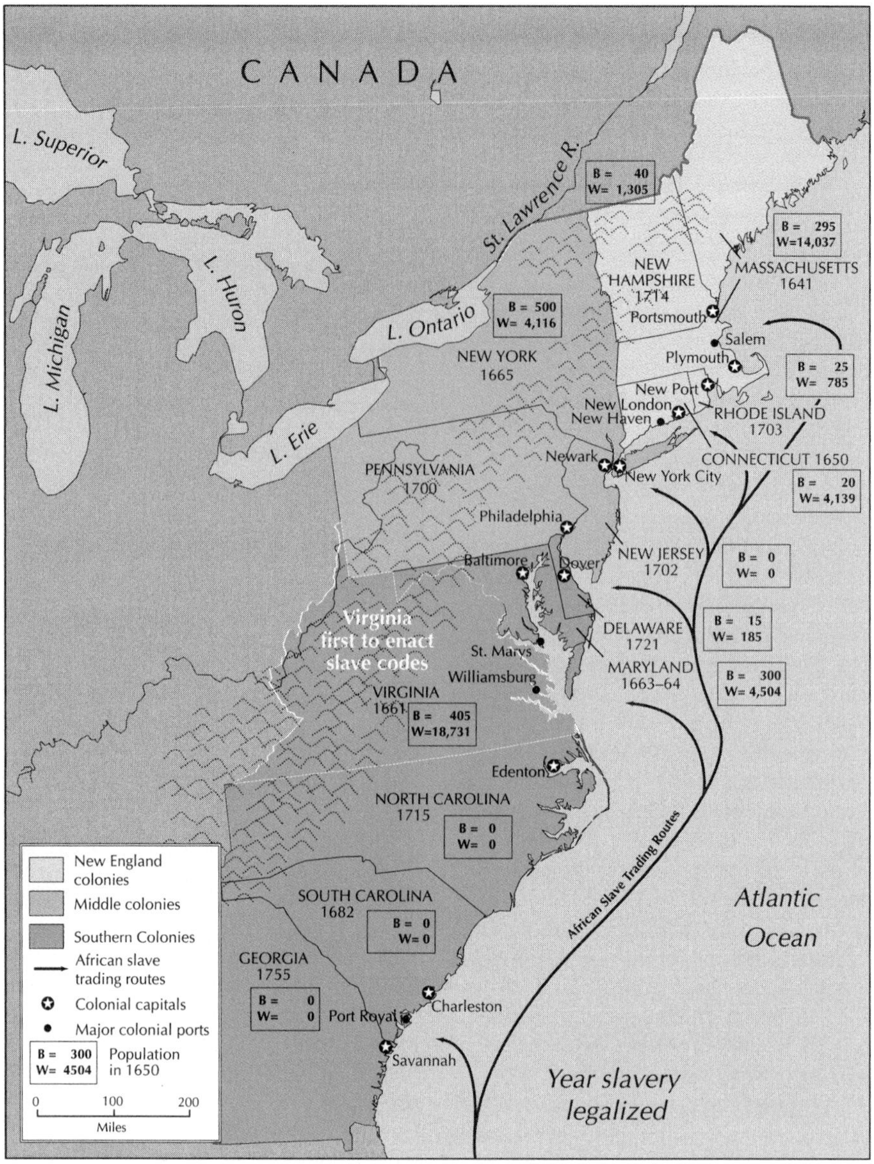
CANADA
L. Superior
L. Michigan
L. Huron
L. Ontario
L. Erie
St. Lawrence R.
B = 40 W = 1,305
B = 295 W = 14,037
MASSACHUSETTS 1641
NEW HAMPSHIRE 1714
Portsmouth
B = 500 W = 4,116
NEW YORK 1665
Salem
Plymouth
B = 25 W = 785
New Port
New London
New Haven
RHODE ISLAND 1703
Newark
New York City
CONNECTICUT 1650
B = 20 W = 4,139
PENNSYLVANIA 1700
Philadelphia
Baltimore
Dover
NEW JERSEY 1702
B = 0 W = 0
Virginia first to enact slave codes
St. Marys
Williamsburg
DELAWARE 1721
B = 15 W = 185
MARYLAND 1663–64
B = 300 W = 4,504
VIRGINIA 1661
B = 405 W = 18,731
Edenton
NORTH CAROLINA 1715
B = 0 W = 0
African Slave Trading Routes
SOUTH CAROLINA 1682
B = 0 W = 0
GEORGIA 1755
B = 0 W = 0
Port Royal
Charleston
Savannah
Atlantic Ocean
Year slavery legalized
New England colonies
Middle colonies
Southern Colonies
African slave trading routes
Colonial capitals
Major colonial ports
B = 300 W = 4504 Population in 1650
0 100 200
Miles

MAP 22

Bacon's Rebellion in Colonial Virginia and Its Impact on the Growth of the Slave Population in Virginia (1676–1680)

In 1676 in Virginia, a rebellion broke out which drastically changed Chesapeake society. Nathaniel Bacon, a white plantation owner, led a renegade attack on neighboring friendly Indians and subsequently a large armed revolt against the colonial governor of Virginia, William Berkeley. From the start of the rebellion, a number of enslaved blacks and indentured whites joined Bacon's revolt. Bacon's Rebellion, which proved successful in destroying Jamestown and terrorizing the Virginia colony, revealed two important facts about colonial Virginia. First, black slaves and white indentured servants were displeased with their condition and did not accept it freely. Second, poor whites who had finished their indentures, which usually lasted 4 to 7 years, were becoming a threat to the social and economic structure of colonial Virginia. As a result, when Bacon's revolt was finally extinguished, two significant changes occurred. Additional black slaves were brought to the colony instead of white indentured servants, and stricter laws governing slaves were enacted to control the movement and behavior of both slaves and free blacks in spite of the fact that blacks had also fought *for* Governor Berkeley during the rebellion. By 1680 there were 6,971 Africans in the thirteen colonies out of a total population of 151,507. By 1680 Virginia had overtaken New York to be the largest slaveholding colony with a total African population of 3,000. ■

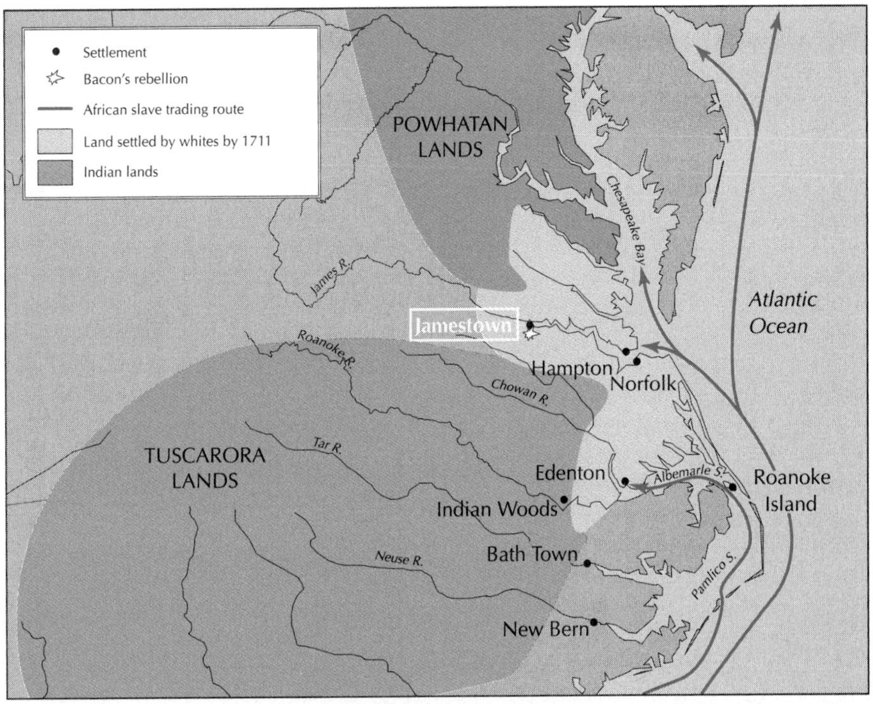
Settlement
Bacon's rebellion
African slave trading route
Land settled by whites by 1711
Indian lands
POWHATAN LANDS
Chesapeake Bay
James R.
Jamestown
Atlantic Ocean
Roanoke R.
Hampton
Norfolk
Chowan R.
TUSCARORA LANDS
Tar R.
Edenton
Albemarle S.
Roanoke Island
Indian Woods
Neuse R.
Bath Town
Pamlico S.
New Bern

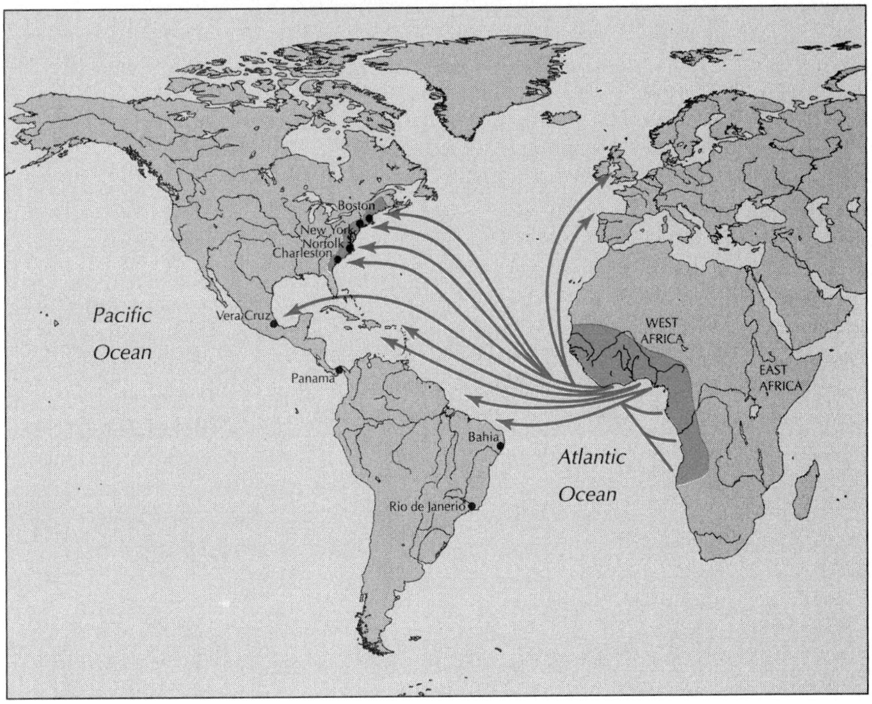
Boston
New York
Norfolk
Charleston
Pacific Ocean
Vera Cruz
Panama
WEST AFRICA
EAST AFRICA
Bahia
Atlantic Ocean
Rio de Janerio

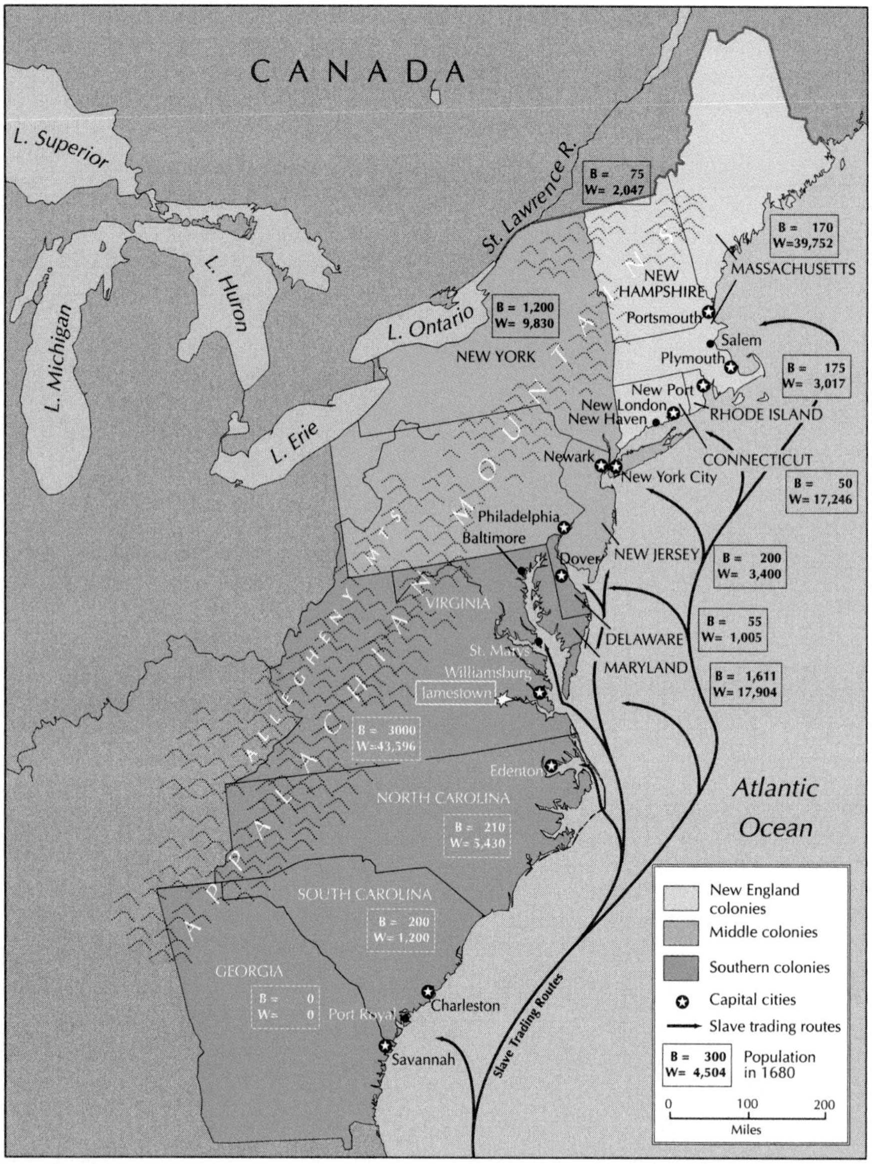
CANADA
L. Superior
L. Michigan
L. Huron
L. Ontario
L. Erie
St. Lawrence R.
B = 75
W= 2,047
B = 170
W=39,752
MASSACHUSETTS
NEW HAMPSHIRE
Portsmouth
Salem
Plymouth
B = 175
W= 3,017
New Port
New London
New Haven
RHODE ISLAND
B = 1,200
W= 9,830
NEW YORK
Newark
New York City
CONNECTICUT
B = 50
W= 17,246
Philadelphia
Baltimore
Dover
NEW JERSEY
B = 200
W= 3,400
VIRGINIA
St. Marys
Williamsburg
Jamestown
B = 55
W= 1,005
DELAWARE
MARYLAND
B = 1,611
W= 17,904
B = 3000
W=43,596
ALLEGHENY MTS
APPALACHIAN MOUNTAINS
Edenton
NORTH CAROLINA
B = 210
W= 5,430
Atlantic
Ocean
SOUTH CAROLINA
B = 200
W= 1,200
GEORGIA
B = 0
W= 0
Port Royal
Charleston
Savannah
Slave Trading Routes
New England colonies
Middle colonies
Southern colonies
Capital cities
Slave trading routes
B = 300
W= 4,504
Population in 1680
0
100
200
Miles

MAP 23

The Slave Tituba and the Origins of the Salem Witch Trials (1692)

In 1692 in Salem, Massachusetts, an event occurred which shocked and terrified the residents of the Puritan community. The niece and daughter of minister Samuel Parris began to have fits and proclaim they were possessed and being tormented by the devil. Historians have continued to debate the cause of the hysteria, but one thing is certain. Central to this controversy was a slave woman called Tituba, who was originally from the West Indies and was a slave in the Parris family. Tituba practiced West Indian voodoo and, at the time of the scare, attempted to forecast the futures of the girls involved in the "possessions." Voodoo was practiced by many West Africans, and brought to the Americas and the Caribbean during the Atlantic slave trade. In the Caribbean, slaves combined voodoo with Catholicism, while continuing to practice their native religions. Even today, blacks still practice voodoo in the Gullah Islands of South Carolina and Georgia. Likewise, in New Orleans, similar religious practices have been documented. Perhaps what occurred in Salem can be explained as a political, economic, social, or sexual dilemma, but the ties to West Africa seem undeniable. ■

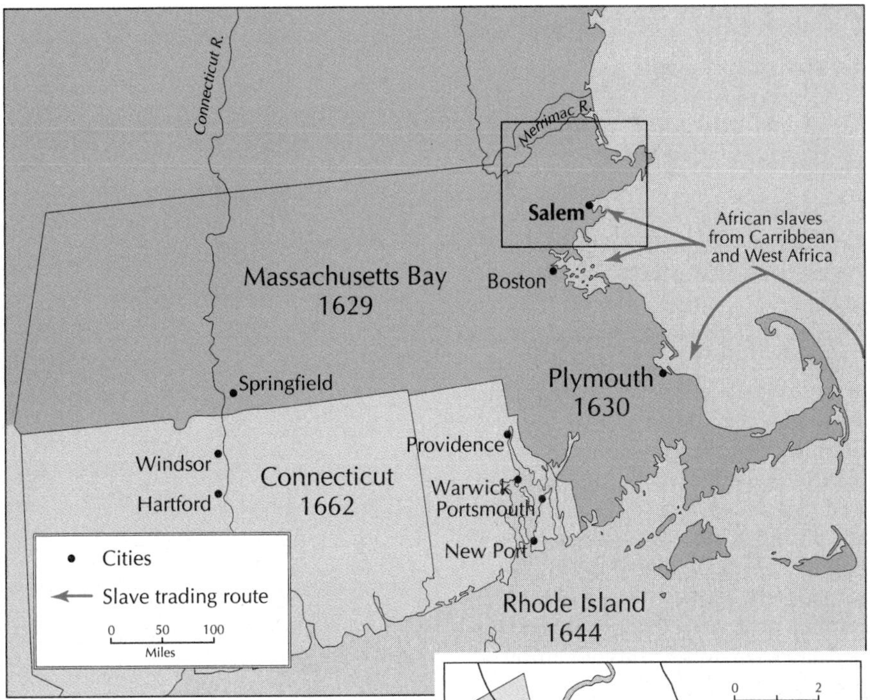
Connecticut R.
Merrimac R.
Salem
African slaves from Carribbean and West Africa
Massachusetts Bay 1629
Boston
Springfield
Plymouth 1630
Providence
Windsor
Hartford
Connecticut 1662
Warwick
Portsmouth
New Port
Rhode Island 1644
Cities
Slave trading route
0 50 100
Miles

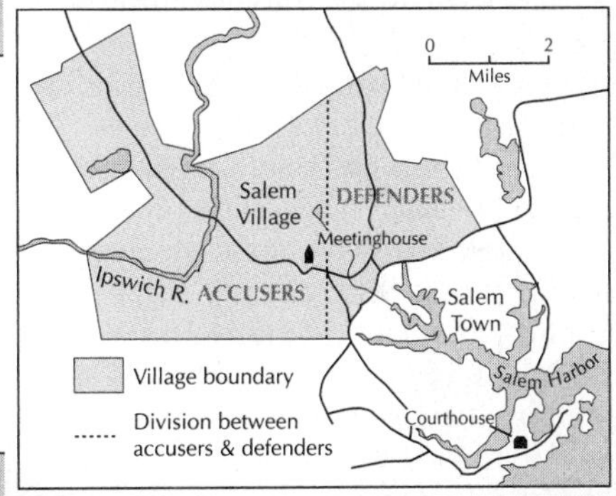
0 2
Miles
Salem Village
DEFENDERS
Meetinghouse
Ipswich R.
ACCUSERS
Salem Town
Salem Harbor
Courthouse
Village boundary
Division between accusers & defenders

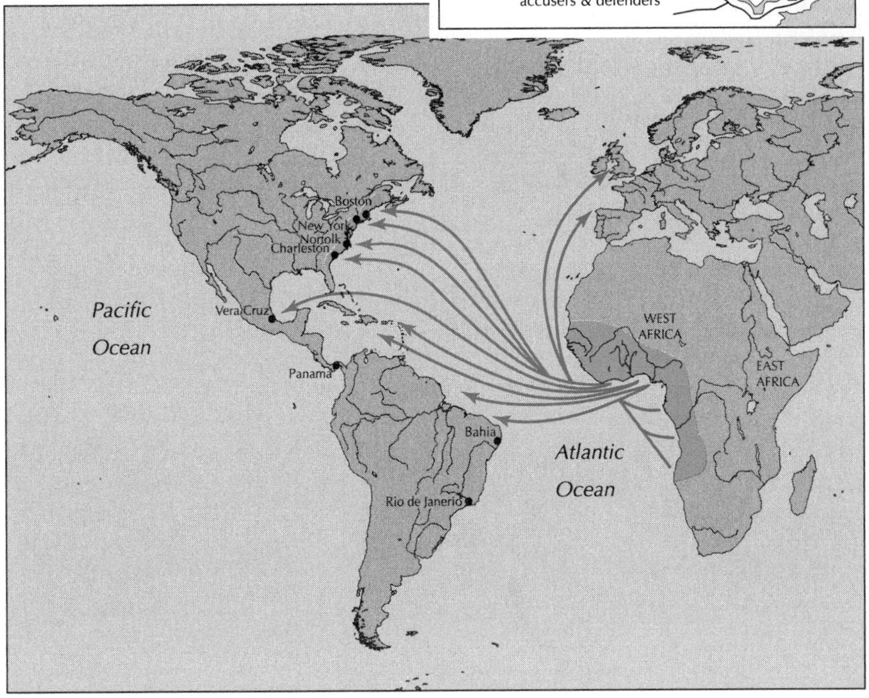
Boston
New York
Norfolk
Charleston
Pacific Ocean
Vera Cruz
Panama
WEST AFRICA
EAST AFRICA
Bahia
Atlantic Ocean
Rio de Janerio

MAP 24

The Slave Revolts and Maroon Communities in the Americas and the Caribbean (1700–1800)

By the start of the eighteenth century, slavery was well established throughout the Western Hemisphere. It stretched from present-day Argentina to Canada. African slaves worked the mines of South America; the sugar plantations of the Caribbean; the rice and indigo fields of Georgia and South Carolina; and the tobacco fields of North Carolina, Virginia, and Maryland. And they toiled as servants and skilled and unskilled laborers in cities from Bahia to Quebec. The 100 years that passed from 1700 to 1800 witnessed the creation of the first democratic republic in America and the institutionalization of slavery in that republic, which would become the worst form of slavery in human history. As more African slaves were brought to the Americas, maroon communities and slave revolts continued to pose a problem for slave owners throughout the hemisphere. Literally hundreds of maroon communities were scattered throughout the mountains and swamps of the Americas. The best-known maroon communities included the Great Dismal Swamp, located on the northeastern border of North Carolina and Virginia; the Florida everglades and Louisiana bayous; and the most famous, the African state of Palmares, in Brazil. These communities provided shelter, safety, and fellowship for fugitive slaves in the Americas. The slaves not only continued to establish maroon communities, but also continued to revolt in protest. From 1700 to 1800, several major revolts took place which caused loss of property and life for many blacks and whites. ■

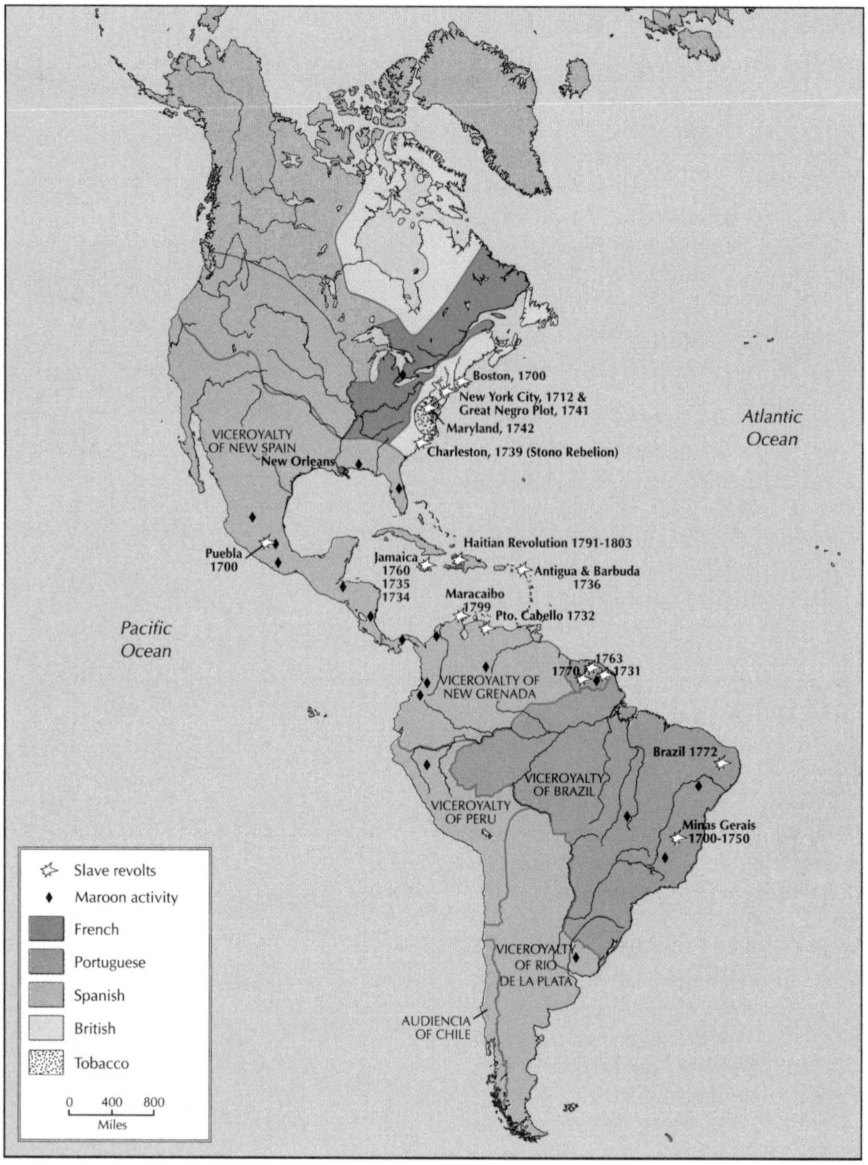
Boston, 1700
New York City, 1712 & Great Negro Plot, 1741
Maryland, 1742
Charleston, 1739 (Stono Rebelion)
Atlantic Ocean
VICEROYALTY OF NEW SPAIN
New Orleans
Haitian Revolution 1791-1803
Puebla 1700
Jamaica 1760 1735 1734
Antigua & Barbuda 1736
Maracaibo 1799
Pto. Cabello 1732
Pacific Ocean
1763
1770
1731
VICEROYALTY OF NEW GRENADA
Brazil 1772
VICEROYALTY OF BRAZIL
VICEROYALTY OF PERU
Minas Gerais 1700-1750
VICEROYALTY OF RIO DE LA PLATA
AUDIENCIA OF CHILE
Slave revolts
Maroon activity
French
Portuguese
Spanish
British
Tobacco
0 400 800
Miles

MAP 25

The British "Triangle of Trade" with Colonial America and the Growth of the African-American Slave Population in North America (1710–1776)

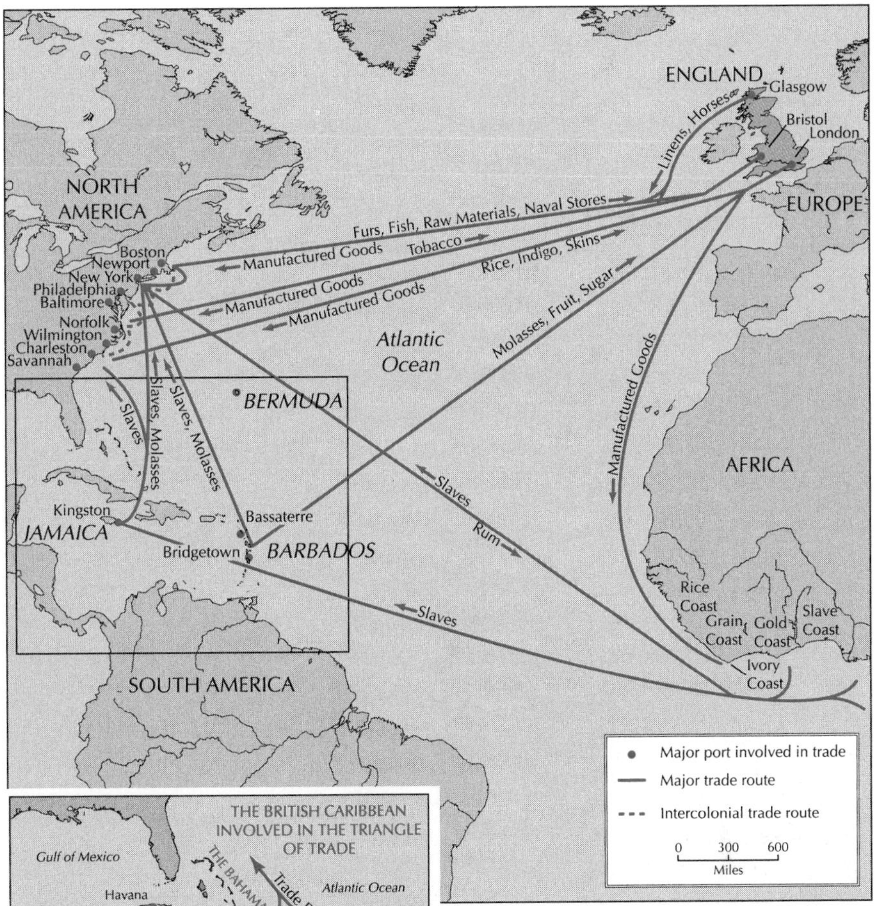

ENGLAND
Glasgow
Bristol
London
EUROPE
NORTH AMERICA
Boston
Newport
New York
Philadelphia
Baltimore
Norfolk
Wilmington
Charleston
Savannah
Linens, Horses
Furs, Fish, Raw Materials, Naval Stores
Manufactured Goods
Tobacco
Manufactured Goods
Manufactured Goods
Rice, Indigo, Skins
Molasses, Fruit, Sugar
Atlantic Ocean
Manufactured Goods
BERMUDA
Slaves
Slaves, Molasses
Slaves, Molasses
AFRICA
Slaves
Rum
Kingston
JAMAICA
Bassaterre
Bridgetown
BARBADOS
Slaves
Rice Coast
Grain Coast
Gold Coast
Slave Coast
Ivory Coast
SOUTH AMERICA
Major port involved in trade
Major trade route
Intercolonial trade route
0 300 600
Miles

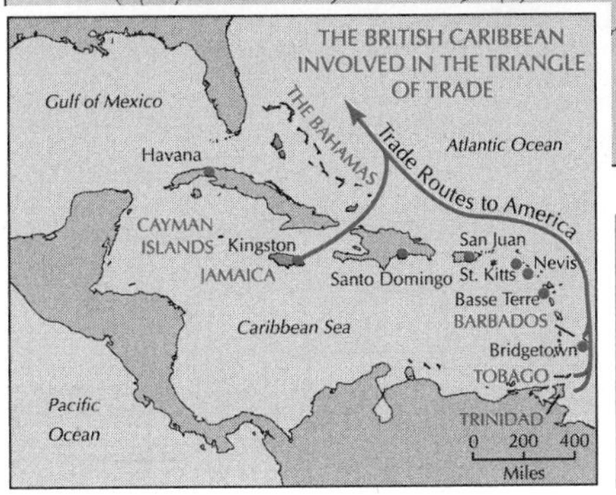

THE BRITISH CARIBBEAN INVOLVED IN THE TRIANGLE OF TRADE
Gulf of Mexico
THE BAHAMAS
Trade Routes to America
Atlantic Ocean
Havana
CAYMAN ISLANDS
Kingston
JAMAICA
San Juan
Santo Domingo
St. Kitts
Nevis
Basse Terre
BARBADOS
Caribbean Sea
Bridgetown
TOBAGO
TRINIDAD
Pacific Ocean
0 200 400
Miles

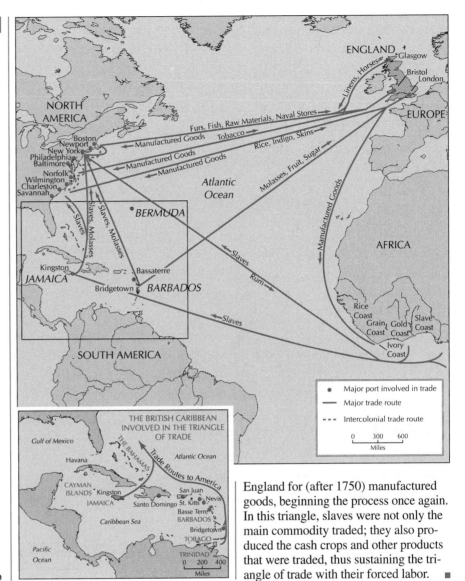

By 1710 there were 44,866 Africans in the thirteen colonies, the overwhelming majority of whom were slaves. The largest number of Africans continued to be in Virginia, which contained 23,118. As slavery became more firmly entrenched in colonial America, it—and the Africans who were a part of it—became the foundation of a very lucrative trade that included the English colonies in North America and the Caribbean, England, and West Africa. This trade across the Atlantic became known as the "triangle of trade," or "triangular trade." Although it was not always a perfect triangle, the trade operated as follows: (1) manufactured goods such as guns were shipped from England to West Africa where they were traded for slaves; (2) the slaves were then traded to the British Caribbean where they were used on sugar plantations and seasoned (trained) before being sold to the English colonies in North America along with sugar cane and molasses in exchange for rice, indigo, tobacco, fish, and hardtack; and (3) raw materials such as sugar cane from the Caribbean and rice, indigo, tobacco, and fish from the thirteen colonies were then traded to England for (after 1750) manufactured goods, beginning the process once again. In this triangle, slaves were not only the main commodity traded; they also produced the cash crops and other products that were traded, thus sustaining the triangle of trade with their forced labor. ■

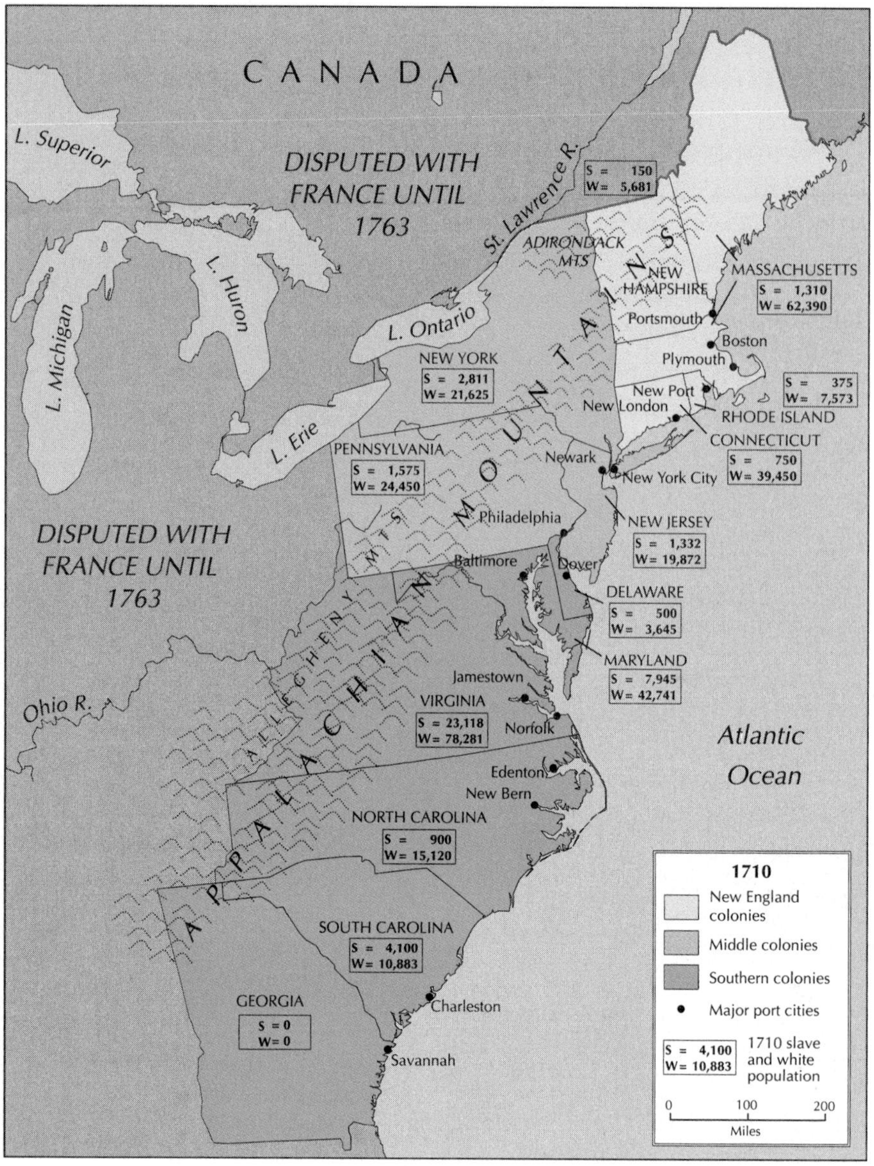
CANADA
L. Superior
DISPUTED WITH FRANCE UNTIL 1763
St. Lawrence R.
S = 150 W= 5,681
L. Michigan
L. Huron
ADIRONDACK MTS
NEW HAMPSHIRE
MASSACHUSETTS
S = 1,310 W= 62,390
Portsmouth
Boston
Plymouth
L. Ontario
NEW YORK
S = 2,811 W= 21,625
New Port
New London
S = 375 W= 7,573
RHODE ISLAND
CONNECTICUT
S = 750 W= 39,450
L. Erie
PENNSYLVANIA
S = 1,575 W= 24,450
Newark
New York City
Philadelphia
NEW JERSEY
S = 1,332 W= 19,872
DISPUTED WITH FRANCE UNTIL 1763
Baltimore
Dover
DELAWARE
S = 500 W= 3,645
APPALACHIAN MOUNTAINS
ALLEGHENY MTS
MARYLAND
S = 7,945 W= 42,741
Jamestown
Ohio R.
VIRGINIA
S = 23,118 W= 78,281
Norfolk
Atlantic Ocean
Edenton
New Bern
NORTH CAROLINA
S = 900 W= 15,120
SOUTH CAROLINA
S = 4,100 W= 10,883
GEORGIA
S = 0 W= 0
Charleston
Savannah
1710
New England colonies
Middle colonies
Southern colonies
Major port cities
S = 4,100 W= 10,883
1710 slave and white population
0 100 200
Miles

MAP 26

The Role of the Tuscarora, the Iroquois Confederacy, and Their Allies in Developing the Underground Railroad in the English Colonies of North America (1711–1803)

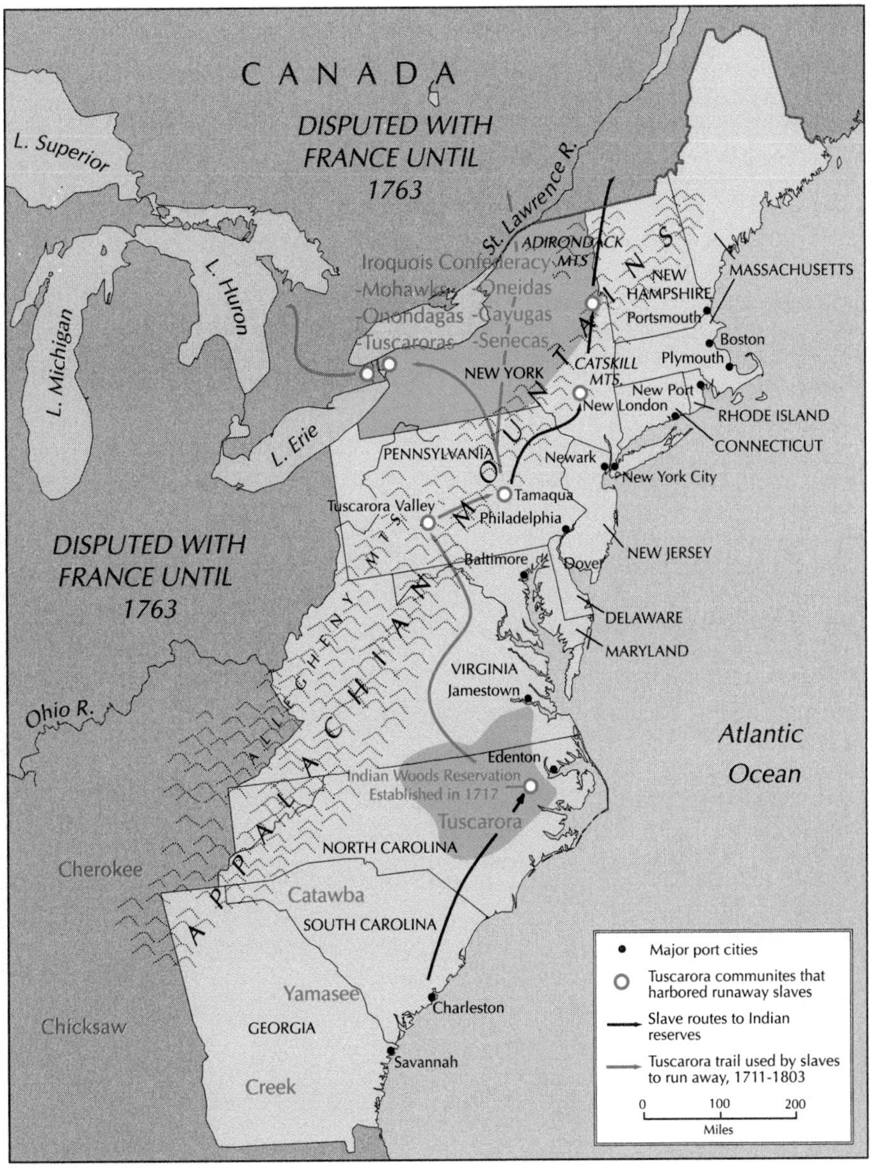
CANADA
DISPUTED WITH FRANCE UNTIL 1763
L. Superior
L. Michigan
L. Huron
L. Erie
St. Lawrence R.
ADIRONDACK MTS
Iroquois Confederacy
-Mohawks
-Oneidas
-Onondagas
-Cayugas
-Tuscaroras
-Senecas
NEW YORK
CATSKILL MTS
NEW HAMPSHIRE
Portsmouth
MASSACHUSETTS
Boston
Plymouth
New Port
New London
RHODE ISLAND
CONNECTICUT
PENNSYLVANIA
Newark
New York City
Tamaqua
Tuscarora Valley
Philadelphia
NEW JERSEY
Baltimore
Dover
DELAWARE
MARYLAND
DISPUTED WITH FRANCE UNTIL 1763
ALLEGHENY MTS
APPALACHIAN MOUNTAINS
VIRGINIA
Jamestown
Ohio R.
Atlantic Ocean
Edenton
Indian Woods Reservation Established in 1717
Tuscarora
NORTH CAROLINA
Cherokee
Catawba
SOUTH CAROLINA
Yamasee
Charleston
Chicksaw
GEORGIA
Savannah
Creek
Major port cities
Tuscarora communites that harbored runaway slaves
Slave routes to Indian reserves
Tuscarora trail used by slaves to run away, 1711-1803
0 100 200
Miles

As slavery spread and the cruelty of slavery became known among Native Americans, many began to sympathize with Africans and despise the institution of slavery. Many Indian nations began to assist and harbor runaway slaves and intermarry with them, just as Native Americans had done in the Caribbean and in Central and South America as early as 1502. Africans began to forge alliances and close friendships with Native Americans such as the Tuscarora of North Carolina and the group of Native Americans that made up the Iroquois Confederacy. This group included the Mohawk, Cayuga, Oneida, Seneca, and Onondaga, and collectively, along with the Tuscarora, was known as the Six Nations. They grew to mistrust whites and hate the institution of slavery since many of the Tuscarora had fallen victim to this illicit institution after their defeat in the Tuscarora War of 1711–1713. As a result, many Iroquois raided frontier plantations, killing whites and allowing Africans to go free or join their nations. Even at the start of the Tuscarora War in 1711, slaves were released by the warring Indians and came to no harm. After the war, from 1717 to 1803, the Tuscarora who remained in North Carolina on a reservation known as Indian Woods began to shelter runaway slaves and sometimes intermarried with them. Many of the Tuscarora and other Iroquois became so mixed that they appeared more African than Indian. Later, as members of the Six Nations were subdued and forced onto reservations, they continued to hide runaway slaves as a part of the Underground Railroad. The Meherrin, Nottoway, Delaware, and Powhatan also assisted runaway slaves. Fearful that Indians and slaves might create alliances that would destroy white settlements, whites informed slaves that Indians were their enemy and not to be trusted, causing many slaves to fear them and remain loyal to their masters for protection. Whites also armed slaves and used them to fight Indians, driving wedges between the two groups as in the Tuscarora War and the Yamasee War of 1715. As well, whites taught Indians to fear Africans and recruited them to serve as slave catchers and slaveholders. Some Indian nations adopted the European type of slavery. Most of these nations were bitter enemies of the Tuscarora and the Iroquois Confederacy, and had been even before the arrival of the Europeans. These nations included what became known as the Five Civilized Tribes: the Seminole, Creek, Choctaw, Chickasaw, and Cherokee. Even though these nations accepted many of the practices of European slaveholders, African slavery among them was never as harsh or restrictive as it was among slaveholding whites. For example, many of these Native Americans intermarried with their African slaves, and the children of slaves were considered free and full members of the nation. The Seminole of Florida became so mixed that, like the Tuscarora and other Iroquois, many of their people became as much African as Indian. The mixing of whites and Indians and Africans and Indians eventually led to civil wars within the Five Civilized Tribes. In these wars, most full-blooded Indians sided with those who were part African because many of the traditional Native American religions and beliefs did not recognize the superiority of any race over another. On the other hand, many part-white Indians accepted the idea of racial superiority along with Christianity, which was taught to them by whites. ■

MAP 27

The Stono Rebellion and the Growth of the African-American Slave Population in British North America (1739–1740)

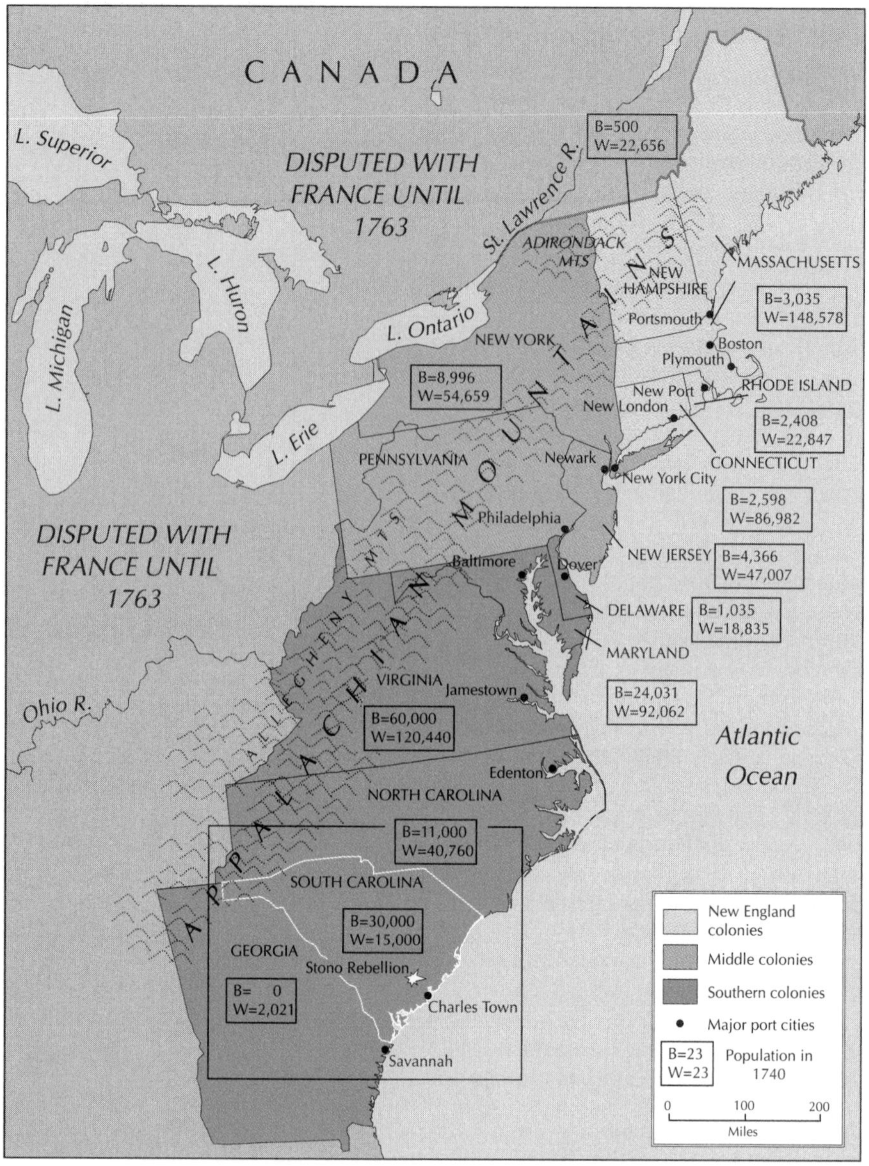
CANADA
L. Superior
DISPUTED WITH FRANCE UNTIL 1763
St. Lawrence R.
B=500
W=22,656
ADIRONDACK MTS
NEW HAMPSHIRE
MASSACHUSETTS
B=3,035
W=148,578
Portsmouth
Boston
Plymouth
L. Huron
L. Michigan
L. Ontario
NEW YORK
B=8,996
W=54,659
New Port
RHODE ISLAND
New London
B=2,408
W=22,847
CONNECTICUT
L. Erie
PENNSYLVANIA
Newark
New York City
B=2,598
W=86,982
Philadelphia
DISPUTED WITH FRANCE UNTIL 1763
NEW JERSEY
B=4,366
W=47,007
Baltimore
Dover
DELAWARE
B=1,035
W=18,835
MARYLAND
B=24,031
W=92,062
Ohio R.
VIRGINIA
Jamestown
B=60,000
W=120,440
Atlantic Ocean
APPALACHIAN MOUNTAINS
ALLEGHENY MTS
Edenton
NORTH CAROLINA
B=11,000
W=40,760
SOUTH CAROLINA
B=30,000
W=15,000
GEORGIA
Stono Rebellion
B= 0
W=2,021
Charles Town
Savannah
New England colonies
Middle colonies
Southern colonies
Major port cities
B=23
W=23
Population in 1740
0
100
200
Miles

In 1739, some 20 miles outside of Charleston, South Carolina, slaves on the Stono Plantation organized one of the most successful slave revolts of that time. It commenced when twenty slaves attacked a local store to secure weapons and ammunition. Once armed, they crossed the Stono River and headed south for Spanish Florida, a haven for runaway slaves. As they traveled south, the slaves raided nearby plantations, killing whites and freeing slaves. They burned homes, barns, and crops, seizing any weapons they could find. By the end of the day, the number of slaves involved in the revolt had grown from twenty to eighty. They adopted a flag and proclaimed their intention to live as free men in Florida. Their hopes, however, were quickly dashed. By day's end, the South Carolina militia caught up to them on the banks of the Savannah River, where all were massacred. The militia then beheaded the dead slaves and lined the road with their heads from that point to Charles Town, in order to discourage other slaves from initiating similar revolts. Despite the above events, for more than a year South Carolina would still suffer from smaller disturbances all over the colony. In all, twenty whites and eighty slaves were killed, several plantations were destroyed, and whites across the colony were terrified. As a result of the Stono Rebellion, South Carolina enacted stricter slave codes to regulate the movement and activities of both slaves and free blacks in the colony. This rebellion had enormous national repercussions. It caused the southern colonies, which had large numbers of African slaves, to enact stricter slave codes, and the northern colonies, which boasted small numbers of slaves, to be concerned about the dangers associated with expanding slavery. The fear of slaves and future slave revolts only grew with the growth of the slave population in the colonies. In 1740 the African population in the thirteen colonies totaled 150,000. In South Carolina, out of a total population of 45,000, two-thirds—30,000—were Africans. ■

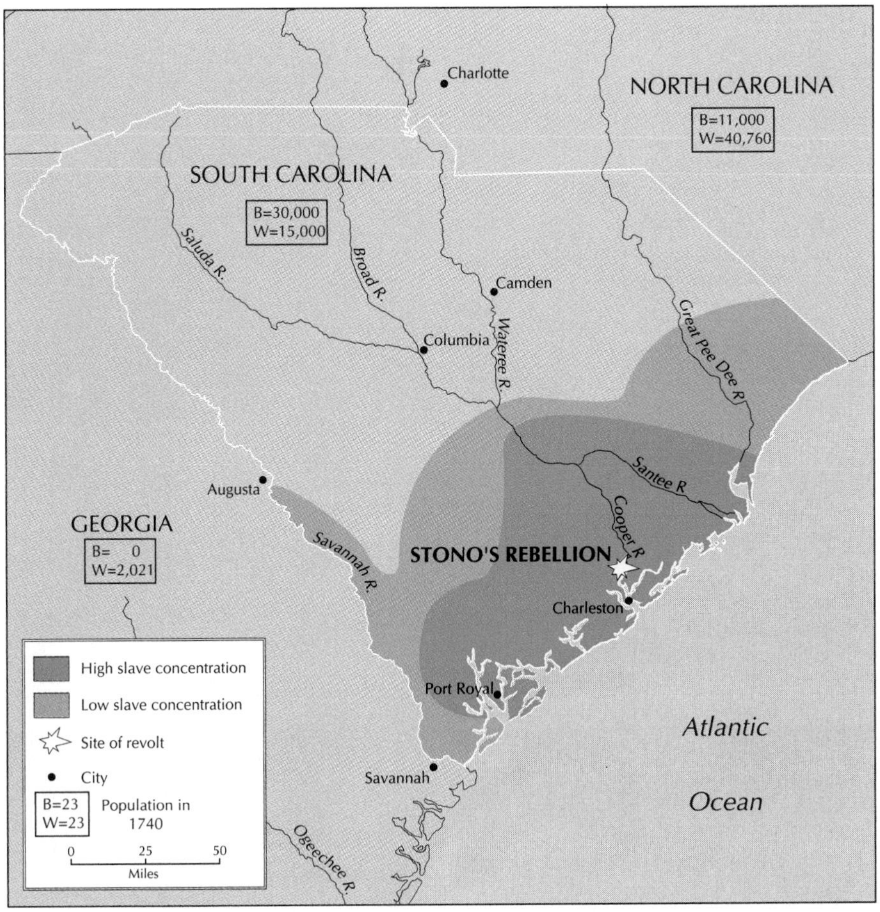
Charlotte
NORTH CAROLINA
B=11,000
W=40,760
SOUTH CAROLINA
B=30,000
W=15,000
Saluda R.
Broad R.
Camden
Columbia
Wateree R.
Great Pee Dee R.
Santee R.
Cooper R.
Augusta
GEORGIA
B= 0
W=2,021
Savannah R.
STONO'S REBELLION
Charleston
Port Royal
Savannah
Ogeechee R.
Atlantic
Ocean
High slave concentration
Low slave concentration
Site of revolt
City
B=23
W=23
Population in 1740
0 25 50
Miles

MAP 28

The Role of Maroons, Slaves, and Free Blacks in the Seven Years' War and Other European World Wars Waged in the Americas and the Caribbean

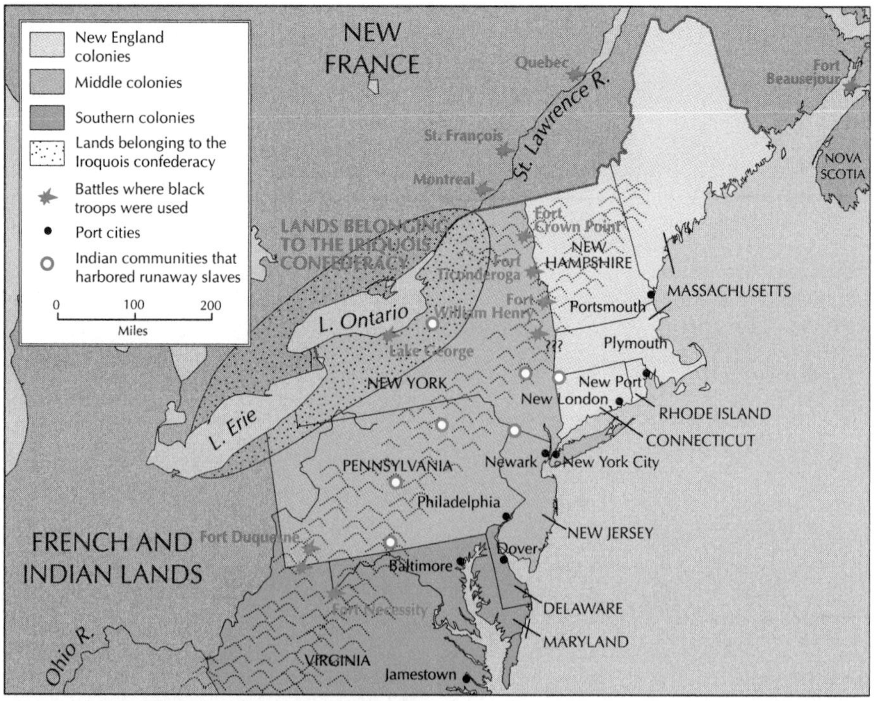
New England colonies
Middle colonies
Southern colonies
Lands belonging to the Iroquois confederacy
Battles where black troops were used
Port cities
Indian communities that harbored runaway slaves
0 100 200
Miles
NEW FRANCE
Quebec
St. Lawrence R.
Fort Beausejour
NOVA SCOTIA
St. François
Montreal
LANDS BELONGING TO THE IROQUOIS CONFEDERACY
Fort Crown Point
Fort Ticonderoga
NEW HAMPSHIRE
MASSACHUSETTS
Portsmouth
Fort William Henry
L. Ontario
Lake George
Plymouth
NEW YORK
New Port
New London
RHODE ISLAND
CONNECTICUT
L. Erie
Newark
New York City
PENNSYLVANIA
Philadelphia
NEW JERSEY
FRENCH AND INDIAN LANDS
Fort Duquesne
Dover
Baltimore
Fort Necessity
DELAWARE
MARYLAND
Ohio R.
VIRGINIA
Jamestown

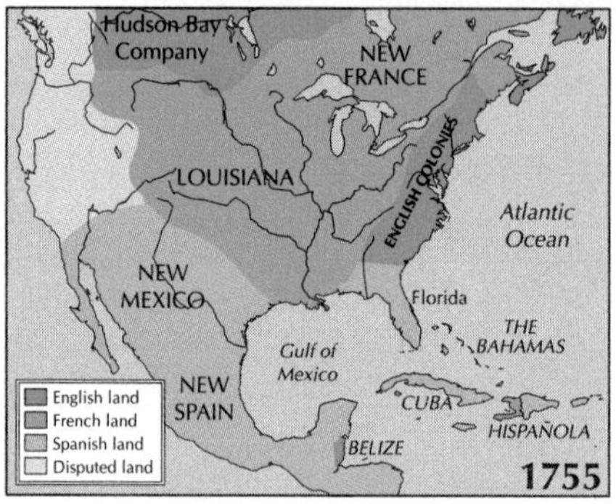
Hudson Bay Company
NEW FRANCE
LOUISIANA
ENGLISH COLONIES
Atlantic Ocean
NEW MEXICO
Florida
THE BAHAMAS
Gulf of Mexico
NEW SPAIN
CUBA
HISPAÑOLA
BELIZE
English land
French land
Spanish land
Disputed land
1755

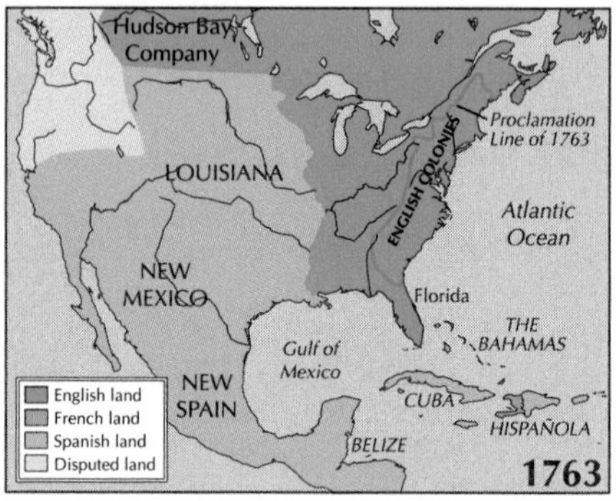
Hudson Bay Company
Proclamation Line of 1763
LOUISIANA
ENGLISH COLONIES
Atlantic Ocean
NEW MEXICO
Florida
THE BAHAMAS
Gulf of Mexico
NEW SPAIN
CUBA
HISPAÑOLA
BELIZE
English land
French land
Spanish land
Disputed land
1763

From 1755 to 1763, France and England fought what became known in Europe as the Seven Years' War and in America as the French and Indian War. The conflict was fought in Europe and in the Americas. Most of the fighting in North America occurred along the western frontier, where many Native American groups aligned themselves with the French and attacked British settlements. In the Caribbean the French and British extensively used African soldiers. The British captured the French islands of Martinique and Guadelupe in 1759, and then captured Havana, Cuba, in 1762. Over 3,000 African soldiers were used by the British and even more by the French and Spanish in the Caribbean, not including maroons, and also not including runaway slaves who served as guides and spies for both sides during the war. Slaves were even armed and used in the thirteen colonies, particularly in South Carolina and Georgia and in frontier areas in New York, Pennsylvania, and Virginia. Many French and English slaveholders used their slaves to assist in protecting their families, farms, and property. In 1763, Great Britain defeated France and Spain, and as a result of the victories of their African troops in the Caribbean, the British were able to win favorable concessions at the Paris Peace in 1763. These concessions included control of all the land west of the Appalachian Mountains to the Mississippi River and possession of France's lands in Canada. Now only two European nations remained in control of North America, Spain and England, and both relied on slavery for economic growth and prosperity. During the Seven Years' War hundreds of Indians and slaves fought for the French and the British in return for their freedom or security. The Seven Years' War was fought mainly in Canada, the Ohio Valley, and western Pennsylvania, New York, and Massachusetts. With the defeat of the French and their Indian allies, many Americans, particularly slave owners, were intent on moving into the new western lands. ■

MAP 29

The British Proclamation Line of 1763 and Its Impact on Slavery in Colonial America (1763)

At the end of the Seven Years' War, the British undertook several actions that upset the colonists greatly, chief of which was the issuance of the Proclamation of 1763. This measure forbade the colonists from crossing the Appalachian Mountains into the newly ceded territory east of the Mississippi River and west of the Appalachian Mountains. The British issued the proclamation with the goal of splitting the new lands between the Southwestern Indians, who were given the Mississippi Territory, and the Northwestern Indians of the new British (formerly French) colony of Quebec, which was a part of the Northwest Territory. The slaveholders in the South were furious. They desired the new lands that were given to the Southwestern Indians for their ever-growing plantations, which were rapidly exhausting the soil in the East. Many northern colonists also wanted to settle in the lands beyond the Appalachians in the Ohio Valley. The Proclamation of 1763 was unacceptable to both northerners and southerners. ■

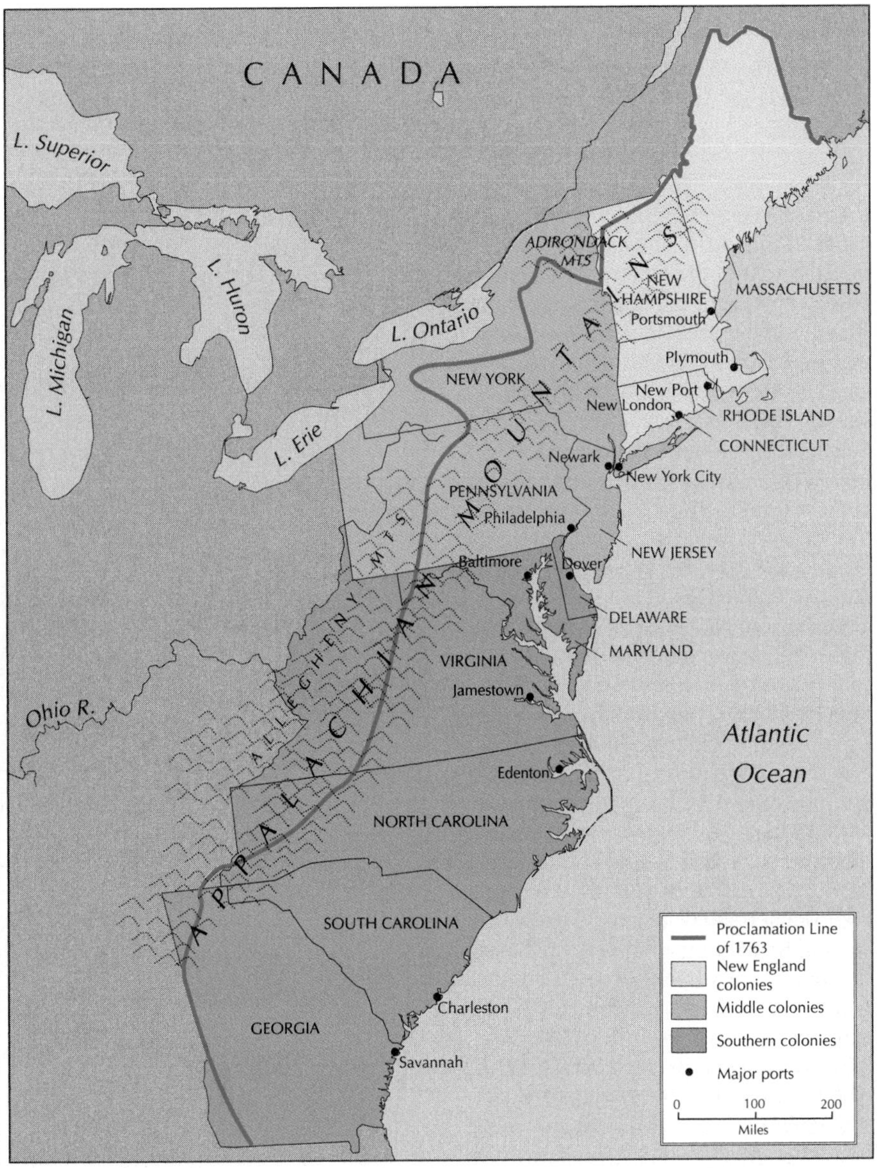
CANADA
L. Superior
L. Michigan
L. Huron
L. Ontario
L. Erie
Ohio R.
ADIRONDACK MTS
NEW HAMPSHIRE
Portsmouth
MASSACHUSETTS
Plymouth
NEW YORK
New Port
New London
RHODE ISLAND
CONNECTICUT
Newark
New York City
PENNSYLVANIA
Philadelphia
NEW JERSEY
Baltimore
Dover
DELAWARE
MARYLAND
VIRGINIA
Jamestown
ALLEGHENY MTS
APPALACHIAN MOUNTAINS
Edenton
NORTH CAROLINA
SOUTH CAROLINA
Charleston
GEORGIA
Savannah
Atlantic Ocean
Proclamation Line of 1763
New England colonies
Middle colonies
Southern colonies
Major ports
0
100
200
Miles

MAP 30

The Free Black and Slave Population of Colonial America (1770)

By 1770, African Americans made up 21 percnt of the colonies' total population. That is, of the 1,688,000 persons living in the thirteen colonies, approximately 459,822 were African Americans. Of this number, 440,000 were slaves. The South, because of its dependence on agriculture, contained the highest number of slaves. These slaves were needed to cultivate the cash crops of tobacco in Delaware, Maryland, Virginia, and northeastern North Carolina and rice and indigo in South Carolina, Georgia, and southeastern North Carolina. The North had fewer slaves because the society and economy that developed there required little or no slave labor; much of the economy was based on family farms, fishing, shipbuilding, and trade with other colonies and England. Although slaves passed through many New England ports and New England Puritans profited from their transport and sale, many New Englanders feared large numbers of blacks in their community. Thus most African Americans, free and slave, in the North could be found in large cities like Boston, Philadelphia, and New York where they worked as servants and as skilled and unskilled laborers. In the South the majority of slaves were located on large isolated plantations scattered along the Atlantic seaboard. Most free African Americans in the South lived in major port cities like Norfolk, Charleston, Savannah, and Baltimore. ■

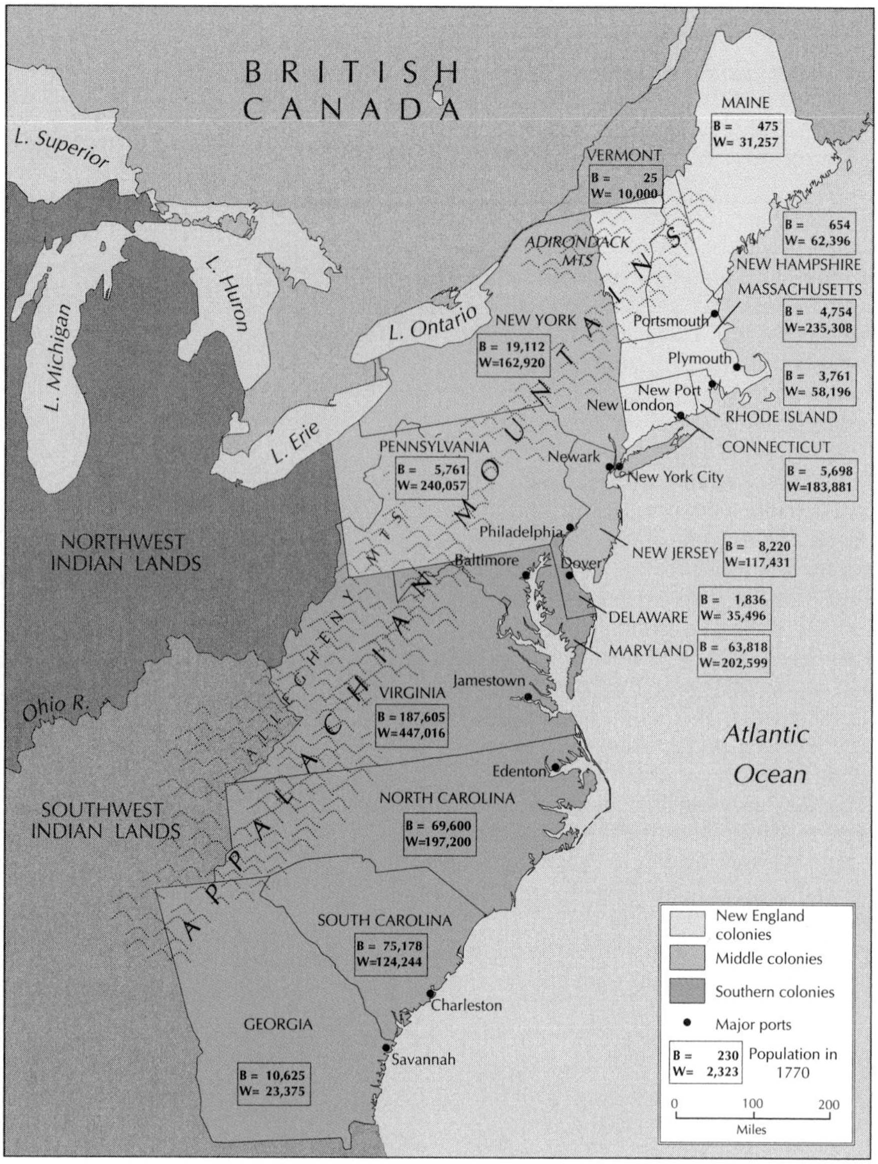
BRITISH CANADA
L. Superior
L. Michigan
L. Huron
L. Ontario
L. Erie
NORTHWEST INDIAN LANDS
SOUTHWEST INDIAN LANDS
Ohio R.
ADIRONDACK MTS
ALLEGHENY MTS
APPALACHIAN MOUNTAINS
MAINE
B = 475
W= 31,257
VERMONT
B = 25
W= 10,000
B = 654
W= 62,396
NEW HAMPSHIRE
MASSACHUSETTS
B = 4,754
W=235,308
B = 3,761
W= 58,196
RHODE ISLAND
CONNECTICUT
B = 5,698
W=183,881
NEW YORK
B = 19,112
W=162,920
Portsmouth
Plymouth
New Port
New London
Newark
New York City
PENNSYLVANIA
B = 5,761
W= 240,057
Philadelphia
Baltimore
Dover
NEW JERSEY
B = 8,220
W=117,431
DELAWARE
B = 1,836
W= 35,496
MARYLAND
B = 63,818
W=202,599
Jamestown
VIRGINIA
B = 187,605
W=447,016
Edenton
NORTH CAROLINA
B = 69,600
W=197,200
SOUTH CAROLINA
B = 75,178
W=124,244
Charleston
GEORGIA
B = 10,625
W= 23,375
Savannah
Atlantic Ocean
New England colonies
Middle colonies
Southern colonies
Major ports
B = 230
W= 2,323
Population in 1770
0
100
200
Miles

Map and Text Sources

15. Blake, William O. *The History of Slavery and the Slave Trade, Ancient and Modern; The Forms of Slavery That Prevailed in Ancient Nations, Particularly in Greece and Rome, the African Slave Trade and the Political History of Slavery in the United States*. Detroit: Negro History Press, 1971.

Curtin, Philip D. *The Atlantic Slave Trade; A Census*. Madison: University of Wisconsin Press, 1969.

Curtin, Philip D. *The Tropical Atlantic in the Age of the Slave Trade*. Washington, DC: American Historical Association, 1991.

Inikori, Joseph E., and Stanley L. Engerman. *The Atlantic Slave Trade: Effects on Economies, Societies, and Peoples in Africa, the Americas, and Europe*. Durham; NC: Duke University Press, 1992.

Manning, Patrick. *Slavery and African Life: Occidental, Oriental and African Slave Trades*. Cambridge: Cambridge University Press, 1990.

Mannix, Daniel. *Black Cargos: A History of the Atlantic Slave Trade, 1518–1865*. New York: Penguin Books, 1976.

Thompson, Vincent Bakpetu. *The Making of the Africian Diaspora in the Americas, 1441–1900*. White Plains, NY: Longman, 1986.

16. Curtin, Philip D. *Africa Remembered: Narratives by West Africans from the Era of the Slave Trade*. Madison: University of Wisconsin Press, 1968.

Curtin, Philip D. *Economic Change in Precolonial Africa: Senegambia in the Era of the Slave Trade*. Madison: University of Wisconsin Press, 1975.

Curtin, Philip D. *Cross-Cultural Trade in World History*. Cambridge: Cambridge University Press, 1984.

Law, Robin. *The Slave Coast of West Africa, 1550–1750: The Impact of the Atlantic Slave Trade on an African Society*. New York: Oxford University Press, 1991.

Mannix, Daniel. *Black Cargos: A History of the Atlantic Slave Trade, 1518–1865*. New York: Penguin Books, 1976.

17. Aptheker, Herbert. *American Negro Slave Revolts*, 6th ed. New York: International Publishers, 1993.

Hine, Darlene Clark and David Barry Gaspar, editors. *More Than Chattel: Black Women and Slavery in the Americas*. Bloomington: Indiana University Press, 1996.

Price, Richard. *Maroon Societies: Rebel Slave Communities in the Americas*. Baltimore: Johns Hopkins University Press, 1979.

Voelz, Peter M. *Slave and Soldier: The Military Impact of Blacks in the Colonial Americas*. New York: Garland, 1993.

18. Bridenbaugh, Carl, and Roberta Bridenbaugh. *No Peace beyond the Line: The English in the Caribbean, 1624–1690*. New York: Oxford University Press, 1972.

Dunn, Richard S. *Sugar and Slaves: The Rise of the Planter Class in the English West Indies, 1624–1713*. New York: Norton, 1973.

Knight, Franklin W., and Peggy K. Liss, eds. *Atlantic Port Cities: Economy, Culture, and Society in the Atlantic World, 1650–1850*. Knoxville: University of Tennessee Press, 1990.

Voelz, Peter M. *Slave and Soldier: The Military Impact of Blacks in the Colonial Americas*. New York: Garland, 1993.

19. Crow, Jeffrey J., Paul D. Escott, and Flora J. Hatley. *A History of African Americans in North Carolina*. Raleigh: North Carolina Division of Archives and History, North Carolina Department of Cultural Resources, 1992.

Hine, Darlene Clark and David Barry Gaspar, editors. *More Than Chattel: Black Women and Slavery in the Americas*. Bloomington: Indiana University Press, 1996.

Hine, Darlene Clark. *Black Women in United States History*. New York: Carlson Publishing, 1990.

Kulikoff, Allan. *Tobacco and Slaves: The Development of Southern Cultures in the Chesapeake, 1680–1800*. Chapel Hill: University of North Carolina Press, 1986.

Sobel, Mechal. *The World They Made Together: Black and White Values in Eighteenth-Century Virginia*. Princeton, NJ: Princeton University Press, 1987.

United States Bureau of the Census. *Historical Statistics of the United States, Colonial Times to 1970, Bicentennial Edition [Part 2]*. Washington, DC: Government Printing Office, 1975.

20. Cohen, David W., and Jack P. Greene, eds. *Neither Slave nor Free; The Freedman of African Descent in the Slave Societies of the New World*. Baltimore: Johns Hopkins University Press, 1972.

Godwyn, Morgan. *The Negro's & Indians Advocate Suing for Their Admission into the Church*. London: Printed for the author by J. D., 1680.

Greene, Jack P. *The American Colonies in the Eighteenth Century, 1689–1763*. Arlington Heights, IL: AHM Publishing Co., 1969.

Greene, Jack P. *Pursuits of Happiness: The Social Development of Early Modern British Colonies and the Formation of American Culture*. Chapel Hill: University of North Carolina Press, 1988.

Hine, Darlene Clark. *Black Women in United States History*. New York: Carlson Publishing, 1990.

Hine, Darlene Clark and David Barry Gaspar, editors. *More Than Chattel: Black Women and Slavery in the Americas*. Bloomington: Indiana University Press, 1996.

McDougall, Marion G. *Fugitive Slaves (1619–1865)*. Boston: Ginn, 1971.

21. Braund, Kathryn E. Holland. "The Creek Indians, Blacks and Slavery," *The Journal of Southern History* 57 (November 1991): 603–636.

Covington, James W. "Some Observations Concerning the Florida-Carolina Indian Slave Trade," *Florida Anthropologist* 20 (1967): 10–18.

Duignan, Peter, and Clarence Clendenen. *The United States and the African Slave Trade, 1619–1862*. Westport, CT: Greenwood Press, 1978.

Hine, Darlene Clark and David Barry Gaspar, editors. *Black Women in United States History*. New York: Carlson Publishing, 1990.

Hine, Darlene Clark and David Barry Gaspar, editors. *More Than Chattel: Black Women and Slavery in the Americas*. Bloomington: Indiana University Press, 1996.

Handler, Jerome S. "The Amerindian Slave Population of Barbados in the Seventeenth and Early Eighteenth Centuries," *Caribbean Studies* 8 (1969): 38–64.

Katz, William Loren. *Black Indians: A Hidden Heritage*. New York: Alladin Paperbacks, 1986.

Katz, William Loren. *Breaking the Chains: African-American Slave Resistance*, 1st ed. New York: Atheneum, 1990.

Leder, Lawrence H., ed. "The Livingston Indian Records, 1666–1723," *Pennsylvania History* 23 (1956): 29–240.

McClain, Kimberly Ann. "From Black to Indian: The Racial Identity of the Haliwa-Saponi Indians of North

Carolina." A.B. honors thesis, Harvard University, 1989.

McDougall, Marion G. *Fugitive Slaves (1619–1865)*. Freeport, NY: Books for Libraries Press, 1971.

Parramore, Thomas C. "Conspiracy and Revivalism in 1802: A Direful Symbiosis," *Negro History Bulletin* 43 (1980): 28–31.

Porter, Kennth W. "Relations between Negroes and Indians within the Present Limits of the United States," *Journal of Negro History* 17 (July 1932): 287–367.

United States Bureau of the Census. *Historical Statistics of the United States, Colonial Times to 1970, Bicentennial Edition [Part 2]*. Washington, DC: Government Printing Office, 1975.

Watson, Alan. *Slave Law in the Americas*. Athens: University of Georgia Press, 1989.

Willis, William S. "Divide and Rule: Red White and Black in the Southeast," *Journal of Negro History* 48 (July 1963); 157–176.

Winston, Sanford. "Indian Slavery in the North Carolina Region," *Journal of Negro History* 19 (October 1934): 431–440

22. United States Bureau of the Census. *Historical Statistics of the United States, Colonial Times to 1970, Bicentennial Edition, [Part 2]*. Washington, DC: Government Printing Office, 1975.

Voelz, Peter M. *Slave and Soldier: The Military Impact of Blacks in the Colonial Americas*. New York: Garland, 1993.

Washburn, Wilcomb E. *The Governor and the Rebel: A History of Bacon's Rebellion in Virginia*. New York: Norton, 1972.

23. Boyer, Paul, and Stephen Nissenbaum. *Salem-Village Witchcraft: A Documentary Record of Local Conflict in Colonial New England*. Boston: Northeastern University Press, 1972.

Hine, Darlene Clark. *Black Women in United States History*. New York: Carlson Publishing, 1990.

Hine, Darlene Clark and David Barry Gaspar editors. *More Than Chattel: Black Women and Slavery in the Americas*. Bloomington: Indiana University Press, 1996.

Lawson, Deodat. *A Brief and True Narrative of Some Remarkable Passages Relating to Sundry Persons Afflicted by Witchcraft at Salem Village*. Boston: Printed for B. Harris, 1692.

Walker, Sheila S. *Ceremonial Spirit Possession in Africa and Afro-America: Forms, Meanings and Functional Significance for Individuals and Social Groups*. Leiden, Netherlands: Brill, 1972.

Williams, Joseph J. *Voodoos and Obeahs; Phases of West Indian Witchcraft*. New York: AMS Press, 1970.

24. Aptheker, Herbert. *American Negro Slave Revolts*, 6th ed. New York: International Publishers, 1993.

Price, Richard. *Maroon Societies: Rebel Slave Communities in the Americas*. Baltimore: Johns Hopkins University Press, 1979.

Voelz, Peter M. *Slave and Soldier: The Military Impact of Blacks in the Colonial Americas*. New York: Garland, 1993.

25. Alderman, Clifford Lindsey. *Rum, Slaves and Molasses: The Story of New England's Triangular Trade*. Folkestone, England: Bailey & Swinfen, 1974.

United States Bureau of the Census. *Historical Statistics of the United States, Colonial Times to 1970, Bicentennial Edition [Part 2]*. Washington, DC: Government Printing Office, 1975.

26. Blockson, Charles L. *The Underground Railroad*. New York: Berkley Publishing Group, 1994.

Dramer, Kim. *Native Americans and Black Americans*. Philadelphia: Chelsea House Publishers, 1997.

Forbes, Jack D. *Black Africans and Native Americans: Color, Race, and Caste in the Evolution of Red-Black Peoples*, New York: Blackwell, 1988.

Forbes, Jack D. *Africans and Native Americans: The Language of Race and the Evolution of Red-Black Peoples*, 2nd ed. Urbana: University of Illinois Press, 1993.

Katz, William Loren. *Black Indians: A Hidden Heritage*. New York: Atheneum, 1986.

Katz, William Loren. *Breaking the Chains: African-American Slave Resistance*, 1st ed. New York: Atheneum, 1990.

McDougall, Marion G. *Fugitive Slaves (1619–1865)*. New York: Ginn, 1971.

Poe, Clarence H. "Indians, Slaves, and Tories: Legislation Regarding Them," *North Carolina Booklet* 9 (July 1909): 3–15.

Smallwood, Arwin D. "A History of Three Cultures: Indian Woods, North Carolina 1585 to 1995." Ph.D. dissertation, The Ohio State University, Columbus, 1997.

Watson, Alan. *Slave Law in the Americas*. Athens: University of Georgia Press, 1989.

27. Littlefield, Daniel C. *Rice and Slaves: Ethnicity and the Slave Trade in Colonial South Carolina*. Urbana: University of Illinois Press, 1991.

United States Bureau of the Census. *Historical Statistics of the United States, Colonial Times to 1970, Bicentennial Edition [Part 2]*. Washington, DC: Government Printing Office, 1975.

Voelz, Peter M. *Slave and Soldier: The Military Impact of Blacks in the Colonial Americas*. New York: Garland, 1993.

Wood, Peter H. *Black Majority: Negroes in Colonial South Carolina from 1670 through the Stono Rebellion*. New York: Norton, 1975.

28. Bird, Harrison. *Battle for a Continent*. New York: Oxford University Press, 1965.

Jennings, Francis. *Empire of Fortune: Crowns, Colonies, and Tribes in the Seven Years' War in America*. New York: Norton, 1988.

Voelz, Peter M. *Slave and Soldier: The Military Impact of Blacks in the Colonial Americas*. New York: Garland, 1993.

29. Sosin, Jack M. *Whitehall and the Wilderness: The Middle West in British Colonial Policy, 1760–1775*. Lincoln: University of Nebraska Press, 1961.

Voelz, Peter M. *Slave and Soldier: The Military Impact of Blacks in the Colonial Americas*. New York: Garland, 1993.

30. United States Bureau of the Census. *Historical Statistics of the United States, Colonial Times to 1970, Bicentennial Edition [Part 2]*. Washington, DC: Government Printing Office, 1975.

MAP 31

African-Americans and the American Revolution (1770–1783)

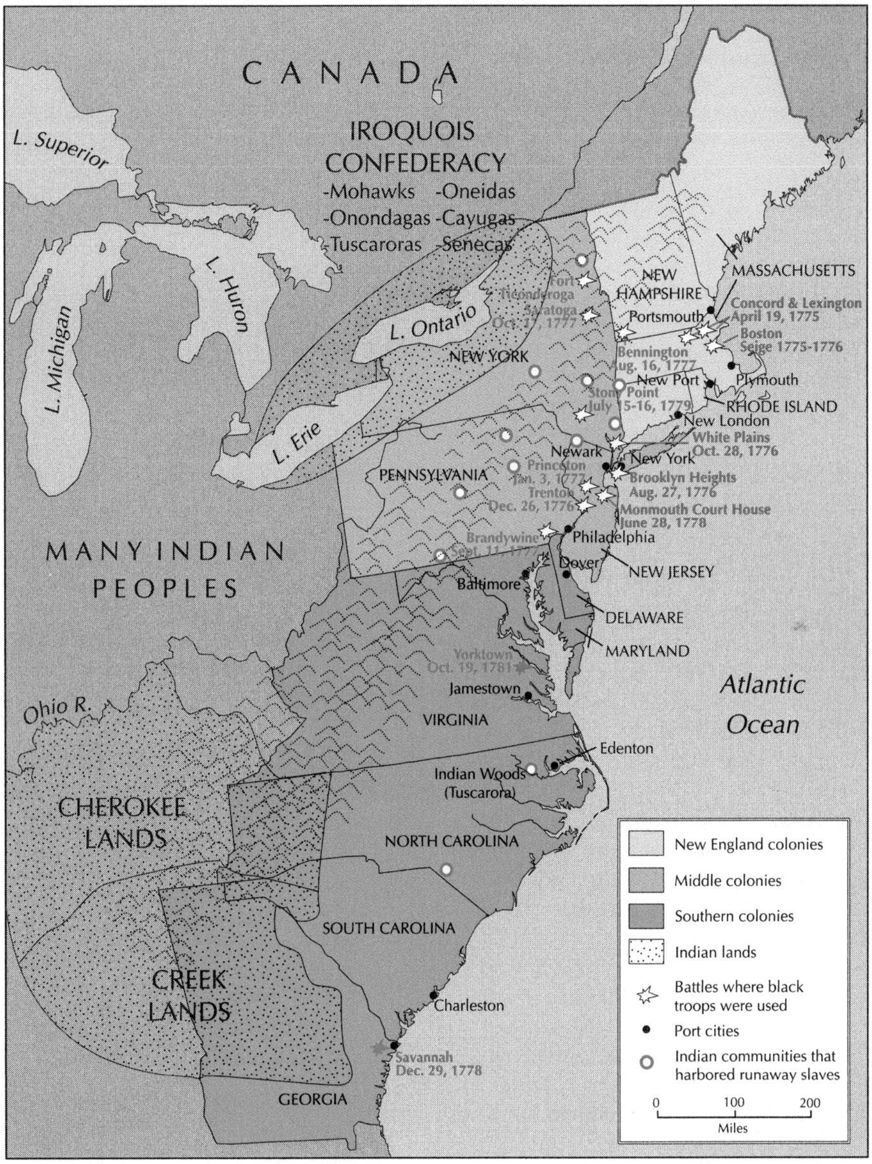
CANADA
IROQUOIS CONFEDERACY
-Mohawks -Oneidas
-Onondagas -Cayugas
-Tuscaroras -Senecas
L. Superior
L. Michigan
L. Huron
L. Ontario
L. Erie
MANY INDIAN PEOPLES
Ohio R.
CHEROKEE LANDS
CREEK LANDS
NEW HAMPSHIRE
MASSACHUSETTS
Portsmouth
Fort Ticonderoga
Saratoga
Oct. 17, 1777
Concord & Lexington
April 19, 1775
Boston
Seige 1775-1776
Bennington
Aug. 16, 1777
NEW YORK
New Port
Plymouth
Stony Point
July 15-16, 1779
RHODE ISLAND
New London
White Plains
Oct. 28, 1776
Newark
New York
Princeton
Jan. 3, 1777
Brooklyn Heights
Aug. 27, 1776
PENNSYLVANIA
Trenton
Dec. 26, 1776
Monmouth Court House
June 28, 1778
Brandywine
Sept. 11, 1777
Philadelphia
Dover
NEW JERSEY
Baltimore
DELAWARE
MARYLAND
Yorktown
Oct. 19, 1781
Jamestown
VIRGINIA
Atlantic Ocean
Edenton
Indian Woods
(Tuscarora)
NORTH CAROLINA
SOUTH CAROLINA
Charleston
Savannah
Dec. 29, 1778
GEORGIA
New England colonies
Middle colonies
Southern colonies
Indian lands
Battles where black troops were used
Port cities
Indian communities that harbored runaway slaves
0
100
200
Miles

As tensions began to increase between Americans and the British over the Quebec Act, the Proclamation of 1763, and the Intolerable Acts, passed from 1763 to 1776, so did the desire of many Americans to be free from England. The Revolutionary spirit soon took hold of many colonists. Like many white citizens, free blacks and slaves were also filled with the revolutionary spirit. Literate blacks studied Thomas Paine, Jean Jacques Rousseau, John Locke, and the other political philosophers of the time. Those blacks who could not read were told of their ideas by literate blacks. As a result, when the British began to impose the Coercive Acts on Boston, black Bostonians were as outraged as white Bostonians. One such outraged black was Crispus Attucks, who in 1770 became the first American to die in what has become known as the Boston Massacre. Attucks was a leader of a group of protesters who spoke out against British soldiers being in Boston. The group was fired on by the British, and Attucks and several others were shot and killed. This event was one of the major events that led to the American Revolution. When the Revolutionary War broke out in 1775, blacks were among the first to join the Continental Army. They found, however, that there was widespread opposition, in both the North and South, to black participation in the war. For this reason, the Continental Congress prohibited blacks from serving in the army. This ruling stood until late 1775, when Lord Dunmore, the royal governor of Virginia and a Loyalist, offered to emancipate any slave who was willing to join the British Army in order to quell the Revolution. This action prompted the Continental Congress to reverse itself and allow at least free blacks to serve. These blacks fought bravely and valiantly throughout the Revolutionary War. During the war over 5,000 free blacks served in the Continental Army, and an equal number of runaway slaves and free blacks in the British Army. ■

MAP 32

The British, Their Indian Allies, and Slaves during the American Revolution (1776–1783)

During the American Revolution over 5,000 slaves and free blacks fought for their freedom as allies of the British. The British also enlisted the aid of the Six Nations (the Mohawk, Seneca, Onondaga, Oneida, Cayuga, and Tuscarora) in the North and the Cherokee and Creek in the South. As a result of this alliance, many Indians and blacks found themselves allies against the Americans. In western New York, Pennsylvania, Maryland, and Virginia, warriors of the Six Nations under Chief Joseph Brant raided plantations, killing whites and freeing slaves as they had done during the French and Indian War from 1755 to 1763. Those slaves who so desired were allowed to become members of the Iroquois Confederacy, and none were ever returned to slave owners, even after repeated requests. The American Revolution was not the first time that members of the Six Nations fought with blacks, nor was it the last. In the South the Cherokee and Creek, who also were aligned with the British, menaced the Carolinas and Georgia. In South Carolina slaveholders on the frontier were constantly losing slaves to the Cherokee and Creek, who had served as slave catchers for the southerners since the Tuscarora War of 1711–1713. When the Revolutionary War ended, thousands of slaves had been taken by Britain and its Indian allies. The British alone took with them over 14,000 Africans—some slave, some free—when they withdrew from the colonies. It is unclear exactly how many blacks their Indian allies freed, but the number is likely to be in the hundreds if not thousands. ■

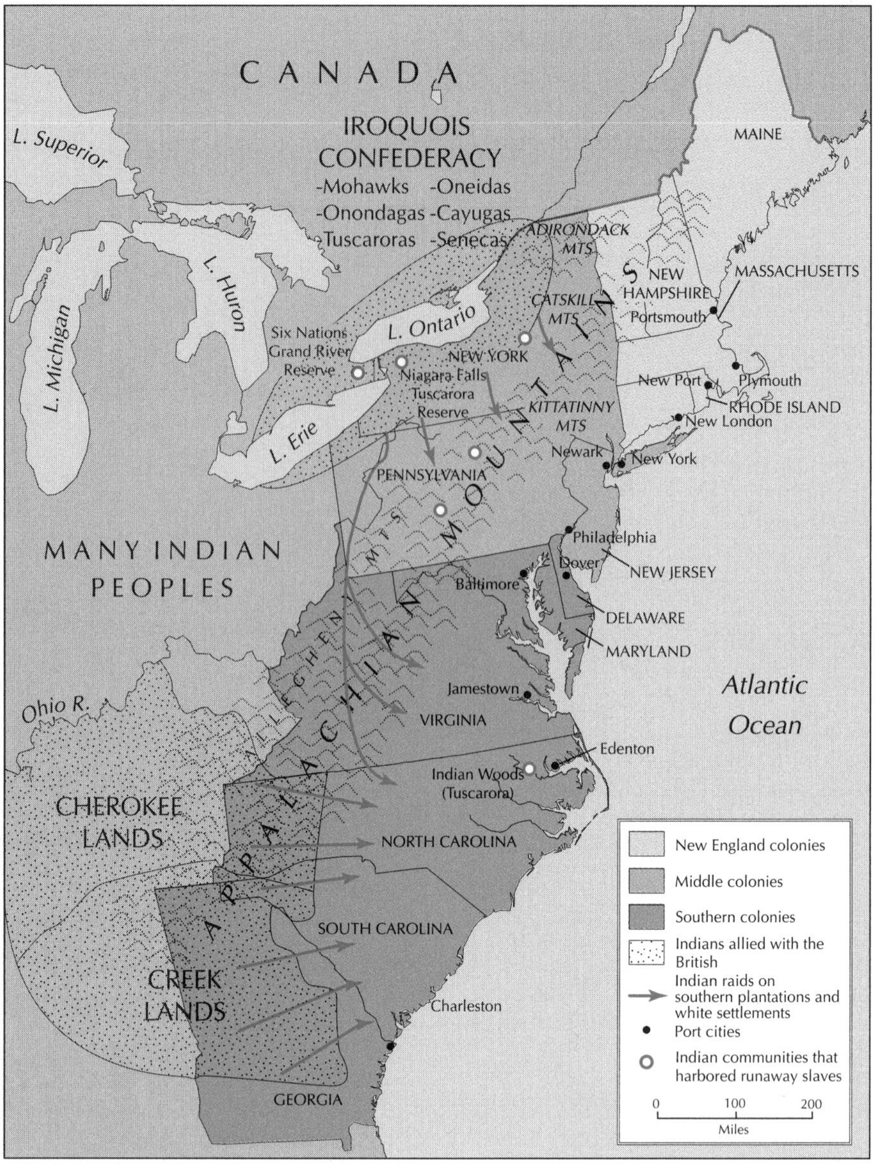
CANADA
IROQUOIS CONFEDERACY
-Mohawks -Oneidas
-Onondagas -Cayugas
-Tuscaroras -Senecas
L. Superior
L. Michigan
L. Huron
L. Ontario
L. Erie
Six Nations Grand River Reserve
Niagara Falls Tuscarora Reserve
NEW YORK
ADIRONDACK MTS
CATSKILL MTS
KITTATINNY MTS
PENNSYLVANIA
ALLEGHENY MTS
APPALACHIAN MOUNTAINS
MANY INDIAN PEOPLES
Ohio R.
CHEROKEE LANDS
CREEK LANDS
MAINE
NEW HAMPSHIRE
Portsmouth
MASSACHUSETTS
New Port
Plymouth
RHODE ISLAND
New London
Newark
New York
Philadelphia
Dover
NEW JERSEY
Baltimore
DELAWARE
MARYLAND
Jamestown
VIRGINIA
Edenton
Indian Woods (Tuscarora)
NORTH CAROLINA
SOUTH CAROLINA
Charleston
GEORGIA
Atlantic Ocean
New England colonies
Middle colonies
Southern colonies
Indians allied with the British
Indian raids on southern plantations and white settlements
Port cities
Indian communities that harbored runaway slaves
0 100 200
Miles

MAP 33

The British Withdrawal and the Resettlement of Black Loyalists Following the American Revolution (1783–1792)

On November 7, 1775, Lord Dunmore, the royal governor of Virginia, issued a proclamation extending freedom to any slave who would join the British in the Revolutionary War. As a result, during the war as many as 5,000 free slaves and blacks decided to fight for the British instead of the Americans, concluding that the promise of freedom was preferable to perpetual slavery. These slaves were rewarded by the British by being freed and taken with them when they withdrew from the colonies. Over 14,000 slaves, free blacks, and former soldiers were evacuated along with white Loyalists from Charleston (6,000), Savannah (4,000), and New York (3,000 to 4,000). The British not only took blacks who were loyal to their cause, but also razed numerous plantations and confiscated slaves before withdrawing to Halifax, (in Nova Scotia), England, and the Caribbean. The former slaves and free blacks who had served in the British Army or Navy were allowed passage to any part of the British Empire, even England. Most chose to go to Halifax, where they were promised they would be cared for. After several years of neglect, Thomas Peters, a black leader in Halifax, traveled to England, where he requested further redress. As a result, in 1792 the black population was moved from Nova Scotia and resettled in Sierra Leone, where they established the settlement of Freetown. These blacks helped to create the first West African state controlled by blacks who were born in what would become the United States. ■

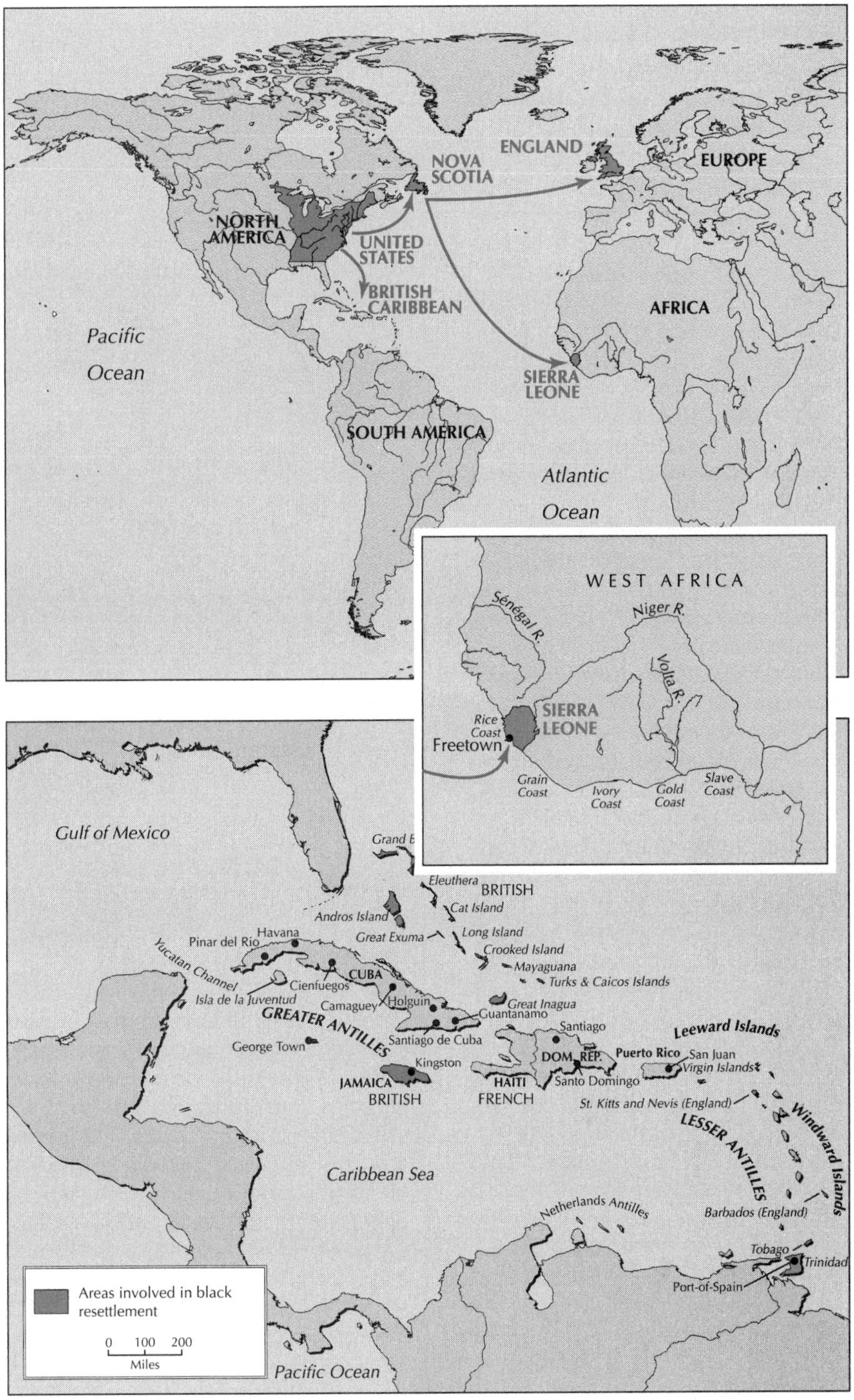
NORTH AMERICA
NOVA SCOTIA
ENGLAND
EUROPE
UNITED STATES
BRITISH CARIBBEAN
AFRICA
Pacific Ocean
SIERRA LEONE
SOUTH AMERICA
Atlantic Ocean
WEST AFRICA
Sénégal R.
Niger R.
Volta R.
Rice Coast
Freetown
SIERRA LEONE
Grain Coast
Ivory Coast
Gold Coast
Slave Coast
Gulf of Mexico
Eleuthera
BRITISH
Cat Island
Andros Island
Great Exuma
Long Island
Crooked Island
Mayaguana
Turks & Caicos Islands
Pinar del Rio
Havana
Yucatan Channel
Cienfuegos
CUBA
Isla de la Juventud
Camaguey
Holguin
Great Inagua
Guantanamo
GREATER ANTILLES
Santiago de Cuba
Santiago
Leeward Islands
George Town
Kingston
DOM. REP.
Puerto Rico
San Juan
Virgin Islands
JAMAICA
BRITISH
HAITI
FRENCH
Santo Domingo
St. Kitts and Nevis (England)
LESSER ANTILLES
Windward Islands
Caribbean Sea
Netherlands Antilles
Barbados (England)
Tobago
Trinidad
Port-of-Spain
Areas involved in black resettlement
0 100 200
Miles
Pacific Ocean

MAP 34

The Emancipation of Slaves in the North and the Expansion of Slavery in the Southern States and Territories of the New American Republic (1777–1800)

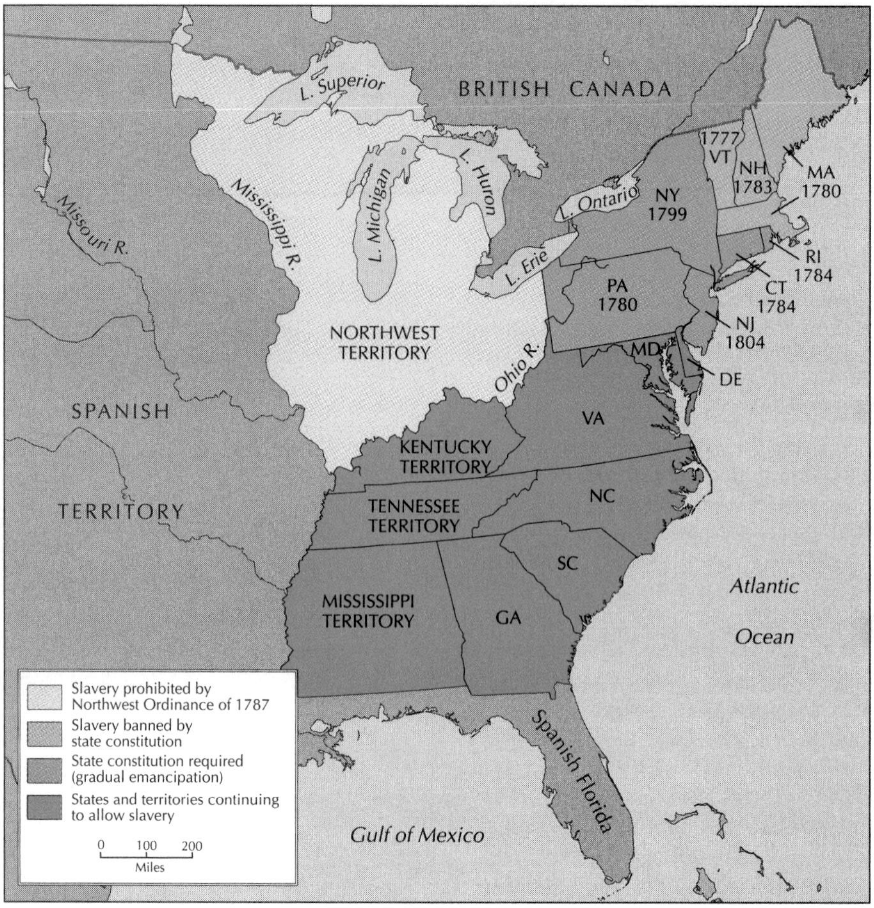
L. Superior
BRITISH CANADA
Mississippi R.
Missouri R.
L. Michigan
L. Huron
Ontario
L. Erie
1777 VT
NH 1783
MA 1780
NY 1799
RI 1784
CT 1784
PA 1780
NJ 1804
MD
DE
NORTHWEST TERRITORY
Ohio R.
SPANISH
TERRITORY
VA
KENTUCKY TERRITORY
TENNESSEE TERRITORY
NC
SC
MISSISSIPPI TERRITORY
GA
Atlantic
Ocean
Spanish Florida
Gulf of Mexico
Slavery prohibited by Northwest Ordinance of 1787
Slavery banned by state constitution
State constitution required (gradual emancipation)
States and territories continuing to allow slavery
0 100 200
Miles

Although slavery existed in both the North and South, it evolved differently in each region during the colonial era. This was due in part to the distinct differences in the colonies themselves. It must be remembered that when the first English settlers arrived in Massachusetts Bay, which would become part of the North, in 1627, they were escaping religious persecution. However, those who settled the Chesapeake Bay area, which would become part of the South, 20 years earlier in 1607, were in search of immediate riches and had no intention of staying. Most New Englanders had traveled to America with their families and were very pious. Their religion required them to be hard workers and do their own work. As a result, few slaves were introduced into these mostly Puritan and later Quaker communities. The few slaves who found their way into the region were employed as servants or hired out as laborers. The South, on the other hand, was made up mostly of white males, many of whom were the children of English aristocracy and were not used to hard work. They attempted to make money from the cultivation of their cash crops of tobacco, rice, and indigo. This kind of agriculturally based economy required large numbers of slaves to work the large tobacco, rice, and indigo plantations. As a result, the South had a greater need for slave labor, and most southern slaves were agricultural laborers. The northern economy, on the other hand, developed around mercantile trade, shipbuilding, and fishing. Most slaves either worked as servants or were allowed to work in the port cities at unskilled jobs such as loading and unloading ships or as skilled laborers building ships, along with other jobs. These early economic differences would lead to future conflicts between the North and South over the expansion of slavery. As early as 1777, slavery was being banned by northern states. The first state to do so was Vermont, which forbade the practice when it drafted its constitution in 1777. Those states that did not ban the practice in the North amended their constitutions to gradually eliminate the institution. By 1800, all northern states had either forbidden slavery or passed laws for gradual emancipation. In contrast, the South continued to expand slavery. Northern emancipation, however, meant that African Americans enslaved in the South could find refuge and allies in the North in the fight to end slavery. ■

MAP 35

The Impact of the Three-Fifths Compromise and the Northwest Ordinance on the Institution of Slavery in America (1787)

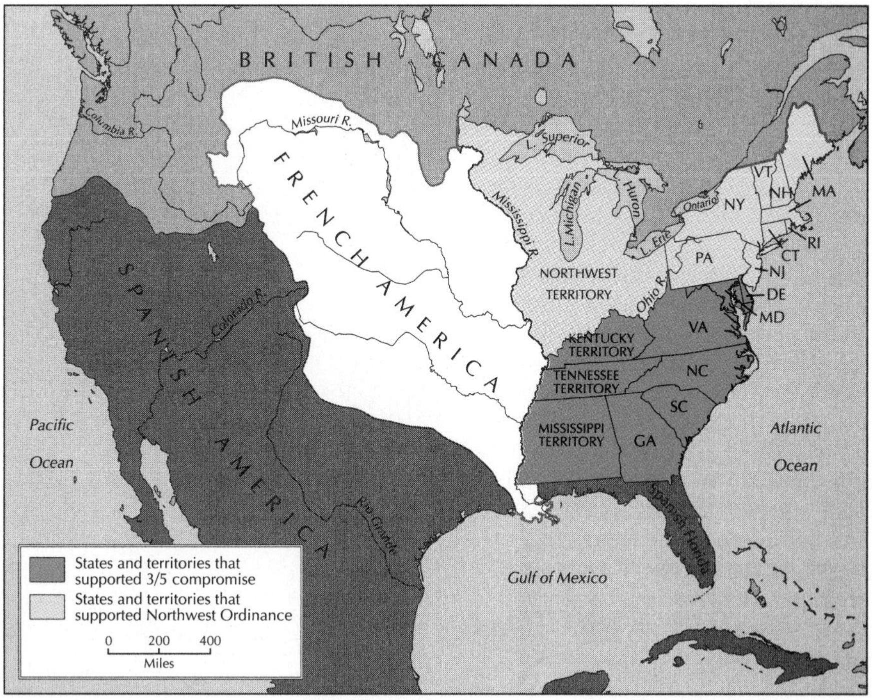
BRITISH CANADA
FRENCH AMERICA
SPANISH AMERICA
Missouri R.
Columbia R.
L. Superior
L. Michigan
Huron
L. Ontario
L. Erie
Mississippi R.
Ohio R.
Colorado R.
Rio Grande
NORTHWEST TERRITORY
KENTUCKY TERRITORY
TENNESSEE TERRITORY
MISSISSIPPI TERRITORY
VT
NH
MA
NY
RI
CT
PA
NJ
DE
MD
VA
NC
SC
GA
Spanish Florida
Pacific Ocean
Atlantic Ocean
Gulf of Mexico
States and territories that supported 3/5 compromise
States and territories that supported Northwest Ordinance
0 200 400
Miles

During the Constitutional Convention of 1787 the issue of slavery figured prominently in the delegates' considerations. The southern slaveholding states, which had large numbers of slaves, demanded that their slaves be added to their overall population for the purpose of determining how many congressmen a state should have in the House of Representatives. The northern states, which boasted larger free labor populations, opposed the move. In what became known as the Three-Fifths Compromise, it was agreed that a slave would be counted as three-fifths of a person, giving the South greater representation in the House of Representatives than it would have had based on the number of free voters. The Constitution also paved the way for the first fugitive slave laws (which would be enacted later) when it defined the duty of one state to another. In another compromise, the North was promised an end to the Atlantic slave trade in 1808—20 years after the ratification of the Constitution. Another piece of legislation that had significant impact was the Northwest Ordinance of 1787. The Northwest Ordinance forbade slavery in the Northwest Territory—what today is Ohio, Indiana, Michigan, Illinois, and Wisconsin. This act and the emancipation of slaves by northern states meant half of the nation was to be free and the other half slave. The decision to create a nation half slave and half free would lead to continuous friction between northern and southern states and to a series of compromises including the Compromise of 1820, the Compromise of 1850, and the Kansas-Nebraska Act of 1854. This friction eventually led to the Civil War in 1861. ■

MAP 36

The Haitian Revolution (1791–1804)

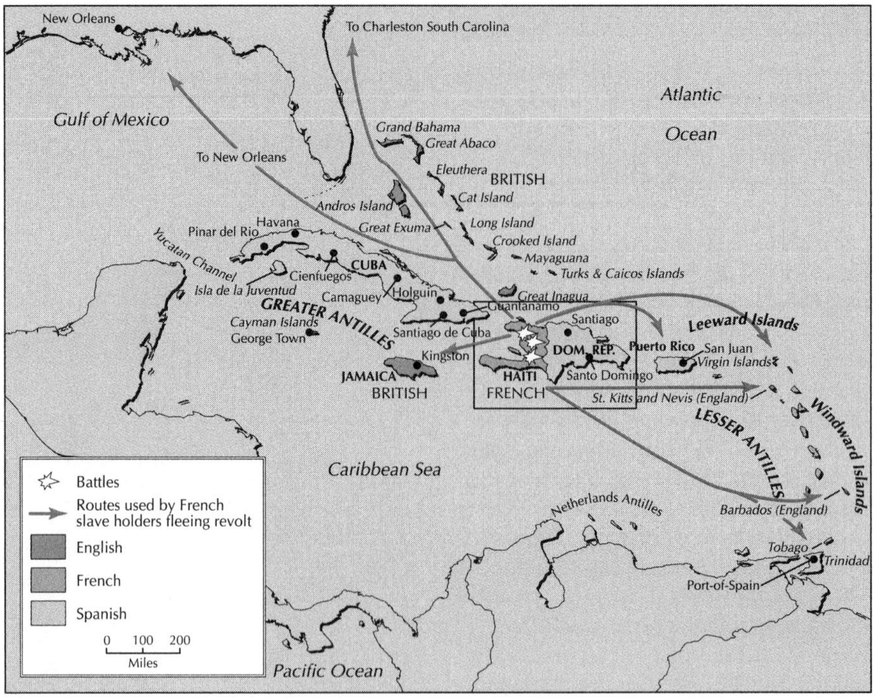
New Orleans
To Charleston South Carolina
Atlantic
Ocean
Gulf of Mexico
To New Orleans
Grand Bahama
Great Abaco
Eleuthera
BRITISH
Cat Island
Andros Island
Great Exuma
Long Island
Crooked Island
Mayaguana
Turks & Caicos Islands
Havana
Pinar del Rio
Yucatan Channel
CUBA
Cienfuegos
Isla de la Juventud
Camaguey
Holguin
Great Inagua
Guantanamo
GREATER ANTILLES
Cayman Islands
George Town
Santiago de Cuba
Santiago
DOM. REP.
Leeward Islands
Puerto Rico
San Juan
Virgin Islands
Kingston
JAMAICA
BRITISH
HAITI
FRENCH
Santo Domingo
St. Kitts and Nevis (England)
LESSER ANTILLES
Windward Islands
Caribbean Sea
Netherlands Antilles
Barbados (England)
Tobago
Trinidad
Port-of-Spain
Pacific Ocean
Battles
Routes used by French slave holders fleeing revolt
English
French
Spanish
0 100 200
Miles

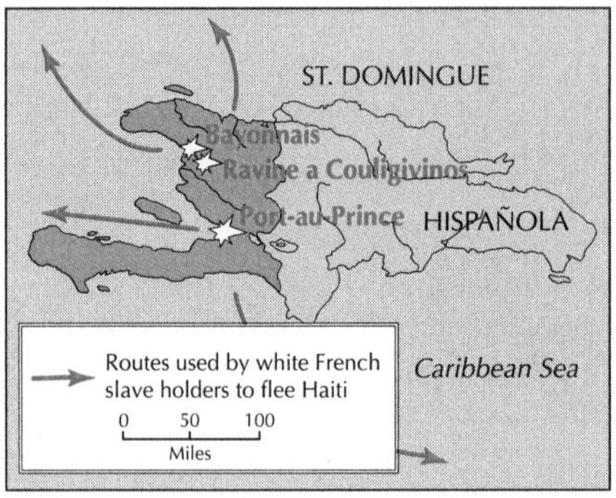
ST. DOMINGUE
Bayonnais
Ravine a Couleuvres
Port-au-Prince
HISPAÑOLA
Routes used by white French slave holders to flee Haiti
0 50 100
Miles
Caribbean Sea

From 1791 to 1803, Haiti was the site of one of the longest, most violent and successful slave revolts in the history of the Americas. Haiti occupies the western half of the island of Hispaniola. At the time of the slave revolt, Haiti was ruled by France. The Spanish, which had introduced African slavery to the island in the 1500s, controlled the island until 1697 when it was given to France in the Treaty of Ryswick. The French called their new colony Saint Domingue and continued to use it to produce sugar, molasses, and rum. They also used African slaves for labor. French slave owners treated the slaves so cruelly, however, that in 1697 the slaves began a long series of revolts that ended in 1804 with their freedom. As a result of the largest and most organized of these revolts, which began in 1791, the French government abolished slavery on the island in 1793. Led by Toussaint L'Ouverture, a former slave, slaves seized control of the colony in 1801. Before the French were forced to flee, L'Ouverture was captured and later imprisoned in France. His generals, Jean-Jacques Dessalines, Henri Christophe, and Alexandre Petion continued the revolution and won Haiti's independence from France in 1804. The Haitian Revolution, which in many ways paralleled the examples of the American and French Revolutions, had a profound impact on America. Because Napoleon needed money after spending large amounts trying to defeat the Haitians, he agreed to sell the Louisiana Territory in 1803 to Thomas Jefferson, an acquisition that doubled the size of the United States. It also led to Haiti becoming the first independent African republic in the Western Hemisphere, and to the mass exodus of white French slaveholders to the United States. The revolution caused widespread fear among southern slaveholders of a similar revolt in the United States. This fear would touch off a major panic in Virginia and North Carolina and lead to the strengthening of slave codes throughout the slaveholding South. ■

MAP 37

The Passage of the First Fugitive Slave Act and the Development of the Underground Railroad (1793)

By 1790, most northern states had either abolished slavery or enacted laws to force gradual emancipation. In response to these laws, many slaves fled to the northern states, where they were free from the horrors of slavery. When the slave states requested assistance from these states in recovering their lost "property," most free states refused. The slave states were infuriated. Thus, at the insistence of southerners, in 1793, Congress enacted the first fugitive slave law. This law required free states to turn over any fugitive slaves requested by their "masters" to slave catchers. Although the issue sparked debate over the application of the law to free blacks, the controversy proved short-lived and the law was enacted. In part, the law was spawned by the fears of white southerners throughout the South that runaway slaves would encourage slave revolts. Their fears were fueled by the ongoing Haitian Revolution. Southern slaveholders were also concerned about the return of their property (slaves) in which they had invested hundreds and sometimes thousands of dollars. The law, however, devastated free blacks, who were excluded from the protection of the Constitution. As a result, many free blacks, along with fugitive slaves, were forced into slavery—or, if they were able to, fled further north into Canada, which had abolished slavery in 1791, or south and west into Spanish Florida and Mexico, out of the legal reach of southern slave catchers.

TO CANADA
BRITISH CANADA
L. Superior
IROQUOIS CONFEDERACY
L. Huron
L. Michigan
L. Ontario
L. Erie
Six Nations Grand River Reserve
Niagara Falls
Tuscarora Reserve
NEW YORK
NEW HAMPSHIRE
Portsmouth
MASSACHUSETTS
Boston
Plymouth
New Port
New London
RHODE ISLAND
CONNECTICUT
Newark
New York City
PENNSYLVANIA
Philadelphia
MIDWESTERN INDIANS
TO INDIANS IN NORTHWEST
Ohio R.
Baltimore
Dover
NEW JERSEY
Washington D. C.
DELAWARE
MARYLAND
Jamestown
VIRGINIA
Atlantic Ocean
Edenton
Indian Woods
KENTUCKY TERRITORY June 1, 1792
CHEROKEE LANDS
TENNESSEE TERRITORY June 1, 1796
NORTH CAROLINA
TO INDIANS IN SOUTHWEST
SOUTH CAROLINA
Charleston
SOUTHWEST TERRITORY
CREEK LANDS
GEORGIA
Savannah
TO SPANISH FLORIDA
Free states and territories affected by fugitive slave act
Slave states and territories
Port cities
Indian communities that harbored runaway slaves
Early Underground Railroad
0
100
200
Miles

MAP 38

The Free Black and Slave Population of the United States (1800)

By 1800, there were 4.3 million whites and over 1 million blacks living in the United States. Blacks had become a well-established part of American society; some were slaves, and some were free. They made up 19 percent of the country's total population and nearly half of the total population of southern slaveholding states. They were necessary to the workings of the American economic and social structure. The vast majority of blacks were slaves and were concentrated in the South Atlantic states of Maryland, Virginia, North Carolina (the eastern part), and South Carolina. Most resided on rural plantations scattered throughout the South, farming tobacco, cotton, and other agricultural crops. The rest, skilled and unskilled free blacks and slaves, could be found in southern and northern port and river cities. By 1800 the majority of African Americans were native born, and many were descendants of the first blacks who were brought to Virginia in 1619. From 1800 to 1830, as a result of the domestic slave trade, the southern black population would shift from the South Atlantic states to the Gulf states of Florida, Alabama, Mississippi, Louisiana, and Texas. ■

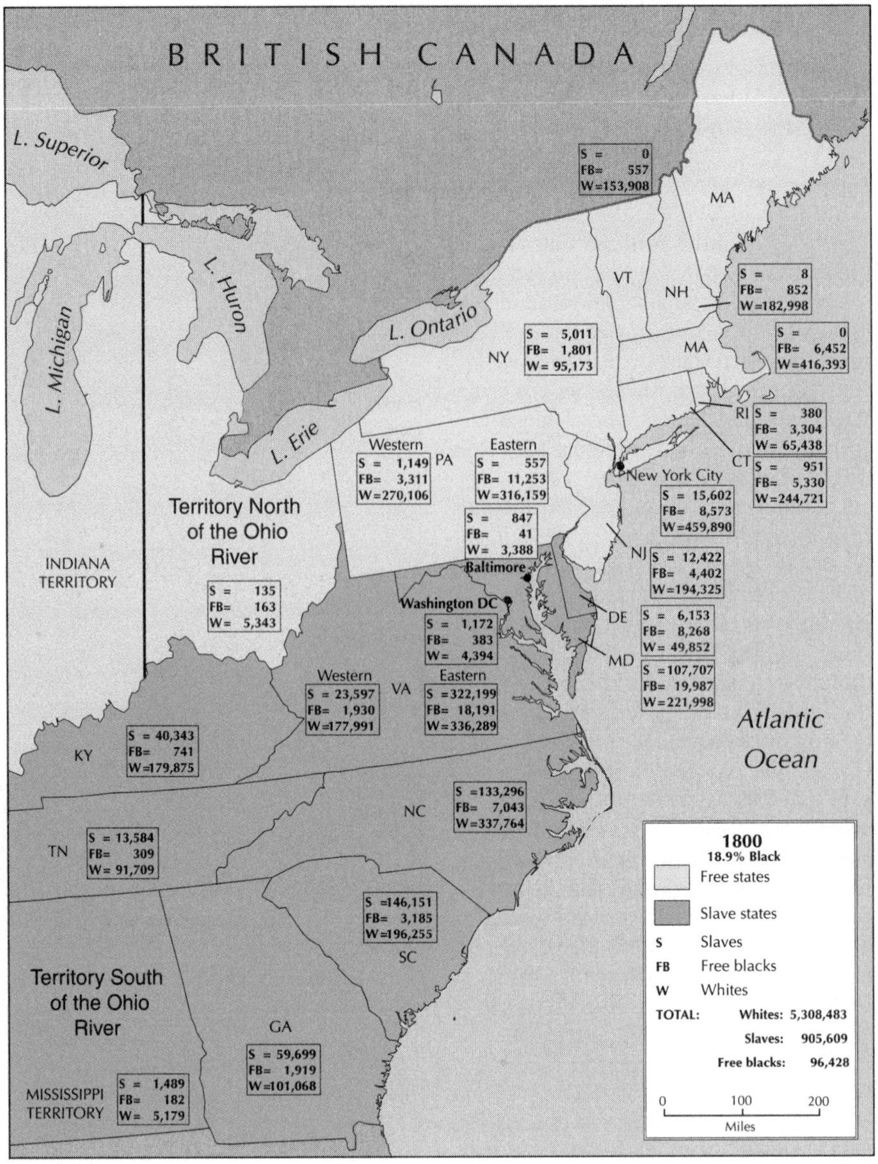
BRITISH CANADA
L. Superior
L. Michigan
L. Huron
L. Ontario
L. Erie
S = 0 FB= 557 W=153,908
MA
VT
NH
S = 8 FB= 852 W=182,998
S = 0 FB= 6,452 W=416,393
MA
NY
S = 5,011 FB= 1,801 W= 95,173
RI
S = 380 FB= 3,304 W= 65,438
CT
S = 951 FB= 5,330 W=244,721
Western
PA
S = 1,149 FB= 3,311 W=270,106
Eastern
S = 557 FB= 11,253 W=316,159
New York City
S = 15,602 FB= 8,573 W=459,890
Territory North of the Ohio River
S = 847 FB= 41 W= 3,388
Baltimore
NJ
S = 12,422 FB= 4,402 W=194,325
INDIANA TERRITORY
S = 135 FB= 163 W= 5,343
Washington DC
S = 1,172 FB= 383 W= 4,394
DE
S = 6,153 FB= 8,268 W= 49,852
MD
S =107,707 FB= 19,987 W=221,998
Western
VA
S = 23,597 FB= 1,930 W=177,991
Eastern
S =322,199 FB= 18,191 W=336,289
Atlantic Ocean
KY
S = 40,343 FB= 741 W=179,875
NC
S =133,296 FB= 7,043 W=337,764
TN
S = 13,584 FB= 309 W= 91,709
S =146,151 FB= 3,185 W=196,255
SC
Territory South of the Ohio River
GA
S = 59,699 FB= 1,919 W=101,068
MISSISSIPPI TERRITORY
S = 1,489 FB= 182 W= 5,179
1800
18.9% Black
Free states
Slave states
S Slaves
FB Free blacks
W Whites
TOTAL: Whites: 5,308,483
Slaves: 905,609
Free blacks: 96,428
0 100 200
Miles

MAP 39

Slave Revolts and Maroon Communities in the United States (1800–1865)

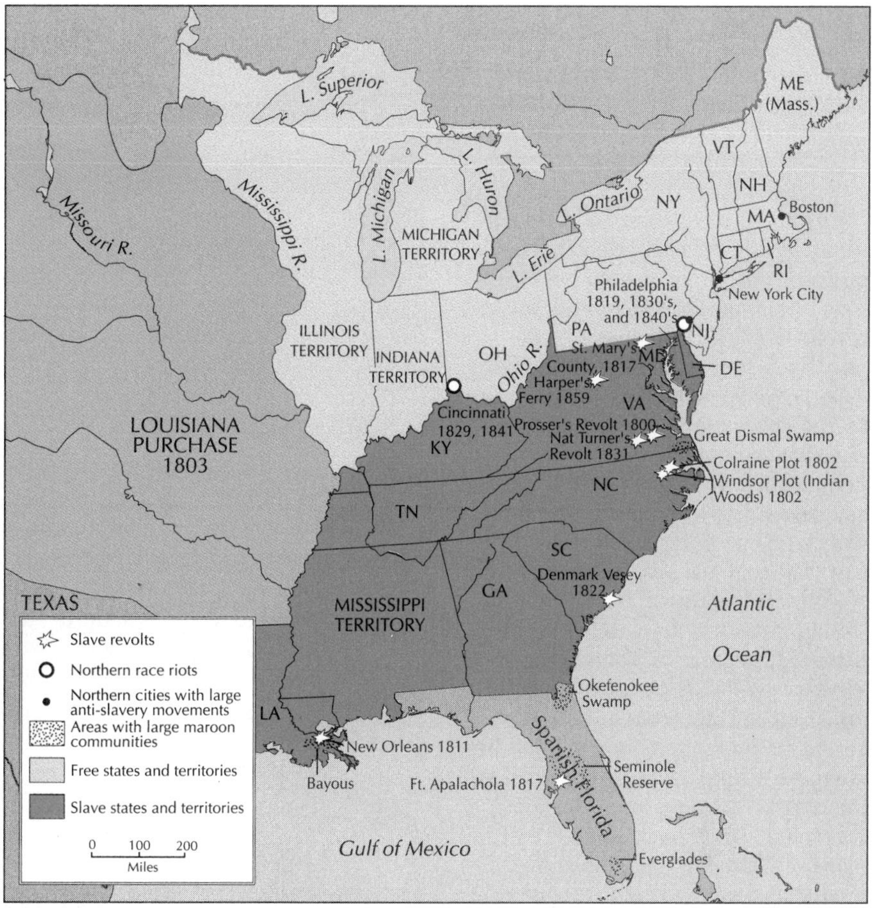
L. Superior
ME (Mass.)
VT
NH
MA
Boston
CT
RI
New York City
NY
Ontario
L. Huron
L. Michigan
MICHIGAN TERRITORY
L. Erie
Mississippi R.
Missouri R.
Philadelphia 1819, 1830's, and 1840's
PA
NJ
St. Mary's County, 1817
MD
DE
ILLINOIS TERRITORY
INDIANA TERRITORY
OH
Ohio R.
Harper's Ferry 1859
VA
Cincinnati 1829, 1841
Prosser's Revolt 1800
Nat Turner's Revolt 1831
Great Dismal Swamp
KY
LOUISIANA PURCHASE 1803
Colraine Plot 1802
Windsor Plot (Indian Woods) 1802
NC
TN
SC
Denmark Vesey 1822
GA
TEXAS
MISSISSIPPI TERRITORY
Atlantic Ocean
Slave revolts
Northern race riots
Northern cities with large anti-slavery movements
Areas with large maroon communities
Free states and territories
Slave states and territories
0 100 200
Miles
LA
Okefenokee Swamp
New Orleans 1811
Spanish Florida
Bayous
Ft. Apalachola 1817
Seminole Reserve
Gulf of Mexico
Everglades

From 1800 to the end of slavery in 1865 in the United States, slaves did whatever they could to express their dissatisfaction with their condition. As was true of the colonial era, slaves continued to escape, organize revolts, and form maroon communities. Indeed, more than a hundred maroon communities were established in the mountains, swamps, and bayous of the United States. Slaves on the Underground Railroad made their way to free states in the North, to unorganized territory in the West, and to Canada, Mexico, and the Caribbean. Native Americans also offered runaway slaves protection from capture by giving them refuge on their reservations. The Great Dismal Swamp on the northeastern border of North Carolina and Virginia, the bayous of southern Louisiana, and the Florida everglades were the three best-known areas for maroon communities in the United States. Revolts were also organized, some of which were led by free blacks and others which were orchestrated by the slaves themselves. From 1800 to 1865 several such revolts and conspiracies in the United States included those led by Gabriel Prosser in 1800, Denmark Vesey in 1822, Nat Turner in 1831, and John Brown in 1859. Although slave revolts in the United States were not as successful as those in the Caribbean or South America, they did cause southern whites a great deal of anxiety and fear. By 1859 they also began to polarize the North and South over the issue of slavery, as was the case for John Brown's raid, which made him a martyr in the North and a murderer in the South. ■

MAP 40

Gabriel Prosser's Revolt and White Fear in Virginia and North Carolina (1800–1802)

Although southerners were successful in making the institution of slavery profitable, they remained in a constant state of fear over the possibility of slave revolts. The greater the number of slaves in a state or county, the greater the fear. Slaveholders had good reason to fear slave revolts, for earlier uprisings that occurred during the colonial period had resulted in great loss of life and destruction of property. The Haitian Revolution of 1791 to 1803 fueled that fear. Although the revolt occurred outside the United States, the death, the destruction, and the flight to the United States of hundreds of former French slave owners was evidence of what could happen and brought back memories of the Stono Rebellion of 1739. In August of 1800, the fear of revolt was realized when, a few miles outside of Richmond, Virginia, an African by the name of Gabriel Prosser assembled more than a thousand slaves in preparation for a march on Richmond. Governor James Monroe summoned the state militia to crush the revolt. As a result, the revolt was put down, and Prosser was captured several days later in Norfolk, Virginia. This rebellion, although unsuccessful, caused widespread panic in Virginia and North Carolina. From 1800 to 1805 hundreds of slaves and free blacks would be tried and executed in southeastern Virginia and northeastern North Carolina merely as a result of rumored slave conspiracies, like the one in Indian Woods, Bertie County, North Carolina. Ultimately the scare would lead to tighter restrictions being placed on slaves and free blacks throughout the region and the denial of many slaves from worshiping without white supervision. ■

L. Superior
BRITISH CANADA
VT
NH
MA
RI
CT
NY
L. Ontario
L. Huron
L. Michigan
Mississippi R.
Missouri R.
PA
NJ
TERRITORY NW OF THE OHIO RIVER
INDIANA TERRITORY
Ohio R.
MD
DE
VA
Prosser's Revolt
Norfolk
"Colraine Plot"
"Windsor Plot"
NC
LOUISIANA PURCHASE 1803
KENTUCKY TERRITORY
TENNESSEE TERRITORY
SC
MISSISSIPPI TERRITORY
GA
Atlantic Ocean
Spanish Florida
Gulf of Mexico
Free states and territories
Slave states and territories
0 100 200
Miles

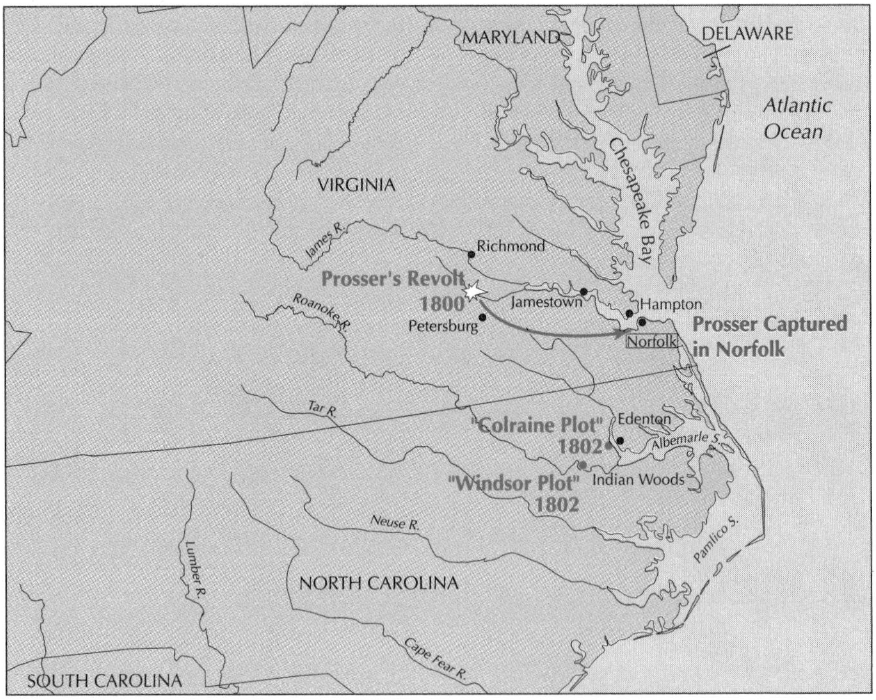
MARYLAND
DELAWARE
Atlantic Ocean
Chesapeake Bay
VIRGINIA
James R.
Richmond
Prosser's Revolt 1800
Jamestown
Hampton
Roanoke R.
Petersburg
Norfolk
Prosser Captured in Norfolk
Tar R.
"Colraine Plot" 1802
Edenton
Albemarle S.
"Windsor Plot" 1802
Indian Woods
Neuse R.
Pamlico S.
Lumber R.
NORTH CAROLINA
Cape Fear R.
SOUTH CAROLINA

MAP 41

The Rise of Antislavery Societies in the North and the Growth of the Underground Railroad (1800–1865)

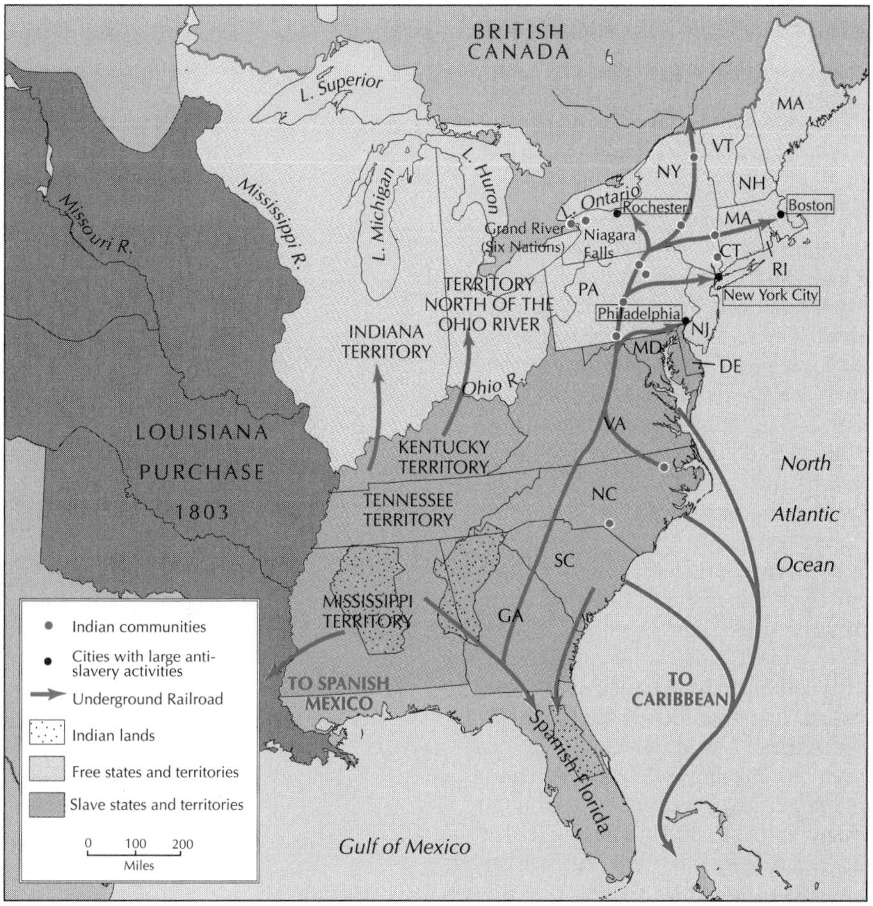
BRITISH
CANADA
L. Superior
L. Michigan
L. Huron
L. Ontario
Mississippi R.
Missouri R.
Ohio R.
MA
VT
NH
NY
Rochester
Boston
MA
CT
RI
Grand River
(Six Nations)
Niagara
Falls
PA
New York City
Philadelphia
NJ
MD
DE
TERRITORY
NORTH OF THE
OHIO RIVER
INDIANA
TERRITORY
LOUISIANA
PURCHASE
1803
KENTUCKY
TERRITORY
TENNESSEE
TERRITORY
VA
NC
SC
GA
MISSISSIPPI
TERRITORY
TO SPANISH
MEXICO
Spanish Florida
TO
CARIBBEAN
North
Atlantic
Ocean
Gulf of Mexico
Indian communities
Cities with large anti-slavery activities
Underground Railroad
Indian lands
Free states and territories
Slave states and territories
0 100 200
Miles

The earliest abolition society was organized by the Quakers in 1775, who had been active in the cause for abolition since 1688. Quakers throughout the colonies from 1688 to 1758 held slaves but were required by their church to treat them humanely. By 1693 Quaker George Keith published the first antislavery literature in America. Eventually the church forced its members to end slavery. As a result of this, not only would Quakers organize and run the first abolition societies, but they would also start and remain an important part of the Underground Railroad in both the North and the South. By the early nineteenth century, the morality of slavery was being questioned throughout the world. England and France were moving toward abolition in their colonies and would do so in the mid-1800s—England in 1838 and France in 1848. In America, many free blacks, mulattos, and northern whites became abolitionists and denounced the institution of slavery. These abolitionists were dedicated to ending slavery in the United States. They raised money to help runaway slaves, printed antislavery newspapers and flyers, and lobbied Congress to end the institution of slavery in America. As the movement grew, so did disagreements among abolitionists on what strategies should be used to end slavery. There were three basic groups: the conservatives, like William Lloyd Garrison; the moderates, like Frederick Douglass; and the radicals, like David Walker. The conservatives and moderates chose protest and other nonviolent means, while radicals advocated violence in the form of uprisings and slave revolts. Members of all three groups agreed on and supported smuggling slaves out of the South to freedom in the North on the Underground Railroad. The earliest known routes of the Underground Railroad were conducted by the Quakers, who often used their homes, churches, and Indian reservations to hide runaway slaves from slave catchers. ■

MAP 42

Slave Revolts and Maroon Communities in the Caribbean and the Americas (1800–1888)

Africans never accepted their enslavement and resisted the institution of slavery until 1888 when it was finally abolished everywhere in the Western Hemisphere. As in previous centuries slaves resisted enslavement by staging revolts throughout the Americas and the Caribbean. In the United States from 1800 to 1865 there were several major revolts and conspiracies including Gabriel Prosser's revolt in 1800, Nat Turner's revolt in 1831, and John Brown's raid in1859. There were also major revolts in the Caribbean, Spanish South America, and Brazil, all of which were violent and destructive. Slaves also continued to run away and form maroon communities in the swamps and mountains of the Americas. These communities developed their own government, militia, and economy. Although many of these communities flourished and became independent, they remained under constant threat of attack by slaveholding nations. This threat increased with the independence of Spanish America. Even after slavery was abolished, many of the maroon communities that had been created in isolated, hard-to-reach areas continued to exist into the early twentieth century. ■

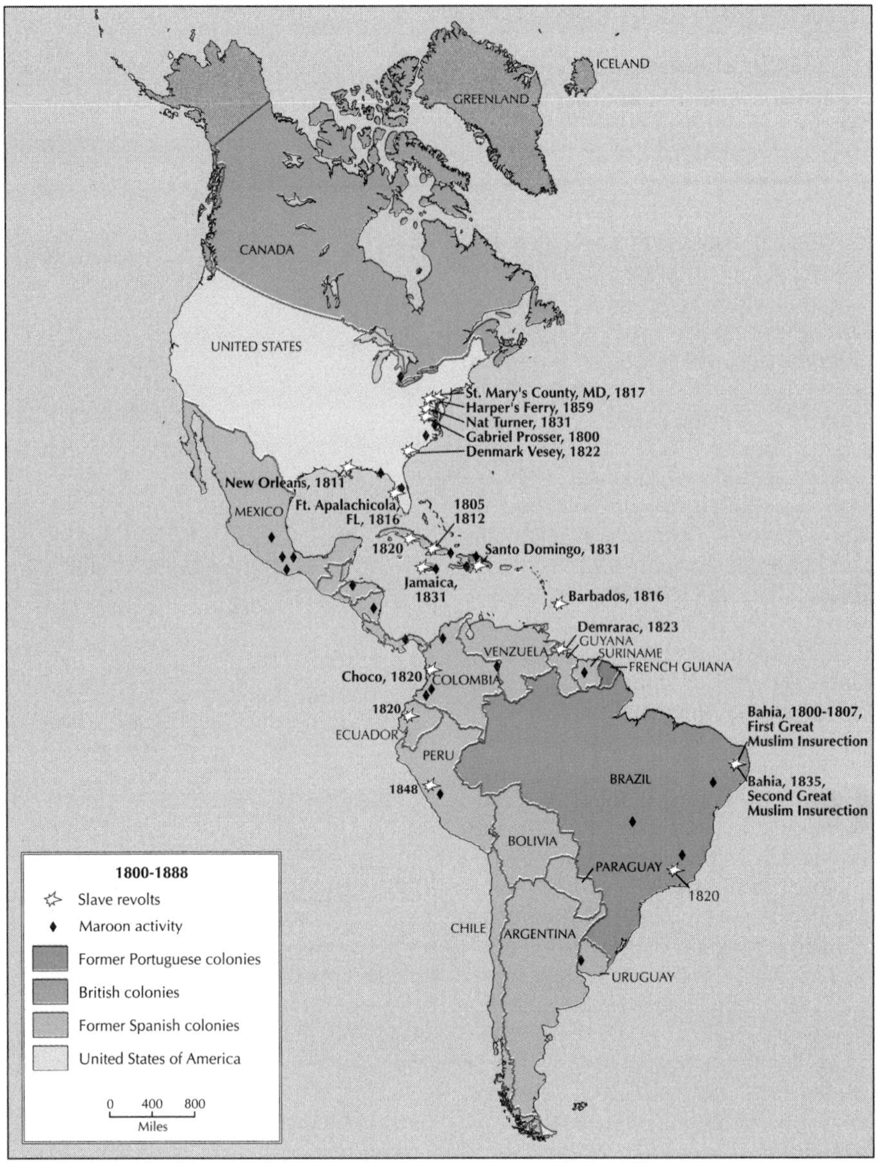
ICELAND
GREENLAND
CANADA
UNITED STATES
St. Mary's County, MD, 1817
Harper's Ferry, 1859
Nat Turner, 1831
Gabriel Prosser, 1800
Denmark Vesey, 1822
New Orleans, 1811
MEXICO
Ft. Apalachicola, FL, 1816
1805
1812
1820
Santo Domingo, 1831
Jamaica, 1831
Barbados, 1816
Demrarac, 1823
GUYANA
VENZUELA
SURINAME
FRENCH GUIANA
Choco, 1820
COLOMBIA
1820
ECUADOR
PERU
1848
BRAZIL
Bahia, 1800-1807, First Great Muslim Insurection
Bahia, 1835, Second Great Muslim Insurection
BOLIVIA
PARAGUAY
1820
CHILE
ARGENTINA
URUGUAY
1800-1888
Slave revolts
Maroon activity
Former Portuguese colonies
British colonies
Former Spanish colonies
United States of America
0 400 800
Miles

MAP 43

Manifest Destiny and Blacks on the Western Frontier in the United States (1800–1860)

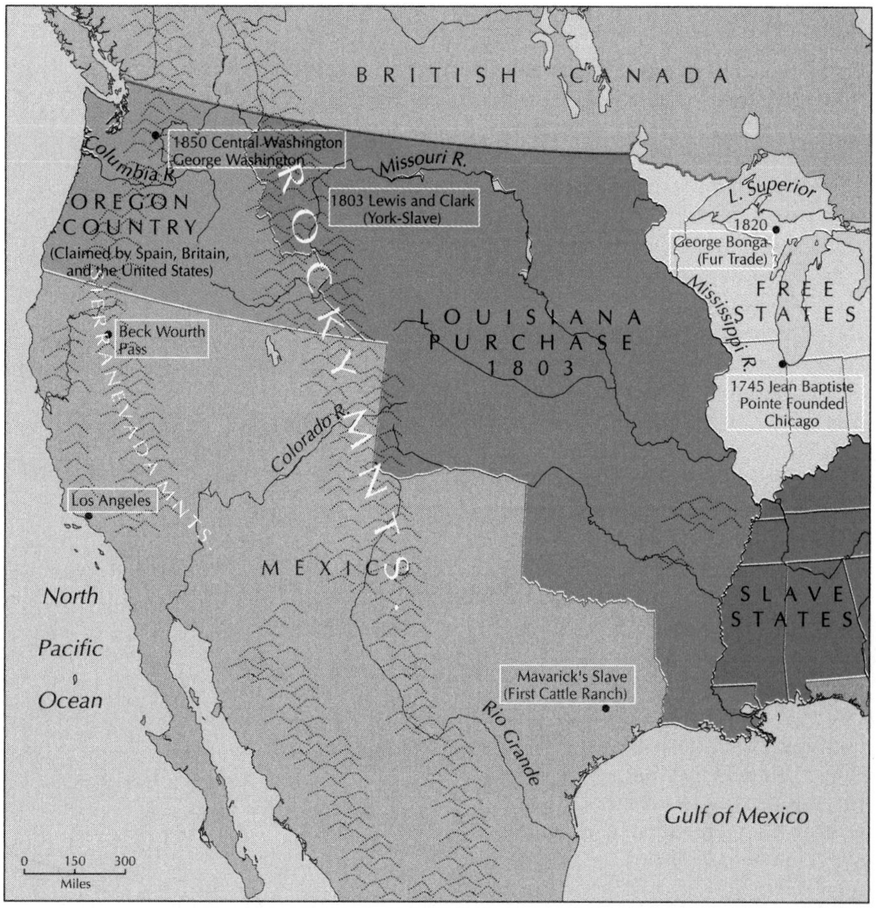
BRITISH CANADA
1850 Central Washington George Washington
Columbia R.
Missouri R.
1803 Lewis and Clark (York-Slave)
OREGON COUNTRY
(Claimed by Spain, Britain, and the United States)
ROCKY MNTS.
L. Superior
1820 George Bonga (Fur Trade)
Mississippi R.
FREE STATES
LOUISIANA PURCHASE 1803
Beck Wourth Pass
1745 Jean Baptiste Pointe Founded Chicago
Colorado R.
Los Angeles
MEXICO
North Pacific Ocean
SLAVE STATES
Mavarick's Slave (First Cattle Ranch)
Rio Grande
Gulf of Mexico
0 150 300
Miles

Although most Americans saw the West as an untamed and uncivilized hinterland, the region was home to whites, Indians, and blacks who lived and traded there for over 300 years before America's westward march. From 1500 to 1803 much of the West was under Spanish and French rule. Africans were used by first the Spanish and later the French as soldiers, slaves, and servants. Many individual Africans became pioneers, fur traders, guides, gold miners, and whalers (in the north Pacific). Vigorous exchanges were carried on between the native inhabitants, Africans, and Europeans. These black frontiersmen did not fear the unknown but met its challenges in the West. Both the English and the Spanish used blacks to explore and settle lands in the West and to protect colonies on the frontier from European and Indian attacks. For example, blacks were used by the English to help defeat the Yamasee in 1715, and by the Spanish to protect Florida from the English in the War of Spanish Succession in 1702. Thus when the Americans began to move west in the 1800s, Africans were already there and had been there for over two centuries. Although most were in the Southwest, they maintained a significant presence in the Northwest as well. Several of these great black frontiersmen helped to open the floodgate for the settlers who poured over the Appalachians and headed west. When President Thomas Jefferson sent Lewis and Clark to explore the Louisiana Purchase in the West between 1804 and 1806, an American slave by the name of York accompanied them. In fact, York was responsible for the expedition being a success by assisting the expedition in many ways, including actually saving the members of the expedition from death. As a result of his bravery, York was granted his freedom. ■

MAP 44

Slave Smuggling in the United States (1808–1865)

Although the Atlantic slave trade officially ended in the United States in 1808, slaves from Africa and the West Indies still found their way to southern auction blocks as late as 1860. Some slaves were brought directly from West Africa to southern ports; others were brought from the Caribbean. Although it was illegal to do so, many slave owners readily bought slaves from smugglers for use on their cotton plantations. Slave smuggling had two profound impacts on blacks in the South. First, it contributed to the increase in the black population in the lower South. Second, it helped to maintain African culture in places like the Gullah Sea Islands in South Carolina and coastal Georgia and in New Orleans, Louisiana. Because smuggling continued until the start of the Civil War, Africans fresh from West Africa and the West Indies came into close contact with American blacks in these areas. As a result, today in these places, many of the blacks still practice some of the religions, music, and speech patterns that are West African in origin. ■

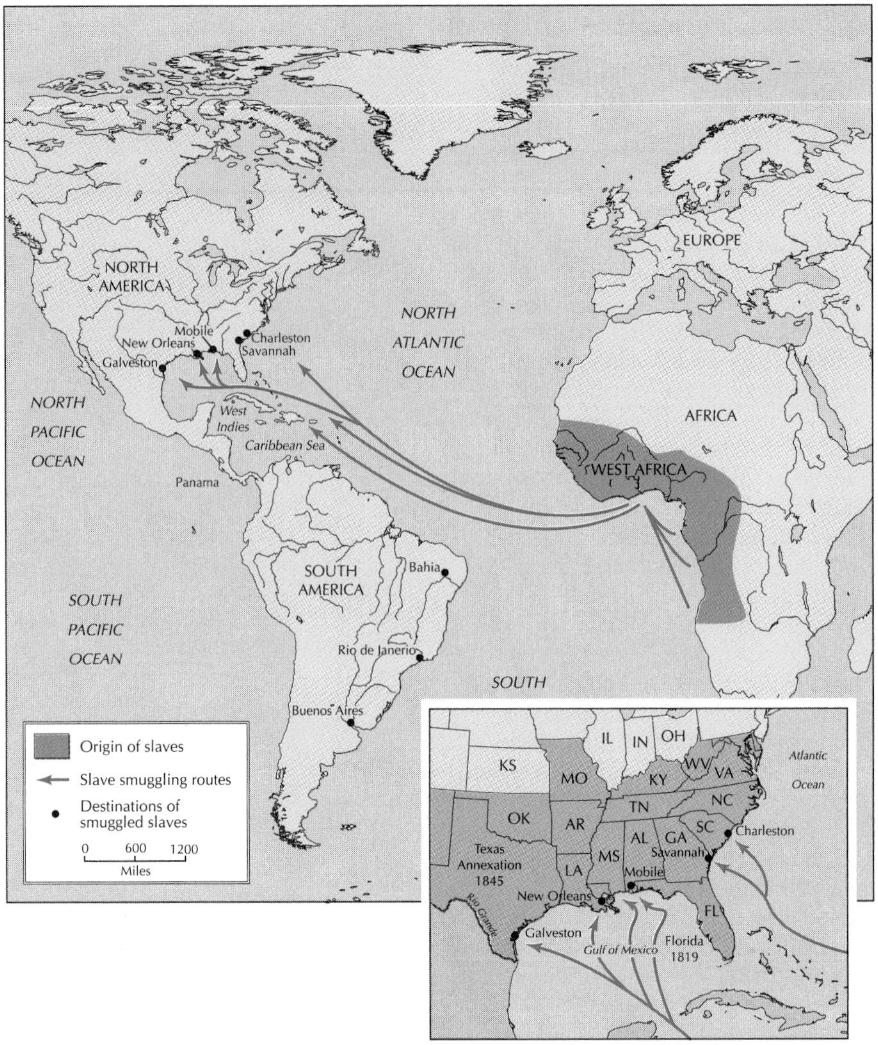

NORTH AMERICA
EUROPE
NORTH ATLANTIC OCEAN
AFRICA
WEST AFRICA
NORTH PACIFIC OCEAN
SOUTH PACIFIC OCEAN
SOUTH AMERICA
SOUTH
Mobile
New Orleans
Galveston
Charleston
Savannah
West Indies
Caribbean Sea
Panama
Bahia
Rio de Janeiro
Buenos Aires
Origin of slaves
Slave smuggling routes
Destinations of smuggled slaves
0 600 1200
Miles
KS
MO
IL
IN
OH
WV
VA
KY
NC
TN
OK
AR
SC
AL
GA
MS
LA
Texas Annexation 1845
Rio Grande
FL
Florida 1819
Gulf of Mexico
Atlantic Ocean

MAP 45

The Upper and Lower South and the Domestic Slave Trade (1808–1865)

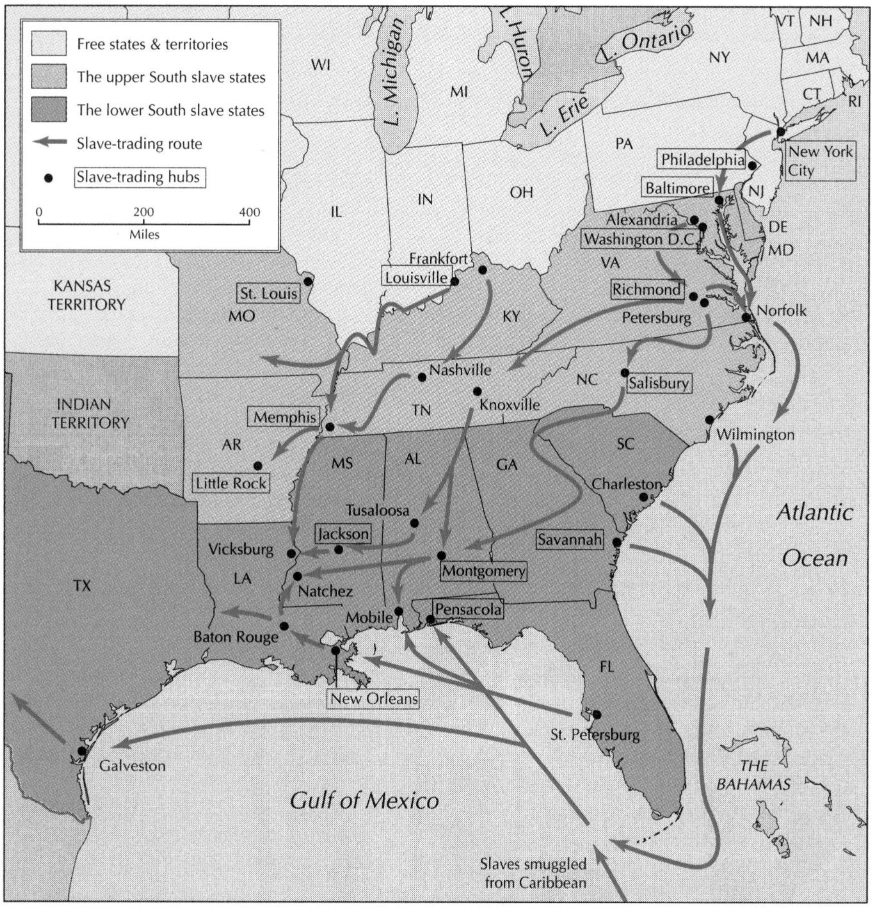
Free states & territories
The upper South slave states
The lower South slave states
Slave-trading route
Slave-trading hubs
0 200 400
Miles
WI
L. Michigan
L. Huron
L. Ontario
L. Erie
MI
NY
VT
NH
MA
CT
RI
PA
New York City
Philadelphia
Baltimore
NJ
DE
MD
IL
IN
OH
Alexandria
Washington D.C.
VA
Frankfort
Louisville
KANSAS TERRITORY
St. Louis
MO
Richmond
Petersburg
Norfolk
KY
Nashville
Knoxville
NC
Salisbury
INDIAN TERRITORY
Memphis
TN
Wilmington
AR
Little Rock
MS
AL
GA
SC
Charleston
Tusaloosa
Jackson
Vicksburg
LA
Savannah
Montgomery
Atlantic Ocean
TX
Natchez
Mobile
Pensacola
Baton Rouge
New Orleans
FL
St. Petersburg
Galveston
THE BAHAMAS
Gulf of Mexico
Slaves smuggled from Caribbean

In 1808, as specified by the Constitution, the foreign slave trade was officially ended. It continued, however, on a lesser scale, as an "outlawed occupation" until 1861. The closing of the Atlantic slave trade in 1808 came at the same time that the need for slaves in the lower South was on the rise. In the 1800s, cotton became king in the lower South. Just as tobacco, rice, and indigo had fueled colonial slavery in the upper South, cotton fueled antebellum slavery in the lower South. Developing what became known as the Cotton Kingdom, the lower South grew and prospered. The upper South did not share in this prosperity since it was unable to grow large quantities of cotton because of the soil. It could not compete with the lower South agriculturally. As a result, many southerners left the upper South for the economic prosperity of the lower South. This exodus caused a major population and financial drain on the upper South. This drain together with the closing of the Atlantic slave trade led to the birth of the domestic slave trade. With the close of the Atlantic slave trade, the deep South found it more difficult to secure the slaves they needed for cotton production. In response to the lower South's need, the upper South began the sale of surplus slaves and the notorious practice of slave breeding. The practice used female slaves, sometimes as young as thirteen, to breed, over a lifetime, as many as fourteen children. These children were sold into slavery in the deep South. The domestic slave trade would last from 1808 until the end of the Civil War in 1865. ■

Map and Text Sources

31. Bergman, Peter M., and Jean McCarroll. *The Negro in the Continental Congress. Journals of the Continental Congress, 1774–1789*. New York: Bergman, 1969.

Berlin, Ira, and Ronald Hoffman, eds. *Slavery and Freedom in the Age of the American Revolution*. Urbana: University of Illinois Press, 1986.

Quarles, Benjamin. *The Negro in the American Revolution*. New York: Norton, 1973.

Voelz, Peter M. *Slave and Soldier: The Military Impact of Blacks in the Colonial Americas*. New York: Garland, 1993.

32. Beatty, Erkuries. *Journal of Lieut. Erkuries Beatty in the Expedition against the Six Nations under Gen. Sullivan, 1779*. Harrisburg: Pennsylvania State Library, 1974.

Dramer, Kim E. *Native Americans and Black Americans*. Philadelphia: Chelsea House Publishers, 1997.

Graymont, Barbara. *The Iroquois in the American Revolution*. Syracuse, NY: Syracuse University Press, 1972.

Hatley, M. Thomas. *The Dividing Paths: Cherokees and South Carolinians through the Era of Revolution*. New York: Oxford University Press, 1993.

Heard, Joseph N. *The Black Frontiersmen: Adventures of Negroes among American Indians, 1528–1918*. New York: John Day Company, 1969.

Katz, William Loren. *Black Indians: A Hidden Heritage*. New York: Atheneum, 1986.

Kelsay, Isabel Thompson. *Joseph Brant, 1743–1807, Man of Two Worlds*. Syracuse, NY: Syracuse University Press, 1986.

Wilson, Ellen Gibson. *The Loyal Blacks*. New York: Capricorn Books, 1976.

33. Johnson, Howard. *The Bahamas from Slavery to Servitude, 1783–1933*. Gainesville: University of Florida, 1996.

Walker, James W. S. G. *The Black Loyalists: The Search for a Promised Land in Nova Scotia and Sierra Leone, 1783–1870*. Toronto: University of Toronto Press, 1992.

Wilson, Ellen Gibson. *The Loyal Blacks*. New York: Capricorn Books, 1976.

34. *The Constitution of the United States, with the Acts of Congress, Relating to Slavery, Embracing the Constitution, the Fugitive Slave Act of 1793, the Missouri Compromise Act of 1820, the Fugitive Slave Law of 1850, and the Nebraska and Kansas Bill, Carefully Compiled*. Rochester, NY: D. M. Dewey, 1854.

Eaton, Clement. *The Growth of Southern Civilization, 1790–1860*. New York: Harper & Row, 1963.

Litwack, Leon F. *North of Slavery: The Negro in the Free States, 1790–1860*. Chicago: University of Chicago Press, 1970.

McDougall, Marion G. *Fugitive Slaves (1619–1865)*. Freeport, NY: Books for Libraries Press, 1971.

McManus, Edgar J. *Black Bondage in the North*. Syracuse, NY: Syracuse University Press, 1973.

35. Ellis, William D. *The Ordinance of 1787: The Nation Begins*. Dayton, OH: Landfall Press, 1987.

Farrand, Max. *The Fathers of the Constitution: A Chronicle of the Establishment of the Union*. New York: United States Publishers Association, 1975.

Galbreath, Charles B. *The Ordinance of 1787, Its Origin and Authorship*. Columbus, OH: F. J. Heer Printing Co., 1924.

McDougall, Marion G. *Fugitive Slaves (1619–1865)*. Freeport, NY: Books for Libraries Press, 1971.

Robinson, Donald L. *Slavery in the Structure of American Politics, 1765–1820*. New York: Norton, 1979.

36. James, Cyril Lionel Roberts. *The Black Jacobins: Toussaint L'Ouverture and the San Domingo Revolution*, 2nd ed., rev. New York: Vintage Books, 1989.

Korngold, Ralph. *Citizen Toussaint*. London: Victor Gollancz, 1945.

Ott, Thomas O. *The Haitian Revolution, 1789–1804*. Knoxville: University of Tennessee Press, 1973.

37. *The Constitution of the United States, with the Acts of Congress, Relating to Slavery, Embracing the Constitution, the Fugitive Slave Act of 1793, the Missouri Compromise Act of 1820, the Fugitive Slave Law of 1850, and the Nebraska and Kansas Bill, Carefully Compiled*. Rochester, NY: D. M. Dewey, 1854.

Blockson, Charles L. *The Underground Railroad*. New York: Berkley Publishing Group, 1994.

Hilty, Hiram, H. *By Land and By Sea: Quakers Confront Slavery and Its Aftermath in North Carolina*. Greensboro: North Carolina Friends Historical Society, 1993.

Hilty, Hiram H. *North Carolina Quakers and Slavery*. Ph.D. dissertation, Durham, NC: Duke University, 1968.

McDougall, Marion G. *Fugitive Slaves (1619–1865)*. Freeport, NY: Books for Libraries Press, 1971.

United States. Congress. House. *A Bill to Amend the Act, Intituled, An Act Respecting Fugitives from Justice, and Persons Escaping from the Service of Their Masters*. United States: Duane, Printer, 1801.

38. Aptheker, Herbert. *American Negro Slave Revolts*, 6th ed. New York: International Publishers, 1993.

Carroll, Joseph C. *Slave Insurrections in the United States, 1800–1865*. New York: Negro Universities Press, 1968.

Price, Richard, ed. *Maroon Societies: Rebel Slave Communities in the Americas*, 2nd ed. Baltimore: Johns Hopkins University Press, 1979.

39. United States Bureau of the Census. *Historical Statistics of the United States, Colonial Times to 1970, Bicentennial Edition [Part 2]*. Washington, DC: Government Printing Office, 1975.

40. Egerton, Douglas R. *Gabriel's Rebellion: The Virginia Slave Conspiracies of 1800 and 1802*. Chapel Hill: University of North Carolina Press, 1993.

Mullin, Gerald. *Flight and Rebellion: Slave Resistance in Eighteenth-Century Virginia*. New York: Oxford University Press, 1975.

Parramore, Thomas C. "Conspiracy and Revivalism in 1802: A Direful Symbiosis," *Negro History Bulletin* 43 (1980): 28–31.

Parramore, Thomas C. "The Great Slave Conspiracy," *The State: A Weekly Survey of North Carolina* 39 (August 15, 1971): 7–10.

41. Blockson, Charles L. *The Underground Railroad*. New York: Berkley Publishing Group, 1994.

Filler, Louis. *Crusade against Slavery, 1830–1860*. Algonac, MI: Reference Publications, 1986.

Locke, Mary S. *Anti-slavery in America from the Introduction of African Slaves to the Prohibition of the Slave Trade (1619–1808)*. New York: Johnson Reprint Corp., 1968.

Mathieson, William Law. *British Slavery and Its Abolition, 1823–1838*. New York: Octagon Books, 1967.

Mathieson, William Law. *British Slave Emancipation, 1838–1849*. New York: Octagon Books, 1967.

Quarles, Benjamin. *Black Abolitionists*. New York: Da Capo Press, 1991.

Schwartz, Rosalie. *Across the Rio to Freedom: U.S. Negroes in Mexico*. El Paso: Texas Western Press, University of Texas at El Paso, 1974.

Shyllon, Folarin O. *Black People in Britain 1555–1833*. New York: Oxford University Press, 1977.

42. Aptheker, Herbert. *American Negro Slave Revolts*, 6th ed. New York: International Publishers, 1993.

Perez, Louis A. *Slaves, Sugar, and Colonial Society: Travel Accounts of Cuba, 1801–1899*. Wilmington, DE: Scholarly Resources, 1992.

Price, Richard. *Maroon Societies: Rebel Slave Communities in the Americas*. Baltimore: Johns Hopkins University Press, 1979.

43. Billington, Ray A. *America's Frontier Heritage*. Albuquerque: University of New Mexico Press, 1993.

Cashin, Joan E. *A Family Venture: Men and Women on the Southern Frontier*. Baltimore: Johns Hopkins University Press, 1994.

Hardaway, Roger D. *A Narrative Bibliography of the African-American Frontier: Blacks in the Rocky Mountain West, 1535–1912*. Lewiston, NY: Edwin Mellen Press, 1995.

Heard, Joseph N. *The Black Frontiersmen: Adventures of Negros among American Indians, 1528–1918*. New York: John Day Company, 1969.

Katz, William Loren. *Black People Who Made the Old West*. Trenton, NJ: Africa World Press, 1992.

Katz, William Loren. *The Black West: A Documentary and Pictorial History of the African American Role in the Westward Expansion of the United States*, 4th ed. New York: Simon & Schuster, 1996.

Porter, Kenneth W. *The Negro on the American Frontier*. New York: Arno Press, 1971.

Weinberg, Albert K. *Manifest Destiny: A Study of Nationalist Expansionism in American History*. New York: AMS Press, 1979.

44. Du Bois, William Edward Burghardt. *The Suppression of the African Slave Trade to the United States*. New York: Longmans, Green, 1896.

Howard, Warren S. "The United States Government and the African Slave Trade, 1837–1862." Ph.D. dissertation, University of California, Los Angeles, 1959.

45. Bancroft, Frederic. *Slave Trading in the Old South*. New York: Ungar, 1969.

Collins, Winfield H. *The Domestic Slave Trade of the Southern States*. Port Washington, NY: Kennikat Press, 1969.

MAP 46

African Americans in the War of 1812

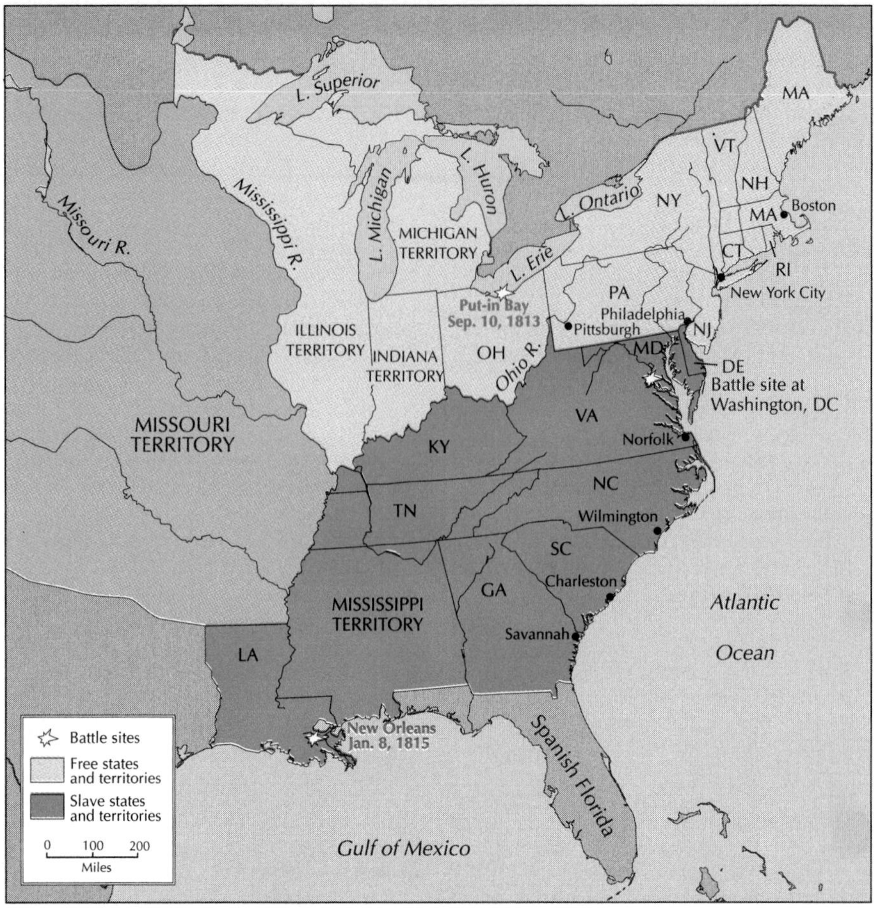
L. Superior
L. Michigan
L. Huron
Ontario
L. Erie
Mississippi R.
Missouri R.
Ohio R.
MICHIGAN TERRITORY
ILLINOIS TERRITORY
INDIANA TERRITORY
OH
Put-in Bay Sep. 10, 1813
MISSOURI TERRITORY
KY
TN
VA
NC
SC
GA
MISSISSIPPI TERRITORY
LA
New Orleans Jan. 8, 1815
Spanish Florida
Gulf of Mexico
Atlantic Ocean
PA
Philadelphia
Pittsburgh
NJ
MD
DE
Battle site at Washington, DC
Norfolk
Wilmington
Charleston
Savannah
NY
VT
NH
MA
Boston
CT
RI
New York City
Battle sites
Free states and territories
Slave states and territories
0 100 200
Miles

As with the American Revolution, free blacks and slaves were willing to serve their country in the War of 1812. The blacks who fought for the United States served in both the Navy and Army. In fact, it is estimated that 20 percent of the men who served in the Navy during the war were black. Northern states, however, were more willing to use blacks than the South. Many Southern states refused to arm any blacks for fear of slaves and free blacks turning their guns on them. As a result, many blacks joined northern state militias, where they served with distinction. These black sailors and soldiers made significant contributions during the war, two of which are most notable. On September 10, 1813, Captain Oliver H. Perry and the black sailors under his command defeated the British at Put-in-Bay on Lake Erie. They seized control of the lake, forcing the British to abandon their plans to capture Detroit. Black soldiers also distinguished themselves for their efforts in defending the city of New Orleans. Indeed, on January 8, 1815, black troops, under the command of General Andrew Jackson, were instrumental in the defeat of British forces in the Battle of New Orleans. So impressive were their heroics, that they drew strong praise from General Jackson for their valor. When the British withdrew to Halifax, Nova Scotia, they razed southern plantations, taking over 2,000 slaves with them. Most of them went willingly in hopes of being freed by the British once out of America. For those free blacks and slaves who helped America defend its independence from Britain, little changed with regard to their condition in America. In spite of the contributions by black troops in the War of 1812, the War Department—some five years after the conflict—issued a general order prohibiting the recruitment of blacks or mulattos into the armed forces. This order would remain in effect until January 1, 1863, when it would be lifted by President Abraham Lincoln's Emancipation Proclamation. ■

MAP 47

The Missouri Compromise and Its Impact on Slavery in the United States (1819–1821)

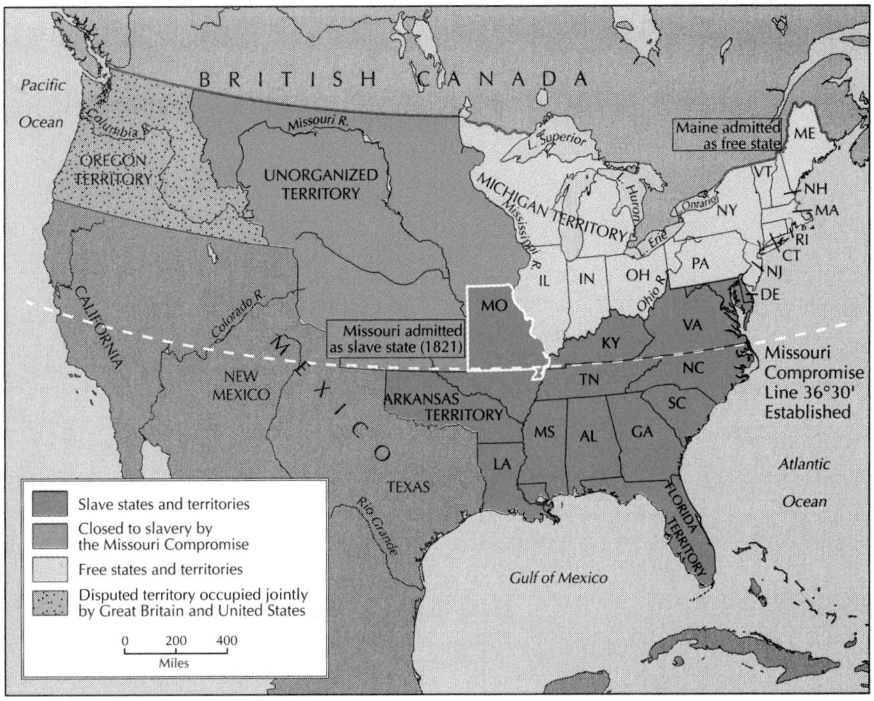
BRITISH CANADA
Pacific Ocean
Columbia R.
OREGON TERRITORY
Missouri R.
UNORGANIZED TERRITORY
L. Superior
Maine admitted as free state
ME
NH
MA
RI
CT
VT
NY
NJ
DE
PA
MICHIGAN TERRITORY
Mississippi R.
Huron
Ontario
Erie
IL
IN
OH
Ohio R.
MO
Missouri admitted as slave state (1821)
KY
VA
NC
TN
SC
GA
AL
MS
LA
Missouri Compromise Line 36°30' Established
CALIFORNIA
Colorado R.
NEW MEXICO
MEXICO
ARKANSAS TERRITORY
TEXAS
Rio Grande
FLORIDA TERRITORY
Atlantic Ocean
Gulf of Mexico
Slave states and territories
Closed to slavery by the Missouri Compromise
Free states and territories
Disputed territory occupied jointly by Great Britain and United States
0 200 400
Miles

The issue of slavery remained a bitterly divisive one in America until the end of the Civil War. Since 1787, northern states had routinely demanded that slavery be prohibited in the Northwest and Southwest territories of the United States, while southern states demanded its extension. The issue was settled in 1787 with the passage of the Northwest Ordinance, which closed the Northwest Territory to slavery but allowed the Southwest to practice the institution. When President Thomas Jefferson purchased the vast land area of Louisiana from France in 1803, the debate was resumed. At issue was how much, if any, of the new territory would be slave and how much would be free. The nation fell into a crisis over the debate in 1819, when Missouri applied for admission into the Union as a slave state. At the time, America had eleven slave states and eleven free states. The North, fearing a loss of power, opposed Missouri's admission into the Union. Finally, in 1820, it was agreed that Missouri would be admitted as a slave state, while Maine would be admitted as a free state. The remaining territory north of the 36°30' parallel would remain free, while the Arkansas territory south of the 36°30' parallel would be slave territory. Although the northern territory was three times the size of the Arkansas territory, most of the northern territory was inhabited by Native Americans and was seen as too cold and isolated to be inhabitable by U.S. settlers. The compromise was momentarily stalled when Missouri refused to allow free blacks to settle in its boundaries, even though free blacks were granted the status of citizens in other states. The crisis was finally resolved in 1821, when Henry Clay expanded the compromise to include a clause prohibiting Missouri from passing laws forbidding U.S. citizens from settling in the state. While the measure did not clarify whether free blacks were legally citizens or not, it did end the argument over where slavery could be practiced, with the 36°30' parallel being the agreed-upon dividing line. ■

MAP 48

The Cotton Kingdom and Cotton Production in the Deep South (1820–1860)

In 1793, the cotton gin was introduced in the South. The invention greatly increased cotton production. Cotton moved from being less than 5 percent of all U.S. exports in 1790, to 32 percent in 1820, to 51.6 percent in 1840, and by 1860 to over 57.5 percent, in the United States. In other words, cotton production in the South increased from only 3,135 bales a year in 1790 to 3,841,000 (3.8 million) bales a year in 1860. The price of slaves also rose, reflecting their importance to the cotton-producing South, from an average price of $600 per slave to $1,800 per slave. With the use of the gin the United States became the largest producer and the largest exporter of cotton in the world. The invention also was largely responsible for reviving the institution of slavery in the South. With the declining market in Europe for tobacco, the institution had been dying. In fact, without the cotton gin, slavery might have proved unprofitable and been abandoned. Indeed, the War between the States might never have been fought. However, as cotton became an integral part of England's textile industry and production continued to increase in the South from 1820 to 1860, so did the demand for slaves. Cotton helped to make the South rich, to institutionalize slavery, and to develop a social structure that would separate the North from the South, even today. The Cotton Kingdom, or Black Belt, as it came to be known, ran from Virginia through the coastal plains of North Carolina, South Carolina, Georgia, Alabama, Mississippi, Louisiana, and eastern Texas and up the Mississippi River Valley into eastern Arkansas and Missouri and western Kentucky and Tennessee. As a result of the rich soil of the coastal plains and the Mississippi River Valley, slaveholders and their slaves from the upper South and south Atlantic states rapidly moved west and south into these areas to grow cotton. ■

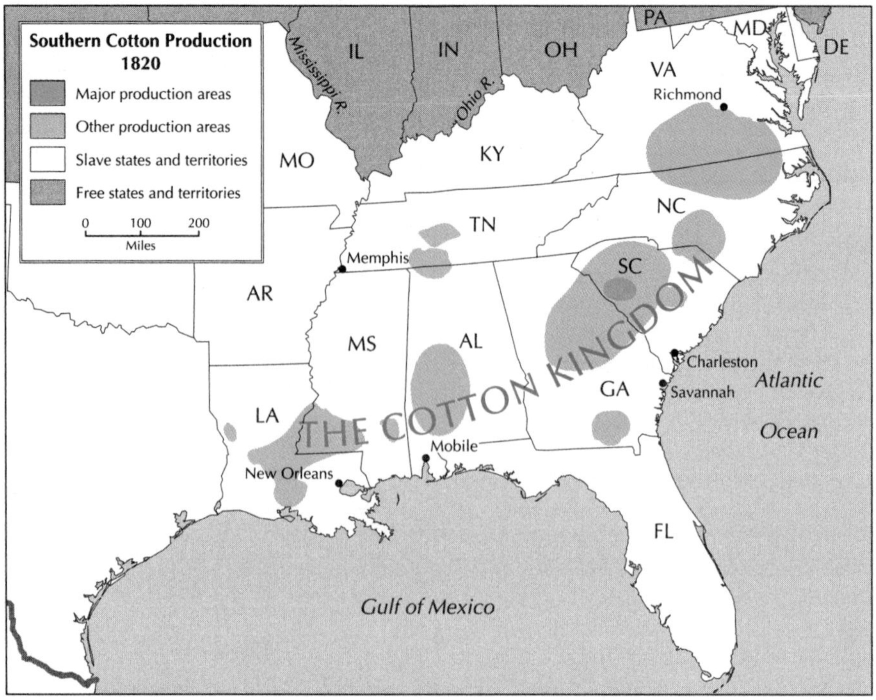
Southern Cotton Production 1820
Major production areas
Other production areas
Slave states and territories
Free states and territories
0 100 200
Miles
THE COTTON KINGDOM
IL
IN
OH
PA
MD
DE
VA
Richmond
Mississippi R.
Ohio R.
MO
KY
NC
TN
Memphis
SC
AR
MS
AL
Charleston
GA
Savannah
Atlantic
Ocean
LA
Mobile
New Orleans
FL
Gulf of Mexico

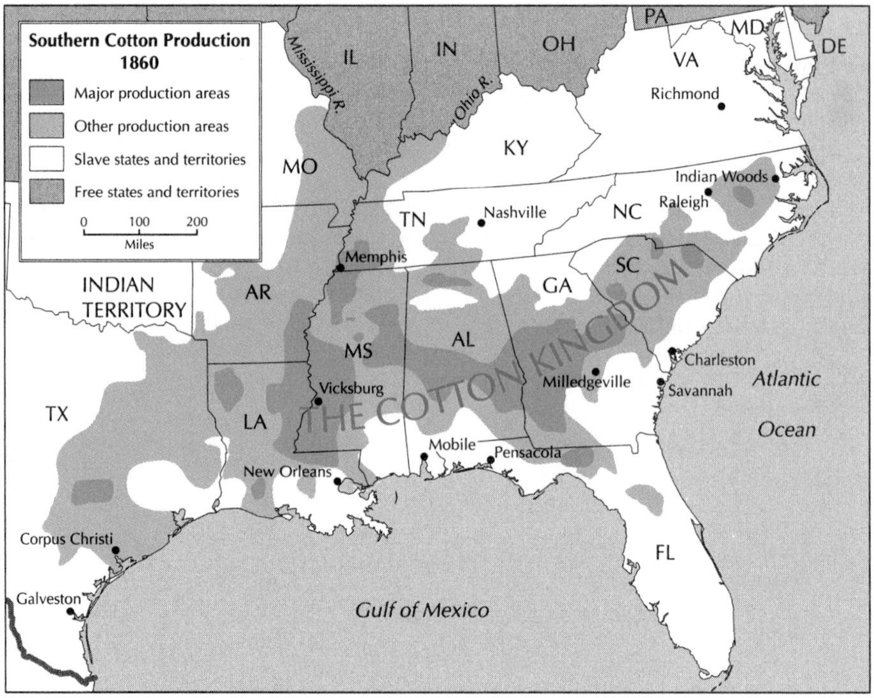
Southern Cotton Production 1860
Major production areas
Other production areas
Slave states and territories
Free states and territories
0 100 200
Miles
THE COTTON KINGDOM
IL
IN
OH
PA
MD
DE
VA
Richmond
Mississippi R.
Ohio R.
MO
KY
Indian Woods
Raleigh
NC
TN
Nashville
Memphis
SC
GA
INDIAN TERRITORY
AR
MS
AL
Charleston
Milledgeville
Savannah
Atlantic
Ocean
Vicksburg
TX
LA
Mobile
Pensacola
New Orleans
Corpus Christi
FL
Galveston
Gulf of Mexico

MAP 49

The American Colonization Movement and the Resettlement of African Americans to Liberia (1815–1834)

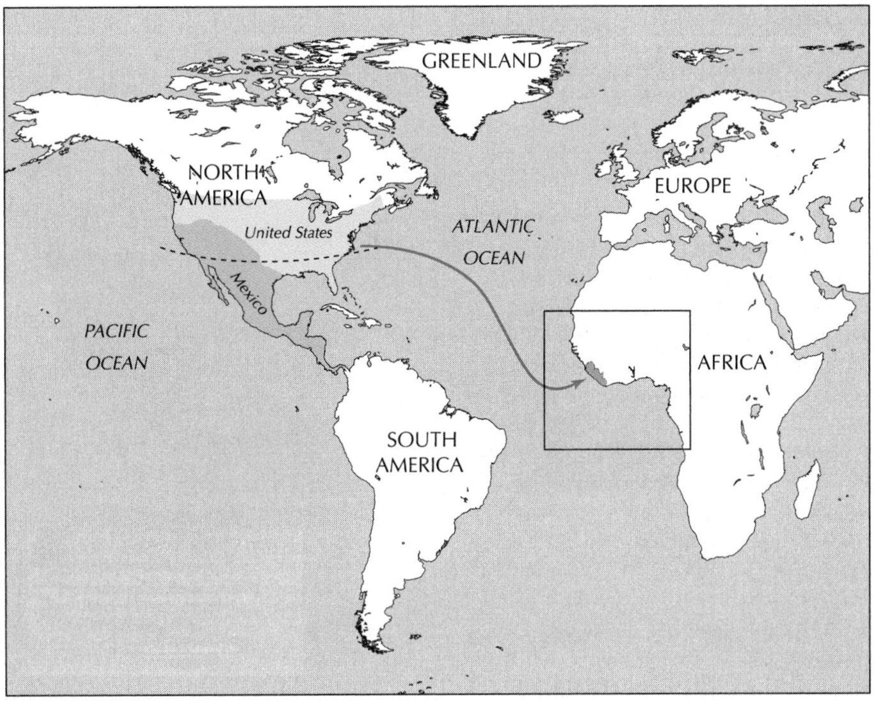
GREENLAND
NORTH AMERICA
EUROPE
United States
ATLANTIC OCEAN
Mexico
PACIFIC OCEAN
AFRICA
SOUTH AMERICA

By 1815, many free blacks became convinced that it was not possible for blacks and whites to live together in the United States. These blacks, with the backing of some whites, established the American Colonization Society and began preparations to leave the United States and return to Africa. Paul Cuffe, a wealthy black, helped to fund the first group of blacks who went back to Africa during this period. By the 1820s hundreds of blacks were pooling their money to purchase ships to carry as many blacks as desired to go back to Africa. Most of those who left from 1815 to 1834 would end up in the West African nation today known as Liberia. Many of the early emigrants stopped in Freetown, Sierra Leone, and later were resettled in Monrovia, Liberia. In 1822, with the help of President James Monroe, Liberia became the second independent African Republic founded and governed by blacks from the United States, the first being Sierra Leone. The settlers of Liberia, like those of Sierra Leone, worked to create a community similar to the one they had left behind in the United States. The settlers proceeded to Christianize and educate as many of the native Africans as possible while dismissing their native religions and languages. As a result of this, many native Africans were alienated by American blacks and resentful of their presence. Although some blacks relocated to Liberia, most did not want to leave America and return to an Africa they had never known. Also, the expense of relocating large numbers of free blacks prevented the program from being successful. ■

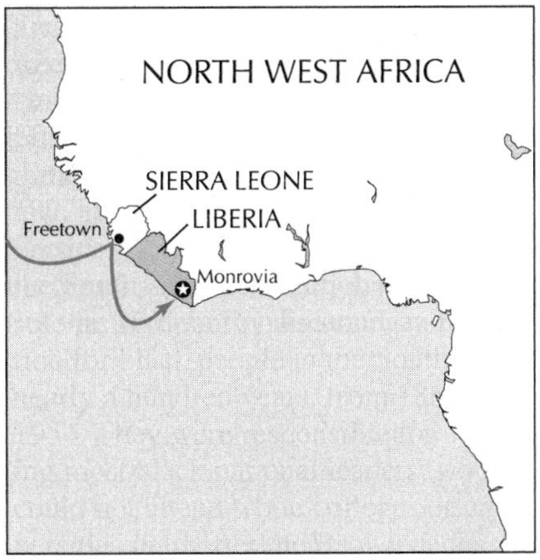
NORTH WEST AFRICA
SIERRA LEONE
LIBERIA
Freetown
Monrovia

MAP 50

The Denmark Vesey Slave Revolt and Revolutions in Spanish America (1822–1830)

In 1822, Denmark Vesey, a former slave turned preacher and carpenter, planned a slave revolt in Charleston, South Carolina. Vesey, an African Methodist Episcopal (AME) Church minister, developed a large following in his church, where he often preached on the evils of slavery. During the revolt Vesey planned to seize the city's arsenal and give the arms to slaves in and around Charleston. However, his efforts were thwarted when whites were informed by loyal slaves of his scheme. Although in the end Vesey and his followers were captured, tried, and executed by the state of South Carolina for this failed rebellion, the revolt profoundly altered life for blacks and whites all over the nation. As with the Stono Rebellion of 1739, South Carolinians were shocked by their vulnerability to slave revolts. The revolt forced South Carolina, the leader in support of maintaining and extending the institution of slavery, to become more fearful of the dangers large numbers of slaves posed for the state's white population, and to become defensive and sensitive to attacks on the institution by abolitionists. The revolt brought praise and support from radical blacks and white abolitionists, who, along with conservatives and moderates, lobbied Congress to both limit and abolish slavery everywhere in the United States. Thus the revolt increased the gulf between the North and South over the issue of slavery and moved the two regions closer to war. While the United States struggled with the Vesey revolt and the troubles it wrought, other areas in the Americas were also undergoing problems. In Spanish America from Mexico to Argentina, slaves, mulattos, free blacks, Indians, and Creoles joined forces to end Spanish rule. These revolutions began as early as 1810 and 1811 with Argentina and Paraguay and by 1821 engulfed all of Spanish America. When

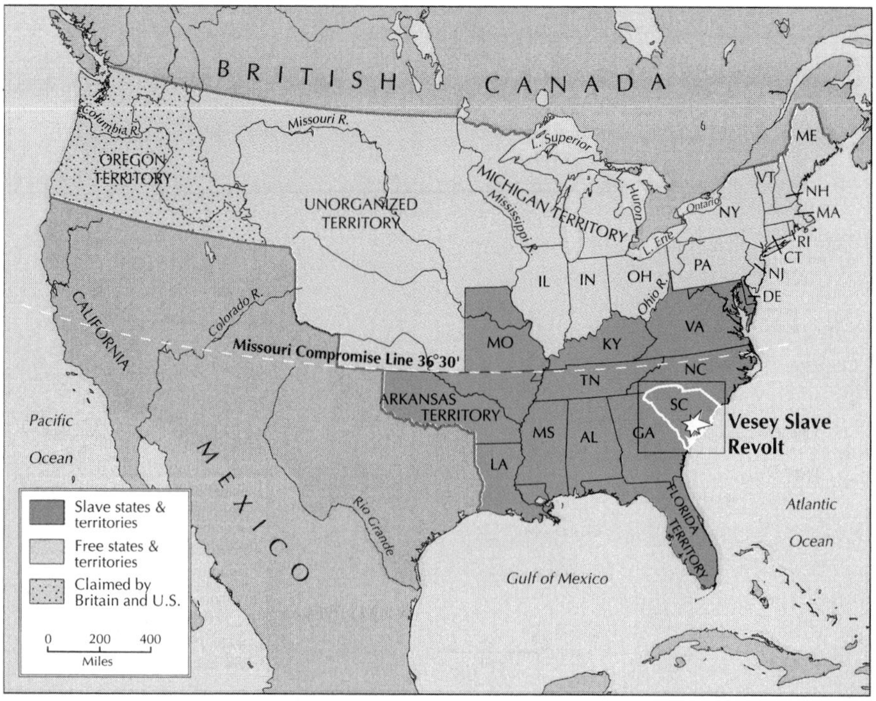
BRITISH CANADA
Missouri R.
Columbia R.
OREGON TERRITORY
UNORGANIZED TERRITORY
MICHIGAN TERRITORY
L. Superior
Mississippi R.
Huron
Ontario
L. Erie
ME
VT
NH
MA
NY
RI
CT
PA
NJ
DE
IL
IN
OH
Ohio R.
VA
KY
MO
NC
TN
SC
CALIFORNIA
Colorado R.
Missouri Compromise Line 36°30'
ARKANSAS TERRITORY
MS
AL
GA
LA
Vesey Slave Revolt
Pacific Ocean
MEXICO
Rio Grande
FLORIDA TERRITORY
Atlantic Ocean
Gulf of Mexico
Slave states & territories
Free states & territories
Claimed by Britain and U.S.
0 200 400
Miles

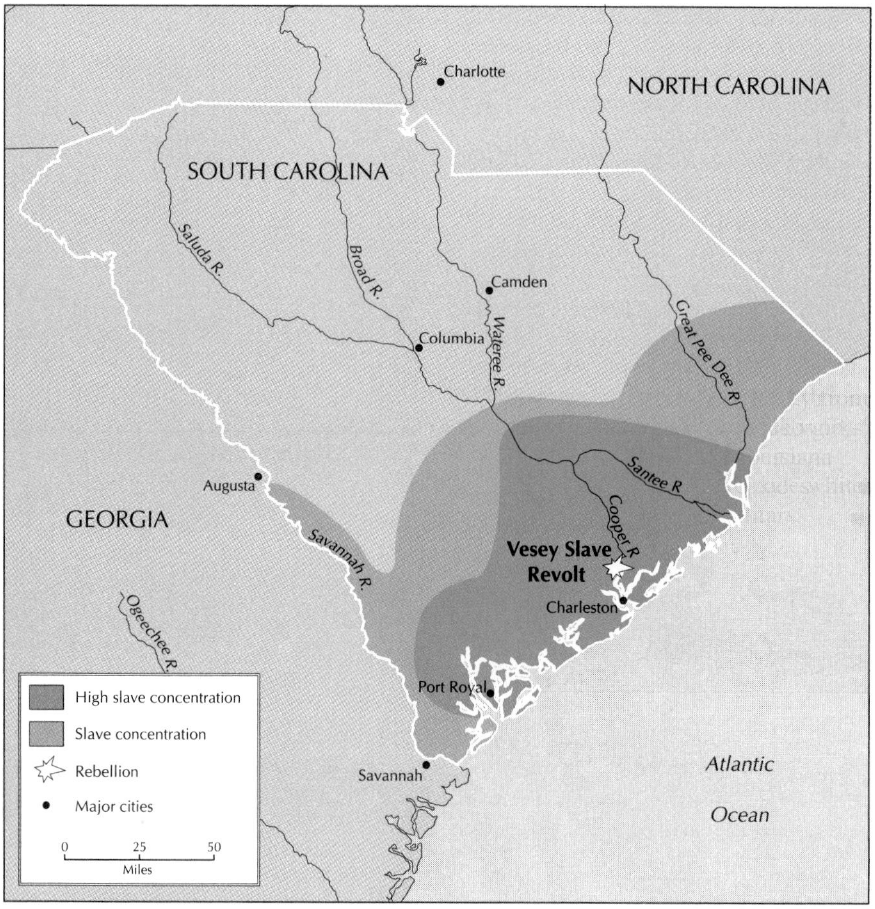
Charlotte
NORTH CAROLINA
SOUTH CAROLINA
Saluda R.
Broad R.
Camden
Columbia
Wateree R.
Great Pee Dee R.
Santee R.
Augusta
GEORGIA
Savannah R.
Cooper R.
Vesey Slave Revolt
Charleston
Ogeechee R.
Port Royal
Savannah
High slave concentration
Slave concentration
Rebellion
Major cities
0 25 50
Miles
Atlantic Ocean

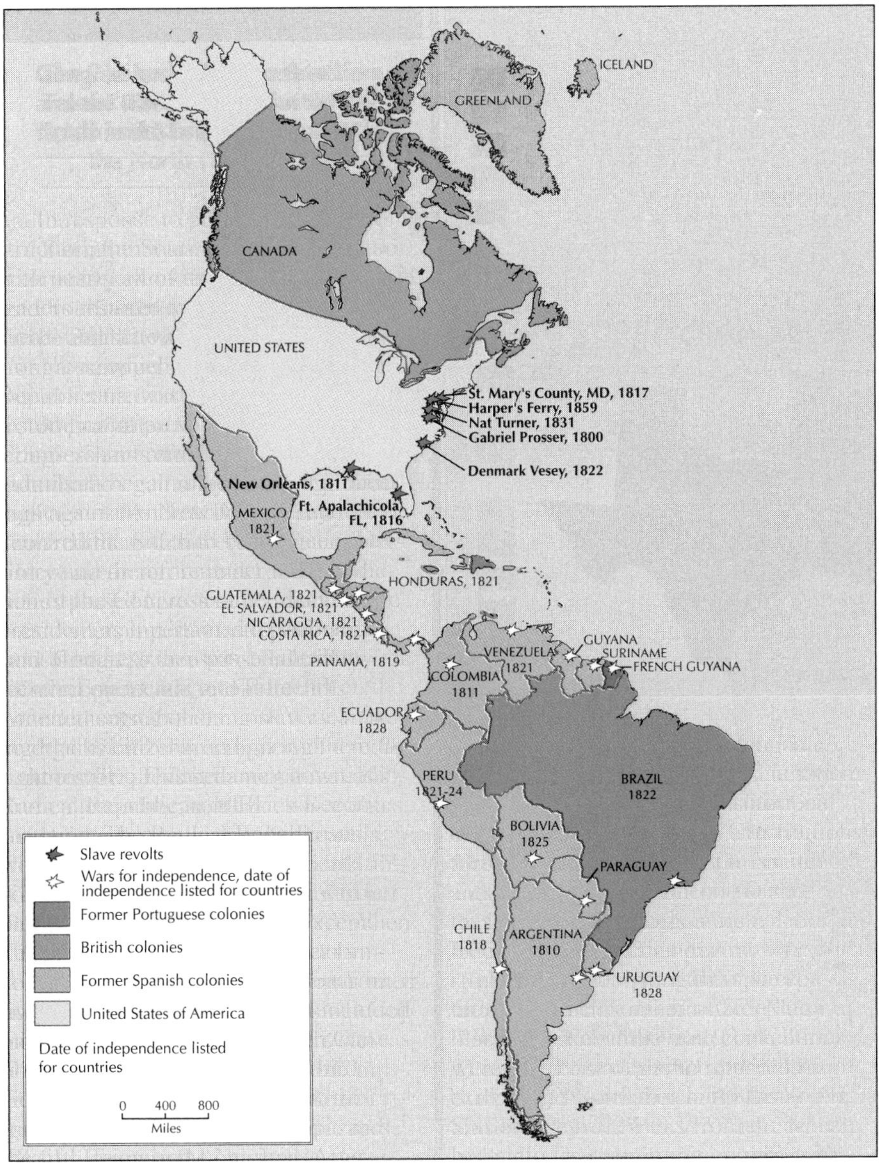
ICELAND
GREENLAND
CANADA
UNITED STATES
St. Mary's County, MD, 1817
Harper's Ferry, 1859
Nat Turner, 1831
Gabriel Prosser, 1800
Denmark Vesey, 1822
New Orleans, 1811
Ft. Apalachicola, FL, 1816
MEXICO 1821
HONDURAS, 1821
GUATEMALA, 1821
EL SALVADOR, 1821
NICARAGUA, 1821
COSTA RICA, 1821
PANAMA, 1819
GUYANA
SURINAME
FRENCH GUYANA
VENEZUELA 1821
COLOMBIA 1811
ECUADOR 1828
PERU 1821-24
BRAZIL 1822
BOLIVIA 1825
PARAGUAY
CHILE 1818
ARGENTINA 1810
URUGUAY 1828
Slave revolts
Wars for independence, date of independence listed for countries
Former Portuguese colonies
British colonies
Former Spanish colonies
United States of America
Date of independence listed for countries
0 400 800
Miles

the revolutions were over by 1828, there were a total of seventeen new republics in the Western Hemisphere. Many of these early nations, including Mexico, Guatemala, El Salvador, Honduras, Nicaragua, Costa Rica, Panama, and Chile, immediately abolished slavery to reward their slaves who had fought in their wars of independence. Other nations like Brazil would betray their slave allies and continue to practice slavery until the late nineteenth century. ■

MAP 51

The Free Black and Slave Population of the United States (1830)

By 1830, the United States had a total population of 12,866,000. Of this total the black population in the United States numbered about 2.3 million and made up around 18 percent of the nation's population and nearly half of the South's population. The vast majority of blacks were slaves living in the slaveholding states of the South, but there were also free blacks living in northeastern and midwestern cities like New York, Philadelphia, Boston, Chicago, Cleveland, and Cincinnati and southern cities like Richmond, Norfolk, Charleston, Savannah, Atlanta, New Orleans, Mobile, and Montgomery. Beginning in 1800 the slave population of the South shifted from the south Atlantic states of Maryland, Virginia, North Carolina, South Carolina, and Georgia to the Gulf states of Florida, Alabama, Mississippi, Louisiana, and Texas. The majority of free blacks during this period continued to live in southern cities. Most free blacks, North and South, worked as carpenters, blacksmiths, or servants for whites, while the majority of slaves toiled on farms and plantations throughout the South. Because the Atlantic slave trade was outlawed by the U.S. Constitution in 1808, the growth of the black population during this period was primarily due to slave breeding. This was used to provide cotton growers in the lower South with slaves. ■

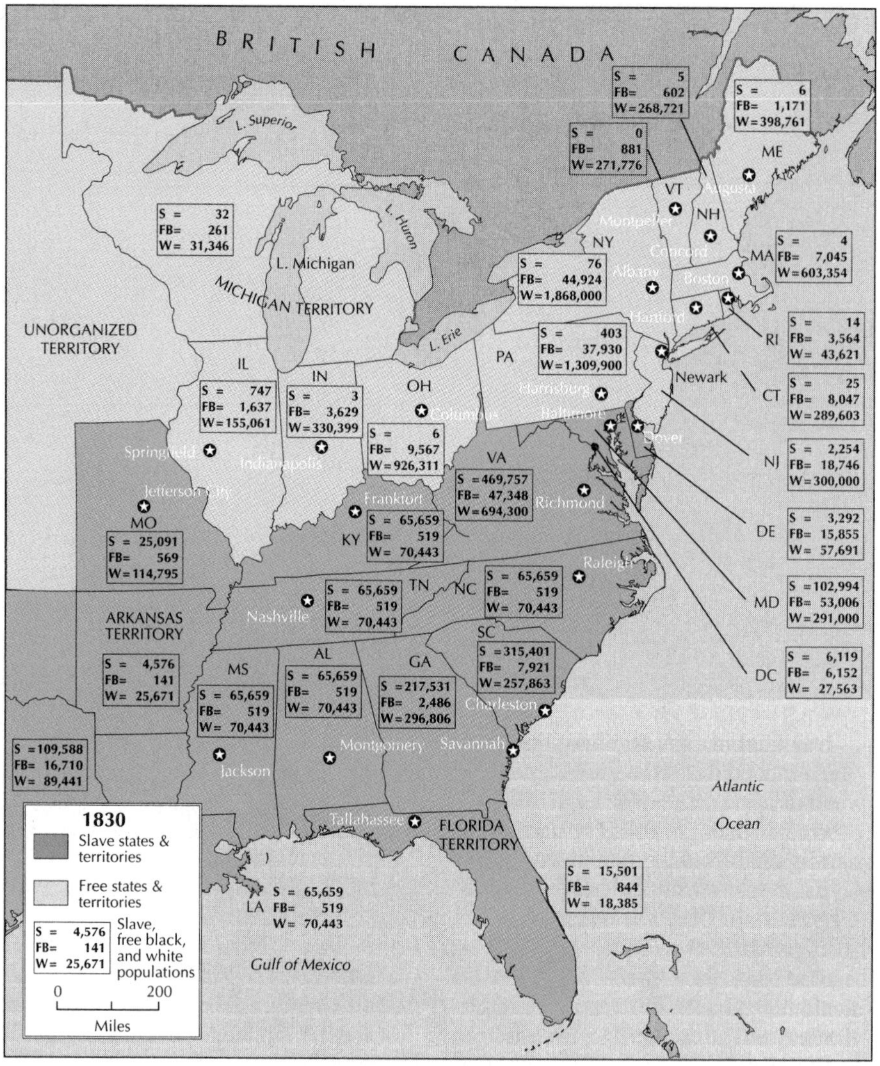
BRITISH CANADA
L. Superior
L. Michigan
L. Huron
L. Erie
UNORGANIZED TERRITORY
MICHIGAN TERRITORY
ARKANSAS TERRITORY
FLORIDA TERRITORY
IL
IN
OH
PA
NY
VT
NH
ME
MA
RI
CT
NJ
DE
MD
DC
VA
KY
TN
NC
SC
GA
AL
MS
LA
MO
S = 5 FB= 602 W=268,721
S = 6 FB= 1,171 W=398,761
S = 0 FB= 881 W=271,776
S = 32 FB= 261 W= 31,346
S = 76 FB= 44,924 W=1,868,000
S = 4 FB= 7,045 W=603,354
S = 403 FB= 37,930 W=1,309,900
S = 14 FB= 3,564 W= 43,621
S = 25 FB= 8,047 W=289,603
S = 747 FB= 1,637 W=155,061
S = 3 FB= 3,629 W=330,399
S = 6 FB= 9,567 W=926,311
S = 2,254 FB= 18,746 W=300,000
S =469,757 FB= 47,348 W=694,300
S = 65,659 FB= 519 W= 70,443
S = 3,292 FB= 15,855 W= 57,691
S = 25,091 FB= 569 W=114,795
S = 65,659 FB= 519 W= 70,443
S = 65,659 FB= 519 W= 70,443
S =102,994 FB= 53,006 W=291,000
S = 4,576 FB= 141 W= 25,671
S = 65,659 FB= 519 W= 70,443
S =315,401 FB= 7,921 W=257,863
S = 6,119 FB= 6,152 W= 27,563
S = 65,659 FB= 519 W= 70,443
S =217,531 FB= 2,486 W=296,806
S = 65,659 FB= 519 W= 70,443
S =109,588 FB= 16,710 W= 89,441
S = 15,501 FB= 844 W= 18,385
S = 65,659 FB= 519 W= 70,443
Augusta
Montpelier
Concord
Albany
Boston
Hartford
Newark
Harrisburg
Baltimore
Dover
Columbus
Indianapolis
Springfield
Jefferson City
Frankfort
Richmond
Raleigh
Nashville
Charleston
Montgomery
Savannah
Jackson
Tallahassee
Atlantic Ocean
Gulf of Mexico
1830
Slave states & territories
Free states & territories
S = 4,576 FB= 141 W= 25,671
Slave, free black, and white populations
0 200
Miles

MAP 52

Indian "Removal" and the Expansion of Slavery into Former Indian Lands in the South (1830–1860)

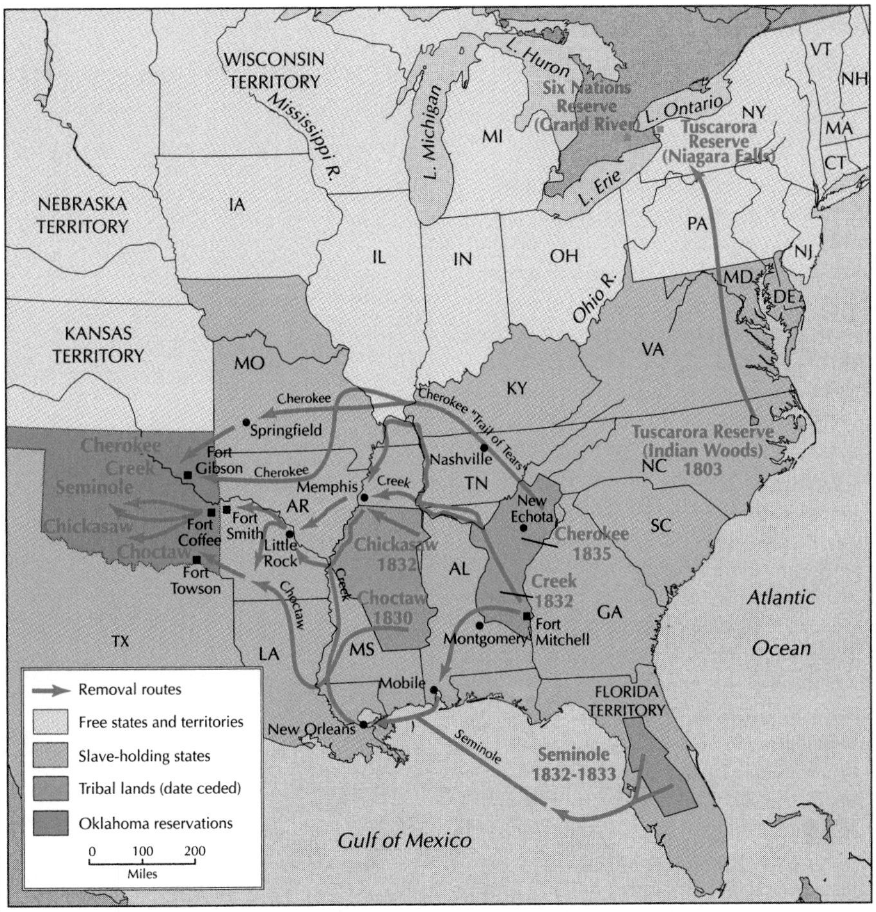
WISCONSIN TERRITORY
Mississippi R.
L. Michigan
L. Huron
Six Nations Reserve (Grand River)
L. Ontario
NY
Tuscarora Reserve (Niagara Falls)
VT
NH
MA
CT
MI
L. Erie
NEBRASKA TERRITORY
IA
PA
NJ
IL
IN
OH
Ohio R.
MD
DE
KANSAS TERRITORY
VA
MO
KY
Cherokee
Springfield
Cherokee "Trail of Tears"
Tuscarora Reserve (Indian Woods)
NC 1803
Fort Gibson
Cherokee
Nashville
Cherokee
Creek
Seminole
Memphis
Creek
TN
AR
New Echota
Chickasaw
Fort Coffee
Fort Smith
Little Rock
SC
Cherokee 1835
Choctaw
Chickasaw 1832
Fort Towson
AL
Creek 1832
Atlantic Ocean
Choctaw 1830
Creek
Choctaw
GA
TX
Fort Mitchell
Montgomery
MS
LA
Mobile
FLORIDA TERRITORY
New Orleans
Seminole
Seminole 1832-1833
Gulf of Mexico
Removal routes
Free states and territories
Slave-holding states
Tribal lands (date ceded)
Oklahoma reservations
0 100 200
Miles

The institution of slavery affected every aspect of American life. It divided the nation into proslavery and antislavery forces and threatened the future of the country. By 1830, slavery had also impacted many Native American peoples as well, particularly the Five Civilized Tribes (Seminoles, Creeks, Choctaws, Chickasaws, and Cherokees), who by 1830 had been practicing African slavery on their lands for over a hundred years. Although the Five Civilized Tribes had been the allies of southerners dating back to the Tuscarora War of 1711, served as slave catchers, and actually adopted African slavery at the insistence of their southern neighbors, they were never fully accepted by southerners. As cotton production became more profitable and land employed for cotton production began to be exhausted from the overcultivation of the cash crop, southern whites started to demand the removal of these tribes from their fertile lands located on the coastal plains of the lower South. They accused the Indians of harboring runaway slaves, encouraging slave rebellions, and straying off their reservations onto the farms of nearby whites. In 1830, two years after the election of President Andrew Jackson, the federal government, with little opposition, began to forcibly remove these Indians from their ancestral lands to lands west of the Mississippi River—to what was then called Indian Territory and today is Oklahoma. The uprootings continued from 1830 to about 1840. The journey was long and difficult, and many people died traveling the "Trail of Tears." On these forced marches the Indians were accompanied by their African slaves, who also endured the great hardships of the marches. Southern plantation owners quickly moved their slaves onto the former Indian lands, cleared the areas, and prepared the lands for the production of cotton. ■

MAP 53

Nat Turner's Slave Revolt (1831)

In 1831, in Southampton County, Virginia, former slave Nat Turner led one of the most successful slave revolts in American history. Turner, a Baptist minister, would often preach sermons to slaves, who would steal away from their plantations to hear him. He also was known by slaves to have visions and the power of prophecy. In August 1831, Turner and about fifty slaves went from plantation to plantation, wantonly killing white men, women, and children. By the time they were captured, Turner and his followers had killed fifty-five whites. The revolt engendered panic throughout Virginia and North Carolina and caused many states to pass stricter slave codes to control the movements and actions of free blacks and slaves. The revolt was especially worrisome because of the Vesey revolt in Charleston, South Carolina, nine years earlier. Although Turner was captured and hanged, his connection to the church caused many Virginia and North Carolina slaveholders to prohibit their slaves from worshiping together unsupervised. In fact, slaves were allowed to worship only in white churches with whites present and white ministers delivering the sermons. As with the Prosser revolt in 1800, free blacks and slaves in southeastern Virginia, from Richmond to Norfolk, and northeastern North Carolina, from Murfreesboro to Edenton, were arrested, imprisoned, and executed for suspicion of plotting slave revolts. It would take months before calm would be restored. ■

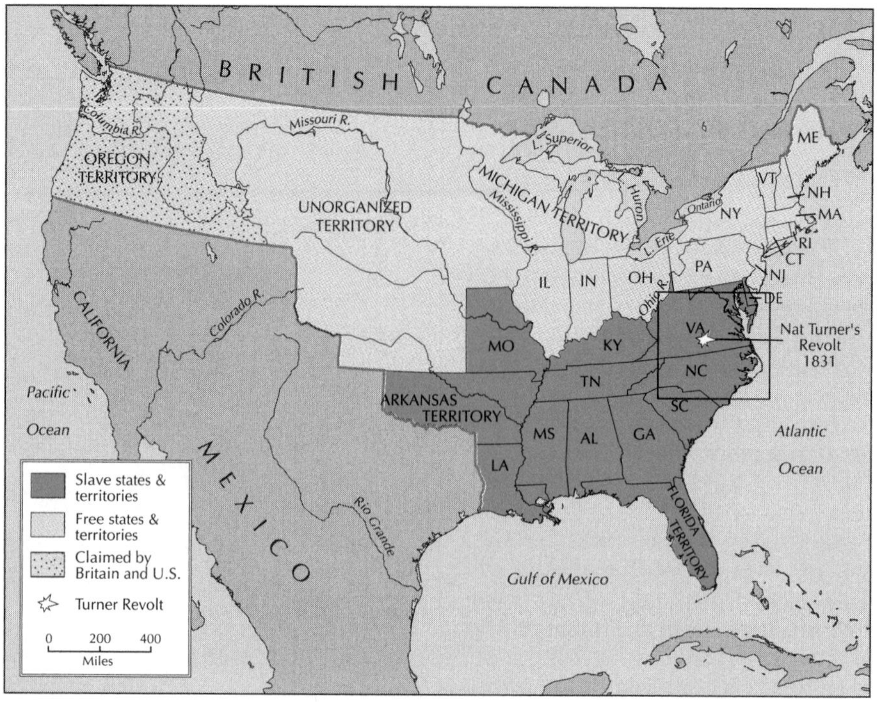
BRITISH CANADA
OREGON TERRITORY
UNORGANIZED TERRITORY
MICHIGAN TERRITORY
CALIFORNIA
MEXICO
Missouri R.
Columbia R.
Colorado R.
Rio Grande
Mississippi R.
Ohio R.
L. Superior
Huron
Ontario
L. Erie
ME
VT
NH
MA
RI
CT
NY
PA
NJ
DE
IL
IN
OH
MO
KY
VA
NC
TN
SC
ARKANSAS TERRITORY
MS
AL
GA
LA
FLORIDA TERRITORY
Nat Turner's Revolt 1831
Pacific Ocean
Atlantic Ocean
Gulf of Mexico
Slave states & territories
Free states & territories
Claimed by Britain and U.S.
Turner Revolt
0 200 400
Miles

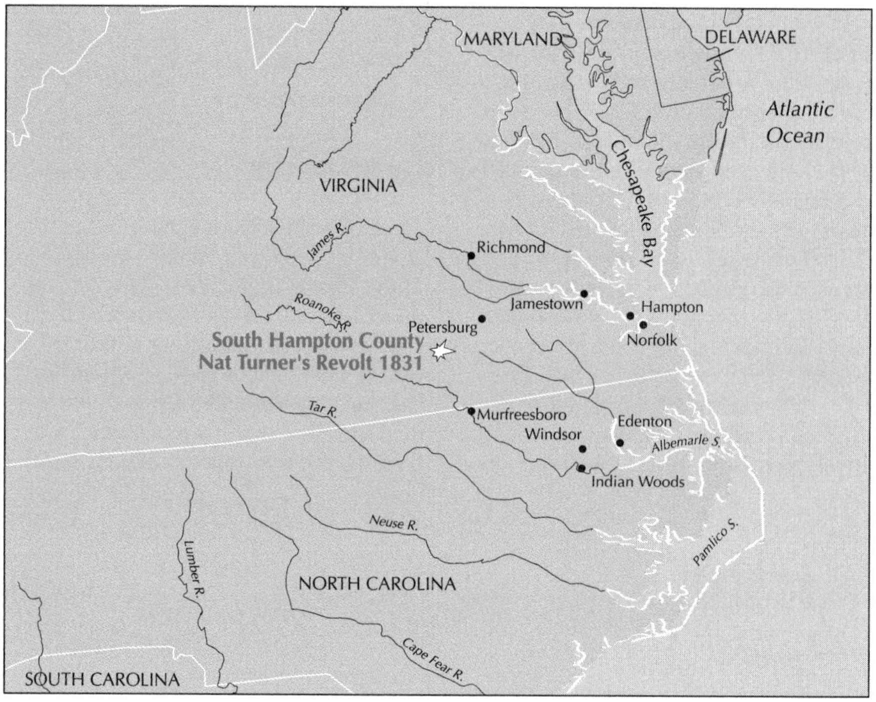
MARYLAND
DELAWARE
Atlantic Ocean
VIRGINIA
Chesapeake Bay
James R.
Richmond
Jamestown
Hampton
Norfolk
Roanoke R.
Petersburg
South Hampton County
Nat Turner's Revolt 1831
Tar R.
Murfreesboro
Windsor
Edenton
Albemarle S.
Indian Woods
Neuse R.
Pamlico S.
Lumber R.
NORTH CAROLINA
Cape Fear R.
SOUTH CAROLINA

MAP 54

The Mexican-American War, the Wilmot Proviso, and the Expansion of Slavery into the Southwest (1846–1853)

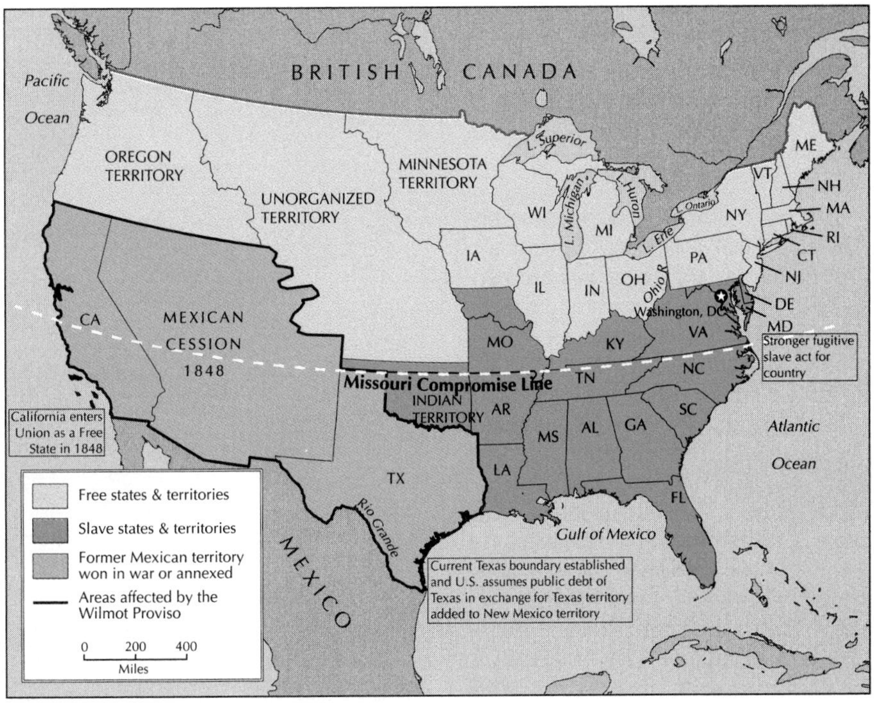
Pacific Ocean
BRITISH CANADA
L. Superior
OREGON TERRITORY
MINNESOTA TERRITORY
UNORGANIZED TERRITORY
WI
L. Michigan
L. Huron
MI
Ontario
NY
VT
ME
NH
MA
RI
CT
NJ
DE
MD
IA
IL
IN
OH
Ohio R.
L. Erie
PA
Washington, DC
VA
KY
MO
CA
MEXICAN CESSION 1848
Missouri Compromise Line
INDIAN TERRITORY
AR
TN
NC
SC
MS
AL
GA
LA
TX
FL
Rio Grande
MEXICO
Gulf of Mexico
Atlantic Ocean
Stronger fugitive slave act for country
California enters Union as a Free State in 1848
Current Texas boundary established and U.S. assumes public debt of Texas in exchange for Texas territory added to New Mexico territory
Free states & territories
Slave states & territories
Former Mexican territory won in war or annexed
Areas affected by the Wilmot Proviso
0 200 400
Miles

In 1835, Texans declared their independence from Mexico in the Texas Revolution. One of the major causes of this revolution was the abolition of slavery by the new Mexican nation and the gift of land and protection to runaway slaves and free blacks from the Texas province and the slaveholding South. Thus, when war broke out, the southern slaveholding states quickly began to support the revolution with men and supplies. By 1836, Texas had defeated Mexico, preserved the institution of slavery, and established the Republic of Texas, with Sam Houston as president. Nine years later, after being annexed by the United States, Texas would be allowed to join the Union as a slave state. In 1846, after Mexico refused to recognize Texas's independence, the United States declared war on Mexico, in an attempt to fulfill its "manifest destiny." During the war, northern abolitionists and Democrats adamantly opposed U.S. involvement and believed the war to be orchestrated by southerners to gain Mexican territory for the expansion of slavery. When the United States defeated Mexico in 1848, it acquired control over the vast southwest territory from Texas to California. The debate over slavery in this new territory resurfaced. Southerners assumed that the new territory, or at least that portion beneath the 36°30' parallel, would be open to slavery. However, northern senators vehemently opposed extending slavery to any of the new territory. In 1848, Democratic Senator David Wilmot from Pennsylvania proposed a controversial amendment, which became known as the "Wilmot Proviso," to a bill that had been introduced in the House of Representatives. The bill provided an appropriation of $2 million for peace negotiations with Mexico. The money was to be used to purchase new territory from Mexico. The Wilmot Proviso declared that slavery should be forbidden in any territory that was obtained with the $2 million. The House of Representatives approved the amendment, but the Senate refused to pass the proviso. Wilmot's amendment caused an uproar in the southern states, reopening a chasm between the North and South which had been bridged by the Missouri Compromise of 1820. ■

MAP 55

The Compromise of 1850 and Its Impact on Slavery in the United States

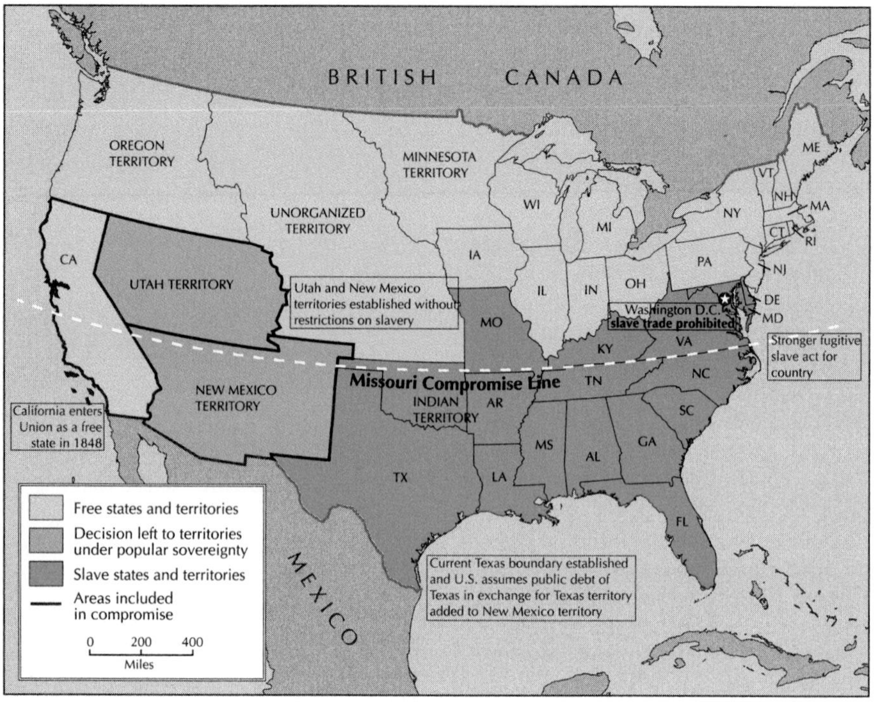
BRITISH CANADA
OREGON TERRITORY
MINNESOTA TERRITORY
UNORGANIZED TERRITORY
CA
UTAH TERRITORY
Utah and New Mexico territories established without restrictions on slavery
NEW MEXICO TERRITORY
California enters Union as a free state in 1848
Missouri Compromise Line
INDIAN TERRITORY
Washington D.C. slave trade prohibited
Stronger fugitive slave act for country
Current Texas boundary established and U.S. assumes public debt of Texas in exchange for Texas territory added to New Mexico territory
MEXICO
ME
VT
NH
MA
NY
CT
RI
NJ
PA
DE
MD
WI
MI
IA
IL
IN
OH
MO
KY
VA
NC
TN
AR
SC
MS
AL
GA
TX
LA
FL
Free states and territories
Decision left to territories under popular sovereignty
Slave states and territories
Areas included in compromise
0 200 400
Miles

For the fourth time in American history, a crisis arose over the expansion of slavery. Earlier, the nation had escaped disaster with the Northwest Ordinance and Three-Fifths Compromise in 1787 and the Missouri Compromise in 1820. In 1850, the United States attempted to settle the issue, as it related to its territorial acquisitions, once and for all. The result was the Compromise of 1850, which permitted California to enter the Union as a free state and introduced the policy of "popular sovereignty," a policy that allowed the new territories of New Mexico and Utah to decide the issue of slavery for themselves. Finally, the Compromise of 1850 banned slave trading in the District of Columbia, which was viewed as an international embarrassment by the free states. The South was successful in having a stricter Fugitive Slave Law passed by Congress to aid in recovering the increasing number of slaves being smuggled out of the South on the Underground Railroad. The law required northern states to assist in the apprehension and return of these slaves to their masters. As a result of the Compromise of 1850, the Oregon Territory, Minnesota Territory, and the Unorganized Territory remained closed to slavery, while the New Mexico and Utah Territories were opened to slavery. ■

MAP 56

The Kansas-Nebraska Act (1854)

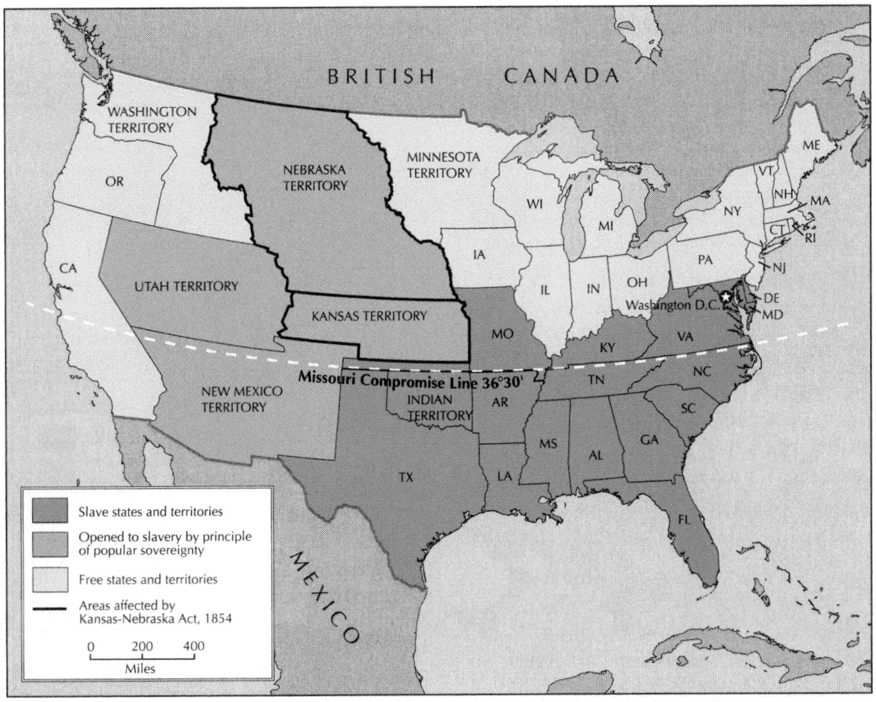
BRITISH CANADA
WASHINGTON TERRITORY
OR
CA
NEBRASKA TERRITORY
MINNESOTA TERRITORY
UTAH TERRITORY
KANSAS TERRITORY
NEW MEXICO TERRITORY
INDIAN TERRITORY
Missouri Compromise Line 36°30'
WI
MI
IA
IL
IN
OH
PA
NY
VT
NH
ME
MA
CT
RI
NJ
DE
MD
Washington D.C.
VA
KY
MO
TN
NC
SC
AR
MS
AL
GA
LA
TX
FL
MEXICO
Slave states and territories
Opened to slavery by principle of popular sovereignty
Free states and territories
Areas affected by Kansas-Nebraska Act, 1854
0 200 400
Miles

For several years, it looked as if the Compromise of 1850 had ended the friction over slavery. Business leaders wanted peace so that prosperity would continue. However, many northerners thought that the Fugitive Slave Law was too harsh, and some states interfered with its enforcement. Of special concern was the policy of popular sovereignty, which allowed the Utah Territory and the New Mexico Territory to decide whether they wished to be free or slave states. Many slaveholders and "Free Soilers" began to flood the territories in the hope of deciding the fate of the new territories. The controversy was fanned when the Kansas-Nebraska bill was proposed in 1854 by Democratic Senator Stephen A. Douglas from Illinois. It provided that two new territories, Kansas and Nebraska, were to be created from the Indian land that lay west of the bend of the Missouri River and north of 37 degrees north latitude. Midwesterners had been trying to organize a new territory in Nebraska for four years. They wanted to see the region opened for settlement. Douglas was influenced by the midwesterners, especially Missourians, and may also have been influenced by his desire for a railroad from Chicago to the Pacific Coast. Douglas included in his bill a provision for popular sovereignty in Kansas and Nebraska. This measure stated that all questions of slavery in the new territories were to be decided by the settlers. It was designed to win the support of the southern congressmen. The slavery provision was directly contrary to the Missouri Compromise of 1820, which had declared that all land in the Louisiana Purchase north of 36°30' was to be free. Douglas also was persuaded by southerners to declare the Missouri Compromise "inoperative and void." The Kansas-Nebraska bill was attacked furiously by antislavery forces. The debate in Congress was long and bitter. However, President Franklin Pierce supported the bill, and it became law. The Kansas-Nebraska Act made slavery legally possible in a vast new area. It also revived the bitter quarrel over the expansion of slavery which had died down after the Compromise of 1850. Most historians believe that the Kansas-Nebraska Act hastened the War between the States. ■

MAP 57

Bleeding Kansas: The Sack of Lawrence, and the Pottawatomie Massacre (1856)

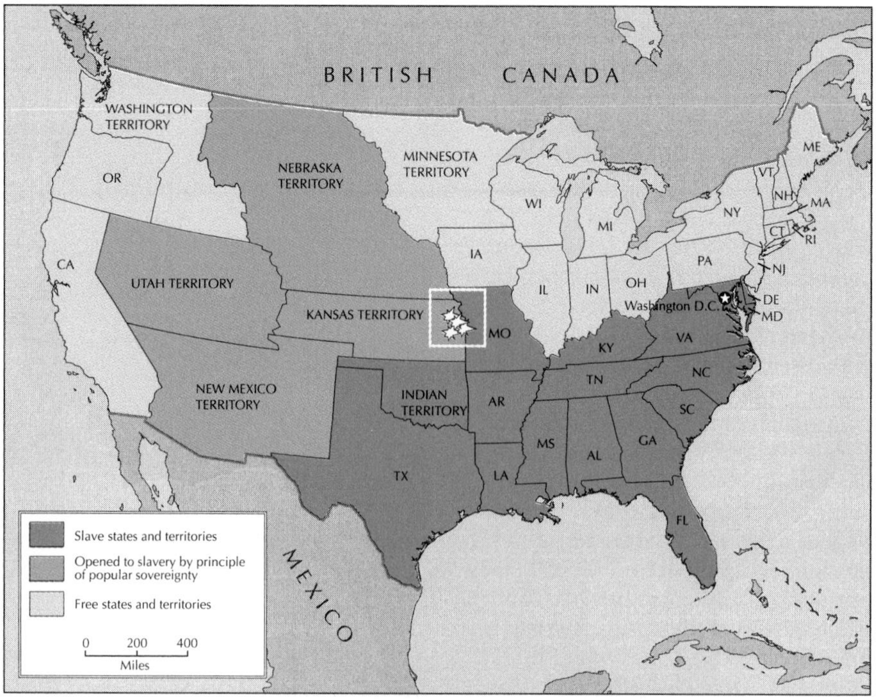
BRITISH CANADA
WASHINGTON TERRITORY
OR
CA
NEBRASKA TERRITORY
MINNESOTA TERRITORY
UTAH TERRITORY
KANSAS TERRITORY
NEW MEXICO TERRITORY
INDIAN TERRITORY
TX
IA
MO
AR
LA
WI
MI
IL
IN
OH
KY
TN
MS
AL
GA
FL
SC
NC
VA
PA
NY
ME
VT
NH
MA
CT
RI
NJ
DE
MD
Washington D.C.
MEXICO
Slave states and territories
Opened to slavery by principle of popular sovereignty
Free states and territories
0 200 400
Miles

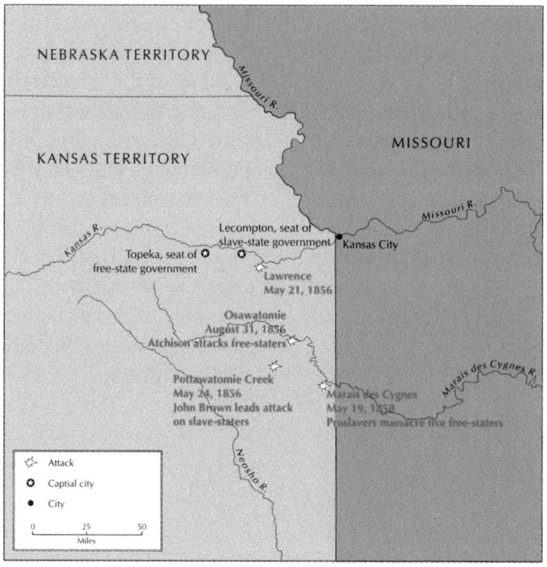
NEBRASKA TERRITORY
Missouri R.
KANSAS TERRITORY
MISSOURI
Missouri R.
Kansas R.
Lecompton, seat of slave-state government
Kansas City
Topeka, seat of free-state government
Lawrence
May 21, 1856
Osawatomie
August 31, 1856
Atchison attacks free-staters
Pottawatomie Creek
May 24, 1856
John Brown leads attack on slave-staters
Marais des Cygnes R.
Marais des Cygnes
May 19, 1858
Neosho R.
Attack
Captial city
City
0 25 50
Miles

The mid-1850s was a troubled time for America. Despite repeated attempts, the nation still could not shake the deeply divisive issue of slavery. Africans had been in America for nearly 250 years, and the country still had not come to grips with their presence. They had worked the fields and cleared the forests, but were still seen by whites as chattel property. Even free blacks were seen as slaves without masters. Sectional divisions over slavery became acute after the passage of the Kansas-Nebraska Act in 1854. This Act repealed for the first time an act of Congress—the Missouri Compromise of 1820, opening territory previously closed to slavery. The furor that was aroused by this act helped to permanently split northern and southern Democrats, and led to the creation of the northern-based Republican party, which in just a few years would nominate and elect Abraham Lincoln as president of the United States. Tensions were at an all-time high when in May of 1856 Senator Charles Sumner of Massachusetts, a Republican and staunch opponent of slavery, gave an impassioned speech on the Senate floor condemning the practice of slavery, the Kansas-Nebraska Act, and southerners defending the institution of slavery. He specifically named Senator Andrew Butler of South Carolina, provoking the wrath of Butler's cousin, Democratic congressman Preston Brooks, also of South Carolina. Two days after the speech, Representative Brooks approached Senator Sumner and struck him on the head several times with his cane, permanently crippling the senator and nearly killing him. This incident further split northerners and southerners, even of the same party, between proslavery and antislavery factions. The level of hostility was so intense that a number of members of the House and Senate began to carry knives, clubs, and guns due to fear of being attacked by their opponents in Congress. This event marked the beginning of open violence between proslavery and antislavery forces around the nation. In Kansas, proslavery and antislavery forces (Free-Soilers) poured into the state swelling the population to more than 100,000. Elections were held and the proslavery side won, but the results were disputed. Free-Soilers charged that proslavery Missourians had crossed over into Kansas and voted in the election illegally, thus nullifying the victory. Proslavery forces declared Kansas a slave state and established Topeka as its capital. Antislavery forces responded by declaring Kansas a free state and establishing the capital at Lawrence. On May 21, 1856, proslavery forces from Lecompton attacked the antislavery city of Lawrence. Although no one was killed, the proslavery forces burned most of the city and destroyed the abolitionist printing presses. This clash between proslavery and antislavery factions became known as the Sack of Lawrence. In response to this attack, John Brown, a self-ordained minister and staunch abolitionist, led an attack at Pottawatomie Creek, where five men he suspected of supporting the proslavery government were killed. This event became known as the Pottawatomie Massacre. ■

MAP 58

The Dred Scott Decision (1857)

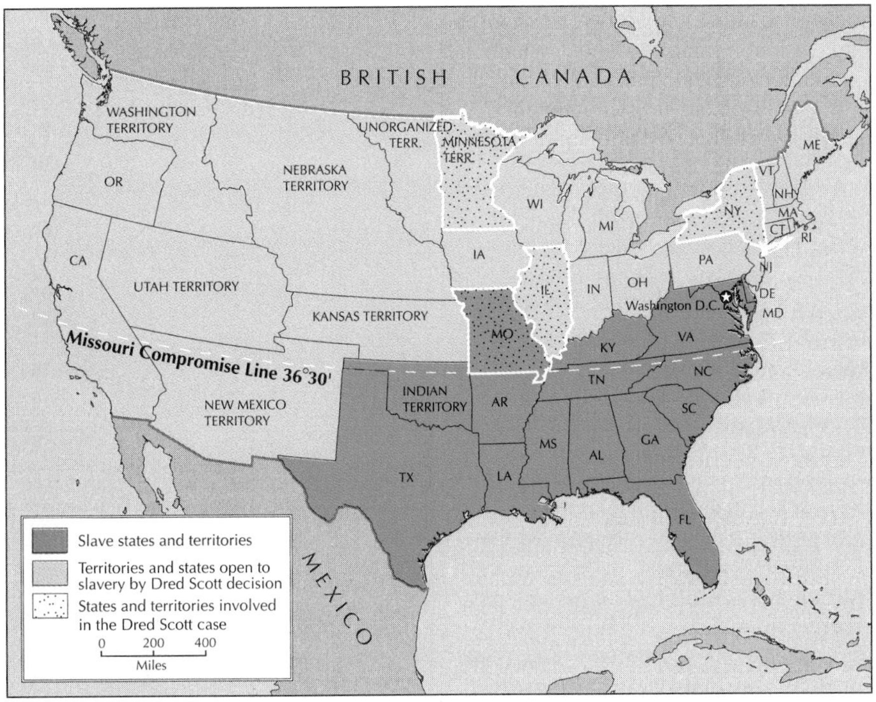
BRITISH CANADA
WASHINGTON TERRITORY
OR
CA
UTAH TERRITORY
NEBRASKA TERRITORY
UNORGANIZED TERR.
MINNESOTA TERR.
KANSAS TERRITORY
NEW MEXICO TERRITORY
INDIAN TERRITORY
Missouri Compromise Line 36°30'
WI
IA
MI
IL
IN
OH
MO
KY
TN
AR
MS
AL
GA
SC
NC
VA
LA
TX
FL
PA
NY
ME
VT
NH
MA
CT
RI
NJ
DE
MD
Washington D.C.
MEXICO
Slave states and territories
Territories and states open to slavery by Dred Scott decision
States and territories involved in the Dred Scott case
0 200 400
Miles

In regard to the issue of slavery, the 1850s were among the most difficult years in American history. Arguments and violence over slavery led to bloodshed in Kansas and on the floor of the U.S. Congress. Before the wounds could heal, the issue of slavery once again exploded when the Dred Scott decision was announced by the Supreme Court in 1857. Dred Scott was the slave of an army surgeon, Dr. John Emerson of Missouri. Dr. Emerson first took Scott to the free state of Illinois and then to that part of the Wisconsin Territory that later became the state of Minnesota, a region in which slavery was forbidden by the Missouri Compromise. In 1838, Scott was taken back to Missouri, a slave state. Scott's master then moved from Missouri. Scott was left behind, hired out, and later sold to John F. A. Sandford. Meanwhile, Scott had been told by interested persons that his residence in a free state made him a free man. He sued for his freedom in 1846, and the state circuit court of St. Louis County issued a verdict in his favor. However, the state supreme court reversed the decision. The case was then taken to the federal courts and eventually reached the U.S. Supreme Court. In the end, the Supreme Court held that it had no jurisdiction in the Dred Scott case. The Court noted that Scott was still a slave. As a slave, argued the Court, he was a citizen neither of Missouri nor of the United States, and therefore could not sue in federal court. The Court might well have stopped at this, but it did not. Seven of the nine justices, including five southerners, were Democrats. They seized the chance to record the opinion that the Missouri Compromise was unconstitutional and that slavery could not be excluded from the territories. The two Republicans held that this part of the decision was merely the opinion of a majority of the justices on a matter that was not before the Court, and that it therefore had no legal force. The announcement of the decision by Chief Justice Roger B. Taney on March 6, 1857, aroused a violent public reaction. The Dred Scott decision fueled the tense feeling between the North and the South, and was another of the important factors that led to the Civil War. ■

MAP 59

John Brown's Raid (1859)

John Brown, one of America's most famous abolitionists, was born in Torrington, Connecticut, in 1800. As a young man, he wandered aimlessly about the country, living at different times in Connecticut, Ohio, and New York. He married early in life, but he was unwilling to settle in any one place or to follow any trade for long. He earned only a modest living for his large family. He arrived in Kansas in 1855 after the Kansas-Nebraska Act had been passed. This law gave the settlers the right to decide whether Kansas would be a slave or free territory. In the fierce warfare that was carried on for several years in Kansas and Missouri, Brown proved to be an expert guerrilla fighter. By 1859, Brown had left Kansas with his sons and had relocated in the Appalachian Mountains of Virginia. He still condemned the immorality of slavery and advocated its end by any means necessary. On October 16, 1859, fortified by the belief that God had called him to organize a slave revolt, Brown led a group of twenty-one men to Harper's Ferry, Virginia (now in West Virginia), with the goal of seizing the federal arsenal and arming the slaves in the area. He believed that this would result in an immediate slave uprising. He planned an ambitious campaign across Virginia and the South, with the intent of liberating slaves and killing their owners. His plan failed, however, since the slaves refused to revolt. Brown was subsequently captured at Harper's Ferry by federal troops, led by Colonel Robert E. Lee. Brown and his supporters were arrested, convicted of treason, and hanged on December 2, 1859. The Harper's Ferry revolt terrified and infuriated southerners, but was heralded by black and white abolitionists as a "glorious undertaking." Brown's subsequent execution made him a martyr for the abolitionist movement.

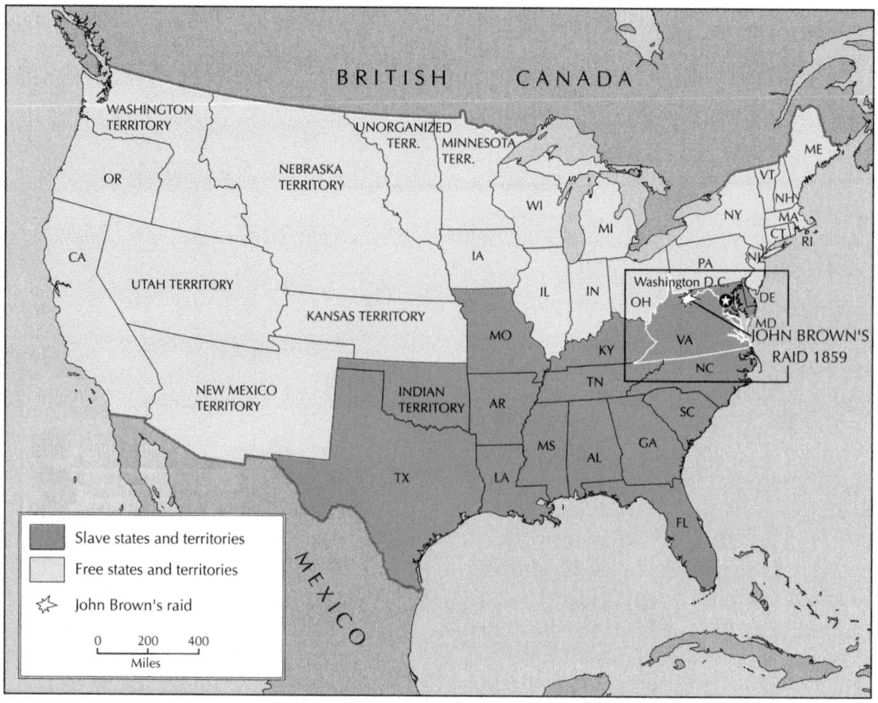
BRITISH CANADA
WASHINGTON TERRITORY
UNORGANIZED TERR.
MINNESOTA TERR.
OR
NEBRASKA TERRITORY
ME
VT
NH
MA
CT
RI
NY
WI
MI
IA
PA
CA
UTAH TERRITORY
IL
IN
Washington D.C.
OH
DE
MD
KANSAS TERRITORY
MO
VA
JOHN BROWN'S RAID 1859
KY
NC
TN
NEW MEXICO TERRITORY
INDIAN TERRITORY
AR
SC
MS
AL
GA
TX
LA
FL
MEXICO
Slave states and territories
Free states and territories
John Brown's raid
0 200 400
Miles

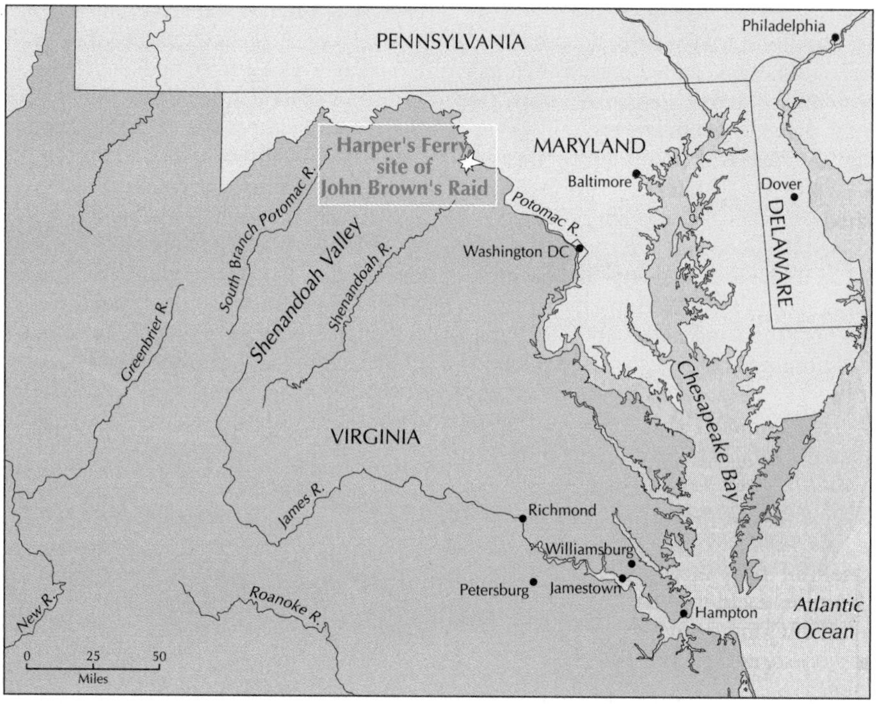
PENNSYLVANIA
Philadelphia
MARYLAND
Harper's Ferry site of John Brown's Raid
Baltimore
Dover
DELAWARE
Potomac R.
South Branch Potomac R.
Shenandoah Valley
Shenandoah R.
Washington DC
Greenbrier R.
Chesapeake Bay
VIRGINIA
James R.
Richmond
Williamsburg
Petersburg
Jamestown
Roanoke R.
New R.
Hampton
Atlantic Ocean
0 25 50
Miles

Map and Text Sources

46. Nalty, Bernard C. *Strength for the Fight: A History of Black Americans in the Military*. New York: Free Press, 1986.
Nell, William C. *Services of Colored Americans in the Wars of 1776 and 1812*. Photocopy. New Haven, CT: Yale University Library, n.d.
Smith, Zachariah Frederick. *The Battle of New Orleans Including the Previous Engagements between the Americans and the British, the Indians, and the Spanish Which Led to the Final Conflict on the 8th of January, 1815*. Louisville, KY: Morton, 1983.
Wilson, Ellen Gibson. *The Loyal Blacks*. New York: Capricorn Books, 1976.

47. *The Constitution of the United States, with Acts of Congress, Relating to Slavery, Embracing the Constitution, the Fugitive Slave Act of 1793, the Missouri Compromise Act of 1820, the Fugitive Slave Law of 1850, and the Nebraska and Kansas Bill, Carefully Compiled*. Rochester, NY: D. W. Dewey, 1854.
McDougall, Marion G. *Fugitive Slaves (1619–1865)*. Freeport, NY: Books for Libraries Press, 1971.
Moore, Glover. *The Missouri Controversy, 1819–1821*. Lexington: University of Kentucky Press, 1966.

48. Dodd, William E. *The Cotton Kingdom: A Chronicle of the Old South*. New York: United States Publishers Association, 1978.
Moore, John Hebron. *The Emergence of the Cotton Kingdom in the Old Southwest: Mississippi, 1770–1860*. Baton Rouge: Louisiana State University Press, 1988.
Stampp, Kenneth M. *The Peculiar Institution: Slavery in the Ante-Bellum South*. New York: Vintage Books, 1989.
Woodman, Harold D. *King Cotton and His Retainers: Financing and Marketing the Cotton Crop of the South, 1800–1925*. Columbia: University of South Carolina Press, 1990.

49. Shick, Tom W. *Behold the Promised Land: A History of Afro-American Settler Society in Nineteenth-Century Liberia*. Baltimore: Johns Hopkins University Press, 1980.
Staudenraus, P. J. *The African Colonization Movement, 1816–1865*. New York: Octagon Books, 1980.

50. Cockcroft, James D. *Latin America: History, Politics, and U.S. Policy*, 2nd ed. Chicago: Nelson-Hall Publishers, 1996.
Lofton, John. *Denmark Vesey's Revolt: The Slave Plot That Lit a Fuse to Fort Sumter*. Kent, OH: Kent State University Press, 1983.
Robertson, William S. *Rise of the Spanish-American Republics, As Told in the Lives of Their Liberators*. New York: Free Press, 1966.
Starobin, Robert S., ed. *Denmark Vesey: The Slave Conspiracy of 1822*. Englewood Cliffs, NJ: Prentice-Hall, 1970.

51. United States Bureau of the Census. *Historical Statistics of the United States, Colonial Times to 1970, Bicentennial Edition [Part 2]*. Washington, DC: Government Printing Office, 1975.

52. Baker, Julie P. *Black Slavery among the American Indians*. Clifton, NJ: AB Bookman's Weekly, 1992.
Dinnerstein, Leonard, Roger Nichols, and David Reimers. *Natives and Strangers: Blacks, Indians, and Immigrants in America*. New York: Oxford University Press, 1990.
Foreman, Grant. *The Five Civilized Tribes: Cherokee, Chickasaw, Choctaw, Creek, Seminole*. Norman: University of Oklahoma Press, 1977.
Foreman, Grant. *Indian Removal: The Emigration of the Five Civilized Tribes of Indians*. Norman: University of Oklahoma Press, 1986.
Foster, Laurence. *Negro-Indian Relationships in the Southeast*. New York: AMS Press, 1978.
Halliburton, R. *Red over Black: Black Slavery among the Cherokee Indians*. Westport, CT: Greenwood Press, 1977.
Littlefield, Daniel F. *Africans and Creeks: From the Colonial Period to the Civil War*. Westport, CT: Greenwood Press, 1979.
Littlefield, Daniel F. *Africans and Seminoles: From Removal to Emancipation*. Westport, CT: Greenwood Press, 1977.
Littlefield, Daniel F. *The Cherokee Freedmen: From Emancipation to Citizenship*. Westport, CT: Greenwood Press, 1980.
Littlefield, Daniel F. *The Chickasaw Freedmen: A People without a Country*. Westport, CT: Greenwood Press, 1980.
Porter, Kenneth Wiggins. *The Black Seminoles: History of a Freedom-Seeking People*. Gainesville: University Press of Florida, 1996.

53. Aptheker, Herbert. *Nat Turner's Slave Rebellion*. New York: Grove Press, 1968.
Greenberg, Kenneth S., ed. *The Confessions of Nat Turner and Related Documents*. Boston: Bedford Books, 1996.
Tragle, Henry Irving. *The Southampton Slave Revolt of 1831: A Compilation of Source Material, Including the Full Text of The Confessions of Nat Turner*. New York: Vintage Books, 1973.

54. Connor, Seymour and Odie Faulk. *North America Divided: The Mexican War, 1846–1848*. New York: Oxford University Press, 1971.
Merk, Frederick, and Lois Bannister Merk. *Slavery and the Annexation of Texas*. New York: Knopf, 1972.
Potter, David M. *The Impending Crisis, 1848–1861*. New York: Harper & Row, 1976.
Schwartz, Rosalie. *Across the Rio to Freedom: U.S. Negroes in Mexico*. El Paso: Texas Western Press, University of Texas at El Paso, 1974.
The Constitution of the United States, with Acts of Congress, Relating to Slavery, Embracing the Constitution, the Fugitive Slave Act of 1793, the Missouri Compromise Act of 1820, the Fugitive Slave Law of 1850, and the Nebraska and Kansas Bill, Carefully Compiled. Rochester, NY: D. W. Dewey, 1854.

55. Foner, Philip S. *History of Black Americans from the Emergence of the Cotton Kingdom to the Eve of the Compromise of 1850*. Westport, CT: Greenwood Press, 1983.
Freehling, William W. *The Road to Disunion: Secessionists at Bay, 1776–1854*. vol. 1. New York: Oxford University Press, 1990.
McDougall, Marion G. *Fugitive Slaves (1619–1865)*. Freeport, NY: Books for Libraries Press, 1971.
Rozwenc, Edwin Charles. *The Compromise of 1850*. Boston: D. C. Heath, 1968.
Stegmaier, Mark Joseph. *Texas, New Mexico, and the Compromise of 1850: Boundary Dispute & Sectional Crisis*. Kent, OH: Kent State University Press, 1996.

56. Holt, Michael F. *The Political Crisis of the 1850s*. New York: Norton, 1983.
Malin, James Claude. *The Nebraska Question, 1852–1854*. Magnolia, MA: Peter Smith, 1973.

57. Nichols, Alice. *Bleeding Kansas*. New York: Oxford University Press, 1954.
Rawley, James A. *Race & Politics: "Bleeding Kansas" and the Coming of*

the Civil War. Lincoln: University of Nebraska Press, 1979.

Sharpe, Jon. *Bleeding Kansas*. New York: Penguin Books, 1990.

58. Fehrenbacher, Don E. *Slavery, Law, and Politics: The Dred Scott Case in Historical Perspective*. New York: Oxford University Press, 1981.

Fehrenbacher, Don E. *The South and Three Sectional Crises*. Baton Rouge: Louisiana State University Press, 1980.

Finkelman, Paul. *Dred Scott v. Sandford: A Brief History with Documents*. Boston: Bedford Books, 1997.

Stampp, Kenneth M. *America in 1857: A Nation on the Brink*. New York: Oxford University Press, 1990.

59. Hinton, Richard J. *John Brown and His Men*. New York: Arno Press, 1968.

Quarles, Benjamin. *Allies for Freedom: Blacks and John Brown*. New York: Oxford University Press, 1974.

Rossbach, Jeffrey S. *Ambivalent Conspirators: John Brown, the Secret Six, and a Theory of Slave Violence*. Philadelphia: University of Pennsylvania Press, 1982.

MAP 60

The Free Black and Slave Population of the United States (1860)

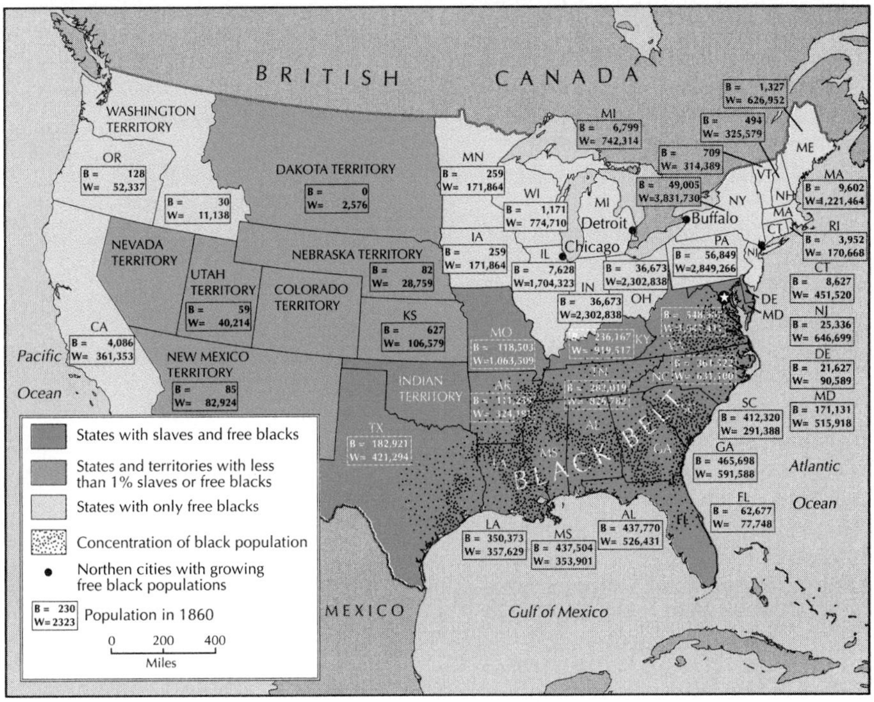
BRITISH
CANADA
WASHINGTON TERRITORY
OR
B = 128
W= 52,337
B = 30
W= 11,138
DAKOTA TERRITORY
B = 0
W= 2,576
NEVADA TERRITORY
UTAH TERRITORY
B = 59
W= 40,214
NEBRASKA TERRITORY
B = 82
W= 28,759
COLORADO TERRITORY
KS
B = 627
W= 106,579
CA
B = 4,086
W= 361,353
Pacific
Ocean
NEW MEXICO TERRITORY
B = 85
W= 82,924
INDIAN TERRITORY
TX
B = 182,921
W= 421,294
MN
B = 259
W= 171,864
WI
B = 1,171
W= 774,710
MI
B = 6,799
W= 742,314
IA
B = 259
W= 171,864
IL
B = 7,628
W=1,704,323
IN
B = 36,673
W=2,302,838
OH
B = 36,673
W=2,302,838
MO
B = 118,503
W=1,063,509
KY
B = 236,167
W= 919,517
TN
B = 283,019
W= 826,782
AR
NC
VA
PA
B = 56,849
W=2,849,266
NY
B = 49,005
W=3,831,730
B = 709
W= 314,389
B = 494
W= 325,579
B = 1,327
W= 626,952
ME
VT
NH
MA
B = 9,602
W=1,221,464
RI
B = 3,952
W= 170,668
CT
B = 8,627
W= 451,520
NJ
B = 25,336
W= 646,699
DE
B = 21,627
W= 90,589
MD
B = 171,131
W= 515,918
SC
B = 412,320
W= 291,388
GA
B = 465,698
W= 591,588
FL
B = 62,677
W= 77,748
AL
B = 437,770
W= 526,431
MS
B = 437,504
W= 353,901
LA
B = 350,373
W= 357,629
BLACK BELT
Detroit
Chicago
Buffalo
Atlantic
Ocean
Gulf of Mexico
MEXICO
States with slaves and free blacks
States and territories with less than 1% slaves or free blacks
States with only free blacks
Concentration of black population
Northen cities with growing free black populations
B = 230
W= 2323
Population in 1860
0 200 400
Miles

By 1860, the population of the United States numbered 31,365,000. Blacks made up 14.1 percent of the nation's population, or 4,442,000. Of this number, over 4 million were slaves, living in the slaveholding states of the South. The remaining 400,000 were free blacks, roughly half of whom lived in large southern cities like Richmond, Atlanta, and Charleston. The other half were scattered throughout northeastern, midwestern, and far western cities like New York, Philadelphia, Boston, Chicago, Cincinnati, Cleveland, Detroit, Los Angeles, and San Francisco. African Americans living in the South made up over 40 percent of the region's total population of 9 million. In the North, free blacks barely made up 1 percent of the 21 million people living there. Most free blacks living in the South either had purchased their freedom, were given it as a reward for meritorious service, or were born to free parents. The same was true for free blacks in the North. In addition, the North was also home to a considerable number of fugitive slaves, who were sought in the South by their masters. ■

MAP 61

Free States and Territories and Slave States and Territories before the Civil War (1860)

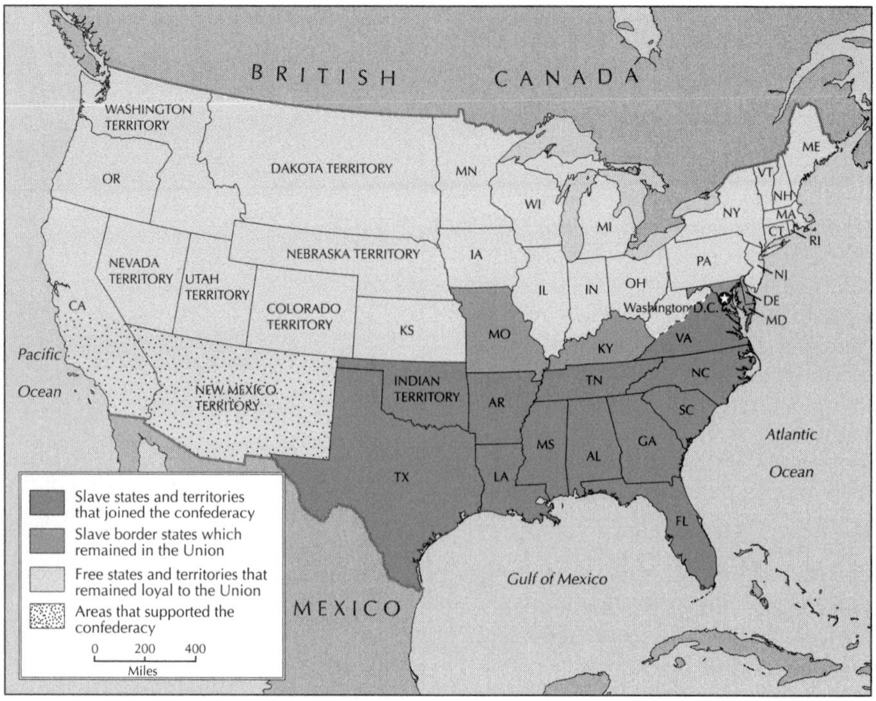
BRITISH CANADA
WASHINGTON TERRITORY
OR
DAKOTA TERRITORY
MN
WI
MI
ME
VT
NH
MA
NY
CT
RI
NEVADA TERRITORY
UTAH TERRITORY
NEBRASKA TERRITORY
IA
PA
NJ
IL
IN
OH
CA
COLORADO TERRITORY
KS
MO
Washington D.C.
DE
MD
VA
KY
Pacific Ocean
NEW MEXICO TERRITORY
INDIAN TERRITORY
AR
TN
NC
SC
GA
AL
MS
LA
TX
FL
Atlantic Ocean
Gulf of Mexico
MEXICO
Slave states and territories that joined the confederacy
Slave border states which remained in the Union
Free states and territories that remained loyal to the Union
Areas that supported the confederacy
0 200 400
Miles

In 1860 the United States consisted of thirty-four states—fifteen slave states and nineteen free states. It contained several territories including Washington, Nebraska, Utah, and New Mexico, all of which were opened to slavery by 1860. The United States also contained the Indian Territory which was occupied by slaveholding Indians including the Cherokee, Creek, Choctaw, Seminole, and Chickasaw. The fifteen slaveholding states, all in the South, were split into two groups. South Carolina, Georgia, Florida, Alabama, Mississippi, Louisiana, and Texas made up the lower South. The upper South included the border states of Delaware, Maryland, Kentucky, and Missouri—the states that bordered the free states—along with Virginia, North Carolina, Tennessee, and Arkansas. The states in the upper South were reluctant to secede from the United States before April 1861. These upper southern states tended to have similar interests and generally supported slavery. The northern free states also had similar interests, which included opposing the spread of slavery into the western territories. By 1860 the nation was polarized over the issue of slavery. The proslavery states of the South and the antislavery states of the North were poised to do battle over the extension of the institution of slavery in the western territories and over the future of the institution of slavery itself in the United States. ■

MAP 62

The South's Largest Slave Plantations on the Eve of the Civil War (1861)

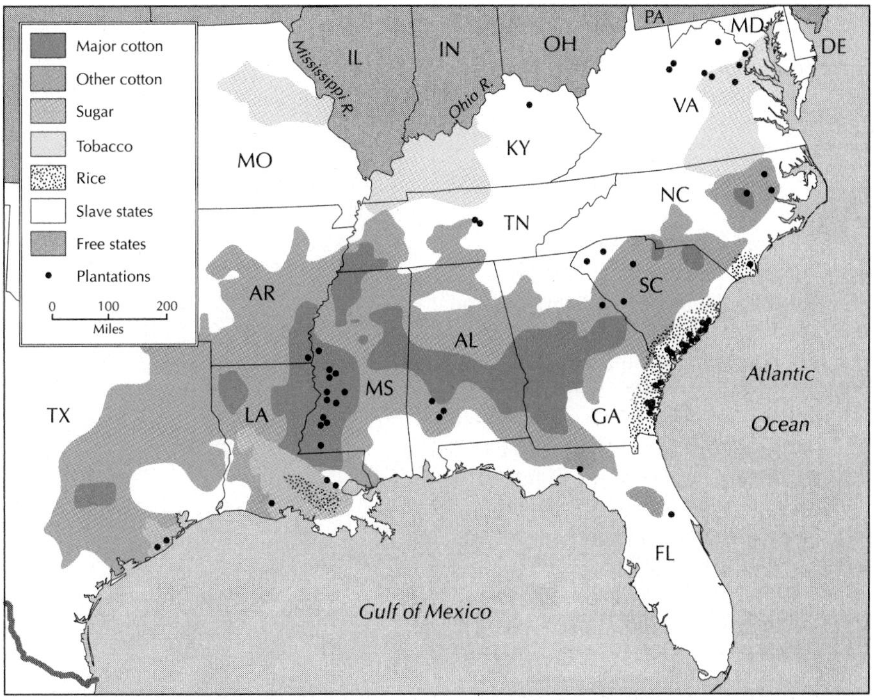

Major cotton
Other cotton
Sugar
Tobacco
Rice
Slave states
Free states
Plantations
0 100 200
Miles
Mississippi R.
Ohio R.
IL
IN
OH
PA
MD
DE
VA
KY
MO
NC
TN
AR
SC
AL
MS
GA
LA
TX
FL
Atlantic
Ocean
Gulf of Mexico

On the eve of the Civil War, there were approximately 4 million slaves in the South, more than 40 percent of the region's total population of 9 million. Of the 5 million whites, about 385,000 owned slaves. About 88 percent of slave owners owned fewer than 20 slaves each. This meant that roughly 12 percent of southerners owned the majority of slaves in the South. This 12 percent owned the South's largest plantations, which usually had over 100 slaves. The plantations were located mainly in the eastern seaboard states and the Gulf states that made up the Cotton Kingdom. These plantations and the individuals who owned them shaped the South socially, economically, and politically. When South Carolina decided to secede from the Union in 1860, it was a decision made by these wealthy white plantation owners, who controlled the state's general assembly. When from 1860 to April 1861 the rest of the states in the South followed South Carolina's lead, the decision to secede was made by large plantation owners. In the newly organized Confederate government and military, these plantation owners were the only ones who could run for or hold political office or lead troops as officers. These men—and their sons—became lieutenants, captains, majors, colonels, and generals. They also became the congressmen, senators, and high-ranking civilians in the new Confederate government on both state and national levels. These plantation owners manipulated the mass of poor and yeomen whites of the South into fighting a war that protected plantation owners' privilege and wealth—and that, after four years of war and the emancipation of slaves, brought financial ruin to the entire region. Thus by noting the existence of these plantations, we acknowledge the most powerful families of the South in the years before the Civil War, families who controlled the institution of slavery and were directly responsible for causing the American Civil War. ■

MAP 63

Pro-Lincoln States in the 1860 Presidential Election

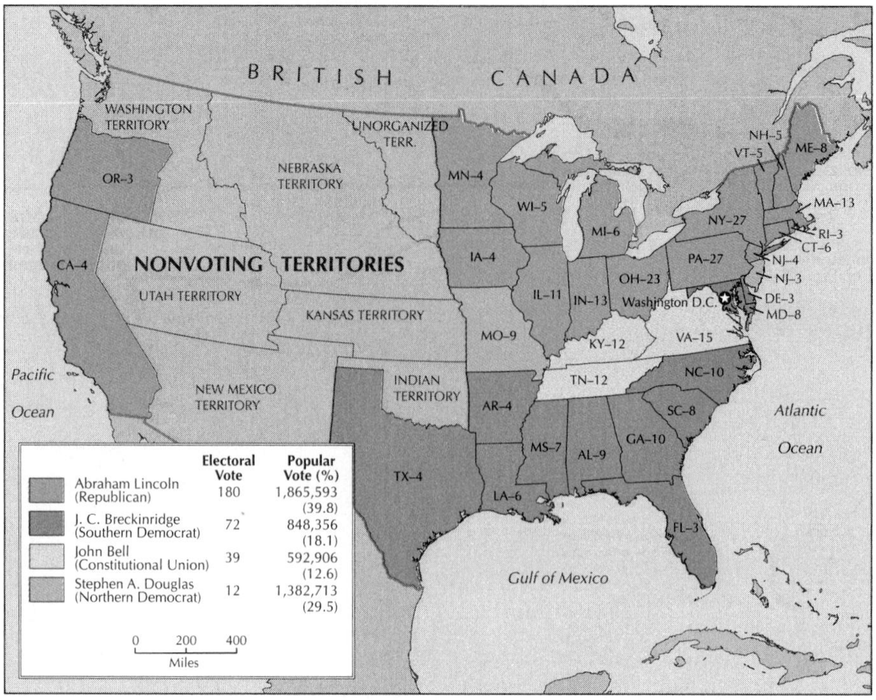
BRITISH CANADA
WASHINGTON TERRITORY
UNORGANIZED TERR.
NEBRASKA TERRITORY
OR-3
MN-4
WI-5
MI-6
NH-5
VT-5
ME-8
MA-13
NY-27
RI-3
CT-6
NONVOTING TERRITORIES
CA-4
UTAH TERRITORY
KANSAS TERRITORY
IA-4
IL-11
IN-13
OH-23
PA-27
NJ-4
NJ-3
Washington D.C.
DE-3
MD-8
MO-9
KY-12
VA-15
Pacific Ocean
NEW MEXICO TERRITORY
INDIAN TERRITORY
TN-12
NC-10
AR-4
SC-8
Atlantic Ocean
MS-7
AL-9
GA-10
TX-4
LA-6
FL-3
Gulf of Mexico
Electoral Vote
Popular Vote (%)
Abraham Lincoln (Republican) 180 1,865,593 (39.8)
J. C. Breckinridge (Southern Democrat) 72 848,356 (18.1)
John Bell (Constitutional Union) 39 592,906 (12.6)
Stephen A. Douglas (Northern Democrat) 12 1,382,713 (29.5)
0 200 400
Miles

In the fall election of 1860, four candidates sought the presidency. Abraham Lincoln represented the Republican Party. The Democratic Party was divided over the issue of slavery and ran two candidates, John C. Breckinridge for the southern wing and Stephen A. Douglas for the northern wing. The fourth candidate, John Bell, represented the Constitutional Union Party. Due in part to the large number of candidates, which caused the vote to be split among four people, Abraham Lincoln won the election. Although no great sympathizer with blacks, Lincoln did feel that slavery had to be contained in the South. He did not believe that slavery should be allowed in the remaining territories. Lincoln's goal was to allow southerners to keep their slaves and continue practicing slavery in the South, but to nullify the Compromise of 1850 and the Kansas-Nebraska Act by prohibiting slavery in the western territories and to not enforce the Dred Scott decision by refusing to allow slave owners to carry their slaves into free states. In spite of his promises not to interfere with slavery in the South if elected, many southern states threatened secession if he won the election of 1860 and refused to include his name on their presidential ballots. When, on November 2, 1860, Abraham Lincoln was elected the sixteenth President of the United States, free blacks and northerners were overjoyed, while white southerners were outraged. For southerners the election of Lincoln without the support of a single slaveholding state meant that the South could no longer influence national elections. With Lincoln planning to close the West to slavery, the South also saw no future slave states to restore their political power in future elections. The balance of power that had been maintained since the Constitutional Convention of 1787 now weighed heavily in favor of the North, and as future free states were sure to be cut out of the western territories, it appeared the balance of power would remain in favor of the North. Faced with these facts, many southern states believed that secession was the only logical answer. Thus, beginning in December of 1860 with South Carolina, outraged southern states began to leave the United States and form the Confederate States of America. ■

MAP 64

The Secession of Southern States (1860–1861)

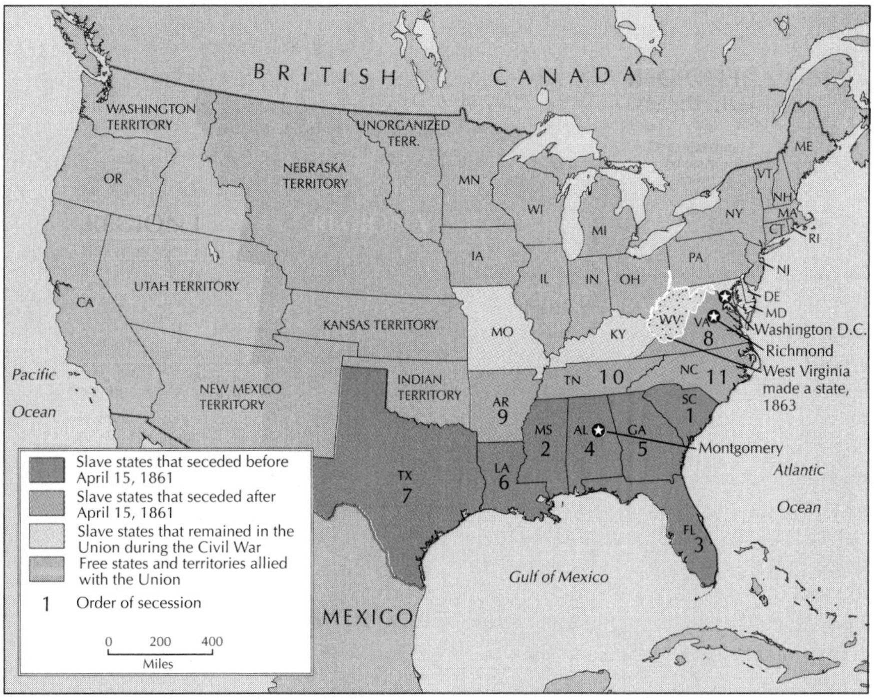
BRITISH CANADA
WASHINGTON TERRITORY
UNORGANIZED TERR.
NEBRASKA TERRITORY
OR
MN
WI
MI
NY
VT
NH
ME
MA
CT
RI
PA
NJ
IA
IL
IN
OH
UTAH TERRITORY
CA
KANSAS TERRITORY
MO
KY
WV
VA 8
DE
MD
Washington D.C.
Richmond
West Virginia made a state, 1863
NC 11
TN 10
INDIAN TERRITORY
AR 9
NEW MEXICO TERRITORY
Pacific Ocean
SC 1
MS 2
AL 4
GA 5
Montgomery
Atlantic Ocean
TX 7
LA 6
FL 3
Gulf of Mexico
MEXICO
Slave states that seceded before April 15, 1861
Slave states that seceded after April 15, 1861
Slave states that remained in the Union during the Civil War
Free states and territories allied with the Union
1 Order of secession
0 200 400
Miles

On December 20, 1860, South Carolina became the first state to secede from the Union. By February 1 of the following year, Alabama, Mississippi, Florida, Georgia, Louisiana, and Texas had also seceded. On February 4, 1861, these seven states met in Montgomery, Alabama, and established the Confederate States of America, electing Jefferson Davis, a senator from Mississippi, as their first president. The upper southern states of Arkansas, Tennessee, North Carolina, Virginia, Missouri, Kentucky, Maryland, and Delaware refused to secede. Instead they chose to work in Congress to reach a compromise that would bring the lower South back into the Union and once more save the Union as had the Great Compromise of 1787, the Missouri Compromise of 1820, and the Compromise of 1850. Lincoln and northern Republicans, however, refused any attempt at a compromise suggested by these moderate states and instead chose to resupply and fortify federal forts in the seceding states. In response to this, on April 12, 1861, South Carolina, rather than allow the federal installation at Charleston to be resupplied, bombed Fort Sumter, beginning the bloodiest war in American history. After the bombing of Fort Sumter, Lincoln requested 75,000 federal troops from loyal states to put down the insurrection. As a result of his request, four more slave states seceded: Virginia, Arkansas, Tennessee, and North Carolina. The border states of Maryland and Kentucky also attempted to convene their legislatures to consider secession but were prevented from doing so by federal troops. Missouri erupted into its own internal civil war over whether to secede or not, and Delaware remained wary of talk of abolishing slavery by northern states and Lincoln for the duration of the conflict. The seceding states quickly organized a government and a military for defense and voted to move their capital from Montgomery, Alabama, to Richmond, Virginia. ■

MAP 65

Slave Contraband Camps during the Civil War (1861–1863)

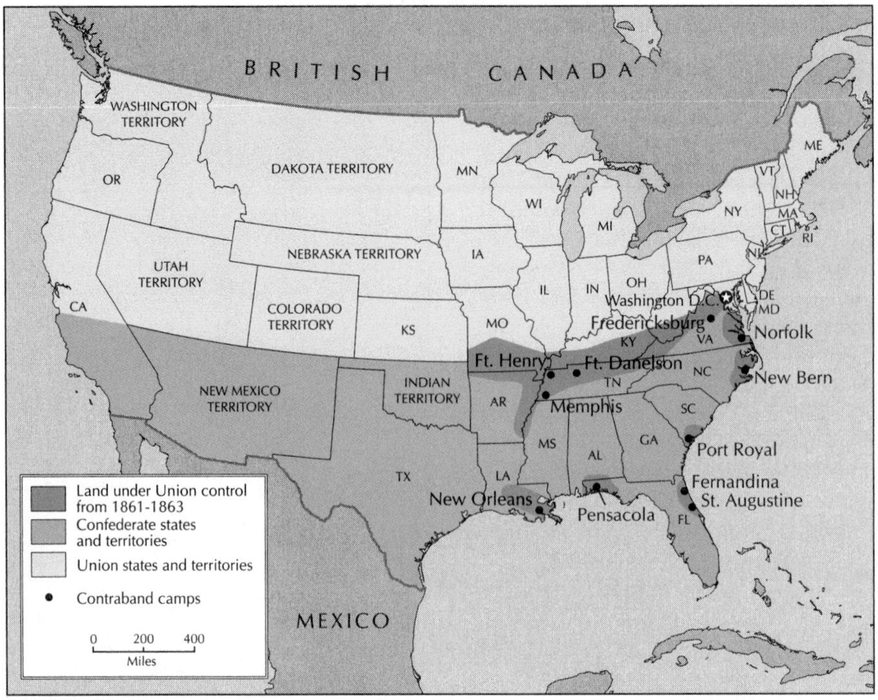
BRITISH
CANADA
WASHINGTON TERRITORY
OR
DAKOTA TERRITORY
MN
WI
MI
ME
VT
NH
NY
MA
CT
RI
PA
NJ
IA
NEBRASKA TERRITORY
UTAH TERRITORY
CA
COLORADO TERRITORY
KS
MO
IL
IN
OH
Washington D.C.
DE
MD
Fredericksburg
KY
VA
Norfolk
Ft. Henry
Ft. Danelson
NC
New Bern
TN
Memphis
INDIAN TERRITORY
AR
NEW MEXICO TERRITORY
SC
MS
AL
GA
Port Royal
TX
LA
Fernandina
St. Augustine
New Orleans
Pensacola
FL
MEXICO
Land under Union control from 1861-1863
Confederate states and territories
Union states and territories
Contraband camps
0 200 400
Miles

From 1861 to 1863 the Union struggled to deal not only with their military defeats at the hands of the Confederacy, but also with the "Negro Question," as the Union Army advanced and the Civil War intensified. Hundreds of runaway slaves streamed into Union lines in Missouri, Tennessee, Virginia, coastal North Carolina, South Carolina, and southeastern Louisiana. At the start of the war, Lincoln required his troops to return these slaves to their masters. He insisted that this was not a war to end slavery, but to bring the South back into the Union. Many Union generals, however, found returning slaves to their masters, the enemy, problematic, and they began to enlist the slaves as soldiers and laborers. Lincoln took issue with this because it indeed gave the impression that the war was about slavery. A compromise of sorts was reached in 1862 with the passage of the Contraband Act by Congress. Slaves were then viewed as contraband of war and were placed in internment camps, where they were held rather than returned to the southerners but forbidden to be used by Union generals to support the war effort as either troops or laborers. There were several of these camps in territory occupied by the Union between 1862 and 1863. Conditions in the camps were terrible, and hundreds of slaves died from disease, lack of proper shelter, and poor diet. In response to these problems a number of religious and social groups traveled to these camps and supervised improvements such as better sanitation, food, and living conditions. These groups also lobbied Congress and the president to dismantle the camps, something that would not happen until January of 1863. ■

MAP 66

Black Spy Activity during the Civil War (1861–1865)

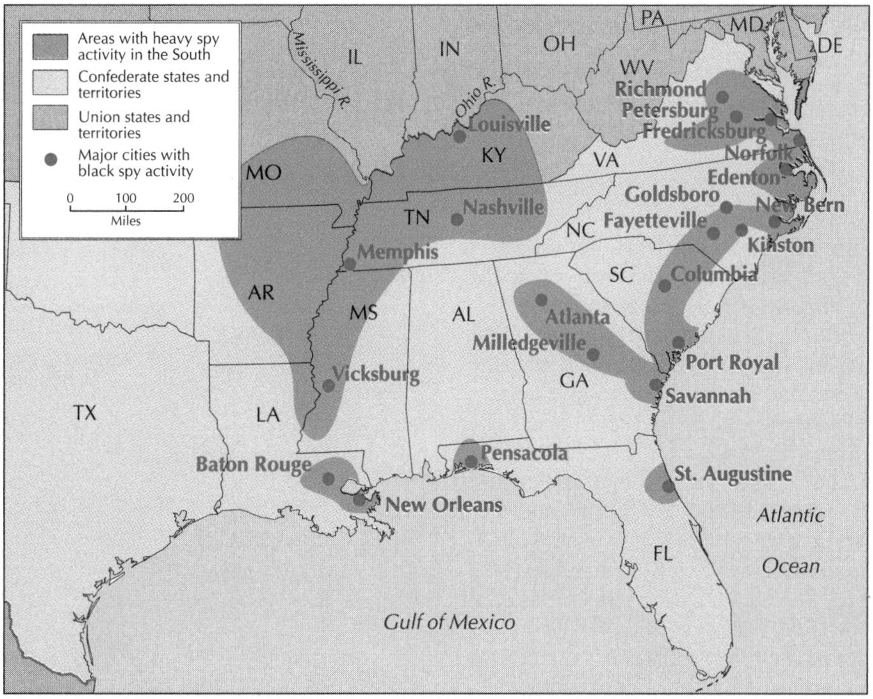
Areas with heavy spy activity in the South
Confederate states and territories
Union states and territories
Major cities with black spy activity
0 100 200
Miles
Mississippi R.
Ohio R.
IL
IN
OH
PA
MD
DE
WV
MO
KY
VA
TN
NC
SC
AR
MS
AL
GA
TX
LA
FL
Louisville
Richmond
Petersburg
Fredricksburg
Norfolk
Edenton
Goldsboro
New Bern
Fayetteville
Kinston
Nashville
Memphis
Columbia
Atlanta
Milledgeville
Port Royal
Savannah
Vicksburg
Pensacola
Baton Rouge
New Orleans
St. Augustine
Atlantic
Ocean
Gulf of Mexico

Just as they did during previous wars, slaves, free blacks, and maroons (runaway slaves) assisted both Union and Confederate Armies, as laborers, soldiers, guides, and spies. These spies were servants, field hands, skilled craftsmen, and unskilled laborers. They were male and female, slave and free, adults and children. They passed between the two armies and learned a great deal about both. In northeastern North Carolina, which was occupied early in the war, the slaves of Bertie, Hertford, and neighboring counties provided information to occupying Union forces that was useful in tracking Confederate movements. They also gave inaccurate or misleading information to enemy armies. Throughout the South, white civilian and military leaders openly discussed secret plans and strategies in front of the slaves and free blacks who served them, believing them to be ignorant and unable to comprehend what was being revealed. These blacks, however, often were fully aware of what was being discussed; and through the "grapevine," which kept slaves on neighboring plantations informed, they passed this information to advancing troops. These slaves and servants also served as guides, leading Union troops through hostile territory, including swamps, forests, and unmapped areas. It is difficult to calculate how important African-American spies were to both armies, but based on the evidence, they made important contributions and significantly influenced the outcome of numerous battles fought during the war. ■

MAP 67

The Underground Railroad during the Civil War (1861–1865)

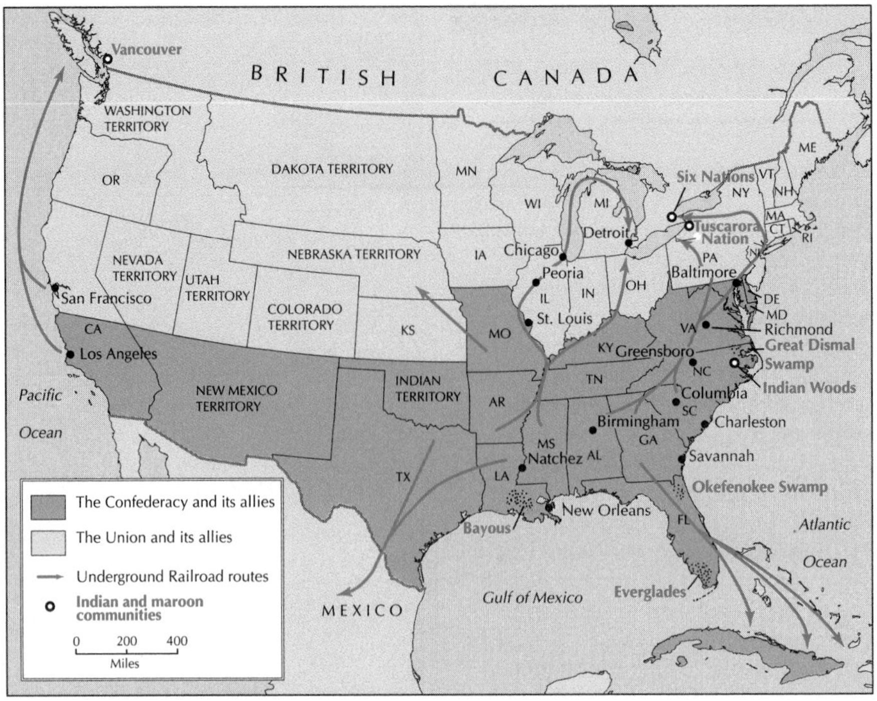
Vancouver
BRITISH CANADA
WASHINGTON TERRITORY
OR
DAKOTA TERRITORY
MN
ME
Six Nations
VT
NY
NH
WI
MI
Detroit
Tuscarora Nation
MA
CT
RI
NEVADA TERRITORY
UTAH TERRITORY
NEBRASKA TERRITORY
IA
Chicago
PA
Peoria
Baltimore
IL
IN
OH
San Francisco
COLORADO TERRITORY
St. Louis
DE
MD
KS
MO
VA
Richmond
CA
KY
Greensboro
Great Dismal Swamp
Los Angeles
NC
INDIAN TERRITORY
TN
NEW MEXICO TERRITORY
AR
Columbia
Indian Woods
Pacific Ocean
SC
Birmingham
Charleston
MS
GA
Natchez
AL
Savannah
TX
LA
Okefenokee Swamp
New Orleans
Bayous
FL
Atlantic Ocean
Gulf of Mexico
Everglades
MEXICO
The Confederacy and its allies
The Union and its allies
Underground Railroad routes
Indian and maroon communities
0 200 400
Miles

By 1860, the Underground Railroad was running at full steam. It had been officially started in 1804, but was active as early as 1775. In the early years of the railroad, most slaves settled in northern cities that had free black populations who looked after them once they were free. But as fugitive slave laws were tightened in the 1850s, many slaves chose to move further north to Canada. Slaves also sought refuge in Mexico and Haiti. By far the most favorable destinations, however, were northern cities like Boston, New York, and Cleveland. During the confusion of the Civil War, over 100,000 slaves found their way to freedom on the Underground Railroad. For example, the four border states of Missouri, Kentucky, Maryland, and Delaware lost well over half of their slaves by the war's end. Southern states in the Confederacy also suffered increasing losses in the number of slaves who ran away as the Union Army advanced. As Union troops neared plantations, slaves fled to their positions. Initially these slaves were returned or held in contraband camps, but by 1863 both practices were abandoned and many runaway slaves began forming towns such as James City near New Bern, North Carolina. Other slaves continued to flee north with the help of conductors of the Underground Railroad such as Harriet Tubman, who made a number of trips into the Confederacy and guided slaves and their families to free states in the North. The Underground Railroad operated until the end of the Civil War in 1865 and over its life helped free hundreds of slaves. ■

MAP 68

The Emancipation Proclamation (1862–1863)

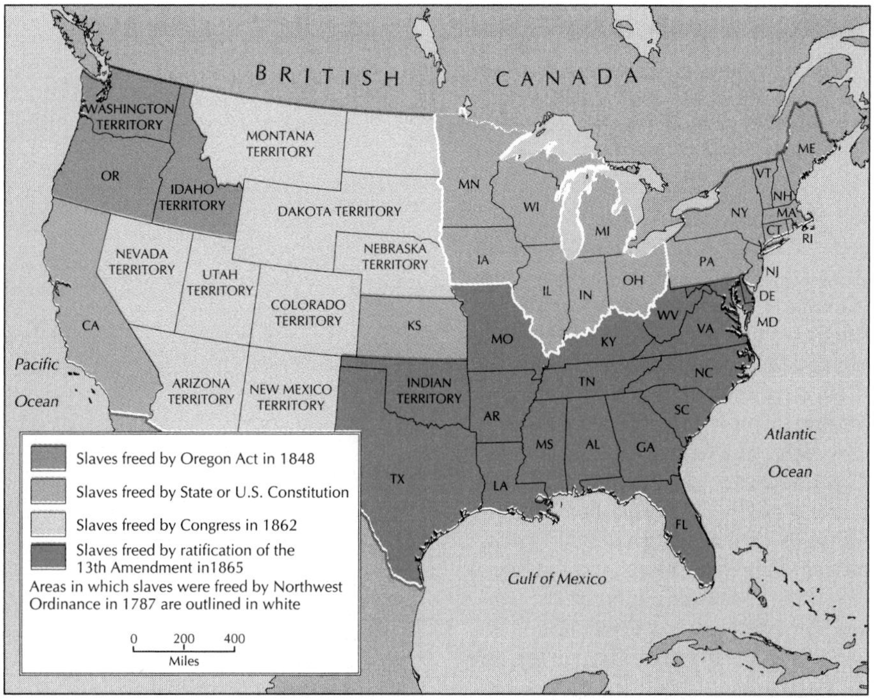
BRITISH CANADA
WASHINGTON TERRITORY
OR
IDAHO TERRITORY
MONTANA TERRITORY
DAKOTA TERRITORY
NEVADA TERRITORY
UTAH TERRITORY
COLORADO TERRITORY
NEBRASKA TERRITORY
CA
ARIZONA TERRITORY
NEW MEXICO TERRITORY
INDIAN TERRITORY
KS
MN
WI
MI
IA
IL
IN
OH
MO
KY
TN
AR
MS
AL
GA
LA
TX
FL
SC
NC
VA
WV
PA
NY
VT
NH
ME
MA
CT
RI
NJ
DE
MD
Pacific Ocean
Atlantic Ocean
Gulf of Mexico
Slaves freed by Oregon Act in 1848
Slaves freed by State or U.S. Constitution
Slaves freed by Congress in 1862
Slaves freed by ratification of the 13th Amendment in1865
Areas in which slaves were freed by Northwest Ordinance in 1787 are outlined in white
0 200 400
Miles

On September 23, 1862, after the Confederate loss at Antietam, Maryland, Lincoln issued his Emancipation Proclamation, which he felt was a necessary war measure to convince the South to return to the Union and stop fighting. In essence, the proclamation declared that all slaves in territories and states controlled by the Confederate States of America were free. The proclamation did not, however, free slaves in the border states of Missouri, Kentucky, Maryland, West Virginia (which by now had split off from Virginia), or Delaware. Nor did it free slaves in states or territories belonging to the Confederacy taken by the Union in battle, which included most of Tennessee, eastern Virginia, North Carolina, South Carolina, and eastern Louisiana, including New Orleans. Since the Confederate government did not recognize the authority of the United States government to free slaves in its states and territories and the United States government refused to free slaves in the border states and portions of the Confederacy taken in battles, no slaves were freed by the proclamation. Furthermore, Lincoln gave the South until January 1, 1863, to stop hostilities and return to the Union, after which it could keep its slaves. No southern states accepted this offer, however, and after the aforementioned deadline, slavery was still very much alive in the Confederacy, the border states, and the areas under Union occupation. Slaves who became aware of the proclamation did run away to Union lines, only to be returned to their masters or placed in internment camps until 1863. ■

MAP 69

Major African American Battle Sites during the Civil War (1863–1865)

When the Civil War broke out in 1861, African Americans were among the first to volunteer for service, as they had in previous American wars. Thousands wanted to fight but were prohibited by the U.S. government, which barred them from service in the U.S. military following the War of 1812. It was also believed by Lincoln and others that this was a white man's war, a war to preserve the Union, not end slavery as many abolitionists and blacks believed. In spite of this, Union officers fighting in the South ignored the ban and the president's order to return slaves by arming slaves and using them in battles as early as 1861 in South Carolina and Louisiana. When the ban on black troops was finally lifted in 1863, over 186,000 fought for the United States, 36,000 of whom died of disease or in battle or were massacred by Confederate soldiers. Many of these blacks, like Joseph Cherry, were runaway slaves who served in units like the Thirty-Seventh Colored Infantry, the Thirty-Fifth Colored Heavy Artillery, and the Thirty-First Colored Infantry. The courage displayed by these soldiers is all the more extraordinary when it is considered that unlike white troops who were taken prisoner after a Confederate victory, black soldiers in uniform were massacred as they surrendered, because the Confederate government refused to take black prisoners. In spite of the massacres of black troops at sites like Fort Pillow, Fort Wagner, Plymouth, and Petersburg, blacks continued to volunteer and fight throughout the conflict. By the end of the war blacks had fought in over 200 battles all over the South, and by April of 1865 even the Confederate Congress had authorized the raising of 200,000 black troops to defend the faltering Confederacy. Of this 200,000, over 5,000 black confederate soldiers were killed in battles with Union troops in the last days of the war in Virginia. ■

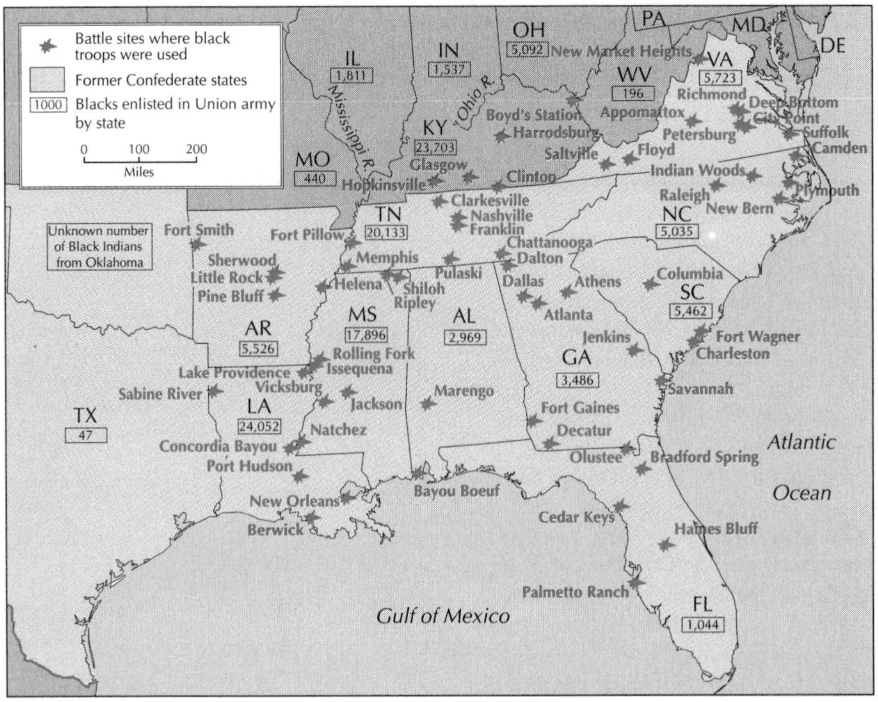
Battle sites where black troops were used
Former Confederate states
1000 Blacks enlisted in Union army by state
0 100 200
Miles
IL 1,811
IN 1,537
OH 5,092
PA
MD
DE
VA 5,723
WV 196
KY 23,703
MO 440
TN 20,133
NC 5,035
SC 5,462
GA 3,486
AL 2,969
MS 17,896
AR 5,526
LA 24,052
TX 47
FL 1,044
Unknown number of Black Indians from Oklahoma
Mississippi R.
Ohio R.
New Market Heights
Richmond
Deep Bottom
City Point
Suffolk
Camden
Appomattox
Petersburg
Boyd's Station
Harrodsburg
Saltville
Floyd
Indian Woods
Plymouth
Glasgow
Hopkinsville
Clinton
Clarkesville
Nashville
Franklin
Raleigh
New Bern
Fort Smith
Fort Pillow
Chattanooga
Dalton
Memphis
Sherwood
Little Rock
Pine Bluff
Helena
Shiloh
Ripley
Pulaski
Dallas
Athens
Columbia
Atlanta
Jenkins
Fort Wagner
Charleston
Rolling Fork
Issequena
Lake Providence
Vicksburg
Sabine River
Jackson
Marengo
Savannah
Natchez
Fort Gaines
Decatur
Concordia Bayou
Port Hudson
Olustee
Bradford Spring
Atlantic Ocean
Bayou Boeuf
New Orleans
Berwick
Cedar Keys
Haines Bluff
Palmetto Ranch
Gulf of Mexico

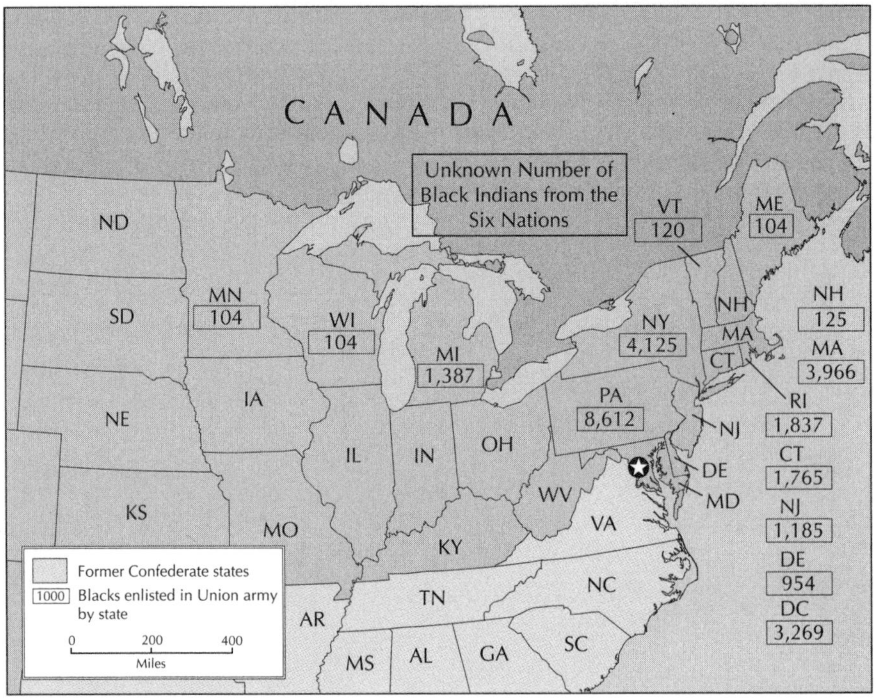
CANADA
Unknown Number of Black Indians from the Six Nations
ND
SD
NE
KS
MN 104
WI 104
IA
MO
MI 1,387
IL
IN
OH
PA 8,612
NY 4,125
VT 120
ME 104
NH
MA
CT
RI
NJ
DE
MD
WV
VA
KY
TN
NC
SC
GA
AL
MS
AR
NH 125
MA 3,966
RI 1,837
CT 1,765
NJ 1,185
DE 954
DC 3,269
Former Confederate states
1000 Blacks enlisted in Union army by state
0 200 400
Miles

MAP 70

William T. Sherman's March to the Sea (1864–1865)

On September 2, 1864, General William T. Sherman drove the Confederates, under General John Bell Hood, out of Atlanta and proceeded to burn the city to the ground. This began his infamous march to the sea. As Sherman moved through southern Georgia and the Carolinas, he destroyed millions of dollars' worth of property. He burned houses, ruined rail lines, looted, killed livestock, and destroyed crops. Anything that he felt might aid the Confederate Army he either destroyed or took with him. After reaching Savannah, Georgia, he turned north and began to march through South Carolina. As Sherman marched through the South, he liberated large numbers of slaves left on plantations by fleeing slave owners. These slaves followed Sherman wherever he went, fearful of being returned to slavery by Confederate soldiers. They offered to fight, spy, or just work as laborers to assist Sherman's advance. On April 19, 1865, several days after the surrender of General Robert E. Lee's Army of Northern Virginia, at Appomattox, Confederate General Joseph E. Johnston surrendered the last of the Confederate Army to Sherman at Durham Station, North Carolina. ■

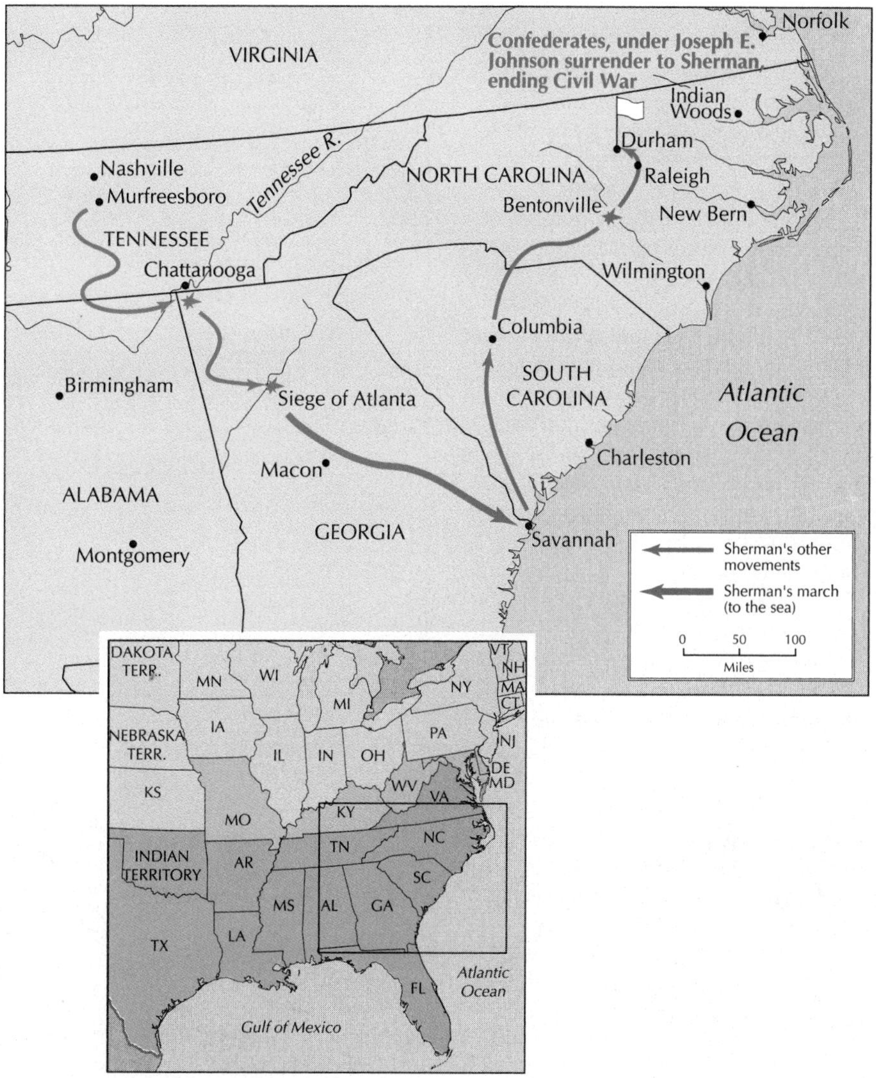
VIRGINIA
Confederates, under Joseph E. Johnson surrender to Sherman, ending Civil War
Norfolk
Indian Woods
Durham
Raleigh
New Bern
Nashville
Murfreesboro
Tennessee R.
NORTH CAROLINA
Bentonville
TENNESSEE
Chattanooga
Wilmington
Columbia
SOUTH CAROLINA
Birmingham
Siege of Atlanta
Atlantic Ocean
Charleston
Macon
ALABAMA
GEORGIA
Savannah
Montgomery
Sherman's other movements
Sherman's march (to the sea)
0 50 100
Miles
DAKOTA TERR.
MN
WI
MI
NY
VT
NH
MA
CT
IA
NEBRASKA TERR.
IL
IN
OH
PA
NJ
DE
MD
KS
MO
WV
VA
KY
NC
INDIAN TERRITORY
AR
TN
SC
MS
AL
GA
TX
LA
FL
Atlantic Ocean
Gulf of Mexico

MAP 71

Major Southern Cities Destroyed by the End of the Civil War (1865)

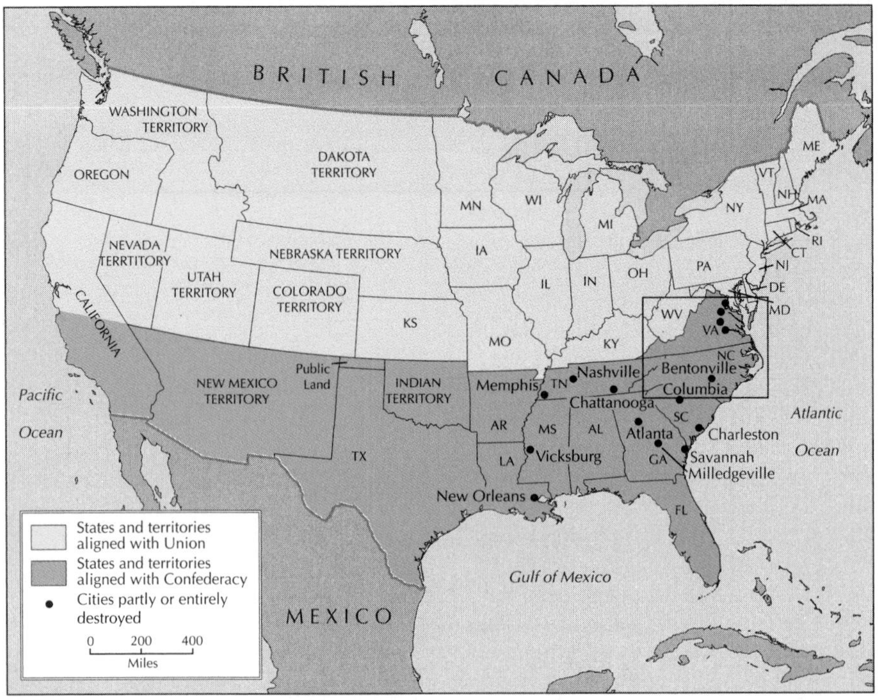
BRITISH CANADA
WASHINGTON TERRITORY
OREGON
DAKOTA TERRITORY
NEVADA TERRITORY
UTAH TERRITORY
NEBRASKA TERRITORY
COLORADO TERRITORY
CALIFORNIA
NEW MEXICO TERRITORY
Public Land
INDIAN TERRITORY
KS
TX
MN
IA
MO
WI
MI
IL
IN
OH
KY
PA
NY
ME
VT
NH
MA
RI
CT
NJ
DE
MD
WV
VA
NC
TN
AR
MS
AL
GA
SC
LA
FL
Nashville
Memphis
Chattanooga
Bentonville
Columbia
Vicksburg
Atlanta
Charleston
Savannah
Milledgeville
New Orleans
Pacific Ocean
Atlantic Ocean
Gulf of Mexico
MEXICO
States and territories aligned with Union
States and territories aligned with Confederacy
Cities partly or entirely destroyed
0 200 400
Miles

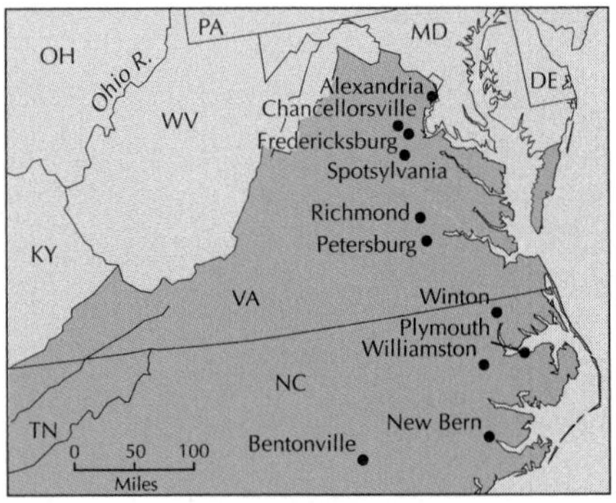
PA
MD
OH
Ohio R.
DE
WV
Alexandria
Chancellorsville
Fredericksburg
Spotsylvania
Richmond
Petersburg
KY
VA
Winton
Plymouth
Williamston
NC
New Bern
TN
Bentonville
0 50 100
Miles

During the Civil War, a number of southern cities were partially or wholly destroyed. The destruction of these cities adversely affected both whites and blacks. The widespread devastation created hundreds of thousands of homeless and starving people, both black and white. Most southern towns and cities that had been burned or otherwise destroyed by the Union Army had black sections, which contained black homes and businesses. Cities like Atlanta, Richmond, Petersburg, Vicksburg, and Charleston, which had been major centers of commerce and trade, lay in ruin. Nor was it just the cities that had been destroyed. Throughout the countryside slave cabins as well as plantation houses had been reduced to rubble. Even the livestock and crops in the countryside were destroyed, without any distinction being made to whether the owners were black or white. With the destruction of southern towns and cities, the potential for prosperity among the South's black population, which also lived and worked in these cities, was severely hampered. The Civil War therefore impoverished the South and impacted the lives of all who lived there, rich and poor, white and black, for decades. It caused many whites to flee to Texas, Kansas, Arizona, and New Mexico and many former slaves and free blacks to turn to the federal government and troops, the Freedmen's Bureau, white northern philanthropists, and religious organizations for needed clothing, food, shelter, and protection from hostile southern whites. ■

MAP 72

The Wealth of Northern and Southern States before and after the Civil War

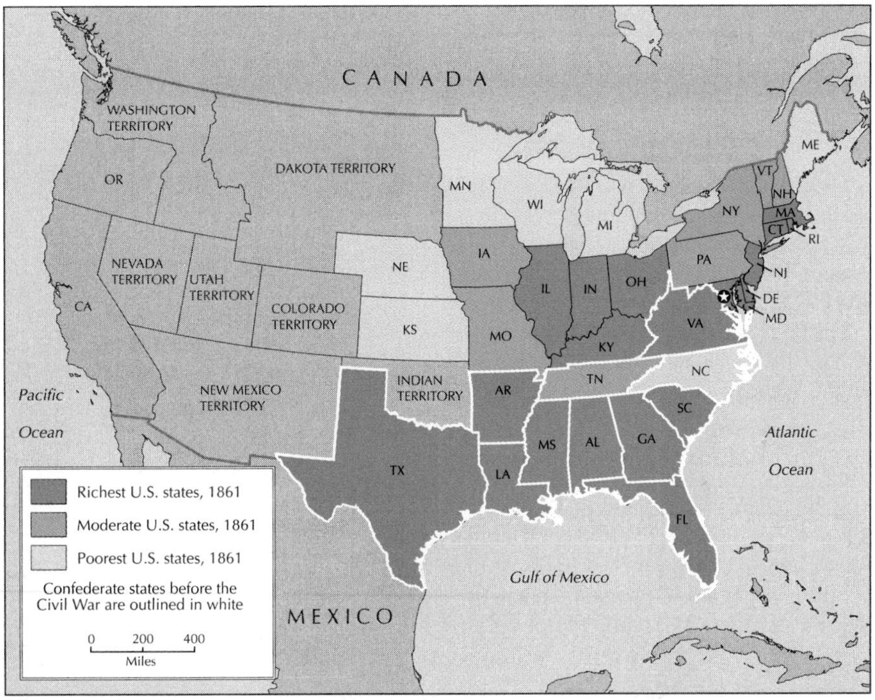
CANADA
WASHINGTON TERRITORY
OR
DAKOTA TERRITORY
MN
WI
MI
ME
VT
NH
NY
MA
CT
RI
IA
NE
IL
IN
OH
PA
NJ
DE
MD
NEVADA TERRITORY
UTAH TERRITORY
CA
COLORADO TERRITORY
KS
MO
KY
VA
NC
TN
INDIAN TERRITORY
AR
SC
NEW MEXICO TERRITORY
Pacific Ocean
MS
AL
GA
Atlantic Ocean
TX
LA
FL
Richest U.S. states, 1861
Moderate U.S. states, 1861
Poorest U.S. states, 1861
Confederate states before the Civil War are outlined in white
0 200 400
Miles
Gulf of Mexico
MEXICO

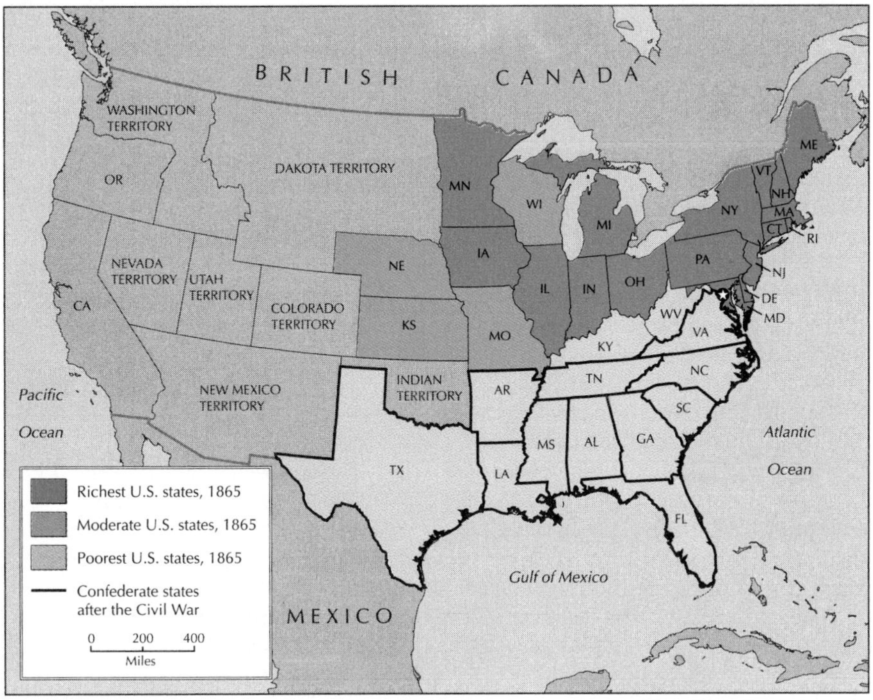
BRITISH CANADA
WASHINGTON TERRITORY
OR
DAKOTA TERRITORY
MN
WI
MI
ME
VT
NH
NY
MA
CT
RI
IA
NE
IL
IN
OH
PA
NJ
DE
MD
NEVADA TERRITORY
UTAH TERRITORY
CA
COLORADO TERRITORY
KS
MO
WV
VA
KY
TN
NC
INDIAN TERRITORY
AR
SC
NEW MEXICO TERRITORY
Pacific Ocean
MS
AL
GA
Atlantic Ocean
TX
LA
FL
Richest U.S. states, 1865
Moderate U.S. states, 1865
Poorest U.S. states, 1865
Confederate states after the Civil War
0 200 400
Miles
Gulf of Mexico
MEXICO

At the start of the Civil War, the South had an economy that was based on agriculture, specifically cotton. Those states that produced the most cotton were the wealthiest in the South and the nation. The North's economy, on the other hand, was very diverse. There was grain farming in the Midwest, and shipping, fishing, and the burgeoning textile industries in the Northeast. Rather than industrialize, the South chose to send its cotton to the North or to Europe, in particular England, for processing. The South's economy was also based on slavery. In southern cities, skilled free black and slave craftsmen aided economic growth. On the cotton and tobacco plantations, slave labor was used exclusively. Many historians who study southern slavery contend that this institution was not as profitable as the wage-labor system of northern industry. In fact, this was also believed by many contemporaries of the period living in the North. It has been argued that if Southern slave owners paid their slaves a wage and forced them to feed, clothe, and house themselves, the slave owners would have saved large sums of money. Furthermore, it was believed that because of these expenses and the expense of medical care, southerners were actually losing money compared with what they could have earned using a wage-labor system. Many northerners of the time, along with later historians, therefore concluded that slavery was not profitable and retarded the economic growth of the South. If owning slaves was not profitable, as many historians contend, four years of war and the loss of over 4 million slaves was devastating to the southern economy. The South spent billions of dollars on slavery and on the establishment and defense of the Confederate States of America. When the war ended in April 1865, the destruction of towns, cities, rail lines, telegraph lines, crops and livestock and the emancipation of 4 million slaves crippled the South and reduced what had been one of the wealthiest regions in the world to one of the poorest. Even with millions of dollars in investments by the federal government and northern industrialists during Reconstruction and the early twentieth century, it would take the South as a region nearly 130 years to overcome this legacy of poverty—a legacy that had a significant impact on the millions of African Americans who shared this economic condition. ■

MAP 73

The End of Slavery in the Western Hemisphere

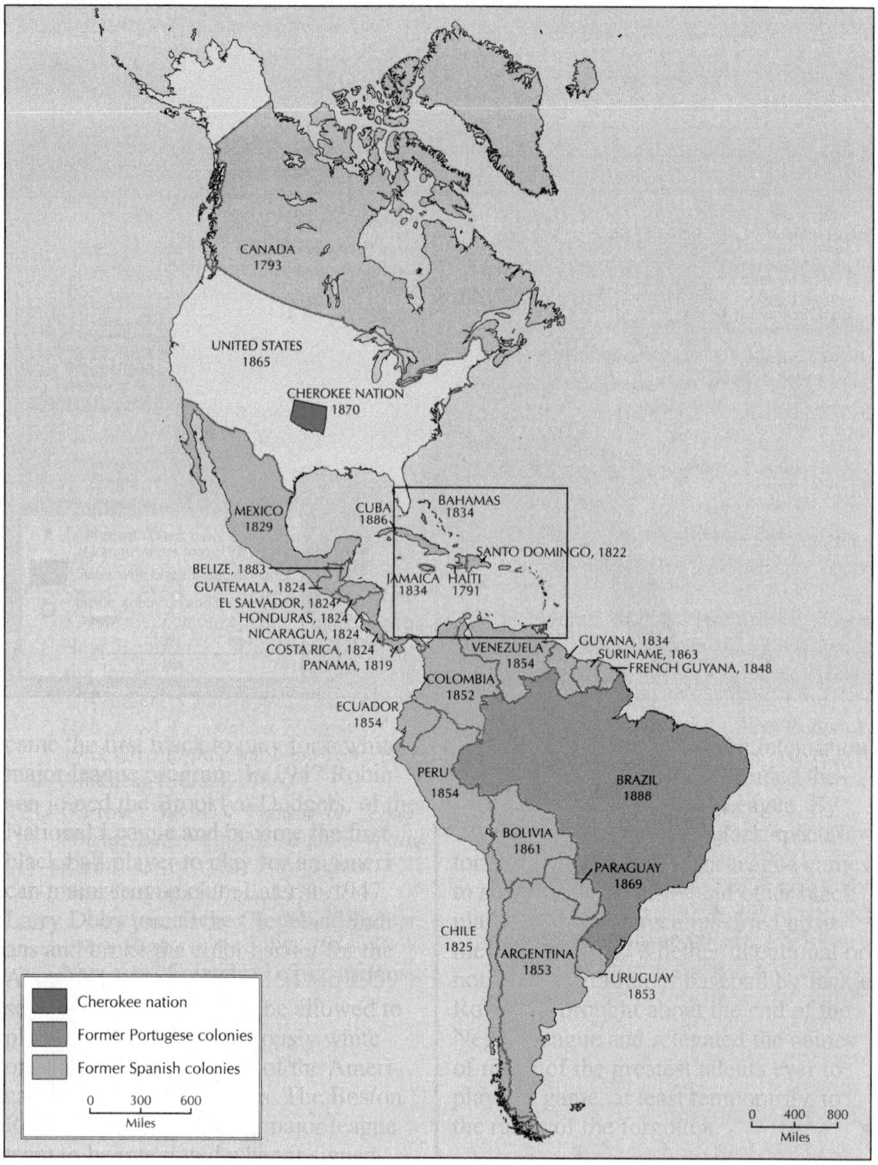
CANADA
1793
UNITED STATES
1865
CHEROKEE NATION
1870
MEXICO
1829
CUBA
1886
BAHAMAS
1834
SANTO DOMINGO, 1822
JAMAICA
1834
HAITI
1791
BELIZE, 1883
GUATEMALA, 1824
EL SALVADOR, 1824
HONDURAS, 1824
NICARAGUA, 1824
COSTA RICA, 1824
PANAMA, 1819
VENEZUELA
1854
GUYANA, 1834
SURINAME, 1863
FRENCH GUYANA, 1848
COLOMBIA
1852
ECUADOR
1854
PERU
1854
BRAZIL
1888
BOLIVIA
1861
PARAGUAY
1869
CHILE
1825
ARGENTINA
1853
URUGUAY
1853
Cherokee nation
Former Portugese colonies
Former Spanish colonies
0 300 600
Miles
0 400 800
Miles

On May 10, 1865, with the passage of the Thirteenth Amendment, slavery officially ended everywhere in the United States, except the Indian Territory where the Cherokee practiced the institution until 1870. The United States, however, was not the first nation in the Western Hemisphere to end slavery, nor was it the last. Slavery continued to be practiced in the Western Hemisphere until 1888 when Brazil officially ended the institution. The New England states of Vermont, New Hampshire, and Massachusetts were the first to abolish slavery in this hemisphere at the start of the American Revolution in 1777. They were followed by the mid-Atlantic states of New York, Pennsylvania, and New Jersey, all of which enacted laws beginning in 1783 to gradually emancipate their slaves. During the Constitutional Convention in Philadelphia in 1787, it was agreed that slavery would be banned in the Northwest Territory in what would become the midwestern states of Ohio, Indiana, Michigan, Illinois, and Wisconsin. This would lead to emancipation in British Canada in 1793 because of the large numbers of Canadian slaves who sought refuge in the Northwest Territory and northern free states. In 1791 during the Haitian Revolution, France abolished slavery in Haiti, creating the first black republic in the Western Hemisphere. Slavery began to collapse throughout the hemisphere when from 1802 to 1818 all European slave-trading nations outlawed the international slave trade. Then, beginning with Britain in 1838 and France in 1848, slavery itself was outlawed and slaves emancipated. During Latin America's wars for independence, which lasted from 1811 to 1828, several newly independent Central American and South American nations also emancipated their slaves, including Mexico, Guatemala, Honduras, El Salvador, Nicaragua, Costa Rica, Panama, Venezuela, Ecuador, Peru, and Chile. Meanwhile from 1820 to 1865, through the Missouri Compromise of 1820 and the Compromise of 1850, the United States would evolve half slave and half free. From 1820 to 1886 the Netherlands and Spain would abolish the institution in the Latin American countries they controlled. Brazil held on the longest due to its economic reliance on slavery. Finally, in 1888, it became the last nation to abolish the institution in the Western Hemisphere. ■

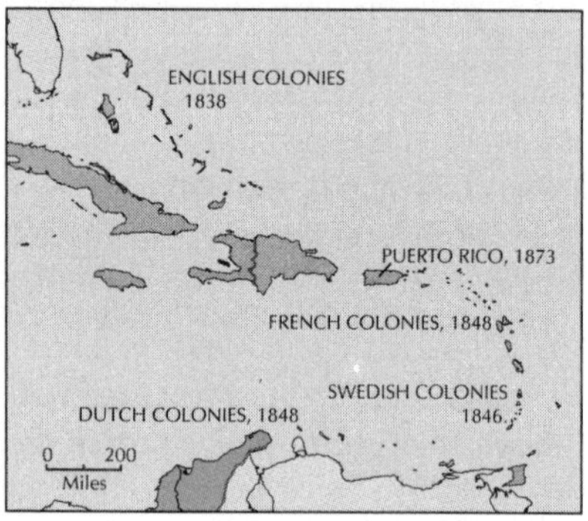
ENGLISH COLONIES
1838
PUERTO RICO, 1873
FRENCH COLONIES, 1848
SWEDISH COLONIES
1846
DUTCH COLONIES, 1848
0 200
Miles

Map and Text Sources

60. United States Bureau of the Census. *Historical Statistics of the United States, Colonial Times to 1970, Bicentennial Edition* [Part 2]. Washington, DC: Government Printing Office, 1975.

61. Potter, David M. *The Impending Crisis, 1848–1861.* New York: Harper & Row, 1976.
Stampp, Kenneth M. *And the War Came: The North and the Secession Crisis, 1860–1861.* Westport, CT: Greenwood Press, 1980.

62. Stampp, Kenneth M. *The Peculiar Institution: Slavery in the Antebellum South.* New York: Vintage Books, 1989.
Schipper, Martin Paul, Kenneth M. Stampp, and Radolph Boehm, ed. *A Guide to Records of Antebellum Southern Plantations from the Revolution through the Civil War.* Frederick, MD: University Publications of America, 1985.

63. Crenshaw, Ollinger. *The Slave States in the Presidential Election of 1860.* Gloucester, MA: P. Smith, 1969.
Hamilton, Joseph Gregoire de Roulhac. *Lincoln's Election an Immediate Menace to Slavery in the States?* New York: Macmillan, 1932.
McPherson, James M. *Abraham Lincoln and the Second American Revolution.* New York: Oxford University Press, 1992.
Quarles, Benjamin. *Lincoln and the Negro.* New York: Da Capo Press, 1991.

64. Stampp, Kenneth M. *And the War Came: The North and the Secession Crisis, 1860–1861.* Westport, CT: Greenwood Press, 1980.
Thomas, Emory M. *The Confederate Nation, 1861–1865.* New York: Harper & Row, 1979.

65. Gerteis, Louis S. *From Contraband to Freedman: Federal Policy toward Southern Blacks, 1861–1865.* Westport, CT: Greenwood Press, 1973.

66. Aptheker, Herbert. *The Negro in the Civil War.* New York: International Publishers, 1962.
Axelrod, Alan. *The War between the Spies: A History of Espionage during the American Civil War.* New York: Atlantic Monthly Press, 1992.
Brockett, Linus P. *Scouts, Spies, and Heroes of the Great Civil War.* Augusta, ME: Badge, 1893.
Jordan, Ervin L. *Black Confederates and Afro-Yankees in Civil War Virginia.* Charlottesville: University Press of Virginia, 1995.
Kane, Harnett Thomas. *Spies for the Blue and Gray.* New York: Ace Books, 1954.
Markle, Donald E. *Spies and Spymasters of the Civil War.* New York: Hippocrene Books, 1994.
Nalty, Bernard C. *Strength for the Fight: A History of Black Americans in the Military.* New York: Free Press, 1986.
Spies, Scouts, and Raiders: Irregular Operations. Alexandria, VA: Time-Life Books, 1993.

67. Aptheker, Herbert. *The Negro in the Civil War.* New York: International Publishers, 1962.
Blockson, Charles L. *The Underground Railroad.* New York: Berkley Publishing Group, 1994.
Schwartz, Rosalie. *Across the Rio to Freedom: U.S. Negroes in Mexico.* El Paso: Texas Western Press, University of Texas at El Paso, 1974.
Siebert, Wilbur Henry. *The Underground Railroad from Slavery to Freedom.* Gloucester, MA: P. Smith, 1968.

68. Aptheker, Herbert. *The Negro in the Civil War.* New York: International Publishers, 1962.
Durden, Robert F. *The Gray and the Black; The Confederate Debate on Emancipation.* Baton Rouge: Louisiana State University Press, 1972.
Franklin, John Hope. *The Emancipation Proclamation.* Wheeling, IL: Harlan Davidson, 1995.
Trefousse, Hans. *Lincoln's Decision for Emancipation.* Philadelphia: Lippincott, 1975.

69. Aptheker, Herbert. *The Negro in the Civil War.* New York: International Publishers, 1962.
Bergeron, Arthur W., Jr. *Black Southerners in Gray: Essays on Afro-Americans in Confederate Armies.* Murfreesboro, TN: Southern Heritage Press, 1994.
Berlin, Ira, Joseph P. Reidy, and Leslie S. Rowland, eds. *The Black Military Experience.* Cambridge: Cambridge University Press, 1982.
Johnson, Jesse J., ed. *A Pictorial History of Black Soldiers in the United States (1619–1969).* Hampton, VA: Johnson, 1973.
Jordan, Ervin L. *Black Confederates and Afro-Yankees in Civil War Virginia.* Charlottesville: University Press of Virginia, 1995.
Hauptman, Laurence M. "Into the Abyss," *Civil War Times* 35 (February 1997): 46–59.
Hauptman, Laurence M. *The Iroquois in the Civil War: From Battlefield to Reservation.* Syracuse, NY: Syracuse University Press, 1993.
Nalty, Bernard C. *Strength for the Fight: A History of Black Americans in the Military.* New York: Free Press, 1986.
Quarles, Benjamin. *The Negro in the Civil War.* New York: Da Capo Press, 1989.
Richter, Daniel K. Hauptman, "The Iroquois in the Civil War," *The Western Historical Quarterly* 24 (November 1993): 571.

70. Ellis, Jerry. *Marching through Georgia: My Walk with Sherman.* New York: Delacorte Press, 1995.
Miers, Earl Schenck. *The General Who Marched to Hell; William Tecumseh Sherman and His March to Fame and Infamy.* New York: Dorset Press, 1990.
Nalty, Bernard C. *Strength for the Fight: A History of Black Americans in the Military.* New York: Free Press, 1986.
Walters, John Bennett. *Merchant of Terror: General Sherman and Total War.* Indianapolis: Bobbs-Merrill, 1973.

71. Schweninger, Loren. *Black Property Owners in the South, 1790–1915.* Urbana: University of Illinois Press, 1990.
Trowbridge, John Townsend. *The Desolate South, 1865–1866; A Picture of the Battlefields and of the Devastated Confederacy.* Freeport, NY: Books for Libraries Press, 1970.

72. Pessen, Edward. *Riches, Class, and Power: America before the Civil War.* New Brunswick, NJ: Transaction Publishers, 1990.

73. Azevedo, Mario, ed. *Africana Studies: A Survey of Africa and the African Diaspora.* Durham, NC: Carolina Academic Press, 1993.
Blackburn, Robin. *The Overthrow of Colonial Slavery, 1776–1848.* New York: Verso, 1988.
Davis, Darien J., ed. *Slavery and Beyond: The African Impact on Latin America and the Caribbean.* Wilmington, DE: SR Books, 1995.

Mellafe, Rolando. *Negro Slavery in Latin America.* Berkeley: University of California Press, 1975.

Morner, Magnus. *Recent Research on Negro Slavery and Abolition in Latin America.* Pittsburgh: Center for International Studies, University Center for International Studies, University of Pittsburgh, 1979.

Okihiro, Gary Y., ed. *In Resistance: Studies in African, Caribbean, and Afro-American History.* Amherst: University of Massachusetts, 1986.

Riddel, William Renwick. "Additional Notes on Slavery: Reciprocity of Slaves between Michigan and Canada," *Journal of Negro History* 17 (July 1932): 368–377.

Toplin, Robert B. *Slavery and Race Relations in Latin America.* Westport, CT: Greenwood Press, 1974.

MAP 74

The Freedmen's Bureau and Blacks during Reconstruction (1865–1877)

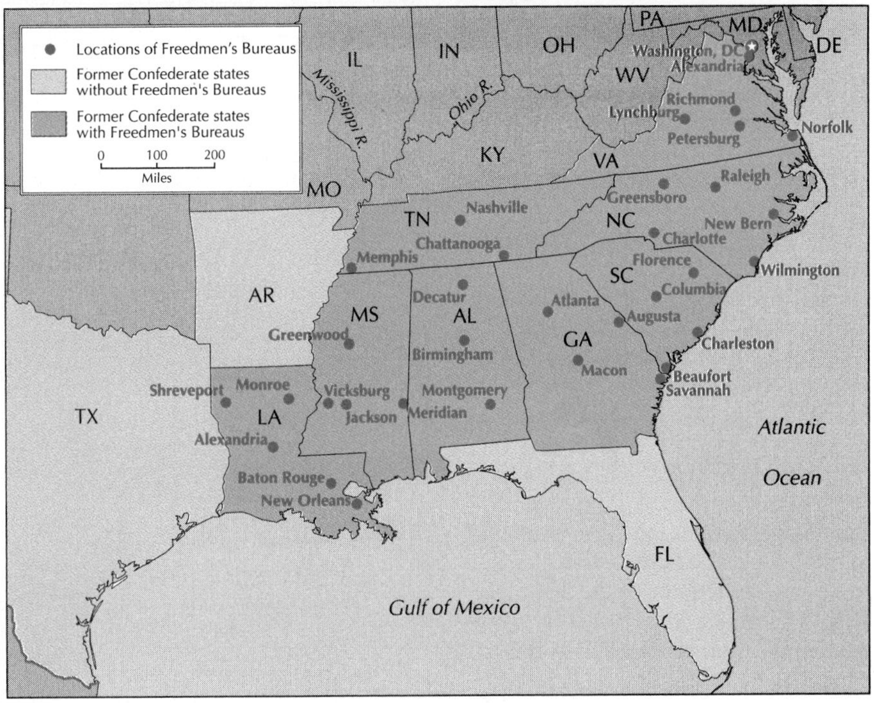
Locations of Freedmen's Bureaus
Former Confederate states without Freedmen's Bureaus
Former Confederate states with Freedmen's Bureaus
0
100
200
Miles
IL
IN
OH
PA
MD
DE
WV
KY
VA
MO
TN
NC
SC
AR
MS
AL
GA
LA
TX
FL
Mississippi R.
Ohio R.
Washington, DC
Alexandria
Richmond
Lynchburg
Petersburg
Norfolk
Raleigh
Greensboro
Nashville
New Bern
Charlotte
Chattanooga
Memphis
Florence
Wilmington
Columbia
Decatur
Atlanta
Augusta
Greenwood
Birmingham
Charleston
Macon
Beaufort
Savannah
Shreveport
Monroe
Vicksburg
Montgomery
Jackson
Meridian
Alexandria
Baton Rouge
New Orleans
Atlantic
Ocean
Gulf of Mexico

By the end of the Civil War the South had been devastated. Crops had been destroyed or never planted; cities were either totally ravaged or a number rendered unlivable. Many former slaves and white refugees faced starvation and lacked basic needs such as food, clothing, and shelter. During the last days of the Confederacy, Union soldiers began to provide for the thousands of refugees who streamed into the few remaining functioning cities and Union camps. It soon became apparent to the U.S. government that additional aid was needed to end the suffering in the South and help whites and blacks to rebuild their lives. In response to this need, Congress passed the Freedmen's Bureau Act in 1865. This act established several Freedmen's Bureau offices in areas with high populations of freed slaves and poor white refugees. Although the bureau's primary concern was the welfare of former slaves, it actually served more poor whites than blacks. The agency provided food, clothing, and shelter for hungry and homeless whites and blacks. The bureau was also responsible for assisting former slaves in negotiating fair labor contracts with whites and establishing schools to help educate their children and themselves. With the assistance of the Freedmen's Bureau, many blacks and whites were given a start toward building a new South. ■

MAP 75

Southern Peonage and the Specialization of American Agriculture after the Civil War (1865–1900)

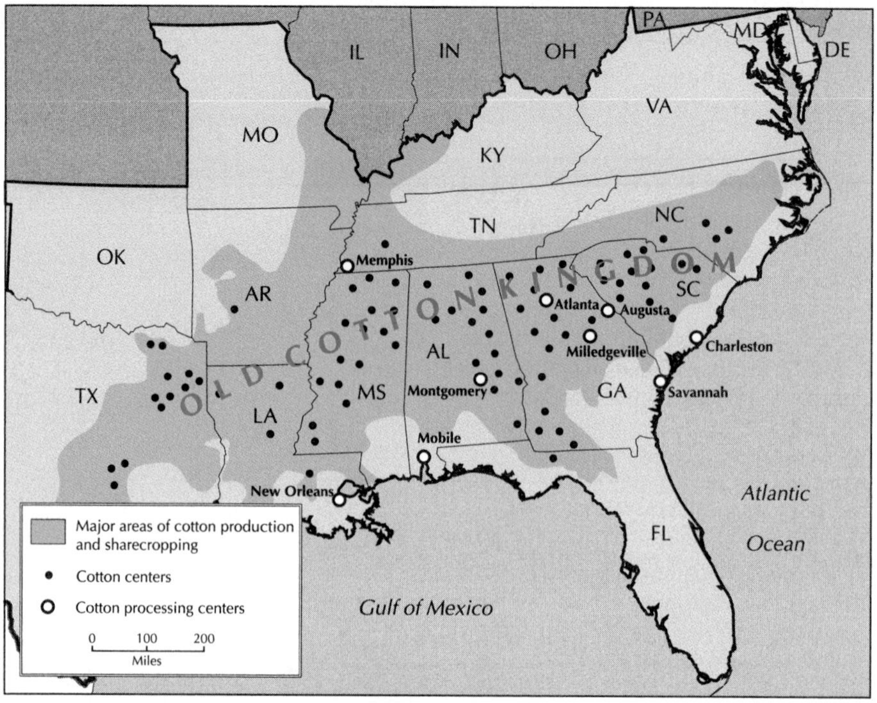
PA
MD
DE
IL
IN
OH
VA
MO
KY
TN
NC
OK
AR
SC
TX
LA
MS
AL
GA
FL
OLD COTTON KINGDOM
Memphis
Atlanta
Augusta
Milledgeville
Charleston
Montgomery
Savannah
Mobile
New Orleans
Atlantic Ocean
Gulf of Mexico
Major areas of cotton production and sharecropping
Cotton centers
Cotton processing centers
0 100 200
Miles

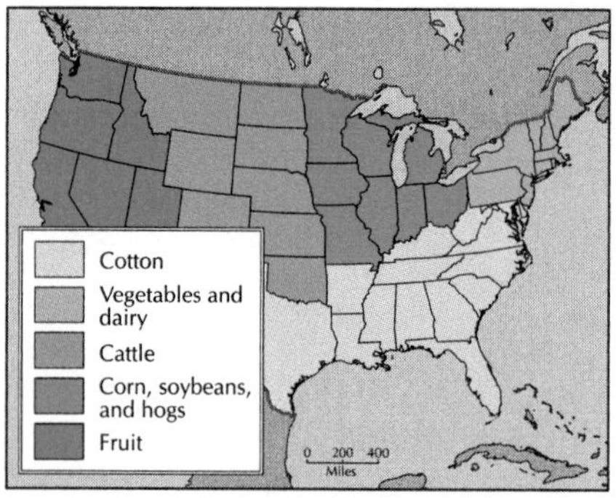
Cotton
Vegetables and dairy
Cattle
Corn, soybeans, and hogs
Fruit
0 200 400
Miles

Although the Civil War changed many things in the South, others remained the same. Before the Civil War, the South had developed the Cotton Kingdom, which stretched from North Carolina to Texas in what is still referred to as the Black Belt. During the war years from 1861 to 1865, very little cotton was grown in the Black Belt. What was harvested was destroyed by southerners in their failed "cotton diplomacy." The rest was ruined by Union forces marching through the South. By 1865 it became critical that cotton production be resumed, preferably at its prewar level. In response to this need, Southern planters and merchants helped to develop the southern sharecropping system. Sharecropping was actually introduced to the South on a large-scale basis by the Freedmen's Bureau. After emancipation and the abolition of the plantation system, the Freedmen's Bureau assisted blacks in negotiating contracts for pay or a share of what they produced for their former masters. Southern planters and merchants insisted that their sharecroppers grow only cotton, the South's most profitable cash crop. Since blacks had little or no money to buy seed, tools, or food stuffs and could only obtain credit extended by these merchants and landowners, they had no choice but to comply. Thus by 1880, the sharecropping and tenant farming system was firmly entrenched in the South. The system in effect reenslaved many blacks living in the South whose former masters, now landowners and merchants, controlled local politics, law enforcement, and the earning potential of blacks. These landowners and merchants balanced the books at the end of the year and often cheated blacks out of their shares. Since they also sold blacks their food, clothing, and supplies, they often overcharged blacks for these goods, causing many to go into debt. They also extended blacks credit at inflated interest rates to force them to become further indebted and then refused to allow them to stop their sharecropping until these debts were paid. Since few blacks could read, write, or calculate very well, there was little they could do to stop from being treated unfairly. If they left their farms, the local sheriff forced them to return to work. Others who stood up to the merchants and landowners were intimidated, beaten, and often lynched to frighten other blacks into remaining quiet. The hardships that most blacks endured under sharecropping in the South were in many ways equal to those of slavery. ■

MAP 76

The Establishment of Historically Black Colleges and Universities in the South during Reconstruction (1865–1877)

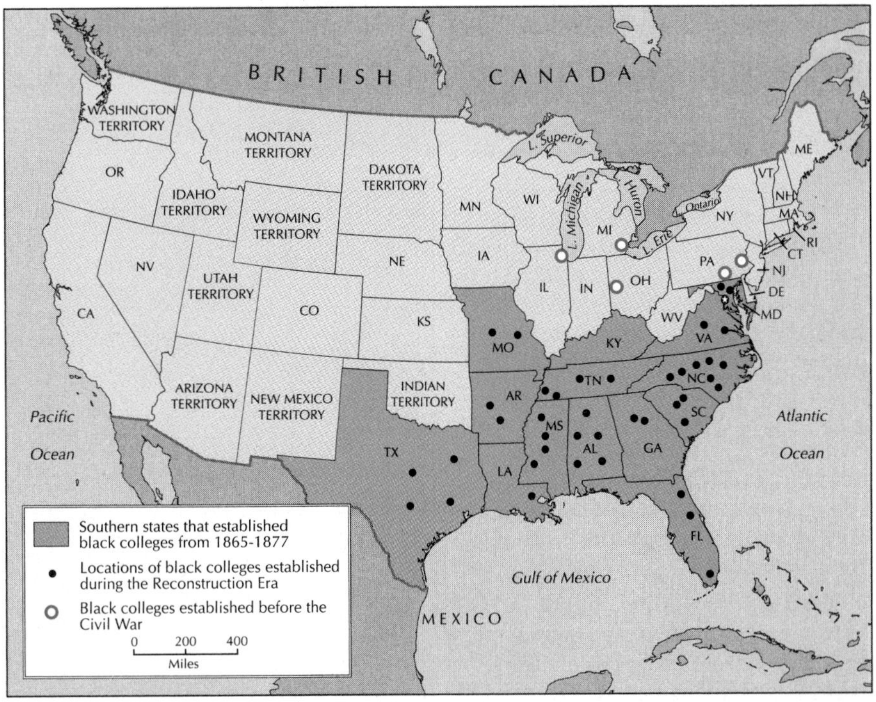
BRITISH CANADA
WASHINGTON TERRITORY
MONTANA TERRITORY
OR
IDAHO TERRITORY
WYOMING TERRITORY
DAKOTA TERRITORY
MN
WI
L. Superior
L. Michigan
L. Huron
L. Ontario
L. Erie
MI
NY
VT
NH
ME
MA
RI
CT
NJ
DE
MD
PA
IA
NE
NV
UTAH TERRITORY
CO
CA
IL
IN
OH
WV
VA
KY
KS
MO
TN
NC
SC
ARIZONA TERRITORY
NEW MEXICO TERRITORY
INDIAN TERRITORY
AR
MS
AL
GA
TX
LA
FL
Pacific Ocean
Atlantic Ocean
Gulf of Mexico
MEXICO
Southern states that established black colleges from 1865-1877
Locations of black colleges established during the Reconstruction Era
Black colleges established before the Civil War
0 200 400
Miles

During Reconstruction many institutions were created to assist former slaves in adjusting to their freedom. Perhaps the most lasting and influential of these, excluding the black church, was the black college. Missionaries, educators, and whites of goodwill immediately saw the importance of education to the betterment of the conditions of blacks in the South. Throughout the period of slavery in the South, blacks had been denied an education. In fact, to educate a slave in many southern states was punishable by public whipping and even death. Thus when slavery was finally abolished by the Thirteenth Amendment, over 4 million former slaves emerged from the institution illiterate. In response to this overwhelming need, schools sprang up everywhere and were used by everyone. Many of these early schools were actually churches that served as schools during the week. They were often constructed by local black residents with what little money they could raise. The freed slaves' craving for knowledge was insatiable. Although most early primary and secondary schools were concerned with basic reading, writing, and arithmetic, it soon became evident that colleges and universities were needed. One of the first black colleges created during the Reconstruction period was Howard University, founded in 1865 by General H. H. Howard, who was the first head of the Freedmen's Bureau. From 1865 to 1877 nearly fifty black colleges and universities were established throughout the South. These institutions were the sole providers of postsecondary education for black people in the South for nearly a hundred years, from 1865 to 1954. They were responsible for educating most black national leaders, who could not attend white colleges or universities until after the Brown decision of 1954. Leaders who attended black schools included Booker T. Washington, who graduated from Hampton Institute; Dr. W.E.B. Du Bois, who completed his undergraduate work at Fisk University; and Dr. Martin Luther King, Jr., who completed his undergraduate work at Morehouse College. These early colleges and universities established the educational foundation for a black middle class and continued to be the primary producers of black doctors, lawyers, professors, and private-sector employees well into the late 1990s. ■

MAP 77

Presidential Reconstruction and the Enactment of Black Codes in the South (1865–1866)

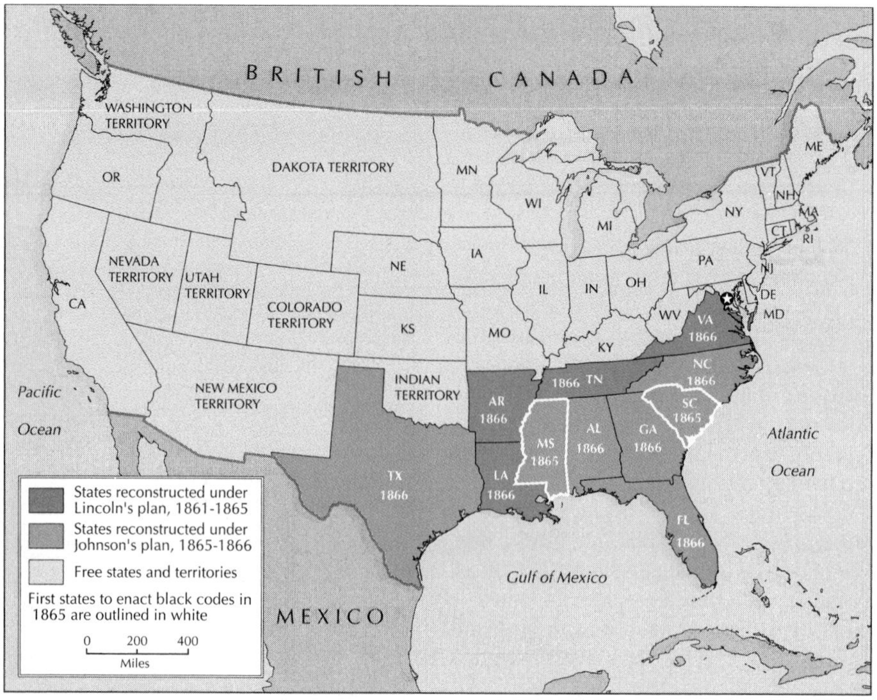
BRITISH CANADA
WASHINGTON TERRITORY
OR
DAKOTA TERRITORY
MN
WI
MI
NY
ME
VT
NH
MA
CT
RI
PA
NJ
DE
MD
IA
NE
IL
IN
OH
WV
VA 1866
NEVADA TERRITORY
UTAH TERRITORY
COLORADO TERRITORY
CA
KS
MO
KY
NEW MEXICO TERRITORY
INDIAN TERRITORY
1866 TN
NC 1866
SC 1865
AR 1866
MS 1865
AL 1866
GA 1866
TX 1866
LA 1866
FL 1866
Pacific Ocean
Atlantic Ocean
Gulf of Mexico
MEXICO
States reconstructed under Lincoln's plan, 1861-1865
States reconstructed under Johnson's plan, 1865-1866
Free states and territories
First states to enact black codes in 1865 are outlined in white
0 200 400
Miles

Presidential Reconstruction of the South began as early as December 1863 when Abraham Lincoln announced his Ten-Percent Plan. Lincoln had formulated a plan that allowed a state to regain recognition after 10 percent of its voters in the 1860 presidential election took an oath of allegiance to the United States and accepted emancipation. Under Lincoln's Ten-Percent Plan, Tennessee would become the first southern state reconstructed under presidential Reconstruction. On April 14, 1865, President Abraham Lincoln was assassinated in Ford's Theater in Washington, D.C. With his death, hopelessness and despair flooded the black community in the South. Blacks feared abandonment, and many felt they had lost a powerful protector. After Lincoln's assassination, newly sworn-in President Andrew Johnson, a native southerner, unveiled his own plan for Reconstruction and immediately went to work implementing it. This plan validated the fears of southern blacks. Unlike Lincoln's plan, it did not protect or provide for the needs of the freedmen. Johnson's plan was more generous to the South than Lincoln's controversial Ten-Percent Plan. When Johnson presented his plan in May 1865, only seven states remained to be reconstructed: North Carolina, South Carolina, Georgia, Florida, Alabama, Mississippi, and Texas. Four states, Arkansas, Louisiana, Virginia, and Tennessee, had already reentered the Union under Lincoln's plan. By the winter of 1865, not only had every southern state been returned to the Union under Johnson's plan, but so had nearly every elected official, as if there had never been a Civil War. This meant that former Confederates who were considered traitors by the rest of the country would be seated in Congress next to those who had remained loyal to the Union. By the start of 1866 the former Confederate states had resumed many of their prewar policies, including attempting to reenslave their black population, refusing to ratify the Thirteenth Amendment, and ignoring the laws of the federal government. The most notorious policy of these reconstructed states was embodied in the black codes these states passed. By enacting black codes, southern states reasserted their control over their former slaves. Black codes were amazingly similar to the slave codes that had existed in the South since the colonial era. They forced blacks to carry passes, forbade interracial marriages, disallowed blacks to testify against whites in court, and instituted vagrancy laws that forced blacks to work or face imprisonment. Like slave codes, the black codes varied in their severity from state to state. South Carolina, Georgia, Mississippi, Alabama, and Louisiana had some of the most severe codes. ■

MAP 78

Congressional Reconstruction and the Rise of Black Elected Officials in the South (1866–1877)

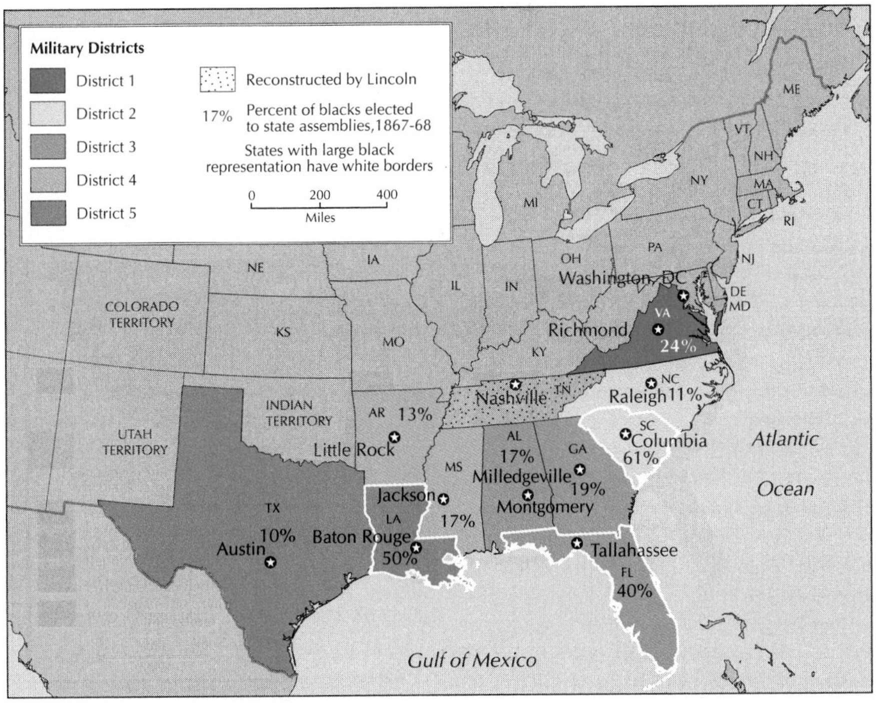
Military Districts
District 1
District 2
District 3
District 4
District 5
Reconstructed by Lincoln
17% Percent of blacks elected to state assemblies, 1867-68
States with large black representation have white borders
0 200 400
Miles
COLORADO TERRITORY
UTAH TERRITORY
INDIAN TERRITORY
NE
KS
IA
MO
IL
IN
OH
MI
PA
NY
KY
VA
Richmond
24%
Washington, DC
NC
Raleigh 11%
SC
Columbia
61%
Nashville
TN
AR 13%
Little Rock
MS
Jackson
17%
AL
17%
Montgomery
GA
Milledgeville
19%
LA
Baton Rouge
50%
TX
10%
Austin
FL
Tallahassee
40%
Gulf of Mexico
Atlantic Ocean
ME
VT
NH
MA
CT
RI
NJ
DE
MD

In response to presidential Reconstruction, the South reentered the Union with nearly all of its former Confederate leaders restored to their old congressional and state assembly positions. Congress, which was led by the Radical Republicans, was outraged over the restoration of prewar southern leaders to Congress and refused to seat these individuals. It began impeachment proceedings against Andrew Johnson and declared the South to be conquered territory and therefore under the jurisdiction of the Congress rather than the president as it pertained to reconstruction. Congress then passed the Thirteenth, Fourteenth, and Fifteenth Amendments abolishing slavery, making blacks citizens, and giving them the right to vote. This became known as Radical Republican or Black Reconstruction. The Radical Republicans were not as forgiving as President Lincoln or Johnson. After expelling from the Union all southern states except Tennessee, which entered under Lincoln's plan, they divided the South into five military districts. The first included only Virginia; the second North Carolina and South Carolina; the third Georgia, Florida, and Alabama; the fourth Arkansas and Mississippi; and the fifth Texas and Louisiana. After these districts were established, each with a military governor, Union troops were sent in to maintain order and enforce the new right to vote given to blacks by the Fifteenth Amendment. Former high ranking Confederate military officers and civilians were barred from voting or running for national, state, or local office, and the states were forced to convene state constitutional conventions and draft new constitutions that included the Thirteenth, Fourteenth, and Fifteenth Amendments. During these conventions large numbers of blacks were elected and were very instrumental in rewriting the state constitutions of each southern state. Many blacks present at the state conventions were former slaves who returned from exile in the North to rebuild the South. Some were free blacks from the North, born into free communities, who traveled south to offer their assistance. Most, however, were southerners who had never left the South. Whether former slaves, teachers, or ministers, all were well educated and determined to do what they could to uplift their race and their home states. Congressional Reconstruction lasted for eleven years, from 1866 to 1877. During those years blacks made great strides in education, economics, and voting rights. From 1866 to 1870, for example, blacks and progressive whites ensured that southern state constitutions provided for public education, granted universal male suffrage, and eliminated property requirements for voting. All southern states incorporated these provisions into their constitutions, which benefited blacks and poor whites. However, by the end of Reconstruction, nearly all blacks were denied these rights, with the political support of poor whites. Ironically, Jim Crow laws like the poll tax, literacy test, and property requirements that disenfranchised blacks disenfranchised just as many poor whites. ■

MAP 79

The Radical Republican Governors of the South and Their Negro State Militias during Reconstruction (1866–1877)

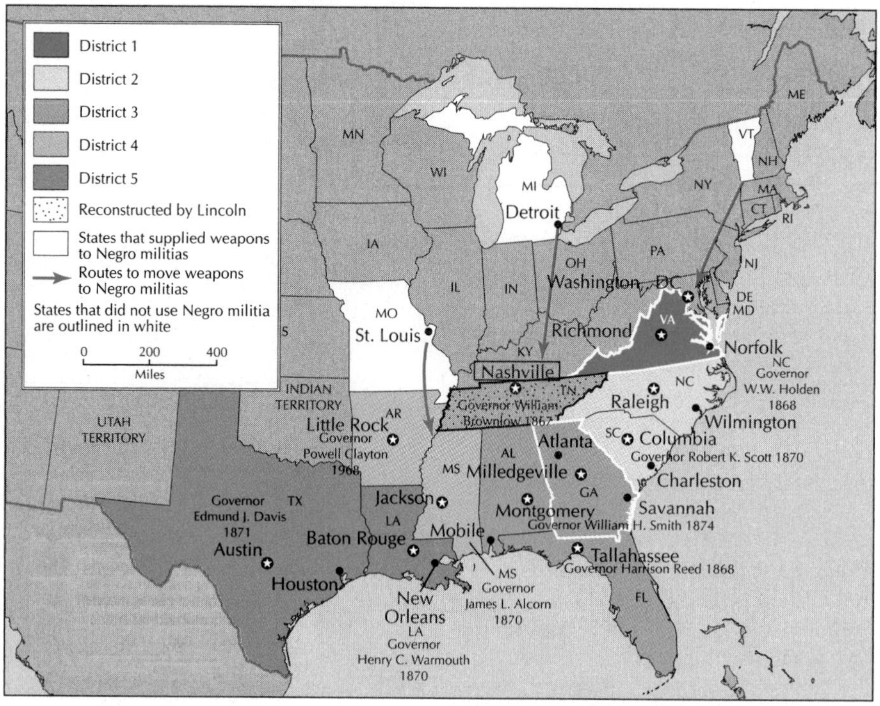
District 1
District 2
District 3
District 4
District 5
Reconstructed by Lincoln
States that supplied weapons to Negro militias
Routes to move weapons to Negro militias
States that did not use Negro militia are outlined in white
0 200 400
Miles
MN
WI
MI
Detroit
IA
IL
IN
OH
PA
NY
VT
NH
ME
MA
CT
RI
NJ
DE
MD
Washington, DC
MO
St. Louis
KY
Richmond
VA
Norfolk
NC
Governor
W.W. Holden
1868
Nashville
TN
Governor William Brownlow 1867
Raleigh
Wilmington
INDIAN TERRITORY
UTAH TERRITORY
AR
Little Rock
Governor
Powell Clayton
1968
SC
Columbia
Governor Robert K. Scott 1870
Atlanta
AL
MS
Milledgeville
GA
Charleston
Savannah
Montgomery
Governor William H. Smith 1874
Jackson
LA
Governor
Edmund J. Davis
1871
TX
Austin
Baton Rouge
Mobile
Tallahassee
Governor Harrison Reed 1868
MS
Governor
James L. Alcorn
1870
Houston
New Orleans
LA
Governor
Henry C. Warmouth
1870
FL

By the end of the Civil War more than 186,000 African Americans had enlisted and served in the Union Army. Over half of these soldiers came from the South, mostly former slaves who aided the Union in defeating the Confederacy and in so doing freed themselves and their families from slavery. When the Civil War ended, these soldiers also assisted the North in reestablishing order in the South. Due to congressional opposition to presidential Reconstruction, Congress assumed control of Reconstruction in 1867 and began congressional or Radical Republican Reconstruction of the South. Military governors and Union troops occupied the state capitals and major centers of commerce in the South. Black troops assisted and were used to protect the newly freed African Americans, northerners helping to reconstruct the South, and southerners who had remained loyal to or reaffirmed their loyalty to the Union. Black troops were also used to protect the members of the state constitutional conventions during the rewriting of state constitutions. Following the conventions, they oversaw the general elections in the South, where many blacks were voting for the first time. During these elections, Republicans gained control of all the reconstructed state assemblies and their governorships. Several of these Republican governors included W. W. Holden of North Carolina; Robert K. Scott, Frank J. Moses, Jr., and Daniel H. Chamberlain of South Carolina; James L. Alcorn and Adelbert Ames of Mississippi; Edmund J. Davis of Texas; William G. Brownlow of Tennessee; Powell Clayton of Arkansas; and Henry C. Warmouth of Louisiana, whose Negro militia was led by General James Longstreet, one of Robert E. Lee's leading generals during the Civil War. Longstreet created and used Negro state militias to keep order and enforce new laws in their states. These militias were also used to fight white terrorist groups that sought to undermine the new state governors and reestablish the old order. The black state militias were a source of pride for many African Americans living in the postwar South. The militias protected the rights of all southerners, black and white, to vote and to live without fear of harm from terrorist groups. They enforced curfews and new laws passed by the new state assemblies. The use of blacks in state militias appalled rebellious and racist white southerners, who continued to see African Americans as the property of whites. As a result, southern racists used the presence of black militias to inflame white fears of "Negro rule," fears that had existed since the Stono Rebellion. These fears led to the birth of the first Ku Klux Klan, which held as its sole purpose to end Reconstruction and put blacks back "in their place." These fears also resulted in violent clashes between armed whites and black militiamen throughout the South from 1868 to 1877. ■

MAP 80

Southern White Resistance to Reconstruction and the Birth of the Ku Klux Klan (1866–1877)

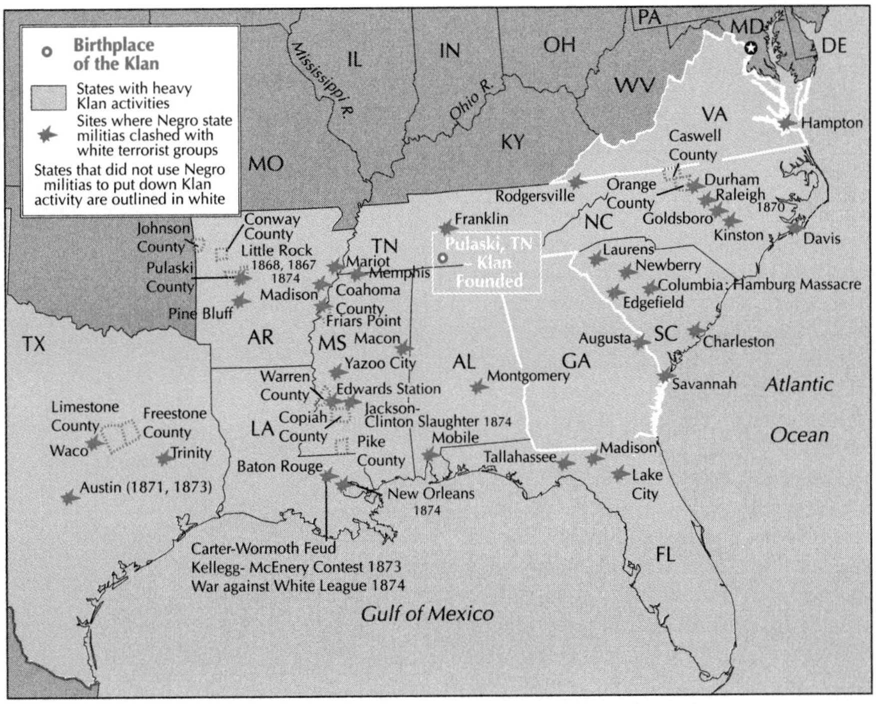
Birthplace of the Klan
States with heavy Klan activities
Sites where Negro state militias clashed with white terrorist groups
States that did not use Negro militias to put down Klan activity are outlined in white
PA
MD
DE
IL
IN
OH
WV
Mississippi R.
Ohio R.
VA
Hampton
Caswell County
KY
MO
Rodgersville
Orange County
Durham
Raleigh 1870
NC
Goldsboro
Kinston
Davis
Franklin
Johnson County
Pulaski County
Conway County
Little Rock 1868, 1867 1874
TN
Mariot
Memphis
Pulaski, TN – Klan Founded
Laurens
Newberry
Columbia
Hamburg Massacre
Edgefield
Madison
Coahoma County
Friars Point
Pine Bluff
AR
MS
Macon
Augusta
SC
Charleston
TX
Yazoo City
AL
GA
Montgomery
Warren County
Edwards Station
Savannah
Atlantic Ocean
Limestone County
Freestone County
Waco
Trinity
LA
Copiah County
Jackson-Clinton Slaughter 1874
Pike County
Mobile
Tallahassee
Madison
Baton Rouge
Lake City
Austin (1871, 1873)
New Orleans 1874
Carter-Wormoth Feud
Kellegg- McEnery Contest 1873
War against White League 1874
FL
Gulf of Mexico

The Civil War officially ended in April of 1865. The war, however, never truly ended for renegade Confederates turned fugitives, such as Jesse James. These men fought on, terrorizing the West and earning the admiration of the white southern populus. White supremacist organizations sworn to keep blacks "in their place" sprang up all over the South. The most popular and well known was the Ku Klux Klan (KKK), founded in Pulaski, Tennessee, in 1866 by Nathan Bedford Forrest. The Klan beat, raped, and murdered hundreds of blacks who attempted to either exercise or enforce their new rights guaranteed by the Fourteenth and Fifteenth Amendments. Negro state militias, which were used by Republican governors to protect blacks, and pro-Union whites fought protracted wars with the organization throughout the old Confederacy. The organization targeted former slaves, black politicians, educators, and religious leaders. Southern and northern whites who assisted blacks were also targets of the Klan's violence. The extensive terrorism, violence, and armed combat with Negro militias prompted Congress to pass the Ku Klux Klan Act in 1871. Under the act the United States Army attempted to eradicate the Klan and restore order in the South. Although the most defiant and murderous actions of the Klan were stopped and hundreds of members arrested and jailed, the organization was never fully eliminated. As late as 1877 armed whites and Negro militias battled in the streets of Charleston, New Orleans, and other cities in the South. Although the Klan was originally made up entirely of southerners who were fighting to take away blacks' rights and to end northern military occupation of the South, by 1915 the organization began to gain national acceptance by Anglo-Saxon Protestants around the country who did not like the large numbers of blacks, Jews, Catholics, Irish, Germans, and southern Europeans who were migrating to the Midwest and the Northeast. ■

MAP 81

Black Cowboys and the Cattle Kingdom of the Southwest (1865–1890)

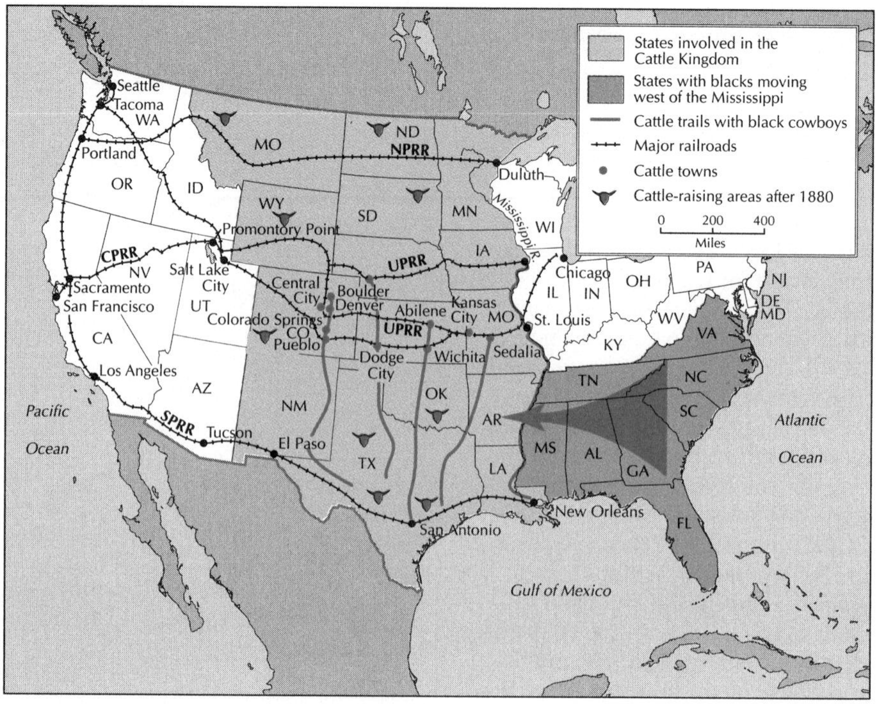
States involved in the Cattle Kingdom
States with blacks moving west of the Mississippi
Cattle trails with black cowboys
Major railroads
Cattle towns
Cattle-raising areas after 1880
0 200 400
Miles
Seattle
Tacoma
WA
Portland
OR
ID
MO
ND
NPRR
Duluth
WY
Promontory Point
SD
MN
Mississippi R.
WI
CPRR
NV
Salt Lake City
UPRR
IA
Chicago
PA
NJ
Sacramento
San Francisco
UT
Central City
Boulder
Denver
Abilene
Kansas City
MO
IL
IN
OH
DE
MD
Colorado Springs
CO
Pueblo
UPRR
St. Louis
WV
VA
CA
Wichita
Sedalia
KY
Los Angeles
Dodge City
TN
NC
AZ
OK
NM
AR
SC
Pacific
Ocean
SPRR
Tucson
El Paso
TX
MS
AL
GA
Atlantic
Ocean
LA
New Orleans
FL
San Antonio
Gulf of Mexico

Blacks had been living in the West in small numbers since the 1500s. They explored the region for the Spanish as early as 1526 and were used as slaves and soldiers to conquer, and protect the region and to provide labor until the arrival of American settlers in the 1800s. During the colonial period they also assisted the French in trading and in defending their forts along the St. Lawrence, the Illinois, and the Mississippi Rivers and assisted in building the multiethnic city of New Orleans, which they helped Andrew Jackson defend from the British in 1815. From 1800 to 1860 more American blacks settled in the West. Some were free; others were fugitive slaves. These blacks were the first to settle in Los Angeles, California, and in New Mexico. They were miners in Colorado, Montana, Idaho, and Nevada. They joined the nations of western Indians like the Apache, Navajo, Comanche, Crow, Arapaho, Cheyenne, and Sioux. They also worked on Spanish haciendas as vaqueros, where they herded and branded cattle and learned to ride horses. Initially, white Americans were not very interested in cattle ranching; thus the first recorded American cowboy was an African slave who was given charge of a herd of 400 cattle by his master, Samuel A. Maverick. Maverick was not as interested in raising cattle as in practicing law, so he sold his cattle in 1856 to A. Toutant Beauregard. Beauregard began what became known as the Cattle Kingdom. Most of the first black cowboys who herded and looked after cattle were slaves who were taught their trade by Mexican vaqueros, Indians, and their white masters. They were brought to Texas from the South by their masters to launch the Cattle Kingdom. In the early years, from 1856 to 1865, there were few black cowboys except in east Texas because most who were slaves could easily escape to freedom across the Rio Grande (south Texas to Mexico). After the Civil War and emancipation, hundreds of blacks moved to the West in search of work and protection from southern racism and violence. As many as 3,000 blacks became cowboys and herded cattle on the western trails to the railroads in Kansas, Wyoming, Nebraska, Colorado, and Missouri. These trails included the Goodnight–Loving Trail, the Western Trail, the Chisholm Trail, and the Sedalia Trail. The most famous of the black cowboys were Bronco Sam, Bill Pickett, Nat Love, Bose Ikard, Bob Lemmons, Cherokee Bill, Ben Hodge, Isom Dart, Jim Young, and Charlie Smith. ■

MAP 82

The Buffalo Soldiers: Black Soldiers and the Indian Wars of the West (1866–1890)

BRITISH CANADA
WA
OR
CA
NE
IDAHO TERRITORY
UTAH TERRITORY
ARIZONA TERRITORY
CO
DAKOTA TERRITORY
MN
WI
MI
IA
IL
IN
KS
MO
KY
TN
INDIAN TERRITORY
TX
AR
MS
AL
LA
MEXICO
Ft. Shaw
Ft. Missoula
Little Big Horn 1876
Ft. Keogh
Fetterman 1866
Ft. Seward
Ft. Ransom
Wounded-Knee 1890
Ft. Snelling
Camp Connor
Chief Dull Knife 1877
Ft. Dodge
Ft. McPhereson
Ft. Madison
Ft. Clark
Presidio of San Francisco
Ft. Kearney II
Ft. Leavenworth
Ft. Orleans
Ft. Osage
Sand Creek 1864
Ft. Wallace
Ft. Lewis
Ft. Dodge
Ft. Baker
Ft. Supply
Ft. Elliot
Ft. Reno
Red River War 1874-1875
Ft. Sill
Little Rock
Ft. Apache
Ft. Thomas
Ft. Grant II
Ft. Stanton
Ft. Bayard
Ft. Griffin II
Ft. Concho
Ft. Houston
Skeleton Canyon Geronimo Surrenders 1886
Ft. Quitman
Ft. Stockton
Ft. McKavett
Ft. Davis
New Orleans
Ft. Jackson
Ft. Clark
Ft. Duncan
Ft. McIntosh
38th and 41st colored infantry combined to form the 24th Buffalo Soldiers
39th and 40th colored infantry combined to form the 25th Buffalo Soldiers
Pancho Villa
0 200 400
Miles
Forts that housed black troops during the Indian Wars
Battle Sites
Soldiers policed Oklahoma before the Land Rush
Lands where Buffalo Soldiers fought and served during the Indian Wars
The South – major source of black troops in the Indian Wars

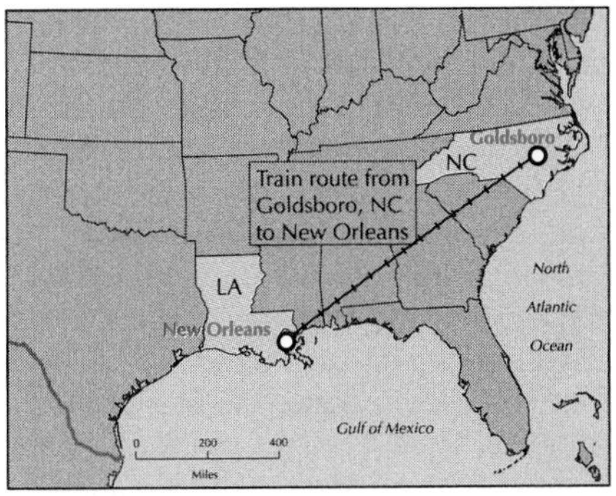
Goldsboro
NC
Train route from Goldsboro, NC to New Orleans
LA
New Orleans
North Atlantic Ocean
Gulf of Mexico
0 200 400
Miles

During the Civil War black troops proved to the Union Army that they were good soldiers. White officers found that they had the character, fortitude, and heart to fight and win. With the Civil War over, America quickly switched its attention to the Indian troubles of the West. These conflicts were brought on primarily by the building of the transcontinental railroad and the thousands of white settlers it brought. As Indian attacks increased on white settlements and rail lines, troops not being used to reconstruct the South were redeployed in the West. These troops were placed under the command of William T. Sherman, arguably the most hated man in the South next to Abraham Lincoln. It was decided in Congress that the best black veterans of the Civil War would be gathered together and sent west to fight the Plains Indians. On July 28, 1866, Congress authorized the establishment of four permanent black military units. The act created two infantry regiments, the U.S. Twenty-Fourth and Twenty-Fifth, and two cavalry regiments, the Ninth and Tenth. Command of these troops was originally offered to General Armstrong Custer. However he refused the command, believing black troops to be inferior in every way, particularly in intelligence, to white troops. These four black units were used extensively in the Indian wars of the West from 1866 to 1880 and earned a reputation for being fierce fighters. White soldiers called them "Brunettes." The Indians called them "Buffalo soldiers" because their skin and hair resembled that of the sacred buffalo. The Buffalo Soldiers fought Indians throughout the West, including the Apache, Navajo, Comanche, Crow, Arapaho, Cheyenne, and Sioux. They were also used to put down Indian rebellions on the western reservations. They fought Crazy Horse and captured Geronimo. They prevented settlers from entering Oklahoma before its opening and protected cattlemen from Indians while they were traveling through Oklahoma on their cattle drives. They were the best and brightest, hand-picked for their intelligence and physical ability. Many of these men joined the Buffalo Soldiers because they believed that they were representing the black race and, that if they fought well, it would help all blacks earn the respect of white Americans. Although these black soldiers did serve their country well, they did not change the attitudes of most white Americans, and their race remained oppressed well into the mid-Twentieth century. ■

MAP 83

The Compromise of 1877 and Its Impact on African Americans Living in the South

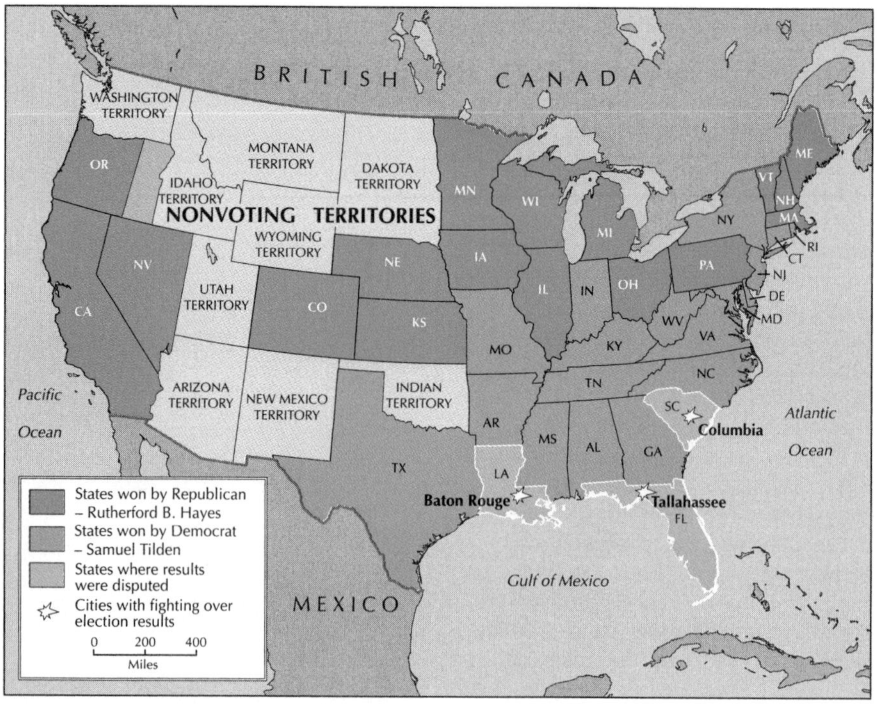
BRITISH CANADA
WASHINGTON TERRITORY
MONTANA TERRITORY
DAKOTA TERRITORY
IDAHO TERRITORY
NONVOTING TERRITORIES
WYOMING TERRITORY
UTAH TERRITORY
ARIZONA TERRITORY
NEW MEXICO TERRITORY
INDIAN TERRITORY
OR
NV
CA
CO
NE
KS
TX
MN
IA
MO
AR
LA
WI
IL
MI
IN
OH
KY
TN
MS
AL
GA
FL
SC
NC
VA
WV
PA
NY
ME
VT
NH
MA
RI
CT
NJ
DE
MD
Columbia
Baton Rouge
Tallahassee
Pacific Ocean
Atlantic Ocean
Gulf of Mexico
MEXICO
States won by Republican - Rutherford B. Hayes
States won by Democrat - Samuel Tilden
States where results were disputed
Cities with fighting over election results
0 200 400
Miles

By November of 1876, after four years of war and twelve years of Reconstruction, the North began to tire of the defiant South. Terrorist organizations like the Ku Klux Klan and the Regulators continued to thrive and torment blacks and pro-Union whites despite the Ku Klux Klan Act of 1871. In spite of the best efforts of the Union Army and Negro state militias, it became increasingly more difficult to control the white southern populus. By the election of 1876 the pre-Civil War southern Democrats had regained control of Virginia (1869), Tennessee (1869), North Carolina (1870), Georgia (1871), Texas (1873), Arkansas (1874), Alabama (1874), and Mississippi (1876). Only three southern states remained in the hands of northern Republicans, South Carolina, Florida, and Louisiana. Northern Republicans still controlled the presidency and held a majority in Congress, but they were increasingly being challenged by southern Democrats returned to Congress from Democrat-controlled southern states. In the election of 1876, however, control of the presidency was seriously threatened by the forging of a new political alliance between northern and southern Democrats. The Democratic candidate, Samuel J. Tilden, needed one more electoral vote to win the presidency. The votes of Louisiana, Florida, and South Carolina were in dispute because of claims in each of the three states of irregular returns. If Tilden could garner the votes of just one of these states, he would become president. The three southern states of Louisiana, Florida, and South Carolina held in their hands the decision of whether there would be a Democratic or Republican president. With the presidency at stake, both Democrats and Republicans in the three states claimed victory. If the dispute was resolved in favor of Rutherford B. Hayes, the Republicans would maintain control of the presidency. If resolved in favor of Samuel Tilden, for the first time in sixteen years the country would see a Democratic president. The dispute erupted into violence in each of the three states. Supporters of both parties fought in the streets of Columbia, South Carolina, Baton Rouge, and Tallahassee. The crisis threatened to rip the nation apart once again, with South Carolina calling for secession and former Confederate states rallying to her side. Tragedy was averted, however, when northern Republicans and southern Democrats struck what has become known as the Compromise of 1877. In exchange for the electoral votes of the three disputed states to elect Rutherford B. Hayes as president, Republicans agreed to withdraw federal troops from the South and to end Reconstruction. The compromise ended twelve years of Reconstruction and resulted in the abandonment of southern blacks, who had been protected by the federal troops, leaving them at the mercy of angry, vindictive whites, who immediately returned blacks to a position of servitude. ■

MAP 84

The "Exodusters": African-American Migration to Kansas and the American Far West (1879)

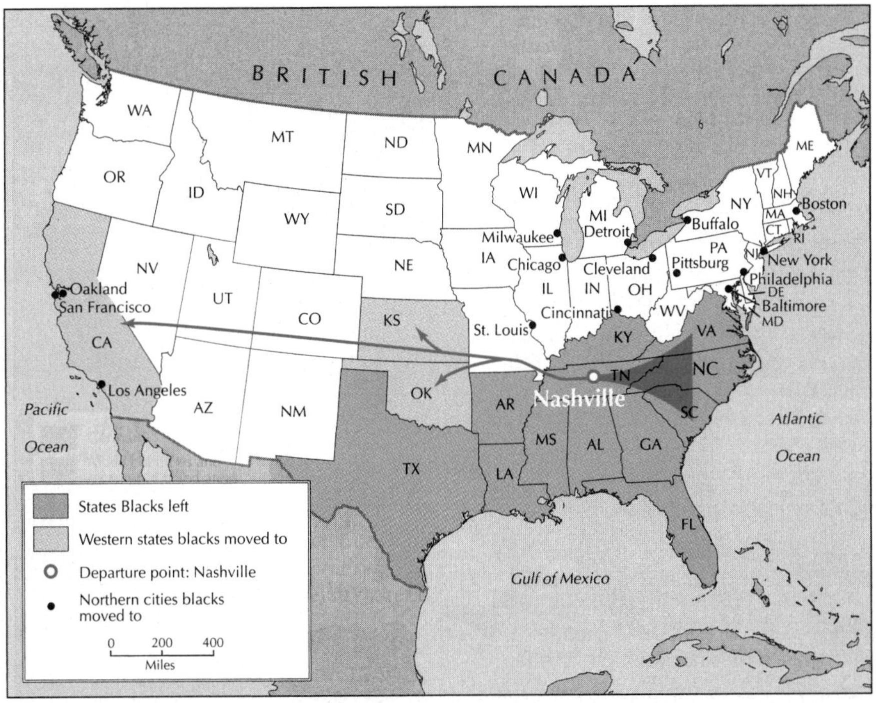
BRITISH CANADA
WA
OR
ID
MT
WY
ND
SD
NE
MN
WI
MI
IA
IL
IN
OH
PA
NY
ME
VT
NH
MA
CT
RI
NJ
DE
MD
WV
VA
KY
TN
NC
SC
GA
AL
MS
AR
LA
TX
OK
KS
CO
NM
AZ
UT
NV
CA
FL
Oakland
San Francisco
Los Angeles
Milwaukee
Chicago
Detroit
Cleveland
Cincinnati
St. Louis
Buffalo
Pittsburg
New York
Philadelphia
Baltimore
Boston
Nashville
Pacific Ocean
Atlantic Ocean
Gulf of Mexico
States Blacks left
Western states blacks moved to
Departure point: Nashville
Northern cities blacks moved to
0 200 400
Miles

Following the departure of federal troops and the collapse of Reconstruction in 1877, blacks found southern white oppression and terrorism unbearable. Conditions for many blacks in the South were worse than during slavery. Terrorist groups such as the Ku Klux Klan roamed the South, lynching, beating, and raping with impunity. Some blacks, like Henry McNeal Turner, began to encourage their fellow blacks to leave the United States and return to Africa. Others like Pap Singleton, a minister, sent out a call for all blacks to go west to make a new start away from the racial persecution of the South. In 1879 Singleton issued flyers that were distributed all over the South, encouraging unhappy blacks to follow him to Kansas. In 1880 over 60,000 blacks gathered in Nashville, Tennessee, and began a massive exodus to Kansas. Thousands more moved to Oklahoma and California. Newspapers called these blacks "Exodusters." Whatever their title, they left the South in massive numbers from 1880 to 1890. Many blacks were also willing to leave because the sharecropping and tenant farming that replaced the plantation system seemed little different from slavery. The few blacks who acquired land of their own lived under constant threat of having their land taken or their crops destroyed by local whites. Because there was no protection of blacks by the law—in fact, authorities were often the perpetrators of atrocities against blacks, or at least gave their approval—many blacks saw no future in the South. As more and more blacks joined the exodus, both black leaders and southern white planters became alarmed—needless to say, for different reasons. Black leaders like Booker T. Washington, who proclaimed, "Cast your bucket down where you are," believed that it did not matter where blacks moved. They were still likely to encounter white racism. Therefore it was better for blacks to face it in the South and build their homes, churches, schools, and businesses there, rather than take a chance somewhere else. The Baptist Church also encouraged its members to stay, pray, work hard, and let God be their strength. As a result, most blacks chose not to leave their homes, schools, churches, and businesses. White planters became concerned about who was going to plant and harvest their crops. They needed black labor. As a result, some whites promised better treatment and wages; others threatened blacks with violence if they moved. The black exodus to the West (Kansas, Oklahoma, and California) would be the first mass movement of blacks in post-Civil War America, but it would not be the last. By the start of the twentieth century, blacks would again begin leaving the South, this time by the millions. They headed not only west but also north, to the Northeast and Midwest. ■

MAP 85

The Partitioning of Africa: Africa before and after 1880

While America dealt with the Civil War, the Indian wars, the collapse of Reconstruction, the black exodus, and the rise of Jim Crow, the rest of the world did not stand still. Germany was united in 1871, with "blood and steel," by Otto Von Bismarck. In central Europe, France's Third Republic was established in 1871. Italy was unified, and Great Britain built an industrial empire that stretched around the world. Industrialized European nations like Germany, France, and England expanded colonialism and began to race against one another for additional colonies. By 1880 one of the only uncolonized continents that remained was Africa. During the first phase of European colonialism, Africa furnished the slave labor to clear the land and plant and harvest the cash crops—tobacco, rice, indigo, sugar, and cotton—of the Americas and the Caribbean. In the second phase of European colonialism, Africa furnished the labor and raw materials to fuel the European Industrial Revolution. Before 1880 the interior of Africa had remained independent and untouched by Europeans, mostly because Europeans found it difficult to penetrate the interior of Africa. Fierce resistance from well-armed natives and tropical diseases like dysentery and malaria provided formidable defenses against European efforts to colonize the continent. However, by the 1880s new drugs that protect against tropical diseases, better weapons, and military alliances with local African nations helped Europeans conquer the entire continent. The need for raw materials such as coal, oil, and iron to sustain the Industrial Revolution in Europe and Europe's love of gold, silver, and diamonds increased Europeans' interest in the interior of Africa. In 1880 only four non-African nations held territory in Africa, all of it being coastal territory. Great Britain held Sierra Leone, the Gold Coast, and Lagos on the west coast and South Africa at the southern tip. France held Gambia, Senegal, and Gabon in West Africa and Algeria to the north. Portugal held Angola and Portuguese Guinea in West Africa and

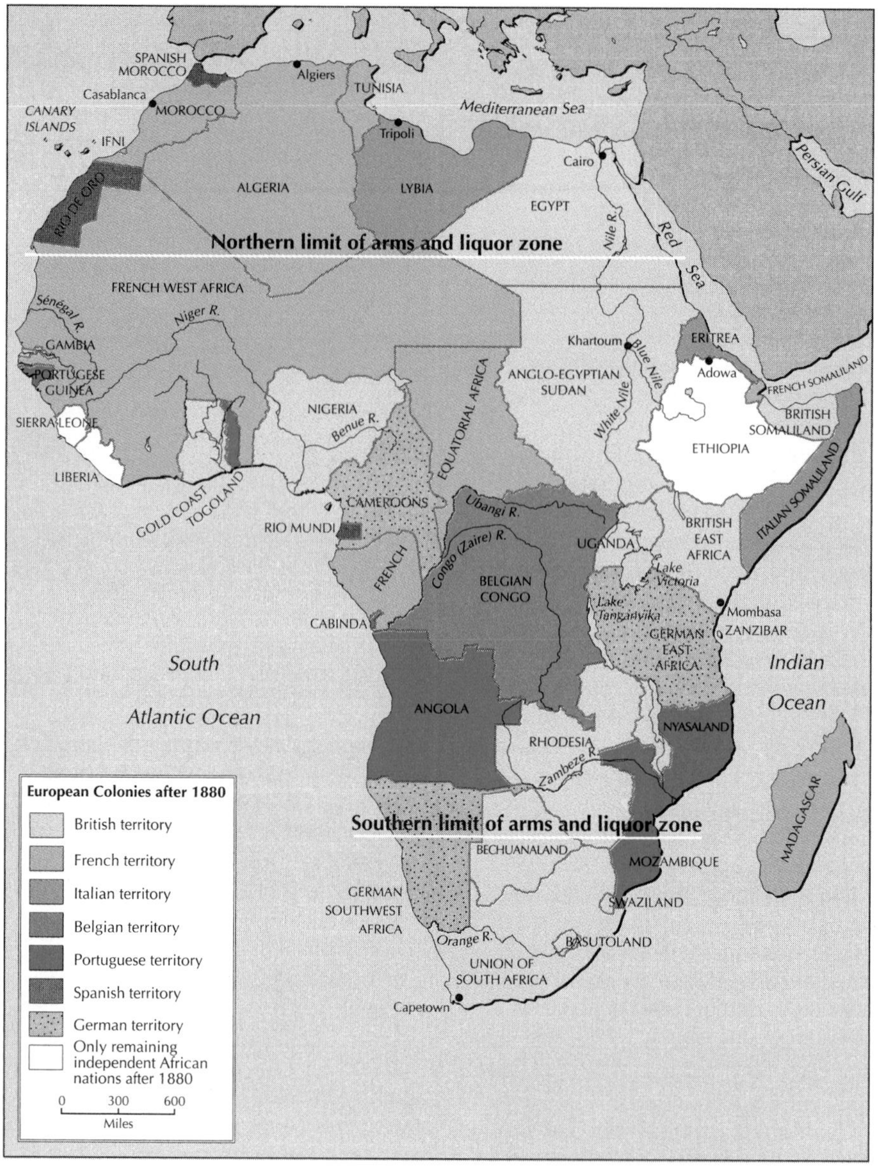

SPANISH MOROCCO
Algiers
TUNISIA
Casablanca
MOROCCO
CANARY ISLANDS
IFNI
Mediterranean Sea
Tripoli
Cairo
Persian Gulf
RIO DE ORO
ALGERIA
LYBIA
EGYPT
Nile R.
Red Sea
Northern limit of arms and liquor zone
FRENCH WEST AFRICA
Sénégal R.
Niger R.
GAMBIA
PORTUGESE GUINEA
SIERRA LEONE
LIBERIA
GOLD COAST
TOGOLAND
NIGERIA
Benue R.
EQUATORIAL AFRICA
Khartoum
ERITREA
Adowa
ANGLO-EGYPTIAN SUDAN
Blue Nile
White Nile
FRENCH SOMALILAND
BRITISH SOMALILAND
ETHIOPIA
ITALIAN SOMALILAND
CAMEROONS
RIO MUNDI
Ubangi R.
Congo (Zaire) R.
FRENCH
BELGIAN CONGO
UGANDA
BRITISH EAST AFRICA
Lake Victoria
Lake Tanganyika
Mombasa
ZANZIBAR
GERMAN EAST AFRICA
CABINDA
South Atlantic Ocean
Indian Ocean
ANGOLA
NYASALAND
RHODESIA
Zambeze R.
Southern limit of arms and liquor zone
BECHUANALAND
MOZAMBIQUE
MADAGASCAR
GERMAN SOUTHWEST AFRICA
SWAZILAND
Orange R.
BASUTOLAND
UNION OF SOUTH AFRICA
Capetown
European Colonies after 1880
British territory
French territory
Italian territory
Belgian territory
Portuguese territory
Spanish territory
German territory
Only remaining independent African nations after 1880
0 300 600
Miles

Mozambique in East Africa. Finally, Turkey controlled Northeast Africa from Algeria to Ethiopia. After 1880 a total of seven European nations would race to capture and colonize almost all of Africa. Britain, France, and Portugal were joined by Germany, Italy, Belgium, and Spain. To avoid warfare among the various European nations vying for control of Africa, France and Germany called for an international conference to be held in Berlin where the fate of Africa would be decided. Begun in November 1884, the conference lasted four months, ending in March 1885. At the conference it was decided that international navigation of the Niger and Congo Rivers would be respected and that an arms and spirituous

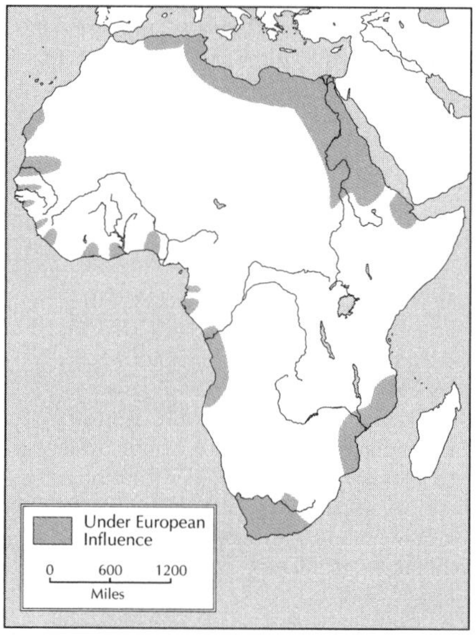

Under European Influence
0 600 1200
Miles

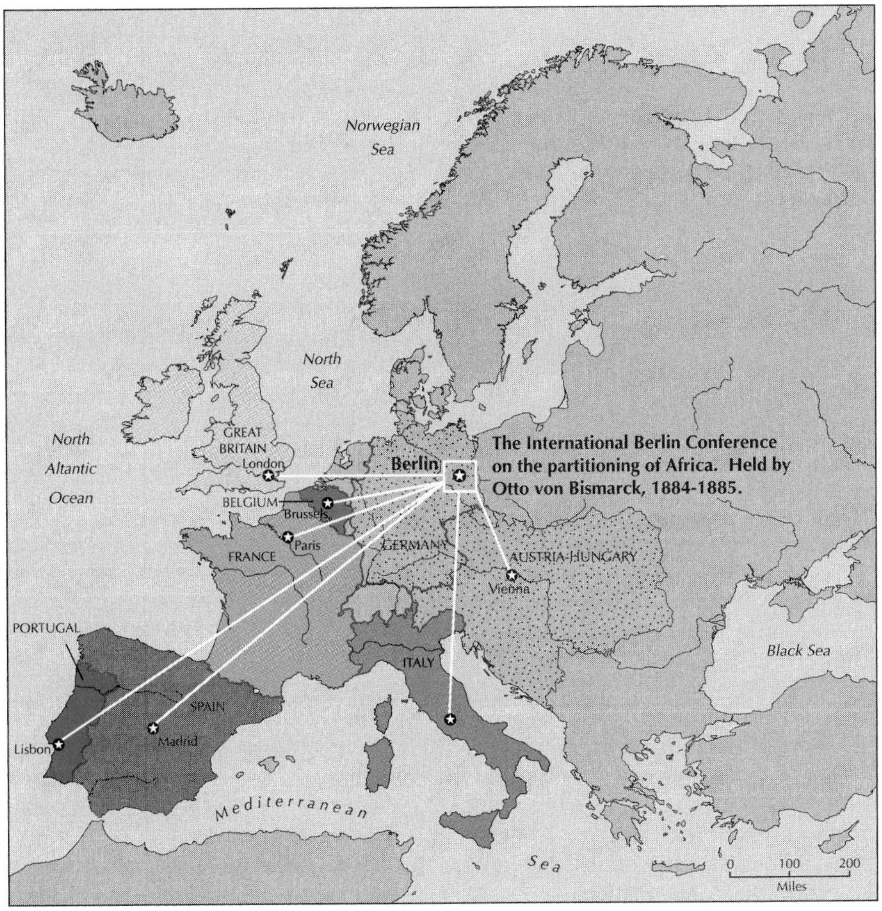
Norwegian Sea
North Sea
North Atlantic Ocean
GREAT BRITAIN
London
Berlin
The International Berlin Conference on the partitioning of Africa. Held by Otto von Bismarck, 1884-1885.
BELGIUM
Brussels
Paris
FRANCE
GERMANY
AUSTRIA-HUNGARY
Vienna
PORTUGAL
ITALY
Black Sea
SPAIN
Lisbon
Madrid
Mediterranean
Sea
0 100 200
Miles

liquor zone would be established, where neither weapons nor hard liquor were to be sold to African peoples. Another important outcome was the development of the protectorate system. However, the most important outcome was the division of Africa among the nations present. As a result of this conference, Europeans succeeded in carving up Africa among themselves and by 1890 began the systematic exploitation of the continent that persisted until the African wars for independence following World War II. Under the agreement reached at the Berlin conference Belgium received the Congo, and Great Britain received Egypt, Sudan, Togoland, the Union of South Africa, North and South Rhodesia, Gambia, British Somalia, Basutoland, Swaziland, Nyasaland, Liberia, the Gold Coast, Nigeria, and modern-day Kenya. France received Morocco, Algeria, French Somalia, and French West Africa, and Germany received Cameroon, Southwest Africa, and German East Africa. Italy received Libya, Eritrea, and Italian Somalia, Portugal received Mozambique and Angola, and Spain received Spanish Guinea, and the Spanish Sahara. Only Ethiopia and Liberia remained independent. ■

MAP 86

The Populist Movement: Blacks and the "Farmers' Revolt" (1887–1898)

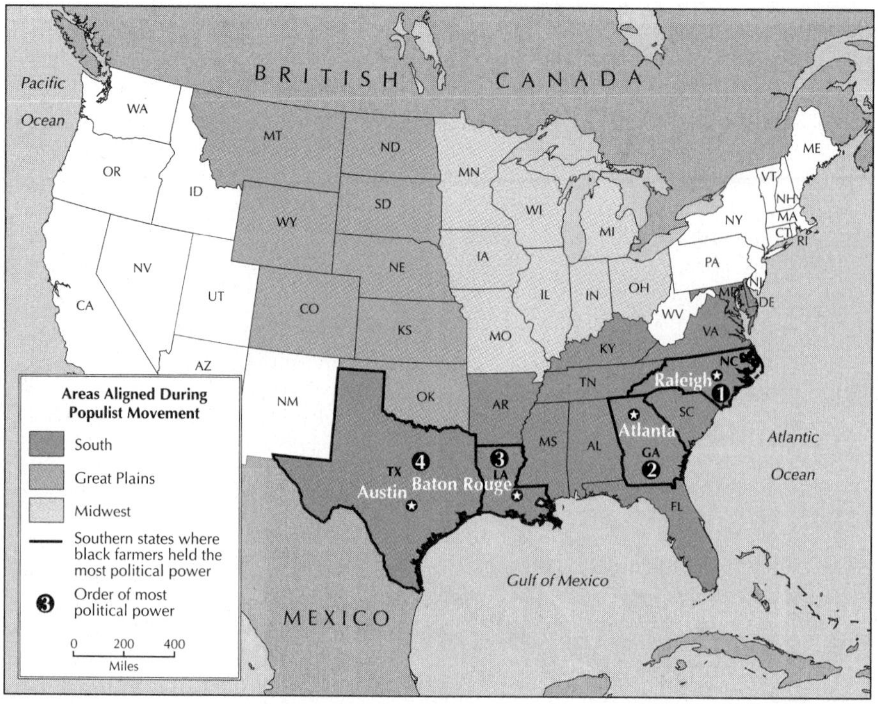
Pacific Ocean
BRITISH CANADA
WA
OR
CA
NV
ID
MT
WY
UT
AZ
NM
CO
ND
SD
NE
KS
OK
TX
MN
IA
MO
AR
LA
WI
IL
MI
IN
OH
KY
TN
MS
AL
GA
FL
SC
NC
VA
WV
PA
NY
ME
VT
NH
MA
CT
RI
NJ
MD
DE
Raleigh
Atlanta
Austin
Baton Rouge
Atlantic Ocean
Gulf of Mexico
MEXICO
Areas Aligned During Populist Movement
South
Great Plains
Midwest
Southern states where black farmers held the most political power
Order of most political power
0 200 400
Miles

The Populist movement, or farmers' revolt, which occurred in the United States in the 1880s and 1890s, arose in response to the growing power and influence of American industry. During the Civil War northern industry expanded rapidly as a result of the production of war goods such as boots, guns, and uniforms. Railroads also grew and became the primary way in which Americans traveled and transported their manufactured goods and agricultural products. From the end of the Civil War until the mid-1880s the West boomed, with midwestern and western farmers growing and selling large amounts of grain and corn. At this time, the South was struggling to return to prewar levels of cotton production. Farming in the South had moved from the plantation system, which used large amounts of slave labor, to the sharecropping and tenant farming system, in which a number of small plots owned by white landowners and merchants were farmed by former slaves and poor white families. In the West cheap lands, sold by the railroads and the U.S. government under the Homestead Act, were farmed by small independent farmers who owned their land. By 1888, however, the boom in the West went bust. Drought caused crops to fail, and high shipping rates charged by the railroads devastated small western farmers. Things were no better in the South. The high cost of fertilizer and farm implements and the falling price of cotton caused many white and black sharecroppers to go into debt . Few railroads had been rebuilt in the South, and the ones that had been rebuilt overcharged southern farmers to ship their goods. Frustrated, many farmers, black and white, began to organize and as a result developed one of America's most amazing and dramatic movements, the Populist movement. The Populist movement was not limited to a particular geographical region or racial group; it was instead a poor people's movement. It spawned organizations like the Farmers' Alliance and the Colored Farmers' Alliance and gave rise to a new political party, the Populist Party, which undermined both the Democratic and Republican Parties. In the South the Populists threatened the ruling southern Democrats of the old Confederacy by forging alliances between black and white tenant farmers and sharecroppers and poor black and white small farmers. The movement was also successful in Texas, Louisiana, Georgia, and North Carolina. In North Carolina, for example, the Populist Party was particularly effective in fusing poor black and white farmers together as a voting bloc, which allowed them to gain control of the state legislature in 1892. In other states similar efforts were successful, and in the presidential election of 1892 black and white voters showed their power by nominating and voting in large numbers for the Populist candidate, James B. Weaver. By the presidential election of 1898, however, the Democrats had added the concerns of these farmers to their national platform, thus giving voters less reason to vote for the Populist Party. At the same time, southern Democrats succeeded in driving wedges between poor whites and blacks by stirring their old fear of "Negro rule." These tactics destroyed the fragile alliance between black and white farmers and with it any chance of black political or economic advancement until the last quarter of the twentieth century. ■

Map and Text Sources

74. Bentley, George R. *A History of the Freedmen's Bureau.* New York: Octagon Books, 1974.

Nieman, Donald G. *The Freedmen's Bureau and Black Freedom.* New York: Garland Publishing, 1994.

Oubre, Claude F. *Forty Acres and a Mule: The Freedmen's Bureau and Black Land Ownership.* Baton Rouge: Louisiana State University Press, 1978.

Pierce, Paul S. *The Freedman's Bureau; A Chapter in the History of Reconstruction.* St. Clair Shores, MI: Scholarly Press, 1970.

75. Daniel, Pete. *Breaking The Land: The Enclosure of Cotton, Tobacco, and Rice Cultures.* Urbana: University of Illinois Press, 1984.

Daniel, Pete. *The Shadow of Slavery: Peonage in the South, 1901–1969.* Urbana: University of Illinois Press, 1990.

Hurt, R. Douglas. *American Agriculture: A Brief History.* Ames: Iowa State University Press, 1994.

Raper, Arthur Franklin, and Ira De A. Reid. *Share Croppers All.* New York: Russell & Russell, 1971.

Royce, Edward Cary. *The Origins of Southern Sharecropping.* Philadelphia: Temple University Press, 1993.

76. Bowman, J. Wilson. *Americas Black & Tribal Colleges.* South Pasadena, CA: Sandcastle Publishing, 1994.

Holmes, Dwight Oliver W. *The Evolution of the Negro College.* New York: AMS Press, 1970.

77. Berry, Mary Frances. *Military Necessity and Civil Rights Policy: Black Citizenship and the Constitution, 1861–1868.* Port Washington, NY: Kennikat Press, 1977.

Perman, Michael. *Reunion without Compromise; The South and Reconstruction: 1865–1868.* Cambridge: Cambridge University Press, 1973.

Wilson, Theodore B. *The Black Codes of the South.* Montgomery: University of Alabama Press, 1965.

78. Broderick, Francis L. *Reconstruction and the American Negro, 1865–1900.* New York: Macmillan, 1969.

Clay, William L. *Just Permanent Interests: Black Americans in Congress, 1870–1992* New York: Amistad Press, 1993.

Cox, LaWanda C. Fenlason, and John H. Cox, eds. *Reconstruction: The Negro, and the New South.* New York: Harper & Row, 1973.

Cruden, Robert. *The Negro in Reconstruction.* Englewood Cliffs, NJ: Prentice-Hall, 1969.

Du Bois, William Edward Burghardt. *Black Reconstruction in America.* New York: Maxwell Macmillan International, 1992.

Fitzgerald, Michael W. *The Union League Movement in the Deep South: Politics and Agricultural Change During Reconstruction.* Baton Rouge: Louisiana State University Press, 1989.

Foner, Eric. *Freedom's Lawmakers: A Directory of Black Officeholders during Reconstruction,* rev. ed. Baton Rouge: Louisiana State University Press, 1996.

Foner, Eric. *Reconstruction: America's Unfinished Revolution, 1863–1877.* New York: Harper & Row, 1989.

Franklin, John Hope. *Reconstruction after the Civil War,* 2nd ed. Chicago: University of Chicago Press, 1994.

Litwack, Leon F. *Been in the Storm So Long: The Aftermath of Slavery.* New York: Knopf, 1979.

Maltz, Earl M. *Civil Rights, the Constitution, and Congress, 1863–1869.* Lawrence: University Press of Kansas, 1990.

Rabinowitz, Howard N., ed. *Southern Black Leaders of the Reconstruction Era.* Urbana: University of Illinois Press, 1982.

Ransom, Roger L., and Richard Sutch. *One Kind of Freedom: The Economic Consequences of Emancipation.* New York: Cambridge University Press, 1977.

Shapiro, Herbert. *White Violence and Black Response: From Reconstruction to Montgomery.* Amherst: University of Massachusetts Press, 1988.

Smith, Samuel Denny. *The Negro in Congress, 1870–1901.* Port Washington, NY: Kennikat Press, 1966.

79. Coulter, E. Merton. *The South during Reconstruction, 1865–1877.* Baton Rouge: Louisiana State University Press, 1965.

Pfanz, Harry W. "Soldiering in the South during the Reconstruction Period, 1865–*1877.*" Ph.D. dissertation, The Ohio State University, Columbus, 1958.

Rabinowitz, Howard N. *Race Relations in the Urban South, 1865–1890.* Urbana: University of Illinois Press, 1980.

Singletary, Otis A. *Negro Militia and Reconstruction.* Westport, CT: Greenwood Press, 1984.

United States, National Archives and Records Service. *Preliminary Inventory of the Records of United States Army Continental Commands, 1821–1920, Record Group 393.* Washington, DC: National Archives & Records Service, General Services Administration, 1973.

United States, President Johnson. *Message from the President of the United States.* Washington, DC: Government Printing Office, 1867.

United States War Department. *General Orders—Reconstruction.* Washington, DC, 1868.

80. Chalmers, David M. *Hooded Americanism: The First Century of the Ku Klux Klan,* 3rd ed. Durham, NC: Duke University Press, 1991.

Horn, Stanley F. *Invisible Empire: The Story of the Ku Klux Klan, 1866–1871.* New York: Haskell House, 1973.

Katz, William Loren. *The Invisible Empire: The Ku Klux Klan Impact on History.* Seattle, WA: Open Hand Publishing, 1987.

Lester, John C., and D. L. Wilson. *The Ku Klux Klan: Its Origin, Growth, and Disbandment.* New York: Neale Publishing Co., 1905.

Rable, George C. *But There Was No Peace: The Role of Violence in the Politics of Reconstruction.* Athens: University of Georgia Press, 1984.

Tourgee, Albion Winegar. *The Invisible Empire.* Baton Rouge: Louisiana State University Press, 1989.

Trelease, Allen W. *White Terror: The Ku Klux Klan Conspiracy and Southern Reconstruction.* Baton Rouge: Louisiana State University Press, 1995.

Wellman, Paul Iselin. *Spawn of Evil: The Invisible Empire of Soulless Men Which for a Generation Held the Nation in a Spell of Terror.* London: Fireside Press, 1964.

81. Davis, Lenwood G. *Blacks in the American West: A Working Bibliography,* 2nd ed. Monticello, IL: Council of Planning Librarians, 1976.

Durham, Philip, and Everett L. Jones, *The Negro Cowboys.* Lincoln: University of Nebraska Press, 1983.

Dusard, Jay. *The North American Cowboy: A Portrait.* Prescott, AZ: Consortium Press, 1983.

Hardaway, Roger D. *A Narrative Bibliography of the African-American Frontier: Blacks in the Rocky Mountain West, 1535–1912.* Lewiston, NY: Edwin Mellen Press, 1995.

Savage, W. Sherman. *Blacks in the West.* Westport, CT: Greenwood Press, 1976.

opment in the Trans-Appalachian West, 1877–1915. Urbana: University of Illinois Press, 1991.

Painter, Nell. *Exodusters: Black Migration to Kansas after Reconstruction.* New York: Norton, 1992.

Redkey, Edwin S. *Black Exodus: Black Nationalist and Back-to-Africa Movements, 1890–1910.* New Haven, CT: Yale University Press, 1969.

85. Collins, Robert O., ed. *The Partition of Africa: Illusion or Necessity?* New York: Wiley, 1969.

Forster, Stig, Wolfgang J. Mommsen, and Ronald Robinson, eds. *Bismarck, Europe, and Africa: The Berlin Africa Conference 1884–1885 and the Onset of Partition.* New York: Oxford University Press, 1988.

Gann, Lewis H., and Peter Duignan, *Colonialism in Africa, 1870–1960,* vol. 1. Cambridge: Cambridge University Press, 1969.

Hauptman, Laurence M., ed. *Reports of the Lake Mohonk Conferences on International Arbitration, 1895–1910.* Lake Mohonk, NY: The Conference, 1916.

Hauptman, Laurence M., ed. *The Lake Mohonk Conference on the Negro Question: Guide to the Annual Reports.* New York: Clearwater Publishing Company, 1975.

Hill, Adelaide Cromwell, and Martin Kilson, eds. *Apropos of Africa: Sentiments of Negro American Leaders on Africa from the 1800s to the 1950s.* London: Cass Library of African Studies, 1969.

Lewis, David Levering. T*he Race to Fashoda: European Colonialism and African Resistance in the Scramble for Africa.* London: Bloomsbury, 1988.

Maddox, Gregory. *Conquest and Resistance to Colonialism in Africa.* New York: Garland, 1993.

Mittlebeeler, Emmet V. *European Colonialism in Africa.* Washington, DC: Georgetown University, Institute of Ethnic Studies, 1961.

Wesseling, H. L. *Divide and Rule: The Partition of Africa, 1880–1914.* Westport, CT: Praeger, 1996.

86. Durden, Robert Franklin. *The Climax of Populism: The Election of 1896.* Westport, CT: Greenwood Press, 1981.

Edmonds, Helen G. *The Negro and Fusion Politics in North Carolina, 1894–1901.* Chapel Hill: University of North Carolina Press, 1951.

Goodwyn, Lawrence. *The Populist Moment: A Short History of the Agrarian Revolt in America.* New York: Oxford University Press, 1978.

Hicks, John D. *The Populist Revolt: A History of the Farmers' Alliance and the People's Party.* Westport, CT: Greenwood Press, 1981.

MAP 87

The African-American Population in the United States (1890)

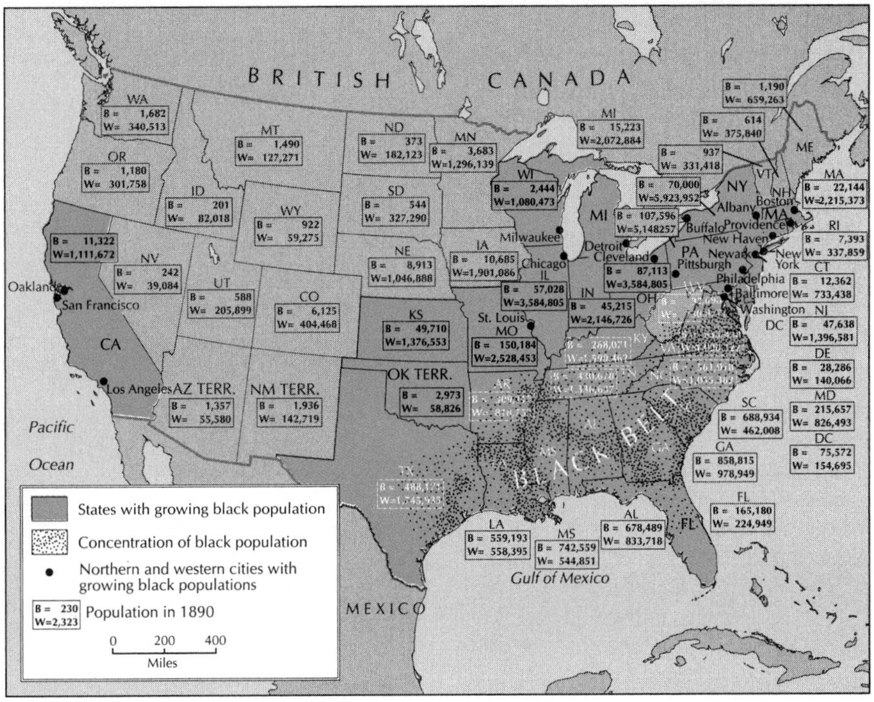
BRITISH
CANADA
WA
B = 1,682
W= 340,513
OR
B = 1,180
W= 301,758
MT
B = 1,490
W= 127,271
ID
B = 201
W= 82,018
WY
B = 922
W= 59,275
ND
B = 373
W= 182,123
SD
B = 544
W= 327,290
MN
B = 3,683
W=1,296,139
B = 11,322
W=1,111,672
NV
B = 242
W= 39,084
UT
B = 588
W= 205,899
CO
B = 6,125
W= 404,468
NE
B = 8,913
W=1,046,888
KS
B = 49,710
W=1,376,553
CA
Oakland
San Francisco
Los Angeles
AZ TERR.
B = 1,357
W= 55,580
NM TERR.
B = 1,936
W= 142,719
OK TERR.
B = 2,973
W= 58,826
Pacific
Ocean
WI
B = 2,444
W=1,080,473
IA
B = 10,685
W=1,901,086
Milwaukee
Chicago
IL
B = 57,028
W=3,584,805
St. Louis
MO
B = 150,184
W=2,528,453
MI
B = 15,223
W=2,072,884
MI
B = 107,596
W=5,148257
Detroit
Cleveland
IN
B = 45,215
W=2,146,726
OH
B = 87,113
W=3,584,805
B = 1,190
W= 659,263
B = 614
W= 375,840
B = 937
W= 331,418
ME
VT
NH
NY
B = 70,000
W=5,923,952
Albany
Boston
MA
B = 22,144
W=2,215,373
Buffalo
Providence
RI
B = 7,393
W= 337,859
New Haven
PA
Newark
New York
CT
B = 12,362
W= 733,438
Pittsburgh
Philadelphia
Baltimore
Washington
NJ
DC
B = 47,638
W=1,396,581
DE
B = 28,286
W= 140,066
MD
B = 215,657
W= 826,493
DC
B = 75,572
W= 154,695
SC
B = 688,934
W= 462,008
GA
B = 858,815
W= 978,949
FL
B = 165,180
W= 224,949
AL
B = 678,489
W= 833,718
MS
B = 742,559
W= 544,851
LA
B = 559,193
W= 558,395
BLACK BELT
Gulf of Mexico
MEXICO
States with growing black population
Concentration of black population
Northern and western cities with growing black populations
B = 230
W=2,323
Population in 1890
0 200 400
Miles

By 1890 African Americans made up 12.3 percent (7,389,000) of the United States's overall population of about 62,490,000 people. Of the approximate 7.4 million African Americans, the vast majority continued to live in the former slaveholding states of the South. They lived in what has become known as the Black Belt, an area that stretched from Maryland through the coastal plains of Virginia, North Carolina, South Carolina, Georgia, Alabama, Mississippi, and Louisiana, to east Texas. Following the Civil War, most blacks chose to remain in the South and lived on or near their old plantations. Protected by occupying Union troops and Negro state militias, most attempted to start new lives near their old homes. By 1877, however, following the collapse of Reconstruction, many blacks found freedom in the South as oppressive as slavery. As a result, beginning in 1879, thousands of blacks began leaving the South for western states like Kansas, Oklahoma, and California and midwestern and northeastern cities like Chicago, Indianapolis, Detroit, Cleveland, Pittsburgh, Philadelphia, Buffalo, New York, and Boston. Thus by 1890, many blacks freed from slavery were convinced that there was no future for them in the South, and they turned to northern and western cities, increasing the black population of these cities initially by thousands and by the turn of the century by hundreds of thousands. In 1890, however, the South still contained the majority of blacks. The lower South included the greatest number of blacks, with South Carolina containing the largest population, followed by Mississippi and Louisiana. ■

MAP 88

Thirty Years of Lynching and the New Ku Klux Klan in America (1889–1918)

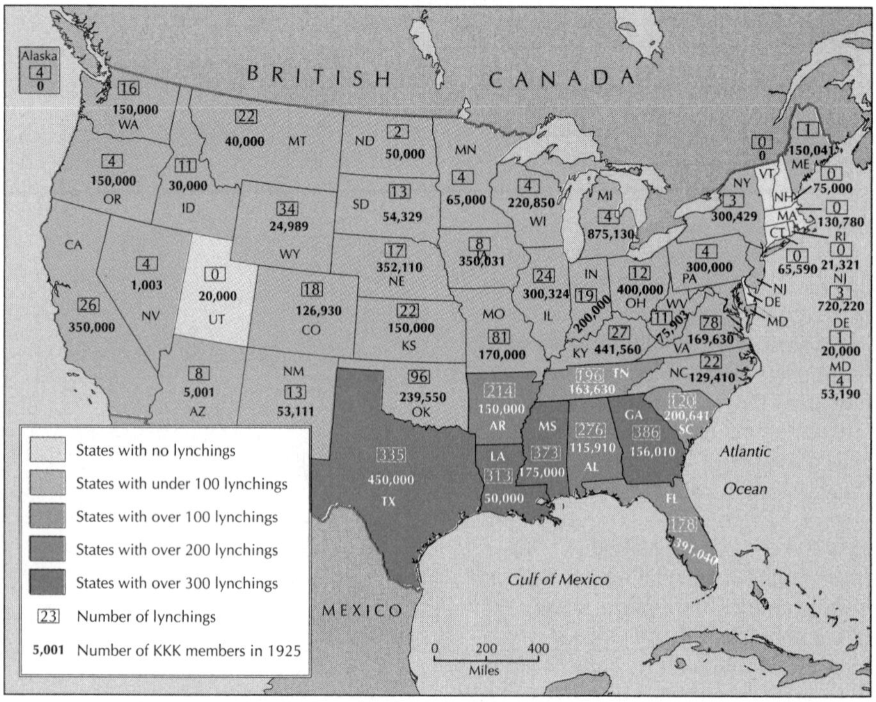
BRITISH CANADA
Alaska 4 0
WA 16 150,000
OR 4 150,000
CA 26 350,000
ID 11 30,000
NV 4 1,003
UT 0 20,000
AZ 8 5,001
MT 22 40,000
WY 34 24,989
CO 18 126,930
NM 13 53,111
ND 2 50,000
SD 13 54,329
NE 17 352,110
KS 22 150,000
OK 96 239,550
TX 335 450,000
MN 4 65,000
IA 8 350,031
MO 81 170,000
AR 214 150,000
LA 313 50,000
WI 4 220,850
IL 24 300,324
MI 4 875,130
IN 19 200,000
OH 12 400,000
KY 27 441,560
TN 196 163,630
MS 373 175,000
AL 276 115,910
GA 386 156,010
FL 178 391,040
SC 120 200,641
NC 22 129,410
VA 78 169,630
WV 11 75,903
PA 4 300,000
NY 3 300,429
VT 0 0
NH 0 75,000
ME 1 150,041
MA 0 130,780
RI 0 21,321
CT 0 65,590
NJ 3 720,220
DE 1 20,000
MD 4 53,190
MEXICO
Gulf of Mexico
Atlantic Ocean
0 200 400 Miles
States with no lynchings
States with under 100 lynchings
States with over 100 lynchings
States with over 200 lynchings
States with over 300 lynchings
23 Number of lynchings
5,001 Number of KKK members in 1925

The Ku Klux Klan was born in the South out of rage, desperation, and racism. It was a terrorist organization with the dual purpose of eliminating northern military rule and forcing blacks back into "their place" as the servants and slaves of white southerners. By the start of the twentieth century, however, the Klan had changed. It was no longer composed only of rebellious southern whites continuing the Civil War, but included northern and western whites as well, concerned about black migrants and European immigrants moving into their neighborhoods, cities, and states and taking their jobs. In 1915 after being glorified in D. W. Griffith's *Birth of a Nation,* the first major American silent film that was viewed by millions of Americans, the Klan emerged as a popular national organization. As a result of the film, black migration, and European immigration, Klan membership grew to 4 million by 1925, with its targets expanded to include organized labor, Germans, Irish Catholics, and Jews. The Klan included prominent elected officials, authorities, and judges. In fact, being a Klan member was almost necessary to win many local, state, and national elections. Two of the most famous and influential members of the Klan during this period were the Twenty-Ninth President of the United States, Warren G. Harding, sworn in as a member in the White House, and Supreme Court Justice Hugo Black, who served on the High Court until 1971. As membership grew, violence against blacks and other targeted groups skyrocketed. The thirty years between 1889 and 1919 saw thousands of lynchings, rapes, beatings, and murders go unprosecuted throughout the United States. During this time white vigilantes, many of whom were Klan members, lynched a total of 3,200 blacks throughout the United States. Black organizations like the National Association for the Advancement of Colored People (NAACP) and the National Urban League (NUL) kept records of these atrocities and pressured the U.S. government to end this lawlessness. ■

MAP 89

Plessy v. Ferguson and the Spread of Jim Crow Laws in the South (1896–1900)

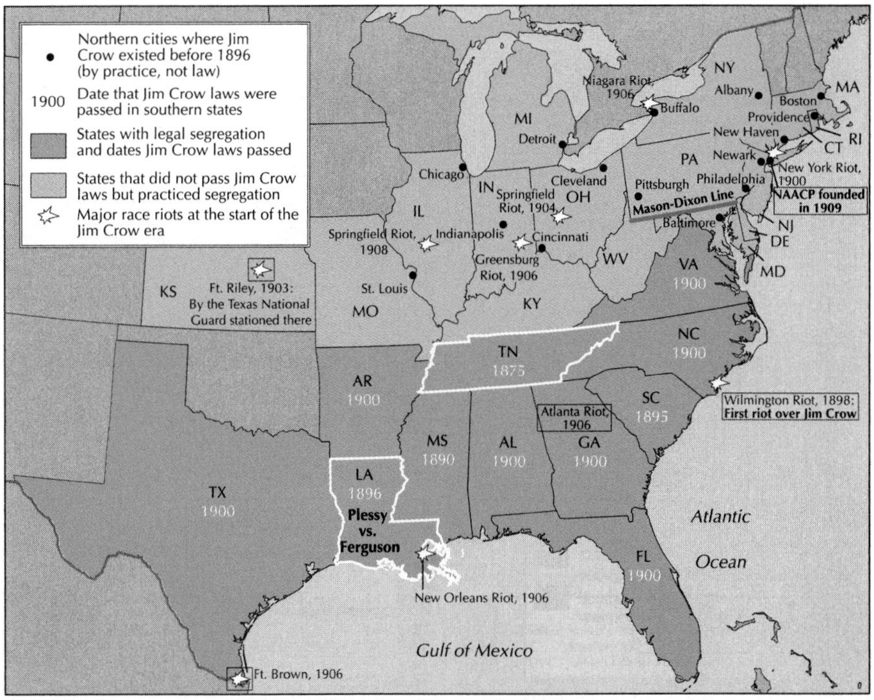
Northern cities where Jim Crow existed before 1896 (by practice, not law)
1900 Date that Jim Crow laws were passed in southern states
States with legal segregation and dates Jim Crow laws passed
States that did not pass Jim Crow laws but practiced segregation
Major race riots at the start of the Jim Crow era
KS
Ft. Riley, 1903: By the Texas National Guard stationed there
MO
St. Louis
IL
Chicago
Springfield Riot, 1908
IN
Indianapolis
Springfield Riot, 1904
Greensburg Riot, 1906
Cincinnati
Cleveland
OH
MI
Detroit
Niagara Riot, 1906
Buffalo
NY
Albany
Boston
MA
Providence
RI
New Haven
CT
Newark
New York Riot, 1900
NAACP founded in 1909
PA
Pittsburgh
Philadelphia
Mason-Dixon Line
Baltimore
NJ
DE
MD
WV
KY
VA
1900
NC
1900
TN
1875
AR
1900
SC
1895
Wilmington Riot, 1898: First riot over Jim Crow
Atlanta Riot, 1906
MS
1890
AL
1900
GA
1900
LA
1896
Plessy vs. Ferguson
TX
1900
New Orleans Riot, 1906
FL
1900
Atlantic Ocean
Gulf of Mexico
Ft. Brown, 1906

On January 1, 1896 the Supreme Court ruled on the *Plessy v. Ferguson* case and established the doctrine of "separate but equal" as the law of the land for the next fifty-eight years. The case involved a black man by the name of Homer Adolph Plessy, who was traveling from New Orleans, Louisiana, to Covington, Louisiana. Plessy refused to ride in a railcar marked for blacks only. He was arrested and brought to trial under one of Louisiana's Jim Crow laws, which mandated separate public facilities, including transportation, for whites and blacks. He was convicted under the Louisiana law in the court of Judge Ferguson and appealed his decision to the Supreme Court. In 1896 the Supreme Court ruled that the Fourteenth Amendment required that accommodations for blacks be equal to those of whites and that as long as Louisiana's separate facilities were equal, they were legal. Later the same year, blacks in North Carolina who had been successful through fusion politics in limiting Jim Crow laws began also to lose power to segregationists as southern Democrats destroyed the Populist Party and fusion politics by frightening southern poor whites with predictions of "Negro rule." These fear tactics turned violent two years later during the Wilmington riot, which began after a black newspaper criticized the tactics of whites to impose Jim Crow laws in North Carolina, which resulted in the destruction of the newspaper along with several black neighborhoods. This bloody and deadly riot was followed by one in New York in 1900 and another in Atlanta in 1906 and violently ushered in the Jim Crow era. These riots and the decision by the U.S. Supreme Court to uphold Louisiana's Jim Crow laws, a decision that legitimized all similar laws throughout the South, began a period of racial segregation that lasted until 1954. ■

MAP 90

"Smoked Yankees": Black Soldiers and the Spanish-American War (1898)

By 1898 America had become a vast continental nation. It was industrialized, and like similar nations in Europe, it had become imperialistic. One of the first tests for this new imperial power was the Spanish-American War. The war increased America's colonial holdings by adding Puerto Rico, the Hawaiian Islands, Guam, and the Philippines, and by placing Cuba under its protection. American journalists, using "yellow journalism" to characterize the Spanish as dark-skinned beasts, were one immediate cause of the war. Under the pretense of liberating the poor subjugated Cubans and Filipinos from the brutal Spanish, and in retaliation for the sinking of the *U.S.S. Maine* in February of 1898, U.S. troops defeated the Spanish in Cuba and the Philippines. Among those troops were members of the all-black Twenty-Fourth and Twenty-Fifth Infantry and the Ninth and Tenth Cavalry, who were known as the Buffalo Soldiers. They were called "Smoked Yankees" by the Spanish because of their dark skin and were respected for their combat ability. In Cuba they fought at Las Guásimas, El Caney, Kettle Hill, and San Juan Hill. The "K" Troop of the Ninth Cavalry is famous for saving Teddy Roosevelt and his Rough Riders at the battle of San Juan Hill. Black troops also fought in the Philippines at Manila Bay. Again black troops served their country courageously, and again they were devalued and their feats unrewarded. Following the war, members of the Twenty-Fourth and Twenty-Fifth Infantry were stationed in the Philippines and Hawaii. In the Philippines they would bear witness to the mistreatment and deaths of over 200,000 Filipinos who rebelled against American rule in 1905. This massive loss of Filipino lives and the mistreatment of black troops by white American soldiers and civilians prompted some black soldiers to mutiny and join the Filipinos in their struggle for freedom. Poor treatment of these soldiers by whites would also lead to a mutiny in Brownsville, Texas, after local whites beat one of their men. Members of the Twenty-Fourth and Twenty-Fifth infantry remained stationed in the Philippines and Hawaii and would be part of America's first line of defense against the Japanese during World War II. ■

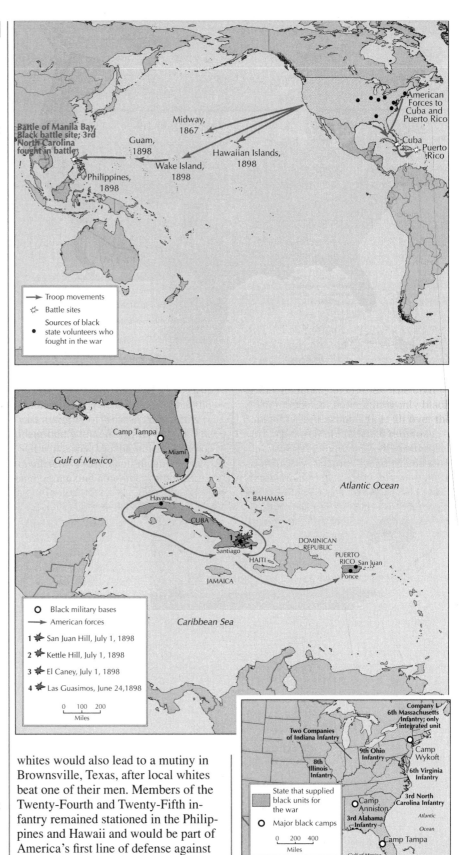

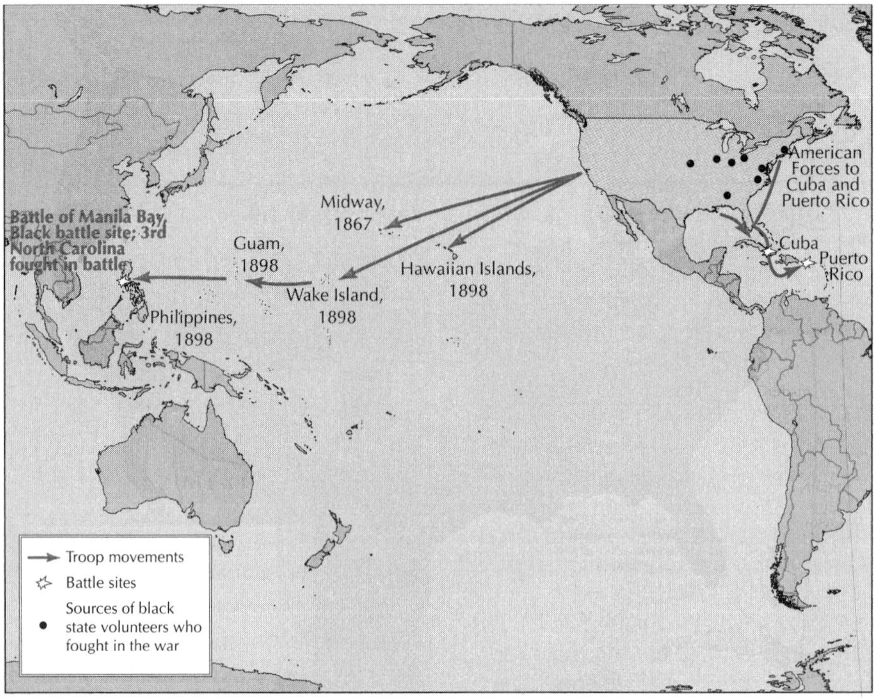

Battle of Manila Bay, Black battle site; 3rd North Carolina fought in battle
Guam, 1898
Midway, 1867
Philippines, 1898
Wake Island, 1898
Hawaiian Islands, 1898
American Forces to Cuba and Puerto Rico
Cuba
Puerto Rico
Troop movements
Battle sites
Sources of black state volunteers who fought in the war

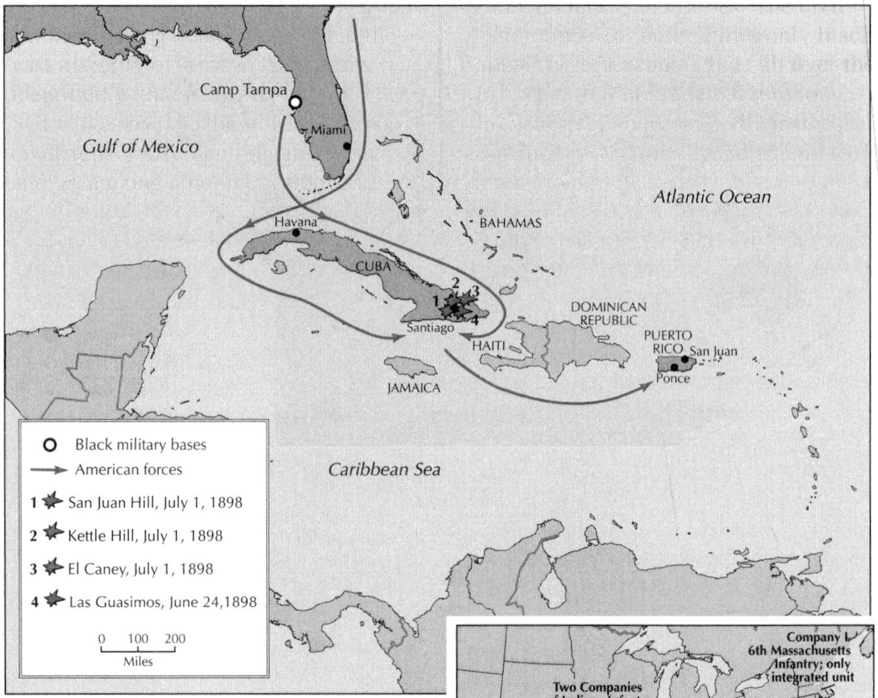

Camp Tampa
Miami
Gulf of Mexico
Atlantic Ocean
Havana
BAHAMAS
CUBA
Santiago
HAITI
DOMINICAN REPUBLIC
PUERTO RICO
San Juan
Ponce
JAMAICA
Caribbean Sea
Black military bases
American forces
1 San Juan Hill, July 1, 1898
2 Kettle Hill, July 1, 1898
3 El Caney, July 1, 1898
4 Las Guasimos, June 24,1898
0 100 200
Miles

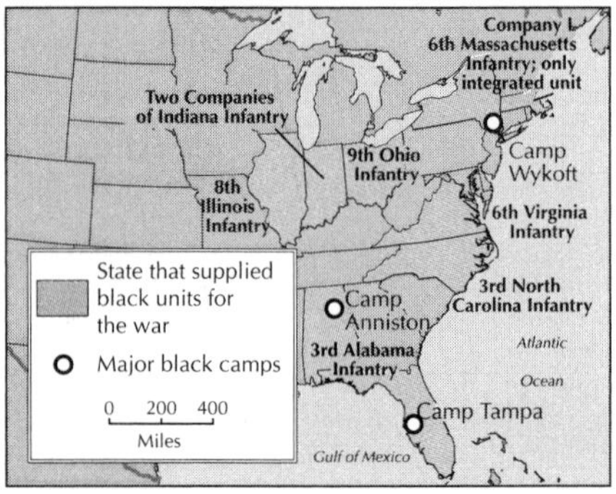

Company L 6th Massachusetts Infantry; only integrated unit
Two Companies of Indiana Infantry
9th Ohio Infantry
Camp Wykoft
8th Illinois Infantry
6th Virginia Infantry
3rd North Carolina Infantry
Camp Anniston
3rd Alabama Infantry
Camp Tampa
State that supplied black units for the war
Major black camps
0 200 400
Miles
Atlantic Ocean
Gulf of Mexico

MAP 91

The Rise of the National Association for the Advancement of Colored People (1909)

In response to Jim Crow laws, lynchings, and black migration to cities, two major organizations were founded between 1909 and 1910. These were started by blacks and whites to improve race relations, end racial violence and discrimination, and assist northern blacks in finding jobs and housing and generally adjusting to urban life. The first organization, founded in 1909 by W. E. B. Du Bois and other prominent leaders, was the National Association for the Advancement of Colored People (NAACP). Begun in 1905 as the Niagara Movement in Niagara Falls, NY by William Monroe Trotter and Du Bois, the organization held its first official meeting in New York City in 1909. Black and white ministers, social workers, publishers, and civil rights activists gathered to revive the old abolitionist fervor. All agreed that conditions for blacks in America were as bad as they had been at any time in American history. They agreed to continue the movement and to pursue, through legal means, the protection of African-American civil rights. Booker T. Washington, one of the most influential black leaders of the time, disagreed with the philosophy of the NAACP and refused to attend. In spite of this, however, the organization grew and spread throughout the United States, with New York City as its national headquarters. By 1980 the NAACP was divided into seven districts in the United States with 1,372 branches. It also had established branches in six foreign countries including India, Sweden, Germany, France, Brazil, and Panama. ■

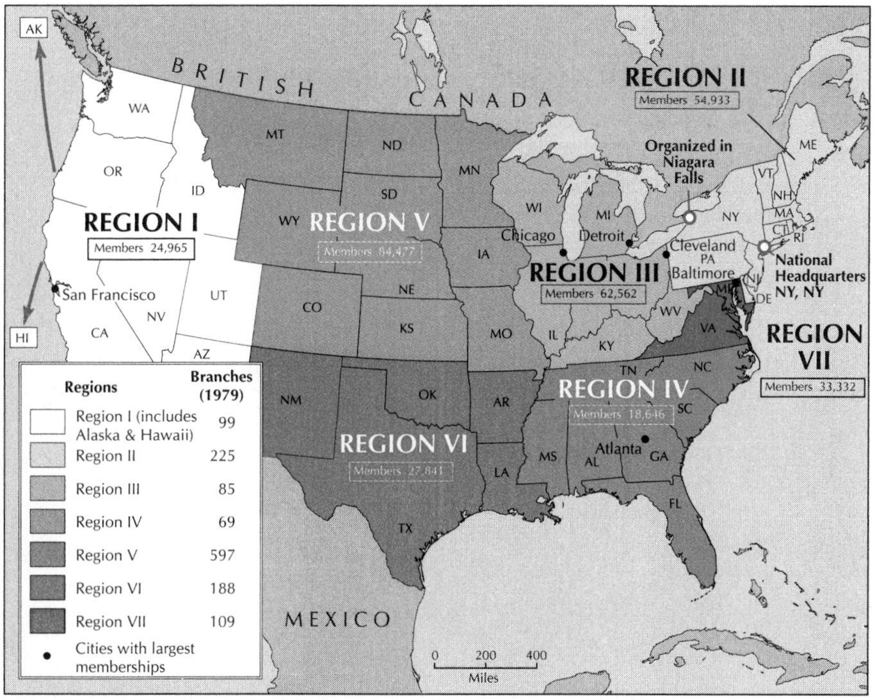
AK
HI
BRITISH
CANADA
MEXICO
REGION I
Members 24,965
REGION II
Members 54,933
REGION III
Members 62,562
REGION IV
Members 18,646
REGION V
Members 84,477
REGION VI
Members 27,841
REGION VII
Members 33,332
Organized in Niagara Falls
National Headquarters NY, NY
San Francisco
Chicago
Detroit
Cleveland
Baltimore
Atlanta
WA
OR
ID
CA
NV
UT
AZ
MT
WY
CO
NM
ND
SD
NE
KS
OK
TX
MN
IA
MO
AR
LA
WI
MI
IL
KY
TN
MS
AL
GA
FL
SC
NC
VA
WV
PA
NY
VT
NH
ME
MA
CT
RI
NJ
DE
MD
Regions
Branches (1979)
Region I (includes Alaska & Hawaii) 99
Region II 225
Region III 85
Region IV 69
Region V 597
Region VI 188
Region VII 109
Cities with largest memberships
0 200 400
Miles

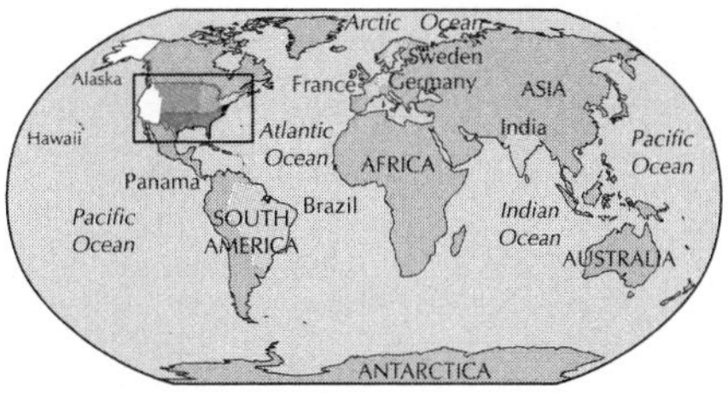
Arctic Ocean
Sweden
Germany
France
ASIA
Alaska
Hawaii
Atlantic Ocean
AFRICA
India
Pacific Ocean
Panama
Brazil
Pacific Ocean
SOUTH AMERICA
Indian Ocean
AUSTRALIA
ANTARCTICA

MAP 92

The Rise of the National Urban League (1910)

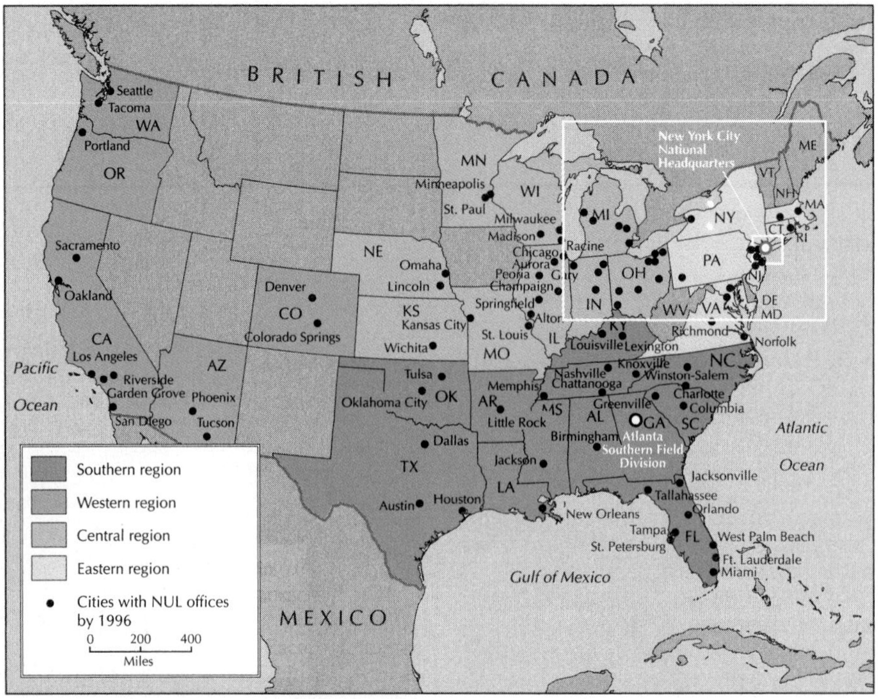
BRITISH CANADA
MEXICO
Pacific Ocean
Atlantic Ocean
Gulf of Mexico
New York City National Headquarters
Atlanta Southern Field Division
Southern region
Western region
Central region
Eastern region
Cities with NUL offices by 1996
0 200 400
Miles
WA
OR
CA
AZ
CO
NE
KS
OK
TX
MN
WI
MI
IL
IN
OH
KY
MO
AR
LA
MS
AL
GA
SC
NC
VA
WV
PA
NY
NJ
DE
MD
CT
RI
MA
VT
NH
ME
FL
Seattle
Tacoma
Portland
Sacramento
Oakland
Los Angeles
Riverside
Garden Grove
San Diego
Phoenix
Tucson
Denver
Colorado Springs
Omaha
Lincoln
Kansas City
Wichita
Tulsa
Oklahoma City
Dallas
Austin
Houston
Minneapolis
St. Paul
Milwaukee
Madison
Racine
Chicago
Aurora
Peoria
Gary
Champaign
Springfield
Alton
St. Louis
Louisville
Lexington
Memphis
Nashville
Knoxville
Chattanooga
Winston-Salem
Charlotte
Columbia
Greenville
Little Rock
Birmingham
Jackson
New Orleans
Tallahassee
Jacksonville
Orlando
Tampa
St. Petersburg
West Palm Beach
Ft. Lauderdale
Miami
Richmond
Norfolk

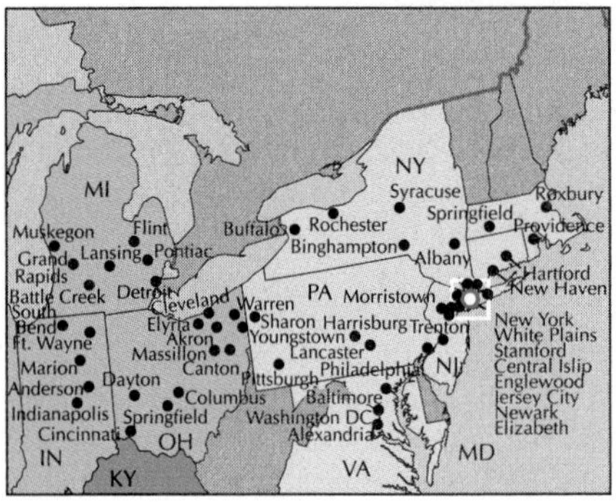
MI
NY
PA
NJ
MD
VA
OH
IN
KY
Muskegon
Flint
Grand Rapids
Lansing
Pontiac
Battle Creek
Detroit
South Bend
Ft. Wayne
Marion
Anderson
Indianapolis
Cincinnati
Springfield
Dayton
Columbus
Cleveland
Elyria
Akron
Massillon
Canton
Warren
Sharon
Youngstown
Pittsburgh
Buffalo
Rochester
Syracuse
Binghampton
Albany
Springfield
Roxbury
Providence
Hartford
New Haven
Morristown
Harrisburg
Trenton
Lancaster
Philadelphia
Baltimore
Washington DC
Alexandria
New York
White Plains
Stamford
Central Islip
Englewood
Jersey City
Newark
Elizabeth

A year after the establishment of the NAACP, the National Urban League (NUL) was founded when three New York-based organizations merged in 1910. The NUL was founded by white and black reformers living in New York City. These men and women became alarmed by the abuses against southern black migrants, particularly young women, who were often taken advantage of and tricked or forced into prostitution by unscrupulous whites and blacks familiar with city life. The first merging organization, founded in 1905 by Mrs. Frances A. Keller, was known as the National League for the Protection of Colored Women (NLPCW). This organization was primarily concerned with keeping black women from the South from being sexually abused or exploited. The second, founded in the same year by Mr. William H. Baldwin, Jr., was called the Committee for Improving the Industrial Conditions of Negroes in New York (CIICN). This organization was made up of a number of local black and white civic, religious, and business leaders who were concerned about the economic needs of the black community. The third, founded earlier in 1910 by Mrs. Ruth Standish Baldwin, the widow of William H. Baldwin, was known as the Committee of Urban Conditions (CUC). The NLPCW and the CIICN both initially worked to discourage southern blacks from moving north by informing southern ministers and southern black newspapers of the horrors of urban living. As it became clear that this was not working, the two organizations began to work to improve the economic, educational, and health problems of those blacks who continued to move north, since many ended up in ghettos where these problems were more acute. When the CUC joined the NLPCW and CIICN to create the NUL in 1910, the newly formed organization held as its mission to assist African Americans migrating to northern, midwestern, and western cities in locating jobs, schooling, and housing. By 1992 there were 112 NUL affiliates in the United States. These affiliates, found in cities all over the United States, are grouped into four basic regions: the Central Region, which contains 40 affiliates; the Eastern Region, which contains 30 affiliates; the Southern Region, which contains 29 affiliates; and the Western Region, which contains 13 affiliates. ■

MAP 93

The Black Exodus: The Great Migration of African Americans from the American South (1900–1929)

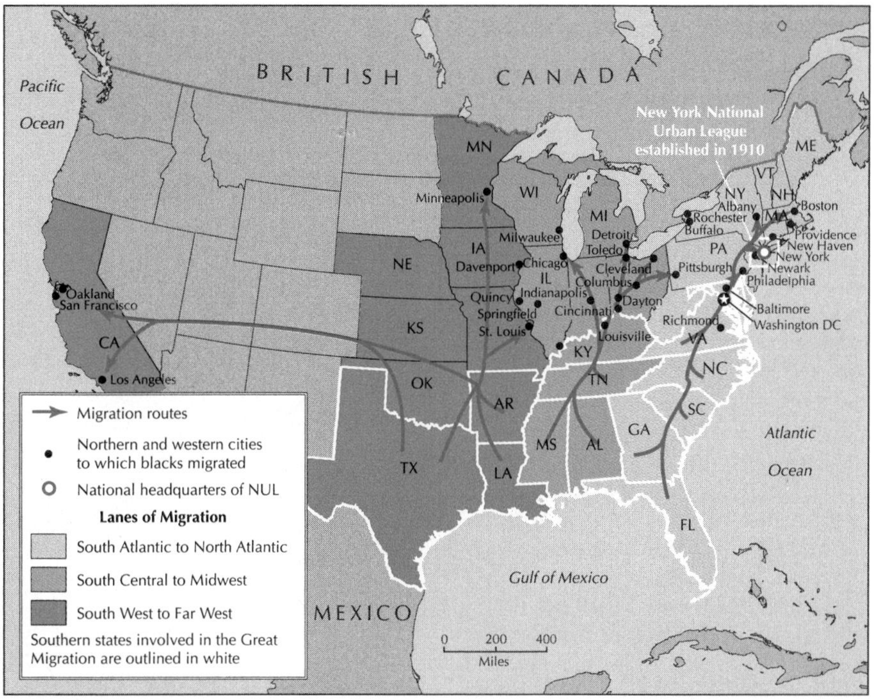
BRITISH CANADA
Pacific Ocean
Atlantic Ocean
Gulf of Mexico
MEXICO
New York National Urban League established in 1910
MN
WI
MI
IA
NE
KS
OK
TX
AR
LA
MS
AL
IL
KY
TN
GA
FL
SC
NC
VA
PA
NY
VT
NH
MA
ME
CA
Minneapolis
Milwaukee
Detroit
Toledo
Davenport
Chicago
Cleveland
Columbus
Indianapolis
Dayton
Quincy
Springfield
St. Louis
Cincinnati
Louisville
Pittsburgh
Richmond
Albany
Rochester
Buffalo
Boston
Providence
New Haven
New York
Newark
Philadelphia
Baltimore
Washington DC
Oakland
San Francisco
Los Angeles
Migration routes
Northern and western cities to which blacks migrated
National headquarters of NUL
Lanes of Migration
South Atlantic to North Atlantic
South Central to Midwest
South West to Far West
Southern states involved in the Great Migration are outlined in white
0 200 400
Miles

After the collapse of Reconstruction in 1877, there was a continuous stream of blacks leaving the South for the promise of a better life in the North or West. Three lanes of migration developed, and by the start of World War I, they were filled with thousands of blacks seeking employment in the growing war industries of northeastern, midwestern, and far western cities. The first lane of black migration was between the Southeast and the Northeast, the second between the middle South and the Midwest, and the third between the old Southwest and the Far West and Western Midwest. In the Southeast, blacks left Virginia, North Carolina, South Carolina, Georgia, and Florida for mid-Atlantic and New England cities like New York, Boston, Newark, Philadelphia, and Washington, D.C. In the middle South, blacks left Kentucky, Tennessee, Alabama, and Mississippi for the midwestern cities of Chicago, Milwaukee, Cincinnati, Cleveland, and Indianapolis. Finally, in the old southwest, they left Texas, Louisiana, and Arkansas for the Pacific coast, including Seattle, Portland (Oregon), and especially Los Angeles. This movement became the flood that made up the first phase of the Great Migration, which lasted from 1914 to 1929. As World War I came to an end in 1918 and whites and blacks returned from Europe, job opportunities declined for blacks. These blacks previously found work due to the lack of manpower at home during the war. As jobs became more scarce, the flood slowed but did not stop. Blacks were still attracted by the wonders of the Harlem Renaissance and driven by a need for security from the brutality of whites in the Jim Crow South. ■

MAP 94

Major African American Training Centers in the United States and Battle Sites in Europe during World War I (1917–1918)

When the United States entered World War I in 1917, as with all previous wars, African Americans were among the first to volunteer to serve. About 2 million blacks registered for the draft, and over 400,000 were inducted into the armed services. These soldiers joined the Army because the Navy, Coast Guard, and Marines refused to allow them to enlist. Of the total who served, 200,000 served overseas, 50,000 of whom saw combat. More than 3,900 were killed or wounded. The majority of black soldiers were forced by racism in the Army to serve in service units such as the quartermasters, the stevedores, and the pioneer infantrymen, who were responsible for cooking, loading and unloading supplies, digging latrines, and burying the dead killed in battle. Most were part of the Twenty-Third Division while in training in the United States before being reassigned to the French or the Ninety-Second and Ninety-Third Divisions of the U.S. Expeditionary Forces in France, under General John J. Pershing. There were several all-black units, including the Twentieth Engineer Regiment, Tenth Cavalry, 805th Pioneer Infantry, 315th Pioneer Regiment, Fifteenth Infantry Regiment, and four combat regiments: the 369th, 370th, 371st, and 372nd. Most of these troops were trained at Camp Wadsworth, in Spartanburg, South Carolina, before being sent to France. All black troops served under white officers due to the Army's lack of interest in training or commissioning black officers. This would not change until late 1917. At that time, the U.S. government started several ROTC and junior ROTC programs at historically black colleges and universities around the country. It also established a separate officers' training school for black officers at Fort Des Moines, Iowa, after being pressured by black civilian leaders to train blacks to lead black troops. By the end of World War I several training camps would be established on military bases around the

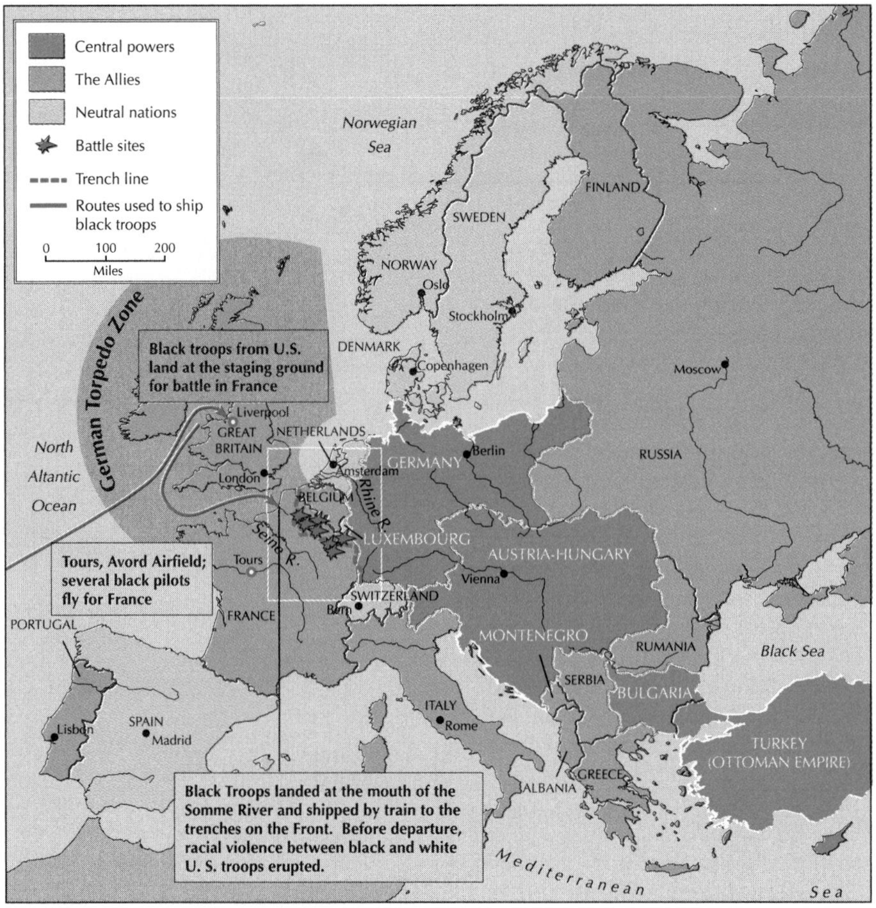
Central powers
The Allies
Neutral nations
Battle sites
Trench line
Routes used to ship black troops
0 100 200
Miles
Norwegian Sea
German Torpedo Zone
Black troops from U.S. land at the staging ground for battle in France
North Atlantic Ocean
Tours, Avord Airfield; several black pilots fly for France
Black Troops landed at the mouth of the Somme River and shipped by train to the trenches on the Front. Before departure, racial violence between black and white U. S. troops erupted.
FINLAND
SWEDEN
NORWAY
Oslo
Stockholm
DENMARK
Copenhagen
Moscow
Liverpool
GREAT BRITAIN
NETHERLANDS
London
Amsterdam
Berlin
GERMANY
RUSSIA
BELGIUM
Rhine R.
Seine R.
LUXEMBOURG
Tours
AUSTRIA-HUNGARY
Vienna
SWITZERLAND
Bern
FRANCE
PORTUGAL
MONTENEGRO
RUMANIA
Black Sea
SERBIA
BULGARIA
ITALY
Rome
SPAIN
Madrid
Lisbon
TURKEY (OTTOMAN EMPIRE)
GREECE
ALBANIA
Mediterranean Sea

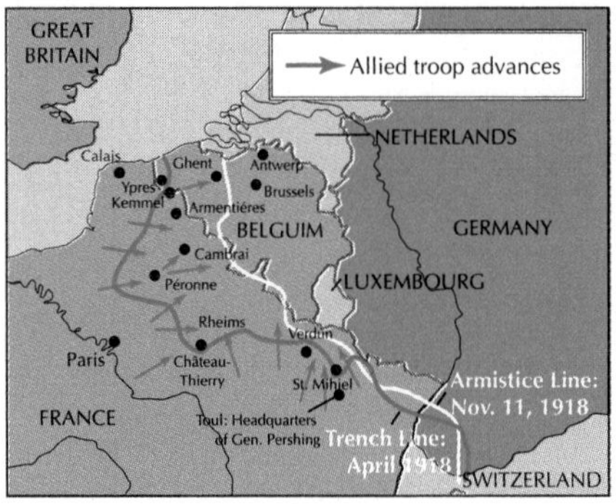
GREAT BRITAIN
Allied troop advances
NETHERLANDS
Calais
Ghent
Antwerp
Ypres
Kemmel
Brussels
Armentières
GERMANY
BELGUIM
Cambrai
Péronne
LUXEMBOURG
Rheims
Verdun
Paris
Château-Thierry
St. Mihiel
Armistice Line: Nov. 11, 1918
FRANCE
Toul: Headquarters of Gen. Pershing
Trench Line: April 1918
SWITZERLAND

country. By the end of the war more than 639 black officers were commissioned and would play a major role in leading black troops during World War II. In 1917, black troops were transported to the battlefields of France from New York by ship to the northern coast of France and then by train to the front. Once there, many, particularly the 369th Harlem Hell Fighters, would eventually fight side by side in the trenches with the French and with African peoples including the Senegalese and the Moroccans, who were also used by the French to defend France. When the Allies began to gain the upper hand in March 1918, the Germans launched a major offensive to drive the Allies out of their trenches and seize France's ports on the English Channel. In the face of disaster the all-black 369th, under the command of the French general Ferdinand Foch, halted the German advance at Cantigny. In May 1918, as the Germans again attempted to break through the Allied lines at Chateau-Thierry and Belleau Wood, they were again stopped with the assistance of the all-black combat units of the Ninety-Third Division. Wherever other American forces traveled in Europe, black soldiers accompanied them as either combat or service units. By June 1918, these troops helped to drive back the Germans at the Meuse River and the Argonne Forest. The 369th not only drove back the Germans but were the first Allied forces to reach the Rhine River in 1918. By the end of the war the 369th had earned the distinction of being in the trenches in France longer than any other American unit, 191 days. At the end of World War I, three of the four regiments of the Ninety-Third Infantry

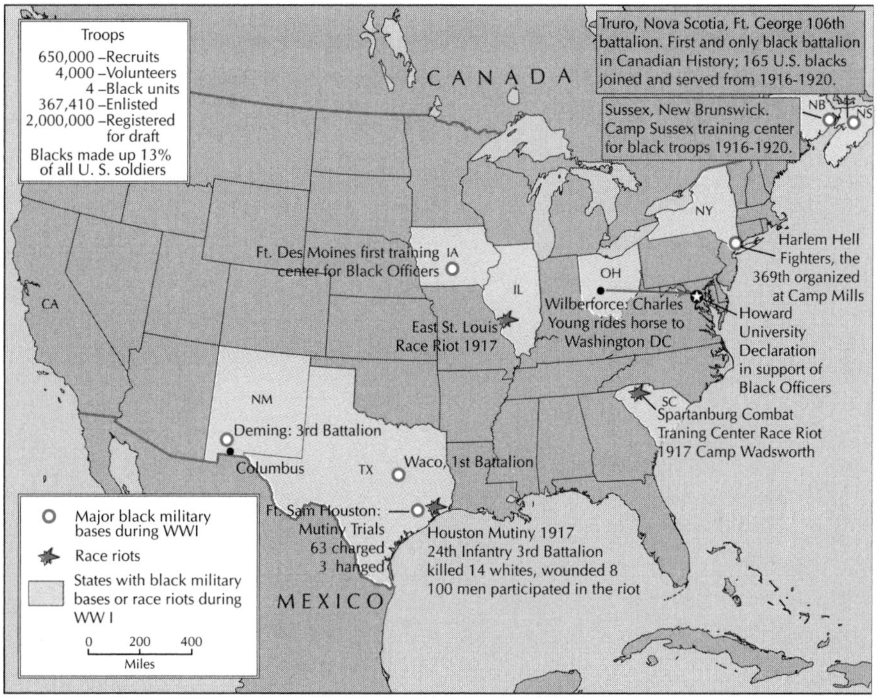
Troops
650,000 –Recruits
4,000 –Volunteers
4 –Black units
367,410 –Enlisted
2,000,000 –Registered for draft
Blacks made up 13% of all U. S. soldiers
CANADA
Truro, Nova Scotia, Ft. George 106th battalion. First and only black battalion in Canadian History; 165 U.S. blacks joined and served from 1916-1920.
Sussex, New Brunswick. Camp Sussex training center for black troops 1916-1920.
NB
NS
NY
Harlem Hell Fighters, the 369th organized at Camp Mills
Ft. Des Moines first training center for Black Officers
IA
IL
OH
CA
Wilberforce: Charles Young rides horse to Washington DC
Howard University Declaration in support of Black Officers
East St. Louis Race Riot 1917
NM
SC
Spartanburg Combat Traning Center Race Riot 1917 Camp Wadsworth
Deming: 3rd Battalion
Columbus
TX
Waco, 1st Battalion
Ft. Sam Houston: Mutiny Trials 63 charged 3 hanged
Houston Mutiny 1917 24th Infantry 3rd Battalion killed 14 whites, wounded 8 100 men participated in the riot
MEXICO
Major black military bases during WWI
Race riots
States with black military bases or race riots during WW I
0 200 400
Miles

Division and a company from the Fourth Regiment received the Croix de Guerre, the French Medal of Honor. Privates Henry Johnson and Needham Roberts of the Ninety-Third's 369th Harlem Hell Fighters each received individual Croix de Guerres for heroism and returned to the United States as international war heroes. The 370th Eighth Illinois commanded by black officers received more citations than any other American regiment in France. The Ninety-Second Division's First Battalion of the 367th Infantry Rattle Snakes also received the French Medal of Honor. Although black troops served with distinction in Europe, at home they were still seen by white Americans as inferior, second-class citizens. The war, however, showed these black soldiers that there were other peoples of the world who respected and valued them. The war introduced many of them for the first time to Europe, particularly France, and enlightened them about the opportunities for blacks outside the borders of the United States. ■

MAP 95

The Red Summer of 1919

During World War I, large numbers of black and white migrants had moved to cities in the North and West to take jobs in the war industries. When the war ended, most Americans wanted a return to "normalcy," which meant that blacks were expected to give up their new high-paying industrial jobs to returning white soldiers and continue their status as second-class citizens. However, black workers were not willing to give up their jobs, and returning black soldiers were not willing to be second-class citizens. The black soldiers who returned from Europe were not the same men who left. In Europe many blacks had experienced life without segregation or American racism for the first time. When not on base, they were allowed to mix freely with the French and others. So profound was this feeling of being free and being treated with respect that some remained in Europe after the war. Although the blacks who did return to the United States had changed significantly, by and large the society they returned to had not changed. Upon returning home, many blacks found themselves unable to wear their uniforms in public for fear of harassment, beatings, and lynchings. Even when news of their heroic feats in France were made known, it served only to enrage whites, rather than to impress them. Many blacks wanted not only social change but political and economic change, and they were prepared to fight to secure those changes. Thus when the two views collided in the summer of 1919, more than 30 violent race riots erupted in major cities all over the United States. The summer, sometimes called the "Red Summer," earned its nickname from the bloody confrontations in which many whites and blacks were injured or killed. ■

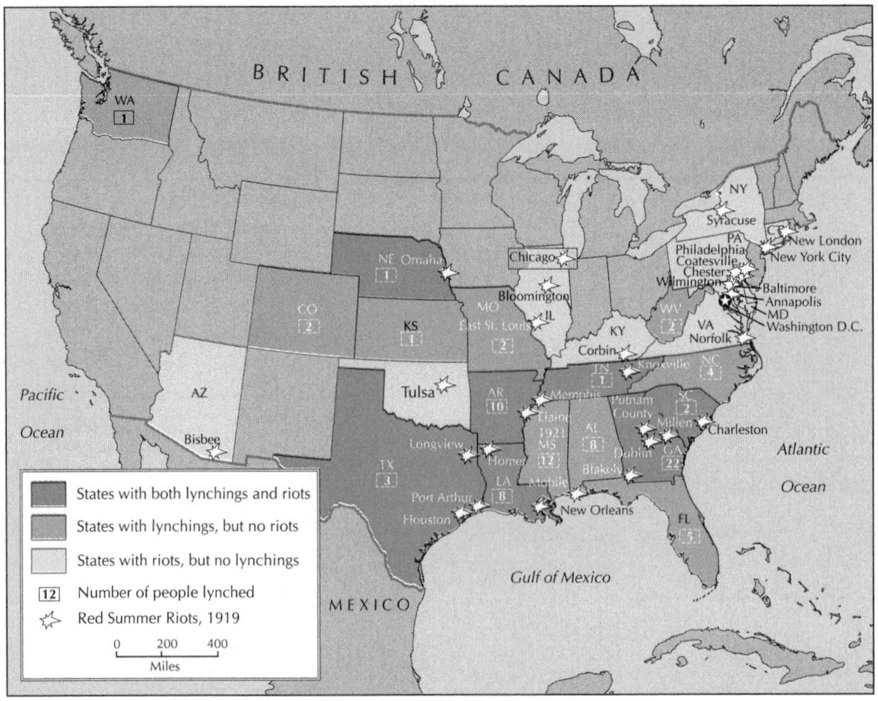
BRITISH CANADA
WA 1
NE Omaha 1
CO 2
KS 1
MO East St. Louis 2
Chicago
Bloomington
IL
KY
Corbin
WV 2
VA Norfolk
NY Syracuse
PA Philadelphia Coatesville Chester Wilmington
CT New London
New York City
Baltimore
Annapolis
MD
Washington D.C.
TN 1 Knoxville
NC 4
SC 2
Charleston
Putnam County
Millen
Dublin
GA 22
Blakely
AL 8
MS 12
Elaine 1921
Memphis
AR 10
Homer
LA 8
Mobile
New Orleans
FL 5
Tulsa
TX 3 Longview Port Arthur Houston
AZ Bisbee
Pacific Ocean
Atlantic Ocean
Gulf of Mexico
MEXICO
States with both lynchings and riots
States with lynchings, but no riots
States with riots, but no lynchings
12 Number of people lynched
Red Summer Riots, 1919
0 200 400 Miles

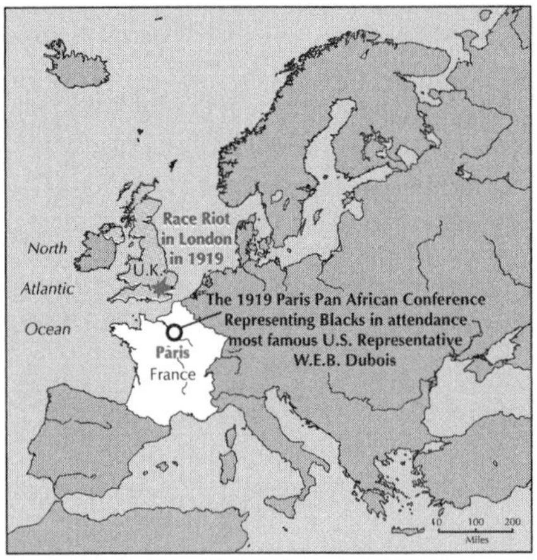
North Atlantic Ocean
Race Riot in London in 1919
U.K.
The 1919 Paris Pan African Conference Representing Blacks in attendance most famous U.S. Representative W.E.B. Dubois
Paris
France
0 100 200 Miles

MAP 96

Black Women, the Suffrage Movement, and the Nineteenth Amendment (1920)

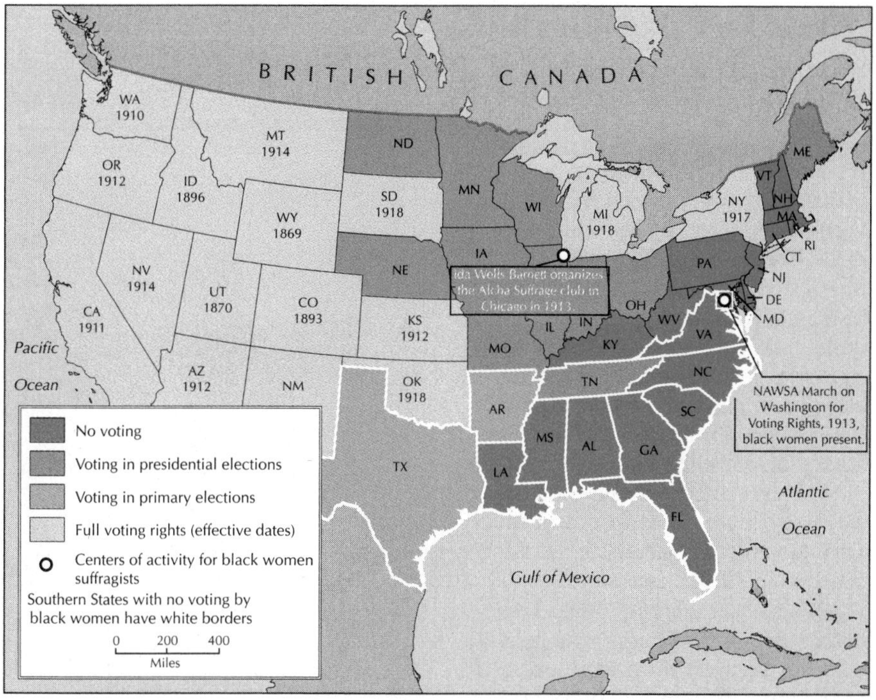
BRITISH
CANADA
WA 1910
OR 1912
ID 1896
MT 1914
WY 1869
NV 1914
UT 1870
CO 1893
CA 1911
AZ 1912
NM
ND
SD 1918
NE
KS 1912
OK 1918
TX
MN
WI
IA
MI 1918
IL
IN
OH
MO
AR
LA
MS
AL
GA
TN
KY
WV
VA
NC
SC
FL
PA
NY 1917
VT
NH
MA
ME
RI
CT
NJ
DE
MD
Ida Wells Barnett organizes the Alpha Suffrage club in Chicago in 1913.
NAWSA March on Washington for Voting Rights, 1913, black women present.
Pacific Ocean
Atlantic Ocean
Gulf of Mexico
No voting
Voting in presidential elections
Voting in primary elections
Full voting rights (effective dates)
Centers of activity for black women suffragists
Southern States with no voting by black women have white borders
0 200 400
Miles

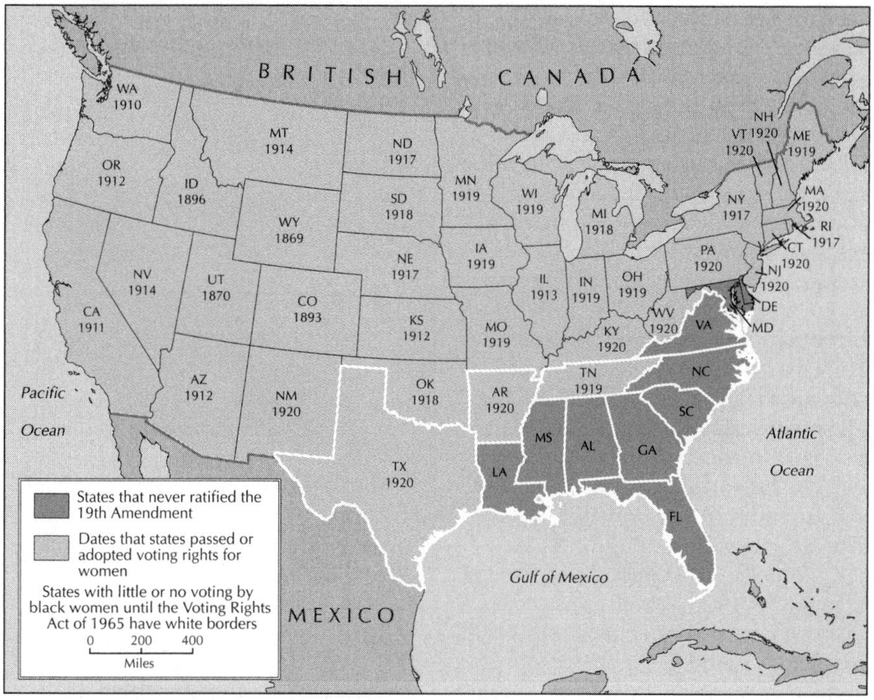
BRITISH
CANADA
MEXICO
WA 1910
OR 1912
ID 1896
MT 1914
WY 1869
NV 1914
UT 1870
CO 1893
CA 1911
AZ 1912
NM 1920
ND 1917
SD 1918
NE 1917
KS 1912
OK 1918
TX 1920
MN 1919
WI 1919
IA 1919
MI 1918
IL 1913
IN 1919
OH 1919
MO 1919
AR 1920
KY 1920
TN 1919
WV 1920
VA
NC
SC
GA
AL
MS
LA
FL
PA 1920
NY 1917
NH
VT 1920
ME 1919
MA 1920
RI 1917
CT
NJ 1920
DE
MD
Pacific Ocean
Atlantic Ocean
Gulf of Mexico
States that never ratified the 19th Amendment
Dates that states passed or adopted voting rights for women
States with little or no voting by black women until the Voting Rights Act of 1965 have white borders
0 200 400
Miles

When the Fifteenth Amendment was ratified in 1870, it gave suffrage to all black and white males in the old Confederacy, most of whom had been denied this privilege before and during the Civil War. The amendment, however, did not cover the millions of black and white women in America. Initially most black women were pleased with the Fifteenth Amendment and supported the right of their husbands to vote, accepting their husbands' vote as their vote. White women, however, many of whom had been abolitionists and supported black suffrage, became outraged that black men had been enfranchised but women had not. As a result, members of the women's movement protested and lobbied state assemblies and Congress for the vote. In spite of the fact that by 1898 nearly all black males in the South had been disenfranchised by poll taxes, literacy tests, property requirements, grandfather clauses, and the actions of terrorist groups like the Ku Klux Klan, white women used the Fifteenth Amendment to chastise white men for enfranchising black men and not their own wives and daughters. Eventually, women won the right to vote, through the efforts of groups such as the National American Women's Suffrage Association (NAWSA) organized in Chicago in 1913, the Alpha Suffrage Club organized by Ida Wells Barnett, and the National Association of Colored Women (NACW). Together these black and white women's organizations organized protests, lobbied states and Congress, marched on Washington, D.C., in 1913, and registered women to vote after the passage of the Nineteenth Amendment in 1920. Although women were granted the right to vote by the Nineteenth Amendment, the new rights were limited in the South by the same literacy tests, grandfather clauses, poll taxes, and terror and violence that disenfranchised southern black men. Some black women voted in western and northern state elections. However, the majority remained disenfranchised until the Voting Rights Act of 1965. It must also be noted that eight of the eleven southern states that made up the Confederacy along with Maryland and Delaware never ratified the Nineteenth Amendment, demonstrating their objection to enfranchising both black and white women. ■

MAP 97

Marcus Garvey and the Universal Negro Improvement Association

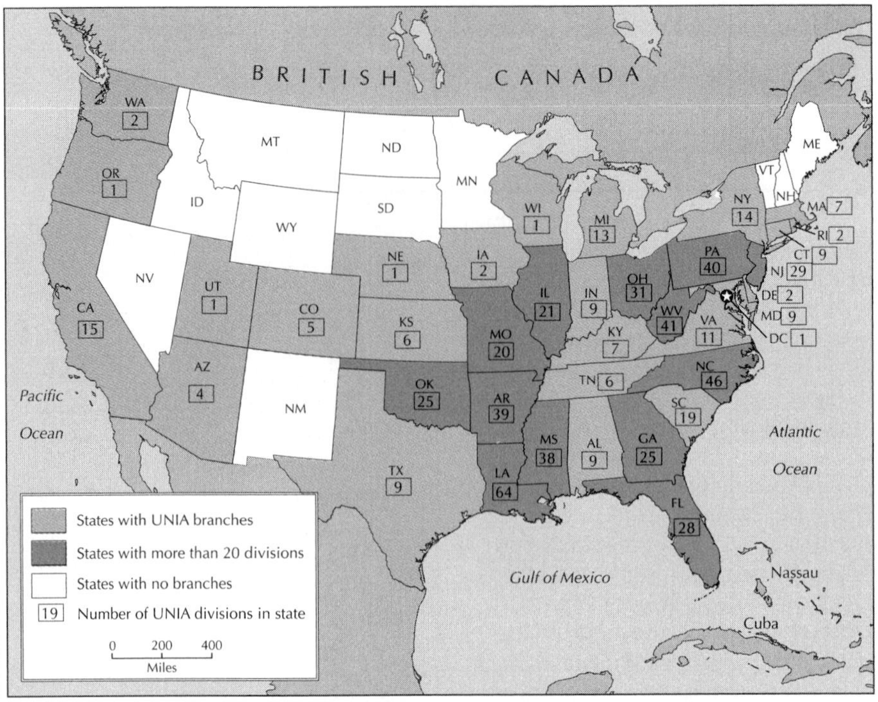
BRITISH CANADA
WA 2
OR 1
ID
MT
ND
SD
WY
MN
WI 1
MI 13
NY 14
VT
NH
ME
MA 7
RI 2
CT 9
NJ 29
DE 2
MD 9
DC 1
PA 40
OH 31
IN 9
IL 21
IA 2
NE 1
NV
UT 1
CO 5
KS 6
MO 20
KY 7
WV 41
VA 11
CA 15
AZ 4
NM
OK 25
AR 39
TN 6
NC 46
SC 19
MS 38
AL 9
GA 25
TX 9
LA 64
FL 28
Pacific Ocean
Atlantic Ocean
Gulf of Mexico
Nassau
Cuba
States with UNIA branches
States with more than 20 divisions
States with no branches
19 Number of UNIA divisions in state
0 200 400
Miles

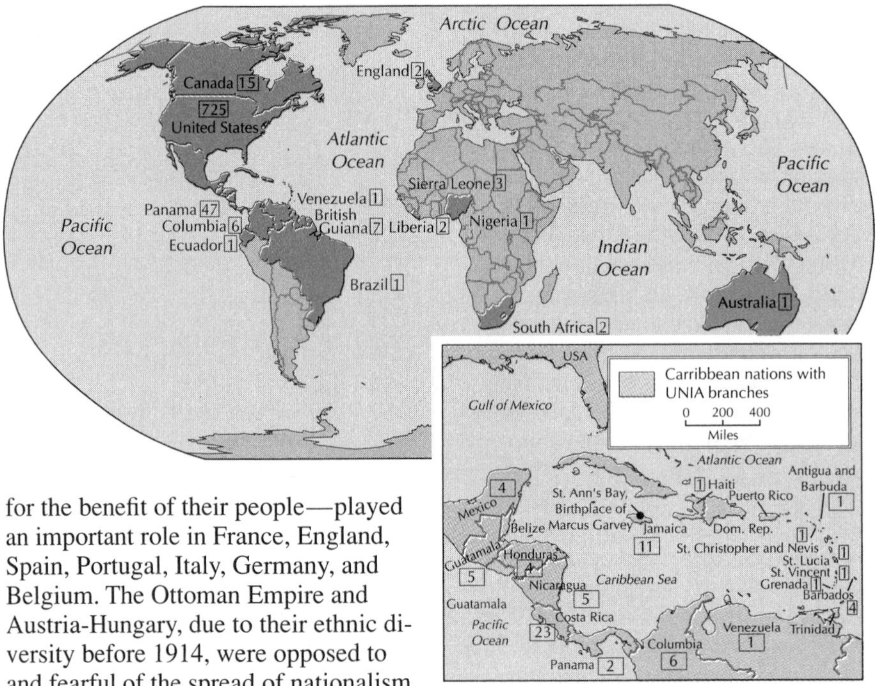
Arctic Ocean
England 2
Canada 15
725
United States
Atlantic Ocean
Pacific Ocean
Sierra Leone 3
Venezuela 1
Panama 47
Columbia 6
Ecuador 1
British Guiana 7
Liberia 2
Nigeria 1
Indian Ocean
Brazil 1
Australia 1
South Africa 2
USA
Gulf of Mexico
Carribbean nations with UNIA branches
0 200 400
Miles
Atlantic Ocean
Antigua and Barbuda
1
Haiti
Puerto Rico
St. Ann's Bay, Birthplace of Marcus Garvey
Mexico
4
Belize
Jamaica
Dom. Rep.
11
St. Christopher and Nevis 1
St. Lucia 1
St. Vincent 1
Grenada 1
Barbados
4
Honduras
4
Guatamala
5
Nicaragua
5
Caribbean Sea
Guatamala
Costa Rica
Pacific Ocean
23
Venezuela
1
Trinidad
Columbia
6
Panama 2

Marcus Garvey was born in Jamaica, in the West Indies, in 1887. He began the Universal Negro Improvement Association (UNIA) there in 1917. In 1919 he moved to Harlem, New York, and expanded and perfected one of the most successful all-black organizations ever to exist. Garvey's message was one of self-help and racial pride. He preached black nationalism—that blacks all over the world were being exploited and the only way to stop this was for them to create their own state with an army to protect it. He did not believe that blacks and whites could live together peaceably, not because blacks were not willing to, but because whites were not willing to allow them to. He pointed to the lynchings of blacks by the thousands since the 1890s and the riots of the Red Summer of 1919 as proof of the savageness of the white race. Garvey appealed to the masses of black people because they could identify with him. He was a proud, dark-skinned man and professed pride for his ebony complexion. In Harlem he held parades in which his followers wore uniforms and marched in formation. Garvey and his Universal Negro Improvement Association became so popular that by 1926 in the United States there were thirty-eight chapters in thirty-seven states and the District of Columbia and numerous branches in over forty-one foreign countries. Sadly, however, his success did not last. Fearing Garvey's nationalistic message, the U.S. government sought to discredit Garvey and his organization. In 1924 he was arrested and charged with mail fraud and sentenced to prison. After serving one year of an eight-year sentence, he was released and deported back to Jamaica. Although Garvey's movement failed, much of his message remained with African Americans and served as the foundation of American black nationalism. In the first decades of the twentieth century, nationalism—the belief that people of the same ethnic group, language, culture, and region should be allowed to establish and operate their own government for the benefit of their people—played an important role in France, England, Spain, Portugal, Italy, Germany, and Belgium. The Ottoman Empire and Austria-Hungary, due to their ethnic diversity before 1914, were opposed to and fearful of the spread of nationalism in their empires. It is important to understand this because the nationalism that caused World War I would greatly impact many African Americans, most notably the scholar W. E. B. Du Bois. Thus European nationalism not only drastically altered Europe, but molded the thinking of America's blacks as well. By the end of World War I, African people all over the world began to demand independence from the European colonial powers that had exploited them since 1880. Citing the creation of ethnic nationalistic states in the Balkans and the Middle East, African colonies demanded their independence as well. Movements to overthrow European rule and win independence for African peoples began in many African countries. ■

MAP 98

Artistic and Intellectual Centers of the Harlem Renaissance (1920–1935)

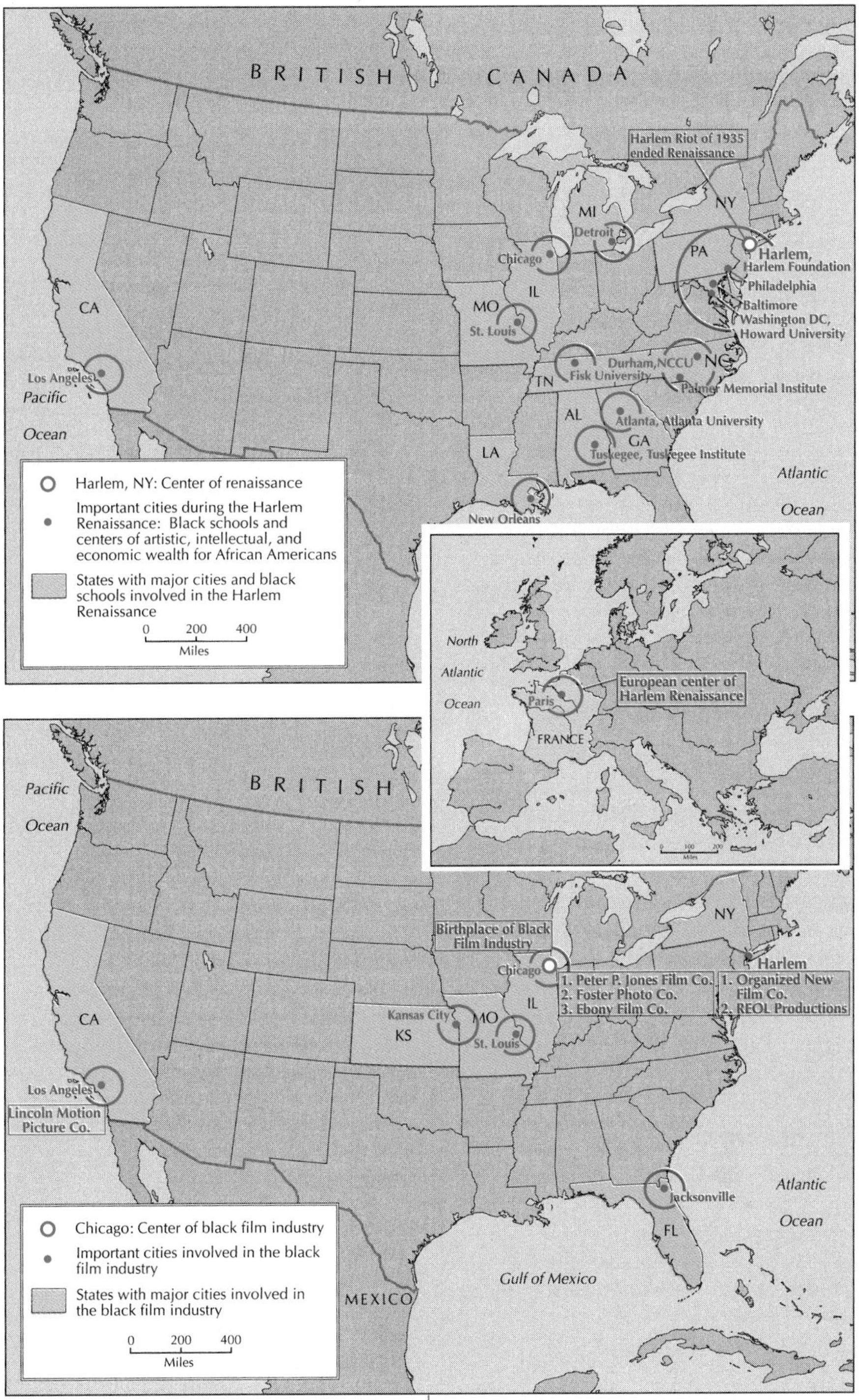
BRITISH
CANADA
Harlem Riot of 1935 ended Renaissance
MI
Detroit
NY
Chicago
PA
Harlem, Harlem Foundation
IL
Philadelphia
MO
Baltimore
St. Louis
Washington DC, Howard University
CA
Durham, NCCU
NC
Fisk University
TN
Los Angeles
Palmer Memorial Institute
Pacific
AL
Atlanta, Atlanta University
Ocean
GA
LA
Tuskegee, Tuskegee Institute
Atlantic
Ocean
New Orleans
Harlem, NY: Center of renaissance
Important cities during the Harlem Renaissance: Black schools and centers of artistic, intellectual, and economic wealth for African Americans
States with major cities and black schools involved in the Harlem Renaissance
0 200 400
Miles
North
Atlantic
Ocean
Paris
European center of Harlem Renaissance
FRANCE
BRITISH
Pacific
Ocean
NY
Birthplace of Black Film Industry
Harlem
Chicago
1. Peter P. Jones Film Co.
2. Foster Photo Co.
3. Ebony Film Co.
1. Organized New Film Co.
2. REOL Productions
IL
Kansas City
MO
KS
St. Louis
CA
Los Angeles
Lincoln Motion Picture Co.
Jacksonville
Atlantic
Ocean
FL
Chicago: Center of black film industry
Important cities involved in the black film industry
States with major cities involved in the black film industry
Gulf of Mexico
MEXICO
0 200 400
Miles

Marcus Garvey and his movement can be said to have directly inspired the Harlem Renaissance with its beautiful art, music, literature, and films. In preaching his message of racial pride, Garvey created a love for anything and everything related to African and African American culture. Although Harlem, in New York City, was the center of the Harlem Renaissance, similar communities arose throughout the United States, fostering this artistic and intellectual explosion. There was activity in the Northeast, South, Midwest, and the Far West. Scholars, musicians, writers, poets, and artists like Carter G. Woodson, James Weldon Johnson, Langston Hughes (the "Shakespeare of Harlem"), and Duke Ellington created new styles of literature, art, and music that were equally popular among whites and blacks and also loved by Europeans, particularly the French. The renaissance was even taken to Paris, France, by painters, writers, and performers. The dancer Josephine Baker, who opened in Paris in 1925, won instant acclaim. The art, music, literature, and history produced during this period were amazing. They enriched the lives of millions of African Americans and caused them to become more aware of their race's talents and abilities. During this period blacks would also see the rise of "race films." Not usually identified as a part of the Harlem Renaissance, the black film industry began to flourish during this period. From 1910 to 1950 over 30 movie companies, most black-owned, produced more than 500 black movies for black audiences. They were shown at over 300 black-owned and run movie houses all over the country. These films dealt with nearly every conceivable issue facing black Americans during this period, including, but not limited to, interracial marriage, dark and light prejudice among blacks, class prejudice within the black community, white racism, and racial violence including riots and lynchings. The first black movie company was begun in Chicago by William Foster in 1910. Eight years later in 1918, to combat negative racial stereotypes of blacks in white films, the first serious black film, *The Homesteader*, was produced. Based on a novel by Oscar Micheaux, the film depicted the life of a hard-working black homesteader in South Dakota. Black films produced during this period did as much to benefit blacks as art, music, literature, and history. The films gave black youth black images to look up to and to strive to be like. They also reached a number of people who did not have access to or the financial resources to benefit from the artistic and intellectual revolution that occurred. However, most blacks could view the many films of the period that helped blacks to escape the horror of their daily lives. The Harlem race riot of 1935 signaled the end of the Harlem Renaissance. ■

MAP 99

The Roaring Twenties and the Rise of the Negro Baseball League and Its Teams (1920–1950)

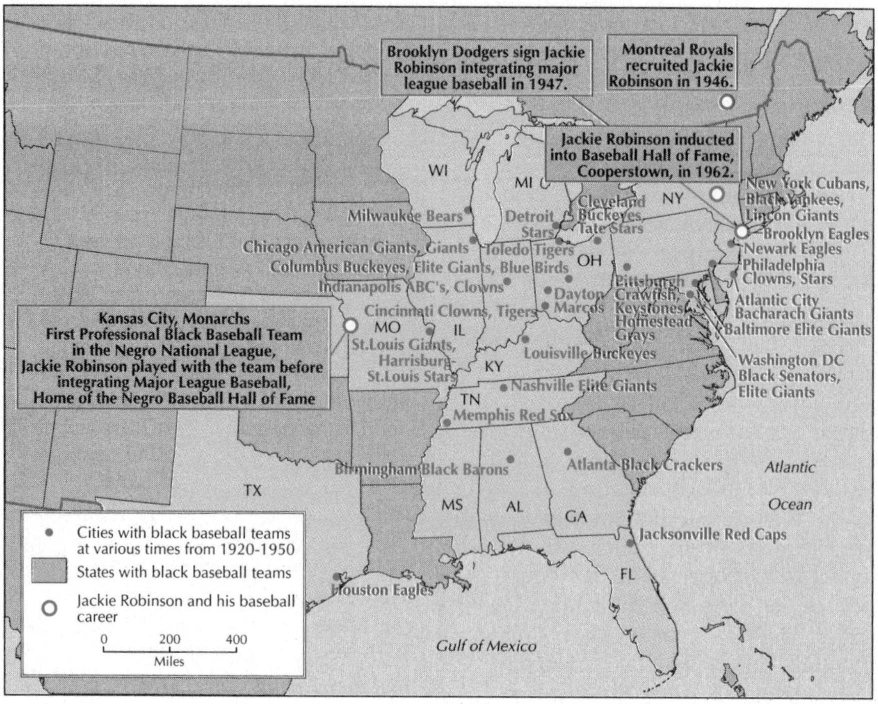
Brooklyn Dodgers sign Jackie Robinson integrating major league baseball in 1947.
Montreal Royals recruited Jackie Robinson in 1946.
Jackie Robinson inducted into Baseball Hall of Fame, Cooperstown, in 1962.
Kansas City, Monarchs First Professional Black Baseball Team in the Negro National League, Jackie Robinson played with the team before integrating Major League Baseball, Home of the Negro Baseball Hall of Fame
WI
MI
NY
OH
MO
IL
KY
TN
TX
MS
AL
GA
FL
Milwaukee Bears
Chicago American Giants, Giants
Columbus Buckeyes, Elite Giants, Blue Birds
Indianapolis ABC's, Clowns
Cincinnati Clowns, Tigers
St.Louis Giants,
Harrisburg-
St.Louis Stars
Detroit Stars
Cleveland Buckeyes, Tate Stars
Toledo Tigers
Dayton Marcos
Pittsburgh Crawfish, Keystones, Homestead Grays
Louisville Buckeyes
Nashville Elite Giants
Memphis Red Sox
Birmingham Black Barons
Atlanta Black Crackers
Jacksonville Red Caps
Houston Eagles
New York Cubans, Black Yankees, Lincon Giants
Brooklyn Eagles
Newark Eagles
Philadelphia Clowns, Stars
Atlantic City Bacharach Giants
Baltimore Elite Giants
Washington DC Black Senators, Elite Giants
Atlantic Ocean
Gulf of Mexico
Cities with black baseball teams at various times from 1920-1950
States with black baseball teams
Jackie Robinson and his baseball career
0 200 400
Miles

By the end of the Civil War, baseball had become a popular sport and was well on its way to becoming the national pastime. During the early twentieth century, it became synonymous with America. While whites praised and admired the home run record of Babe Ruth and the team play of the New York Yankees and the Chicago White Sox, the Negro League helped the sport to grow and flourish in the black community. With teams like the Kings, the Cardinals, and the Chicago Leapers, the league boasted some of the best athletes ever to play the game. It is believed, for example, that Oscar Charleston, a left-handed hitter, outfielder, and sometime first baseman, who played with the Indianapolis ABC's, the Chicago American Giants, the Pittsburgh Crawfords, and several other Negro teams, easily would have shattered Babe Ruth's home run record had he been allowed to play in the major leagues and would have been recognized as one of the greatest players of all times. Charleston was in good company. Fellow players included John Henry Lloyd, Smokey Joe Williams, Bullet Rogan, Dick Redding, and Satchel Paige, all of whom are considered among the best players of any race. When Jackie Robinson joined the Montreal Royals on April 18, 1946, he became the first black to play for a white major league program. In 1947 Robinson joined the Brooklyn Dodgers, of the National League and became the first black ball player to play for an American major league club. Later in 1947, Larry Doby joined the Cleveland Indians and broke the color barrier for the American League. From 1947 to 1959 seventeen players would be allowed to play for the sixteen previously white-only major league teams of the American and National Leagues. The Boston Red Sox became the last major league team to be integrated when it signed Pumpsie Green in 1959. The integration of major league baseball sounded the death knell for the Negro League. By 1950, as more and more black spectators began to attend major league games to see Jackie Robinson and other black players play, gate receipts dried up at the black games. Whether intentional or not, the integration of baseball by Jackie Robinson brought about the end of the Negro League and relegated the names of many of the greatest talents ever to play the game, at least temporarily, to the ranks of the forgotten. ■

Map and Text Sources

87. United States Bureau of the Census. *Historical Statistics of the United States, Colonial Times to 1970, Bicentennial Edition [Part 2].* Washington, DC: Government Printing Office, 1975.

88. Cannon, Margaret. *Invisble Empire: Racism in Canada.* Toronto, Canada: Random House, 1995.
Ginzburg, Ralph. *100 Years of Lynchings.* New York: Lancer Books, 1969.
Jackson, Kenneth T. *The Ku Klux Klan in the City, 1915–1930.* Chicago: Dee, 1992.
Lay, Shawn, ed. *The Invisible Empire in the West: Toward a New Historical Appraisal of the Ku Klux Klan of the 1920s.* Urbana: University of Illinois Press, 1992.
Mecklin, John M. *The Ku Klux Klan: A Study of the American Mind.* New York: Russell & Russell, 1963.
Shay, Frank. *Judge Lynch, His First Hundred Years.* New York: Biblo and Tannen, 1969.
Thirty Years of Lynching in the United States, 1889–1918. New York: National Association for the Advancement of Colored People, 1919.
White, Walter Francis. *Rope and Faggot.* New York: Arno Press, 1969.
Zangrando, Robert L. *The NAACP Crusade Against Lynching, 1909–1950.* Philadelphia: Temple University, 1980.

89. Berry, Mary Frances. *Black Resistance, White Law: A History of Constitutional Racism in America.* New York: Penguin Books, 1995.
Bowen, John W. E., ed. *Africa and the American Negro: Addresses and Proceedings of the Congress on Africa, Held under the Auspices of the Stewart Missionary Foundation for Africa of Gammon Theological Seminary in Connection with the Cotton States and International Exposition, December 13–15, 1895.* Atlanta: Gammon Theological Seminary, 1896.
Olsen, Otto H. *The Thin Disguise: Turning Point in Negro History; Plessy v. Ferguson; A Documentary Presentation, 1864–1896.* New York: Humanities Press, 1967.
Ruderman, Jim, and Bill Fauver. *Keeping Them Apart: Plessy v. Ferguson and the Black Experience in Post-Reconstruction America.* Los Angeles: National Center for History in the Schools, UCLA, 1991.
Thomas, Brook, ed. *Plessy v. Ferguson: A Brief History with Documents.* Boston: Bedford Books, 1997.
Woodward, C. Vann. *The Strange Career of Jim Crow.* New York: Oxford University Press, 1982.

90. Gatewood, Willard, comp. *"Smoked Yankees" and the Struggle for Empire: Letters from Negro Soldiers, 1898–1902.* Fayetteville: University of Arkansas Press, 1987.

91. Ames, Jessie Daniel. *The Changing Character of Lynching; Review of Lynching, 1931–1941, with a Discussion of Recent Developments in This Field.* New York: AMS Press, 1973.
Finch, Minnie. *The NAACP, Its Fight for Justice.* Metuchen, NJ: Scarecrow Press, 1981.
Kellogg, Charles Flint. *NAACP: A History of the National Association for the Advancement of Colored People.* Baltimore: Johns Hopkins University Press, 1973.
St. James, Warren D. *NAACP: Triumphs of a Pressure Group, 1909–1980,* 2nd ed., rev. Smithtown, NY: Exposition Press, 1980.

92. Glaab, Charles N., and A. Theodore Brown. *A History of Urban America,* 3rd ed. New York: Macmillan, 1983.
National Urban League. *70th Anniversary, National Urban League.* New York: The League, 1980.
Parris, Guichard, and Lester Brooks. *Blacks in the City; A History of the National Urban League.* Boston: Little, Brown, 1971.
Weiss, Nancy J. *The National Urban League, 1910–1940.* New York: Oxford University Press, 1974.

93. Bracey, John H., August Meier, Jr., and Elliott M. Rudnick, comps. *The Rise of the Ghetto.* Belmont, CA: Wadsworth Publishing Company, 1971.
Grossman, James R. *Land of Hope: Chicago, Black Southerners and the Great Migration.* Chicago: University of Chicago Press, 1989.
Harrison, Alferdteen, ed. *Black Exodus: The Great Migration from the American South.* Jackson: University Press of Mississippi, 1991.
Scott, Emmett J. *Negro Migration during the War.* New York: Arno Press, 1969.
Trotter, Joe William. *Black Milwaukee: The Making of an Industrial Proletariat, 1915–45.* Urbana: University of Illinois Press, 1988.
Trotter, Joe William, ed. *The Great Migration in Historical Perspective: New Dimensions in Race, Class, and Gender.* Bloomington: Indiana University Press, 1991.

94. Barbeau, Arthur E., and Florette, Henri. *The Unknown Soldiers: African-American Troops in World War I.* New York: Da Capo Press, 1996.
Heywood, Chester D. *Negro Combat Troops in the World War: The Story of the 371st Infantry.* New York: Negro Universities Press, 1969.
Johnson, Jesse J. *A Pictorial History of Black Soldiers in the United States (1619–1969).* Hampton, VA: Johnson Publishing Company, 1973.
Little, Arthur W. *From Harlem to the Rhine: The Story of New York's Colored Volunteers.* New York: Haskell House, 1974.
Padmore, George. *Pan-Africanism or Communism: The Coming Struggle for Africa.* London: Cass Library of African Studies, 1969.
Patton, Gerald W. *War and Race: The Black Officer in the American Military, 1915–1941.* Westport, CT: Greenwood Press, 1981.
Ruck, Calvin W. *Black Battalion: 1916–1920 Canada's Best Kept Military Secret,* rev. ed. Halifax, NS: Nimbus Publishing, 1987.
Sweeney, William A. *History of the American Negro in the Great World War: His Splendid Record in the Battle Zones of Europe, Including a Resume of His Past Services to His Country in the Wars of the Revolution, of 1812, the War of the Rebellion, the Indian Wars on the Frontier, the Spanish-American War, and the Late Imbroglio with Mexico.* Chicago: Cuneo-Henneberry, 1919.
United States Department of Labor, Division of Negro Economics. *The Negro at Work during the World War and during Reconstruction; Statistics, Problems, and Policies Relating to the Greater Inclusion of Negro Wage Earners in American Industry and Agriculture.* New York: Negro Universities Press, 1969.
Williams, Charles H. *Negro Soldiers in World War I: The Human Side.* New York: AMS Press, 1970.
Williams, Charles H. *Sidelights on Negro Soldiers.* Boston: B. J. Brimmer Company, 1923.

95. Haynes, Robert V. *A Night of Violence: The Houston Riot of 1917.* Baton Rouge: Louisiana State University Press, 1976.
Jenkinson, Jacqueline. "The 1919 Race Riots in Britain: Their Background

and Consequences." Ph.D. dissertation, University of Edinburgh, United Kingdom, 1987.

Kerlin, Robert T. *The Voice of the Negro, 1919.* New York: Dutton, 1920.

Lane, Ann J. *The Brownsville Affair; National Crisis and Black Reaction.* Port Washington, NY: Kennikat Press, 1971

Rudwick, Elliot M. *The East St. Louis Race Riot of 1917.* Frederick, MD: University Publications of America, 1985.

Tuttle, William M. *Race Riot. Chicago in the Red Summer of 1919.* New York: Atheneum, 1970.

United States House Committee on the Judiciary. *Hearing January 15 and 29, 1920, Part I, Segregation, Part II, Anti-Lynching (Serial no. 14).* Washington, DC: Government Printing Office, 1920.

Waskow, Arthur I. *From Race Riot to Sit-In, 1919 and the 1960s; A Study in the Connections between Conflict and Violence.* Garden City, NY: Doubleday, 1966.

Waskow, Arthur I. *The 1919 Race Riots: A Study in the Connections between Conflict and Violence.* Madison: University of Wisconsin Press, 1963.

96. Gordon, Ann D., and Bettye Collier-Thomas. *African American Women and the Vote, 1837–1965.* Amherst: University of Massachusetts Press, 1997.

Link, William L., ed. *The Rebuilding of Old Commonwealths and Other Documents of Social Reform in the Progressive Era South.* Boston: Bedford Books, 1996.

Neverdon-Morton, Cynthia. *Afro-American Women of the South and the Advancement of the Race, 1895–1925.* Knoxville: University of Tennessee Press, 1991.

O'Neill, William L. *The Woman Movement; Feminism in the United States and England.* New York: Barnes and Noble, 1969.

Shaw, Stephanie J. *What a Woman Ought to Be and to Do: Black Professional Women Workers during the Jim Crow Era.* Chicago: University of Chicago Press, 1996.

97. Cronon, E. David. *Black Moses: The Story of Marcus Garvey and the Universal Negro Improvement Association,* 2nd ed. Madison: University of Wisconsin Press, 1981.

Draper, Theodore. *The Rediscovery of Black Nationalism.* London: Secker & Warburg, 1971.

Jacques-Garvey, Amy, ed. *Philosophy and Opinions of Marcus Garvey.* New York: Atheneum, 1992.

Link, William L., ed. *The Rebuilding of Old Commonwealths and Other Documents of Social Reform in the Progressive Era South.* Boston: Bedford Books, 1996.

Martin, Tony. *Race First: The Ideological and Organizational Struggles of Marcus Garvey and the Universal Negro Improvement Association.* Dover, MA: Majority Press, 1986.

Wolters, Raymond. *The New Negro on Campus: Black College Rebellions of the 1920s.* Princeton, NJ: Princeton University Press, 1975.

98. Bontemps, Arna, ed. *The Harlem Renaissance Remembered.* New York: Dodd, Mead, 1972.

Candaele, Kerry. *Bound for Glory: From the Great Migration to the Harlem Renaissance, 1910–1930.* New York: Chelsea House Publishers, 1996.

Haskins, James. *The Harlem Renaissance.* Brookfield, CT: Millbrook Press, 1996.

Huggins, Nathan I. *Harlem Renaissance.* New York: Oxford University Press, 1973.

Lewis, David L. *When Harlem Was in Vogue.* New York: Oxford University Press, 1989.

McKay, Claude. *Harlem, Negro Metropolis.* New York: Harcourt Brace Jovanovich, 1968.

Watson, Steven. *The Harlem Renaissance: Hub of African-American Culture, 1920–1930.* New York: Pantheon Books, 1995.

Wintz, Cary D., ed. *The Emergence of the Harlem Renaissance.* New York: Garland Publishing, 1996.

Wintz, Cary D., ed. *Remembering the Harlem Renaissance.* New York: Garland Publishing, 1996.

99. Rader, Benjamin G. *Baseball: A History of America's Game.* Urbana: University of Illinois Press, 1994.

Holway, John. *Voices from the Great Black Baseball Leagues,* rev. ed. New York: Da Capo Press, 1992.

Rogosin, Donn. *Invisible Men: Life in Baseball's Negro Leagues.* New York: Kodansha International, 1995.

MAP 100

From Republican to Democrat: Black Political Realignment 1932–1944

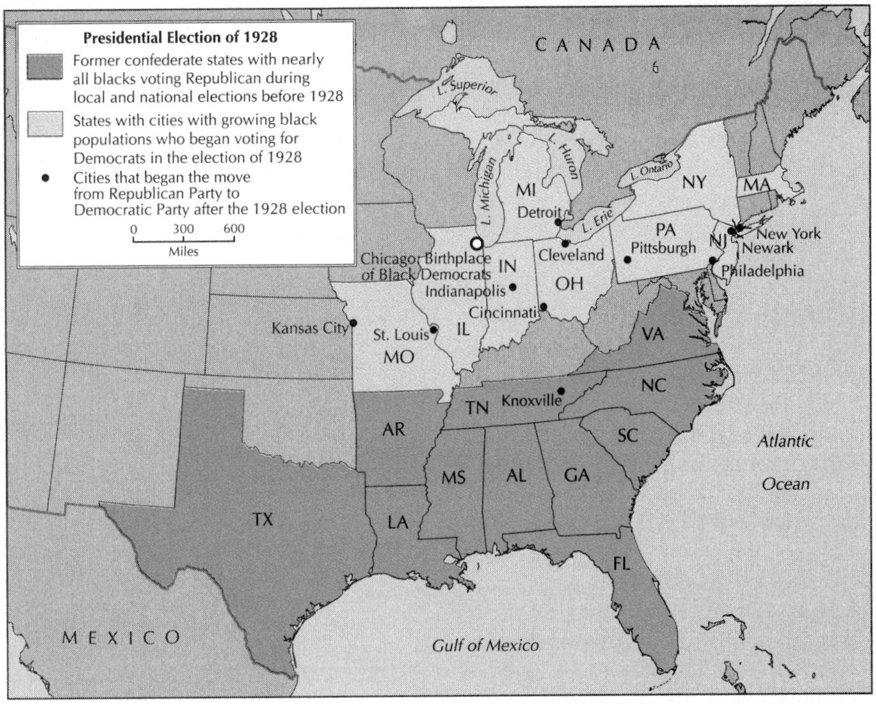
Presidential Election of 1928
Former confederate states with nearly all blacks voting Republican during local and national elections before 1928
States with cities with growing black populations who began voting for Democrats in the election of 1928
Cities that began the move from Republican Party to Democratic Party after the 1928 election
0 300 600
Miles
CANADA
L. Superior
L. Michigan
L. Huron
L. Ontario
L. Erie
MI
Detroit
NY
MA
PA
Pittsburgh
NJ
New York
Newark
Philadelphia
Chicago Birthplace of Black Democrats
IN
Indianapolis
Cleveland
OH
Cincinnati
IL
Kansas City
St. Louis
MO
VA
NC
TN
Knoxville
AR
SC
MS
AL
GA
TX
LA
FL
Atlantic
Ocean
MEXICO
Gulf of Mexico

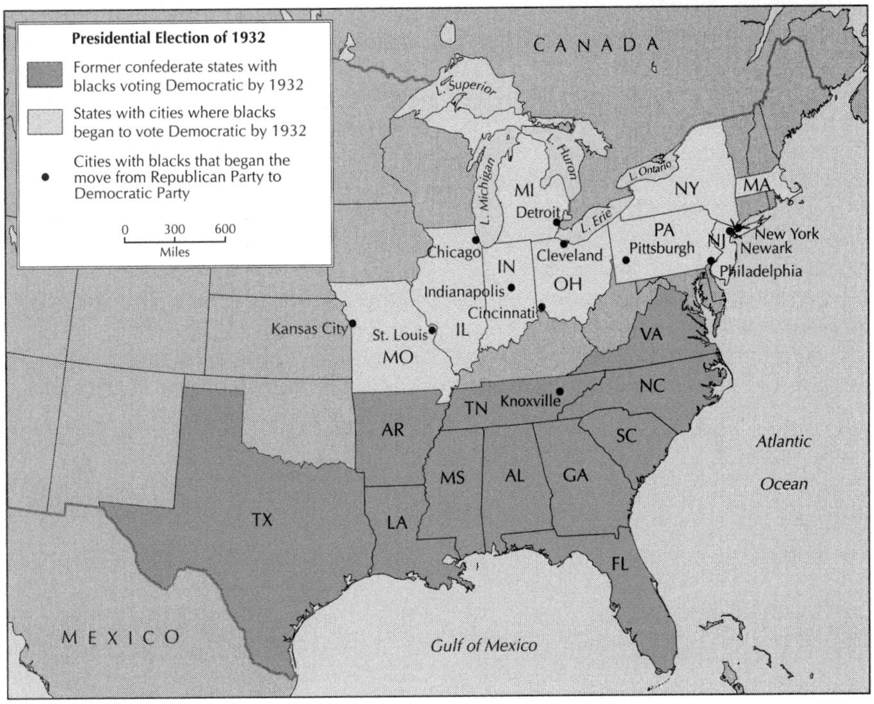
Presidential Election of 1932
Former confederate states with blacks voting Democratic by 1932
States with cities where blacks began to vote Democratic by 1932
Cities with blacks that began the move from Republican Party to Democratic Party
0 300 600
Miles
CANADA
L. Superior
L. Michigan
L. Huron
L. Ontario
L. Erie
MI
Detroit
NY
MA
PA
Pittsburgh
NJ
New York
Newark
Philadelphia
Chicago
IN
Indianapolis
Cleveland
OH
Cincinnati
IL
Kansas City
St. Louis
MO
VA
NC
TN
Knoxville
AR
SC
MS
AL
GA
TX
LA
FL
Atlantic
Ocean
MEXICO
Gulf of Mexico

From the end of the Civil War to the elections of 1928, African Americans overwhelmingly supported the Republican Party. This loyalty to the Republican Party lasted until the "lily-white" movement of the southern branch of the Republican Party in 1928. In every major local, state, and national election, blacks voted (where they were allowed to) overwhelmingly Republican. By 1932, however, blacks were losing faith in the Republican Party as a result of the southern "lily-white" movement. In the election of 1928 in Chicago, blacks began voting for candidates in the Democratic Party. In the Illinois congressional election of 1934, Arthur W. Mitchell, a former Republican, became the first black Democrat elected to Congress replacing Oscar DePriest, the black Republican. This election heralded the start of black political realignment in America. Offering help to blacks suffering from the Great Depression, Democrats primarily in northern cities, like New York and Chicago, campaigned for black votes and received them. African Americans, like most other Americans, turned to Franklin D. Roosevelt and the Democratic Party for relief. As a result of his New Deal program, the creation of his "Black Cabinet," made up of leading blacks from around the nation who advised the president on Negro affairs, and the work of his wife, Eleanor Roosevelt, in promoting black equality, blacks began voting for and running in larger numbers for the Democratic Party. Roosevelt's policies, created a loyal following in the African American community and completed the switch by most African Americans from the Republican Party to the Democratic Party. In spite of this switch by blacks, however, it must be noted that the entrance of blacks into the Democratic Party was not well received by all Democrats. In the South, the Dixiecrats, as they became known, were outraged. Even before the Civil War the South had been a one-party region. The party, like the rest of the South, was religiously, socially, and fiscally conservative. Southerners during the Civil War and Reconstruction grew to loathe Republicans and the Republican Party. They saw the support the Republican Party gave to blacks as detrimental to southern whites and their way of life. Thus the southern Democratic Party promoted white supremacy and segregation throughout the South. As a result of this, many blacks in the South found it difficult to vote for Democrats on the local and state level until late in the civil rights movement, but supported Democrats in presidential elections from 1932 on. ■

MAP 101

Major Black Religious Leaders during the Great Depression: Father Divine, Sweet Daddy Grace, Elder Baker, Wallace D. T. Farad, and Elijah Muhammad (1929–1940)

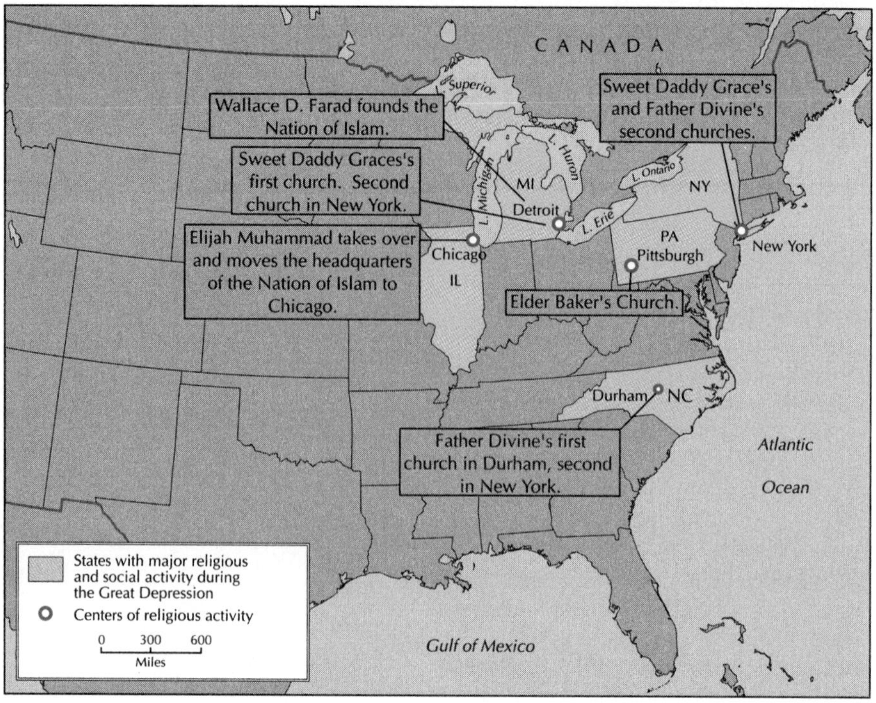
CANADA
Superior
Wallace D. Farad founds the Nation of Islam.
Sweet Daddy Graces's first church. Second church in New York.
Elijah Muhammad takes over and moves the headquarters of the Nation of Islam to Chicago.
Sweet Daddy Grace's and Father Divine's second churches.
L. Michigan
L. Huron
L. Ontario
L. Erie
MI
Detroit
NY
New York
PA
Pittsburgh
Chicago
IL
Elder Baker's Church.
Durham
NC
Father Divine's first church in Durham, second in New York.
Atlantic Ocean
Gulf of Mexico
States with major religious and social activity during the Great Depression
Centers of religious activity
0 300 600
Miles

On October 2, 1929, Black Tuesday, the stock market crashed in New York City. Many traders who were financially ruined threw themselves from buildings or shot themselves. Before long, 30 million Americans lost their jobs and could find no work. The Depression was the most cataclysmic event in American history since the Civil War. Many working- and middle-class white Americans lost everything. They were forced out onto the street and were reduced to eating garbage from trash cans or even eating rats when they could be found. If conditions were this debilitating for many whites during the period, it leaves little to the imagination about what befell America's black population. The Great Depression, coming on the heels of the Harlem Renaissance, was a great blow to African Americans. As in the case of their abandonment after Reconstruction, however, African Americans showed great resilience. They created soup kitchens to care for the starving and demanded equal assistance from the government during the New Deal era. Blacks were assisted by institutions that were as old as emancipation, including the church and fraternal and sororital organizations. Newly created organizations like the NAACP and the NUL also hurried to provide assistance. Perhaps the most remarkable of all the groups that attempted to help African Americans cope with this disaster, however, were the religious sects that developed during the period. Five of the most well known leaders of these sects were (1) Father Divine, (2) Sweet Daddy Grace, (3) Elder Baker, (4) Wallace D. T. Farad, and (5) Elijah Muhammad. These men helped to give many African Americans faith that they could survive the Depression. In cities like Chicago, New York, and Durham, North Carolina, they opened soup kitchens and preached to those who came. These leaders were often criticized by mainstream blacks because of their religious claims—for example, Father Divine believed that he would rise from the dead. In spite of their religious shortcomings, however, these leaders, as did other black groups, provided blacks with the means to survive the Depression. ■

MAP 102

The African American Population in the United States (1930)

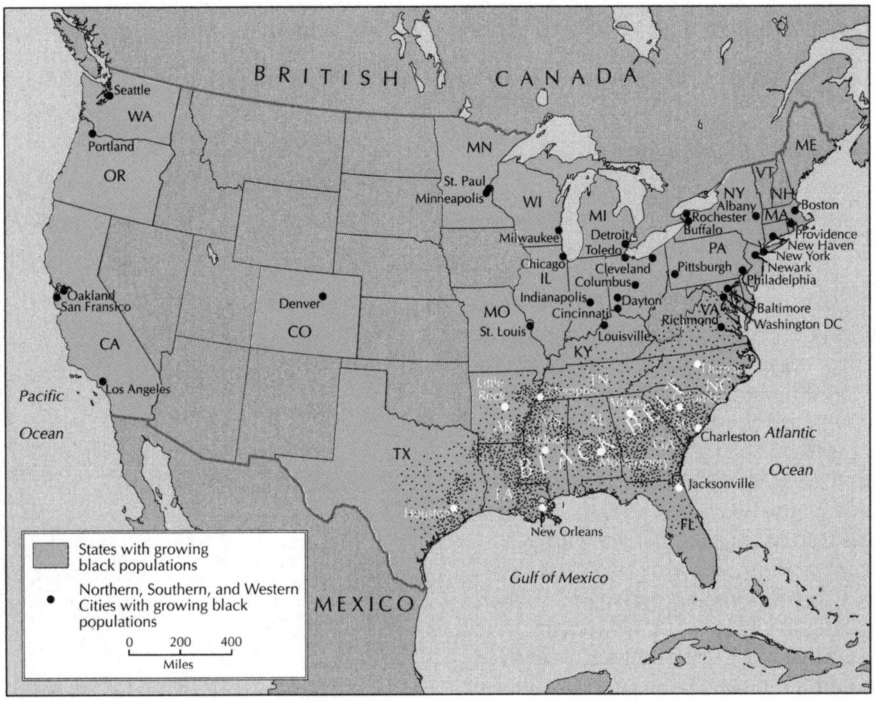
BRITISH CANADA
Seattle
WA
Portland
OR
MN
St. Paul
Minneapolis
WI
MI
ME
VT
NH
NY
Albany
Rochester
Buffalo
MA
Boston
Providence
New Haven
New York
Newark
Philadelphia
PA
Pittsburgh
Milwaukee
Detroit
Toledo
Chicago
IL
Cleveland
Columbus
Indianapolis
Dayton
Cincinnati
MO
St. Louis
Louisville
KY
Richmond
VA
Baltimore
Washington DC
Oakland
San Fransico
Denver
CO
CA
Los Angeles
Pacific Ocean
TX
Charleston
Atlantic Ocean
Jacksonville
New Orleans
FL
Gulf of Mexico
MEXICO
States with growing black populations
Northern, Southern, and Western Cities with growing black populations
0 200 400
Miles

By 1930 approximately 11,891,000 blacks and 108,864,000 whites lived in the United States. Blacks made up about 10 percent of the nation's overall population. Most continued to live in the rural South, but since 1914, black populations in northern cities like Chicago, New York, Detroit, Cleveland, and Pittsburgh and western cities like Los Angeles and Oakland began to increase rapidly. World War I broke out in Europe in 1914, and the war accelerated a migration that had begun as early as 1879. Industries in northeastern, midwestern and western cities geared up to supply the Allied war effort. As more opportunities for employment in the war industries became available, those industries encouraged blacks from the South to fill them. And they did. They flocked to the cities where the jobs were. Termed the Great Migration, this mass movement of hundreds of thousands of blacks from the rural South to the urban North and West lasted from 1914 until 1980. In terms of the numbers of blacks who were relocated from one region to another, the migration could be compared with the Atlantic slave trade. However, it differed from the Atlantic slave trade in that blacks left willingly, and it was an internal migration. The migration, however, would have just as profound an impact on the North as the Atlantic slave trade had on the South. As a result of job opportunities, the Harlem Renaissance, and the absence of lynchings and Jim Crow laws, the northern urban black population continued to increase throughout the 1920s and 1930s. By the time of the 1930 census, nearly 50 percent of America's blacks lived in northern and western cities, reflecting a shift in the black population from the rural South to the urban North. ■

MAP 103

The Second Migration: African Americans Moving North (1930–1980)

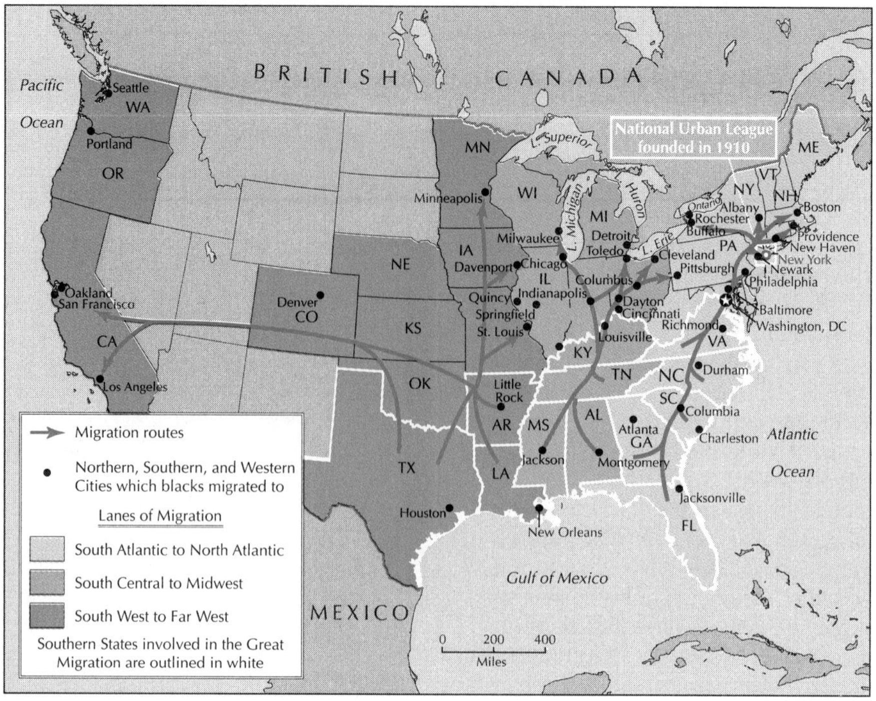
BRITISH CANADA
Pacific Ocean
National Urban League founded in 1910
Seattle
WA
Portland
OR
Oakland
San Francisco
CA
Los Angeles
Denver
CO
NE
KS
OK
TX
Houston
MN
Minneapolis
WI
IA
Davenport
Milwaukee
Chicago
IL
Quincy
Springfield
St. Louis
Indianapolis
MI
Detroit
Toledo
Cleveland
Columbus
Dayton
Cincinnati
Louisville
KY
Pittsburgh
PA
NY
Albany
Rochester
Buffalo
VT
NH
ME
Boston
Providence
New Haven
New York
Newark
Philadelphia
Baltimore
Washington, DC
Richmond
VA
NC
Durham
TN
SC
Columbia
Charleston
Little Rock
AR
MS
Jackson
AL
Atlanta
GA
Montgomery
LA
New Orleans
FL
Jacksonville
Atlantic Ocean
Gulf of Mexico
MEXICO
L. Superior
L. Michigan
L. Huron
L. Erie
L. Ontario
Migration routes
Northern, Southern, and Western Cities which blacks migrated to
Lanes of Migration
South Atlantic to North Atlantic
South Central to Midwest
South West to Far West
Southern States involved in the Great Migration are outlined in white
0 200 400
Miles

Black migration to the North and West never really ended after it began with the black Exodus to Kansas and Oklahoma in 1879. From that time until 1980 there was a steady stream of blacks out of the South. There were two periods in black migration when huge numbers flocked to northern and western cities. The first period occurred from 1914 to 1929. Fueled both by the war industries of World War I and by the Harlem Renaissance, hundreds of thousands of blacks moved north in search of jobs and a better life. Even during the Depression years, rural southern blacks continued to migrate, hoping things would be better in the cities. Many poor blacks turned north for help, not realizing that in most cases black urban dwellers were in a worse state than rural blacks. In fact, the flood of poor blacks that went north and west during the Depression only aggravated an already stressed system developed to assist impoverished blacks. New Deal programs introduced by Roosevelt helped some, but suffering was still the order of the day until 1938. In 1938 Adolf Hitler invaded Poland and engaged half the world in war. France and Britain, due to alliances with Poland, immediately declared war on Germany and the Axis Powers, and World War II began. For America, particularly black America, the war meant economic recovery, for although the United States did not officially enter the war until the end of 1941, it supplied tanks, guns, ships, and other war supplies to Great Britain and to Russia and China also. The jobs created by the growing war industries fueled the second period of massive black migration north and west, from 1938 to 1950. Again encouraged by job openings in the North and West, millions of blacks would leave the South. When the Japanese bombed Pearl Harbor in 1941, white male factory workers were needed for military service, opening up even more jobs for blacks and women. This migration can be said to be responsible for many changes in the black community, including an increase in black influence and political power in the United States. This increase came about because African Americans living in the North and West were allowed to vote and hold local, state, and national offices. Blacks' new political power fostered the development of the Congress on Racial Equality (CORE), the civil rights movement, and the rise of black labor unions and one of the most influential leaders of the period, A. Philip Randolph. By 1960 the black migration also led to the rise of modern urban ghettos, which were linked to the return of white males to northern and western cities after World War II. Their return caused the displacement of millions of black workers who during the war had been encouraged to move north to replace white workers inducted into the military. ■

MAP 104

The Rise and Fall of the Southern Tenant Farmers' Union in the South and Black Labor Unions in the North (1932–1945)

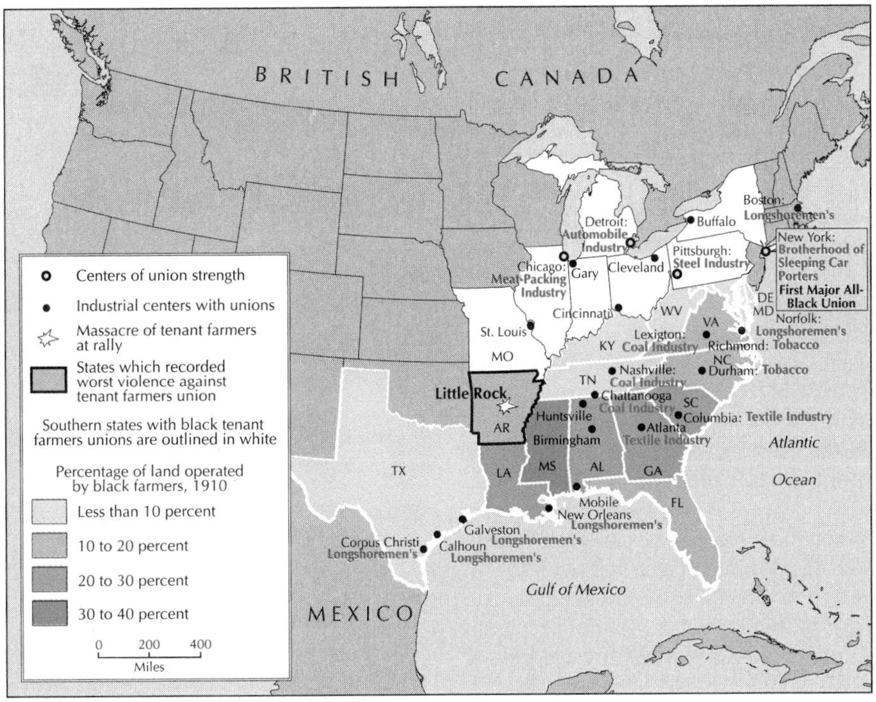
BRITISH CANADA
Centers of union strength
Industrial centers with unions
Massacre of tenant farmers at rally
States which recorded worst violence against tenant farmers union
Southern states with black tenant farmers unions are outlined in white
Percentage of land operated by black farmers, 1910
Less than 10 percent
10 to 20 percent
20 to 30 percent
30 to 40 percent
0 200 400
Miles
Detroit: Automobile Industry
Buffalo
Boston: Longshoremen's
Pittsburgh: Steel Industry
New York: Brotherhood of Sleeping Car Porters First Major All-Black Union
Chicago: Meat-Packing Industry
Gary
Cleveland
Cincinnati
WV
VA
DE
MD
Norfolk: Longshoremen's
St. Louis
MO
Lexigton: Coal Industry
KY
Richmond: Tobacco
NC
Durham: Tobacco
Nashville: Coal Industry
TN
Chattanooga Coal Industry
SC
Little Rock
AR
Huntsville
Birmingham
Columbia: Textile Industry
Atlanta Textile Industry
Atlantic
Ocean
TX
LA
MS
AL
GA
FL
Mobile
New Orleans Longshoremen's
Galveston Longshoremen's
Corpus Christi Longshoremen's
Calhoun Longshoremen's
Gulf of Mexico
MEXICO

During the years from 1930 to 1950, many black workers in both the North and South attempted to organize unions. In the South, where most blacks worked as sharecroppers or tenant farmers, a union seemed to be the only way they could guarantee fair treatment by southern merchants and landowners. Discriminated against by the agricultural policies of the New Deal, many found it more difficult than before to earn a livable wage in agriculture. Southern states passed laws that benefited white landowners but hurt both poor whites and blacks. As a result, black and white sharecroppers and tenant farmers founded segregated unions that worked to organize all sharecroppers and tenant farmers. To prevent the organizations from succeeding, southern white elites, as they had done during the Populist movement, attempted to politically divide poor whites from blacks by pointing to the threat of "Negro rule." When this failed, landowners turned to violence. They beat, burned, and murdered a number of blacks and whites who supported unions. Other supporters were forced off the land and joined the millions of people, black and white, migrating to northern and western cities. Blacks living in the North also attempted to organize unions. Denied entry into major white unions, blacks attempted to start their own in the railroad, meatpacking, iron and steel, coal mining, automobile and aircraft, textiles, clothing and laundry, longshore, and rubber and tire industries in northern and western cities like Chicago, Gary, Indiana, Pittsburgh, Cleveland, Buffalo, New York City, Philadelphia, and San Francisco. One of the most well-known African American labor and civil rights leaders at this time was A. Philip Randolph. Randolph organized the Brotherhood of Sleeping Car Porters in New York in 1925 and orchestrated one of the most successful strikes by black labor in the history of this country when in 1935 he reached a collective bargaining agreement with the Pullman Palace Car Company. With the exception of only a few industries and jobs in the South—the iron and steel mills of Montgomery, Alabama, the coal mines of southern Appalachia, and shipbuilding and longshoremen jobs of southern port cities like Hampton Roads, Virginia; Baltimore; New Orleans; Mobile, Alabama; and Galveston, Beaumont, Orange, Calhoun, and Corpus Christi, Texas—only northern industries were unionized. There were so few black unions in the South because southern industries such as textiles and tobacco were for whites only, and domestics and other unskilled laborers were not allowed to organize in the South. Although some blacks were able to modestly improve their standard of living in the north, most who were unable to join unions were paid extremely low wages and found themselves living in urban slums and earning far less than their white coworkers. ■

MAP 105

Military Training Centers for Blacks in the United States during World War II (1941–1945)

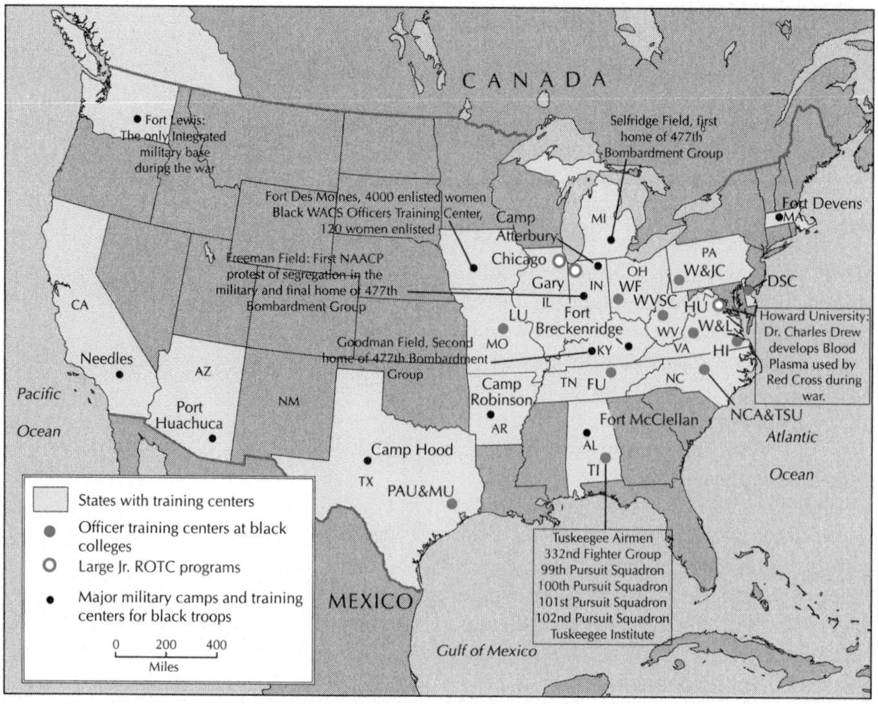
CANADA
Fort Lewis: The only Integrated military base during the war
Fort Des Moines, 4000 enlisted women Black WACS Officers Training Center, 120 women enlisted
Freeman Field: First NAACP protest of segregation in the military and final home of 477th Bombardment Group
Goodman Field, Second home of 477th Bombardment Group
Selfridge Field, first home of 477th Bombardment Group
Camp Atterbury
Chicago
Gary
IN
IL
MI
OH
WF
PA
W&JC
DSC
Fort Devens
MA
WVSC
HU
LU
Fort Breckenridge
WV
W&L
MO
KY
VA
HI
Howard University: Dr. Charles Drew develops Blood Plasma used by Red Cross during war.
TN
FU
NC
Camp Robinson
AR
Fort McClellan
NCA&TSU
AL
TI
Atlantic Ocean
CA
Needles
AZ
Port Huachuca
NM
Pacific Ocean
Camp Hood
TX
PAU&MU
MEXICO
Gulf of Mexico
Tuskeegee Airmen
332nd Fighter Group
99th Pursuit Squadron
100th Pursuit Squadron
101st Pursuit Squadron
102nd Pursuit Squadron
Tuskeegee Institute
States with training centers
Officer training centers at black colleges
Large Jr. ROTC programs
Major military camps and training centers for black troops
0 200 400
Miles

In 1917 several black colleges and universities, along with several military bases, were selected to establish officer training programs for black soldiers. ROTC and junior ROTC programs were established to develop black military officers who could lead black troops into battle. From 1917 until the start of World War II in 1941, these schools and military bases produced a number of black officers for the peacetime military. When the United States entered World War II, it became clear that not only were more of these training centers needed, but additional training centers to prepare the hundreds of thousands of black volunteers and recruits for service in Europe and the Pacific were needed as well. Black soldiers were trained to be antiaircraft gunners, artillerymen, tank destroyers, submarine hunters, truck drivers, engineers, combat soldiers, tank men, sailors, pilots, and, by the end of the war, Marines. With the help of his "Black Cabinet," President Roosevelt attempted to assist African American soldiers by giving black troops, over the objection of southern members of Congress, the opportunity for every imaginable kind of training. With pressure from his wife, he also saw to it that black tank men who served under General George S. Patton, Jr., and black pilots who served in North Africa and Europe saw action. African Americans benefited greatly from the new educational programs and expanded training centers. The most famous of these military training centers was at the Tuskegee Institute, where the Tuskegee Airmen would gain national recognition for their support of American troops in North Africa, Italy, and Germany. Many of the officers trained during this period would return to the United States following the war to become leaders in the effort to integrate the United States armed forces. Many of the black soldiers trained at these centers would go on to have distinguished careers in the Army, Navy, Air Force, and Marines and become the first black captains, majors, colonels, and generals in the United States military. ■

MAP 106

Countries Where Black Troops Were Deployed during World War II (1941–1945)

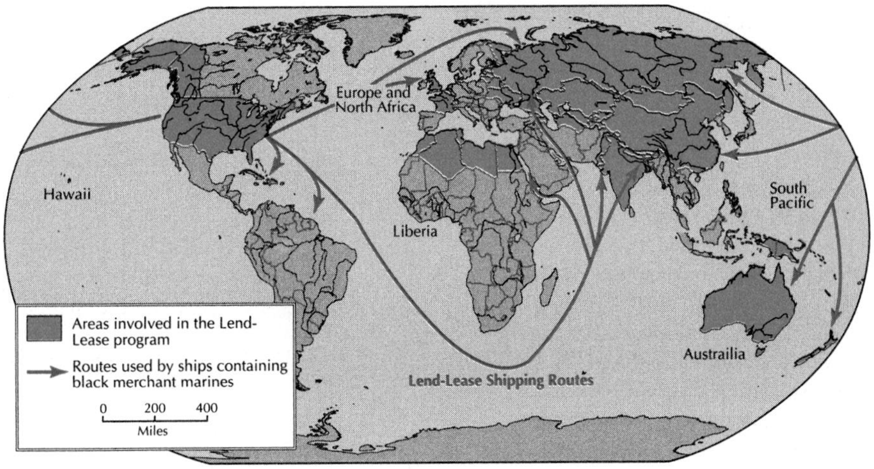
Europe and North Africa
Hawaii
Liberia
South Pacific
Australia
Areas involved in the Lend-Lease program
Routes used by ships containing black merchant marines
0 200 400
Miles
Lend-Lease Shipping Routes

Even before the United States officially entered World War II, blacks were involved in the conflict as both soldiers and merchant marines. People of African descent from French and British colonies in Africa, the Caribbean, Canada, and the United States supplied Great Britain with American weapons and fighting men. On the battlefields of Europe, American blacks, as they had during World War I—when 165 black Americans volunteered to fight with the 106th Battalion of Canada as early as 1916—were already fighting the enemy, some after volunteering to fight in the Spanish Civil War from 1936 to 1939, and others after joining the Canadian Army to fight for Great Britain as early as 1938. When the war broke out in the Pacific, black soldiers who were stationed in the Philippines and Hawaii built and maintained fortifications until reinforcements arrived from the states. Black soldiers were deployed in both the European and Pacific theaters during the war. They were sent to North and West Africa, Italy, France, Germany, England, Australia, Venezuela, Panama, Bermuda, the Caribbean, Burma, Alaska, and the Philippines. Wherever U.S. forces were sent, black soldiers were included. They were used for combat and as support personnel. As in World War I, the vast majority assisted in building bridges and roads as well as restoring communications and electricity. They reburied the dead and helped to construct the Burma Road, which was used to supply the Chinese with American weapons to assist them in driving the Japanese out of China. Black troops also helped to construct the Alaska Highway used by Americans to supply U.S. military bases in Alaska and the Aleutian Islands. Black pilots and air crews were stationed in North Africa and later Italy, and escorted U.S. bombing missions throughout German-held Europe. They were with Patton's Third Army that battled through northern France across Belgium and on to Berlin. They were also with the Seventh Army that landed in southern France and pushed on across Austria and into central Germany, and with U.S. forces in Italy who fought their way through eastern Austria and into southern Germany. By serving in so many countries African American soldiers gained an even greater awareness of the conditions of people of color who were being exploited around the world. As a result, by the end of the war many African Americans would become Pan-Africanists and supporters of black nationalism, sensing a need for African people to unify to gain their independence worldwide. ■

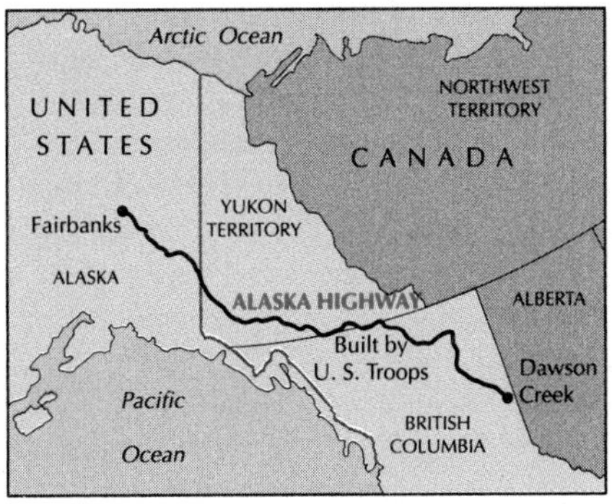
Arctic Ocean
UNITED STATES
NORTHWEST TERRITORY
CANADA
Fairbanks
YUKON TERRITORY
ALASKA
ALASKA HIGHWAY
ALBERTA
Built by U. S. Troops
Dawson Creek
Pacific Ocean
BRITISH COLUMBIA

MAP 107

Race Riots in American Cities during World War II (1943)

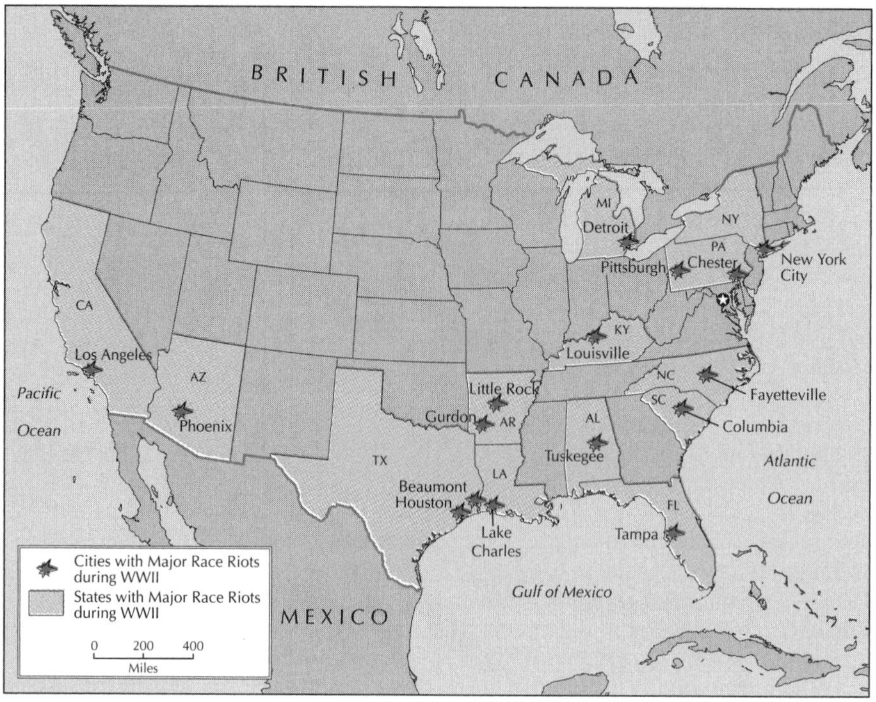
BRITISH
CANADA
MI
Detroit
NY
PA
Pittsburgh
Chester
New York City
CA
KY
Louisville
Los Angeles
AZ
NC
Pacific Ocean
Little Rock
Fayetteville
SC
Gurdon
AR
Columbia
Phoenix
AL
Tuskegee
TX
Atlantic Ocean
LA
Beaumont
Houston
FL
Lake Charles
Tampa
Cities with Major Race Riots during WWII
States with Major Race Riots during WWII
Gulf of Mexico
MEXICO
0 200 400
Miles

During World War II African Americans served their country by both working in the war industries and serving in the armed forces. Although America was fighting a war in Europe and the Pacific to preserve democracy, and ultimately to end the Fascist and Nazi regimes, it became clear to many African Americans that democracy did not extend to them in their home country. Many African Americans had been routinely discriminated against in cities throughout the United States. Civilians and men and women in uniform suffered from racial insults, beatings, and lynchings at the hands of whites. Failing to see the hypocrisy of their actions, many whites, in both the North and the South, wanted to keep blacks in their place as second-class citizens. Many blacks were fed up with unequal pay, harsh treatment, lack of proper housing, and physical attacks that often resulted in the deaths of black men, women, and children by racist whites in towns and cities around the country. Complaints by black leaders went unanswered by local, state, and federal officials. Beginning in Chicago in 1943, race riots erupted on or near military bases and in cities all over the country. These riots caused many injuries and deaths and the destruction of millions of dollars' worth of property. They caused great concern among the white and black communities, civic, and business leaders, and brought to the forefront many of the problems that black civilians and soldiers dealt with on a daily basis. The riots also embarrassed the United States, which was rapidly becoming the leader of the free world. As a result of these riots, interracial committees and organizations were created and expanded to bridge the racial divide in America. ■

MAP 108

Race Riots on United States Military Bases during World War II (1943)

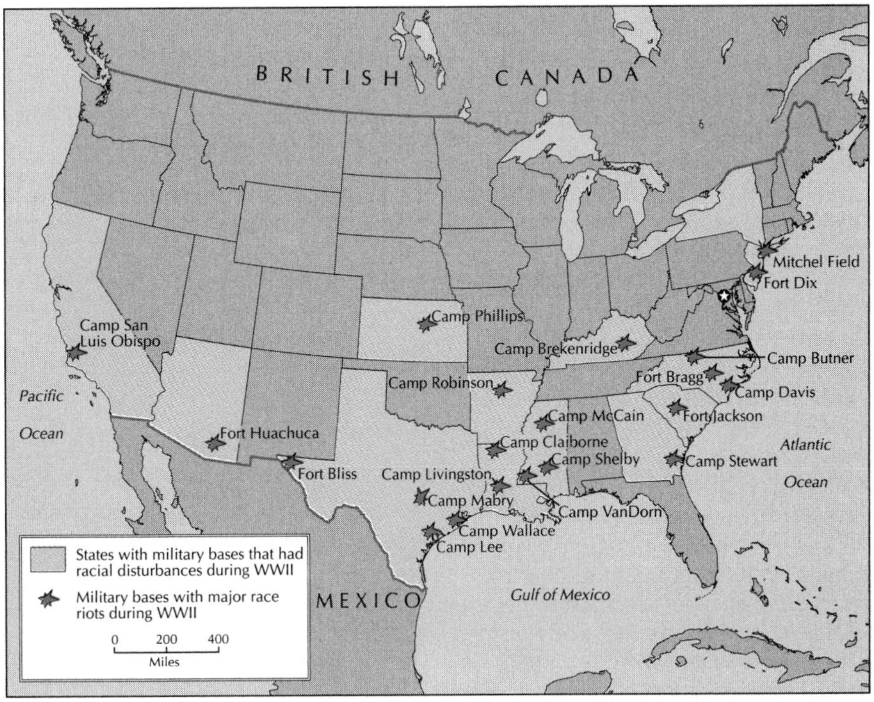
BRITISH
CANADA
Mitchel Field
Fort Dix
Camp Phillips
Camp San Luis Obispo
Camp Brekenridge
Camp Butner
Fort Bragg
Camp Robinson
Camp Davis
Pacific Ocean
Camp McCain
Fort Jackson
Fort Huachuca
Camp Claiborne
Atlantic Ocean
Camp Shelby
Camp Stewart
Fort Bliss
Camp Livingston
Camp Mabry
Camp VanDorn
Camp Wallace
Camp Lee
States with military bases that had racial disturbances during WWII
Military bases with major race riots during WWII
0 200 400
Miles
MEXICO
Gulf of Mexico

Before black troops were sent overseas to fight for America, they were trained and stationed on a number of U.S. military bases in various parts of the country. Beginning with their induction into the military, life for black soldiers was very different from that of their white comrades. When they boarded the trains that took them to their new home, they found that segregation extended to the military. They traveled in the forward railcars because the soot from the coal-powered engine blew into those cars first and covered the riders with its toxic fumes. They were forced to travel night and day with the window shades lowered because southern whites often fired shots at train cars carrying black troops. When they reached their training bases, they found many of their instructors, who were white, baited them, used racial slurs to degrade them, forced them to do demeaning work, and considered them to be inferior. Even black officers were not respected by white officers or enlisted men and often were not allowed to use the base facilities reserved for officers. They were often forbidden to leave the base because their presence upset white civilians who lived nearby. When they were allowed to leave the base, many found it safer not to wear their uniforms because blacks in uniform around the country, especially in the South where most of the bases were located, were often attacked by mobs, beaten, shot, and lynched for merely being in uniform. As a result, black soldiers, who were recruited to fight racism and tyranny in Europe and the Pacific, found their situation unacceptable. Added to this was the knowledge that the U.S. Congress, led by southern congressmen, had no intention of allowing black soldiers to fight in either Europe or the Pacific. All these problems and the emotions associated with them erupted into racial violence on military bases all over the country. Black soldiers battled white soldiers, and the violence threatened to grow. In response to these riots the U.S. government finally began to ship large numbers of black combat troops to both Europe and the Pacific. ■

MAP 109

Major Black Battle Sites during World War II (1943–1945)

During World War II, black soldiers fought and died for America in North Africa, Europe, and the Pacific. They served at Pearl Harbor in Hawaii, defending their country from Japanese bombers on December 7, 1941. They dive-bombed Germans in North Africa and escorted American bombers and battled the German Luftwaffe in the skies over Germany as the Allies began to bomb German cities. African Americans, although relegated at the start of the war to menial tasks, were actively fighting in every theater of the war by the end of the war in 1945. Over three-fourths of the truck drivers who transported fuel, men, guns, bullets, food, and other supplies for U.S. forces in Europe were African Americans. Many of these men, operating what was referred to as the "Red Ball Express," often found themselves behind enemy lines and engaging Germans in hand-to-hand combat. They also often encountered groups of Germans who had been successful in infiltrating the Allied lines and were attempting to disrupt supply lines and slow the Allied advance. Over 15,000 blacks helped to build the Burma Road, which ran from Burma to China and supplied the Chinese forces with badly need supplies to defeat the Japanese. Under miserable conditions —having to contend with gigantic mosquitos and other insects and the frigid weather of Canada and Alaska—over 3,000 black troops helped to build the Alaska Highway. More than 50,000 black nurses served in England, initially forced to treat only black soldiers as white casualties continued to mount, but later, after protesting, were allowed to treat both. Black tank men fighting under the command of General George S. Patton helped to turn the German offensive back at the Battle of the Bulge and saved American paratroopers trapped by the Germans at Bastogne. These soldiers fought in numerous battles and served their country bravely and loyally until the end of the war. When Allied forces entered Berlin, black soldiers fought gallantly against the enemy, and during the military occupation that followed the war, black soldiers remained in both Europe and Japan. It is also important to note the work of Dr. Charles Drew of Howard University. He developed blood plasma, which was used by the Red Cross during the war to save the lives of millions of soldiers on both sides during the conflict. ■

German Reich under seige
Recaptured allied areas by 1945
Neutral countries
Black ground forces
Black battle sites and German-held cities bombed with support of Tuskeegee airmen (routes in white)
Air base for Tuskeegee airmen
0 100 200
Miles
Norwegian Sea
FINLAND
SWEDEN
NORWAY
ESTONIAN S.S.R.
LATVIAN S.S.R.
LITHUANIAN S.S.R.
EAST PRUSSIA
U.S.S.R.
UNITED KINGDOM
DENMARK
North Atlantic Ocean
IRELAND
NETHERLANDS
Berlin
POLAND
WHITE RUSSIAN S.S.R.
London
London 50,000 Black Nurses served in U.S. Army
BELGIUM
GERMANY
Blechhammer
UKRANIAN S.S.R.
LUXEMBOURG
Munich
CZECHOSLOVAKIA
FRANCE
SWITZERLAND
AUSTRIA
HUNGARY
Polesti
PORTUGAL
RUMANIA
Black Sea
Toulon
YUGOSLAVIA
ITALY
BULGARIA
SPAIN
Black Pilots and Soldiers from US join Canadian Royal Airforce and Army and Fight in Spanish Civil War
SARDINIA
ALBANIA
GREECE
TURKEY (OTTOMAN EMPIRE)
Mediterranean Sea
Ramitell AFB Home of Tuskeegee Airmen
MOROCCO
ALGERIA
TUNISIA

Arctic Ocean
UNITED STATES
CANADA
Fairbanks
ALASKA
YUKON TERRITORY
ALASKA HIGHWAY
Built by U.S. Troops
ALBERTA
Dawson Creek
Pacific Ocean
BRITISH COLUMBIA

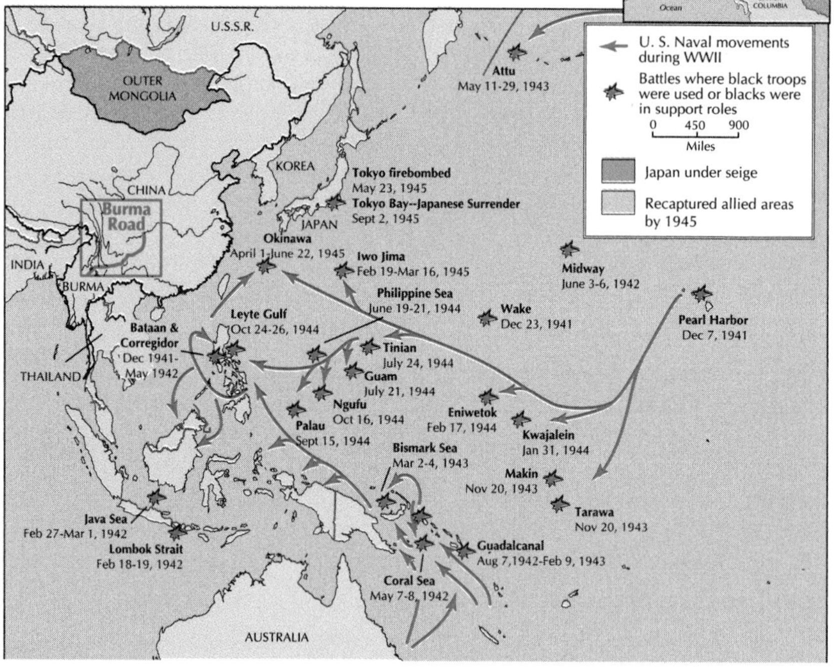
U.S.S.R.
OUTER MONGOLIA
Attu May 11-29, 1943
U. S. Naval movements during WWII
Battles where black troops were used or blacks were in support roles
0 450 900
Miles
Japan under seige
Recaptured allied areas by 1945
KOREA
CHINA
Burma Road
Tokyo firebombed May 23, 1945
Tokyo Bay--Japanese Surrender Sept 2, 1945
JAPAN
Okinawa April 1-June 22, 1945
Iwo Jima Feb 19-Mar 16, 1945
INDIA
BURMA
Midway June 3-6, 1942
Philippine Sea June 19-21, 1944
Leyte Gulf Oct 24-26, 1944
Wake Dec 23, 1941
Pearl Harbor Dec 7, 1941
Bataan & Corregidor Dec 1941-May 1942
Tinian July 24, 1944
THAILAND
Guam July 21, 1944
Ngufu Oct 16, 1944
Palau Sept 15, 1944
Eniwetok Feb 17, 1944
Kwajalein Jan 31, 1944
Bismark Sea Mar 2-4, 1943
Makin Nov 20, 1943
Tarawa Nov 20, 1943
Java Sea Feb 27-Mar 1, 1942
Lombok Strait Feb 18-19, 1942
Guadalcanal Aug 7,1942-Feb 9, 1943
Coral Sea May 7-8, 1942
AUSTRALIA

MAP 110

Buchenwald and Dachau: African American Involvement in the Liberation of Holocaust Survivors (1944–1945)

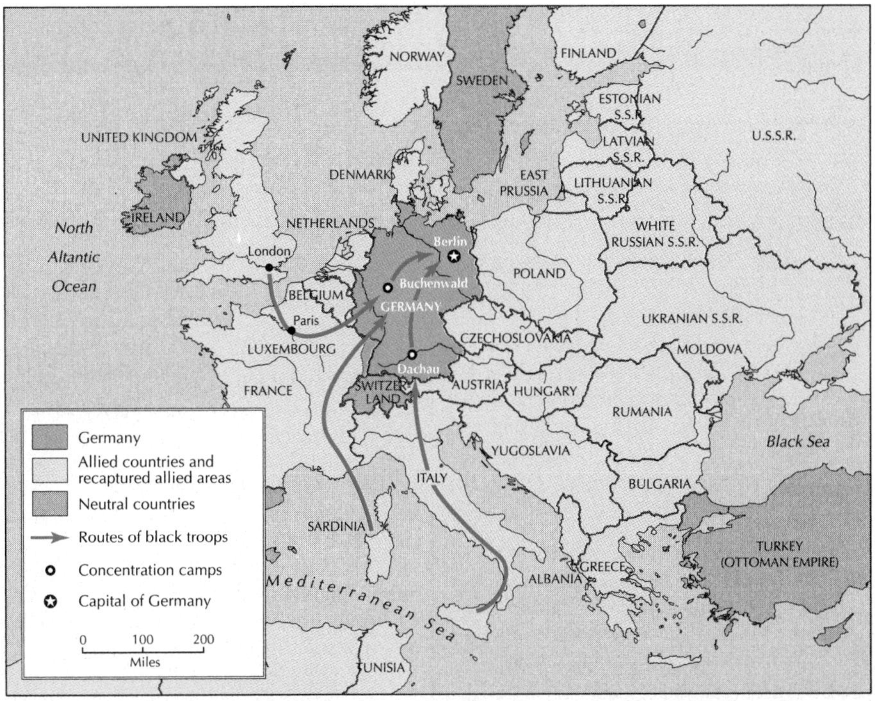
NORWAY
SWEDEN
FINLAND
ESTONIAN S.S.R.
LATVIAN S.S.R.
LITHUANIAN S.S.R.
U.S.S.R.
UNITED KINGDOM
IRELAND
DENMARK
EAST PRUSSIA
North Altantic Ocean
NETHERLANDS
London
Berlin
Buchenwald
GERMANY
POLAND
WHITE RUSSIAN S.S.R.
BELGIUM
Paris
LUXEMBOURG
CZECHOSLOVAKIA
UKRANIAN S.S.R.
MOLDOVA
Dachau
FRANCE
SWITZERLAND
AUSTRIA
HUNGARY
RUMANIA
Black Sea
YUGOSLAVIA
ITALY
BULGARIA
SARDINIA
ALBANIA
GREECE
TURKEY (OTTOMAN EMPIRE)
Mediterranean Sea
TUNISIA
Germany
Allied countries and recaptured allied areas
Neutral countries
Routes of black troops
Concentration camps
Capital of Germany
0 100 200
Miles

As American forces pushed German forces back to Berlin, the Germans left behind a number of concentration camps that were used to imprison Jews and other "undesirable" peoples. The true horrors of racism were about to be uncovered in the concentration camps of the Third Reich. Early in the war, millions of Jews, Poles, Romanians, Gypsies, and others were rounded up and shipped by train or marched into concentration camps all over Germany and in the countries allied with or conquered by Hitler. Then, in 1942, Hitler began to order the implementation of his "final solution," the extermination of these people. When the survivors of the Buchenwald and Dachau concentration camps were liberated in 1944, the first faces they saw were African American. The blacks of the 371st Tank Battalion who entered Buchenwald witnessed the ultimate consequence of racism. They found there the skeleton-like survivors of a concentration camp that had claimed the lives of more than 100.000 Jews. Black soldiers liberated these survivors and those of Dachau and Lambach would not forget the horrors they witnessed. When these men returned to America, they were forever transformed. They resolved not to allow what they witnessed in Germany to happen in America. ■

0 50
Miles
DENMARK
SWEDEN
NETHERLANDS
Schleswig-Holstein
Mecklenburg
Hamburg
Bremen
POLAND
Niedersachsen
GERMANY
Berlin
Brandenburg
Nordrhein-Westfalen
Altmark
BELGIUM
Buchenwald April 4
Thuringia
Saxony
Rhineland-Pfalz
Hessen
Saarland
CZECHOSLOVAKIA
LUXEMBOURG
Bayern
Baden-Wurttemberg
Dachau April 29
FRANCE
AUSTRIA
SWITZERLAND
ITALY

Map and Text Sources

100. Gosnell, Harold F. *Negro Politicians: The Rise of Negro Politics in Chicago.* Chicago: University of Chicago Press, 1967.

Hughes, Cicero Alvin. "Toward a Black United Front: The National Negro Congress Movement." Ph.D. dissertation, Ohio University, 1982.

National Negro Congress. *Resolutions of the National Negro Congress Held in Chicago, Illinois, February 14, 15, 16, 1936.* S. l.: The Congress, 1936.

Nowlin, William Felbert. *The Negro in American National Politics.* New York: Russell & Russell, 1970.

Price, Margaret W. *The Negro Voter in the South.* Atlanta: Southern Regional Council, 1957.

Record, Wilson. *The Negro and the Communist Party.* Westport, CT: Greenwood Press, 1980.

Streater, John B. "The National Negro Congress, 1936–1947." Ph.D. dissertation, University of Cincinnati, 1981.

Weiss, Nancy J. *Farewell to the Party of Lincoln: Black Politics in the Age of FDR.* Princeton, NJ: Princeton University Press, 1983.

Wilson, James Q. *Negro Politics: The Search for Leadership.* New York: Octagon Books, 1980.

101. Albanese, Catherine L. *America, Religions and Religion.* Belmont, CA: Wadsworth Publishing Company, 1981.

Fisher, Robert B. *African-American Christianity.* New Orleans: Xavier University Press, 1993.

Muhammad, Elijah. *History of the Nation of Islam.* Atlanta: Secretarius Memps Publications, 1994.

Watts, Jill. *God, Harlem U.S.A.: The Father Divine Story.* Berkeley: University of California Press, 1992.

Weisbrot, Robert. *Father Divine and the Struggle for Racial Equality.* Urbana: University of Illinois Press, 1983.

Wilmore, Gayraud S. *Black Religion and Black Radicalism: An Interpretation of the Religious History of Afro-American People,* 2nd ed. Maryknoll, NY: Orbis Books, 1993.

102. United States Bureau of the Census. *Historical Statistics of the United States, Colonial Times to 1970, Bicentennial Edition [Part 2].* Washington, DC: Government Printing Office, 1975.

103. Bracey, John H., August Meier, and Elliott Rudwick. *The Rise of the Ghetto.* Belmont, CA: Wadsworth Publishing Company, 1971.

Dennis, Sam Joseph. "Black Exodus and White Migration, 1950 to 1970: A Comparative Analysis of Population Movements and Their Relations to Labor and Race Relations." Ph.D. dissertation, American University, 1984.

Gill, Flora. *Economics and the Black Exodus: An Analysis of Negro Emigration from the Southern United States, 1910–70.* New York: Garland Publishing, 1979.

Goodwin, E. Marvin. *Black Migration in America from 1915 to 1960: An Uneasy Exodus.* Lewiston: E. Mellen Press, 1990.

Grossman, James R. *Land of Hope: Chicago, Black Southerners and the Great Migration.* Chicago: University of Chicago Press, 1989.

Harrison, Alferdteen, ed. *Black Exodus: The Great Migration from the American South.* Jackson: University Press of Mississippi, 1991.

Marks, Carole. *Farewell, We're Good and Gone: The Great Black Migration.* Bloomington: Indiana University Press, 1989.

McMillen, Neil R. *Dark Journey: Black Mississippians in the Age of Jim Crow.* Urbana: University of Illinois Press, 1990.

Scott, Emmet J. *Negro Migration during the War.* New York: Arno Press, 1969.

Trotter, Joe William. *Black Milwaukee: The Making of an Industrial Proletariat, 1915–45.* Urbana: University of Illinois Press, 1985.

Trotter, Joe William, ed. *The Great Migration in Historical Perspective: New Dimensions of Race, Class, and Gender.* Bloomington: Indiana University Press, 1991.

104. Cantor, Milton, comp. *Black Labor in America.* Westport, CT: Negro Universities Press, 1969.

Cayton, Horace R., and George S. Mitchell. *Black Workers and the New Unions.* Westport, CT: Negro Universities Press, 1970.

Conrad, David Eugene. *The Forgotten Farmers: The Story of Sharecroppers in the New Deal.* Urbana: University of Illinois Press, 1965.

Douglas, Ensen X. *A New Deal for Blacks: Suggestions for Salvation.* New York: Exposition Press, 1974.

Dulles, Foster Rhea. *Labor in America: A History.* New York: Crowell, 1963.

Grant, Nancy L. *TVA and Black Americans: Planning for the Status Quo.* Philadelphia: Temple University Press, 1990.

Grubbs, Donald H. *Cry from the Cotton: The Southern Tenant Farmers' Union and the New Deal.* Chapel Hill: University of North Carolina Press, 1971.

Harris, William H. *The Harder We Run: Black Labor Since the Civil War.* New York: Oxford University Press, 1982.

Harris, William H. *Keeping the Faith: A. Philip Randolph, Milton P. Webster, and the Brotherhood of Sleeping Car Porters, 1925–1937.* Urbana: University of Illinois Press, 1991.

Hayes, Laurence John Wesley. *The Negro Federal Governmental Worker: A Study of His Classification Status in the District of Columbia, 1883–1938.* Washington, DC: The Graduate School, Howard University, 1941.

Hill, Timothy Arnold. *The Negro and Economic Reconstruction.* Washington, DC: The Associates in Negro Folk Education, 1937.

Hurt, R. Douglas. *American Agriculture: A Brief History.* Ames: Iowa State University Press, 1994.

Kele, Max H. *Nazis and Workers: National Socialist Appeals to German Labor, 1919–1933.* Chapel Hill: University of North Carolina Press, 1972.

Northrup, Herbert R. *Organized Labor and the Negro.* New York: Harper, 1971.

Pfeffer, Paula F. *A. Philip Randolph, Pioneer of the Civil Rights Movement.* Baton Rouge: Louisiana State University Press, 1990.

Sitkoff, Harvard. *A New Deal for Blacks: The Emergence of Civil Rights as a National Issue. Vol. 1, The Depression Decade.* New York: Oxford University Press, 1981.

Spero, Sterling Denhard. *The Black Worker: The Negro and the Labor Movement.* New York: Atheneum, 1972.

Sterner, Richard M. *The Negro's Share: A Study of Income, Consumption, Housing, and Public Assistance.* Westport, CT: Negro Universities Press, 1971.

Sternsher, Bernard, ed. *The Negro in Depression and War: Prelude to Revolution, 1930–1945.* Chicago: Quadrangle Press, 1969.

United States Department of Labor, Division of Negro Economics. *The Negro at Work during the World War and during Reconstruction; Statistics, Problems, and Policies Relating to the Greater Inclusion of Negro Wage Earners in American Industry and Agriculture.* New York: Negro Universities Press, 1969.

Weaver, Robert C. *Negro Labor: A National Problem.* Port Washington, NY: Kennikat Press, 1969.

Wesley, Charles H. *Negro Labor in the United States, 1850–1925: A Study in American Economic History.* New York: Vanguard Press, 1927.

Williams, Walter E., Loren A. Smith, and Wendell W. Gunn. *Black America and Organized Labor: A Fair Deal?* Washington, DC: Lincoln Institute for Research and Education, 1979.

Wolters, Raymond. *Negroes and the Great Depression: The Problem of Economic Recovery.* Westport, CT: Greenwood Publishing Corperation, 1970.

105. Hawkins, Walter L. *African American Generals and Flag Officers: Biographies of over 120 Blacks in the United States Military.* Jefferson, NC: McFarland, 1993.

Jakeman, Robert J. *The Divided Skies: Establishing Segregated Flight Training at Tuskegee, Alabama, 1934–1942.* Tuscaloosa: University of Alabama Press, 1992.

Johnson, Charles. *African American Soldiers in the National Guard: Recruitment and Deployment during Peacetime and War.* Westport, CT: Greenwood Press, 1992.

Lee, Ulysses. *The Employment of Negro Troops.* Washington, DC: Center of Military History, United States Army, 1994.

Nalty, Bernard C. *Strength for the Fight: A History of Black Americans in the Military.* New York: Free Press, 1986.

106. Johnson, Jesse J. *A Pictorial History of Black Soldiers in the United States (1619–1969).* Hampton, VA: Johnson Publishing Company, 1973.

Lee, Ulysses. *The Employment of Negro Troops.* Washington, DC: Center of Military History, United States Army, 1994.

Nalty, Bernard C. *Strength for the Fight: A History of Black Americans in the Military.* New York: Free Press, 1986.

Patton, Gerald W. *War and Race: The Black Officer in the American Military, 1915–1941.* Westport, CT: Greenwood Press, 1981.

Silvera, John D., comp. *The Negro in World War II.* New York: Arno Press, 1969.

Yancey, Francis, ed. *This Is Our War; Selected Stories of Six War Correspondents Who Were Sent Overseas by the Afro-American Newspapers: Baltimore, Washington, Philadelphia, Richmond and Newark.* Baltimore: The Afro-American Company, 1945.

107. Capeci, Dominic J., and Martha F. Wilkerson. *Layered Violence: The Detroit Rioters of 1943.* Jackson: University of Mississippi Press, 1991.

Lee, Ulysses. *The Employment of Negro Troops.* Washington, DC: Center of Military History, United States Army, 1994.

Nalty, Bernard C. *Strength for the Fight: A History of Black Americans in the Military.* New York: Free Press, 1986.

Shapiro, Herbert. *White Violence and Black Response: From Reconstruction to Montgomery.* Amherst: University of Massachusetts Press, 1988.

Waskow, Arthur I. *From Race Riot to Sit-In, 1919 to the 1960s; A Study in the Connections between Conflict and Violence.* Garden City, NY: Anchor Books, 1967.

108. Johnson, Jesse J., ed. *A Pictorial History of Black Soldiers in the United States (1619–1969).* Hampton, VA: Johnson Publishing Company, 1973.

Lee, Ulysses. *The Employment of Negro Troops.* Washington, DC: Center of Military History, United States Army, 1994.

Nalty, Bernard C. *Strength for the Fight: A History of Black Americans in the Military.* New York: Free Press, 1986.

109. Baldwin, Hanson W. *Battles Lost and Won: Great Campaigns of World War II.* New York: Avon Books, 1968.

Buchanan, A. Russell. *Black Americans in World War II.* Santa Barbara, CA: Clio Books, 1979.

Francis, Charles E. *The Tuskegee Airmen: The Men Who Changed a Nation,* 3rd ed. Boston: Branden Publishing Company, 1993.

Hargrove, Hondon B. *Buffalo Soldiers in Italy: Black Americans in World War II.* Jefferson, NC: McFarland, 1985.

Harris, Jacqueline L. *The Tuskegee Airmen: Black Heroes of World War II.* Parsippany, NJ: Dillon Press, 1996.

Lee, Ulysses. *The Employment of Negro Troops.* Washington, DC: Center of Military History, United States Army, 1994.

MacGregor, Morris J. *Integration of the Armed Forces, 1940–1965.* Washington, DC: Center of Military History, United States Army, 1981.

Motley, Mary Penick, ed. *The Invisible Soldiers: The Experience of the Black Soldier, World War II.* Detroit: Wayne State University Press, 1987.

Nalty, Bernard C. *Strength for the Fight: A History of Black Americans in the Military.* New York: Free Press, 1986.

Spector, Ronald H. *Eagle Against the Sun: The American War with Japan.* New York: Free Press, 1985.

110. Abzug, Robert H. *Inside the Vicious Heart: Americans and the Liberation of Nazi Concentration Camps.* New York: Oxford University Press, 1985.

Gilbert, Martin. *Atlas of the Holocaust.* New York: William Morrow, 1993.

Nalty, Bernard C. *Strength for the Fight: A History of Black Americans in the Military.* New York: Free Press, 1986.

Potter, Lou. *Liberators: Fighting on Two Fronts in World War II,* New York: Harcourt Brace Jovanovich, 1992.

MAP 111

African Americans and the Cold War: The Role of African Americans in Europe, Asia, and Africa (1945–1980)

After World War II ended in September 1945, the United States and the Soviet Union, which had been uneasy allies during the war, became bitter enemies in the cold war that followed. The Allies had divided Germany into four zones: The Russian Zone included all of eastern Germany; the British Zone consisted of west central Germany; the French Zone encompassed northern west Germany; and the United States Zone comprised of southern west Germany. The American Zone was policed by both black and white troops. The capital city of Berlin had likewise been divided into four sectors—one Russian, one French, one British, and one American. American troops, both black and white, also were used to police the American sector of Berlin. Due to Allied-Soviet tensions and the fact that Berlin was located well within the borders of Soviet-controlled East Germany, U.S. troops stationed in Berlin were often in grave danger. One of the most dangerous situations arose between April 1948 and May 1949. In April 1948 Russia blockaded Berlin, refusing to allow food and supplies into the French, English, and American sectors of the city. To avoid confrontation and possible war, the United States turned to the Air Force to keep the Allies supplied in what has become known as the Berlin Airlift. During the crisis, black troops helped to load and unload the planes that flew supplies into Berlin, and these troops were prepared to go to war to defend democracy. When the crisis finally ended in May of 1949, black troops had played an important role in both the

NORWAY
FINLAND
Helsinki
Oslo
Stockholm
SWEDEN
Dublin
North Sea
UNITED KINGDOM
DENMARK
Black Sea
Moscow
SOVIET UNION
NETHERLANDS
IRELAND
London
POLAND
Berlin
EAST GERMANY
Warsaw
Atlantic Ocean
BELGIUM
Bonn
WEST GERMANY
Prague
Paris
Munich
CZECH.
SWITZERLAND
Vienna
Budapest
AUSTRIA
FRANCE
HUNGARY
ROMANIA
Russian occupation zone
British occupation zone
French occupation zone
U.S occupation zone
Capital cities
0 100 200
Miles
ALGERIA
Ankara
CYPRUS
Berlin
Tegel (French)
East Berlin (Soviet)
West Berlin (British)
Tempelhof Airfield
Tempelhof (United States)
Berlin Wall 1961
The Tempelhof Airfield was the site of the U.S. Berlin Airlift in 1948-1949.
0 5 10
Miles

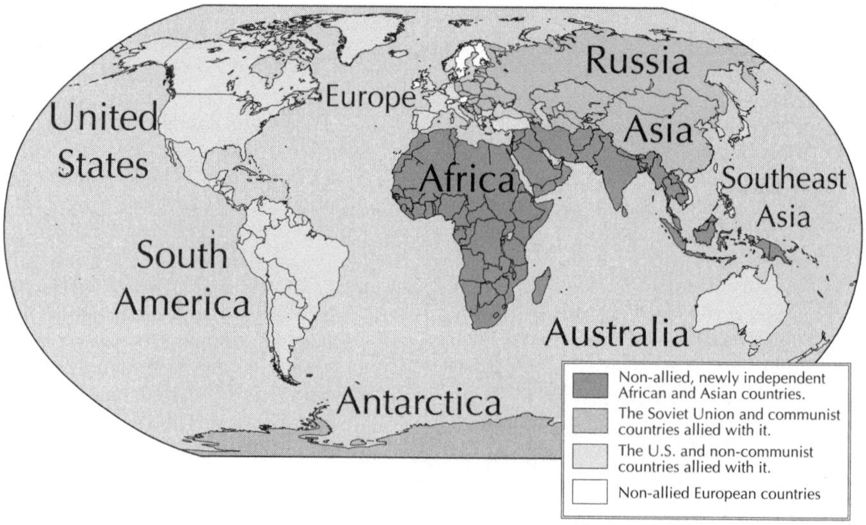
United States
Europe
Russia
Asia
Africa
Southeast Asia
South America
Australia
Antarctica
Non-allied, newly independent African and Asian countries.
The Soviet Union and communist countries allied with it.
The U.S. and non-communist countries allied with it.
Non-allied European countries

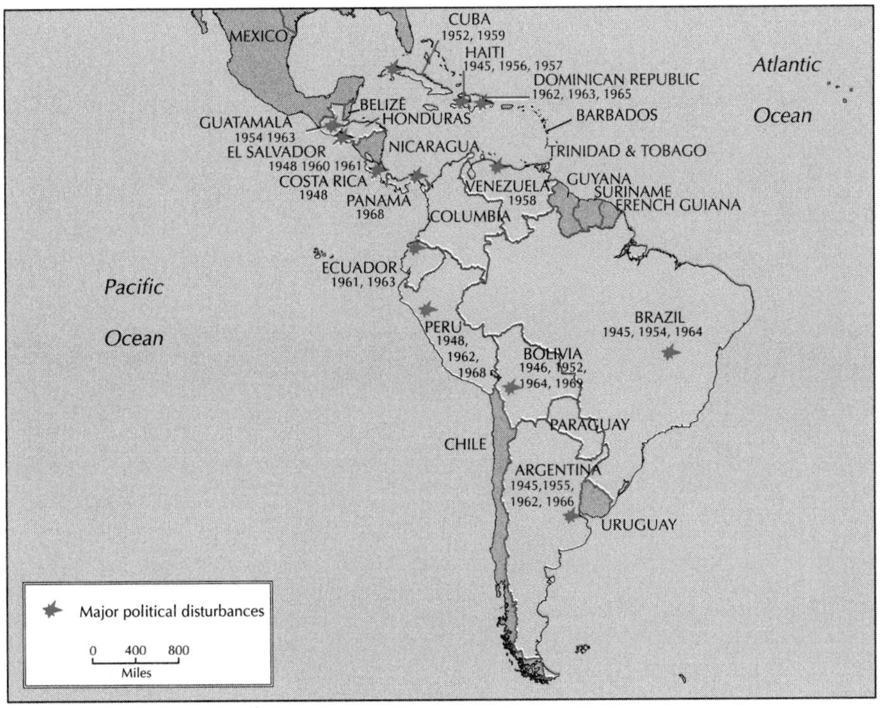
MEXICO
CUBA
1952, 1959
HAITI
1945, 1956, 1957
DOMINICAN REPUBLIC
1962, 1963, 1965
Atlantic
Ocean
BELIZE
HONDURAS
BARBADOS
GUATAMALA
1954 1963
EL SALVADOR
1948 1960 1961
NICARAGUA
TRINIDAD & TOBAGO
COSTA RICA
1948
PANAMA
1968
VENEZUELA
1958
GUYANA
SURINAME
FRENCH GUIANA
COLUMBIA
ECUADOR
1961, 1963
Pacific
Ocean
PERU
1948,
1962,
1968
BRAZIL
1945, 1954, 1964
BOLIVIA
1946, 1952,
1964, 1969
PARAGUAY
CHILE
ARGENTINA
1945,1955,
1962, 1966
URUGUAY
Major political disturbances
0 400 800
Miles

United States and Berlin. During the cold war, the world was polarized into two camps, the free West, led by the United States, and the Communist East, led by the Soviet Union, with many countries of the third world (Africa and Asia) refusing to align themselves with either superpower. Although black soldiers and civilians served the United States faithfully during the Berlin Airlift and the many other crises that followed during the cold war, they became increasingly angry over the double standard set by the U.S. government—freedom abroad, but state-sanctioned segregation, racial violence, and oppression at home. Blacks were also very concerned about the U.S.'s role in suppressing popular revolutions by people of African descent in the Caribbean, Central America, and South America, which was defended by government leaders as necessary to contain the spread of communism in the Americas. ■

MAP 112

Black Nationalism and the Decolonization of Africa (1945–1995)

Nationalism was not conceived by Africans or African Americans but by Europeans. The concept began in Europe during the French Revolution. Though contained and suppressed by the Congress of Vienna in 1815, it rose again in Europe during the Revolutions of 1848, and began to dominate the politics of the major and lesser nations of Europe throughout the late nineteenth and early twentieth century. Nationalism was a major cause of the First World War and was used by the British and French to destroy the multiethnic Ottoman Empire. It was also, at the insistence of Woodrow Wilson, used to redraw the political boundaries of Europe at the Versailles Peace Conference and as the foundation for the creation of the League of Nations in 1919. Out of the old multiethnic Austro-Hungarian Empire was created several new ethnic nations, including Czechoslovakia, Romania, and Yugoslavia in Europe. In the Middle East, the Ottoman Empire was also dismantled to create Palestine (Israel), Syria, Lebanon, Jordan, and Iraq. By the end of the Versailles Peace Conference, nationalism began to spread throughout Africa. It inspired African peoples who had been colonial possessions of European nations to declare their independence and pursue armed resistance if needed in achieving this goal. Black nationalism, which had existed in the United States since 1900, and according to some scholars as early as the 1800s, was expanded by Marcus Garvey and his movement from 1914 to 1928. Garvey believed that people of color around the world were being exploited by Europeans and should unite against them. From 1918 to 1970, Africans, with the support of African Americans throughout the Western Hemisphere, would demand and secure independence through war or diplomacy. American black nationalists began to support African nationalists in demanding independence for Africans and more humane treatment in the United States. This global cooperation would begin a new era of black nationalism for the United States and the world. ■

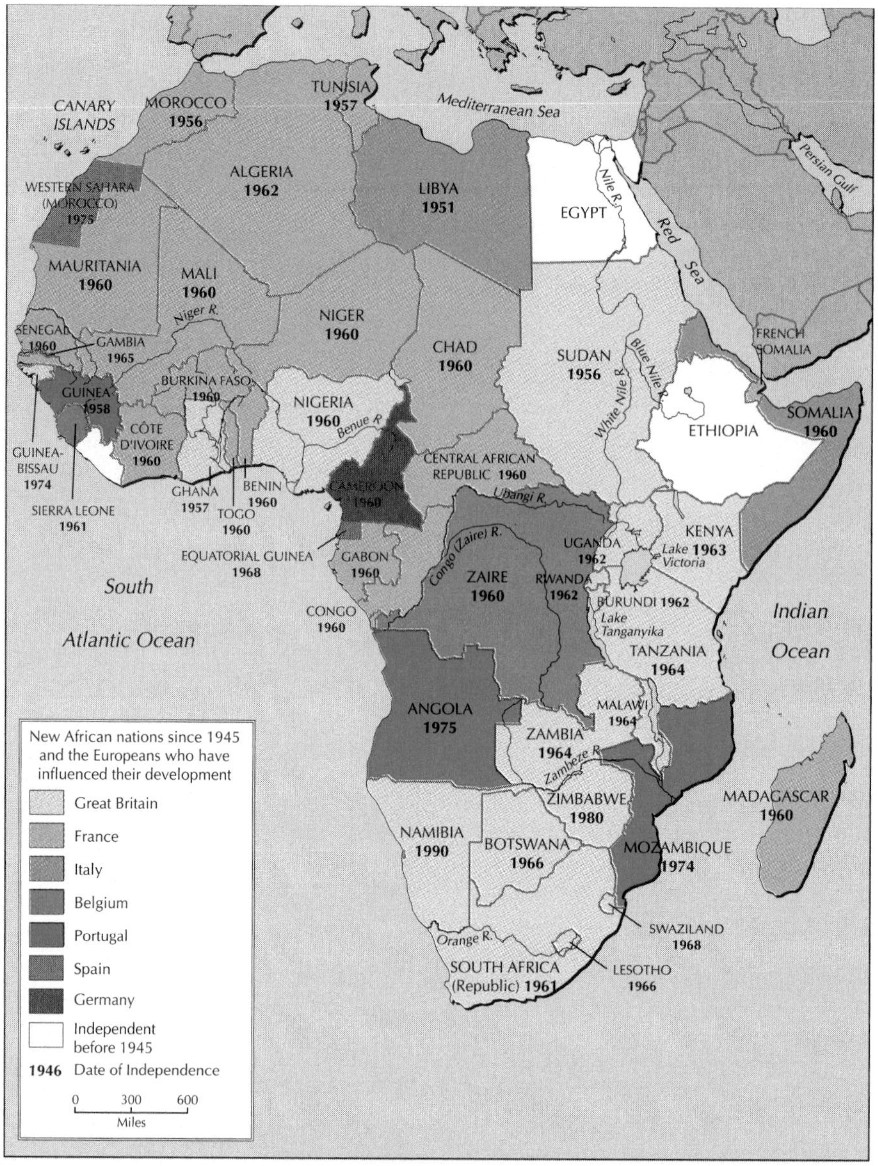

CANARY ISLANDS
MOROCCO 1956
TUNISIA 1957
Mediterranean Sea
ALGERIA 1962
LIBYA 1951
EGYPT
Nile R.
Red Sea
Persian Gulf
WESTERN SAHARA (MOROCCO) 1975
MAURITANIA 1960
MALI 1960
Niger R.
NIGER 1960
CHAD 1960
SUDAN 1956
Blue Nile R.
White Nile R.
FRENCH SOMALIA
SENEGAL 1960
GAMBIA 1965
GUINEA 1958
BURKINA FASO 1960
NIGERIA 1960
Benue R.
ETHIOPIA
SOMALIA 1960
CÔTE D'IVOIRE 1960
GUINEA-BISSAU 1974
SIERRA LEONE 1961
GHANA 1957
BENIN 1960
TOGO 1960
CAMEROON 1960
CENTRAL AFRICAN REPUBLIC 1960
Ubangi R.
EQUATORIAL GUINEA 1968
GABON 1960
Congo (Zaire) R.
ZAIRE 1960
UGANDA 1962
KENYA 1963
Lake Victoria
RWANDA 1962
BURUNDI 1962
Lake Tanganyika
CONGO 1960
South Atlantic Ocean
Indian Ocean
TANZANIA 1964
ANGOLA 1975
MALAWI 1964
ZAMBIA 1964
Zambeze R.
ZIMBABWE 1980
MADAGASCAR 1960
NAMIBIA 1990
BOTSWANA 1966
MOZAMBIQUE 1974
SWAZILAND 1968
Orange R.
SOUTH AFRICA (Republic) 1961
LESOTHO 1966
New African nations since 1945 and the Europeans who have influenced their development
Great Britain
France
Italy
Belgium
Portugal
Spain
Germany
Independent before 1945
1946 Date of Independence
0 300 600
Miles

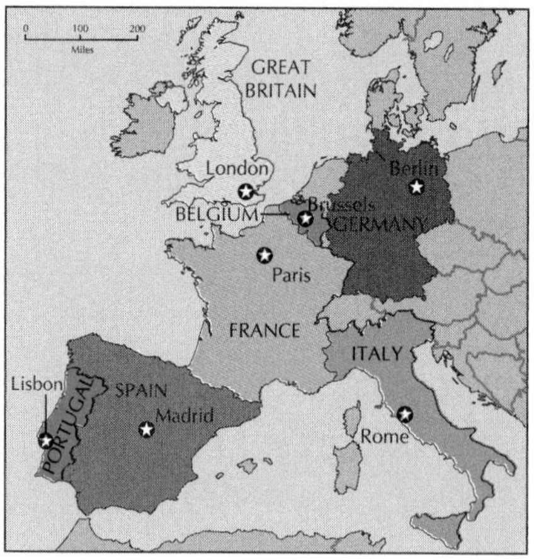

0 100 200
Miles
GREAT BRITAIN
London
BELGIUM
Brussels
GERMANY
Berlin
Paris
FRANCE
ITALY
Lisbon
PORTUGAL
SPAIN
Madrid
Rome

MAP 113

Black Soldiers in the Korean War (1950–1953)

Even though the military's policy still called for segregation in the armed forces, in the closing months of World War II in the last major battle with the Germans, black and white units fought side by side at the Battle of the Rhine. This was the first time that American troops were integrated in battle. The armed forces officially ended segregation in 1948 when President Harry S. Truman issued an Executive Order banning the practice. The Korean War was the first war featuring a fully integrated American military. After the integration of the U.S. military, many African Americans joined the branches of the service that had been closed to them under segregation. Increasing numbers continued to join the Army, but increasingly more began to join the Navy, Air Force, and Marines. From 1948 to the 1980s, larger percentages of blacks than whites, seeking better employment opportunities and education, joined the armed forces. As their numbers rose, so did concerns over the potential for heavy African American casualties in the event of a major war, as in Vietnam. Fear of the domino effect, in which non-Communist countries were expected to fall to communism if not contained, helped to ignite America's first integrated war. When U.S. troops landed in Korea to contain communism, black troops were some of the first to arrive. These troops helped to prove to whites that black troops were just as competent as white troops. They also helped to show that the integration of troops did not hinder the military's ability to do its job. By the end of the war, several thousand blacks had given their lives to prevent the spread of communism in Asia. Many of the black veterans of the war would go on to fight in Vietnam and have noteworthy careers in the armed forces.

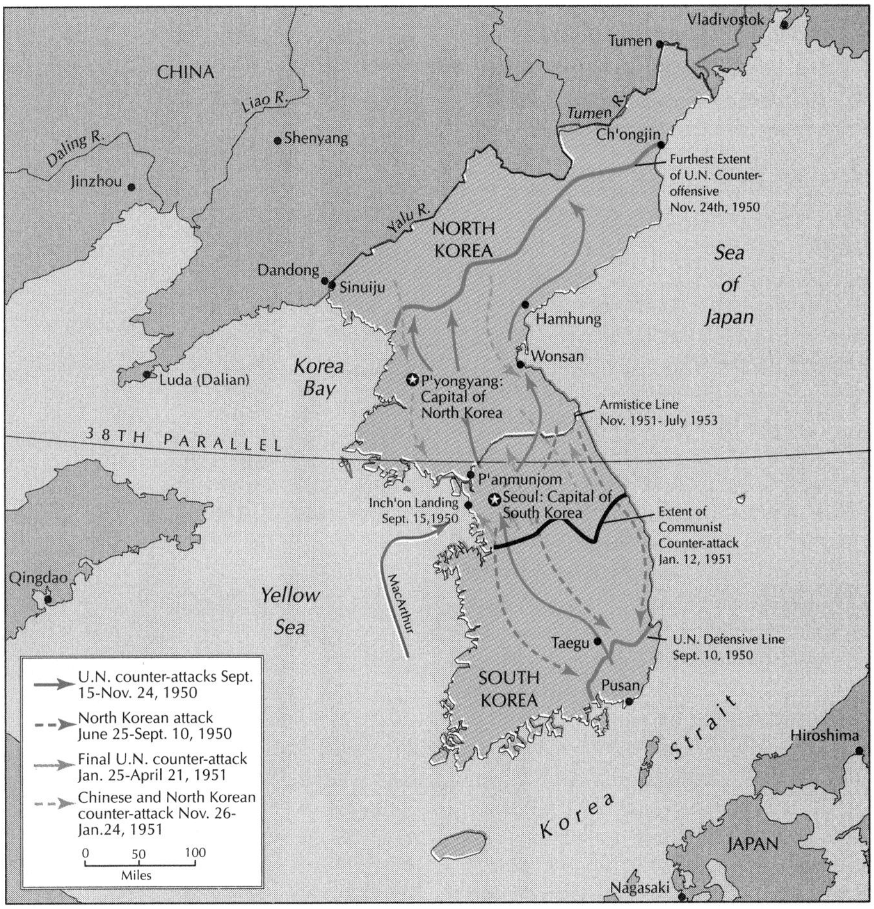

CHINA
Vladivostok
Tumen
Tumen R.
Ch'ongjin
Liao R.
Daling R.
Shenyang
Jinzhou
Yalu R.
NORTH KOREA
Furthest Extent of U.N. Counter-offensive Nov. 24th, 1950
Sea of Japan
Dandong
Sinuiju
Hamhung
Wonsan
Luda (Dalian)
Korea Bay
P'yongyang: Capital of North Korea
Armistice Line Nov. 1951 - July 1953
38TH PARALLEL
P'anmunjom
Inch'on Landing Sept. 15,1950
Seoul: Capital of South Korea
Extent of Communist Counter-attack Jan. 12, 1951
Qingdao
Yellow Sea
MacArthur
Taegu
U.N. Defensive Line Sept. 10, 1950
SOUTH KOREA
Pusan
Korea Strait
Hiroshima
JAPAN
Nagasaki
U.N. counter-attacks Sept. 15-Nov. 24, 1950
North Korean attack June 25-Sept. 10, 1950
Final U.N. counter-attack Jan. 25-April 21, 1951
Chinese and North Korean counter-attack Nov. 26-Jan.24, 1951
0 50 100
Miles

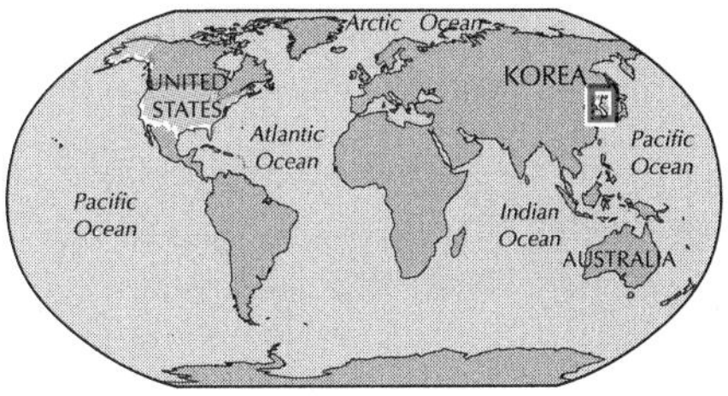

Arctic Ocean
UNITED STATES
KOREA
Atlantic Ocean
Pacific Ocean
Pacific Ocean
Indian Ocean
AUSTRALIA

MAP 114

The Rise of the Black Muslims in the United States (1950–1995)

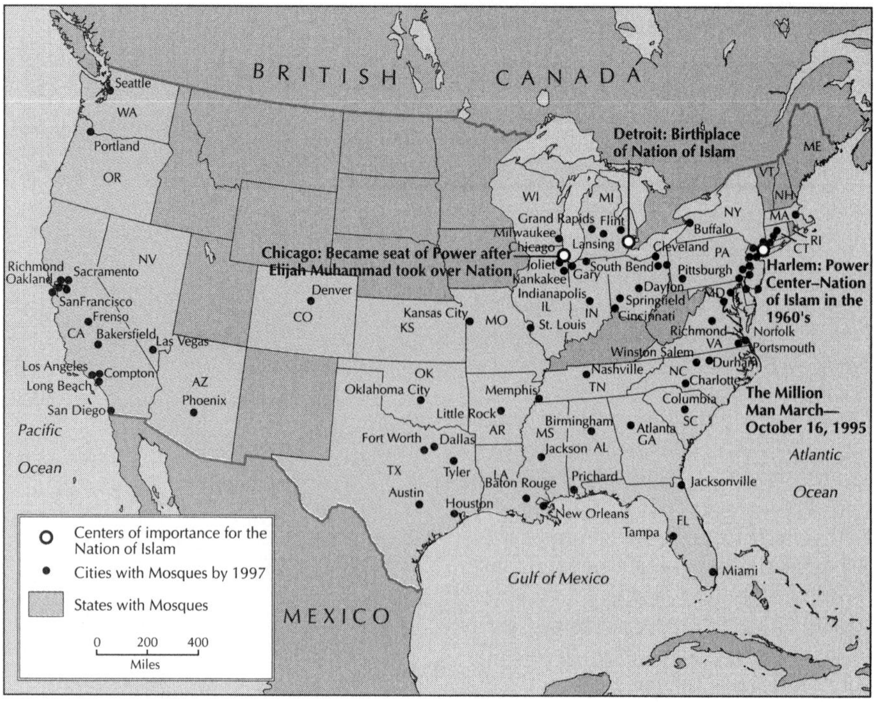
BRITISH CANADA
Detroit: Birthplace of Nation of Islam
Chicago: Became seat of Power after Elijah Muhammad took over Nation
Harlem: Power Center–Nation of Islam in the 1960's
The Million Man March—October 16, 1995
Pacific Ocean
Atlantic Ocean
Gulf of Mexico
MEXICO
Seattle
WA
Portland
OR
NV
Richmond
Oakland
Sacramento
SanFrancisco
Frenso
CA
Bakersfield
Las Vegas
Los Angeles
Compton
Long Beach
San Diego
AZ
Phoenix
Denver
CO
Kansas City
KS
MO
OK
Oklahoma City
TX
Fort Worth
Dallas
Tyler
Austin
Houston
Little Rock
AR
Memphis
LA
Baton Rouge
New Orleans
MS
Jackson
AL
Birmingham
Prichard
Atlanta
GA
Nashville
TN
WI
MI
Milwaukee
Grand Rapids
Flint
Lansing
Chicago
Joliet
Kankakee
Gary
South Bend
IL
IN
Indianapolis
St. Louis
Springfield
Dayton
Cincinnati
Cleveland
PA
Pittsburgh
NY
Buffalo
VT
NH
ME
MA
CT
RI
MD
Richmond
VA
Norfolk
Portsmouth
Winston Salem
Durham
NC
Charlotte
Columbia
SC
Jacksonville
FL
Tampa
Miami
Centers of importance for the Nation of Islam
Cities with Mosques by 1997
States with Mosques
0 200 400
Miles

One of the most notable black nationalist groups in American history was the Nation of Islam, or the Black Muslims. The Black Muslims were founded by the Honorable Wallace D. Farad in Detroit in 1929. The movement at first gained few converts and developed slowly. It was finally taken over by the Honorable Elijah (Poole) Muhammad in 1950. After Farad mysteriously disappeared, Muhammad based the organization in Chicago, and from there established temples in New York, Detroit, and, by the 1960s, in Los Angeles. Elijah Muhammad, using many of the methods of Marcus Garvey, blended Islam with black nationalism and told African Americans that they were superior to whites and that they should be proud of their African heritage. He also told African Americans that whites were devils and were naturally evil. At the same time that black nationalism was spreading throughout Africa and new African nations were being created, the Black Muslims grew in popularity and numbers all over the United States. The best-known member of the Nation of Islam during this period was Malcolm X. As a result of his ability to draw large crowds and communicate with his audience, he helped to increase the membership of the Nation. After Malcolm X's assassination, he would be replaced by Louis Farrakhan, who became the leader of the Nation of Islam. On October 16, 1995, Farrakhan led the Million Man March in Washington, D.C., and offered blacks, particularly those who had fathered illegitimate children or had run-ins with the law and spent time in prison, a chance for a new start during what was referred to as "the Day of Atonement." The organization also offered many blacks hope and security from white racism. Members of the Nation of Islam rejected Christianity as the religion of their white oppressors and embraced Islam as the true faith of African Americans. Members changed their names to remove the influence of their former white slaveholders—the names most African Americans retained following slavery. The Nation also believed in the complete separation of the black and white communities. ■

MAP 115

The Brown Decision, Southern Schools, and the Southern Response to School Integration (1954–1957)

In 1954 the Supreme Court ruled in *Brown v. Board of Education* that segregated schools were unconstitutional. This ruling overturned the "separate but equal" doctrine that had governed southern education since 1896. The Brown decision brought hope and joy to millions of African Americans who had been denied a quality education. For southern whites, however, the decision was a challenge to their right to govern the affairs of their states. Southern states railed at the notion that after 80 years of segregation and states rights the federal government was again intervening into their affairs and forcing its will on the sovereign states of the South. Southern governors refused to obey the decision, and southern congressmen issued the "Southern Manifesto" declaring the decision illegal. In spite of southern opposition, however, southern schools were desegregated when President Dwight D. Eisenhower used federal troops to enforce the Court's decision at Little Rock, Arkansas, in 1957. The civil rights movement grew from the Brown decision to the Montgomery bus boycott in 1955 and to the establishment of the Southern Christian Leadership Conference (SCLC) in 1957. The segregationists found it impossible to stand against federal troops, U.S. marshals, and millions of black and white protestors, who marched, sat in, and legislated an end to the old system of segregation. ■

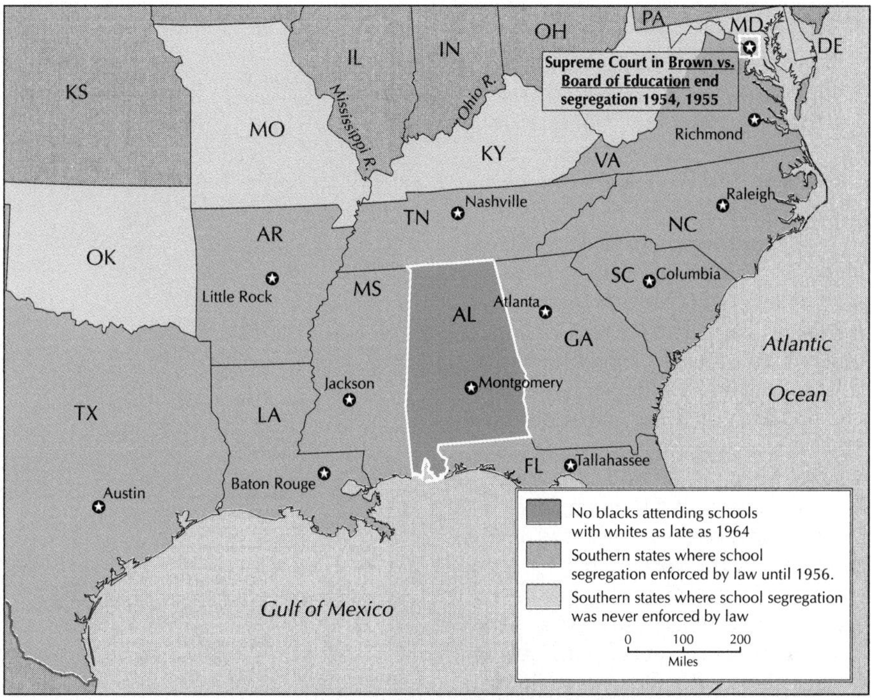
Supreme Court in Brown vs. Board of Education end segregation 1954, 1955
No blacks attending schools with whites as late as 1964
Southern states where school segregation enforced by law until 1956.
Southern states where school segregation was never enforced by law
0 100 200
Miles
KS
MO
IL
IN
OH
PA
MD
DE
KY
VA
Richmond
TN
Nashville
NC
Raleigh
AR
Little Rock
OK
MS
AL
Atlanta
GA
SC
Columbia
Jackson
Montgomery
TX
LA
Baton Rouge
FL
Tallahassee
Austin
Mississippi R.
Ohio R.
Atlantic Ocean
Gulf of Mexico

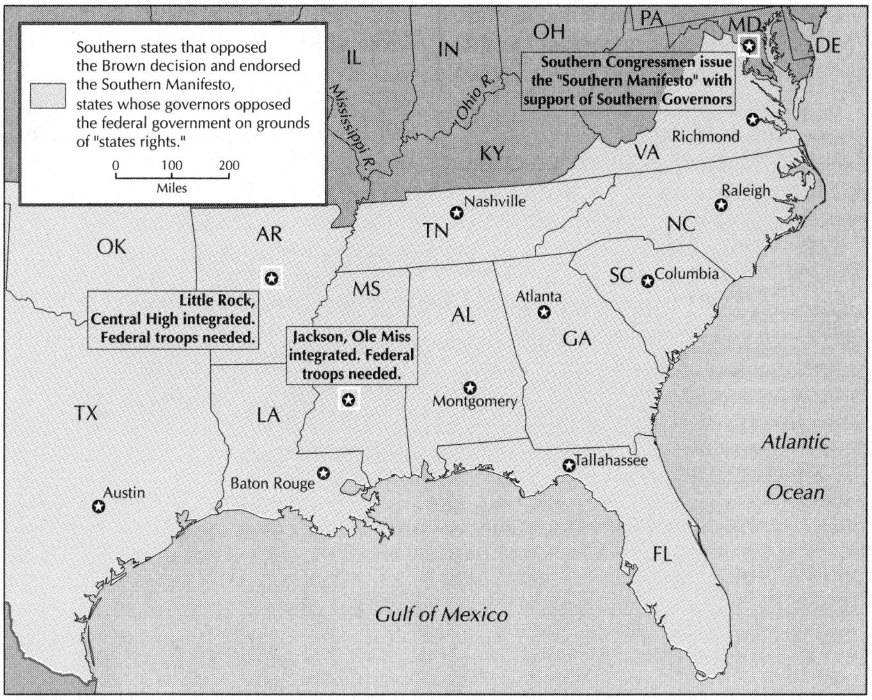
Southern states that opposed the Brown decision and endorsed the Southern Manifesto, states whose governors opposed the federal government on grounds of "states rights."
0 100 200
Miles
Southern Congressmen issue the "Southern Manifesto" with support of Southern Governors
Little Rock, Central High integrated. Federal troops needed.
Jackson, Ole Miss integrated. Federal troops needed.
IL
IN
OH
PA
MD
DE
KY
VA
Richmond
TN
Nashville
NC
Raleigh
AR
OK
MS
AL
Atlanta
GA
SC
Columbia
Montgomery
TX
LA
Baton Rouge
Tallahassee
FL
Austin
Mississippi R.
Ohio R.
Atlantic Ocean
Gulf of Mexico

MAP 116

Rosa Parks, Martin Luther King, Jr., and the Southern Christian Leadership Conference (1955–1957)

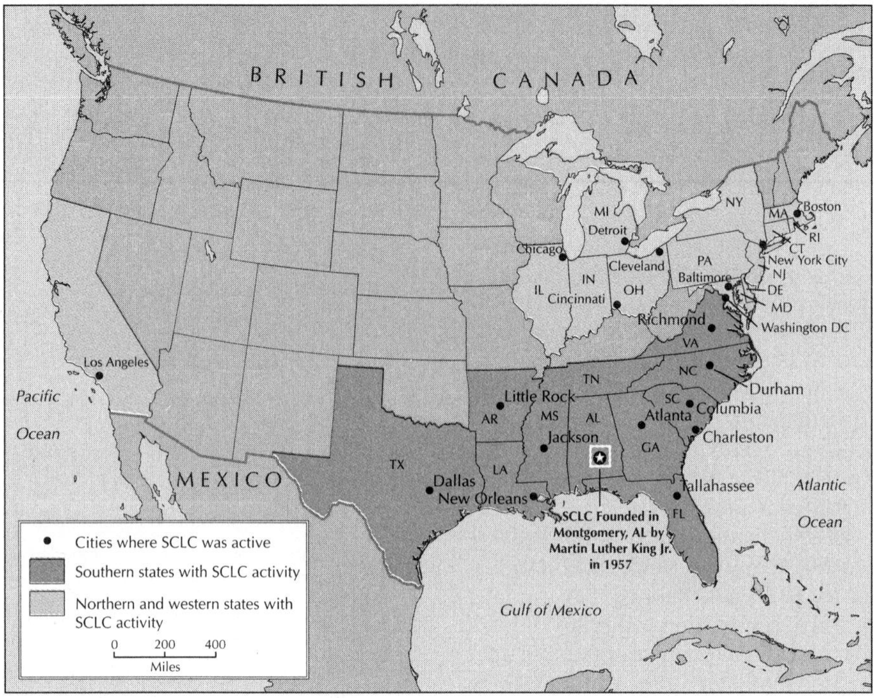
BRITISH CANADA
MEXICO
Pacific Ocean
Atlantic Ocean
Gulf of Mexico
Los Angeles
Chicago
MI
Detroit
Cleveland
IN
IL
Cincinnati
OH
PA
NY
MA
Boston
RI
CT
New York City
NJ
Baltimore
DE
MD
Washington DC
Richmond
VA
NC
Durham
TN
Little Rock
AR
MS
AL
Jackson
SC
Atlanta
Columbia
Charleston
GA
TX
Dallas
LA
New Orleans
Tallahassee
FL
SCLC Founded in Montgomery, AL by Martin Luther King Jr. in 1957
Cities where SCLC was active
Southern states with SCLC activity
Northern and western states with SCLC activity
0 200 400
Miles

On December 1, 1955, Rosa Parks, an African-American woman, refused to give up her seat to a white man on an overcrowded Montgomery, Alabama, city bus. By refusing to give up her seat, she violated a city ordinance. She was arrested and jailed. Her act of defiance, however, touched off a movement that would sweep the nation and forever change the laws of the South concerning race. The arrest of Parks led to a bus boycott by the black community, a boycott organized under the leadership of Reverend Martin Luther King, Jr., who at that time was a young minister at the Dexter Avenue Baptist Church in Montgomery. In 1956, the Supreme Court declared that the Montgomery bus ordinance was unconstitutional—segregation on public transportation was illegal. Spurred on by the success in organizing the boycott in Montgomery, King helped to found the Southern Christian Leadership Conference (SCLC) in 1957. The SCLC was made up of Baptist ministers, a denomination that the vast majority of African Americans identified with during this period. The SCLC was responsible for leading the civil rights movement, raising money, and organizing a number of boycotts, sit-ins, marches, and rallies. The civil rights movement brought not only black Baptists together, but people all over the world of different races and religious, who were prepared to give their lives for justice in America—and an end to segregation. ■

MAP 117

The African American Population in the United States (1960)

By 1960, approximately 15 million African Americans were living in America. Although their economic situation had not changed much, their location did. In 1865, there were around 4.5 million African Americans in the United States. All but about 200,000 lived in the rural South. By 1960 over half of America's 15 million blacks lived in northeastern, midwestern, and far western cities. By 1910, millions of African Americans were fleeing the violence and poor economic opportunities of the South for the promise of industrial jobs in cities like Pittsburgh, Cleveland, and Oakland. From 1910 to 1960 the African American population in the United States continued to grow and move from the rural South. Most migrated to northern cities, where they were forced to live in overcrowded all-black ghettos. This shift in population from the South to the North would continue until the 1980s, when, for the first time, more blacks would return to the South than move to the North.

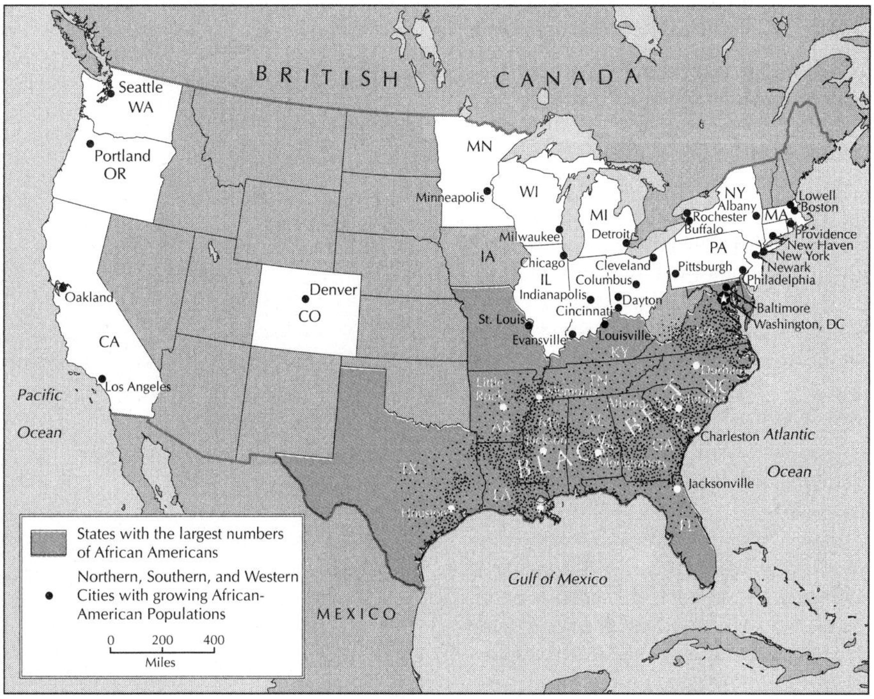
BRITISH CANADA
Seattle
WA
Portland
OR
Oakland
CA
Los Angeles
Pacific Ocean
Denver
CO
MN
Minneapolis
WI
MI
Milwaukee
Detroit
IA
Chicago
IL
Indianapolis
Cleveland
Columbus
Dayton
Cincinnati
St. Louis
Evansville
Louisville
KY
NY
Albany
Rochester
Buffalo
MA
Lowell
Boston
Providence
New Haven
New York
Newark
Philadelphia
PA
Pittsburgh
Baltimore
Washington, DC
Charleston
Atlantic Ocean
Jacksonville
Gulf of Mexico
MEXICO
States with the largest numbers of African Americans
Northern, Southern, and Western Cities with growing African-American Populations
0 200 400
Miles

MAP 118

African American Voter Registration in the South before and after 1960

During the 1960s, blacks focused their efforts on registering blacks to vote. Following the Civil War, blacks used the right to vote to shape southern state constitutions. They elected to state legislatures and to Congress blacks and whites sympathetic to their cause. They also voted in large numbers for presidential candidates who supported their interests. However, blacks were disenfranchised by whites in the South, as early as 1868. In some states very few southern blacks were allowed to vote or even register to vote. Between 1868 and 1965, very few southern blacks were allowed to vote or even register to vote. Then in the 1960s, with the protection of federal officials and the passage of the 1964 Civil Rights Act and the 1965 Voting Rights Act, all this changed. With the aid of courageous civil rights workers such as Medgar Evers, blacks registered to vote and became active participants in national, state, and local politics in the South once again. By the late 1960s, black voters were increasingly becoming powerful voting blocs, deciding major local, state, and national elections. ■

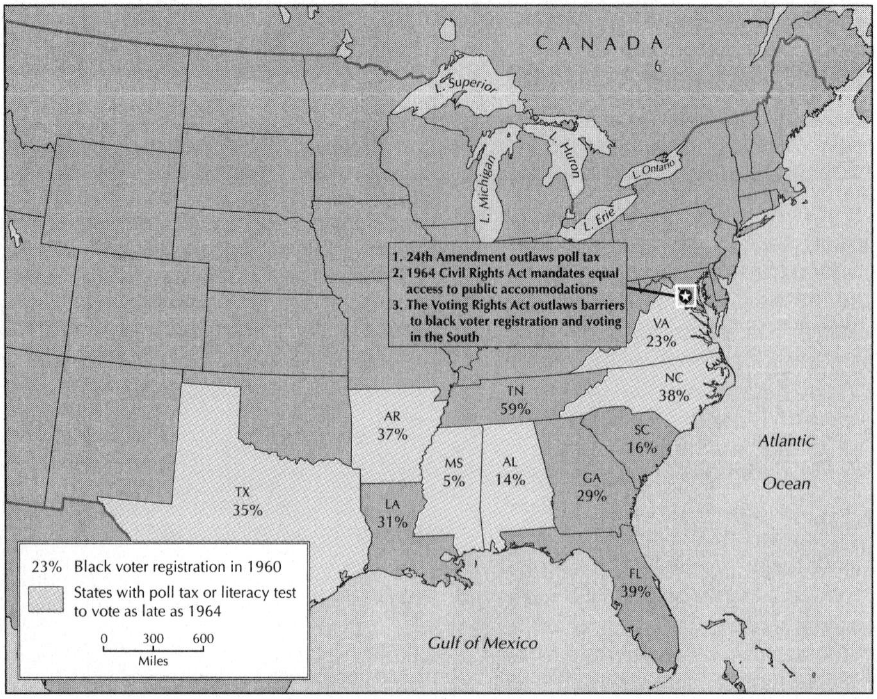
CANADA
L. Superior
L. Michigan
L. Huron
L. Ontario
L. Erie
1. 24th Amendment outlaws poll tax
2. 1964 Civil Rights Act mandates equal access to public accommodations
3. The Voting Rights Act outlaws barriers to black voter registration and voting in the South
VA 23%
NC 38%
TN 59%
AR 37%
SC 16%
MS 5%
AL 14%
GA 29%
TX 35%
LA 31%
FL 39%
Atlantic Ocean
Gulf of Mexico
23% Black voter registration in 1960
States with poll tax or literacy test to vote as late as 1964
0 300 600
Miles

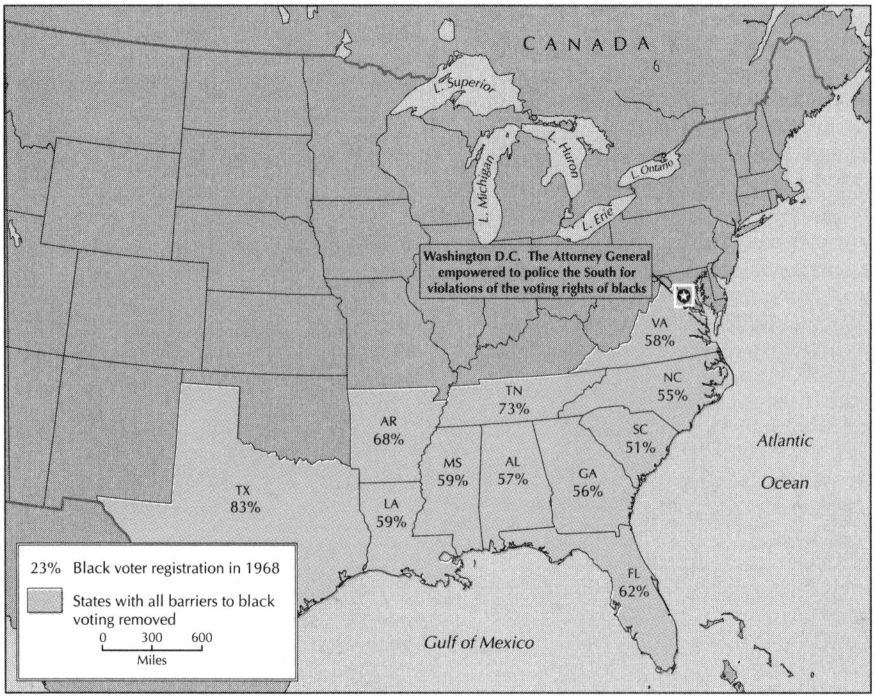
CANADA
L. Superior
L. Michigan
L. Huron
L. Ontario
L. Erie
Washington D.C. The Attorney General empowered to police the South for violations of the voting rights of blacks
VA 58%
NC 55%
TN 73%
AR 68%
SC 51%
MS 59%
AL 57%
GA 56%
TX 83%
LA 59%
FL 62%
Atlantic Ocean
Gulf of Mexico
23% Black voter registration in 1968
States with all barriers to black voting removed
0 300 600
Miles

MAP 119

African Americans and the Vietnam War (1965–1975)

As with all of America's other wars, many African Americans volunteered to fight in the Vietnam War. Large numbers were also drafted. Unlike previous wars, Vietnam was not supported by the majority of the American people. Many wealthy young American men evaded the draft by going to college, leaving the country, or having elected officials provide them with assignments that kept them out of harm's way. Perhaps the most significant difference between Vietnam and other wars, however, was the disproportionate number of poor Americans, white and black, who died in the conflict. Extremely large numbers of blacks died in this war. Most of them were poor, young, uneducated men who were forced to fight in an army where many white soldiers openly made racist comments and discriminated against them. Furthermore, they were fighting overseas while their families, neighbors, and friends were being beaten and killed in riots and violent clashes with the police at home. In 1968, at the Riverside Baptist Church in New York City, Dr. Martin Luther King Jr. publicly condemned America's role in Vietnam causing millions of blacks to turn against the war. ■

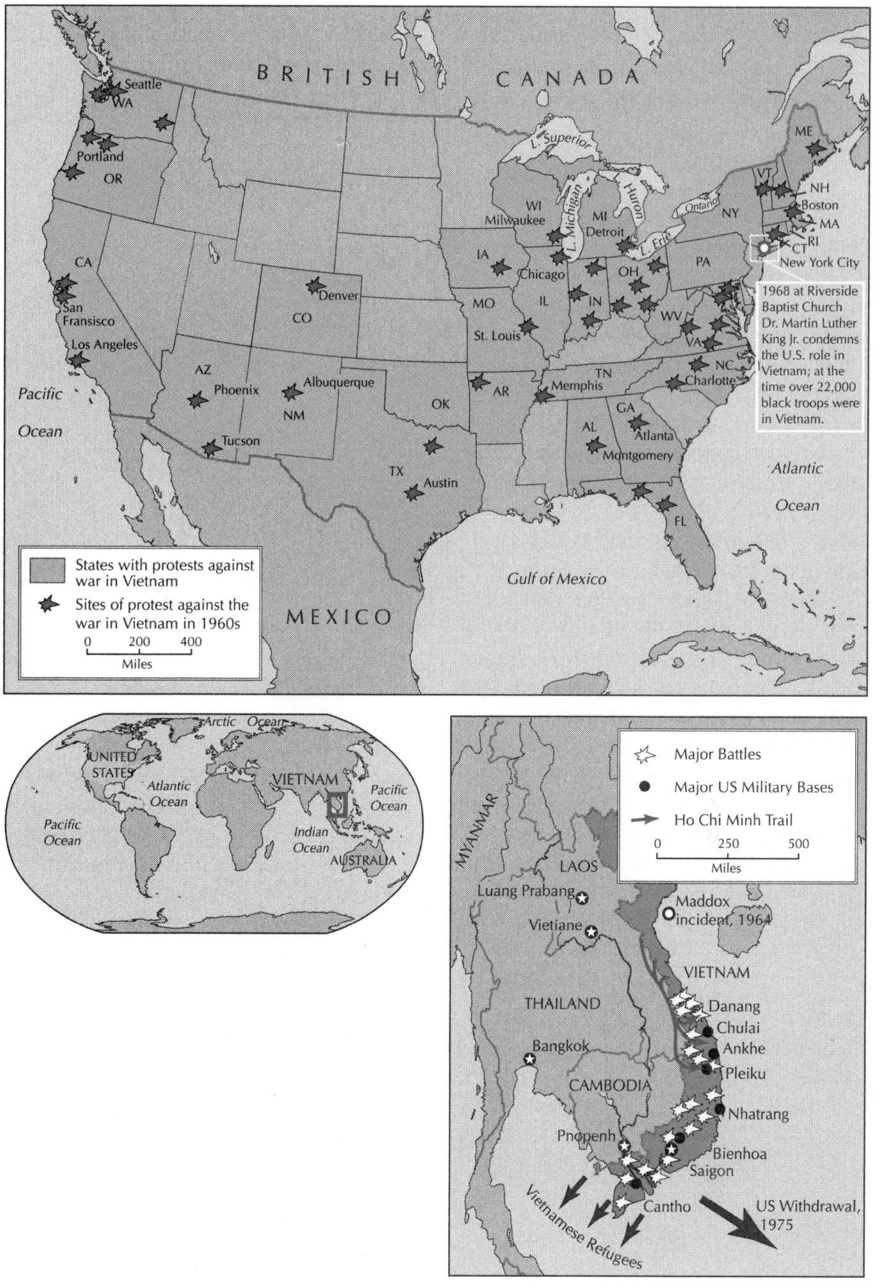
BRITISH
CANADA
MEXICO
Seattle
WA
Portland
OR
CA
San Fransisco
Los Angeles
AZ
Phoenix
Tucson
CO
Denver
NM
Albuquerque
OK
TX
Austin
IA
MO
St. Louis
AR
WI
Milwaukee
IL
Chicago
MI
Detroit
IN
OH
TN
Memphis
AL
Montgomery
GA
Atlanta
FL
PA
WV
VA
NC
Charlotte
NY
VT
ME
NH
Boston
MA
RI
CT
New York City
L. Superior
L. Michigan
L. Huron
L. Erie
L. Ontario
1968 at Riverside Baptist Church Dr. Martin Luther King Jr. condemns the U.S. role in Vietnam; at the time over 22,000 black troops were in Vietnam.
Pacific Ocean
Atlantic Ocean
Gulf of Mexico
States with protests against war in Vietnam
Sites of protest against the war in Vietnam in 1960s
0 200 400
Miles
Arctic Ocean
UNITED STATES
Atlantic Ocean
VIETNAM
Pacific Ocean
Pacific Ocean
Indian Ocean
AUSTRALIA
Major Battles
Major US Military Bases
Ho Chi Minh Trail
0 250 500
Miles
MYANMAR
LAOS
Luang Prabang
Vietiane
Maddox incident, 1964
VIETNAM
THAILAND
Bangkok
CAMBODIA
Danang
Chulai
Ankhe
Pleiku
Nhatrang
Phnopenh
Bienhoa
Saigon
Cantho
US Withdrawal, 1975
Vietnamese Refugees

MAP 120

The Emergence of Sit-Ins and the Student Non-Violent Coordinating Committee (1960)

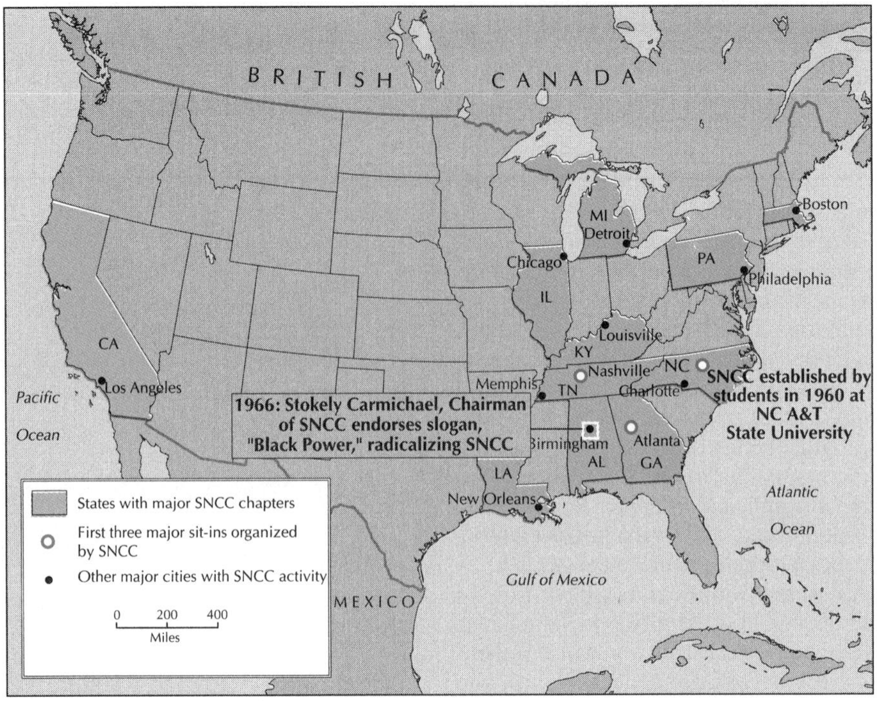
BRITISH
CANADA
Boston
MI
Detroit
Chicago
PA
Philadelphia
IL
Louisville
KY
CA
Nashville
NC
Los Angeles
Memphis
TN
Charlotte
SNCC established by students in 1960 at NC A&T State University
Pacific
Ocean
1966: Stokely Carmichael, Chairman of SNCC endorses slogan, "Black Power," radicalizing SNCC
Birmingham
Atlanta
AL
GA
LA
New Orleans
Atlantic
Ocean
States with major SNCC chapters
First three major sit-ins organized by SNCC
Other major cities with SNCC activity
0 200 400
Miles
MEXICO
Gulf of Mexico

Although Martin Luther King, Jr., and the Southern Christian Leadership Conference organized and led the civil rights movement of the late 1950s and early 1960s, not everyone agreed with their approach. By the mid 1960s, a number of radical groups, led by young blacks, began to emerge. These included the Student Non-Violent Coordinating Committee (SNCC) and the Black Panther Party. SNCC, which was started at North Carolina, Agricultural and Technical State University in Greensboro, North Carolina, grew very quickly and was credited with bringing many young blacks into the movement. SNCC began the sit-ins that would integrate lunch counters and restaurants throughout the South. By 1966, with the election of Stokely Carmichael as chairman of the organization, a supporter of Black Nationalism and "Black Power," SNCC began to adopt the militant slogans of groups like the Black Panthers ("Black Power"), and accepted the philosophy of Malcolm X to fight back if attacked. By 1968, SNCC broke with Dr. King and SCLC and began to push for more immediate and radical changes in America. SNCC represented the frustrations of many young blacks over the persistence of racism and white oppression. The organization also began to reject white support and push only black leadership for black goals. ■

MAP 121

Martin Luther King, Jr.'s U.S. and World Travels (1960–1968)

The African American most synonymous with the civil rights movement was Dr. Martin Luther King, Jr. King organized and led civil rights demonstrations, lobbied Congress for new laws protecting the rights of African Americans, and worked with state and local elected officials to improve the quality of life for black Americans. As the spokesperson for black America, King traveled to Europe, where he received the Nobel Peace Prize; to Africa, where he met with African leaders; and throughout the United States, where he met with governors, senators, presidents, and religious leaders. His travels and worldwide contacts broadened his perspective on race and poverty. Before his death in 1968, he began to espouse the view that the world's greatest problem was not race but economics and the unequal distribution of wealth. This belief led to the organization of the Poor People's Campaign and the establishment of Resurrection City in May 1968, under the leadership of Reverend Ralph David Abernathy of the SCLC. ■

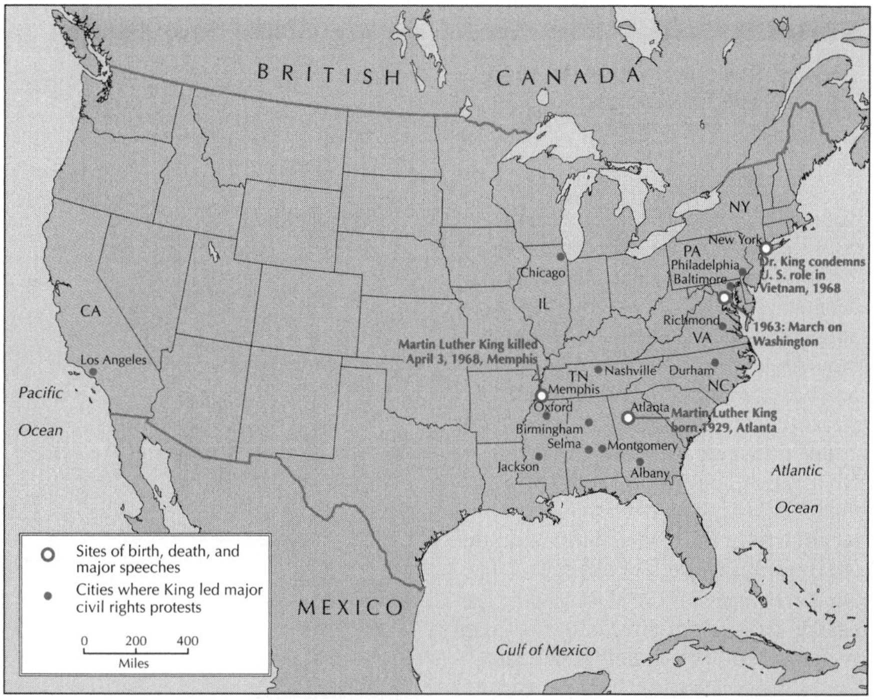
BRITISH CANADA
NY
New York
PA
Philadelphia
Baltimore
Dr. King condemns U.S. role in Vietnam, 1968
Chicago
IL
CA
Richmond
VA
1963: March on Washington
Martin Luther King killed April 3, 1968, Memphis
Los Angeles
TN
Nashville
Durham
NC
Memphis
Oxford
Atlanta
Martin Luther King born 1929, Atlanta
Birmingham
Selma
Montgomery
Jackson
Albany
Pacific Ocean
Atlantic Ocean
Sites of birth, death, and major speeches
Cities where King led major civil rights protests
0 200 400
Miles
MEXICO
Gulf of Mexico

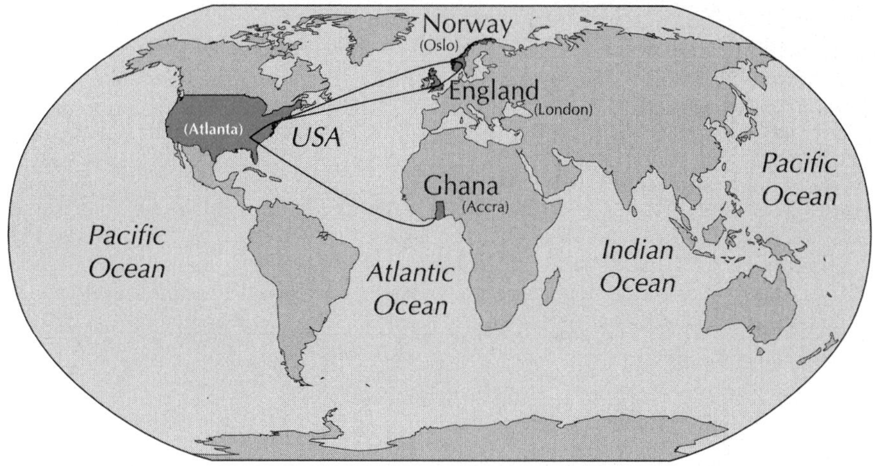
Norway
(Oslo)
England
(London)
(Atlanta)
USA
Ghana
(Accra)
Pacific Ocean
Atlantic Ocean
Indian Ocean
Pacific Ocean

MAP 122

The 1964 Civil Rights Act and the Targeted States

Before the passage of the 1964 Civil Rights Act, the civil and human rights of blacks throughout the South were routinely violated by sheriffs, police officers, and the general southern white population. Blacks were often denied the right to vote, and were beaten, raped, and murdered, receiving virtually no protection from southern lawmakers or law enforcers. Although the 1964 Civil Rights Act applied equally to all fifty states, it was passed to eliminate racial wrongs in eleven states: Virginia, North Carolina, South Carolina, Georgia, Alabama, Florida, Mississippi, Tennessee, Arkansas, Louisiana, and Texas. As a result of the act and federal enforcement of it, schools, universities, restaurants, buses, and workplaces were all opened to blacks. Blacks were also provided protection for civil and human rights, which for years had been ignored by whites in these states. ■

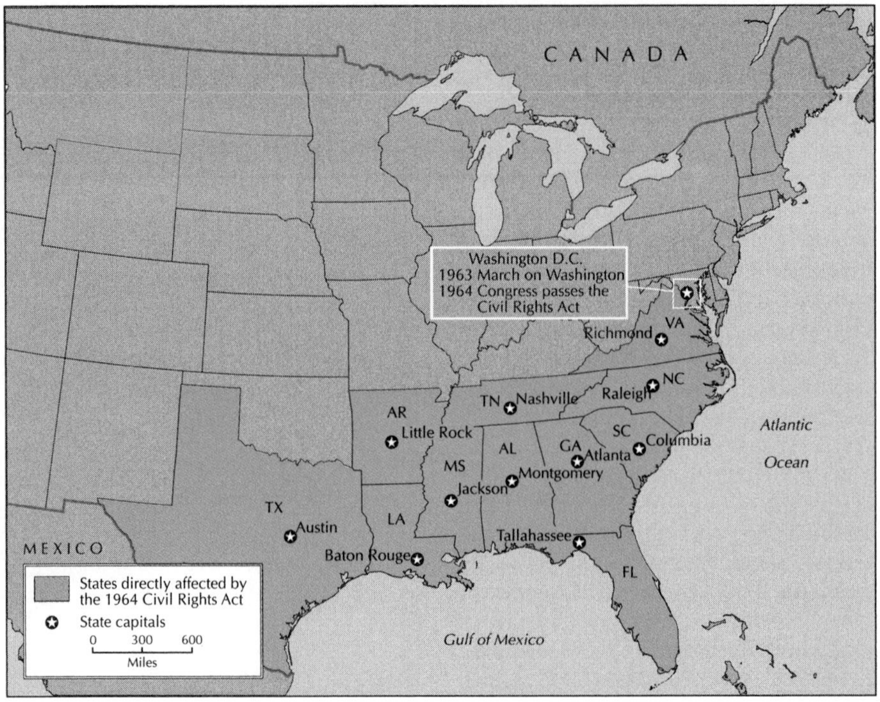
CANADA
Washington D.C.
1963 March on Washington
1964 Congress passes the Civil Rights Act
Richmond
VA
NC
Raleigh
TN
Nashville
AR
Little Rock
SC
Columbia
AL
GA
Atlanta
MS
Montgomery
Jackson
TX
Austin
LA
Baton Rouge
Tallahassee
FL
MEXICO
Atlantic Ocean
Gulf of Mexico
States directly affected by the 1964 Civil Rights Act
State capitals
0 300 600
Miles

MAP 123

The 1965 Voting Rights Act and the Targeted States

Like the Civil Rights Act of 1964, the Voting Rights Act of 1965 targeted the same eleven southern states. Since the end of Reconstruction, these eleven states, through intimidation, violence, and murder, had systematically prevented blacks from exercising their constitutional rights. Although in some states certain blacks were allowed to vote, the majority could not. The Voting Rights Act forced these states and others to repeal poll taxes, grandfather clauses, and other unconstitutional laws to prevent blacks from voting. It also mandated that federal observers be present at polling stations to ensure that blacks were properly registered and not turned away on election day. As a result of the Voting Rights Act, millions of blacks in the South were enfranchised. With their political power restored, they began to shape the politics of the "New South." They would elect blacks as mayors, judges, and members of Congress and heavily influence congressional and presidential elections. ■

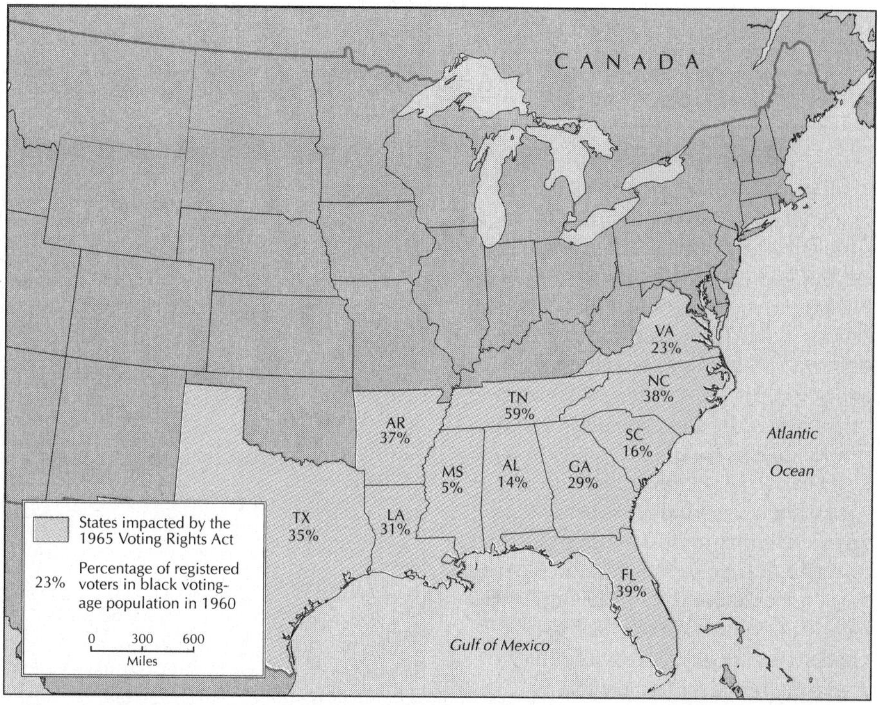
CANADA
VA 23%
NC 38%
TN 59%
SC 16%
AR 37%
MS 5%
AL 14%
GA 29%
TX 35%
LA 31%
FL 39%
Atlantic Ocean
Gulf of Mexico
States impacted by the 1965 Voting Rights Act
23% Percentage of registered voters in black voting-age population in 1960
0 300 600
Miles

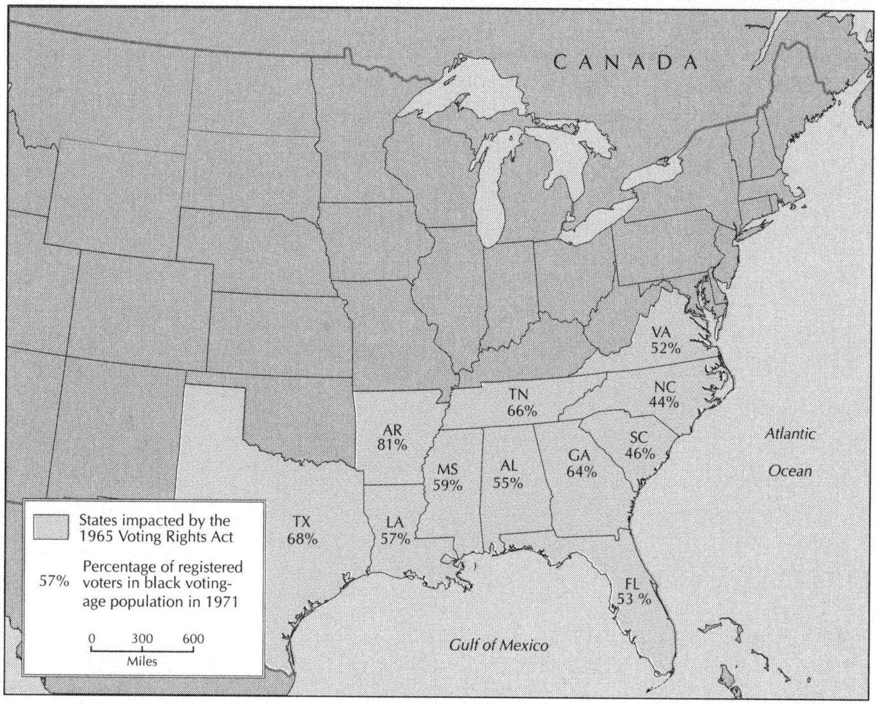
CANADA
VA 52%
NC 44%
TN 66%
SC 46%
AR 81%
MS 59%
AL 55%
GA 64%
TX 68%
LA 57%
FL 53 %
Atlantic Ocean
Gulf of Mexico
States impacted by the 1965 Voting Rights Act
57% Percentage of registered voters in black voting-age population in 1971
0 300 600
Miles

MAP 124

Major Events in the Civil Rights Movement (1955–1970)

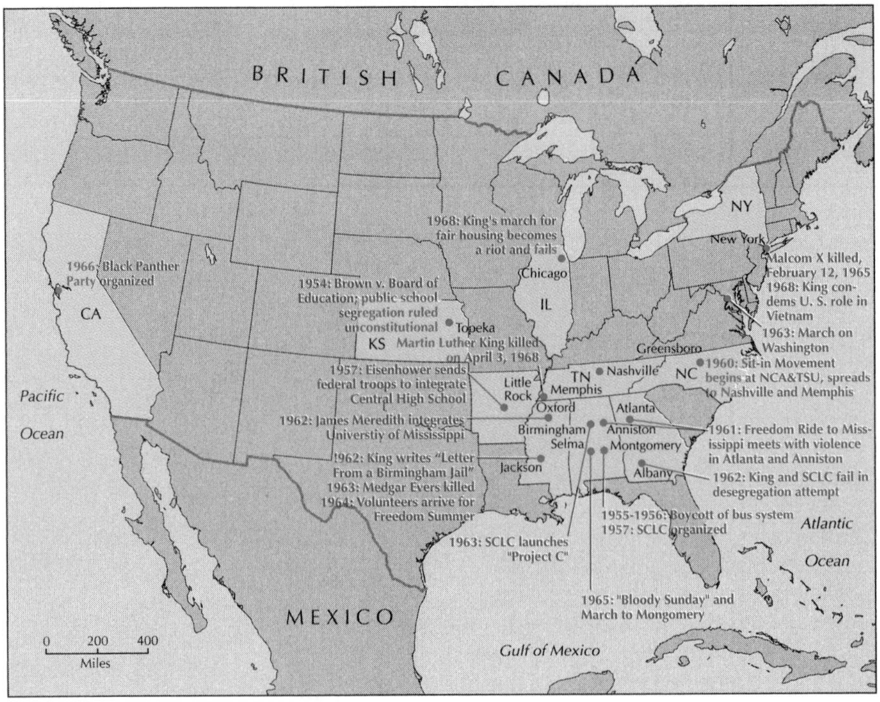
BRITISH CANADA
1968: King's march for fair housing becomes a riot and fails
Chicago
IL
1966: Black Panther Party organized
CA
1954: Brown v. Board of Education; public school segregation ruled unconstitutional
Topeka
KS
Martin Luther King killed on April 3, 1968
1957: Eisenhower sends federal troops to integrate Central High School
Little Rock
TN
Memphis
Nashville
NC
Greensboro
Oxford
1962: James Meredith integrates Universtiy of Mississippi
1962: King writes "Letter From a Birmingham Jail"
1963: Medgar Evers killed
1964: Volunteers arrive for Freedom Summer
Jackson
Birmingham
Selma
Anniston
Montgomery
Atlanta
Albany
1963: SCLC launches "Project C"
1965: "Bloody Sunday" and March to Mongomery
1955-1956: Boycott of bus system
1957: SCLC organized
NY
New York
Malcom X killed, February 12, 1965
1968: King condems U. S. role in Vietnam
1963: March on Washington
1960: Sit-in Movement begins at NCA&TSU, spreads to Nashville and Memphis
1961: Freedom Ride to Mississippi meets with violence in Atlanta and Anniston
1962: King and SCLC fail in desegregation attempt
Pacific Ocean
Atlantic Ocean
Gulf of Mexico
MEXICO
0 200 400
Miles

During the civil rights era a number of events took place which are of historical significance. Included among these are the Montgomery bus boycott; the March on Washington led by Martin Luther King, Jr.; the sit-ins; and freedom rides. These events, along with countless others, in which ordinary people of all races took part, helped to reshape America into a place where legal discrimination, violence, and murder against blacks trying to exercise their civil and human rights were no longer tolerated. These events and the movement impacted not only African Americans, but Asian, Hispanic, Mexican, Native American, and other ethnic groups in this country, as well as women. These events and the people who participated in them have profoundly changed America for all who live here. ■

Map and Text Sources

111. Albrecht-Carriè, Renè. *A Diplomatic History of Europe Since the Congress of Vienna,* rev. ed. New York: Harper & Row, 1973.

Bell, Inge Powell. *CORE and the Strategy of Nonviolence.* New York: Random House, 1968.

Brzezinski, Zbigniew K. *The Soviet Bloc, Unity and Conflict,* rev. and enl. ed. Cambridge, MA: Harvard University Press, 1967.

Horne, Gerald. *Black and Red: W.E.B. Du Bois and the Afro American Response to the Cold War, 1944–1963.* Albany, NY: State University of New York Press, 1986.

LaFeber, Walter. *America, Russia, and the Cold War, 1945–1992,* 7th ed. New York: McGraw-Hill, 1993.

Luxenburg, Norman. *Europe since World War II: The Big Change,* rev. ed. enl. Carbondale: Southern Illinois University Press, 1979.

Meier, August, and Elliott Rudwick. *CORE: A Study of the Civil Rights Movements 1942–1968.* New York: Oxford University Press, 1973.

Nalty, Bernard C. *Strength for the Fight: A History of Black Americans in the Military.* New York: Free Press, 1986.

Turner, Henry Ashby. *The Two Germanies since 1945.* New Haven, CT: Yale University Press, 1987.

112. Beer, George L. *African Questions at the Paris Peace Conference.* New York: Macmillan, 1923.

Crowder, Michael. *West African Resistance: The Military Response to Colonial Occupation.* London: Hutchinson, 1978.

Fieldhouse, David K. *Black Africa, 1945–80: Economic Decolonization and Arrested Development.* London: Allen & Unwin, 1986.

Logan, Rayford W. *The Senate and the Versailles Mandate System.* Washington, DC: Minorities Publishers, 1945.

Mazrui, Ali A. *The Africans: A Triple Heritage.* Boston: Little, Brown, 1986.

Pinkney, Alphonso. *Red, Black, and Green: Black Nationalism in the United States.* Cambridge: Cambridge University Press, 1976.

Rothney, John A. M., and Carter V. Findley. *Twentieth-Century World,* 3rd ed. Boston: Houghton Mifflin, 1994.

113. Blair, Clay. *The Forgotten War: America in Korea, 1950–1953.* New York: Anchor Books, 1989.

Bowers, William T. *Black Soldier, White Army: The 24th Infantry Regiment in Korea.* Washington, DC: Center of Military History, United States Army, 1996.

Bussey, Charles M. *Firefight at Yechon: Courage and Racism in the Korean War.* Washington: Brassey's, 1991.

Dalfiume, Richard M. *Desegregation of the U.S. Armed Forces; Fighting on Two Fronts, 1939–1953.* Columbia: University of Missouri Press, 1969.

Davis, Lenwood G. *Blacks in the Armed Forces, 1776–1983: A Bibliography.* Westport, CT: Greenwood Press, 1985.

Foner, Jack D. *Blacks and the Military in American History; a New Perspective.* New York: Praeger Publishers, 1974.

MacGregor, Morris J. *Integration of the Armed Forces, 1940–1965.* Washington, DC: Center of Military History, United States Army, 1981.

MacGregor, Morris J., and Bernard Nalty, eds. *Blacks in the United States Armed Forces: Basic Documents,* 13 vols. Wilmington, DE: Scholarly Resources, 1977.

Nalty, Bernard C. *Strength for the Fight: A History of Black Americans in the Military.* New York: Free Press, 1986.

National Association for the Advancement of Colored People. *Papers of the NAACP, Part Nine, Discrimination in the U.S. Armed Forces, 1918–1955.* Frederick, MD: University Publications of America, 1989.

114. Lincoln, C. Eric. *The Black Muslims in America,* 3rd ed. Grand Rapids, MI: Africa World Press, 1993.

Marsh, Clifton E. *From Black Muslim to Muslims: The Resurrection, Transformation, and Change of the Lost-Found Nation of Islam in America, 1930–1995,* 2nd ed. Lanham, MD: Scarecrow Press, 1996.

115. Bartley, Numan V., and Hugh B. Gram. *Southern Politics and the Second Reconstruction.* Baltimore: Johns Hopkins University Press, 1976.

Berman, William C. *The Politics of Civil Rights in the Truman Administration.* Columbus: Ohio State University Press, 1970.

Blumberg, Rhoda L. *Civil Rights, the 1960s Freedom Struggle,* rev. ed. Boston: Twayne Publishers, 1991.

Burk, Robert Fredrick. *The Eisenhower Administration and Black Civil Rights.* Knoxville: University of Tennessee Press, 1984.

Huckaby, Elizabeth. *Crisis at Central High, Little Rock, 1957–58.* Baton Rouge: Louisiana State University Press, 1980.

Key, Jr. Valdimer O. *Southern Politics in State and Nation.* New York: Knopf, 1950.

Kirkendall, Richard, ed. *The Truman Period as a Research Field, a Reappraisal, 1972.* Columbia: University of Missouri Press, 1974.

Lachicotte, Alberta M. *Rebel Senator: Strom Thurmond of South Carolina.* New York: Devin-Adair Company, 1966.

Wilkinson, J. Harvie. *From Brown to Bakke: The Supreme Court and School Integration, 1954–1978.* New York: Oxford University Press, 1981.

116. Clayton, Ed, comp. *The SCLC Story.* Atlanta: Southern Christian Leadership Conference, 1964.

Garrow, David J. *Bearing the Cross: Martin Luther King, Jr. and the Southern Christian Leadership Conference.* London: Vintage, 1993.

117. United States Bureau of the Census. *Historical Statistics of the United States, Colonial Times to 1970, Bicentennial Edition [Part 2].* Washington, DC: Government Printing Office, 1975.

118. Lawson, Steven F. *Black Ballots: Voting Rights in the South, 1944–1969.* New York: Columbia University Press, 1976.

Lawson, Steven F. *Running for Freedom: Civil Rights and Black Politics in America since 1941,* 2nd ed. New York: McGraw-Hill, 1997.

Moon, Henry L. *Balance of Power: The Negro Vote.* Garden City, NY: Doubleday, 1948.

Wolk, Allan. *The Presidency and Black Civil Rights; Eisenhower to*

Nixon. Rutherford, NJ: Fairleigh Dickinson University Press, 1971.

119. Alexander, Vern L. "Black Opposition to Participation in American Military Engagements from the American Revolution to Vietnam." M.S. thesis. North Texas State University, 1976.

Millett, Allan R. *A Short History of the Vietnam War.* Bloomington: Indiana University Press, 1978.

Mullen, Robert W. *Blacks in America's Wars: The Shift in Attitudes from the Revolutionary War to Vietnam.* New York: Monad Press, 1974.

Nalty, Bernard C. *Strength for the Fight: A History of Black Americans in the Military.* New York: Free Press, 1986.

Taylor, Clyde, comp. *Vietnam and Black America: An Anthology of Protest and Resistance.* Garden City, NY: Anchor Press, 1973.

Wallace, Terry. *Blood, an Oral History of the Vietnam War.* New York: Ballantine, 1985.

The Civil Rights Movement and the Vietnam Era 1964–1975. New York: Macmillan, 1992.

120. Carson, Clayborne. *In Struggle: SNCC and the Black Awakening of the 1960s.* Cambridge, MA: Harvard University Press, 1995.

Schmeidler, Emilie. "Shaping Ideas and Actions: CORE, SCLC, and SNCC in the Struggle for Equality, 1960–1966." Ph.D. dissertation, University of Michigan, 1980.

Wolff, Miles. *Lunch at the 5 & 10,* rev. and exp. ed. Chicago: Dee, 1990.

Zinn, Howard. *SNCC, the New Abolitionists.* Westport, CT: Greenwood Press, 1985.

121. Bishop, Jim. *The Days of Martin Luther King Jr.* New York: Putman, 1971.

Branch, Taylor. *Parting the Waters: America in the King Years, 1954–63.* New York: Simon & Schuster, 1988.

Cone, James H. *Martin & Malcolm & America: A Dream or a Nightmare.* Charlotte: University of North Carolina at Charlotte, 1993.

Lewis, David L. *King: A Biography,* 2nd ed. Urbana: University of Illinois Press, 1978.

Oates, Stephen B. *Let the Trumpet Sound: The Life of Martin Luther King, Jr.* New York: New American Library, 1982.

122. Stern, Mark. *Calculating Visions: Kennedy, Johnson, and Civil Rights.* New Brunswick, NJ: Rutgers University Press, 1992.

Whalen, Charles W. *The Longest Debate: A Legislative History of the 1964 Civil Rights Act.* New York: New American Library, 1986.

123. Garrow, David J. *Protest at Selma: Martin Luther King, Jr., and the Voting Rights Act of 1965.* New Haven, CT: Yale University Press, 1978.

Lawson, Steven F. *Black Ballots: Voting Rights in the South, 1944–1969.* New York: Columbia University Press, 1976.

Moon, Henry L. *Balance of Power: The Negro Vote.* Garden City, NY: Doubleday, 1969.

The Voting Rights Act: Unfulfilled Goals. Washington, DC: United States Commission on Civil Rights, 1981.

124. Bell, Inge Powell. *CORE and the Strategy of Nonviolence.* New York: Random House, 1968.

Graham, Hugh Davis. *The Civil Rights Era: Origins and Development of National Policy, 1960–1972.* New York: Oxford University Press, 1990.

Harding, Vincent. *Hope and History: Why We Must Share the Story of the Movement.* Maryknoll, NY: Orbis Books, 1990.

Lomax, Louis E. *The Negro Revolt.* New York: Harper, 1963.

McAdam, Doug. *Freedom Summer.* New York: Oxford University Press, 1990.

Meier, August, John, Bracey, Jr., and Elliott Rudwick, eds. *Black Protest in the Sixties.* New York: Markus Wiener Publishing, 1991.

Meier, August, and Elliott Rudwick. *CORE: A Study of the Civil Rights Movement, 1942–1968.* New York: Oxford University Press, 1973.

Peck, James. *Freedom Ride.* New York: Simon & Schuster, 1962.

Sitkoff, Harvard. *The Struggle for Black Equality, 1954–1992,* rev. ed. New York: Hill and Wang, 1993.

MAP 125

Malcolm X's U.S. and World Travels (1960–1965)

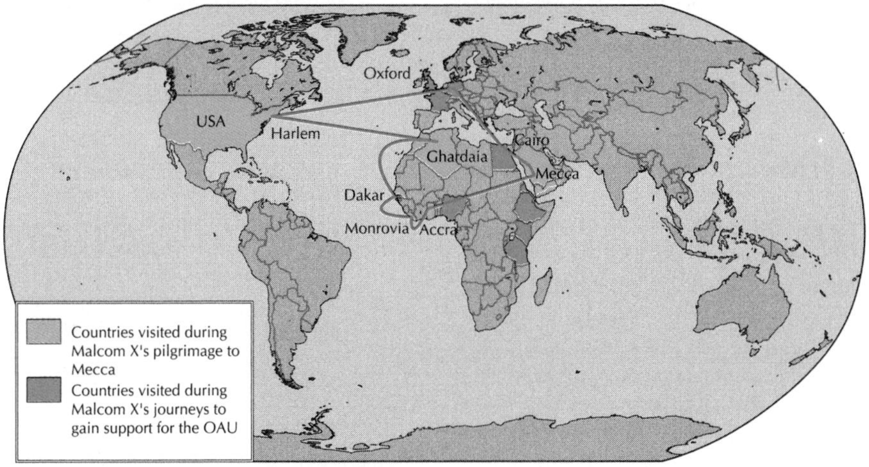
Oxford
USA
Harlem
Cairo
Ghardaia
Mecca
Dakar
Monrovia
Accra
Countries visited during Malcom X's pilgrimage to Mecca
Countries visited during Malcom X's journeys to gain support for the OAU

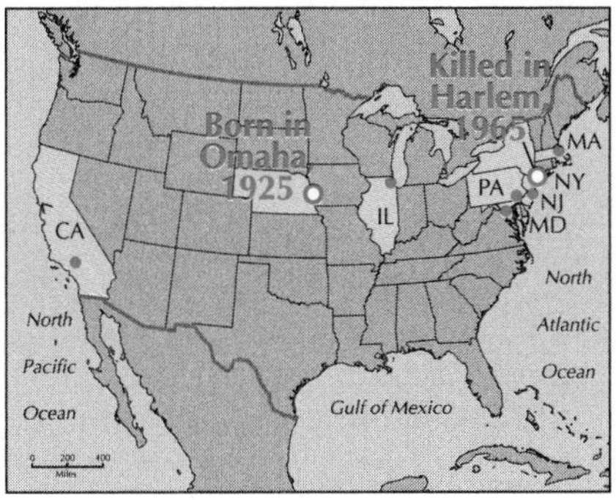
Killed in Harlem 1965
Born in Omaha 1925
MA
NY
NJ
MD
PA
IL
CA
North Atlantic Ocean
North Pacific Ocean
Gulf of Mexico

The decade of the 1960s was a turbulent time in America's history. For conservative, wealthy, and middle-class Americans, their world seemed to fall apart. The women's movement was rising in popularity, the sexual revolution was under way, drug use was rampant, and rock 'n' roll music was "corrupting the morals" of the nation's youth. The Vietnam War raged in Asia, and protests against the war were staged on college campuses and in the streets of America. In the South, the civil rights movement threatened the very foundation of southern society, the supremacy of whites. Added to this mix was the radical black power and black nationalist movements. For many, the American way of life was under siege. At the center of this chaos was Malcolm X. Malcolm X was hated by whites, feared as an extremist by the black middle-class, and loved by the poor blacks of America's depressed urban ghettos. Although Malcolm X has been both glorified and demonized, it is clear that no black leader since Marcus Garvey had been so revered by America's black urban poor. Malcolm X traveled extensively around America as a spokesperson for the growing Nation of Islam. After being expelled from the group, he traveled to Europe and Africa and founded the Organization of African Unity (OAU), with the belief that people of color share such common problems as racism and poverty. Malcolm's travels convinced him that America's racial problems were uniquely American and a result of centuries of legalized prejudice dating back to the colonial era. Through his travels, Malcolm X, like Martin Luther King, Jr., began to realize that the real evil was economic inequality and that racial divisions only helped to maintain the economic status quo. ■

MAP 126

The Rise of the Black Power Movement and the Emergence of the Black Panther Party (1966)

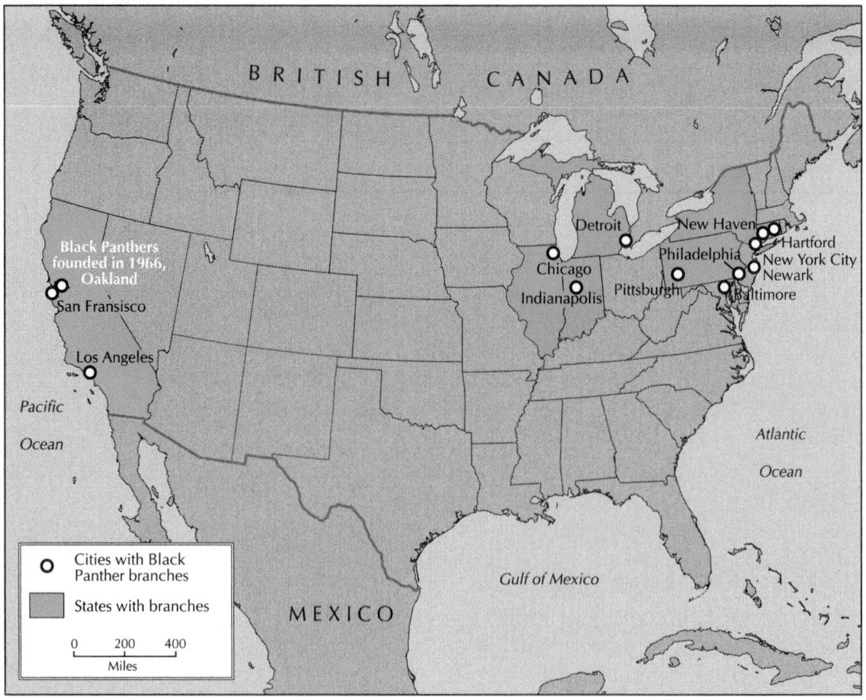
BRITISH CANADA
Black Panthers founded in 1966, Oakland
San Fransisco
Los Angeles
Pacific Ocean
Detroit
Chicago
Indianapolis
Pittsburgh
New Haven
Hartford
Philadelphia
New York City
Newark
Baltimore
Atlantic Ocean
Gulf of Mexico
MEXICO
Cities with Black Panther branches
States with branches
0 200 400
Miles

On May 19, 1966, in Oakland, California, Bobby Seale and Huey P. Newton organized the Black Panther Party. It was organized in response to the killing of a local black man by the Oakland Police Department. The party was established with two major purposes. One was to protect blacks from abuse by the police, and the other was to help feed and educate black children who were living in the inner city. Because the Black Panthers chose to exercise their constitutional right to carry unconcealed weapons, they incurred the fear and wrath of whites and local police, who viewed the Panthers as a threat. With the help of the Federal Bureau of Investigation under the direction of J. Edgar Hoover, the Black Panthers were eliminated as a viable group in America. Many of the members were gunned down in shoot-outs with the FBI or local police. However, during the organization's short life, over twenty-five chapters were organized in major cities all over America, and the social programs they administered helped thousands of poor inner-city children. ■

MAP 127

The Worst Race Riots of the 1960s in the United States

By the mid-1960s the civil rights movement began to stall. Young blacks became impatient, believing changes were not coming quickly enough. Many students and inner-city youths became disillusioned with nonviolence. Hundreds of people were being beaten, murdered and harassed by police, and the government was doing nothing to stop it. In response to this, by 1966, the Student Non-Violent Coordinating Committee (SNCC) split with the Southern Christian Leadership Conference (SCLC) and Stokely Carmichael began to preach "black power" to his followers. In California, Huey P. Newton and Bobby Seale organized the Black Panther Party, threatening to meet violence with violence if blacks were brutalized. In the midst of these events came the deaths of America's two most admired black leaders, Malcolm X (1965) and Martin Luther King (1968). Their deaths touched off several years of race riots that rocked the nation and threatened the stability of the country. ■

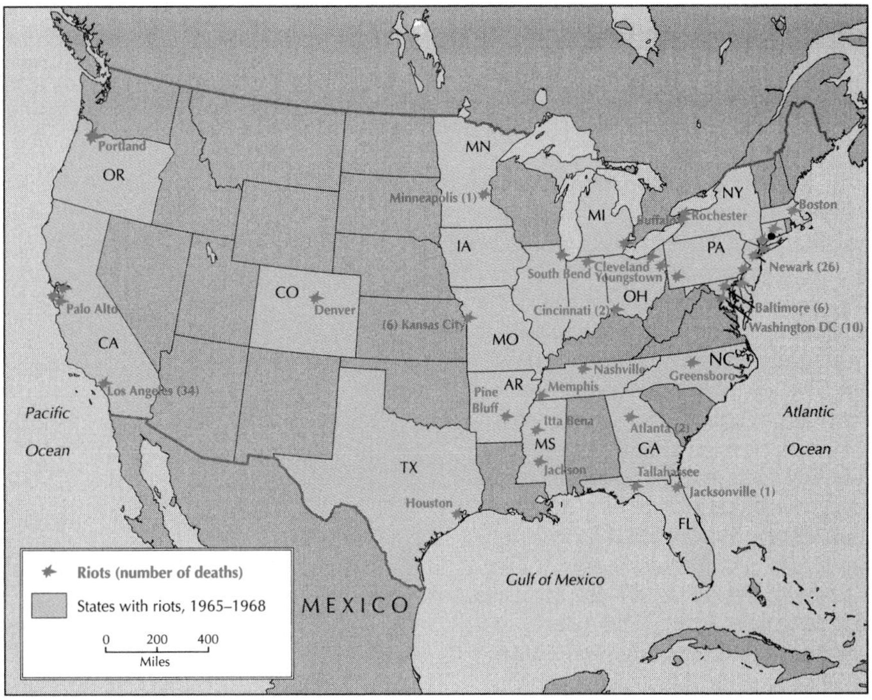
Portland
OR
Palo Alto
CA
Los Angeles (34)
Pacific
Ocean
CO
Denver
MN
Minneapolis (1)
IA
(6) Kansas City
MO
TX
Houston
MI
South Bend
Cleveland
Youngstown
OH
Cincinnati (2)
NY
Buffalo
Rochester
Boston
PA
Newark (26)
Baltimore (6)
Washington DC (10)
NC
Greensboro
Nashville
Memphis
AR
Pine
Bluff
Itta Bena
MS
Jackson
Atlanta (2)
GA
Tallahassee
Jacksonville (1)
FL
Atlantic
Ocean
Gulf of Mexico
MEXICO
Riots (number of deaths)
States with riots, 1965–1968
0 200 400
Miles

MAP 128

The North Carolina A&T State Disturbance (1969)

In 1970 Ohio National Guardsmen opened fire on a group of college students at Kent State University who were protesting the war in Vietnam. News of the shooting was broadcast across the nation and shocked middle-class America. Citizens found it hard to believe Americans were killing other Americans over their political views. What few Americans realized then was that the first time lives were taken in peaceful protest against the state did not occur at Kent State, but at North Carolina Agricultural and Technical State University in Greensboro, North Carolina. Students at the university were tutoring students at the local high school. They also advised the high school student government. The relationship of many university students to the high school students was very supportive. On May 12, 1969, college and high school students began a peaceful protest against conservative black and white leaders at the high school over dress codes. The governor, Robert W. Scott of Alamance County, North Carolina, called out the National Guard, which proceeded to fire at will, damaging a number of buildings on campus, killing one student, Willie Grimes, and wounding several others.

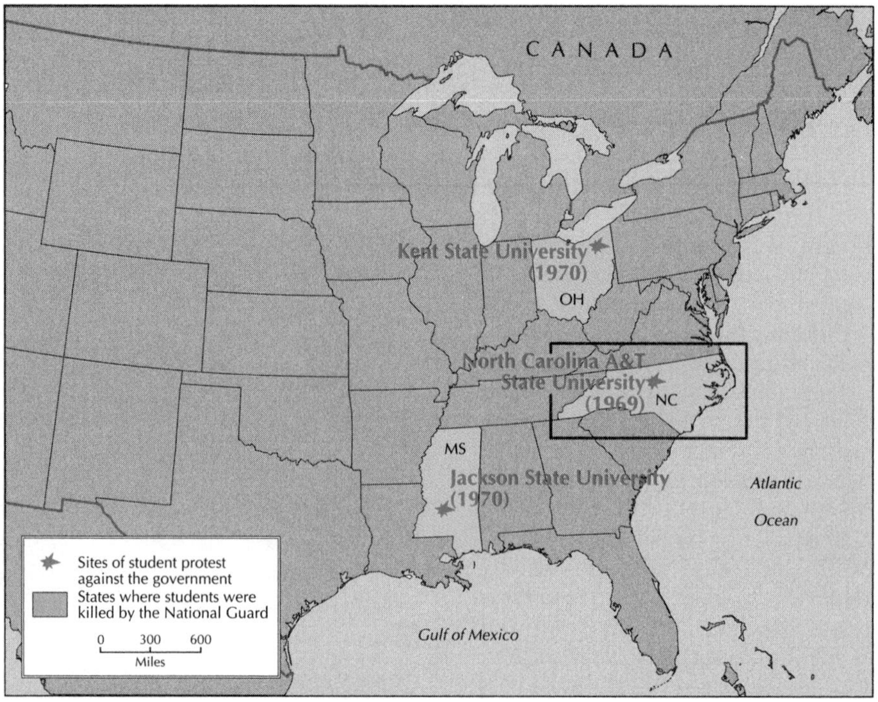
CANADA
Kent State University
(1970)
OH
North Carolina A&T
State University
(1969)
NC
MS
Jackson State University
(1970)
Atlantic
Ocean
Gulf of Mexico
Sites of student protest against the government
States where students were killed by the National Guard
0 300 600
Miles

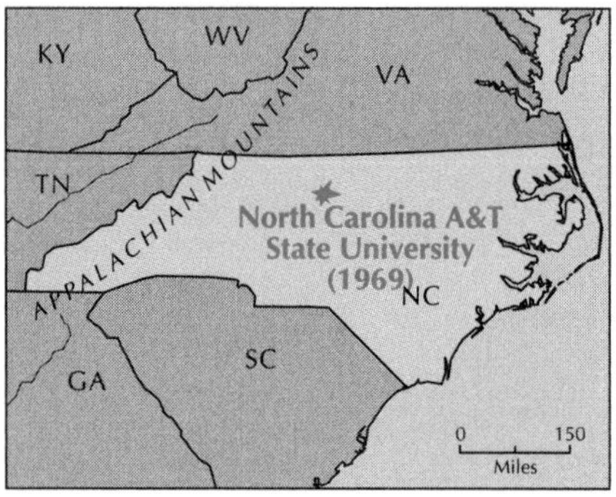
KY
WV
VA
TN
APPALACHIAN MOUNTAINS
North Carolina A&T
State University
(1969)
NC
SC
GA
0 150
Miles

Governor Scott also threatened to permanently close the university if its president did not end the riot begun by the National Guard. There was no national, state, or local outcry, but the result was the same. Middle-class American students had been shot down by the state for their social and political views. ■

MAP 129

Shirley Chisholm's Campaign for the Presidential Nomination of the Democratic Party and the Black National Political Convention in 1972

On May 10, 1972, Democratic congresswoman Shirley Chisholm of New York became the first woman and African American to try to win the nomination for the presidency by a major political party. Although Representative Chisholm's campaign for the nomination was unsuccessful, it symbolized the feeling of frustration many blacks felt with America's two major political parties. It also demonstrated black America's growing political power throughout the South and the rest of the United States. As more blacks were elected to federal, state and local offices, a number of black political organizations were created, including the Congressional Black Caucus. In addition to Representative Chisholm, many other black leaders began to feel a need to meet and discuss issues of major concern to black Americans. This resulted in the first Black National Political Convention held in Chicago in 1972. Both the convention and Representative Chisholm's presidential campaign inspired blacks to become and remain politically active. ■

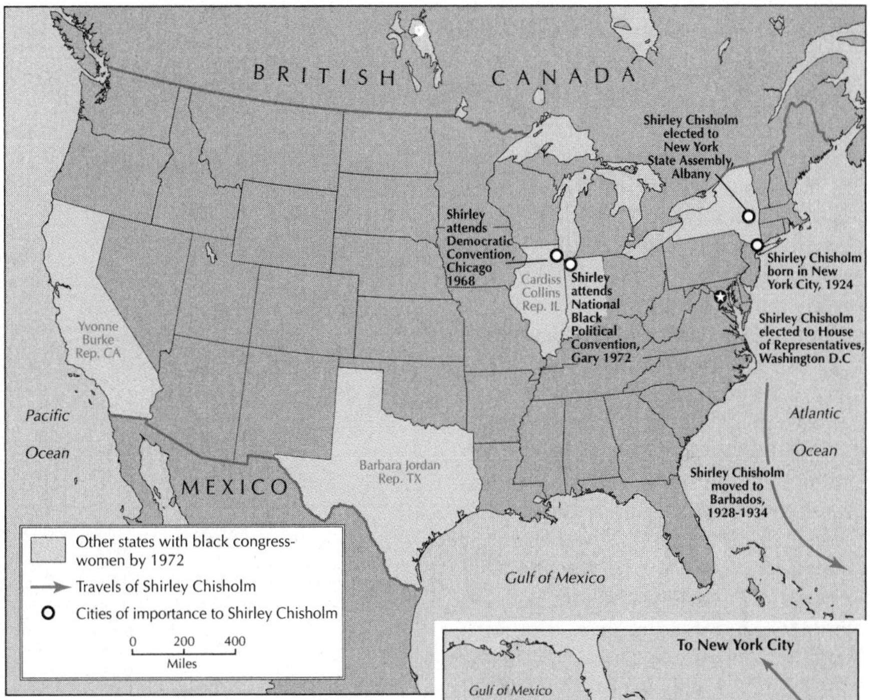
BRITISH CANADA
Shirley Chisholm elected to New York State Assembly, Albany
Shirley attends Democratic Convention, Chicago 1968
Cardiss Collins Rep. IL
Shirley attends National Black Political Convention, Gary 1972
Shirley Chisholm born in New York City, 1924
Shirley Chisholm elected to House of Representatives, Washington D.C
Yvonne Burke Rep. CA
Pacific Ocean
Atlantic Ocean
Barbara Jordan Rep. TX
MEXICO
Shirley Chisholm moved to Barbados, 1928-1934
Gulf of Mexico
Other states with black congresswomen by 1972
Travels of Shirley Chisholm
Cities of importance to Shirley Chisholm
0 200 400
Miles

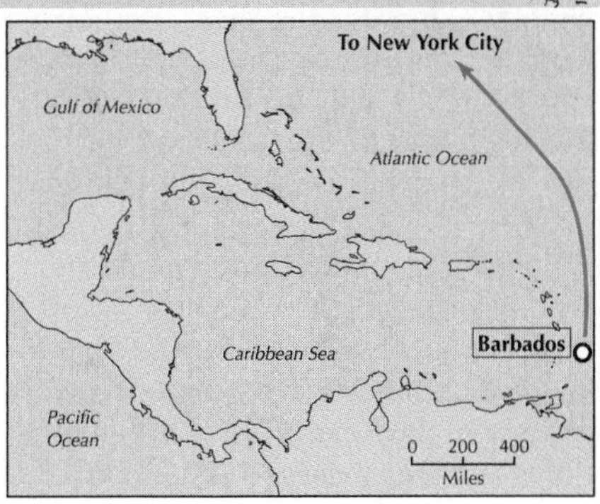
To New York City
Gulf of Mexico
Atlantic Ocean
Caribbean Sea
Barbados
Pacific Ocean
0 200 400
Miles

MAP 130

Black Electoral Gains in Major U.S. Cities and States (1980s)

As a result of the civil rights movement, specifically the 1964 Civil Rights Act and the 1965 Voting Rights Act, blacks voted from 1965 to 1980 in record numbers. More blacks were elected to federal, state, and local offices than at any other time since Reconstruction. Many of these political gains were in cities, northern and southern, where blacks made up over 50 percent of the population. During this period a number of major cities elected their first black mayors. These included Carl Stokes of Cleveland, the first black to be elected mayor of a major U.S. city (the tenth largest at the time); Harold Washington of Chicago; Maynard Jackson of Atlanta; and Marion Barry of Washington, D.C. From 1965 to 1995 over twenty black mayors, thirty black members of Congress, and at least one black governor were elected to office. Numerous black sheriffs, county commissioners, school board members, and state representatives were also elected throughout the South. The civil rights movement meant empowerment for millions of black Americans that would last well into the 1990s. ■

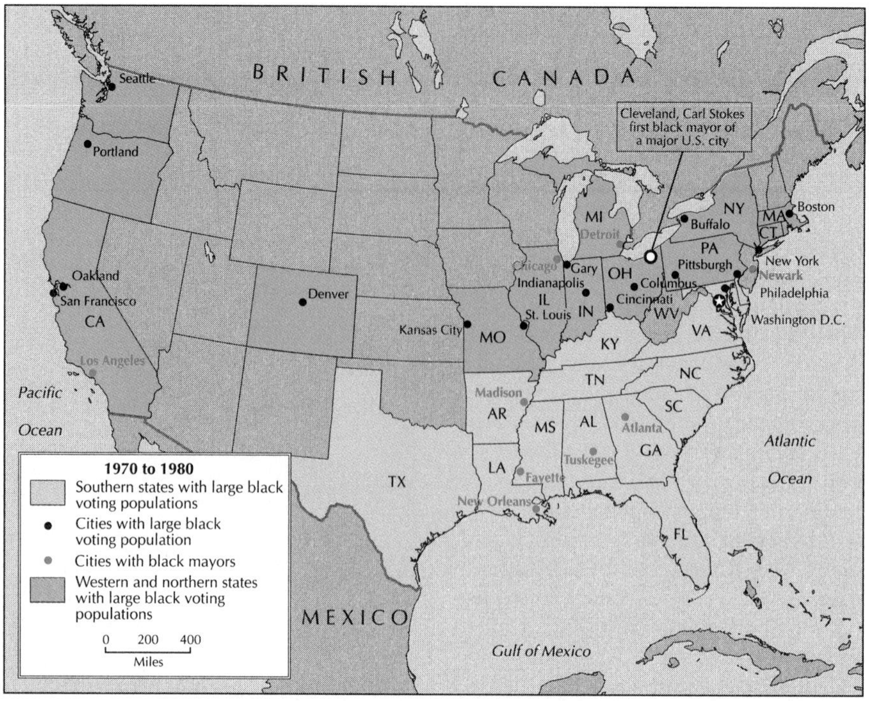
BRITISH
CANADA
Cleveland, Carl Stokes first black mayor of a major U.S. city
Seattle
Portland
Oakland
San Francisco
CA
Los Angeles
Denver
Kansas City
MO
Madison
AR
MS
AL
Atlanta
GA
Tuskegee
LA
Fayette
New Orleans
TX
MI
Detroit
Chicago
Gary
Indianapolis
IL
St. Louis
IN
OH
Columbus
Cincinnati
WV
KY
TN
NC
SC
VA
FL
NY
Buffalo
PA
Pittsburgh
MA
CT
Boston
New York
Newark
Philadelphia
Washington D.C.
Pacific Ocean
Atlantic Ocean
MEXICO
Gulf of Mexico
1970 to 1980
Southern states with large black voting populations
Cities with large black voting population
Cities with black mayors
Western and northern states with large black voting populations
0 200 400
Miles

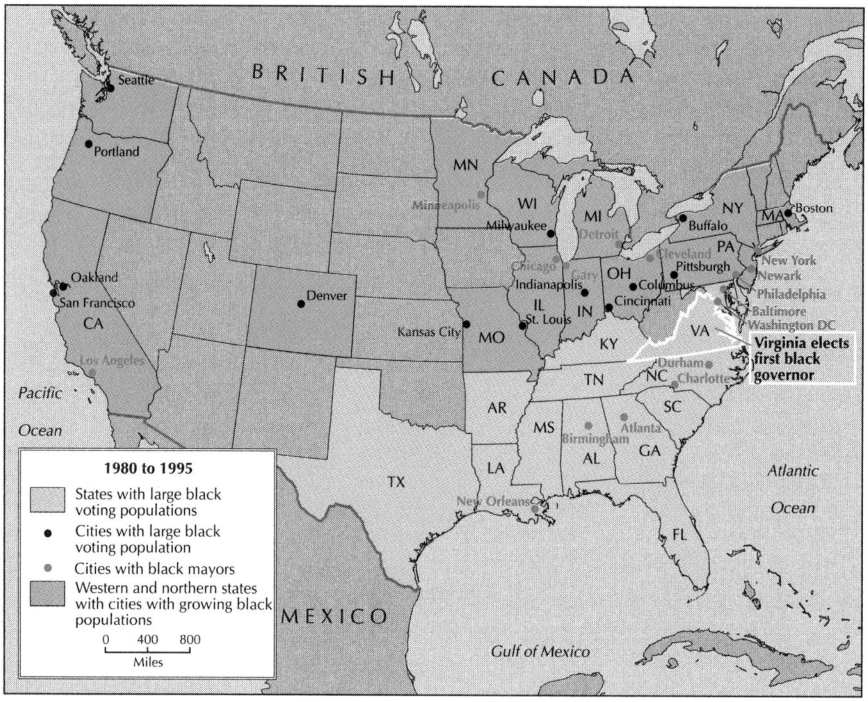
BRITISH
CANADA
Seattle
Portland
Oakland
San Francisco
CA
Los Angeles
Denver
Kansas City
MO
MN
Minneapolis
WI
Milwaukee
MI
Detroit
Chicago
Gary
Indianapolis
IL
St. Louis
IN
OH
Columbus
Cincinnati
Cleveland
PA
Pittsburgh
NY
Buffalo
MA
Boston
New York
Newark
Philadelphia
Baltimore
Washington DC
VA
Virginia elects first black governor
KY
TN
Durham
NC
Charlotte
SC
AR
MS
Birmingham
AL
Atlanta
GA
LA
New Orleans
TX
FL
Pacific Ocean
Atlantic Ocean
MEXICO
Gulf of Mexico
1980 to 1995
States with large black voting populations
Cities with large black voting population
Cities with black mayors
Western and northern states with cities with growing black populations
0 400 800
Miles

MAP 131

The Dixiecrats and the Election of Ronald Reagan (1980)

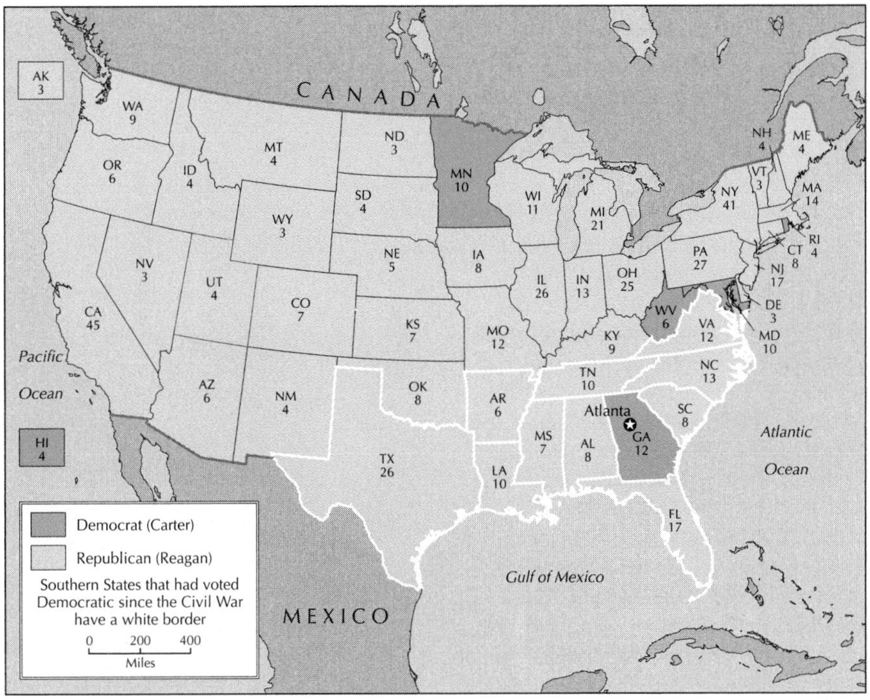
CANADA
MEXICO
Pacific Ocean
Atlantic Ocean
Gulf of Mexico
AK 3
HI 4
WA 9
OR 6
CA 45
ID 4
NV 3
MT 4
WY 3
UT 4
AZ 6
CO 7
NM 4
ND 3
SD 4
NE 5
KS 7
OK 8
TX 26
MN 10
IA 8
MO 12
AR 6
LA 10
WI 11
IL 26
MI 21
IN 13
OH 25
KY 9
TN 10
MS 7
AL 8
GA 12
Atlanta
FL 17
SC 8
NC 13
VA 12
WV 6
PA 27
NY 41
VT 3
NH 4
ME 4
MA 14
RI 4
CT 8
NJ 17
DE 3
MD 10
Democrat (Carter)
Republican (Reagan)
Southern States that had voted Democratic since the Civil War have a white border
0 200 400
Miles

As black power increased and states and businesses were required to account for past discriminatory practices, white resentment grew. Southerners continued to rebel against forced integration and the enfranchisement of blacks, just as they had during Reconstruction. The composition of the Democratic Party, however, the party that had dominated politics in the South since the Civil War, was changing. It was becoming increasingly liberal because of the increasing number of white male liberals, blacks and other minorities, and women who had become active in the party. All of them were more liberal than the white, conservative, Christian "Dixiecrats," as they became known, who had been the backbone of the party in the South. As early as 1964 conservative southern Democrats revolted against the rise of liberals, minorities, and feminists in "their" party. Southern Democrats like Senator J. Strom Thurmond of South Carolina switched parties, becoming Republicans, who tended to be as conservative and against civil rights as southern Democrats. Conservative southern Democrats also condemned President Lyndon B. Johnson, who was a Texan by birth, as a traitor to the South and to America for his support of civil rights. Northern whites, alarmed by the increasing number of poor blacks flooding into their cities and threatening their jobs, also began to become concerned by the late 1970s. As a result, by the 1980 presidential election, conservative southern Democrats broke with their party and joined forces with the Republicans to slow the growth of black political power. Together they elected President Ronald Reagan. The Reagan administration effectively ended thirty years of political gains by blacks and attempted to undo many of the programs enacted in the 1960s and 1970s to help blacks. The election was therefore significant for black America for two reasons. (1) It was the first time that large numbers of white southerners voted Republican, and (2) it was the first time since the beginning of the civil rights movement that blacks lost economic and political ground. The election of Reagan signaled the rise of conservativism in America and represented the white backlash against the civil rights movement. ■

MAP 132

Jesse Jackson for President: The Democratic Presidential Primaries of 1984 and 1988

As the conservative Republican revolution, which combined southern Dixiecrats, northern and western urban Republicans, and the new religious right, grew in popularity and political strength, black political, economic, and social gains made from 1954 to 1980 began to erode. Initially the Democratic Party, which had been responsible for many of these gains, battled conservative Republicans who lashed out against what they saw as "social liberalism." However, by the 1980s, as more southern Democrats abandoned the Democratic Party for the Republican Party, more conservative Democrats also questioned whether the party should continue to advocate social liberalism, which benefited women, the poor, and various ethnic minorities, especially blacks. In response to this conservative movement in the Democratic Party and as a result of the political strength blacks gained from their programs, Jesse Jackson, with the support of his broad-based Rainbow Coalition, ran for the Democratic presidential nomination in 1984 and 1988. Although both campaigns were unsuccessful in winning him the nomination, they were successful in demonstrating the new political power of African Americans. With his broad support among the poor, labor, farmers, and other groups, he was successful in keeping the Democratic Party committed to social liberalism until the election of William Jefferson Clinton in 1992. The election of Clinton ushered in a new age of Democratic conservativism to counter the rise of the Republican Party. ■

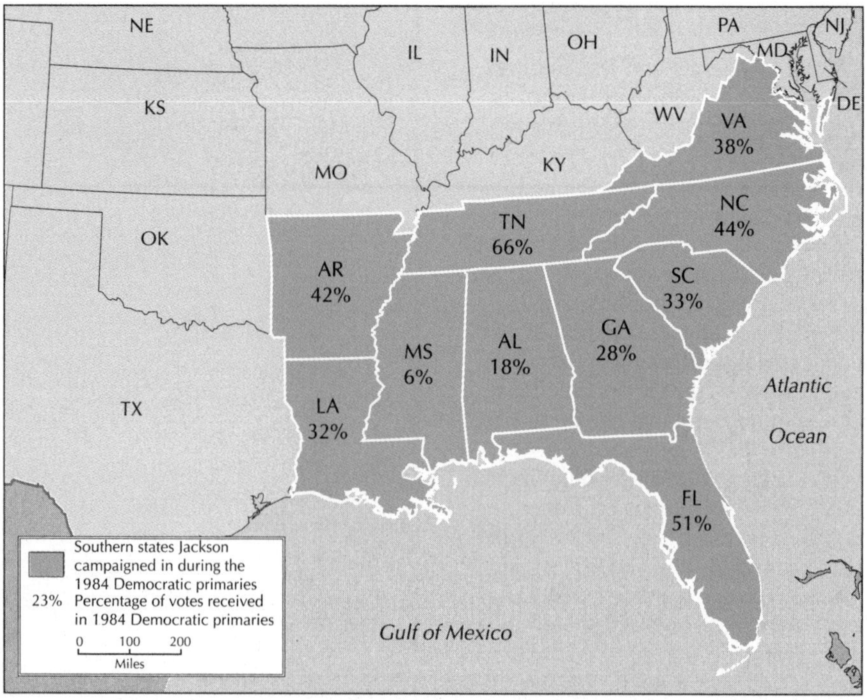
NE
IL
IN
OH
PA
NJ
MD
DE
KS
WV
VA
38%
MO
KY
OK
TN
66%
NC
44%
AR
42%
SC
33%
GA
28%
MS
6%
AL
18%
TX
LA
32%
Atlantic
Ocean
FL
51%
Gulf of Mexico
Southern states Jackson campaigned in during the 1984 Democratic primaries
23% Percentage of votes received in 1984 Democratic primaries
0 100 200
Miles

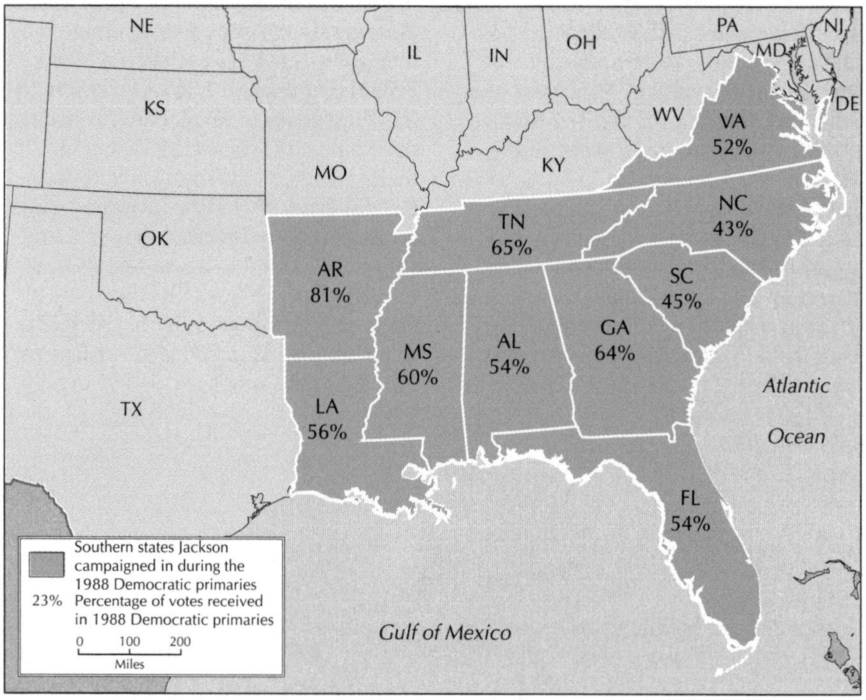
NE
IL
IN
OH
PA
NJ
MD
DE
KS
WV
VA
52%
MO
KY
OK
TN
65%
NC
43%
AR
81%
SC
45%
GA
64%
MS
60%
AL
54%
TX
LA
56%
Atlantic
Ocean
FL
54%
Gulf of Mexico
Southern states Jackson campaigned in during the 1988 Democratic primaries
23% Percentage of votes received in 1988 Democratic primaries
0 100 200
Miles

MAP 133

Reverse Migration: The Return of African Americans to the South (1980–1995)

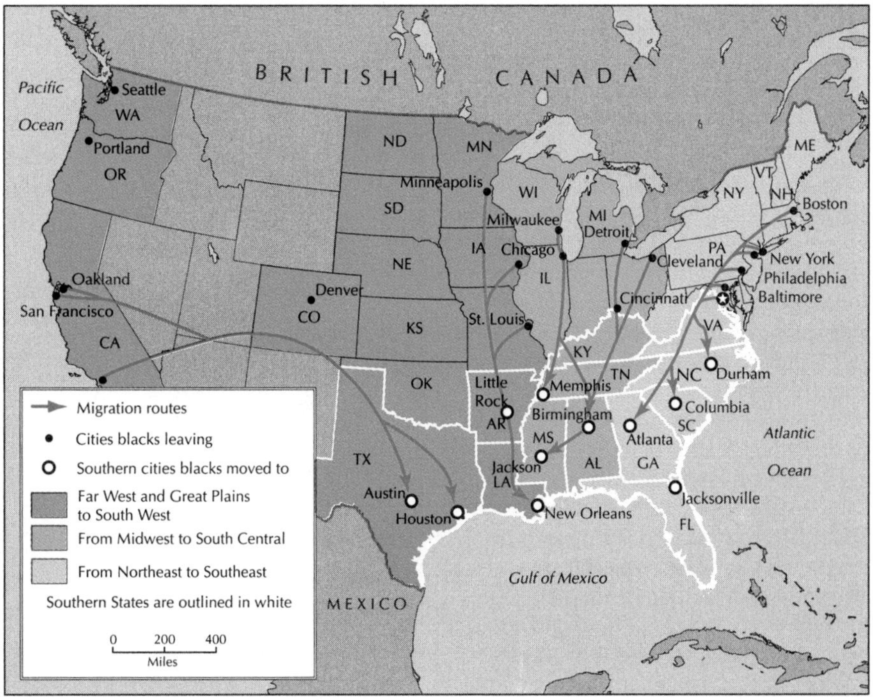
BRITISH CANADA
Pacific Ocean
Atlantic Ocean
Gulf of Mexico
MEXICO
Seattle
WA
Portland
OR
Oakland
San Francisco
CA
ND
MN
Minneapolis
SD
NE
Denver
CO
KS
OK
TX
Austin
Houston
WI
Milwaukee
MI
Detroit
IA
Chicago
IL
St. Louis
Little Rock
AR
Memphis
TN
KY
Birmingham
MS
Jackson
LA
New Orleans
AL
Atlanta
GA
Cincinnati
Cleveland
PA
NY
VT
NH
ME
Boston
New York
Philadelphia
Baltimore
VA
NC
Durham
Columbia
SC
Jacksonville
FL
Migration routes
Cities blacks leaving
Southern cities blacks moved to
Far West and Great Plains to South West
From Midwest to South Central
From Northeast to Southeast
Southern States are outlined in white
0 200 400
Miles

The twentieth century in America has been characterized by a number of events that have profoundly changed the way Americans live and work. For African Americans, perhaps the single greatest event has been the Great Migration of southern blacks to urban ghettos in the North and West. Not since the trans-Atlantic slave trade had such large numbers of people of African descent moved, this time voluntarily, to another region. In 1865 over 90 percent of all African Americans lived in the South. Beginning in 1877, with the exodus west to Kansas, blacks left the South in search of a better life in the North or West. When World War I broke out, this migration was accelerated because of the availability of jobs in northern war industries, and a similar movement began at the start of World War II. By 1960 nearly 50 percent of all African Americans had moved from the rural South to the urban North. But by 1960, northern industries began to move out of northern cities and into northern suburbs and the South, even as millions of poor, uneducated, jobless blacks were moving to those cities in search of work. By 1980, however, many southern blacks no longer saw the North as the promised land and, as Booker T. Washington had advocated a century before, began to "cast their buckets where they were." Many found more political power also meant more economic power in the South. They also began to benefit from the relocated industrial jobs that were coming into the South. Finally, many middle-class and upper-middle-class blacks began to relocate in the South, preferring the overt racism of the South to the covert racism of the North. Some of these blacks had been born in the North and West, but the majority had been born and educated in the South and had moved away to find better jobs. Blacks and progressive southern whites worked to build a new, more urban South. In fact, there were now two "Souths:" one poor, rural, uneducated, and racist; and the other urban, well educated, and progressive on matters of race, like Atlanta, Georgia, and Durham, North Carolina. ■

MAP 134

Rap Music and the Virginia Beach Race Riot (1989)

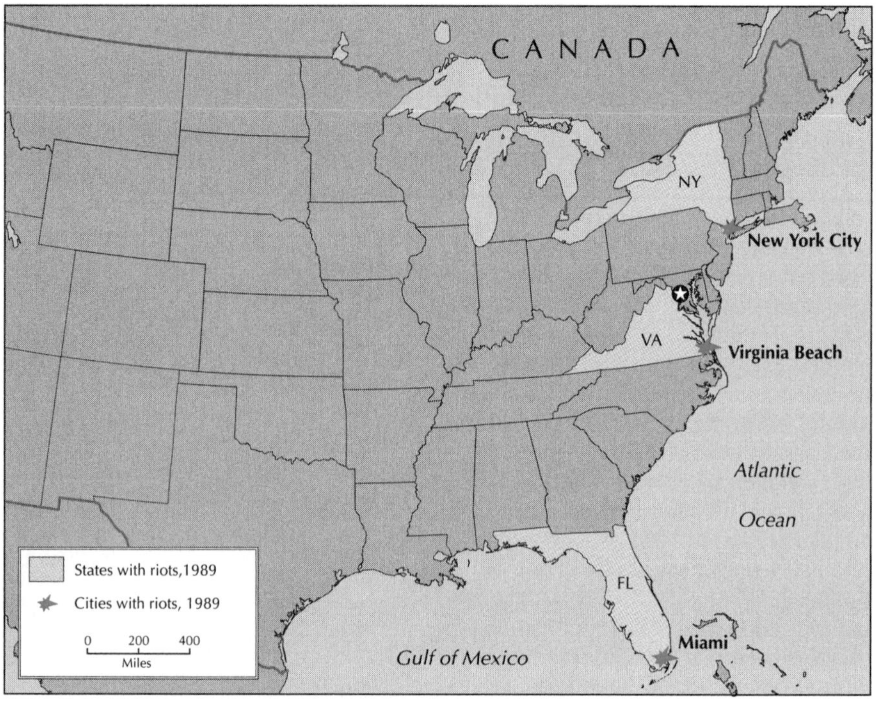
CANADA
NY
New York City
VA
Virginia Beach
FL
Miami
Atlantic Ocean
Gulf of Mexico
States with riots,1989
Cities with riots, 1989
0 200 400
Miles

From 1980 to 1989, blacks would see many of the legal, political, and economic gains they had made since 1954 threatened by a growing conservative Republican movement. The election of Ronald Reagan as president in 1980 and 1984 and the election of his vice president, George Bush, as president in 1988 brought twelve years of constant attacks on the advances made as a result of the civil rights movement. African Americans responded to these attacks in many ways. They voted for candidates who supported their causes, like Jesse Jackson and Senator Edward Kennedy. They also lobbied for and continued to advocate equal rights for all people. Many young African Americans became more nationalistic and turned to the new, radical, antiestablishment music called rap. This music began in the poor ghettos of northern and western urban cities but quickly spread all over the United States. This music and new racial tensions between blacks and whites, fueled in part by the rise of conservativism, led to a major race riot in 1989 at Virginia Beach. The Virginia Beach riot was different from other riots in U.S. history in that it included middle class *black* college students. It occurred after college students celebrating "Greek Fest" were overcharged for their hotel rooms and for items they purchased from local white merchants. The students were harassed and ticketed by police for loitering and playing loud music. When one student playing his car stereo put on a rap song called "Fuck the Police" by a rap group named NWA (Niggers with Attitudes), a group of students gathered and began to chant the song. Many of the police, who had been brought in from rural Virginia only for the weekend, responded negatively to this, causing the first riot over rap music. Because of increased racial tensions, two additional riots also occurred in Florida and New York. The Bensonhurst, New York, and Miami riots occurred after blacks were killed by white police officers. ■

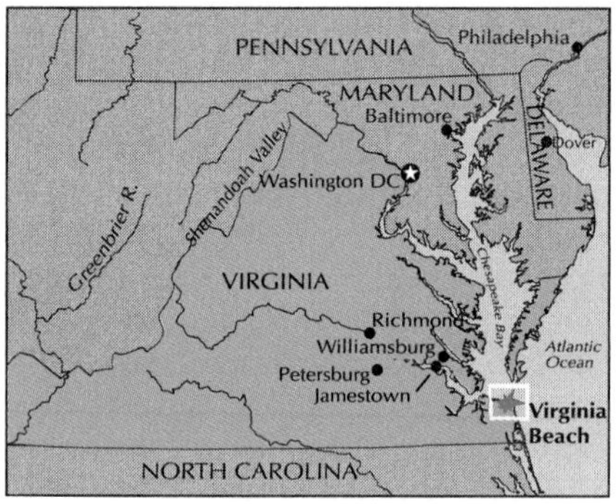
PENNSYLVANIA
Philadelphia
MARYLAND
Baltimore
Dover
DELAWARE
Washington DC
Shenandoah Valley
Greenbrier R.
VIRGINIA
Chesapeake Bay
Richmond
Williamsburg
Petersburg
Jamestown
Atlantic Ocean
Virginia Beach
NORTH CAROLINA

MAP 135

The African American Population in the United States (1980)

By 1980 there were approximately 31 million African Americans living in America, out of a total population of 226 million. The Great Migration, which lasted from 1910 to 1980, saw half of that population leave its native South for northeastern, midwestern, and far western cities. By 1980, however, the African American migration drew to a close. The black population in America began to show profound demographic differences. Urban blacks in the North tended to be overwhelmingly poor and desperate. Poor urban blacks in the South also did not have much, but most blacks in the South were middle-class, with Maryland, Virginia, North Carolina, South Carolina, Georgia, Florida, Alabama, Mississippi, Louisiana, and Texas being the most prosperous states for blacks. As the black population continued to grow, the African-American community continued to diversify and come to grips with that diversity. ■

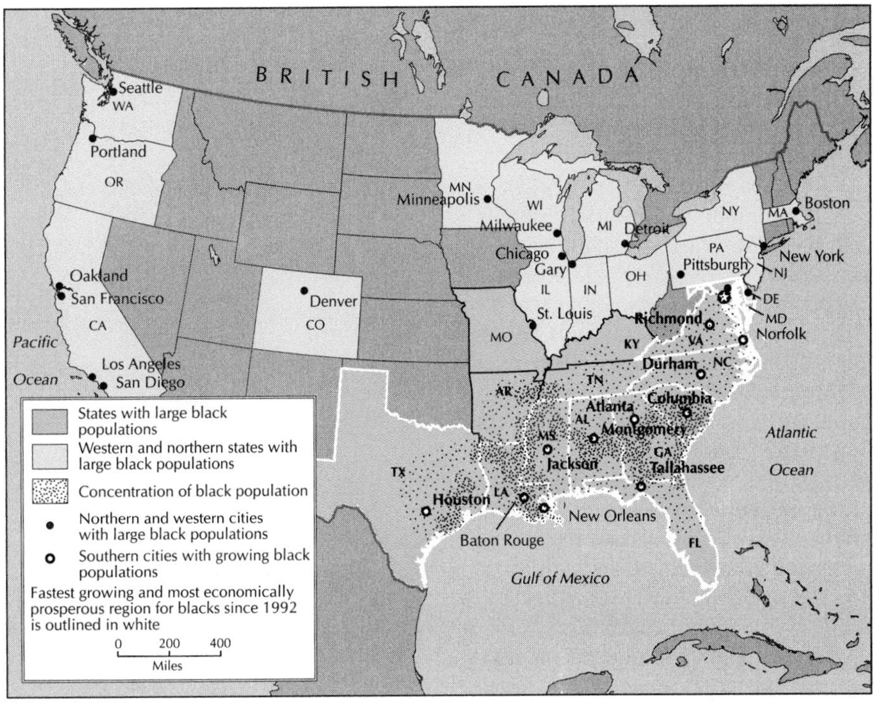
BRITISH CANADA
Seattle
WA
Portland
OR
Oakland
San Francisco
CA
Los Angeles
San Diego
Pacific Ocean
Denver
CO
MN
Minneapolis
WI
Milwaukee
MI
Detroit
Chicago
Gary
IL
IN
OH
St. Louis
MO
NY
PA
Pittsburgh
MA
Boston
New York
NJ
DE
MD
Richmond
VA
KY
Norfolk
Durham
NC
TN
AR
Atlanta
Columbia
AL
Montgomery
MS
Jackson
GA
Tallahassee
TX
Houston
LA
New Orleans
Baton Rouge
FL
Gulf of Mexico
Atlantic Ocean
States with large black populations
Western and northern states with large black populations
Concentration of black population
Northern and western cities with large black populations
Southern cities with growing black populations
Fastest growing and most economically prosperous region for blacks since 1992 is outlined in white
0 200 400
Miles

MAP 136

Race Riots in Major American Cities Following the Rodney King Verdict (1991)

Throughout the 1980s as Republican conservatism grew, so did racial tensions between whites and blacks, particularly in American cities where there had always been tensions between poor blacks and the local police. In 1990, this tension reached a breaking point when an onlooker, who was white, videotaped four members of the Los Angeles Police Department beating a black motorist, Rodney King, while a number of other officers watched. This tape was shown on television throughout the world. Although King had a criminal record and had led police on a high-speed chase minutes before, many people felt that the tape showed that the police overreacted, and the beating brought worldwide condemnation of the officers involved. It was also brought to light that the Los Angeles police routinely beat blacks who were stopped and suspected of committing crimes. In the trial of the police officers that followed, all four officers were acquitted of any wrongdoing by a suburban jury on which no blacks served. The acquittal touched off several days of rioting in Los Angeles and in several other major cities where there had been ongoing tensions with police—New York, Chicago, Detroit, Miami, and Oakland, California. While the officers involved were retried and convicted by the federal government for violating King's civil rights, a huge chasm opened between the black urban class and white police. In Los Angeles, all respect and trust between the police and the city's black community was gone. The beating and subsequent riot brought about major changes in the Los Angeles Police Department, the most notable being the hiring of a new black police chief. ■

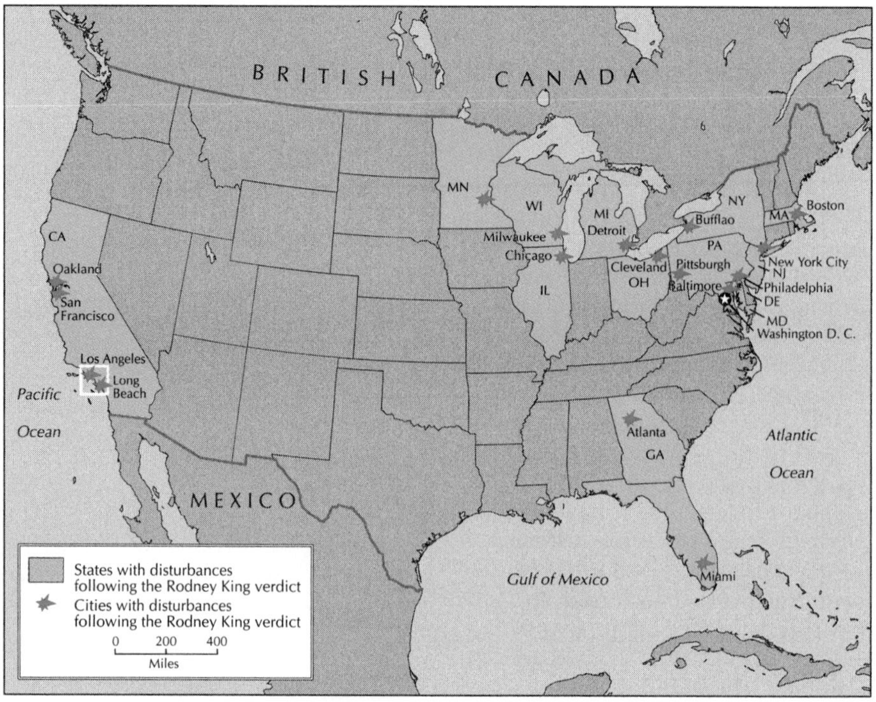
BRITISH
CANADA
MN
WI
MI
Detroit
Milwaukee
Chicago
IL
NY
Bufflao
MA
Boston
PA
Cleveland
OH
Pittsburgh
New York City
NJ
Baltimore
Philadelphia
DE
MD
Washington D. C.
CA
Oakland
San Francisco
Los Angeles
Long Beach
Pacific
Ocean
Atlanta
GA
Atlantic
Ocean
MEXICO
Gulf of Mexico
Miami
States with disturbances following the Rodney King verdict
Cities with disturbances following the Rodney King verdict
0 200 400
Miles

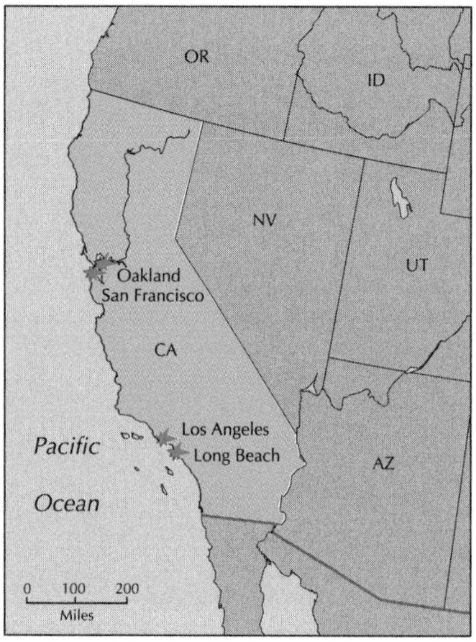
OR
ID
NV
UT
Oakland
San Francisco
CA
Los Angeles
Long Beach
Pacific
Ocean
AZ
0 100 200
Miles

Map and Text Sources

125. Carson, Clayborne. *Malcolm X: The FBI File*. New York: Ballantine Books, 1995.
Haley, Alex. *The Autobiography of Malcolm X*. New York: Ballantine Books, 1965.
Perry, Bruce. *Malcolm: The Life of a Man Who Changed Black America*. New York: Station Hill, 1991.

126. Bell, Derrick A. *Faces at the Bottom of the Well: The Permanence of Racism*. New York: Basic Books, 1992.
Bracey, John H., comp. *Black Nationalism in America*. Indianapolis: Bobbs-Merrill, 1970.
Breines, Wini. *Counterculture and Social Transformation: Essays on Negativistic Themes in Sociological Theory*. Springfield, IL: Thomas, 1982.
Brisbane, Robert H. *Black Activism: Racial Revolution in the United States, 1954–1970*. Valley Forge, PA: Judson Press, 1974.
Carmichael, Stokely, and Charles Hamilton. *Black Power: The Politics of Liberation in America*. Harmondsworth, England: Penguin, 1969.
Cleaver, Eldridge. *Soul on Ice*. New York: Bantam, 1992.
Hilliard, David, and Lewis Cole. *This Side of Glory: The Autobiography of David Hilliard and the Story of the Black Panther Party*. Boston: Little, Brown, 1993.
Hough, Joseph C. *Black Power and White Protestants: A Christian Response to the New Negro Pluralism*. New York: Oxford University Press, 1969.
Seale, Bobby. *Seize the Time: The Story of the Black Panther Party and Huey P. Newton*. Baltimore: Black Classic Press, 1991.
Pinkney, Alphonso. *Red, Black, and Green: Black Nationalism in the United States*. Cambridge: Cambridge University Press, 1976.

127. Baraka, Imamu, A., and Billy, Albernathy. *In Our Terribleness*. Indianapolis: Bobbs-Merrill, 1970.
Bennett, Lerone. *Confrontation: Black and White*. Chicago: Johnson Publishing Company, 1969.
Button, James W. *Black Violence: Political Impact of the 1960s Riots*. Princeton, NJ: Princeton University Press, 1978.
Connery, Robert H., ed. *Urban Riots: Violence and Social Change*. New York: Vintage Books, 1969.
Cruse, Harold. *Rebellion or Revolution?* New York: Morrow, 1968.
Holt, Len. *The Summer That Didn't End: The Story of the Mississippi Civil Rights Project of 1964*. New York: Da Capo Press, 1992.
Kerner Commission. *Report of the National Advisory Commission on Civil Disorders*. Washington, DC: U.S. Government Printing Office, 1968.
Waskow, Arthur I. *From Race Riot to Sit-In, 1919 and the 1960s: A Study in the Connections between Conflict and Violence*. Gloucester, MA: Peter Smith, 1975.

128. Chafe, William H. *Civilities and Civil Rights: Greensboro, North Carolina, and the Black Struggle for Freedom*. New York: Oxford University Press, 1981.
McEvoy, James. *Black Power and Student Rebellion*. Belmont, CA: Wadsworth Publishing Co., 1969.

129. Brownmiller, Susan. *Shirley Chisholm; a Biography*. Garden City, NY: Doubleday Books, 1971.
Chisholm, Shirley. *Unbought and Unbossed*. New York: Avon Books, 1972.
Haskins, James. *Fighting Shirley Chisholm*. New York: Dial Press, 1975.
Ross, Pat, comp. *Young and Female: Turning Points in the Lives of Eight American Women*. New York: Random House, 1972.

130. Cole, Leonard A. *Blacks in Power: A Comparative Study of Black and White Elected Officials*. Princeton, NJ: Princeton University Press, 1976.
Elliot, Jeffrey M. *Black Voices in American Politics*. San Diego: Harcourt Brace Jovanovich, 1986.
Joint Center for Political Studies. *Black Elected Officials: A National Roster, 1993*. 21st ed. Washington, DC: Joint Center for Political Studies Press, 1994.
Karnig, Albert K. *Black Representation and Urban Policy*. Chicago: University of Chicago Press, 1980.
Nelson, William E. *Electing Black Mayors; Political Action in the Black Community*. Columbus: Ohio State University Press, 1977.
Swain, Carol M. *Black Faces, Black Interests: The Representation of African Americans in Congress*, enl. ed. Cambridge, MA: Harvard University Press, 1995.

131. Ashmore, Harry S. *Civil Rights and Wrongs: A Memoir of Race and Politics 1944–1994*. New York: Pantheon Books, 1994.
Barrett, Laurence I. *Gambling with History: Ronald Reagan in the White House*. New York: Penguin Books, 1984.
Bartley, Numan V. *The New South, 1945–1980*. Baton Rouge: Louisiana State University Press, 1996.
Boyer, Paul. *Reagan as President: Contemporary Views of the Man, His Politics, and His Policies*. Chicago: I.R. Dee, 1990.
Hayden, Thomas. *The Power of the Dixiecrats*. Nashville, TN: Southern Student Organizing Committee, 1966.
Johnson, Haynes B. *Sleep walking through History: America in the Reagan Years*. New York: Anchor Books, 1992.
Southern Negro: 1952: Warning to Ike and the Dixiecrats. New York: The Nation, 1952.
White, Theodore H. *America in Search of Itself: The Making of the President, 1956–1980*. Norwalk, CT: Easton Press, 1986.

132. Henry, Charles P. *Jesse Jackson: The Search for Common Ground*. Oakland, CA: Black Scholar Press, 1991.
Reed, Adolph L. *The Jesse Jackson Phenomenon: The Crisis in Afro-American Politics*. New Haven, CT: Yale University Press, 1986.
Reynolds, Barbara A. *Jesse Jackson: America's David*. Washington, DC: JFJ Associates, 1985.
Reynolds, Barbara A. *Jesse Jackson, the Man, the Movement, the Myth*. Chicago: Nelson-Hall, 1975.

133. Chance, Tibbitt Marvin. *The Return Migration of Blacks to North Carolina: A Study in Motivations*. Raleigh: North Carolina State University, 1977.
Harrison, Alferdteen, ed. *Black Exodus: The Great Migration from the American South*. Jackson: University Press of Mississippi, 1991
Johnson, Daniel M., and Rex R. Campbell. *Black Migration in America: A Social Demographic History*. Durham, NC: Duke University Press, 1981.
Stack, Carol. *Call to Home: African Americans Reclaim the Rural South*. HarperCollins, 1996.
Trotter, Joe William. *The Great Migration in Historical Perspective: New Dimensions of Race, Class, and Gender*. Bloomington: Indiana University Press, 1991.

134. Baker, Houston A. *Black Studies, Rap, and the Academy*. Chicago: University of Chicago Press, 1993.

Eighmey, Kathleen M. *The Beach: A History of Virginia Beach, Virginia*, rev. ed. Virginia Beach, VA: City of Virginia Beach, Department of Public Libraries, 1996.

Gregory, Georgie Ruth. *Beyond the Veil.* Virginia Beach, VA: Cornerstone Publishing, 1993.

Kitwana, Bakari. *The Rap on Gangsta Rap: Who Run It?: Gangsta Rap and Visions of Black Violence.* Chicago: Third World Press, 1994.

Proceedings: National Leadership Summit Labor Day Event, 1990. Norfolk, VA: Norfolk State University, 1990.

Rose, Patricia L. *Black Noise: Rap Music & Black Cultural Resistance in Contemporary American Popular Culture.* 1993

Southern, Eileen. *The Music of Black Americans: A History,* 3rd ed. New York: Norton, 1997.

Labor Day Review Commission. *Final Report of the Labor Day Review Commission, January 26, 1990.* Virginia Beach, VA: City of Virginia Beach, 1990.

Labor Day Community Coordination Committee. *Committee Minutes.* Virginia Beach, VA: City of Virginia Beach, 1990.

135. United States Bureau of the Census. *State and Metropolitan Area Data Book 1982, a Statistical Abstract Supplement.* Washington, DC: U.S. Government Printing Office, 1982.

136. Hunt, Darnell M. *Screening the Los Angeles "Riots": Race, Seeing, and Resistance.* Cambridge: Cambridge University Press, 1996.

Los Angeles Times. Understanding the Riots: Los Angeles before and after the Rodney King Case. Los Angeles, CA: Los Angeles Times, 1992.

Vargas, Joao Helion Costa. *Crystal Myths, Silent Politics: The 1992 L.A. Rebellions, The Los Angeles Times' Portrayals, and the American Democracy: (An Essay on Differences).* La Jolla: University of California, San Diego, Department of Anthropology, 1995.

MAP 137

The Fight over the Dixiecrats: The Election of William Jefferson Clinton and Southern Black Voters in the 1992 and 1996 Presidential Elections

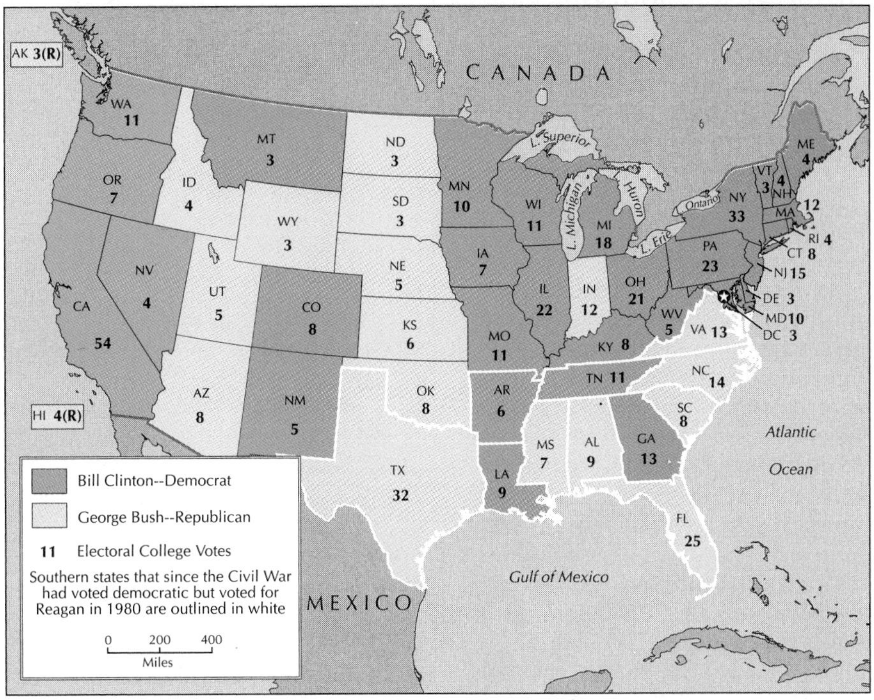

CANADA
MEXICO
Atlantic Ocean
Gulf of Mexico
L. Superior
L. Michigan
L. Huron
L. Erie
L. Ontario
AK 3(R)
HI 4(R)
WA 11
OR 7
CA 54
ID 4
NV 4
MT 3
WY 3
UT 5
AZ 8
CO 8
NM 5
ND 3
SD 3
NE 5
KS 6
OK 8
TX 32
MN 10
IA 7
MO 11
AR 6
LA 9
WI 11
IL 22
MI 18
IN 12
OH 21
KY 8
TN 11
MS 7
AL 9
GA 13
FL 25
SC 8
NC 14
VA 13
WV 5
PA 23
NY 33
VT 3
NH 4
ME 4
MA 12
RI 4
CT 8
NJ 15
DE 3
MD 10
DC 3
Bill Clinton--Democrat
George Bush--Republican
11 Electoral College Votes
Southern states that since the Civil War had voted democratic but voted for Reagan in 1980 are outlined in white
0 200 400
Miles

In the election of 1992, two southern Democrats, Governor William Jefferson Clinton from Arkansas and his running mate Senator Al Gore from Tennessee, did what had not been done since before the Civil War. They gained control of the nation's two highest offices. Although Clinton received the support of a great majority of the nation's black voters, he was successful in winning the election for two other reasons: (1) the entrance into the race of the third-party candidate, Ross Perot, and (2) the movement of the Democratic Party to the political right. With promises of tax relief for the middle class and the end of welfare, Clinton began to bring many white southern Democrats back to the party, while alienating the more liberal wing of the party at the same time. He maintained the support of the liberal wing only because the alternative was four more years of conservative Republican rule under George Bush. The Clinton campaign and first two years of his administration stunned many blacks, who became disillusioned with the Clinton presidency and the Democratic Party. As a result, a well-organized Republican Party won a landslide in the congressional elections of 1994, giving the Republicans control of the House and Senate for the first time since the 1920s. These conservative Republicans, along with conservative southern Democrats, systematically dismantled many of the social, educational, and economic programs of the 1960s and 1970s. Under attack from all sides, black Americans once again looked to one another, as they did at the end of Reconstruction, for the help that seemed to be rapidly ending. In response to these forces, on October 16, 1995, Muslim leader Louis Farrakhan called for one million black men to march on Washington, D.C. The event was billed as a "day of atonement" for black men and the rebirth of the self-help movement begun by Booker T. Washington, Marcus Garvey, Elijah Muhammad, and Malcolm X. ■

MAP 138

America's Black Religious Denominations (Regional Churches) and Southern Black Church Burnings (1995–1997)

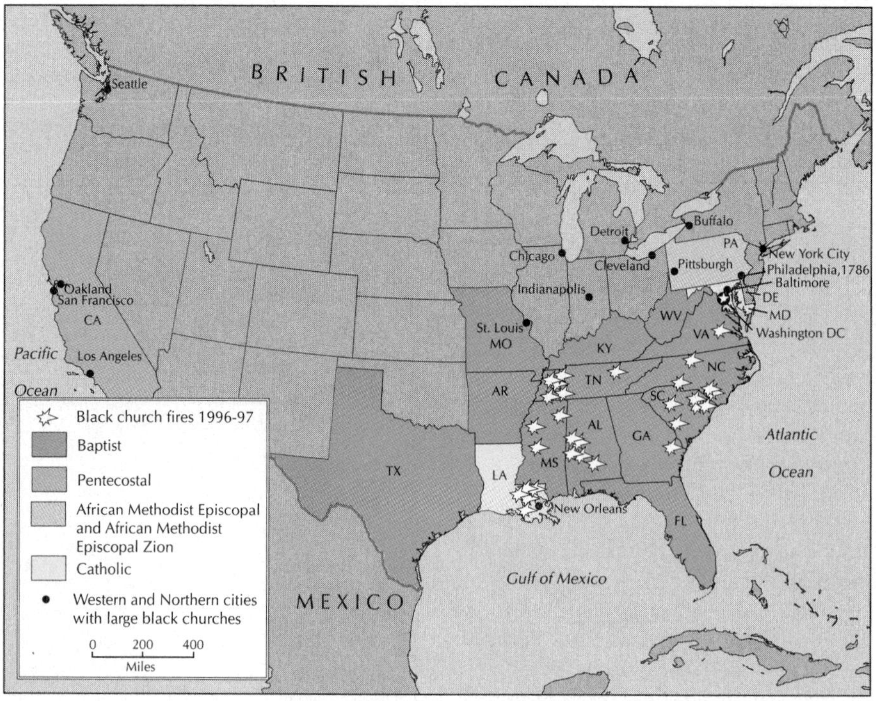
BRITISH
CANADA
Seattle
Oakland
San Francisco
CA
Los Angeles
Pacific Ocean
Detroit
Buffalo
Chicago
Cleveland
PA
Pittsburgh
New York City
Philadelphia,1786
Baltimore
DE
MD
Washington DC
Indianapolis
St. Louis
MO
KY
WV
VA
NC
TN
SC
AR
AL
GA
MS
LA
TX
New Orleans
FL
Atlantic Ocean
Gulf of Mexico
MEXICO
Black church fires 1996-97
Baptist
Pentecostal
African Methodist Episcopal and African Methodist Episcopal Zion
Catholic
Western and Northern cities with large black churches
0 200 400
Miles

Religion has always played a major role in the lives of African Americans. When Africans were enslaved in the Americas, some were allowed to continue their native faiths in the Caribbean, and Central and South America. However, particularly in the American South, slaves were most often deprived of an opportunity to practice either their native faiths or Christianity, which was the religion of their masters. In spite of this, slaves often converted to Christianity and worshiped in secret. Following the Civil War, many former slaves built churches. The vast majority of these slaves were Baptist, but some were also African Methodist Episcopal (AME), African Methodist Episcopal Zion (AMEZ), Muslim, Catholic or followers of other, smaller denominations. The black church has always been at the center of black progress and activism. Abolitionists used religion to point out the immorality of slavery, thus helping to bring about its end. Early black churches served as schools and ministers served as teachers for newly freed slaves. In the 1960s, the Baptist Church, the nation's largest black church, led the civil rights movement and transformed America. However, by the 1990s church membership had declined in most black churches, even as problems in the black community, such as crime, drugs, and teenage pregnancy, rose. This led to a call by religious leaders for a return to the church. At about this same time, from 1995 to 1997, black churches began to be targets of arson as white hate groups grew more violent. During this period more than thirty black churches were burned across the South. ■

MAP 139

America's More Than 100 Historically Black Colleges and Universities (1997)

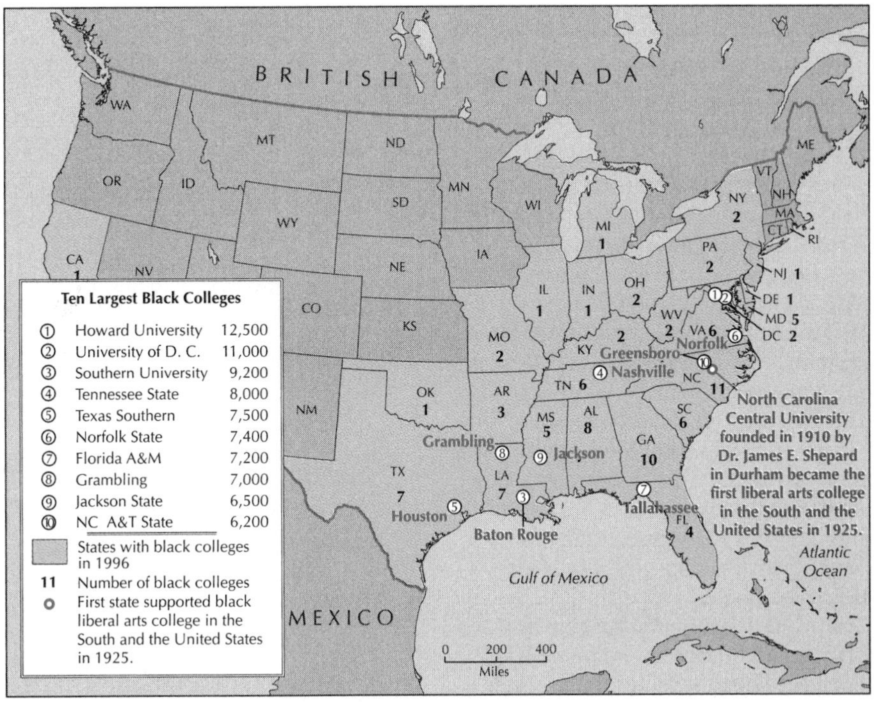
BRITISH
CANADA
MEXICO
Ten Largest Black Colleges
① Howard University 12,500
② University of D. C. 11,000
③ Southern University 9,200
④ Tennessee State 8,000
⑤ Texas Southern 7,500
⑥ Norfolk State 7,400
⑦ Florida A&M 7,200
⑧ Grambling 7,000
⑨ Jackson State 6,500
⑩ NC A&T State 6,200
States with black colleges in 1996
11 Number of black colleges
First state supported black liberal arts college in the South and the United States in 1925.
WA
OR
CA 1
NV
ID
MT
WY
CO
NM
ND
SD
NE
KS
OK 1
TX 7
MN
IA
MO 2
AR 3
LA 7
WI
IL 1
MI 1
IN 1
OH 2
KY 2
TN 6
MS 5
AL 8
GA 10
FL 4
SC 6
NC 11
VA 6
WV 2
PA 2
NY 2
NJ 1
DE 1
MD 5
DC 2
ME
VT
NH
MA
CT
RI
Houston
Grambling
Jackson
Baton Rouge
Tallahassee
Nashville
Greensboro
Norfolk
North Carolina Central University founded in 1910 by Dr. James E. Shepard in Durham became the first liberal arts college in the South and the United States in 1925.
Atlantic Ocean
Gulf of Mexico
0 200 400
Miles

By 1997 America had over 100 predominantly black colleges and universities. Most of these schools were in the South. Nearly half of these black colleges and universities were founded before or during Reconstruction. All serve the same purpose: to give African Americans the opportunity for a quality education in an environment that provides for their cultural needs. In the late 1980s, many Americans questioned the importance and necessity of historically black colleges. Even many black leaders believed that these institutions in some ways contributed to many of the remaining schisms between blacks and whites in America. By 1990, however, important statistics were compiled on black colleges. Of the 300,000 bachelor of arts degrees received by blacks, most were from black colleges. A large portion of blacks who received Ph.D.s, law degrees, and M.B.A.s earned their B.A.s from black colleges. Furthermore, most blacks attending predominantly white universities dropped out after their second year, and those who remained took at least five years or longer to finish their B.A. degrees. ■

MAP 140

America's Major Black Fraternities and Sororities (1997)

As with many other black institutions that were developed during the Jim Crow years and before to promote, protect, and assist the black community, social and service organizations served a major function in the lives of African Americans. Historically, blacks were denied entrance into many white organizations. As a result, as early as 1787, Prince Hall organized the first black Masons in Boston. This organization soon spread across the nation. The Masons provided blacks an opportunity to fellowship together and serve in leadership positions denied them elsewhere. By the early 1900s, with increasing numbers of African Americans attending all-black colleges and universities in the South and integrated northern universities, the first all-black college Greek fraternities and sororities were founded, but not without controversy. The first black Greek college fraternity was begun as a study group because white students refused to allow black students to study in their groups. It was started at Cornell University, in Ithaca, New York, on December 4, 1906, and was named Alpha Phi Alpha. The first black Greek college sorority was founded at Howard University, in Washington, D.C., on January 15, 1908, and was named Alpha Kappa Alpha. These two fraternities and sororities were followed by Omega Psi Phi, Delta Sigma Theta, Phi Beta Sigma, Zeta Phi Beta, Kappa Alpha Psi, Sigma Gamma Rho, and Iota Phi Theta. Many blacks believed these organizations were unnecessary and would take students away from their studies. Others felt the organizations would give black students a sense of belonging that many needed, especially on majority-white campuses. Both good and bad have come from these organizations, but collectively they have all served the black community. ■

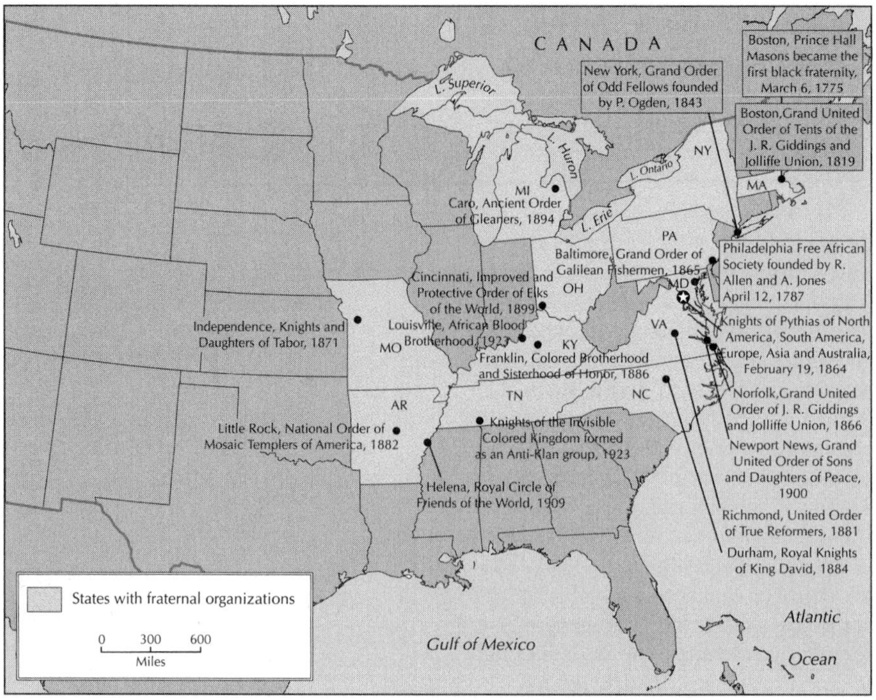
CANADA
L. Superior
L. Huron
L. Ontario
L. Erie
Boston, Prince Hall Masons became the first black fraternity, March 6, 1775
New York, Grand Order of Odd Fellows founded by P. Ogden, 1843
Boston, Grand United Order of Tents of the J. R. Giddings and Jolliffe Union, 1819
NY
MA
MI
Caro, Ancient Order of Gleaners, 1894
PA
Philadelphia Free African Society founded by R. Allen and A. Jones April 12, 1787
Baltimore, Grand Order of Galilean Fishermen, 1865
MD
OH
Cincinnati, Improved and Protective Order of Elks of the World, 1899
Independence, Knights and Daughters of Tabor, 1871
Louisville, African Blood Brotherhood, 1923
MO
KY
VA
Knights of Pythias of North America, South America, Europe, Asia and Australia, February 19, 1864
Franklin, Colored Brotherhood and Sisterhood of Honor, 1886
TN
NC
AR
Norfolk, Grand United Order of J. R. Giddings and Jolliffe Union, 1866
Little Rock, National Order of Mosaic Templers of America, 1882
Knights of the Invisible Colored Kingdom formed as an Anti-Klan group, 1923
Newport News, Grand United Order of Sons and Daughters of Peace, 1900
Helena, Royal Circle of Friends of the World, 1909
Richmond, United Order of True Reformers, 1881
Durham, Royal Knights of King David, 1884
States with fraternal organizations
0 300 600
Miles
Gulf of Mexico
Atlantic Ocean

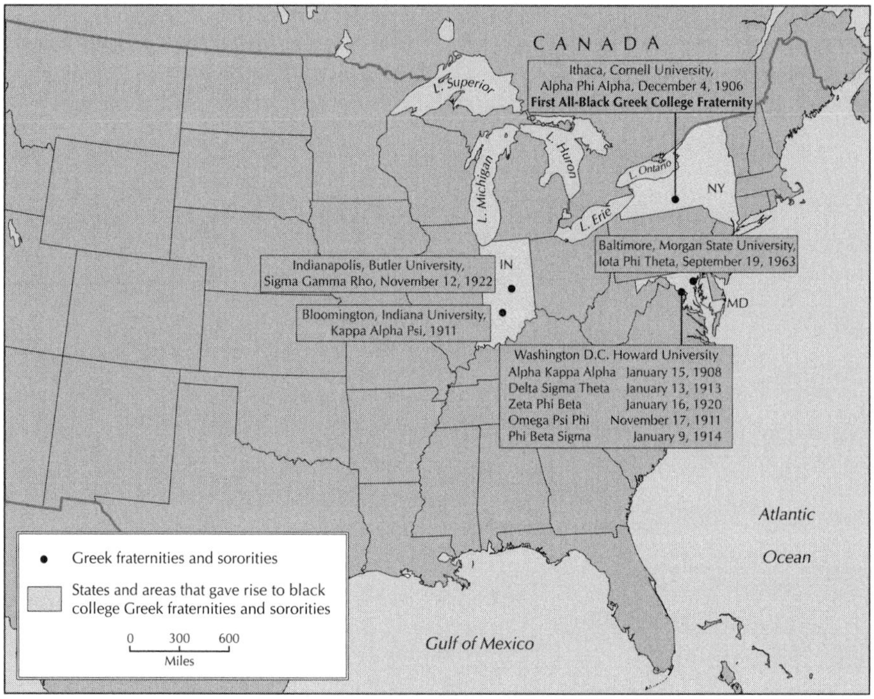
CANADA
L. Superior
L. Michigan
L. Huron
L. Ontario
L. Erie
Ithaca, Cornell University, Alpha Phi Alpha, December 4, 1906
First All-Black Greek College Fraternity
NY
Baltimore, Morgan State University, Iota Phi Theta, September 19, 1963
Indianapolis, Butler University, Sigma Gamma Rho, November 12, 1922
IN
MD
Bloomington, Indiana University, Kappa Alpha Psi, 1911
Washington D.C. Howard University
Alpha Kappa Alpha January 15, 1908
Delta Sigma Theta January 13, 1913
Zeta Phi Beta January 16, 1920
Omega Psi Phi November 17, 1911
Phi Beta Sigma January 9, 1914
Greek fraternities and sororities
States and areas that gave rise to black college Greek fraternities and sororities
0 300 600
Miles
Gulf of Mexico
Atlantic
Ocean

MAP 141

America's Largest Black-Owned Corporations in 1997

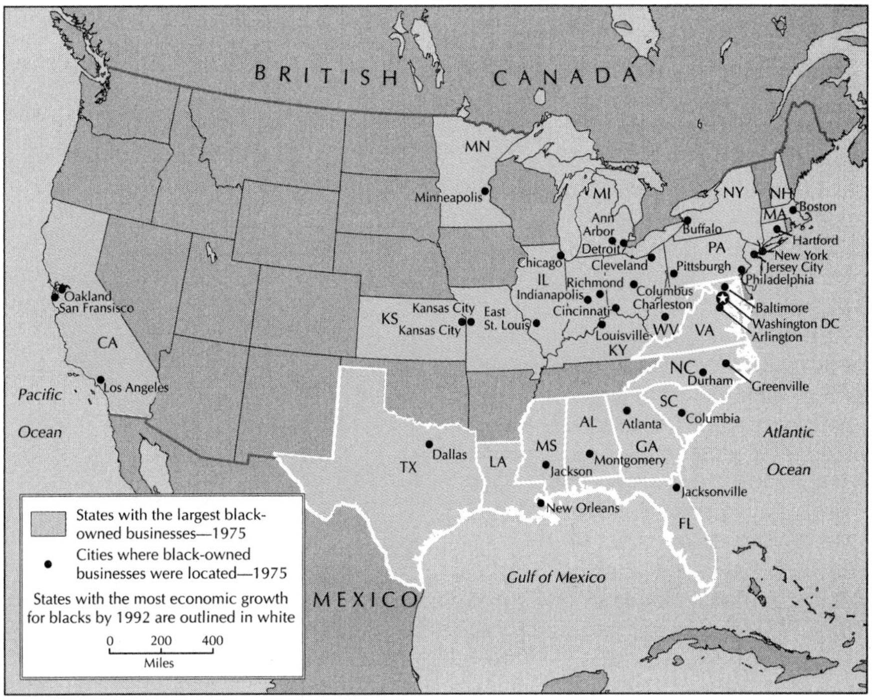
BRITISH
CANADA
MN
Minneapolis
MI
Ann Arbor
Detroit
Chicago
IL
Cleveland
Richmond
Indianapolis
Columbus
Charleston
Cincinnati
Louisville
KY
WV
VA
NY
Buffalo
PA
Pittsburgh
NH
MA
Boston
Hartford
New York
Jersey City
Philadelphia
Baltimore
Washington DC
Arlington
NC
Durham
Greenville
SC
Columbia
AL
Atlanta
GA
Montgomery
MS
Jackson
LA
New Orleans
FL
Jacksonville
KS
Kansas City
Kansas City
East St. Louis
TX
Dallas
CA
Oakland
San Fransisco
Los Angeles
Pacific Ocean
Atlantic Ocean
Gulf of Mexico
MEXICO
States with the largest black-owned businesses—1975
Cities where black-owned businesses were located—1975
States with the most economic growth for blacks by 1992 are outlined in white
0 200 400
Miles

The mid-1990s was a turbulent time for African Americans across the United States. Increased racial tensions, the end of civil rights programs, and the increased stratification of the black community along economic lines caused friction and division within black America. In spite of this, black businesses, some that had been in existence since the 1800s, grew and prospered. One of the nation's largest and most popular companies was the Johnson Products Company. Millions of Americans grew up utilizing Johnson's products, not realizing the company was one of black America's greatest assets. In addition to this company, there was also *Essence* magazine, and Black Entertainment Television (BET), among others. As conservatives grew in power in the 1990s, the importance of black-owned and -operated businesses became a major part of the rhetoric of black leaders. It was viewed as the only way blacks could rebuild their communities and their economic independence from white America. ■

MAP 142

America's Largest Black-Owned Banks (1997)

Although black banks had been in existence since the 1800s and maintained a loyal following in the South, their existence, like that of many other black institutions in the 1970s and 1980s, was threatened, as large numbers of blacks withdrew their funds and deposited their money in larger white-owned institutions. These banks were saved by wise investment strategies and a core of loyal black depositors who were from old money and refused to allow the institutions to die that were created and sustained by their ancestors. As a result of these individuals, more than 100 black-owned banks are still viable and flourishing in America. Most are found in southern cities like Atlanta, Richmond, Durham, and Charlotte, cities with large numbers of black middle-class wage earners. A number are also located in northern and western cities with large black populations, including New York, Chicago, and Detroit. ■

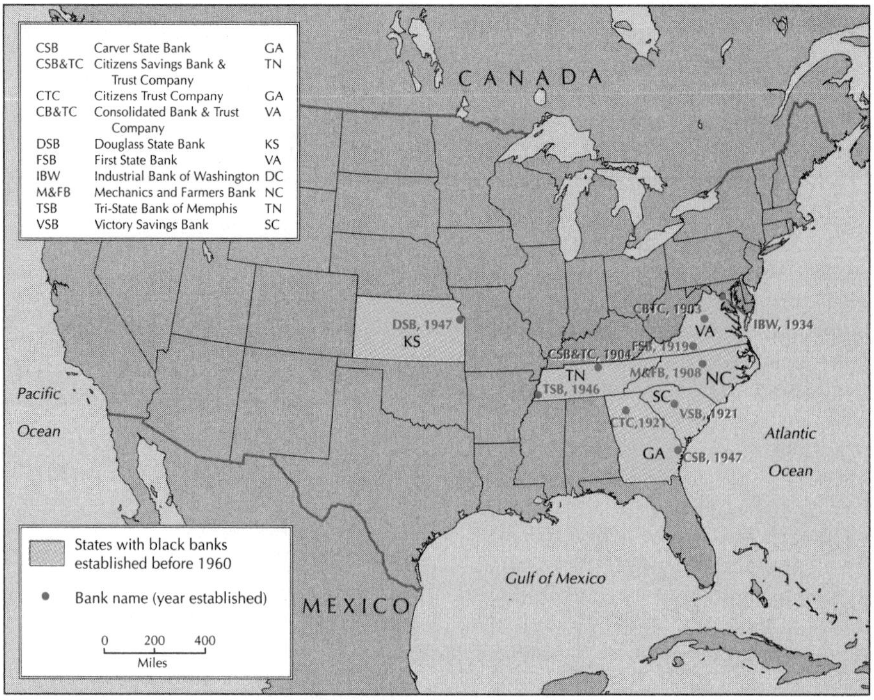
CSB Carver State Bank GA
CSB&TC Citizens Savings Bank & Trust Company TN
CTC Citizens Trust Company GA
CB&TC Consolidated Bank & Trust Company VA
DSB Douglass State Bank KS
FSB First State Bank VA
IBW Industrial Bank of Washington DC
M&FB Mechanics and Farmers Bank NC
TSB Tri-State Bank of Memphis TN
VSB Victory Savings Bank SC
CANADA
MEXICO
Pacific Ocean
Atlantic Ocean
Gulf of Mexico
DSB, 1947
KS
CB&TC, 1903
VA
IBW, 1934
CSB&TC, 1904
FSB, 1919
TN
TSB, 1946
M&FB, 1908
NC
SC
VSB, 1921
CTC, 1921
GA
CSB, 1947
States with black banks established before 1960
Bank name (year established)
0 200 400
Miles

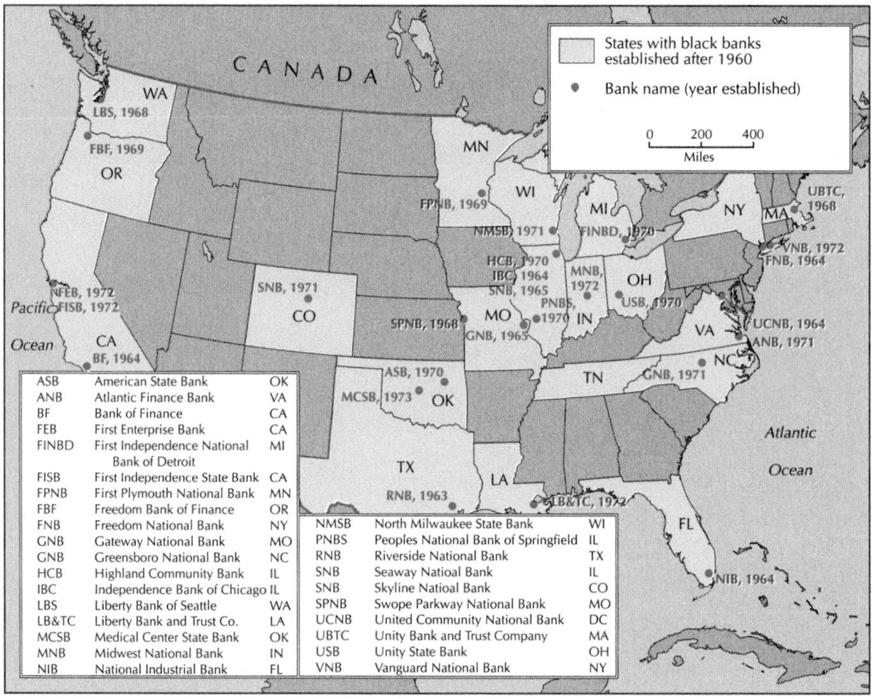
States with black banks established after 1960
Bank name (year established)
0 200 400
Miles
CANADA
Pacific Ocean
Atlantic Ocean
WA
LBS, 1968
FBF, 1969
OR
FEB, 1972
FISB, 1972
CA
BF, 1964
SNB, 1971
CO
MN
FPNB, 1969
WI
NMSB, 1971
MI
FINBD, 1970
HCB, 1970
IBC, 1964
SNB, 1965
MNB, 1972
PNBS, 1970
IN
OH
USB, 1970
MO
SPNB, 1968
GNB, 1965
NY
MA
UBTC, 1968
VNB, 1972
FNB, 1964
VA
UCNB, 1964
ANB, 1971
NC
GNB, 1971
TN
ASB, 1970
MCSB, 1973
OK
TX
RNB, 1963
LA
LB&TC, 1972
FL
NIB, 1964
ASB American State Bank OK
ANB Atlantic Finance Bank VA
BF Bank of Finance CA
FEB First Enterprise Bank CA
FINBD First Independence National Bank of Detroit MI
FISB First Independence State Bank CA
FPNB First Plymouth National Bank MN
FBF Freedom Bank of Finance OR
FNB Freedom National Bank NY
GNB Gateway National Bank MO
GNB Greensboro National Bank NC
HCB Highland Community Bank IL
IBC Independence Bank of Chicago IL
LBS Liberty Bank of Seattle WA
LB&TC Liberty Bank and Trust Co. LA
MCSB Medical Center State Bank OK
MNB Midwest National Bank IN
NIB National Industrial Bank FL
NMSB North Milwaukee State Bank WI
PNBS Peoples National Bank of Springfield IL
RNB Riverside National Bank TX
SNB Seaway Natioal Bank IL
SNB Skyline Natioal Bank CO
SPNB Swope Parkway National Bank MO
UCNB United Community National Bank DC
UBTC Unity Bank and Trust Company MA
USB Unity State Bank OH
VNB Vanguard National Bank NY

MAP 143

America's Largest Black-Owned Insurance Companies (1997)

Along with the rebirth and growth of America's black colleges and universities, businesses, and banks, by 1995 nearly 100 black-owned and -operated insurance companies thrived and prospered. Many of these insurance companies were founded following the Civil War and reached their zenith during the Jim Crow years in the South, when blacks were not insured by white companies. These insurance companies saved thousands of families, who had lost their breadwinners, from financial ruin. They provided safety nets to millions of black Americans and provided jobs for thousands of agents, secretaries, and executives, who would, along with university professors, schoolteachers, ministers, and small-business people, help create a thriving black middle-class in many southern cities in spite of Jim Crow. One of the nation's largest insurance companies, founded in 1898, is the North Carolina Mutual Life Insurance Company, based in Durham, North Carolina. It holds the title of the world's largest black-owned insurance company.

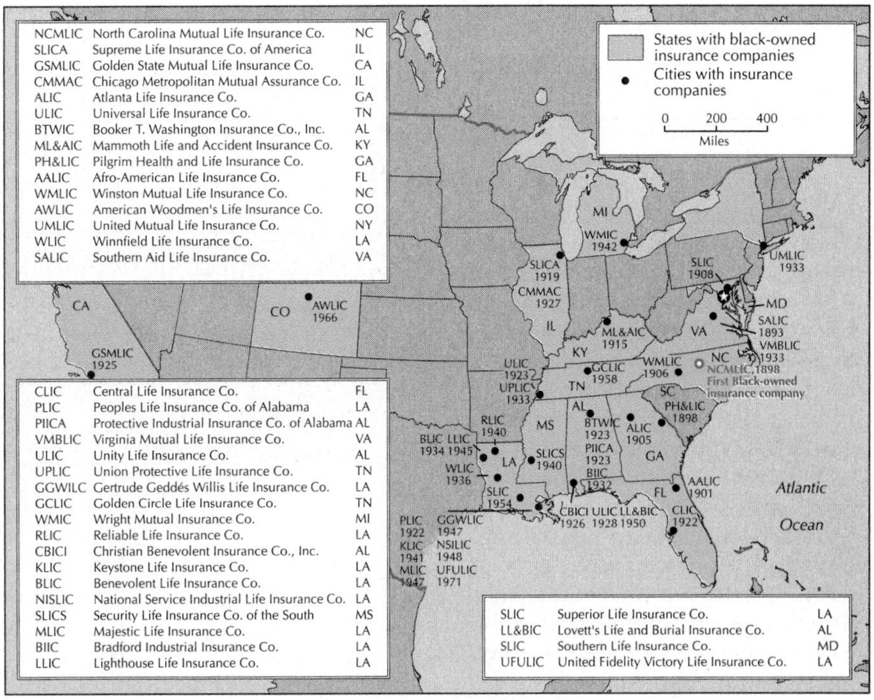
NCMLIC North Carolina Mutual Life Insurance Co. NC
SLICA Supreme Life Insurance Co. of America IL
GSMLIC Golden State Mutual Life Insurance Co. CA
CMMAC Chicago Metropolitan Mutual Assurance Co. IL
ALIC Atlanta Life Insurance Co. GA
ULIC Universal Life Insurance Co. TN
BTWIC Booker T. Washington Insurance Co., Inc. AL
ML&AIC Mammoth Life and Accident Insurance Co. KY
PH&LIC Pilgrim Health and Life Insurance Co. GA
AALIC Afro-American Life Insurance Co. FL
WMLIC Winston Mutual Life Insurance Co. NC
AWLIC American Woodmen's Life Insurance Co. CO
UMLIC United Mutual Life Insurance Co. NY
WLIC Winnfield Life Insurance Co. LA
SALIC Southern Aid Life Insurance Co. VA
CLIC Central Life Insurance Co. FL
PLIC Peoples Life Insurance Co. of Alabama LA
PIICA Protective Industrial Insurance Co. of Alabama AL
VMBLIC Virginia Mutual Life Insurance Co. VA
ULIC Unity Life Insurance Co. AL
UPLIC Union Protective Life Insurance Co. TN
GGWILC Gertrude Geddés Willis Life Insurance Co. LA
GCLIC Golden Circle Life Insurance Co. TN
WMIC Wright Mutual Insurance Co. MI
RLIC Reliable Life Insurance Co. LA
CBICI Christian Benevolent Insurance Co., Inc. AL
KLIC Keystone Life Insurance Co. LA
BLIC Benevolent Life Insurance Co. LA
NISLIC National Service Industrial Life Insurance Co. LA
SLICS Security Life Insurance Co. of the South MS
MLIC Majestic Life Insurance Co. LA
BIIC Bradford Industrial Insurance Co. LA
LLIC Lighthouse Life Insurance Co. LA
SLIC Superior Life Insurance Co. LA
LL&BIC Lovett's Life and Burial Insurance Co. AL
SLIC Southern Life Insurance Co. MD
UFULIC United Fidelity Victory Life Insurance Co. LA
States with black-owned insurance companies
Cities with insurance companies
0 200 400
Miles
CA
GSMLIC 1925
CO
AWLIC 1966
MI
WMIC 1942
SLICA 1919
CMMAC 1927
IL
SLIC 1908
UMLIC 1933
MD
SALIC 1893
VMBLIC 1933
VA
ML&AIC 1915
KY
ULIC 1923
UPLIC 1933
GCLIC 1958
TN
WMLIC 1906
NC
NCMLIC, 1898 First Black-owned insurance company
SC
PH&LIC 1898
AL
MS
BTWIC 1923
PIICA 1923
BIIC 1932
ALIC 1905
GA
RLIC 1940
BLIC LLIC 1934 1945
LA
SLICS 1940
WLIC 1936
SLIC 1954
PLIC 1922
KLIC 1941
MLIC 1947
GGWLIC 1947
NSILIC 1948
UFULIC 1971
CBICI ULIC LL&BIC 1926 1928 1950
FL
AALIC 1901
CLIC 1922
Atlantic Ocean

MAP 144

The Impact of Drugs and Crime on African Americans in the United States (1997)

Beginning in the 1960s, drugs flooded into many black urban communities. In spite of the cries for help by many of the residents of these poor communities, the flow of drugs was allowed to continue unchecked, and by the 1980s drugs began to move out of the black community into the middle-class and wealthy communities of white America. With the introduction of the highly addictive drug, crack cocaine, America experienced an epidemic of drug-related crime—murders, robberies, assaults, prostitution, and very violent gang activity. This crime became a problem in all American neighborhoods. It prompted a national war on drugs, complete with a drug czar, William Bennett, in the 1980s. By the mid-1990s, in spite of the millions of dollars spent in fighting the war on drugs, the drug problem seemed no closer to being solved. Drugs and drug-related crime had destroyed America's poor inner-city areas, where there seemed to be little hope of obtaining the American dream. It also led to attempts by black leaders to reclaim their communities by personally becoming involved in the war on drugs. These drugs entered the U.S. primarily from South America through major airports in Los Angeles, Chicago, New York, and Miami. They were spread all over America by way of the U.S.'s interstate highway system. ■

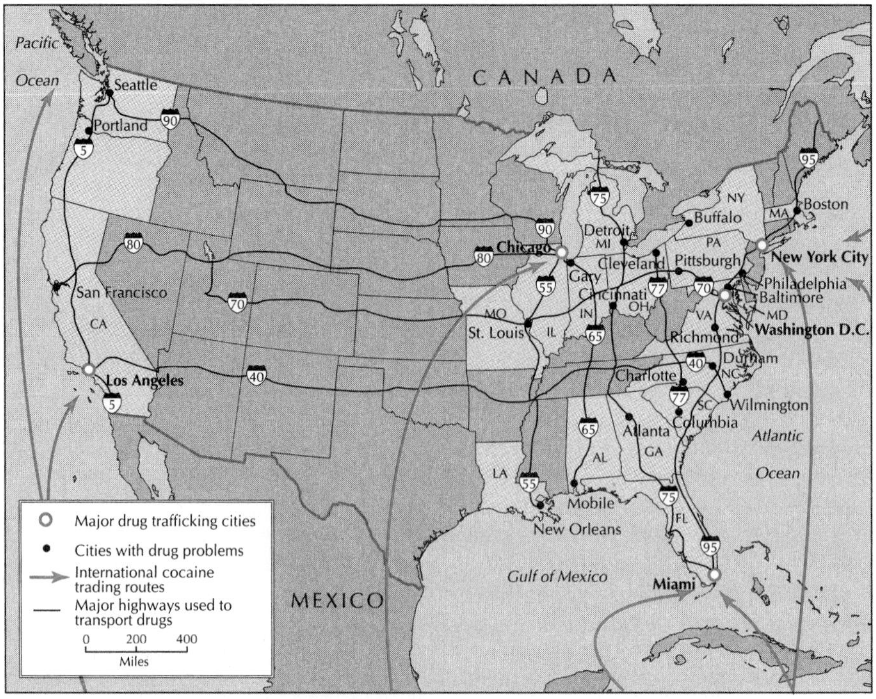

Pacific Ocean
CANADA
Seattle
Portland
San Francisco
CA
Los Angeles
Chicago
Detroit
MI
Gary
Cleveland
Pittsburgh
PA
Buffalo
NY
Boston
MA
New York City
Philadelphia
Baltimore
MD
Washington D.C.
Cincinnati
OH
IN
IL
St. Louis
MO
VA
Richmond
Durham
NC
Charlotte
SC
Wilmington
Columbia
Atlanta
GA
AL
Mobile
LA
New Orleans
FL
Miami
Gulf of Mexico
Atlantic Ocean
MEXICO
Major drug trafficking cities
Cities with drug problems
International cocaine trading routes
Major highways used to transport drugs
0 200 400
Miles

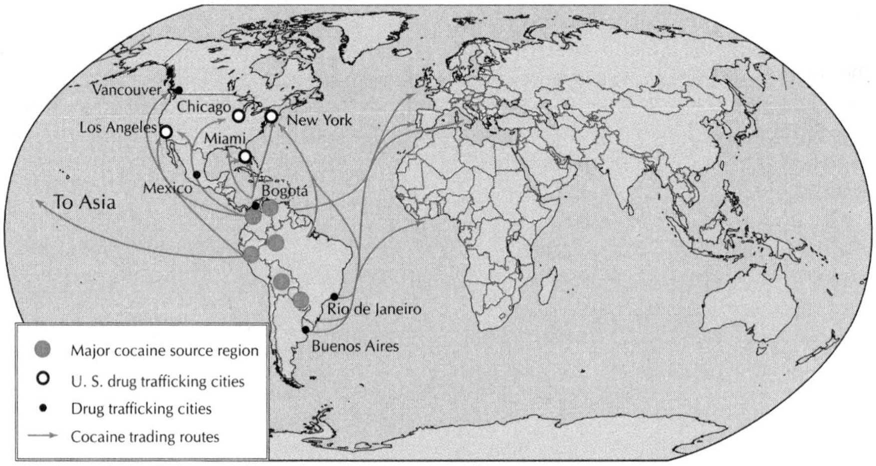

Vancouver
Chicago
New York
Los Angeles
Miami
Mexico
Bogotá
To Asia
Rio de Janeiro
Buenos Aires
Major cocaine source region
U. S. drug trafficking cities
Drug trafficking cities
Cocaine trading routes

MAP 145

Africa in the Post-apartheid Era (1997)

By 1993 Africa contained fifty-three ethnically diverse, independent African-ruled countries, with a total population of 817,000,000. It included several nations with cities of over 2 million people, including Cairo, Egypt, at 10,099,000; Lagos, Nigeria, at 7,998,000; Kinshasa, Zaire, at 3,747,000; and Casablanca, Morocco, at 2,941,000. On May 10, 1994, Nelson Mandela became the first black elected president of South Africa. His triumph reflected nearly ten years of protest by African Americans and international pressure for white South Africans to relinquish control of a country that they had ruled since about 1800. South Africa gained an international reputation for its apartheid system that began in 1946. It was the equivalent of America's Jim Crow system. In 1961, with the help of the United States' CIA, Mandela was arrested and charged with inciting insurrection and spent the following thirty years in prison. Mandela refused to allow his imprisonment to alter his commitment to racial equality. His successful run for the South African presidency made South Africa the last black-majority African nation to win its independence from white-minority rule.

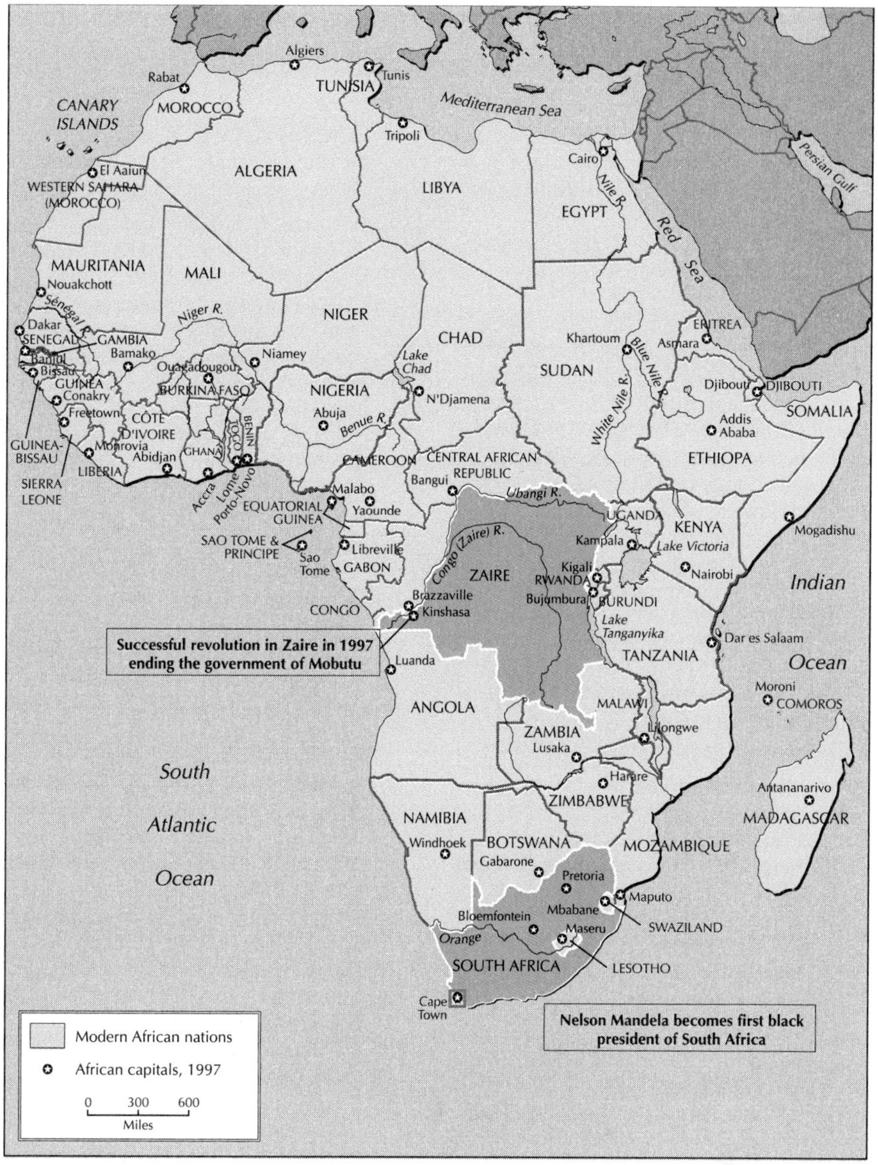
Algiers
Rabat
Tunis
TUNISIA
MOROCCO
CANARY ISLANDS
Mediterranean Sea
Tripoli
Cairo
El Aaiun
WESTERN SAHARA (MOROCCO)
ALGERIA
LIBYA
EGYPT
Persian Gulf
Nile R.
Red Sea
MAURITANIA
Nouakchott
MALI
Sénégal R.
Niger R.
NIGER
CHAD
Dakar
SENEGAL
GAMBIA
Banjul
Bamako
Bissau
Ouagadougou
Niamey
Lake Chad
Khartoum
SUDAN
Asmara
ERITREA
GUINEA
Conakry
BURKINA FASO
NIGERIA
N'Djamena
Blue Nile
White Nile R.
Djibouti
DJIBOUTI
Freetown
CÔTE D'IVOIRE
Abuja
Benue R.
Addis Ababa
SOMALIA
GUINEA-BISSAU
Monrovia
Abidjan
GHANA
TOGO
BENIN
ETHIOPIA
SIERRA LEONE
LIBERIA
Accra
Lome
Porto-Novo
CAMEROON
CENTRAL AFRICAN REPUBLIC
Bangui
Ubangi R.
Malabo
Yaounde
EQUATORIAL GUINEA
UGANDA
KENYA
Mogadishu
SAO TOME & PRINCIPE
Sao Tome
Libreville
GABON
Congo (Zaire) R.
Kampala
Lake Victoria
Kigali
RWANDA
Nairobi
ZAIRE
Indian
Bujumbura
BURUNDI
CONGO
Brazzaville
Kinshasa
Lake Tanganyika
Dar es Salaam
Successful revolution in Zaire in 1997 ending the government of Mobutu
Luanda
TANZANIA
Ocean
Moroni
COMOROS
ANGOLA
MALAWI
Lilongwe
ZAMBIA
Lusaka
South
Harare
Antananarivo
ZIMBABWE
MADAGASCAR
NAMIBIA
Atlantic
Windhoek
BOTSWANA
Gabarone
MOZAMBIQUE
Ocean
Pretoria
Maputo
Mbabane
Bloemfontein
Maseru
SWAZILAND
Orange
SOUTH AFRICA
LESOTHO
Cape Town
Nelson Mandela becomes first black president of South Africa
Modern African nations
African capitals, 1997
0 300 600
Miles

Map and Text Sources

137. Ashmore, Harry S. *Civil Rights and Wrongs: A Memoir of Race and Politics 1944–1994*. New York: Pantheon Books, 1994.

Bartley, Numan V. *The New South, 1945–1980*. Baton Rouge: Louisiana State University Press, 1996.

Brown, Floyd G. *"Slick Willie": Why America Cannot Trust Bill Clinton*. Annapolis, MD: Annapolis-Washington Book Publishers, 1993.

Cavanagh, Thomas E. *The Impact of the Black Electorate*. Washington, DC: Joint Center for Political Studies, 1984.

Hayden, Thomas. *The Power of the Dixiecrats*. Nashville, TN: Southern Student Organizing Committee, 1966.

Solomon, Norman. *False Hope: The Politics of Illusion in the Clinton Era*. Monroe, ME: Common Courage Press, 1994.

Southern Negro: 1952: Warning to Ike and the Dixiecrats. New York: The Nation, 1952.

Swain, Carol M. *Black Faces, Black Interests: The Representation of African Americans in Congress*. enl. ed. Cambridge, MA: Harvard University Press, 1995.

Tate, Katherine. *From Protest to Politics: The New Black Voters in American Elections*. Cambridge, MA: Harvard University Press, 1993.

138. Bucke, Emory Stevens. *The History of American Methodism*. New York: Abingdon Press, 1964.

Cone, James H. *For My People: Black Theology and the Black Church*. Maryknoll, NY: Orbis Books, 1984.

Gillard, John Thomas. *The Catholic Church and the American Negro*. Baltimore: St. Joseph's Society Press, 1968.

Morrow, Ralph E. *Northern Methodism and Reconstruction*. East Lansing: Michigan State University Press, 1956.

Phillips, Charles Henry. *The History of the Colored Methodist Episcopal Church in America Comprising Its Organization, Subsequent Development and Present Status,* 3rd ed. Jackson, TN: Publishing House C. M. E. Church, 1925.

Richardson, Harry Van Buren. *Dark Salvation: The Story of Methodism as It Developed among Blacks in America*. Garden City, NY: Anchor Press, 1976.

Washington, Joseph R. *Black Sects and Cults*. Lanham: University Press of America, 1984.

Woodson, Carter G. *The History of the Negro Church,* 3rd ed. Washington, DC: Associated Publishers, 1992.

139. Bowman, J. Wilson. *America's Black & Tribal Colleges*. South Pasadena, CA: Sandcastle Publishing, 1994.

Cook, Steven J. "Promoting Better Outcomes for Black Students in Predominantly White Colleges and Universities" M.A. thesis, University of New Hampshire, 1996.

Davis, Lenwood G. *A History of Blacks in Higher Education, 1875–1975: A Working Bibliography*. Monticello, IL: Council of Planning Librarians, 1975.

Fleming, Jacqueline. *Blacks in College*. San Francisco: Jossey-Bass Publishers, 1984.

Hazzard, Terry L. "Factors Influencing the Decisions of White Students to Attend Historically Black Colleges and Universities in the South." Ed.D., thesis, Florida State University, 1996.

Jones, Larry G. *Black Students Enrolled in White Colleges and Universities: Their Attitudes and Perceptions*. Atlanta: Southern Regional Education Board, 1979.

McGrath, Earl J. *The Predominantly Negro Colleges and Universities in Transition*. New York: Bureau of Publications, Teachers College, Columbia University, 1965.

Neyland, Leedell W. *Historically Black Land-Grant Institutions and the Development of Agriculture and Home Economics, 1890–1990*. Tallahassee: Florida A & M University Foundation, 1990.

Standley, Nancy V. *White Students Enrolled in Black Colleges and Universities: Their Attitudes and Perceptions*. Atlanta: Southern Regional Education Board, 1978.

Thompson, Daniel C. *Private Black Colleges at the Crossroads*. Westport, CT: Greenwood Press, 1973.

Whiting, Albert N. *Guardians of the Flame: Historically Black Colleges Yesterday, Today, and Tomorrow*. Washington, DC: American Association of State Colleges and Universities, 1991.

140. Grimshaw, William H. *Official History of Free Masonry among the Colored People in North America*. Kila, MT: Kessinger Publishing Company, 1995.

Wesley, Charles H. *The History of Alpha Phi Alpha: A Development in College Life, 1906–1979,* 16th ed. Baltimore: Foundation Publishers, 1996.

Whalen, William J. *Handbook of Secret Organizations*. Milwaukee: Bruce Publishing Company, 1966.

141. Bates, Timothy Mason. *Black Capitalism in America: Historical Foundations, Present Orientations, and Future Prospects*. New York: MSS Modular Publications, 1974.

Marable, Manning. *How Capitalism Underdeveloped Black America: Problems in Race, Political Economy, and Society*. Boston: South End Press, 1983.

U.S. Bureau of the Census, *Survey of Minority-Owned Businesses*. Washington, DC: 1972.

142. Emeka, Mauris Lee Porter. *Black Banks, Past and Present*. Kansas City, MO: 1971.

Gilbert, Abby L. *Black Banks: A Bibliographic Survey*. Washington, DC: Office of the Comptroller of the Currency, 1971.

Osthaus, Carl R. *Freedmen, Philanthropy, and Fraud: A History of the Freedman's Saving Banks*. Urbana: University of Illinois Press, 1976.

143. *Survey of Minority-Owned Businesses*. Washington, DC: U.S. Bureau of the Census, 1972.

Weare, Walter B. *Black Business in the New South: A Social History of the North Carolina Mutual Life Insurance Company*. Durham, NC: Duke University Press, 1993.

144. Gugliotta, Guy, and Jeff Leen. *Kings of Cocaine: An Astonishing True Story of Murder, Money, and Corruption*. New York: Harper & Row, 1990.

Hacker, Andrew. *Two Nations: Black and White, Separate, Hostile, Unequal*. New York: Ballantine Books, 1995.

Langone John, ed. *AIDS: The Facts, Perceptions and Myths*. New Orleans: Louisiana State Medical Society, 1985.

Shilts, Randy. *And the Band Played On: Politics, People, and the AIDS Epidemic*. New York: Quality Paperback Book Club, 1993.

Walker, William O., III., ed. *Drugs in the Western Hemisphere: An Odyssey of Cultures in Conflict*. Wilmington, DE: Scholarly Resources, 1996.

145. Achebe, Chinua. *Things Fall Apart*. Oxford: Heinemann Educational, 1996.

Afigbo, A. E. *The Making of Modern Africa*. New York: Longman, 1986.

Davis, Hunt R. *Mandela, Tambo, and the African National Congress: The Struggle against Apartheid, 1948–1990: A Documentary Survey*. New York: Oxford University Press, 1991.

Fanon, Frantz. *The Wretched of the Earth: The Handbook of the Third-World Revolution.* New York: Ballantine Books, 1973.

Hallett, Robin. *Africa since 1875: A Modern History.* Ann Arbor: University of Michigan Press, 1974.

Mazrui, Ali A. *The Africans: A Triple Heritage.* Boston: Little, Brown, 1986.

McEwan, Peter J. M., and R. B. Sutcliffe, eds. *Modern Africa.* New York: Cronwell, 1965.

Ottaway, David. *Chained Together: Mandela, De Klerk, and the Struggle to Remake South Africa.* New York: Times Books, 1993.

Robottom, John. *Africa and the Middle East.* Harlow, England: Longman, 1972.

Rodney, Walter. *How Europe Underdeveloped Africa*, rev. ed. London: Bogle-L'Ouverhure Publications, 1988.

Worden, Nigel. *The Making of Modern South Africa: Conquest, Segregation, and Apartheid*, 2nd ed. Oxford: Blackwell, 1995.

Index